Child Abuse:
Commission and Omission

edited by

Joanne Valiant Cook
Research Associate, Trent University

and

Roy Tyler Bowles
Professor of Sociology, Trent University

Butterworths

Toronto

© 1980 Butterworth and Company (Canada) Limited
2265 Midland Avenue
Scarborough, Ontario, Canada   M1P 4S1

The Butterworth Group of Companies:

Canada: Butterworth & Co. (Canada) Ltd., Toronto, Vancouver
United Kingdom: Butterworth & Co. (Publishers) Ltd., London, Borough Green
Australia: Butterworth Pty. Ltd., Sydney, Melbourne, Brisbane
New Zealand: Butterworths of New Zealand, Ltd., Wellington
South Africa: Butterworth & Co. (South Africa) Pty. Ltd., Durban
United States: Butterworth Inc., Boston
                 Butterworth (Legal) Inc., Seattle

Canadian Cataloguing in Publication Data

Main entry under title:

Child abuse

Bibliography: p.
ISBN 0-409-82410-0

1. Child abuse—Addresses, essays, lectures.
I. Cook, Joanne Valiant.   II. Bowles, Roy Tyler.

HV713.C3815   362.7′1   C80-094008-3

To Our Parents
Who Cared.

. . . any act of commission or omission by individuals, institutions or society as a whole, and any conditions resulting from such acts or inaction, which deprive children of equal rights and liberties, and/or interfere with their optimal development, constitute by definition abusive or neglectful acts or conditions.

David G. Gil. "Unraveling Child Abuse."

Preface

This edition began as a modest enterprise: to gather literature on child abuse which might serve as source material for community based committees on prevention and for students pursuing studies of the Sociology of the Family. Relevant papers were widely scattered throughout several professional journals and edited volumes. While certain key ideas ran through much of the material, research findings were limited and often contradictory. There seemed to be a need for an organized, readily accessible, source of current scholarly knowledge of the contributions and limitations of research on the problem. Therefore, articles published within the last five years predominate here; relevant previous work is generally noted in the references. The most widely used description of child abuse states that those acts of commission or omission which harm or threaten to harm the welfare of a child constitute abuse. Thus, papers which reflect the range of abuse from physical and sexual assault (commission) to neglect and/or failure to protect children (omission) are included. Also selected were those papers which critically address the controversial issues of causation and social policy.

The material is organized within four main parts representing key areas of both research and professional interest:

1) The Forms of Abuse.
2) The Sources of Abuse.
3) Social Policy Issues.
4) The Victims and The Consequences of Abuse.

Papers dealing with specific treatment and prevention programmes have not been included. Instead a selected, abstracted bibliography of such literature is provided in the Appendix.

Although all the articles stand on their own merit, they have been arranged in complementary order so that insights and problems posed in one paper are often picked up and explored in the next. The introductions to each Part provide abstracts of the articles. They are deliberately brief to allow the authors to speak for themselves. All papers are reprinted as originally published, including the reference citations.

Acknowledgments

We gratefully recognize the contributions of the following special people:

The authors for their gracious consent to include their works;

Mrs. Mary Martin of the Sociology Resource Centre, Trent University, for her cheerful assistance and selfless enthusiasm;

Mrs. Fran Fraser for her skill, efficiency, and sense of responsibility in putting together the manuscript well in advance of the publisher's deadline;

Mrs. Jean Wilson for her help with the correspondence;

and Ms. Sherry Henderson of Butterworths for being so good at her job.

Table of Contents

Prologue

Commission and Omission

Child abuse and neglect are viewed as acts of commission and omission which interfere with the chances of children to develop their potential as human beings. Such interference must be judged in terms of the conditions which permit and encourage the healthy development of potential in each child. To the extent that abuse and neglect result from the conduct of parents, understanding the etiology of neglect requires an understanding of the parenting process. Short term questions about child abuse and neglect probably must focus on pathology: What kinds of damage to a child's development result from the experience of being abused or neglected? What factors predict or cause the inappropriate parental conduct leading to commissions or omissions? In what ways do broader social agencies or institutions (schools, welfare agencies, the legal system, mechanisms of income distribution) interfere with or fail to provide for the development of children? However, those questions capable of guiding efforts to reach long term solutions must focus on health. What are the conditions and experiences which make it possible for a child to develop his potential? How can such conditions be assured for children? What kinds of personal and familial strengths make it possible for parents to effectively provide the nurture which children need? How can such strengths be developed? How can the institutions of society be organized to support most effectively the development of children?

There are three broad questions to be asked about child abuse and neglect which occur in families. First, what is the nature of abuse as experience for the child? Second, what acts are committed or omitted by parents? Third, what social and psychological characteristics discriminate those parents who abuse or neglect their children from those who properly care for their children?

Experience of a Child

An incident of child abuse or neglect is at one very fundamental level an experience for a child. In fact, it is only after identifying that which a child needs and

1

that to which a child has a right that we can articulate those commissions and omissions which constitute abuse. Experience which is good for a child must be considered in its own right and not merely left as a residual category signifying the absence of abuse and neglect.

Gil has offered a useful normative definition of child abuse.

> Every child, despite his individual differences and uniqueness is to be considered of equal intrinsic worth, and hence should be entitled to equal social, economic, civil and political rights, so that he may fully realize his inherent potential and share equally in life, liberty, and happiness.

Society should strive for "circumstances of living which facilitate the optimal development of children," and it should evaluate treatment of children in terms of its effect on "a child's right to develop freely and fully [3]."

Enabling nurture might be a useful concept to describe this set of conditions encouraging optimal development. Nurture is defined as that which promotes the development of the child by providing nourishment, support, and encouragement. Use of the modifier enabling calls attention to the child as a person in becoming and to the objective of facilitating his or her development. Viewing the life experiences of a child, we can use the terms abuse, neglect, and maltreatment to refer to those experiences which deprive the child of things he needs to realize his potential or which directly affect him in such a way that his development is inhibited. Ultimately, criteria for judging child abuse and neglect should be based on norms rooted in knowledge of the processes of child development. The contrast between enabling nurture and maltreatment is schematically presented below.

Enabling Nurture	*Abuse and Neglect*
Conditions which permit and encourage development of potential.	Conditions which inhibit development of potential.
Treatment and responses by caretakers which stimulate healthy development.	Acts by caretakers which inhibit or interfere with healthy development.

The use of "enabling nurture" suggests that programs for the prevention of abuse and the treatment of abusing families need to focus not just on how families can avoid abuse and neglect, but also on what parents can provide as experiences for their children.

Acts By Parents

An incident of child abuse or neglect is an action (commission) or a failure to act (omission) on the part of some adult or adults who have responsibility for the provision of those things to which the child is rightfully entitled. These acts occur in the process of parenting. Green, Gaines, and Sandgrund refer to child abuse and neglect as a "dysfunction in parenting[4]" and Giesmar calls them "the most virulent kinds of faulty socialization[2]." These phrasings imply a notion of properly functioning parenting and proper socialization. Thus, child abuse and neglect as acts by parents must be placed in the total context of parenting behaviour or parenthood as a role. Understanding child abuse requires a more general understanding of parenting.

Parenthood can be characterized as a job with heavy responsibilities but limited possibilities for meeting those responsibilities. These responsibilities are evident to parents because they receive a child into their home when he is both helpless and plastic. They know that in about two decades they will release him to the world as an independent human being. The responsibilities are emphasized by the mass media, churches, schools, and the helping professions all of which carry content which makes parents feel keenly that they are responsible for the kinds of persons their children turn out to be. Because of the distribution of income in the society, and because of the way in which work and other spheres are organized, many parents must rear their children with inadequate resources, inadequate systems of social support, and conflicting demands for time and energy.

When parenthood is viewed as a role or job, and the demands and conditions of that job are reviewed, the marvel may be not so much the number of abused and neglected children, but the number of well cared for and adequately socialized children. The fundamental question is: Why are some parents able to provide enabling nurture for their children while others neglect and abuse their children?

Causation

In cases of child abuse and neglect, as in cases of action and inaction of all kinds, one can pose the question of causation or explanation: Why, in terms of the internal and external forces operating on him, did the person in question act in the way that he did or fail to act in some expected manner? Parke usefully focuses the search for an answer to this question: "Abuse . . . is an orderly outcome of a network of cultural and community forces that, in turn, affect the development of family interaction patterns leading to abusive incidents[6]."

The explanation of child abuse and neglect is inevitably complicated. For one thing, child abuse is probably only one symptom or outcome of a set of underlying forces. Other symptoms may include other forms of interpersonal aggressiveness or even quite dissimilar behaviour. In addition, different incidents of child abuse can result from quite different sets of causal forces. It is probably the case that no single social or psychological factor is either necessary or sufficient as a cause of child abuse. Research has produced substantial insights or understanding into those family processes related to abuse. These insights can usefully be examined as hypotheses of the factors related to the probability of abuse.

Stress

The probability of child abuse or neglect occurring in a family increases with the level of stress experienced. Families lower in the income structure of the society have fewer economic resources with which to meet family needs and are subjected to insecurities of numerous kinds. Large families place more demands on parents than do small families. Children who require special care, perhaps due to handicaps or hyperactivity, place heavy demands on parents. Life changes such as moves and job changes disrupt routines and require new energy for adjustment. The stress hypothesis sees parenting as a role requiring substantial energy and the parent as playing many roles each of which require energy. Some portion of people in stressful circumstances are not able to meet all of the demands placed on them. As a result, they may fail to perform some expected task, such as child care, or express their frustration in the form of aggression.

Stress can explain why some parents do not meet all of their role obligations. However, it cannot explain why persons under equal stress respond to their children in different ways.

Learned Abusive Models

Clinical studies indicate that individuals who have learned abusive parenting models from their own parents are more likely to abuse their children than those who have not. Some authors have advanced psychodynamic explanations for this relationship: The abusing mother identifies with her own mother and hence acts in the same way; the person abused as a child has a resulting pool of frustration which is later expressed as aggression against his or her own child. Role learning is a simpler explanation. A child learns many fundamentals of parental style by interacting in a role set with his own parents. Hence, the child who is abused learns an abusive parenting style.

Cultural Tolerance For Physical Punishment

Child abuse is more likely to occur in families where the use of physical punishment as a disciplinary tactic is culturally approved than in families where it is not. If the repertoire of acceptable parental reactions to children includes physical aggression, then the parent who is angry can, with little hesitation, select a violent act to vent his feelings. It is easier for a parent to escalate from mild physical discipline to injurious action than from verbal discipline to physical injury. It should be noted that this hypothesis also emphasizes learning — learning to use physical action in interpersonal relations as a consequence of membership in a particular subculture.

It may be that the visibility of corporal punishment and clearly inflicted injuries accounts in part for researchers' emphasis on physical punishment. Other routine forms of discipline could also be escalated. Do some parents move from disciplinary isolation to prolonged confinement of a child? Do some move from denial of a favourite food to food and water deprivation? The question needs to be phrased to encompass both physical and non-physical punishment. Under what circumstances do items from the disciplinary practices of parents get magnified so that they are injurious to the child's development?

Inappropriate Expectations of a Child

Parents who expect a child to perform in ways or at levels which are beyond his capability are more likely to abuse than those who have more age appropriate expectations. This hypothesis takes different forms. Incidents of abuse may begin as discipline administered to correct or punish some act, such as bed-wetting, which is relatively common among children of a certain age. Some parents (mothers are most frequently mentioned) expect emotional support and responsiveness from a child which is beyond that child's capacity and abuse may occur when the child fails to provide it. Though not emphasized in the literature, neglect through failure to provide adequate food, hygiene or emotional support may result from the absence of information about what a child actually needs and the extent to which he can independently meet these needs.

Thus, parents, as a result of faulty learning, may develop inappropriate expectations of a child's capacity to care for himself, to comply with adult norms, and to respond to others. Their reaction is often frustration and a perception that the child is misbehaving.

Lack of Social Support

Child abuse is more likely to occur in those families which are socially isolated than it is in those families which are emeshed in a network of social support. This hypothesis relates to the issue of stress. It is assumed that families with social support are more likely to have occasional relief from child-rearing duties, more likely to have listeners to whom they can articulate their stress, and more likely to have sympathetic observers who will alert them to danger signals in their own behaviour. Hence, if social support is present families are less likely to build up stress in child-rearing and less likely to express the stress they do experience in abusive and neglectful treatment of children.

Social support also relates to learning appropriate expectations of children. Parents who are involved in a social network have day-to-day reality checks, in the form of reactions from others, on the normality or expectancy of particular acts by their children. Isolated parents must depend on more impersonal and remote sources for such information. Finally, social support serves as a normative check against extremes of parental behaviour. An isolated parent who becomes excessively punitive or negligent toward his children has only his personal and internal mechanisms to stop him before damage is done to the child. The parent in a supportive social network can be reminded or sanctioned before such extremes are reached. In short, a supportive social network can both reduce stress and shape the parent's behaviour into non-destructive directions.

Defects in Character Structure

There is major disagreement among authors over the role psychological disturbances play in child abuse. The most useful formulation may be: Some instances of child abuse and neglect have roots in psychopathology or in character structure.

Simplistically defined, character structure consists of "a set of attitudes and mechanisms [which] are habitually adopted by the ego to deal with instinctual forces, assure satisfaction, reconcile conflicts, and achieve adjustment within a particular environment[1]." Individuals can differ significantly in their capacity to organize and meet the demands of their daily environment. These differences affect the capacity to provide adequate child care and to deal with the stresses produced by child care.

It should be remembered that even in those circumstances where social and demographic characteristics predict highest abuse rates only a minority of parents abuse their children. Psychological characteristics may distinguish between abusers and non-abusers in comparable social situations.

A broad overview of the attempts to develop a causal explanation of parental neglect and abuse of children, suggests that a parent be regarded as an actor in a total life situation. The way he performs his parenting role depends on the stresses placed on him by that situation, the cultural norms and expectations he has learned (particularly as they pertain to children), and his capacity to manage those demands placed on him by that situation.

Needs of Future Research

Research on child abuse began with a clinical focus on pathology. Child abuse was considered a special kind of disease. Both the abused child and the abusing parents were considered to be sick. Clinical studies gathered data about the characteristics of both groups of sick people. As researchers began to conduct more extensive studies, abused or neglected (i.e. sick) children were compared to children who had *not* been maltreated. Abusing and neglecting (i.e. sick) parents were compared to parents who had *not* mistreated their children. Health has been indicated only by the absence of disease.

Research on child abuse will make more long term contributions if there is a shift from a framework of pathology to a framework of health. It was suggested above that abuse and neglect can be understood only in comparison to enabling nurturance. Newberger argues that further policy advances depend on a better knowledge of those "realities associated with family competency and strength[5]." Future research can contribute to this knowledge if quality of child care is clearly conceptualized as a variable with enabling nurture as a positive value and neglect and abuse as negative values. Studies should then positively identify families who provide children with care which encourages optimal development and compare them to families who abuse and neglect their children. Such comparisons should provide more definitive results. This type of research would be more useful in guiding social policy toward the betterment of life for children.

Roy Tyler Bowles

REFERENCES

1.   FISCHHOFF, Joseph, WHITTEN, Charles F., and PETTIT, Marvin C. "Psychiatric Study of Mothers of Infants With Growth Failure Secondary to Maternal Deprivation." Chapter 14 in this volume.

2.   GEISMAR, Ludwig L. "Family Disorganization: A Sociological Perspective." Chapter 21 in this volume.

3.   GIL, David. "Unraveling Child Aubse." Chapter 12 in this volume.

4. GREEN, Arthur H., GAINES, Richard W., and SANDGRUND, Alice. "Child Abuse: Pathological Syndrome of Family Interaction." Chapter 25 in this volume.

5. NEWBERGER, Eli H. "Child Abuse and Neglect: Toward A Firmer Foundation for Practice and Policy." Chapter 31 in this volume.

6. PARKE, Ross D. "Socialization Into Child Abuse." Chapter 27 in this volume.

Part One

Forms of Abuse

The prevalent practice in the literature on the maltreatment of children is to distinguish between child abuse and neglect. This arbitrary division leads to inconsistency in definitions of the problem. The authors whose work appears in this section effectively argue that neglect and sexual abuse may be equally as damaging to the development of a child as the physical abuse which attracts more public attention.

The readings which follow are not exhaustive of the range of abuse to which children are subjected, but they are illustrative of general categories of misuse. As well, they demonstrate that these modes of expression of indifference or aggression toward children often constitute a continuum.

The phenomenon of child abuse received its widest public and professional interest following the identification of "the battered child syndrome". This first section deals with the roots and nature of physical assault.

A. Physical Assault

M. Lystad

Physical assault against children is one type of violence which occurs within the family. The factors which explain child abuse are probably similar to those which explain violence between other family members. Lystad reviews the research material on family violence. She concludes that to understand violent acts by one member of a family against other members we must examine,

> . . . the individual functioning within the social group and within the cultural norms by which the group operates. Thus, violence at home occurs when social needs and expectations of the individual are unsupported by either the family or by other social institutions, and when such a mode of expression seems eminently available and legitimate to the individual.

This formulation calls attention to several variables which appear in many papers in this book: (1) personality or psychological characteristics; (2) stress generated within the family dynamics themselves; (3) stress arising because of the family's location in the socioeconomic structure; (4) childrearing and interpersonal styles characteristic of the particular family; and (5) the general cultural norms governing the use of violence and the relations between family members.

R. Gelles

In contrast to Lystad's general review on family violence, Richard Gelles examines the incidence of physical force by parents against children. Such data has typically come from studies of childrearing practices entailing corporal punishment, or from clinical studies of battered children. Gelles reviews the literature on incidence of abuse, delineating the methodological inadequacies of studies yielding estimates. He concludes "that most projections . . . are educated guesses," based primarily on "caught cases of abuse." Further, the definition of abuse varies with the investigator. Gelles conducted a large survey to identify more accurately the full range of physical aggression, emphasizing that which goes beyond routine discipline but would not necessarily result in a clinical diagnosis of battering. A major advantage of his report is that he clearly outlines his method of data collection. The data are analyzed in terms of sex of the abuser, and sex and age of the abused. It was found that violence is extensive and patterned, mothers are more likely than fathers to use violence, and males and younger children are the most likely victims. Because of the sampling techniques and the problem of under-reporting, Gelles believes his estimates of incidence most likely underrepresent the extent of violence toward children.

C. H. Kempe et al.

This paper by Kempe and his associates is now a classic and much of the material on child abuse refers back to it. The term "battered child syndrome" refers to a clinical condition in children who have been deliberately injured by physical assault. Often the assaulter is the parent, but it may be another caretaker or a sibling. The authors clearly describe the symptoms associated with battering and the diagnostic techniques required to distinguish deliberately inflicted injuries from those resulting from other causes.

T. Solomon

Theo Solomon considers the issue of child abuse from two perspectives. The first is historical: he shows that such practices as infanticide and child labour have, over long periods, been harmful to or destructive of children in many societies. The second is institutional: he demonstrates that the legal system is willing to inflict punishments on children that would be unacceptable for adults, the economic system permits the manufacture and sale of dangerous toys, and the ideological system (as represented in literature for children) is willing to convey disaster for children as a relatively normal state of affairs. He presents a composite demographic picture of the abused, the abuser and the abusing family. As well, his final section introduces neglect as a form of abuse.

B. Neglect

V. J. Fontana

Fontana suggests that "maltreatment syndrome" reflects a broader range of concerns about the well-being of children than do other terms. "Maltreatment" is useful because it calls attention to a range of omissions or patterns of neglect (such as food or water deprivation, or inadequate hygiene) which may be as injurious to the child as the commissions referred to in battering. He includes a check list for physicians suspicious of maltreatment and provides guidelines for diagnosis.

B. S. Koel

That neglect may indeed be part of a pattern of abuse is indicated in the final sentence of this report: "Fattening a puny infant is satisfying to the staff, but the child remains at risk of subsequent violence if he is sent back to untreated parents." Koel reports on three cases which illustrate that when a clinical diagnosis of "failure to thrive" is made and no underlying pathogenic cause is evident, then emotional and/or nutritional neglect must be considered. However, as his studies show, the continuum between neglect and physical abuse is such that correcting the nutritional and developmental deficits within the hospital is not sufficient insurance for the child's well-being. The infant often returns to hospital either near death or dead due to assault. The paper illustrates that neglect may not be indicative of indifference, ignorance or paucity of resources but a fundamental, severe disturbance in the expected nurturing role of parents. He recommends that caretakers be included in all stages of restorative treatment and provided with extensive after-care service.

J. W. Polier

This article discusses another dimension of neglect, that which involves society itself and in particular those professionals who are charged with the duty of ensuring children's welfare. (It may be useful in this regard to note Gelles' paper in Part Three wherein he examines the gatekeepers —those who identify children at risk—and the processes by which they attach labels.) Polier states that professionals may neglect children by shifting them from agency to agency, effectively leaving them without the services they need. They also neglect children when, for reasons of their own, they concentrate on delivering high quality care to a few clients and leave others without any care. By implication, Polier agrees with Gil's argument (in the final paper in Part One) that children have a right to those conditions which permit them to develop their full potential. Justice Polier notes that protective case workers, in particular, are faced with a dilemma when the funding available for services falls short of the promises made by politicians, leaving a "gap between rhetoric and practice."

A. B. Bergman

Dr. Bergman's brief commentary recognizes the dilemma just mentioned. Treatment resources and service workers are scarce but money is available for repetitive research and for conferences which provide media hype, honoraria for professional speakers, and exposure for politicians. As he states,

Why bother funding expensive child protective services, foster homes and mental health treatment when media messages provide the illusion of meaningful activity? Mandatory reporting laws are cheap. Doing something about the cases that are reported is not.

L. H. Pelton

Leroy Pelton's thesis touches on the concerns raised by both Polier and Bergman. He states that the myth that child abuse is classless

. . . persists not on the basis of evidence or logic, but because it serves certain professional and political interests. These interests do not further the task of dealing with the real problem underlying abuse and neglect; adherence to the myth diverts attention from the nature of the problems and diverts resources from their solution.

Pelton's paper is a critique of current expositions of abuse, an examination of the motives and ideology underlying those ideas and a description of the consequences for policies and programmes of the conceptualization of abuse as a classless phenomenon. His concern is that the strong evident relationship between poverty and misuse must not be overlooked if effective ameliorative programmes are to be developed.

C. Sexual Abuse

C. H. Kempe

The abuse of children through sexual exploitation is what Kempe terms a "hidden pediatric problem." He believes however that it is as common a problem as physical abuse and the failure to thrive syndrome. As this paper indicates, sexual abuse, whether in the form of pornographic exploitation, incest, violent molestation, rape, or pedophilic contact, can have severe developmental consequences and therefore warrants inclusion in studies of maltreatment. In Kempe's comprehensive paper case histories are used to illustrate the nature of sexual assault on children, the personality of both the active and the complicitous abuser, and the consequences for the child's development. Kempe's orientation toward diagnosis, protection and treatment of victims, as well as treatment and punishment of offenders, focuses on the healthy development of the individuals involved. In this regard, criminal prosecution is seen as a possible tool in the therapeutic process.

I. Nakashima and G. Zakus

Nakashima and Zakus focus on one aspect of sexual abuse, reviewing cases of incest diagnosed in an Adolescent Clinic. They discuss the types and characteristics of families where incest has occurred, the consequences of such abuse for the victims and for the sometimes resulting offspring. They make suggestions for clinicians in terms of recognizing and diagnosing, evaluating and treating such cases. The interference with the opportunity for healthy development caused by sexual abuse is described.

D. Definitions of the Nature of Abuse

D. Gil

David Gil's paper helps to put the previous articles in a new perspective. He redefines child abuse "as inflicted gaps or deficits between circumstances of living which would facilitate the optimal development of children . . . and their actual circumstances, irrespective of the sources or agents of the deficit." This implies that we must look not just at what parents directly do to children, but also at the experiences created for children by other aspects of the social environment. It must also be recognized that individual acts of aggression associated with psychopathology are "not independent of societal forces." Hence, according to Gil, no amount of specific focus on the conduct of abusing parents will eliminate child abuse. Effective prevention programmes require a recognition of the interaction of several causal dimensions, and ultimately depend upon more fundamental social change. Gil's concepts of the levels of manifestation and levels of causation make an effective transition from the description of the modes of maltreatment in Part One to the examination of sources of abuse in Part Two.

1

*Violence at Home: A Review of the Literature**

Mary Hanemann Lystad, Ph.D.

If the function of the family is to love and to nurture and to support its members, then violence in the family would seem to be incompatible with its function. Why does violence occur? How often does it occur, and who are its victims?

For the purpose of this paper, violence in the family is defined as a mode of behavior involving the direct use of physical force against other family members. The "family" referred to is primarily the nuclear family of mother, father, and children. Physical force in the family varies in severity from homicide at one extreme to mild spankings at the other. It also varies by intent; in some cases the intent is to control people's behavior, in others it is to vent personal hostility, and in still others it is a mixture of both. In addition, family violence varies by societal interpretation; homicide is rarely considered legitimate in any society, while spankings are considered by some to be necessary to the socialization process.

This paper will review several types of studies relating to family violence: those raising theoretical issues; incidence studies of family violence; studies of violence as it relates to particular family members—husband and wife, parent and child, siblings; studies of violence related to social structure; and, finally, studies concerning needed services, and their effectiveness—services to discordant families employing a wide variety of professional help, from neighborhood policeman to emergency-ward physician.

---

* Mary Hanemann Lystad, "Violence at Home: A Review of the Literature", *American Journal of Orthopsychiatry*, 45(3):328-345. Copyright © 1975 the American Orthopsychiatric Association, Inc. Reproduced by permission.

Theoretical Studies

Theoretical studies have explored many different types of variables—psychological, sociological, and cultural. A number of the studies interrelate several types of variables, but the majority analyze only a single type.

In terms of psychological and psychopathological variables, many factors have been studied, particularly that of intimate social contact in the family. Goode[59] pointed out that one reason intimates commit violence against one another is that they are in each other's presence a lot, and few others can anger one so much as those who are close. Goode maintained that it is probable that intimate emotional links among human beings have their own effects independent of pervasive pressures from the larger culture. A number of other authors[39, 83] noted the feeling of rejection which aggressive children have in the family situation because of separation from parents, birth of another sibling, or parental indifference.

Several studies point to a special interpersonal relationship between murderers and their victims, in which violence is the result of antagonisms that have been tolerated for years while the victim teased, taunted, or suppressed his eventual murderer until a breaking point was reached. On the other hand, the killers are sometimes described as submissive and passive, desiring to avoid conflict whenever possible, particularly if playing a masochistic role results in gaining their affection.[71, 126] Wolfgang[156] pointed out the suicidal nature of some homicide victims, who so aggressively provoke attack upon themselves that they can be viewed as suicides. As for children who murder, Sargent[122] supports the hypothesis that sometimes the child who kills is acting as the unwitting lethal agent of an adult, usually a parent, who unconsciously prompts the child to kill so that the adult can vicariously enjoy the benefits of the act.

In discussing child abuse, a number of authors point to the presence of psychoses among parents.[111, 113, 119, 143] Zalba[159] reported that child battering and severe child abuse are inflicted by parents with a variety of difficult problems, from violent and episodic schizophrenia to impulse-ridden character disorder. These parents displace and act out their anger over marital conflicts onto their children, the common element among them being that children are used as targets of abuse and injury in the process of displacing and denying interpsychic and other-object-oriented hostility and aggression.

On the other hand, Gelles[54] criticized those who look on the phenomenon of child abuse strictly from a psychopathological model. He feels a more fruitful approach to this problem is to focus on sociological and contextual variables associated with abuse: since unemployment and social class are important contextual variables, then strategies to prevent child abuse should aim at alleviating the disastrous effects of being poor in an affluent society; since there appears to be an association between child abuse and unwanted pregnancy, programs should be developed to aid in planned parenthood.

By far the most frequently discussed social structural theory of family violence is that involving the socialization of aggression. The theory states that parents who punish more severely produce children who are more aggressive. And *they* in turn tend to punish *their* children more severely. This is particularly well documented in the study of child abuse, where the abused child often becomes the abusing parent. Punishment both frustrates the child and provides him a model.[72, 88, 129]

On the other hand, Yarrow *et al*,[158] in analyzing theories and correlates of child aggression, concluded that many of the hypotheses relating the child's aggression to punishments and rewards in rearing practices of the mother are not supported in interview studies. The authors cautioned that several methodological factors complicate interpretation of such studies of child rearing: the unknowns and inadequacies in instruments, and the nonstandard, uncertainly equivalent, and uncertainly suitable conceptual labels in the data. The authors concluded that interpretations of consistency between research findings of a number of studies have slighted a great deal of evidence and have given theoretical expectations too compelling an influence.

Not all groups in our society socialize children to the same degree by means of violent behavior. Gelles[51] and Gil[55] found a higher incidence of violence against children among families with lower educational achievements and lower socioeconomic status, among broken families, and among families with four or more children. Eron,[40] to the contrary, did not find class differences.

Why do some parents socialize their children more aggressively? Eron[40] cited evidence that those who do have fewer mobility aspirations for their children. Straus[138] found that such punishment varies with the sex of the child and with the traits parents value in their children. His findings are interpreted as supporting a "linkage theory" explanation of the use of physical punishment. This theory holds that the use of physical punishment by parents is influenced by the parents' conception of the roles the child is to play as an adult. If the child is expected to become an aggressive, competitive adult, to be upwardly mobile, he is encouraged to be aggressive, to win as a child, and he is not punished for aggressive behavior.

Two other social structural aspects of family violence that have been explored are 1) power structure of the family, and 2) power structure of the larger society. With regard to power structure of the family, Curtis,[31] Goode,[60] Phillips,[112] and Reiss[117] pointed out that the family, like all social groups, consists of a hierarchy of interpersonal relations, with superordinate and subordinate roles, rivalries, and use of force. These variables can be measured and analyzed in the study of the family as a social group. Straus[139] offered a general systems theory approach to the study of violence between family members. His paradigm begins with family group characteristics affecting violence in the family, including organization, position in the social structure, values, and belief. Straus carried his analysis through individual characteristics of family members, precipitating factors, societal values of opportunity and power, and the violent act and its consequences for child, family, and society.

In discussing roles between family members and inevitable conflict situations, a number of family sociologists point out that conflict is itself not bad; it can be a positive force in making for equitable exchange of rewards and benefits.[125] Sprey,[132, 133] asserting that the conventional treatment of family harmony and conflict is inadequate, suggested as an alternative and more fruitful theoretical approach a view of the family as a system in conflict.

Unlike the social theories of violence, which hold that the source of the problem lies within the family, the cultural theories hold that the source of the problem lies outside of the family. Gil focused on the power structure within the society as it affects violence in the family, and drew attention to what he considers massive societal abuse of children as a more serious problem than individual abuse of children.[55] Societal abuse, Gil wrote, is manifested in the statistics on infant hunger and malnutrition, mortality, poverty, inadequate medical care, poor education, and officially sanctioned abuse in schools, correctional institutions, childcare facilities, and juvenile court.

Abrahamsen[1] and Gil[56] discussed the attitudes and values of the culture which sanction violence as a way of life. Gil wrote that the reason there is considerable child abuse in American society is because our cultural norms of child rearing allow the use of a certain amount of physical force toward children by adults caring for them. Such use tends to be encouraged by some professional experts in child rearing, education, and medicine, and by some members of the press, radio, and television. Furthermore, Gil pointed out, children are not protected by law in our society against bodily attack in the same way as are adults.

Owens and Straus[106] discussed the complementarity of social and cultural theories of violence. These authors did, however, point out the implications of each for the reduction of violence. The culture-of-violence theory assumes that there is a system of values which justifies and supports violent behavior among segments of the society with high levels of violence; the implication: an educational program designed to change these values is needed. The structural theory of violence assumes that the more violence present in the social structure during childhood, the more the person learns to use it; the implication: alternation of this underlying social behavior of violence is needed. Both of these needs, the authors argued, are actually involved in the reduction of family violence.

Incidence Studies

Data on frequency of violence among family members are hard to come by. No one wants to admit to such behavior, and, of course, except for homicide and severe child abuse, it is relatively easy behavior to hide.

At the extreme end of the spectrum—homicide—a number of investigators have found a high proportion of victim-offender pairs to be relatives. Boudouris,[17] in a study of homicide cases in Detroit over a 42-year period, found that 30% of the pairs were related. Voss and Hepburn[146] found that almost half of the victims in the city of Chicago in 1965 were related to their offenders. Willie[153] found a high proportion of relationships in the state of Michigan, as did Field and Field[43] in a study of murders in the United States as a whole. Wolfgang[157] found that friends, relatives, and acquaintances made up the major types of specific relationships between this nation's homicide victims and offenders—69% of violence-precipitated homicide. Outside of this country, Maldonado,[95] in a study in northern and central Portugal, found that 71% of those who committed murder did so in their place of residence; McClintock,[98] in a study in London, accounted for 30% of homicides as domestic disputes; Siciliano,[128] in a study in Denmark, found a predominance of murders occurring among family members, as did McCarthy,[97] who analyzed murders committed by children in Ireland.

Wolfgang[155] broke down the frequency of homicidal relationships in the United States by race (and found that whites are more likely to be slain by relatives) and by sex (and found that primary group contact amounts to 59% of all victim-offended relatives for males and 84% for females).

The statistics on frequency of child abuse vary considerably, partly of course because of the wide differences in definition of child abuse among researchers. For some researchers, child abuse is defined as severe battering; for other researchers, child abuse involves any use of physical force or acts of omission causing physical injury to a child.

Kempe[79] estimated that child abuse may occur as often as six times for every 1000 births. Zalba[161] estimated conservatively that, of 200,000 to 250,000 children in need of protective services in the United States each year, 30,000 may have been badly hurt. Gil and Noble[57] asserted that reported cases in this country are only a fraction of the actual number, which they estimated at between 2.5 and 4.1 million per year. A nationwide study of child abuse in New Zealand by Fergusson *et al.*[41] showed that 41% of the abused children were under five years of age; the largest number were children under one year old. Younger age groups as more frequent victims were also reported by Gil.[53]

With respect to other violent crimes, some interesting differences are found. As the degree of violence decreases, the percentage of strangers committing the offense increases. Mulvihill *et al.*[102] reported that, among recent violent crimes in this country involving strangers, 16% were homicide, 21% aggravated assault, 53% forcible rape, and 78% armed robbery. The popularly held fear that an attacker will be a stranger is therefore strongly justified for robbery and relevant for rape, but is much less valid for aggravated assault and generally inappropriate for homicide.

Violence Between Husbands and Wives

The occurrence of adult violence in the home usually involves males as aggressors toward females. It is repeatedly cited as a cause for marital unhappiness and discord and for divorce.[25, 29, 130] In analyzing complaints of husbands and wives seeking divorce, Levinger[91] wrote that wives complain about neglect, physical or verbal abuse, lack of love, or other matters included under the catch-all term of "mental cruelty." While husbands are also disturbed by neglect, emotional cruelty, and lack of love, they are more prone to express complaints about in-law intervention or sexual mismatching. Whitehurst[149] reported that one reason for increasing jealousy among husbands is the trend toward economic and social equality of women, which often leads the male to feel threatened. A further problem arises with the wife who violates the sexual norms of a double-standard society.

Bergen[13] gave a detailed account of the effect upon a child of violence between parents. In this case, a four-year-old child observed the killing of her mother by her father. In a way she had been prepared for this event by her father's previous threats to her mother, and had therefore to deal less with the unexpectedness of the murder than with its confirmation of her fears and anxieties. The effect on children of violence among parents has not really been explored to any significant extent, even though it in itself is a form of child abuse and is also a part of the socialization process.

Abuse of Children

The first thing to be learned from the literature is that child abuse is not a unique product of our time and place. Kellum[78] discussed the existence of massive infanticide during the Middle Ages. Langer[84] wrote that, except among Christians and Jews, infanticide has from time immemorial been an accepted procedure for disposing not only of deformed or sickly infants, but of all such newborns as might strain the resources of the individual family or the larger community. Langer noted that infanticide is still employed by so-called "underdeveloped peoples" in an effort to keep the population in reasonable adjustment to the available food supply.

In the nineteenth century, the Society for the Prevention of Cruelty to Animals succeeded in removing a maltreated child from his parents on the grounds that he was a member of the animal kingdom and entitled to protection under the laws against animal cruelty.[115] This action precipitated the formulation in 1871 of the Society for Prevention of Cruelty to Children. More recent interest in child abuse, particularly in the battered-child syndrome, has its origin in the discipline of pediatric radiology, begun in 1906. From x-rays it is possible to document repeated injuries to a child over time, and to confirm suspicions of abuse.

A number of typologies have been developed in relation to child abuse; some focus on the degree of battering (*i.e.*, controllable abuse to enraged battering),[16] some on the reasons for child abuse (*i.e.*, altruistic to revenge), [44, 118, 127] and some of the effect of child abuse on the child (*i.e.*, psychological and physical).[14, 15] Many studies point out clearly that child abuse occurs with other forms of dysfunction in the family. From within the family, there is marital conflict between parents;[74, 76, 140] from without, there are social pressures of economic adversity and social isolation.[21, 69]

Some studies have found socioeconomic differences among abusers of children, a preponderance of abusers being lower-class.[18, 26, 162] Other studies[48, 67] have not found such differences. Reliable data on socioeconomic differences are difficult to obtain, because, as a number of studies have pointed out, upper-class persons are able to get help from private doctors who are sometimes willing to let the abuse go unreported, while lower-class persons must go to the public hospital, which is required to make a report.[22]

What, then, are some of the real problems in family functioning, particularly in child care, that cause parents to abuse their children? There are, first of all, emotional problems. Because of confusion in identities between the mother and the baby, post-partum depression can lead to infanticide in place of suicide.[5] The relationship of infanticide to later actual or attempted suicide of parents is mentioned by a number of investigators[65, 94, 101, 145] Severe personality problems of parents are discussed, and psychoses, including both manic depressive and schizophrenic behaviors, are reported.[12, 18, 45] Other social-psychological problems referred to are alcoholism[46, 47, 110, 137] and drug addiction.[46, 47] Finally, Elmer[36] and Grumet[63] mentioned a combination of physical and emotional problems of parents leading to child abuse.

Some studies point to problems between mother-father as related to child abuse.[11, 69, 74, 140] The husband or wife displaces hostility onto the child. Still other researchers have found child abuse to be related to the stress of mothering.

Elmer[34, 35, 36] and others[58, 76, 143] pointed out that child abuse is usually the result of accumulated stresses within the family, often associated with the lower socioeconomic classes. Among factors involved in the stress are the birth of several children close together, prematurity, and special physical or emotional problems of children. With the increasing isolation of the nuclear family from relatives, and the increasing number of one-parent families, parents, most often mothers, are on call 24 hours a day, seven days a week, fifty-two weeks of the year. When there is no relief from the pressures of this job, the stresses result in blow-ups of one sort or another.

Researchers in this field have noted still another problem leading to child abuse: parental ignorance.[75, 131] Many parents do not know age-appropriate behavior for young children. They also have mistaken notions of how to rear children, how to encourage and guide them at different ages. They see recalcitrant behavior as wilful naughtiness. Laury[87] and Steel[134] both noted that battering is often the result of the child's failure to meet various parental expectations.

A number of studies of child abuse have found a generational pattern of abuse. The battered child tends to become a battering parent in the classical battered-child syndrome. Social anthropologists and psychologists have long recognized that patterns of child-rearing, both good and bad, are passed from one generation to the next in relatively unchanged form. Psychologically speaking, one could describe this phenomenon as an identification with the aggressive parent, this identification occurring despite strong wishes of the person to be different.[73, 81, 86, 100, 105, 131, 135] Some mothers who beat their children have themselves been beaten not only during childhood but, as adults, in weeks immediately prior to their own battering behavior.[148] Some children, likewise, batter other younger children after their own battering.

Abuse by Children

Extreme violence by children occurs rarely. When it occurs, it is viewed primarily as a pathological response to very poor relationships between parent and child. A number of studies show that children who kill or attempt to kill usually choose parents as victims.[24, 77, 99, 121] Hellsten and Katila[68] reported that such children are encouraged by one parent to agress against the other. Duncan[32] reported cases where a history of parental brutality is a significant consideration in cases of homicidal adolescents' abrupt loss of control.

In addition to abusing adults, children also abuse other children. Adelson,[2] in his study of homicide by children eight years old or younger, reminded us that the preschool child is capable of homicidal rage when he is provoked by what he considers to be a threat to his position in the family unit or in the immediate human environment. Sargent[123] presented a case study of two children who killed siblings and who, it is suggested, were the recipients of both overt and covert commands from their adult environment to commit murder. In all the studies mentioned, the child abuser is viewed as the recipient of poor models of social behavior and of overstressful social situations, which cause him to lash out as he has been told or in the only way he can.

Family Violence and Social Structure

The majority of empirical work in the area of family violence has focused upon social structural variables hypothesized to be related to such family disharmony. These include not only the demographic variables of sex, race, and class, but also functional variables of relationships within and outside of the family. In terms of sex, research on family groups[85, 141, 150] and on television and fiction portrayals of family groups[50, 52, 64] show men to be more violent than women. Women may be verbally aggressive, but men are physically aggressive, and such behavior is related to the masculine ideal of violence in Western culture. Feshbach[42] has also found six-year-old boys to be more physically aggressive then six-year-old girls in our society. Whiting[152] analyzed both non-Western and Western societies, and found a higher frequency of physical violence, as a form of protest masculinity, in those societies where the male has lower salience in infancy but higher prestige and salience from childhood on. Levine[90] found Yoruba students' memories of childhood rewards and punishments more heavily related to physical punishment for boys than for girls.

Information on the difference in the amount of family violence between racial groups is scanty. Rosenberg[120] reported violence among Puerto Ricans in New York to be present because of family relationships—parents hit to punish children; parents and children fight to defend one another against outsiders. Campbell[23] stated that the impact of slavery and segregation on the black family has often had a debilitating effect on its ability to socialize its children. The shattering of family control typically causes the family to be replaced as the primary norm-setter by the street culture—in the streets of a crime-ridden, violence-prone, and poverty stricken world. Erlanger[38] wrote that, insofar as differences in social patterns are found between races, they are at least in part related to social class—working-class whites and blacks report more frequently that they were spanked as children than do middle-class whites and blacks.

Class differences in family violence are frequently reported. These differences have to do primarily with differences in socialization practices among middle- and lower-class persons. Brody[19] pointed out that middle-class mothers tend to use a more stimulating and emotionally warm mode of childrearing, with emphasis upon the child's achieving through satisfactions from his own efforts rather than through material rewards and punishments. Working-class mothers, on the other hand, tend to play a more passive and less stimulating role with the child, with more emphasis upon control through rewards and punishments. Brofenbrenner,[20] Coles,[27] and Lewis[92] reported similar class differences in patterns of socialization. Cooney[28] found middle-class mothers more permissive than are lower-class mothers.

Why are middle-class mothers more gentle and more permissive than lower-class mothers? Kohn[82] related the differences in disciplinary practices to the degree of self-direction valued in the two classes, which is in turn related to characteristics of occupations in the two social classes—middle-class occupations demanding self-direction and creativity, lower-class occupations demanding conformity. Steinmetz,[136] agreeing with Kohn, focused on a methodological issue in the study of class differences. She asserted that the widespread practice of using social class as an independent variable in socialization research suppresses important relationships between occupational groups and socialization practices. Her own findings suggest that differences in the verbal, interpersonal, and attitudinal tasks and orientations required by an individual's occupational roles are related to differences in his socialization techniques and personality outcomes. Her findings indicate furthermore that these occupational requirements are better indexed not by social class but by a system of "Occupational Environments" which cuts across social classes to directly index the types of occupationally induced behaviors and values that are only indirectly indexed by social class.

A number of researchers emphasize the necessity of giving children some controls in the process of socializing them. Havens,[66] in looking at new trends in family structure, concluded that there is a need for a better combination of the balance between parental firmness and gentleness. Campbell[23] found that parents of delinquents tend to be more punitive than do parents of nondelinquents, although they do not differ in extent of firmness of socialization and home demands. Gallenkamp[49] reported that delinquents tend to see their parents as more sanctioning of antisocial behavior than the parents see themselves. In measuring aggression in children, Gordon *et al.*[62] found that 1) the stricter the girl's mother, the more aggressive the daughter, if the mother uses physical punishment; and 2) the stricter the boy's mother, the less aggressive the son, especially if physical punishment was not used. Winder,[154] in a study of social deviance among preadolescent boys, found aggression, dependency, withdrawal, depression, and likability correlated with certain parental attitudes. Low self-esteem and high ambivalence in mothers, high punitiveness and physical punishment in fathers, were associated with deviance among children.

Still another structural element that has been explored in the study of family violence is the process by which parent and adolescent are separated. In discussing parent-youth conflict, Goode[61] maintained that even when much of the argument centers upon the sexual behavior of the adolescent, the youngster is not merely disobeying old rules because of temptation. Rather, he or she is asserting the right to behave in that fashion; hence the conflict may be fierce and often breaks, either temporarily or permanently, the attachment of parents and children. Edwards[33] also discussed the breakdown of exchange between parents and adolescent children which can lead to violent conflict. He asserted that such breakdown can also lead to more social independence from parents when children accept fewer benefits and rewards from them. Peer groups, in particular, serve as alternative suppliers for a variety of services needed by adolescents.

Finally, nontraditional and changing family structures have been studied in relation to family violence. In a study of six communes, Leigh[89] wrote that a large majority of commune members report much less hostility and competition and much more cooperation and meaningful communication between men and women in the communal situation than in their former situation. Whitehurst[151] suggested that alternative family structures, those which contain more people than the traditional husband-wife-children combination, may reduce the potential for family violence. He bases his discussion on the assumption that alternative family systems allow more autonomy to the individual than does the nuclear family system. Such an assumption is still to be tested.

Services to Violent Families

There is a considerable amount of literature on delivery of services to adult family members who are in physical combat. A number of articles discuss family-crisis intervention using police teams.[6, 7, 8, 9, 77, 104, 107, 108, 144] They focus upon the application of social-psychological principles to increase the policeman's effectiveness in handling such disputes, and to increase the policeman's own personal safety. There is an emphasis, too, on improving police-community relations, especially in minority group communities. Many of the articles discuss training programs designed to sensitize police workers to social problems and help them resolve conflict, rather than carry out traditional police roles or authoritarianism and arrest.

In addition to this material on services to adults in violence, there is a considerable amount of material related to child abuse. A number of authors point out that parents who abuse children present themselves in many different ways.[3, 30] Most often the child is brought as the problem, and the parents may sincerely believe the difficulty rests with him. No matter how the parents appear, their expectations are that they will be used, attacked, and accused of being bad parents. The worker's immediate and continuing response must be to the underlying fear, hurt, and frustration that the parents are feeling.

A number of authors point out the diversity of problems and of solutions.[96, 103, 116, 160] Treatment, it is urged, must be related to both the child's needs and the basic family situation. Most of the writers suggest the need for interdisciplinary teams to provide services to the whole family, the abuser as well as the abused.[4, 70, 80, 124] Many services are needed, including emergency medical services and legal counseling. As Wasserman[147] pointed out, battering families generally suffer from community exclusion and require intervention by community agencies to break the cycle of reciprocal aggression in the family.

The most important services mentioned are, of course, those that relate to prevention. Educational programs in parenthood are suggested strongly, since it has been amply documented that parents who abuse children often are woefully ignorant about child development.[54, 93, 142] Gill and others[51, 54, 55, 65] also urge certain basic social reforms, such as comprehensive family planning programs, the elimination of poverty, and the assurance of economic security as a right to all individuals and families by means of mother's wages, children's allowances, a negative income tax, or some other mechanism. No doubt such reforms are only a partial answer to the complex issue of preventing violence toward children, but perhaps a very important part of the total answer, and certainly that part without which other preventive efforts may be useless.

Intervention programs are also discussed. Paulson[109] stated that preventive intervention requires that the caseworker or therapist consider not only the abused child but the relationship of the parent to this child and the relationship of the family to the community. The caseworker must be able to identify high-risk families and take steps to help the parents. Bean[10] described a group-therapy demonstration project designed to aid parents in families showing patterns of child abuse. The major treatment method is group therapy, with parent participation encouraged in supervised child day care.

Finally, legal matters are discussed by a number of authors. Elmer mentions the need for sufficient personnel to back new child-abuse laws. Polier *et al.*[114] wrote that the authority of the juvenile court or family court should be invoked when there is evidence of abuse and when voluntary cooperation of the parent is inadequate to safeguard the welfare of the child. The court has a two-fold responsibility at the initial fact-finding hearing. It must see that the constitutional rights of the parent are protected, and it must also safeguard the welfare of the child. When a fact-finding hearing warrants a finding, the court must be able to call upon the probation officers for a full investigation and to call upon its psychiatric staff for an evaluation of the parents, when that is indicated, before disposition is made. Above all, the court must be committed to determining, in accordance with all available information, what is truly in the best interest of the child.

Discussion

Studies on family violence have explored the phenomenon from psychological, social, and cultural levels of analyses. Examination of psychological variables indicates the importance of the factor of long term, intimate social contact, which can evoke anger, and the factor of psychopathology, which can result in uncontrollable social behavior. Social factors found to have a high relationship with violence at home include demeaning and debilitating social statuses, such as unemployment and poverty, and the socialization of aggression, in which the child learns aggressive behavior from an aggressive parent or caretaker. Cultural analysis points to cultural norms of the society, which allow violent behavior, and to attitudes and values, which sometimes condone, sometimes extol violent behavior.

By and large the available evidence is not contradictory, leading to the conclusion that a comprehensive theory of violence at home must take into account factors at these several levels, placing individual funtioning within the social group and within the culture norms by which the group operates. Thus, violence at home occurs when social needs and expectations of the individual are unsupported by either the family or by other social institutions, and when such a mode of expression seems eminently available and legitimate to the individual.

Study of violent behavior in the family should begin with a focus on basic individual needs. What are such needs? What is the role of the family in responding to such needs? What is the interplay (or lack of interplay) of the family with other social institutions in responding to needs? From such perspective one may ask further questions on how the frustrations and stresses on the individual of economic insecurity, community isolation, illness, and overwork contribute to child abuse and to violence between husband and wife; why there is violence rather than passive withdrawal or some other mode of displacement; what are the processual modes of development leading to the violent act; how the participants define the situation.

There is need for study of the changes in relationships between individuals in the family and changing relationships of the family with support institutions of church, school, and work. Not only new family forms but the restructuring of old forms should receive attention. Of particular importance is study of the child-rearing function in our society. Who is to care for the child, attend to his physical needs, socialize him, teach him? Who is to love the child?

There are difficult methodological issues in the study of family functioning. While it is relatively easy to obtain basic demographic data on families, especially those who are not functioning well and are being seen by public agencies which collect records, it is not easy to obtain data on the interpersonal relationships, attitudes, and values among a community sample of families. Important in this research is the analysis of data by class, occupational, racial, and ethnic groups, for such groups receive different societal opportunities and rewards, and they also share different social beliefs and goals. Clear definitions of what constitutes violent behavior, particularly with regard to child abuse, are required of all such research. Sensitive instrument measures that achieve both reliability and validity, and adequate measures for protecting human subjects in this research, still must be devised.

Even with methodological problems, it is essential that research be continued on family functioning and on family violence as a major form of dysfunction. It is important not only for theoretical reasons but for the humane reasons of defining and evaluating services that the society should be providing all families, and those it should be providing special families in distress. For it is within the family that societal stress affects each individual most immediately. It is here that the child's capacity to grow and develop is nurtured. And it is here that the child learns future adult roles of a violent or non-violent character.

REFERENCES

1.   ABRAHAMSEN, D. 1970. *Our Violent Society*. Funk and Wagnalls, New York.

2.   ADELSON, L. 1972. "The battering child." *JAMA* 222(2):159-161.

3.   ALEXANDER, H. 1972. "The social worker and the family." In *Helping the Battered Child And His Family*, C. Kempe and R. Helfer, eds. J. B. Lippincott, Philadelphia.

4.   AMERICAN HUMANE ASSOCIATION (Children's Division). 1967. The Protective Services Center. American Humane Association, Denver.

5.   ASCH, S. 1968. "Crib deaths: their possible relationship to post-partum depression and infanticide." *J. Mt. Sinai Hosp. New York* 35:214-220.

6.   BARD, M. 1969. "Family intervention police teams as a community mental health resource." *J. Crim. Law, Criminol. Police Sci.* 60(2):247-250.

7.   BARD, M. AND BERKOWITZ, B. 1969. "Family disturbance as a police function." In *Law Enforcement Science and Technology—II*, S. Cohn, ed. I.T.T. Research Institute, Chicago.

8.   BARD, M. AND ZACKER, J. 1971. "The prevention of family violence: dilemmas of community intervention." *J. Marr. Fam.* 33(4):677-682.

9.   BAROCAS, H. 1973. "Urban policemen: crisis mediators or crisis creators?" *Amer. J. Orthopsychiat.* 43(4):632-639.

10. BEAN, S. 1971. "The parent's center project: a multiservice approach to the prevention of child abuse." *Child Welfare* 59(5):277-282.

11. BECKER, W. "The problem of maltreatment of the child." *Therapie der Gegenwart* (Berlin) 107(2):135-136, 138-140, 142-144, 147-149.

12. BENNIE, E. AND SCLARE, A. 1969. "The battered child syndrome." *Amer. J. Psychiat.* 125(7):975-979.

13. BERGEN, M. 1958. "The effect of severe trauma on a 4-year-old child." *Psychoanal. Study of the Child* 13:407-429.

14. BIRRELL, R. AND BIRRELL, J. 1968. "The maltreatment syndrome in children: a hospital survey." *Med. J. Austral.* 522(23):1023-1029.

15. BLOCH, D. 1966. "Some dynamics of suffering: effect of the wish for infanticide in a case of schizophrenia." *Psychoanal. Rev.* 53(4):31-54.

16. BOISVERT, M. 1972. "The battered-child syndrome." *Soc. Casewk* 53(8):475-480.

17. BOUDOURIS, J. 1971. "Homicide and the family." *J. Marr. Fam.* 33(4):667-676.

18. BRITISH MEDICAL JOURNAL. 1969. "Battered babies." *Brit. Med. J.* (London) 5672:667-668.

19. BRODY, G. 1968. "Socioeconomic differences in stated maternal child-rearing practices and in observed maternal behavior." *J. Marr. Fam.* 30(4):656-660.

20. BRONFENBRENNER, U. 1958. "Socialization and social class through time and space." In *Readings in Social Psychology*, E. Maccoby, et al., eds. Holt, Rinehart and Winston, New York.

21. BROWN, J. AND DANIELS, R. 1968. "Some observations on abusive parents." *Child Welfare* 47(2):89-94.

22. CAFFEY, J. ET AL. 1972. "Child battery: seek and save." *Med. World News* 13(22):21-25, 28, 32, 33.

23. CAMPBELL, J. 1969. "The family and violence." In *Law and Order Reconsidered: A Staff Report to the National Commission on the Causes and Prevention of Violence*, Vol. 10, J. Campbell, J. Sahid, and D. Strong, eds. U.S. Government Printing Office, Washington, D.C.

24. CAMPBELL, R. 1967. "Violence in adolescence." *J. Analyt. Psychol.* 12(2):161-173.

25. CHESTER, R. AND STREATHER, J. "Cruelty in English divorce: some empirical findings." *J. Marr. Fam.* 34(4):706-710.

26. COHEN, M., PHILBRICK, E. AND MULFORD, R. 1967. *Neglecting Parents: A Study of Psychosocial Characteristics*. American Humane Association, Children's Division, Denver.

27. COLES, R. 1968. "Violence in ghetto children." In *Annual Progress in Child Psychiatry and Child Development*, S. Chess and A. Thomas, eds. Brunner/Mazel, New York.

28. COONEY, N. 1967. "Control of aggression in child rearing in Puerto Rico: a study of professed practices used with boys and girls in two socioeconomic urban groups." *Dissertation Abstracts* 28(2)-A:777.

29. CORMIER, B. 1962. "Psychodynamics of homicide committed in a marital relationship." *Corrective Psychiat. J. Soc. Ther.* 8(4):187-194.

30. COURT, J. AND KERR, A. 1971. "The battered child syndrome—2." *Nursing Times* 67(4):187-194.

31. CURTIS, G. 1963. "Violence breeds violence—perhaps?" *Amer. J. Psychiat.* 120(4):386-387.

32. DUNCAN, J. AND DUNCAN, G. 1971. "Murder in the family: a study of some homicidal adolescents." *Amer. J. Psychiat.* 127(11):74-78.

33. EDWARDS, J. AND BRAUBRUGER, M. 1973. "Exchange and parent-youth conflict." *J. Marr. Fam.* 35(1):101-108.

34. ELMER, E. 1971. "Child abuse: a symptom of family crisis." In *Crisis of Family Disorganization*, E. Pavenstedt, ed. Behavioral Publications, New York.

35. ELMER, E. 1967. "Child abuse: the family's cry for help." *J. Psychiat. Nursing* 5(4):332-341.

36. ELMER, E. 1971. "Studies of child abuse and infant accidents." In *The Mental Health of the Child,* U.S. National Institute of Mental Health. U.S. Government Printing Office, Washington, D.C. (343-370).

37.   ELMER, E. 1967. "Abused children and community resources." *Inter. J. Offender Ther.* 11(1):16-23.

38.   ERLANGER, H. 1971. *The Anatomy of Violence: An Empirical Examination of Sociological Theories of Aggression.* University Microfilms, Ann Arbor, Mich.

39.   ERON, L. 1959. "Symposium: the application of role and learning theories to the study of the development of aggression in children." *Proceedings of the Rip Van Winkle Clinic* 10(1-2):3-61.

40.   ERON, L. ET AL. 1963. "Social class, parental punishment for aggression, and child aggression." *Child Devlpmnt* 34:849-867.

41.   FERGUSSON, D., FLEMING, J. AND O'NEILL, D. 1972. *Child Abuse in New Zealand.* A. R. Shearer, Government Printer, Wellington.

42.   FESHBACH, N. AND FESHBACK, S. 1973. "The young aggressors." *Psychol. Today* 6(11): 90-95.

43.   FIELD, M. AND FIELD, H. 1973. "Marital violence and the criminal process: neither justice nor peace." *Soc. Serv. Rev.* 47(2): 221-240.

44.   FLAMMANG, C. 1970. "The neglected child." In *The Police and the Under-protected Child.* Charles C. Thomas, Springfield, Ill.

45.   FLYNN, W. 1970. "Frontier justice: a contribution to the theory of child battery." *Amer. J. Psychiat.* 127(3):375-379.

46.   FONTANA, V. 1971. "Social manifestations." In *The Maltreated Child.* Charles C. Thomas, Springfield, Ill.

47.   FONTANA, V. 1971. "Which parents abuse children?" *Med. Insight* 3(10):16-21.

48.   GALDSTON, R. 1965. "Observations on children who have been physically abused and their parents." *Amer. J. Psychiat.* 122(4):440-443.

49.   GALLENKAMP, C. AND RYCHLAK, J. 1968. "Parental attitudes of sanction in middleclass adolescent male delinquency." *J. Soc. Psychol.* 75: 255-260.

50.   GECAS, V. 1962. "Motives and aggressive acts in popular fiction: sex and class differences." *Amer. J. Sociol.* 77(4): 680-696.

51.   GELLES, R. 1973. "Child abuse as psychopathology: a sociological critique and reformulation." *Amer. J. Orthopsychiat.* 43(4):611-621.

52.   GERBNER, G. 1972. "Violence in television drama. Trends and symbolic functions." In *Television and Social Behavior: Reports and Papers, Volume 1.* G. Comstock and E. Rubinstein, eds. U.S. Government Printing Office, Washington, D.C.

53.   GIL, D. 1968. *Nationwide Survey of Legally Reported Physical Abuse of Children.* Brandeis University, Waltham, Mass.

54.   GIL, D. 1969. "Physical abuse of children: findings and implications of a nationwide survey." *Ped. Suppl.* 44(5)-II:857.

55.   GIL, D. 1970. *Violence Against Children: Physical Child Abuse in the United States.* Harvard University Press, Cambridge.

56.   GIL, D. 1971. "Violence against children." *J. Marr. Fam.* 33(4):637-648.

57.   GIL, D. AND NOBLE, H. 1967. "Public knowledge, attitudes and opinions about physical abuse in the U.S.; No. 14." *Papers in Social Welfare.* Florence Heller Graduate School for Advanced Studies in Social Welfare, Brandeis University, Waltham, Mass.

58.   GIOVANNONI, J. 1971. "Parental mistreatment: perpetrators and victims." *J. Marr. Fam.* 33(4):649-657.

59. GOODE, W. 1969. "Violence among intimates." U.S. National Commission on the Causes and Prevention of Violence. Task force on Individual Acts of Violence. *Crimes and Violence* 13:941-977.

60. GOODE, W. 1971. "Force and violence in the family." *J. Marr. Fam.* 33(4):624-636.

61. GOODE, W. 1971. "Family disorganization." In *Contemporary Social Problems (Third Ed.)*, R. Merton and R. Nisbet, eds. Harcourt Brace Jovanovich, New York.

62. GORDON, J. AND SMITH, E. 1965. "Children's aggression, parental attitudes, and the effects of an affiliation-arousing story." *J. Pers. Soc. Psychol.* 1(6):654-659.

63. GRUMET, B. 1970. "The plaintive plaintiffs: victims of the battered child syndrome." *Fam. Law Quart.* 4(3): 296-317.

64. HALLORAN, J. AND CROLL, P. 1972. "Television programs in Great Britain: content and control." In *Television and Social Behavior: Reports and Papers, Volume I*, G. Comstock and E. Rubinstein, eds. U.S. Government Printing Office, Washington, D.C.

65. HARDER, T. 1967. "The psychopathology of infanticide." *Acta Psychiatrica Scandinavica* 43(2):196-245.

66. HAVENS, L. 1972. "Youth, violence and the nature of family life." *Psychiatric Annals* 2(2):18-21, 23-25, 29.

67. HELFER, R. AND KEMPE, C. eds. 1968. *The Battered Child*. University of Chicago Press, Chicago.

68. HELLSTEN, P. AND KATILA, O. 1965. "Murder and other homicide, by children under 15 in Finland." *Psychiat. Quart. Suppl.* 39(1):54-74.

69. HOLTER, J. AND FRIEDMAN, S. 1969. "Etiology and management of severely burned children: psychosocial considerations." *Amer. J. Disturbed Child* 118:680-686.

70. HOLTER, J. AND FRIEDMAN, S. 1968. "Principles of management in child abuse cases." *Amer. J. Orthopsychiat.* 38(1):127-136.

71. HOUTS, M. 1970. *They Asked for Death*. Cowles, New York, 241 p.

72. ILFELD, F., JR. 1970. "Environmental theories of violence." In *Violence and the Struggle for Existence*, D. Danield, M. Gilula, and F. Ochberg, eds. Little, Brown, Boston.

73. JENKINS, R. ET AL. 1970. "Interrupting the family cycle of violence." *J. Iowa Med. Society* 60(2):85-89.

74. JOHNSON, B. AND MORSE, H. 1968. "Injured children and their parents." *Children* 15(4):147-152.

75. JOHNSON, B. AND MORSE, H. 1968. *The Battered Child: A Study of Children with Inflicted Injuries*. Colorado Welfare Department, Denver.

76. JOURNAL OF THE TENNESSEE MEDICAL ASSOCIATION. 1971. "The battered-child syndrome." *J. Tenn. Med. Assoc.* 64(4):346-347.

77. KATZ, M. 1973. "Family crisis training: upgrading the police while building a bridge to the minority community." *J. Police Sci. Admin.* 1(1):30-35.

78. KELLUM, B. 1974. "Infanticide in England in the later Middle Ages." *History of Childhood Quart.* 1(3):367-389.

79. KEMPE, C. 1971. "Pediatric implications of the battered baby syndrome." *Arch. Dis. Childhood (London)* 46(245):28-37.

80. KEMPE, C. AND HELPER, R., eds. 1972. *Helping the Battered Child and His Family*. Lippincott, Philadelphia.

81. KEMPE, C. ET AL. 1962. "The battered child syndrome." *JAMA* 181(1):17-24.

82. KOHN, M. 1969. *Class and Conformity*. The Dorsey Press, Homewood, N.J.

83. KOPERNIK, L. 1964. "The family as a breeding ground of violence." *Corrective Psychiat. Journal Soc. Ther.* 10(6).

84. LANGER, W. 1974. "Infanticide: a historical survey." *History of Childhood Quart.* 1(3):353-367.

85. LANSKY, L. 1961. "Sex differences in aggression and its correlates in middle class adolescents." *Child Devlpmnt* 32:45-58.

86. LASCARI, A. 1972. "The abused child." *J. Iowa Med. Society* 62:229-232.

87. LAURY, G. 1970. "The battered-child syndrome; parental motivation, clinical aspects." *Bull. N.Y. Acad. Med.* 46(9): 676-685.

88. LEFKOWITZ, M., WALDER, L. AND ERON, L. 1963. "Punishment, identification and aggression." *Merrill-Palmer Quart.* 9(3):159-174.

89. LEIGH, M. 1974. "The peaceful communities." In *NATO Conference on "Determination and Origins of Aggressive Behavior,"* J. De Wit and W. Hartup, eds. Mouton, The Hague.

90. LEVINE, B. 1962. *Yoruba Students' Memories of Childhood Rewards and Punishments*. Ibadan University Press, Ibadan.

91. LEVINGER, G. 1966. "Sources of marital dissatisfaction among applicants for divorce." *Amer. J. Orthopsychiat.* 36(5):803-807.

92. LEWIS, R. 1971. "Socialization into national violence: familial correlates of hawkish attitudes toward war." *J. Marr. Fam.* 33(4):699-598.

93. LIGHT, R. 1973. "Abused and neglected children in America: a study of alternative policies." *Harvard Ed. Rev.* 43(4):556-598.

94. LUKIANOWICZ, N. 1972. "Attempted infanticide." *Psychiatria Clinica* 5(1):1-16.

95. MALDONADO, M. 1968. "Study of certain socio-criminological aspects of a group of homicides." *Boletim Da Administracao Penitenciaria E Dos Institutos De Criminologia* 23(2):5-34.

96. MCCAGHY, C. 1968. "Drinking and deviance disavowal: the case of child molesters." *Soc. Problems* 16(1):43-49.

97. MCCARTHY, P. 1974. "Summary for assessment by 'papers committee': youth who murder." In *NATO Conference on "Determinants and Origins of Aggressive Behavior,"* J. De Wit, and W. Hartup, eds. Mouton, The Hague.

98. MCCLINTOCK, F. 1963. *Crimes of Violence*. St. Martin's Press, New York.

99. MECIR, J. 1968. "Homicidal behavior of minors directed against their parents." *Ceskoslovenska Psychaitrie (Praha)* 64(5):319-325.

100. MEINICK, B. AND HURLEY, J. 1969. "Distinctive personality attributes of child-abusing mothers." *J. Cons. Clin. Psychol.* 33(6):746-749.

101. MOHR, J. AND MCKNIGHT, C. 1971. "Violence as a function of age and relationship with special reference to matricide." *Canad. Psychiat. Assoc. J.* 16(1):29-53.

102. MULVIHILL, D., TUMIN, M. AND CURTIS, L. 1969. "The interpersonal relationship between victim and offender." In *Crimes of Violence: A Staff Report to the National Commission on the Causes and Prevention of Violence, Vol. 11*. U.S. Government Printing Office, Washington, D.C.

103. NEWBERGER, E., HAAS, G. AND MULFORD, R. 1973. "Child abuse in Massachusetts." *Mass. Physician* 32(1):31-38.

104. NEWMAN, C. 1972. "Police and families: factors affecting police intervention." *Police Chief* 39(3):25-26, 28, 30.

105. OLIVER, J. ET AL. 1971. "Five generations of ill-treated children in one family pedigree." *Brit. J. Psychiat.* 119:473-480.

106. OWENS, D. AND STRAUS, M. 1973. "The social structure of violence in childhood and approval as an adult." Presented to the 1973 annual meeting of the American Orthopsychiatric Association, New York.

107. PARNAS, R. "Police discretion and diversion of incidence of intrafamily violence." *Law and Contemporary Problems* 36(4): 539-565, 171.

108. PARNAS, R. 1973. "Prosecutorial and judicial handling of family violence." *Crim. Law Bull.* 9(9): 733-769.

109. PAULSON, M. AND BLAKE, P. 1969. "The physically abused child: a focus on prevention." *Child Welfare* 48(2):86-95.

110. PAWLIKOSKI, A. 1972. "Fates of children from families of alcoholics." *Problemy Alkoholizmu (Warszawa)* 7(7):4-6.

111. PENNSYLVANIA MEDICINE. 1970. "M.D. has role in child abuse cases." *Penn. Med.* 73(9):102.

112. PHILLIPS, C. 1966. "Power relationships in marital discord." *Dissertation Abstracts* 27(5)-A:1457-1458.

113. POHLEN, M. 1968. "The psychosis of a family." *Zeitschrift Fur Psychosomatische Medizin Und Psychoanalyse (Gottingen)* 14(4):257-274.

114. POLIER, J. AND MCDONALD, K. 1972. "The family court in an urban setting." In *Helping the Battered Child and His Family*, C. Kempe and R. Helfer, eds. Lippincott, Philadelphia.

115. REDBILL, S. 1968. "A history of child abuse and infanticide." In *The Battered Child*, R. Helfer, ed. University of Chicago Press, Chicago.

116. RAFFALLI, H. AND CHRISTIAN. 1970. "The battered child: an overview of a medical, legal, and social problem." *Crime and Delinq.* 16(2):139-150.

117. REISS, D. AND SHERIFF, W. JR. 1970. "A computer-automated procedure for testing some experiences of family membership." *Behav. Sci.* 15(5):431-433.

118. RESNIK, P. 1969. "Child murder by parents: a psychiatric review of fillicide." *Amer. J. Psychiat.* 126(3):325-334.

119. RICHETTE, L. 1969. "Cheated out of childhood." In *The Throw-away Children*. Lippincott, Philadelphia.

120. ROSENBERG, B. AND SILVERSTEIN, H. 1969. "Fighting." In *The Varieties of Delinquent Experience*, Blaisdell, Waltham, Mass.

121. SADOFF, R. 1971. "Clinical observations on parricide." *Psychiat. Quart.* 45(1):65-69.

122. SARGENT, D. 1971. "Children who kill—a family conspiracy?" In *Theory and Practice of Family Psychiatry*. J. Howells, ed. Brunner-Mazel, New York.

123. SARGENT, D. 1971. "The lethal situation: transmission of urge to kill from parent to child." In *Dynamics of Violence*, J. Fawcett, ed. American Medical Association, Chicago.

124. SAVINDO, A. AND SANDERS, R. 1973. "Working with abusive parents: group therapy and home visits." *Amer. J. Nursing* 73(3):482-484.

125.   SCANZONI, J. 1972. "Marital conflict as a positive force." In *Sexual Bargaining: Power Politics in the American Marriage*. Prentice-Hall, Englewood Cliffs, N.J.

126.   SCHULTZ, L. 1968. "The victim-offender relationship." *Crime and Delinq.* 14(2):135-141.

127.   SCOTT, P. 1973. "Parents who kill their children." *Med. Sci. and Law* 13(2):120-126.

128.   SICILIANO, S. 1968. "Homicide in Denmark." *Annals Internationales De Criminologie (Paris)* 7(2):403-435.

129.   SILVER, L. DUBLIN, C. AND LOURIE, R. 1969. "Does violence breed violence? Contributions from a study of the child abuse syndrome." *Amer. J. Psychiat.* 126(3):152-155.

130.   SNELL, J. ET AL. 1974. "The wifebeater's wife: a study of family interaction." *Arch. Gen. Psychiat.* 11(2):107-112.

131.   SPINETTA, J. AND RIGLER, D. 1972. "The child-abusing parent: a psychological review." *Psychol. Bull.* 77(4):296-304.

132.   SPREY, J. 1969. "The family as a system in conflict." *Marr. Fam.* 31(4):699-706.

133.   SPREY, J. 1971. "On the management of conflict in families." *J. Marr. Fam.* 33(4):722-730.

134.   STEELE, B. AND POLLOCK, C. 1968. "A psychiatric study of parents who abuse infants and small children." In *The Battered Child*. R. Helfer, ed. University of Chicago Press, Chicago.

135.   STEINHAUSEN, H. 1972. "Sociomedical aspects of physical maltreatment of children." *Monatsschrift Für Kinderheilkunde (Berlin)* 120(8):314-318.

136.   STEINMETZ, S. AND STRAUS, M., eds. 1974. *Violence in the Family*. Dodd, Mead, New York.

137.   STETIC, D. 1966. "Treatment of alcoholics at the Pakrac Medical Center." *Psihijatrijska Njega; Casopis Za Srednje Medicinske Kadrove (Zagreb)* 1(3):23-25.

138.   STRAUS, M. 1971. "Some social antecedents of physical punishment: a linkage theory interpretation." *J. Marr. Fam.* 33(4):658-663.

139.   STRAUS, M. 1973. "A general systems theory approach to a theory of violence between family members." *Soc. Sci. Information* 12(3):105-125.

140.   TERR, L. 1970. "A family study of child abuse." *Amer. J. Psychiat.* 127(5):665-671.

141.   TOBY, J. 1966. "Violence and the masculine ideal: some qualitative data." *Annals Amer. Acad. Polit. Soc. Sci.* 364:19-28.

142.   TODAY'S EDUCATION. 1974. The abused child. *Today's Ed.* 63(1):40-43.

143.   U.S. MEDICINE. 1973. "High risk abuse children should be identified in clinical setting." *U.S. Med.* 6-7.

144.   U.S. NATIONAL INSTITUTE OF LAW ENFORCEMENT AND CRIMINAL JUSTICE. 1970. *Training Police as Specialists in Family Crisis Intervention* (submitted by Morton Bard, project director). U.S. Government Printing Office, Washington, D.C.

145.   USKIEWICZOWA, L. 1971. "Child murder by parents in the light of medicoforensic material." *Psychiatria Polska (Gdansk)* 5(2):125-132.

146.   VOSS, H. AND HEPBURN, J. 1968. "Patterns in criminal homicide in Chicago." *J. Crim. Law Criminol. Police Sci.* 59(4):499-508.

147. WASSERMAN, S. 1967. "The abused parent of the abused child." *Children* 14(5):175-179.

148. WESTON, J. 1968. "The pathology of child abuse." In *The Battered Child*, R. Helfer and C. Kempe, eds. University of Chicago Press, Chicago.

149. WHITEHURST, R. 1971. "Violently jealous husbands." *Sexual Behav.* 1(4):32-38, 40-41.

150. WHITEHURST, R, 1971. "Violence potential in extramarital sexual responses." *J. Marr. Fam.* 33(4):683-691.

151. WHITEHURST, R. 1974. "Alternative Family Structures and Violence Reduction." In *Violence in the Family*, S. Steinmetz and M. Straus, eds. Dodd, Mead, New York.

152. WHITING, B. 1965. "Sex identity conflict and physical violence: a comparative study." *Amer. Anthropol.* 67(6)-2: 123-140.

153. WILLIE, W. 1970. "Citizens who commit homicides." *Revista Inter-americana De Psicologia (Buenos Aires)* 4(2):131-144.

154. WINDER, C. AND RAU, L. 1962. "Parental attitudes associated with social deviance in preadolescent boys." *J. Abnorm. Soc. Psychol.* 64(6):418-424.

155. WOLFGANG, M. 1957. "Victim precipitated criminal homicide." *J. Crim. Law Criminol. Police Sci.* 48(1):1-11.

156. WOLFGANG, M. 1969. "Who kills whom." *Psychol. Today* 3(5):54-56, 72-75.

157. WOLFGANG, M. 1958. *Patterns in Criminal Homicide.* John Wiley, New York.

158. YARROW, M., CAMPBELL, J. AND BURTON, R. 1968. "Theories and correlates of child aggression." In *Child Rearing: An Inquiry into Research and Methods.* Jossey-Bass, San Francisco.

159. ZALBA, S. 1966. "The abused child: I. a survey of the problem." *Soc. Wk* 11(4):3-16.

160. ZALBA, S. 1967. "The abused child: II. A typology for classification and treatment." *Soc. Wk* 12(1):70-79.

161. ZALBA, S. 1971. "Battered children." *Transaction* 8(9/10):58-61.

162. ZUCKERMAN, K., AMBUEL, J. AND BANDMAN, R. 1972. "Child neglect and abuse: a study of cases evaluated at Columbus Children's Hospital in 1968-1969." *Ohio State Med. J.*

2

Violence Toward Children in the United States*

Richard J. Gelles, Ph.D.

This paper reports on the incidence, modes, and patterns of parent to child violence in the United States. Despite the considerable attention that has been focused on the issue of child abuse and neglect, and the significant and lengthy discussions concerning the physical punishment of children, valid and reliable data on the incidence and prevalence of the use of violence and aggression on children by their parents are almost nonexistent. The statistics that are available on child abuse and physical punishment do not report on the numerous violent acts that are neither routine physical punishment nor abusive. The wide range of acts between spankings and grievous assault have largely gone unnoticed and unresearched by social scientists.

Available data are often flawed by conceptual, definitional, sampling, and measurement problems. Moreover, the available statistics are usually general estimates of incidence which do not give even the crudest breakdown by age, sex, or demographic characteristics of the children or parents. Nevertheless, the figures on violence and aggression between parents and children do shed *some* light on the scope of the phenomenon.

---

* Richard J. Gelles, ''Violence toward children in the United States'', *American Journal of Orthopsychiatry*, 48(4):580-592. Copyright © 1978 the American Orthopsychiatric Association, Inc. Reproduced by permission. The research is part of a program on intrafamily violence supported by grants from the National Institute of Mental Health (MII27557) and the National Center of Child Abuse and Neglect, Office of Child Development (90-C-425).

Physical Punishment

The most comprehensive research on the use of physical force on children are the studies of physical punishment. Between 84% and 97% of all parents use some form of physical punishment on their children.[3, 9, 23] The advantage of these data is that they are typically based on nationally representative surveys. The disadvantages are that they do not provide age specific rates nor do they examine specific acts of force.

Child Abuse

A variety of research strategies have been employed to investigate the incidence of child abuse in America.

Official statistics. Investigations of official reports of child abuse provide varying degrees of the yearly incidence of abuse. Gil's 1968 survey yielded a figure of 6000 abused children.[16] One problem with the Gil survey is that all fifty states did not have mandatory reporting laws for the period Gil studied. The Children's Division of the American Humane Society documented 35,642 cases of child abuse in 1974, which were reported to its clearinghouse for child abuse and neglect reports.[1] However, only 29 states reported to the clearinghouse.

Estimates derived from official reports suffer from various problems. First, official reports do not cover all possible states and localities. Second, states and localities do not employ uniform definitions of "child abuse." Third, official reports represent only a fraction of the total number of children who are abused and battered by their parents.

Household surveys. In 1965, the National Opinion Research Corporation and David Gil collaborated on a household survey of attitudes, knowledge and opinions about child abuse. Of a nationally representative sample of 1520 individuals, 45, or three percent of the sample, reported knowledge of 48 different incidents of child abuse. Extrapolating this finding to the national population, Gil estimated that between 2.53 and 4.07 million adults knew of families involved in incidents of child abuse.[16] Light,[20] by applying corrective adjustments to Gil's data and considering possible overlap of public knowledge of incidents, revised the estimate to be approximately 500,000 abused children in the United States during the survey year.

Survey of community agencies. Nagi[21] attempted to compensate for the shortcoming of estimates of child abuse based on official records by surveying a national sample of community agencies and agency personnel to ascertain how many cases of child abuse they encountered annually. Nagi's estimate of child abuse was arrived at by extrapolating from reporting rates which would be expected on a national basis using presumed "full reporting rates" found in Florida. Nagi's estimate is that 167,000 cases of abuse are reported annually, while an additional 91,000 cases go unreported.[21]

Statistical projection. Estimates of the incidence of child abuse have also been based on projections from regional, state, city, or single agency samples. The range of these estimates is quite wide. DeFrancis estimated that there are between 30,000 and 40,000 instances of "truely battered children" each year.[28] Fontana[10] proposed that there may be as many as 1.5 million cases of child abuse each year. Kempe[19] set the figure closer to 60,000 cases. Cohen and Sussman[8] used data on reported child abuse from the ten most populous states and projected 41,104 confirmed cases of child abuse in 1973.

Deaths of Children by Violence

Just as estimates of the incidence of child abuse vary, so do estimates of the number of children killed each year by parents or guardians. Fontana[10] provided a conservative estimate of 700 children killed each year. Helfer[28] has stated that, if steps are not taken to curb child abuse, there will be over 5000 deaths a year over the next ten years. *Pediatric News*[22] reported that one child dies each day from abuse—a yearly incidence of 365. Gil[16] cited data from the U.S. Public Health Service, which reported 686 children under fifteen died from attacks by parents in 1967.

Summary of Research

Perhaps the most accurate summary of the research on the incidence and extent of child abuse is provided by Cohen and Sussman,[8] who concluded that:

> the only conclusion which can be made fairly is that information indicating the incidence of child abuse in the United States simply does not exist.

It is evident that most projections of the incidence of child abuse are "educated guesses." Information gleaned from official statistics must be qualified by the fact that they represent only "caught" cases of abuse, which become cases through varied reporting and confirmation procedures.[13] In addition, information on child abuse is difficult to interpret because the term "child abuse" is as much a political concept (designed to draw attention to a social problem) as it is a scientific concept that can be used to measure a specific phenomenon. In other words, child abuse can be broadly and loosely defined in order to magnify concern about this social problem. While some social scientists use the term to cover a wide spectrum of phenomena that hinder the proper development of a child's potential,[17] others use the term to focus attention on the specific case of severely physically injured children.[18]

The lack of valid and reliable data on the incidence of child abuse in the United States led to the inclusion of a clause in the Child Abuse Prevention and Treatment Act of 1974 (PL-93-237) calling for a full and complete study on the incidence of child abuse and neglect. Such a study has already been contracted by the National Center of Child Abuse and Neglect. As an indication of the major problems that arise when one tries to measure the abuse and neglect of children, the contracted study has moved into the third quarter of its two-year existence and no decisions have been made on appropriate definitions of abuse or what research design should be employed in the study.

A Note on Trend Data

It should be pointed out that the problems involved in estimating the incidence of child abuse make the task of interpreting trend data almost hopeless. First, it is impossible to determine if rates of reported abuse are rising due to an actual increase in the true rate of abuse or due to increased sensitivity on the part of professionals who see children and families. Second, the constant change in the definition of abuse and the constant revisions of state child abuse and neglect laws, tend to broaden the definition of child abuse. This means that more families and children are vulnerable to being identified as abusers and abused.

The Need for a Study of Parental Violence

It was after evaluating the available evidence on the extent of force and violence between parents and children that we embarked on a national study of parental and family violence. While physical punishment of children appears to be almost a universal aspect of parent-child relations, and while child abuse seems to be a major social problem, we know very little about the modes and patterns of violence toward children in our society. We know almost nothing about the kinds of force and violence children experience. Are mothers more likely than fathers to hit their children? Who employs the most serious forms of violence? Which age group is most vulnerable to being spanked, slapped, hit with a fist, or "beaten up" by parents? Although answers to these questions will not completely fill in the gaps in our knowledge about child abuse, we see the information we generate in this study as providing an important insight into the extent of force and violence children experience and the numbers of children who are vulnerable to injury from serious violence.

Method

One of the most difficult techniques of studying the extent of parental violence is to employ a household interview that involves the self-reporting of violent acts. Although this technique is difficult and creates the problem of underreporting, we felt that, because of the shortcomings of previous research on child abuse,[14] this was the only research design we could employ to assess the extent and causes of intrafamily violence.

Sample and Procedures

Response Analysis (Princeton, N.J.) was contracted to draw a national probability sample. A national sample of 103 primary areas (counties or groups of counties) stratified by geographic region, type of community, and other population characteristics was generated. Within these primary areas, 300 interviewing locations (census districts or block groups) were selected. Each location was divided into ten to 25 housing units by the trained interviewers. Sample segments from each interviewing location were selected. The last step involved randomly selecting an eligible person to be interviewed in each designated household.

Eligible families consisted of a couple who identified themselves as married or being a "couple" (man and woman living together in a conjugal unit). A random procedure was used so that the sample would be approximately half male and half female.

The final national probability sample produced 2143 completed interviews.* Interviews were conducted with 960 men and 1183 women. In each family where there was at least one child living at home between the ages of three and seventeen, a "referent child" was selected using a random procedure. Of the 2143 families interviewed, 1146 had children between the age of three and seventeen living at home. Our data on parent-to-child violence are based on the analysis of these 1146 parent-child relationships.

The interviews were conducted between January and April 1976. The interview protocol took 60 minutes to complete. The questions on parent-to-child violence were one part of an extensive protocol designed to measure the extent of family violence and the factors associated with violence between family members.

Violence: Defined and Operationalized

For the purposes of this study, violence is nominally defined as "an act carried out with the intention, or perceived intention, of physically injuring another person." The injury can range from slight pain, as in a slap, to murder. The motivation may range from a concern for a child's safety (as when a child is spanked for going into the street) to hostility so intense that the death of the child is desired.[15]

We chose a broad definition of violence (which includes spankings as violent behavior) because we want to draw attention to the issue of people hitting one another in families; we have defined this behavior as "violent" in order to raise controversy and call the behavior into question. In addition, our previous research[12] indicated that almost all acts, from spankings to murder, could somehow be justified and neutralized by someone as being in the best interests of the victim. Indeed, one thing that influenced our final choice of a concept was that acts parents carry out on their children in the name of corporal punishment or acceptable force, could, if done to strangers or adults, be considered criminal assault.

Violence was operationalized in our study through the use of a Conflict Tactics Technique scale. First developed at the University of New Hampshire in 1971, this technique has been used and modified extensively since then in numerous studies of family violence.[2, 6, 25] The Conflict Tactics Technique scales were designed to measure intrafamily conflict in terms of the means used to resolve conflicts of interest.[26] The scale used contains eighteen items in three groups: 1) use of rational discussion and argument (discussed the issue calmly; got information to back up your side; brought in/tried to bring in someone to help settle things), 2) use of verbal and nonverbal expressions of hostility (insulted or swore at the other; sulked or refused to talk about it; stomped out of room or house; cried; did or said something to spite the other; threatened to hit or throw something at other; threw, smashed, hit, or kicked something), and 3) use of physical force or violence as a means of managing the conflict (threw something at the other; pushed, grabbed, shoved the

---

* The completion rate for the entire sample was 65%, varying from a low of 60% in metropolitan areas to a high of 72.3% in other areas.

other; slapped or spanked; kicked, bit, or hit with a fist; hit or tried to hit with something; beat up the other; threatened with a knife or gun; used knife or gun).*

Administration of the Conflict Tactics Technique involves presenting the subjects with the list of eighteen items, in the order enumerated above, and asking them to indicate what they did when they had a disagreement with the referent child in the past year and in the course of their relationship.

Reliability and validity. The reliability and validity of the Conflict Tactics Technique has been assessed over the five-year period of its development and modification. Pretests on more than 300 college students indicated that the indices have an adequate level of internal consistency reliability.[26] Bulcroft and Straus[6] provided evidence of concurrent validity. In addition, evidence of "construct validity" exists, in that data compiled in the pretests of the scale are in accord with previous empirical findings and theories.[26]

Advantages and disadvantages of the violence scale. An advantage of the violence scale, aside from previous evidence of its reliability, "concurrent" validity, and "construct" validity, is that the mode of administration increased the likelihood of the interviewer establishing rapport with the subject. The eight force and violence items came at the end of the list of conflict tactics. Presumably, this enhanced the likelihood that the subject would become committed to the interview and continue answering questions. Our analysis of the responses to the items indicates that there was no noticeable drop in the completion rate of items as the list moved from the rational scale questions to the most violent modes of conflict management.

Two disadvantages of the scale are that it focuses on conflict situations and does not allow for the measurement of the use of violence in situations where there was no "conflict of interest," and that it deals with the *commission* of acts only. We have no idea of the *consequences* of those acts, and thus have only a limited basis for projecting these statistics to the extent of the phenomenon "child abuse," since child abuse normally is thought to have injurious consequences for a child. While we may learn that a parent used a gun or a knife, and we can presume that this has negative consequences for a child, even if the child was not injured, we do not know what the actual consequences were.

Results

As proposed at the outset of this paper, "ordinary" physical punishment and "child abuse" are but two ends of a single continuum of violence toward children. In between are millions of parents whose use of physical force goes beyond mild punishment, but for various reasons does not get identified and labeled as child abuse.

Sixty-three percent of the respondents who had children between the ages of three and seventeen living at home mentioned at least one violent episode during the survey year (1975). The proportion of our sample reporting at least one violent occurrence in the course of raising the child was 73%.

---

* Copies of the scale used, containing questionnaire items and response categories, are available from the author on request.

Table 1

Types of Parent-to-Child Violence (N = 1146)[a]

| | Occurrence In Past Year | | | | |
| | Once | Twice | More Than Twice | Total | Occurrence Ever |
Incident					
Threw Something	1.3%	1.8%	2.3%	5.4%	9.6%
Pushed/Grabbed/Shoved	4.3	9.0	27.2	40.5	46.4
Slapped or Spanked	5.2	9.4	43.6	58.2	71.0
Kicked/Bit/Hit with Fist	0.7	0.8	1.7	3.2	7.7
Hit with Something	1.0	2.6	9.8	13.4	20.0
Beat Up	0.4	0.3	0.6	1.3	4.2
Threatened with Knife/Gun	0.1	0.0	0.0	0.1	2.8
Used Knife or Gun	0.1	0.0	0.0	0.1	2.9

[a] On some items, there were a few responses omitted, but figures for all incidents represent at least 1140 families.

As expected, and reported in TABLE 1, the milder forms of violence were more common. Slaps or spankings were mentioned by 58% of the respondents as having occurred in the previous year and by 71% of the parents as having ever taken place. Forty-one percent of the parents admitted pushing or shoving the referent child during 1975, while 46% stated that pushes or shoves had occurred some time in the past. Hitting with something was reported by thirteen percent of the parents for the last year and by twenty percent for the duration of their raising the referent child. Throwing an object was less common—approximately five percent of the parents did this in the survey year, while fewer than ten percent had ever thrown something at their referent child.

The more dangerous types of violence were the least frequent. However, extrapolating the data to the population of children three to seventeen years of age living with both parents produces an astoundingly large number of children who were kicked, bitten, punched, beat up, threatened with a gun or a knife, or had a gun or a knife actually used on them. First, looking at the number of parents who reported each type of violence, approximately three percent of the parents reported kicking, biting, or hitting the referent child with a fist in 1975; nearly eight percent stated that these acts had occurred at some point in the raising of the child. Slightly more than one percent of the respondents reported "beating up" (operationally defined as more than a single punch) the randomly selected referent child in the last year, and four percent stated that they had ever done this. One-tenth of one percent, or one in a thousand parents, admitted to threatening their child with a gun or a knife in 1975, while nearly three parents in 100 said they had ever threatened their child with such weapons. The same statistics were found for parents admitting actually using a gun or knife—one-tenth of a percent for the year, almost three percent ever.*

---

* We do not know exactly what is meant by *using* a gun or knife. It could mean a parent threw a knife at the child, or it could mean attempting to stab or actually stabbing the child; a gun could have been fired without the child being wounded. However, the fact is that these parents admit using the weapon, not just threatening its use.

One can extrapolate these frequencies to estimate how many children were victims of these serious modes of violence in 1975 and how many ever faced these types of violence. There were nearly 46 million children between the ages of three and seventeen years old who lived with both parents in 1975.[7] Of these children, between 3.1 and 4.0 million have been kicked, bitten, or punched by parents at some time in their lives, while between 1.0 and 1.9 million were kicked, bitten, or punched in 1975. Between 1.4 and 2.3 million children have been "beat up" while growing up, and between 275,000 and 750,000 three- to- seventeen-year-olds were "beat up" in 1975. Lastly, our data suggest that between 900,000 and 1.8 million American children between the ages of three and seventeen have ever had their parents use a gun or a knife on them. Our figures do not allow for a reliable extrapolation of how many children faced parents using guns and knives in 1975, but our estimate would be something close to 46,000 children (based on an incidence of one in 1000 children).

An examination of the data on violence used on children in 1975 indicates that violence typically represents a *pattern* of parent-child relations rather than an isolated event. Only in the case of using a gun or knife was the violent episode likely to be a one-time affair. While it is generally accepted that slaps, spankings, and shoves are frequently used techniques of child rearing, we find that even bites, kicks, punches, and using objects to hit children occur frequently in the families where they are employed.

Children at Risk

As stated earlier, our examination of violent acts without information on the consequences of those acts prevents us from accurately estimating how many children incurred physical harm from violence during any one year. Our problem is compounded by the fact that we rely on the subject's own definition of what is meant by "beating up" a child. In addition, we do not know what objects were used to hit the child (a pipe or a paddle?), and we do not know how the guns or knives were deployed. Nevertheless, we felt it was important to generate an estimate of children-at-risk. We chose to compile an "at-risk" index which combined the items we felt produced the highest probability of injuring or damaging the child (kicked, bit, or hit with a fist; hit with something; beat up; threatened with a knife or a gun; used a knife or a gun). Using this index, we found that 3.6% of the parents admitted to using at least one of these modes of violence at least once in 1975. Assuming the acts we indexed have a high potential of causing harm to the intended victim, between 1.4 million and 1.9 million children were vulnerable to physical injury from violence in 1975.

A Note on the Incidence Data and Extrapolations

The data on the incidence of physical violence between parents and children, and the extrapolations which produced estimates of the number of children who experienced violence and who are at risk of physical injury, ought to be considered *low estimates of violence toward children*. First, we are dealing with self-reports of violence. Although subjects who reported spanking or slapping their children may constitute an accurate estimate of incidence, the desire to give socially acceptable responses is likely to have caused many people to underreport the more serious

Table 2

Parent-to-Child Violence by Sex of Parent[a]

	In Past Year		Ever	
Incident	Father	Mother	Father	Mother
Threw Something	3.6%	6.8%*	7.5%	11.3%*
Pushed/Grabbed/Shoved	29.8	33.4	35.6	39.5
Slapped or Spanked	53.3	62.5**	67.7	73.6*
Kicked/Bit/Hit with Fist	2.5	4.0	6.7	8.7
Hit with Something	9.4	16.7**	15.7	23.6**
Beat Up	0.6	1.8	4.0	4.2
Threatened with Knife/Gun	0.2	0.0	3.1	2.6
Used Knife or Gun	0.2	0.0	3.1	2.7

[a] Reports of 523 fathers and 623 mothers; figures for all incidents represent at least 520 fathers and 619 mothers.
* $\chi^2 \leqslant .05$.
** $\chi^2 \leqslant .01$.

modes of violence. If one subject in a thousand answered that he used a gun or knife, it might be reasonable to assume that at least another one in a thousand used these weapons and did not admit to it in the interview. Second, we interviewed only "intact" families, where both adult males and females were in the household. If, as some believe, parental violence is more common in single-parent families, then our data will underestimate the number of children experiencing potentially damaging acts from their parents. Third, we examined violence used by only one of the two parents on the referent child. Lastly, our lower than expected response rate might mean that some highly violent families refused to be interviewed; if so, our incidence statistics might again be low estimates of violence toward children.

As a result of the sampling frame used and the methodological problems involved in using self-reports of violence, we see our statistics, although they may seem high to some, as being quite conservative and low estimates of the true level of violence toward children in the United States.

Violence Toward Children by Sex of Parent

Sixty-eight percent of the mothers and 58% of the fathers in our sample reported at least one violent act toward their child during the survey year. Seventy-six percent of the mothers and 71% of the fathers indicated at least one violent episode in the course of rearing their referent child. Our data on violence in the survey year indicate a small but significant difference between mothers and fathers using violence on their children. It has been frequently argued that mothers are more prone to use violence because they spend more time with their children. We hypothesize that the explanation for mothers' greater likelihood of using violence goes beyond the simple justification that they spend more time with the children. Our future analyses of the information gathered in our survey of violence in the family will examine this relationship from a number of points of view, including family power, coping ability, resources, and personality traits.

Examining the relationship between sex of the parent and various modes of violence used on children (see TABLE 2), we find that, for both the survey year and

Table 3

Parent-to-Child Violence by Sex of Child[a]

	In Past Year		Ever	
Incident	*Sons*	*Daughters*	*Sons*	*Daughters*
Threw Something	5.9%	4.4%	10.1%	8.8%
Pushed/Grabbed/Shoved	38.1	24.9**	43.9	30.7**
Slapped or Spanked	60.1	56.1	73.9	67.8*
Kicked/Bit/Hit with Fist	3.8	2.6	8.0	7.3
Hit with Something	14.9	11.2	21.5	18.1
Beat Up	1.6	0.7	4.2	4.0
Threatened with Knife/Gun	0.2	0.0	2.4	3.3
Used Knife or Gun	0.2	0.0	2.6	3.3

[a] Reports on 578 sons (responses reported for at least 574) and 547 daughters (responses for at least 545).
* $\chi^2 \leqslant .05$.
** $\chi^2 \leqslant .01$.

the duration of the relationship, mothers are more likely to throw something at the child, slap or spank the child, or hit the child with something. There are no significant differences between mothers and fathers with respect to any of the other forms of violence. It is interesting to note that even for the most serious forms of violence (beating up; kicking, biting, punching; using guns or knives), men and women are approximately equal in their disposition to use of these modes of violence on their children. This is important because it suggests that the management of children is one of the only situations in which women are as likely as men to resort to violence.

Violence Toward Children by Sex of the Child

While females are more likely to use violence in parent-child relations, male children are slightly more likely to be victims. Sixty-six percent of the sons and 61% of the daughters were struck at least once in the survey year, while 76% of the male children and 71% of the females were ever hit by their parents.

Why sons are slightly more likely than daughters to be victims of parental violence is open for debate. Some might argue that boys are more difficult to raise and commit more "punishable offenses" than daughters. Another hypothesis is that our society accepts and often values boys experiencing violence because it serves to "toughen them up." The data from the 1968 National Commission on the Causes and Prevention of Violence Survey seem to bear this out in that seven in ten people interviewed believed that is good for a boy to have a few fist fights while he is growing up.[23] Thus, experiencing violence might be considered part of the socialization process for boys and a less important "character builder" for girls.[24]

Data on violence in the survey year (TABLE 3) show that the only significant difference between boys and girls was whether they were pushed, grabbed, or shoved. The other forms of violence showed no significant differences between the sexes. In the course of growing up, boys are more likely to be pushed, grabbed, shoved, spanked, or slapped.

Table 4

Parent-to-Child Violence in Past Year by Age of Child

Incident	3-4 Years	5-9 Years	10-14 Years	15-17 Years
Threw Something	5.1%	7.0%	3.6%	5.1%
Pushed/Grabbed/Shoved	39.0	39.1	27.9	20.8*
Slapped or Spanked	84.1	79.9	47.9	23.0*
Kicked/Bit/Hit with Fist	6.2	3.2	2.2	2.5
Hit with Something	19.2	19.7	9.6	4.3*
Beat Up	1.1	0.9	1.1	1.7
Threatened with Knife/Gun	0.0	0.0	0.3	0.0
Used Knife or Gun	0.0	0.0	0.3	0.0
	(N = 177)[a]	(N = 346)[a]	(N = 365)[a]	(N = 236)[a]

[a] No more than three responses omitted on any category.
* $\chi^2 \leqslant .01$.

Violence Towards Children by Age of the Child

The literature on physical punishment and abuse of children presents various hypotheses and findings on the relationship between age and being punished or abused. A number of researchers and clinicians have proposed that the most dangerous period in a child's life is from three months to three years of age.[10, 11, 18] Bronfenbrenner[4] proposed that the highest rates of child abuse and battering occur among adolescents. Gil[6] discovered that half of the confirmed cases of child abuse were children over six years of age, while nearly one-fifth of the confirmed reports were children in their teens.

Our survey excluded parental relations with children three years of age or younger, since we also studied child-to-parent violence in the interview. Thus, our data cannot be used to infer the rate of violence used on infants.

During the survey year, younger children were most likely to be victims of some form of physical force. Eighty-six percent of children three and four years old had some mode of force used on them in 1975; 82% of the children five to nine had been hit; 54% of preteens and early teenage children (ten to fourteen years of age) were struck; and 33% of the referent children fifteen to seventeen years old were hit by their parents ($x^2 \leq .01$).

It appears that younger children are vulnerable to a wide range of forceful and violent acts. As shown in TABLE 4, preschoolers and children under nine years old were more likely to be pushed, grabbed, shoved, slapped, spanked, and hit with an object. The older children seemed more vulnerable to the severest types of violence, including being beaten up and having a gun or a knife used on them, although the differences are not statistically significant.

Again, there are a number of reasons why younger children are more frequent victims of parental violence. Parents may perceive difficulties in using reason to punish their younger children. A second reason might be that younger children interfere with their parents' activities more than do older children. Our future analyses of the data will focus on the factors associated with young children's susceptibility to being struck.

Discussion and Conclusions

These data on the incidence of parent-to-child violence only begin to scratch the surface of this very important topic. Our results indicate that violence toward children involves acts that go well beyond ordinary physical punishment and is an extensive and patterned phenomenon in parent-child relations. In addition, we see that mothers are the most likely users of violence, while sons and younger children are the more common victims.

A number of controversial points arise from our presentation. First, disagreement over our nominal and operational definitions of violence may lead some to disagree with our conclusion that violence is widespread in families. If someone views slaps and spankings as acceptable punishment, then they might dispute our statistics as being based on a too broadly constructed definition of violence. Although we believe there are many salient reasons for considering spankings and slaps violent, we would counter this argument by pointing to the statistics for beating up children or using a gun or a knife on a child. If a million or more children had guns or knives used on them in school, we would consider that a problem of epidemic proportions. The fact that these acts occur in the home tends to lessen concern about the impact and consequences. However, the impact and consequences are potentially dramatic, since the child is experiencing violence from those who claim love and affection for him.

A second point that will be raised about our findings is the question of bias and whether our respondents actually told the truth. We have spent seven years developing and testing the instruments used in this study. However, we do not know the actual validity of our findings or whether our subjects "told the truth." The major bias in this study of family violence is likely to be one of underreporting. We doubt that many subjects will report beating up their children or using a gun or a knife on them when they did not. Thus, our statistics are probably underestimates of the true level of parent-child violence in the United States. If one considers the possibility that, for every subject who admitted using a knife or a gun, an additional subject used these weapons but did not admit it, then our estimates of risk could be doubled to produce a true estimate of risk of physical violence.

Another issue that will be pursued after examining our data, and an issue we will pursue in later analyses, is the fact that people actually admitted using severe and dangerous forms of physical violence. Our tentative explanation of this is that many of our subjects did not consider kicking, biting, punching, beating up, shooting, or stabbing their children deviant. In other words, they may have admitted to these acts because they felt they were acceptable or tolerable ways of bringing up children. Thus, it may be that one major factor contributing to the high level of parent-child violence we have found is the normative acceptability of hitting one's children.

Despite the methodological problems, this is the first survey of parent-to-child violence based on a true cross-section of American families. Thus, the data presented here probably come closer to describing the real situation of violence toward children in America than anything available until now.

REFERENCES

1. AMERICAN HUMANE ASSOCIATION. 1974. *Highlights of the 1974 National Data.* American Humane Association, Denver. (mimeo)

2. ALLEN, C. AND STRAUS, M. 1975. "Resources, power, and husband-wife violence." Presented to the National Council on Family Relations, in Salt Lake City.

3. BLUMBERG, M. 1964. "When parents hit out." *Twentieth Century* 173 (Winter):39-44.

4. BRONFENBRENNER. U. 1958. "Socialization and social class throughout time and space." In *Readings in Social Psychology*, E. Macoby, T. Newcomb, and E. Hartley, eds. Holt, New York.

5. BRONFENBRENNER, U. 1974. "The origins of alienation." *Scientif. Amer.* 231:53.

6. BULCROFT, R. AND STRAUS, M. 1975. "Validity of husband, wife, and child reports of conjugal violence and power." Presented to the National Council on Family Relations, Salt Lake City.

7. BUREAU OF THE CENSUS. 1975. "Estimates of the population of the United States by age, sex, and race: 1970-1975." *Current Population Reports,* Series P-25, No. 614, Government Printing Office, Washington, D.C.

8. COHEN, S. AND SUSSMAN, A. 1975. "The incidence of child abuse in the United States." (unpublished)

9. ERLANGER, H. 1974. "Social class and corporal punishment in childrearing: a reassessment." *Amer. Sociol. Rev.* 39 (Feb.): 68-85.

10. FONTANA, V. 1973. *Somewhere a Child is Crying: Maltreatment—Causes and Prevention.* Macmillan, New York.

11. GALDSTON, R. 1965. "Observations of children who have been physically abused by their parents." *Amer. J. Psychiat.* 122(4):440-443.

12. GELLES, R. 1974. *The Violent Home: A Study of Physical Aggression Between Husbands and Wives.* Sage Publications, Beverly Hills, Calif.

13. GELLES, R. 1975. "The social construction of child abuse." *Amer. J. Orthopsychiat.* (April):363-371.

14. GELLES, R. 1978. "Methods for studying sensitive family topics." *Amer. J. Orthopsychiat.* 48(3):408-424.

15. GELLES, R. AND STRAUS, M. 1978. "Determinants of violence in the family: toward a theoretical integration." In *Contemporary Theories About the Family*, W. Burr et al., eds. Free Press, New York.

16. GIL, D. 1970. *Violence Against Children: Physical Child Abuse in the United States.* Harvard University Press, Cambridge, Mass.

17. GIL, D. 1975. "Unraveling child abuse." *Amer. J. Orthopsychiat.* 45(April): 364-358.

18. KEMPE, C. ET AL. 1962. "The battered child syndrome." *JAMA* 181(July 7):17-24.

19. KEMPE, C. 1971: "Pediatric implications of the battered baby syndrome." *Arch. Dis. Children* 46:28-37.

20. LIGHT, R. 1974. "Abused and neglected children in America: a study of alternative policies." *Harvard Ed. Rev.* 43(Nov.):556-598.

21. NAGI, R. 1975. "Child abuse and neglect programs: a national overview." *Children Today* 4(May-June):13-17.

22.   PEDIATRIC NEWS. 1975. "One child dies daily from abuse: parent probably was abuser." *Pediat. News* 9(April):3.

23.   STARK, R. AND MCEVOY, J. 1970. "Middle class violence." *Psychol. Today* 4(Nov.):52-65.

24.   STRAUS, M. 1971. "Some social antecendents of physical punishment: a linkage theory interpretation." *J. Marr. Fam.* 33(Nov.):658-663.

25.   STRAUS, M. 1974. "Leveling, civility, and violence in the family." *J. Marr. Fam.* 36(Feb.):13-30.

26.   STRAUS, M. 1978. "Measuring intrafamily conflict and violence: the conflict tactics (CT) scales." *J. Marr. Fam.* (in press).

27.   STRAUS, M., GELLES, R. AND STEINMETZ, S. 1976. "Violence in the family: an assessment of knowledge and research needs." Presented to the American Association for the Advancement of Science, in Boston.

28.   UNITED STATES SENATE. 1973. Hearing Before the Subcommittee on Children and Youth of the Committee on Labor and Public Welfare. United States Senate, 93rd Congress First Session, on S. 1191 Child Abuse Prevention Act, U.S. Government Printing Office, Washington, D.C.

3

The Battered-Child Syndrome*

C. Henry Kempe, M.D.,
Frederic N. Silverman, M.D.,
Brandt F. Steele, M.D.,
William Droegemueller, M.D.,
and Henry K. Silver, M.D.

The Battered-Child Syndrome is a term used by us to characterize a clinical condition in young children who have received serious physical abuse, generally from a parent or foster parent. The condition has also been described as "unrecognized trauma" by radiologists, orthopedists, pediatricians, and social service workers. It is a significant cause of childhood disability and death. Unfortunately, it is frequently not recognized or, if diagnosed, is inadequately handled by the physician because of hesitation to bring the case to the attention of the proper authorities.

Incidence

In an attempt to collect data on the incidence of this problem, we undertook a nation-wide survey of hospitals which were asked to indicate the incidence of this syndrome in a one-year period. Among 71 hospitals replying, 302 such cases were reported to have occurred; 33 of the children died; and 85 suffered permanent brain

---

* C. H. Kempe, Frederic N. Silverman, Brandt F. Steele, William Droegemueller, and Henry K. Silver, "The Battered Child Syndrome," *JAMA*, 181(1):17-24. Copyright © 1962, American Medical Association; except Figures 2, 3, and 4, copyright © 1962, American Roentgen Ray Society. All matter reproduced by permission.

injury. In one-third of the cases proper medical diagnosis was followed by some type of legal action. We also surveyed 77 District Attorneys who reported that they had knowledge of 447 cases in a similar one-year period. Of these, 45 died, and 29 suffered permanent brain damage; court action was initiated in 46% of this group. This condition has been a particularly common problem in our hospitals; on a single day, in November, 1961, the Pediatric Service of the Colorado General Hospital was caring for 4 infants suffering from the parent-inflicted battered-child syndrome. Two the 4 died of their central nervous system trauma; 1 subsequently died suddenly in an unexplained manner 4 weeks after discharge from the hospital while under the care of its parents, while the fourth is still enjoying good health.

Clinical Manifestations

The clinical manifestations of the battered-child syndrome vary widely from those cases in which the trauma is very mild and is often unsuspected and unrecognized, to those who exhibit the most florid evidence of injury to the soft tissues and skeleton. In the former group, the patients' signs and symptoms may be considered to have resulted from failure to thrive from some other cause or to have been produced by a metabolic disorder, an infectious process, or some other disturbance. In these patients specific findings of trauma such as bruises or characteristic roentgenographic changes as described below may be misinterpreted and their significance not recognized.

The battered-child syndrome may occur at any age, but, in general, the affected children are younger than 3 years. In some instances the clinical manifestations are limited to those resulting from a single episode of trauma, but more often the child's general health is below par, and he shows evidence of neglect including poor skin hygiene, multiple soft tissue injuries, and malnutrition. One often obtains a history of previous episodes suggestive of parental neglect or trauma. A marked discrepancy between clinical findings and historical data as supplied by the parents is a major diagnostic feature of the battered-child syndrome. The fact that no new lesions, either of the soft tissue or of the bone, occur while the child is in the hospital or in a protected environment lends added weight to the diagnosis and tends to exclude many diseases of the skeletal or hemopoietic systems in which lesions may occur spontaneously or after minor trauma. Subdural hematoma, with or without fracture of the skull, is, in our experience, an extremely frequent finding even in the absence of fractures of the long bones. In an occasional case the parent or parent-substitute may also have assaulted the child by administering an overdose of a drug or by exposing the child to natural gas or other toxic substances. The characteristic distribution of these multiple fractures and the observation that the lesions are in different stages of healing are of additional value in making the diagnosis.

In most instances, the diagnostic bone lesions are observed incidental to examination for purposes other than evaluation for possible abuse. Occasionally, examination following known injury discloses signs of other, unsuspected, skeletal involvement. When parental assault is under consideration, radiologic examination of the entire skeleton may provide objective confirmation. Following diagnosis, radiologic examination can document the healing of lesions and reveal the appearance of new lesions if additional trauma has been inflicted.

The radiologic manifestations of trauma to growing skeletal structures are the same whether or not there is a history of injury. Yet there is reluctance on the part of many physicians to accept the radiologic signs as indications of repetitive trauma and possible abuse. This reluctance stems from the emotional unwillingness of the physician to consider abuse as the cause of the child's difficulty and also because of unfamiliarity with certain aspects of fracture healing so that he is unsure of the significance of the lesions that are present. To the informed physician, the bones tell a story the child is too young or too frightened to tell.

Psychiatric Aspects

Psychiatric knowledge pertaining to the problem of the battered child is meager, and the literature on the subject is almost nonexistent. The type and degree of physical attack varies greatly. At one extreme, there is direct murder of children. This is usually done by a parent or other close relative, and, in these individuals, a frank psychosis is usually readily apparent. At the other extreme are those cases where no overt harm has occurred, and one parent, more often the mother, comes to the psychiatrist for help, filled with anxiety and guilt related to fantasies of hurting the child. Occasionally the disorder has gone beyond the point of fantasy and has resulted in severe slapping or spanking. In such cases the adult is usually responsive to treatment; it is not known whether or not the disturbance in these adults would progress to the point where they would inflict significant trauma on the child.

Between these 2 extremes are a large number of battered children with mild to severe injury which may clear completely or result in permanent damage or even death after repeated attack. Descriptions of such children have been published by numerous investigators including radiologists, orthopedists, and social workers. The latter have reported on their studies of investigations of families in which children have been beaten and of their work in effecting satisfactory placement for the protection of the child. In some of these published reports the parents, or at least the parent who inflicted the abuse, have been found to be of low intelligence. Often, they are described as psychopathic or sociopathic characters. Alcoholism, sexual promiscuity, unstable marriages, and minor criminal activities are reportedly common amongst them. They are immature, impulsive, self-centered, hypersensitive, and quick to react with poorly controlled aggression. Data in some cases indicate that such attacking parents had themselves been subject to some degree of attack from their parents in their own childhood.

Beating of children, however, is not confined to people with a psychopathic personality or of borderline socioeconomic status. It also occurs among people with good education and stable financial and social background. However, from the scant data that are available, it would appear that in these cases, too, there is a defect in character structure which allows aggressive impulses to be expressed too freely. There is also some suggestion that the attacking parent was subjected to similar abuse in childhood. It would appear that one of the most important factors to be found in families where parental assault occurs is "to do unto others as you have been done by." This is not surprising; it has long been recognized by psychologists and social anthropologists that patterns of child rearing, both good and bad, are passed from one generation to the next in relatively unchanged form.

Psychologically, one could describe this phenomenon as an identification with the aggressive parent, this identification occurring despite strong wishes of the person to be different. Not infrequently the beaten infant is a product of an unwanted pregnancy, a pregnancy which began before marriage, too soon after marriage, or at some other time felt to be extremely inconvenient. Sometimes several children in one family have been beaten; at other times one child is singled out for attack while others are treated quite lovingly. We have also seen instances in which the sex of the child who is severely attacked is related to very specific factors in the context of the abusive parent's neurosis.

It is often difficult to obtain the information that a child has been attacked by its parent. To be sure, some of the extremely sociopathic characters will say, "Yeah, Johnny would not stop crying so I hit him. So what? He cried harder so I hit him harder." Sometimes one spouse will indicate that the other was the attacking person, but more often there is complete denial of any knowledge of injury to the child and the maintenance of an attitude of complete innocence on the part of both parents. Such attitudes are maintained despite the fact that evidence of physical attack is obvious and that the trauma could not have happened in any other way. Denial by the parents of any involvement in the abusive episode may, at times, be a conscious, protective device, but in other instances it may be a denial based upon psychological repression. Thus, one mother who seemed to have been the one who injured her baby had complete amnesia for the episodes in which her aggression burst forth so strikingly.

In addition to the reluctance of the parents to give information regarding the attacks on their children, there is another factor which is of great importance and extreme interest as it relates to the difficulty in delving into the problem of parental neglect and abuse. This is the fact that physicians have great difficulty both in believing that parents could have attacked their children and in undertaking the essential questioning of parents on this subject. Many physicians find it hard to believe that such an attack could have occurred and they attempt to obliterate such suspicions from their minds, even in the face of obvious circumstantial evidence. The reason for this is not clearly understood. One possibility is that the arousal of the physician's antipathy in response to such situations is so great that it is easier for the physician to deny the possibility of such attack than to have to deal with the excessive anger which surges up in him when he realizes the truth of the situation. Furthermore, the physician's training and personality usually makes it quite difficult for him to assume the role of policeman or district attorney and start questioning patients as if he were investigating a crime. The humanitarian-minded physician finds it most difficult to proceed when he is met with protestations of innocence from the aggressive parent, especially when the battered child was brought to him voluntarily.

Although the technique wherein the physician obtains the necessary information in cases of child beating is not adequately solved, certain routes of questioning have been particularly fruitful in some cases. One spouse may be asked about the other spouse in relation to unusual or curious behavior or for direct description of dealings with the baby. Clues to the parents' character and pattern of response may be obtained by asking questions about sources of worry and tension. Revealing answers may be brought out by questions concerning the baby such as, "Does he cry a lot? Is he stubborn? Does he obey well? Does he eat well? Do you have problems in controlling him?" A few general questions concerning the parents' own ideas of how they themselves were brought up may bring forth illuminating answers; interviews with grandparents or other relatives may elicit additional suggestive data. In some cases, psychological tests may disclose strong aggressive tendencies, impulsive behavior, and lack of adequate mechanisms of controlling impulsive behavior. In other cases only prolonged contact in a psychotherapeutic milieu will lead to a complete understanding of the background and circumstances surrounding the parental attack. Observation by nurses or other ancillary personnel of the behavior of the parents in relation to the hospitalized infant is often extremely valuable.

The following 2 condensed case histories depict some of the problems encountered in dealing with the battered-child syndrome.

Report of Cases

Case 1.—The patient was brought to the hospital at the age of 3 months because of enlargement of the head, convulsions, and spells of unconsciousness. Examination revealed bilateral subdural hematomas, which were later operated upon with great improvement in physical status. There had been a hospital admission at the age of one month because of a fracture of the right femur, sustained "when the baby turned over in the crib and caught its leg in the slats." There was no history of any head trauma except "when the baby was in the other hospital a child threw a little toy at her and hit her in the head." The father had never been alone with the baby, and the symptoms of difficulty appeared to have begun when the mother had been caring for the baby. Both parents showed concern and requested the best possible care for their infant. The father, a graduate engineer, related instances of impulsive behavior, but these did not appear to be particularly abnormal, and he showed appropriate emotional concern over the baby's appearance and impending operation. The mother, aged 21, a high school graduate, was very warm, friendly, and gave all the appearance of having endeavored to be a good mother. However, it was noted by both nurses and physicians that she did not react as appropriately or seem as upset about the baby's appearance as did her husband. From interviews with the father and later with the mother, it became apparent that she had occasionally shown very impulsive, angry behavior, sometimes acting rather strangely and doing bizarre things which she could not explain nor remember. This was their first child and had resulted from an unwanted pregnancy which had occurred almost immediately after marriage and before the parents were ready for it. Early in pregnancy the mother had made statements about giving the baby away, but by the time of delivery she was apparently delighted with the baby and seemed to be quite fond of it. After many interviews, it became apparent that the mother had identified herself with her own mother who had also been unhappy with her first pregnancy and had frequently beaten her children. Despite very strong conscious wishes to be a kind, good mother, the mother of our patient was evidently repeating the behavior of her own mother toward herself. Although an admission of guilt was not obtained, it seemed likely that the mother was the one responsible for attacking the child; only after several months of treatment did the amnesia for the aggressive outbursts begin to lift. She responded well to treatment, but for a prolonged period after the infant left the hospital the mother was not allowed alone with her.

Case 2.—This patient was admitted to the hospital at the age of 13 months with signs of central nervous system damage and was found to have a fractured skull. The parents were questioned closely, but no history of trauma could be elicited. After one week in the hospital no further treatment was deemed necessary, so the infant was discharged home in the care of her mother, only to return a few hours later with hemiparesis, a defect in vision, and a new depressed skull fracture on the other side of the head. There was no satisfactory explanation for the new skull fracture, but the mother denied having been involved in causing the injury, even though the history revealed that the child had changed markedly during the hour when the mother had been alone with her. The parents of this child were a young, middle-class couple who, in less than 2 years of marriage, had been separated, divorced, and remarried. Both felt that the infant had been unwanted and had come too soon in the marriage. The mother gave a history of having had a "nervous breakdown" during her teens. She had received psychiatric assistance because she had been markedly upset early in the pregnancy. Following an uneventful delivery, she had been depressed and had received further psychiatric aid and 4 electroshock treatments. The mother tended to gloss over the unhappiness during the pregnancy and stated that she was quite delighted when the baby was born. It is interesting to note that the baby's first symptoms of difficulty began the first day after its first birthday, suggesting an "anniversary reaction." On psychological and neurological examination, this mother showed definite signs of organic brain damage probably of lifelong duration and possibly related to her own prematurity. Apparently her significant intellectual defects had been camouflaged by an attitude of coy, naïve, cooperative sweetness which distracted attention from her deficits. It was noteworthy that she had managed to complete a year of college work despite a borderline I.Q. It appeared that the impairment in mental functioning was probably the prime factor associated with poor control of aggressive impulses. It is known that some individuals may react with aggressive attack or psychosis when faced with demands beyond their intellectual capacity. This mother was not allowed to have unsupervised care of her child.

Up to the present time, therapeutic experience with the parents of battered children is minimal. Counseling carried on in social agencies has been far from successful or rewarding. We know of no reports of successful psychotherapy in such cases. In general, psychiatrists feel that treatment of the so-called psychopath or sociopath is rarely successful. Further psychological investigation of the character structure of attacking parents is sorely needed. Hopefully, better understanding of the mechanisms involved in the control and release of aggressive impulses will aid in the earlier diagnosis, prevention of attack, and treatment of parents, as well as give us better ability to predict the likelihood of further attack in the future. At present, there is no safe remedy in the situation except the separation of battered children from their insufficiently protective parents.

Techniques of Evaluation

A physician needs to have a high initial level of suspicion of the diagnosis of the battered-child syndrome in instances of subdural hematoma, multiple unexplained fractures at different stages of healing, failure to thrive, when soft tissue swellings or skin bruising are present, or in any other situation where the degree and type of injury is at variance with the history given regarding its occurrence or in any child who dies suddenly. Where the problem of parental abuse comes up for consideration, the physician should tell the parents that it is his opinion that the injury should not occur if the child were adequately protected, and he should indicate that he would welcome the parents giving him the full story so that he might be able to give greater assistance to them to prevent similar occurrences from taking place in the future. The idea that they can now help the child by giving a very complete history of circumstances surrounding the injury sometimes helps the parents feel that they are atoning for the wrong that they have done. But in many instances, regardless of the approach used in attempting to elicit a full story of the abusive incident(s), the parents will continue to deny that they were guilty of any wrongdoing. In talking with the parents, the physician may sometimes obtain added information by showing that he understands their problem and that he wishes to be of aid to them as well as to the child. He may help them reveal the circumstances of the injuries by pointing out reasons that they may use to explain their action. If it is suggested that "new parents sometimes lose their tempers and are a little too forceful in their actions," the parents may grasp such a statement as the excuse for their actions. Interrogation should not be angry or hostile but should be sympathetic and quiet with the psysician indicating his assurance that the diagnosis is well established on the basis of objective findings and that all parties, including the parents, have an obligation to avoid a repetition of the circumstances leading to the trauma. The doctor should recognize that bringing the child for medical attention in itself does not necessarily indicate that the parents were innocent of wrongdoing and are showing proper concern; trauma may have been inflicted during times of uncontrollable temporary rage. Regardless of the physician's personal reluctance to become involved, complete investigation is necessary for the child's protection so that a decision can be made as to the necessity of placing the child away from the parents until matters are fully clarified.

Often, the guilty parent is the one who gives the impression of being the more normal. In 2 recent instances young physicians have assumed that the mother was at fault because she was unkempt and depressed while the father, in each case a military man with good grooming and polite manners, turned out to be the psychopathic member of the family. In these instances it became apparent that the mother had good reason to be depressed.

Radiologic Features

Radiologic examination plays 2 main roles in the problem of child-abuse. Initially, it is a tool for case finding, and, subsequently, it is useful as a guide in management.

The diagnostic signs result from a combination of circumstances: age of the patient, nature of the injury, the time that has elapsed before the examination is carried out, and whether the traumatic episode was repeated or occurred only once.

Age.—As a general rule, the children are under 3 years of age; most, in fact are infants. In this age group the relative amount of radiolucent cartilage is great; therefore, anatomical disruptions of cartilage without gross deformity are radiologically invisible or difficult to demonstrate (Fig. 1a). Since the periosteum of infants is less securely attached to the underlying bone than in older children and adults, it is more easily and extensively stripped from the shaft by hemorrhage than in older patients. In infancy massive subperiosteal hematomas may follow injury and elevate the active periosteum so that new bone formation can take place around and remote from the parent shaft (Figs. 1c and 2).

Nature of Injury.—The ease and frequency with which a child is seized by his arms or legs make injuries to the appendicular skeleton the most common in this syndrome. Even when bony injuries are present elsewhere, e.g., skull, spine, or ribs, signs of injuries to the extremities are usually present. The extremities are the "handles" for rough handling, whether the arm is pulled to bring a reluctant child to his feet or to speed his ascent upstairs or whether the legs are held while swinging the tiny body in a punitive way or in an attempt to enforce corrective measures. The

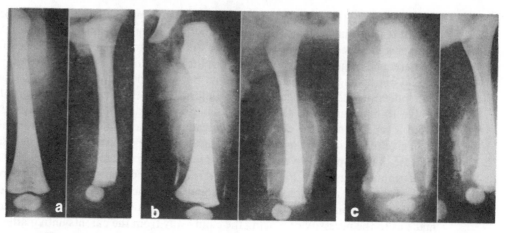

Fig. 1.—Male, 5 months: *a*, Initial films taken 3 to 4 days after onset of knee swelling. Epiphyseal separation shown in lateral projection with small metaphyseal chip shown in frontal projection; *b*, Five days later, there was beginning reparative change; *c*, Twelve days later (16 days after onset), there was extensive reparative change, history of injury unknown, but parents were attempting to teach child to walk at 5 months.

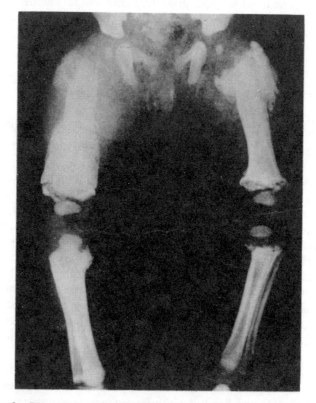

Fig. 2.—Female, 7½ months with a history of recurring abuse, including being shaken while held by legs 4-6 weeks prior to film. Note recent (2-3 weeks) metaphyseal fragmentation, older (4-6 weeks) periosteal reaction, and remote (2-4 months) external cortical thickening. Note also normal osseous structure of uninjured pelvic bones. (By permission of *Amer. J. Roentgenol.*)

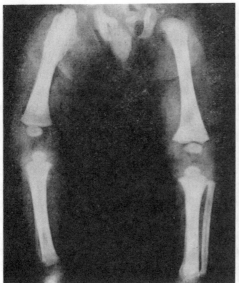

Fig. 3.—Male, 5 months, pulled by legs from collapsing bathinette 6 weeks earlier. Epiphyseal separation, right hip, shown by position of capital ossification center. Healing subperiosteal hematoma adjacent to it. Healing metaphyseal lesions in left knee, healing periosteal reactions (mild) in left tibia. No signs of systemic disease. (By permission of *Amer. J. Roentgenol.*)

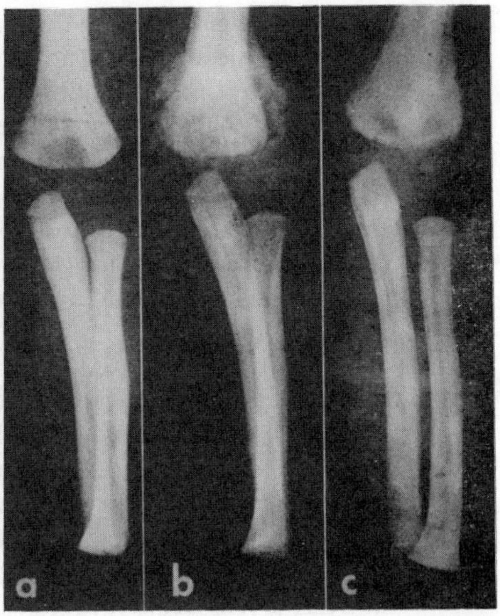

Fig. 4.—Female 7½ months; *a*, Elbow injured 30 hours before, except for thickened cortex from previous healed reactions, no radiologic signs of injury; *b*, Fifteen days after injury, irregular productive reaction, clinically normal joint; *c*, Three weeks after *b*, organization and healing progressing nicely. (By permission of *Amer. J. Roentgenol.*)

forces applied by an adult hand in grasping and seizing usually involve traction and torsion; these are the forces most likely to produce epiphyseal separations and periosteal shearing (Figs. 1 and 3). Shaft fractures result from direct blows or from bending and compression forces.

Time After Injury That the X-Ray Examination Is Made.—This is important in evaluating known or suspected cases of child-abuse. Unless gross fractures, dislocations, or epiphyseal separations were produced, no signs of bone injury are found during the first week after a specific injury. Reparative changes may first become manifest about 12 to 14 days after the injury and can increase over the subsequent weeks depending on the extent of initial injury and the degree of repetition (Fig. 4). Reparative changes are more active in the growing bones of children than in adults and are reflected radiologically in the excessive new bone reaction. Histologically, the reaction has been confused with neoplastic change by those unfamiliar with the vigorous reactions of young growing tissue.

Repetition of Injury.—This is probably the most important factor in producing diagnostic radiologic signs of the syndrome. The findings may depend on diminished immobilization of an injured bone leading to recurring macro-and micro-trauma in the area of injury and healing, with accompanying excessive local reaction and hemorrhage, and ultimately, exaggerated repair. Secondly, repetitive injury may produce bone lesions in one area at one time, and in another area at another, producing lesions in several areas and in different stages of healing (Fig. 3).

Thus, the classical radiologic features of the battered-child syndrome are usually found in the appendicular skeleton in very young children. There may be irregularities of mineralization in the metaphyses of some of the major tubular bones with slight malalignment of the adjacent epiphyseal ossification center. An overt fracture may be present in another bone. Elsewhere, there may be abundant and active but well-calcified subperiosteal reaction with widening from the shaft toward one end of the bone. One or more bones may demonstrate distinctly thickened cortices, residuals of previously healed periosteal reactions. In addition, the radiographic features of a subdural hematoma with or without obvious skull fracture may be present.

Differential Diagnosis.—The radiologic features are so distinct that other diseases generally are considered only because of the reluctance to accept the implications of the bony lesions. Unless certain aspects of bone healing are considered, the pertinent findings may be missed. In many cases roentgenographic examination is only undertaken soon after known injury; if a fracture is found, reexamination is done after reduction and immobilization; and, if satisfactory positioning has been obtained, the next examination is usually not carried out for a period of 6 weeks when the cast is removed. Any interval films that may have been taken prior to this time probably would have been unsatisfactory since the fine details of the bony lesions would have been obscured by the cast. If fragmentation and bone production are seen, they are considered to be evidence of repair rather than manifestations of multiple or repetitive trauma. If obvious fracture or the knowledge of injury is absent, the bony changes may be considered to be the result of scurvy, syphilis, infantile cortical hyperostoses, or other conditions. The distribution of lesions in the abused child is unrelated to rates of growth; moreover, an extensive lesion may be present at the slow-growing end of a bone which otherwise is normally mineralized and shows no evidence of metabolic disorder at its rapidly growing end.

Scurvy is commonly suggested as an alternative diagnosis, since it also produces large calcifying subperiosteal hemorrhages due to trauma and local exaggerations most marked in areas of rapid growth. However, scurvy is a systemic disease in which all of the bones show the generalized osteoporosis associated with the disease. The dietary histories of most children with recognized trauma have not been grossly abnormal, and whenever the vitamin C content of the blood has been determined, it has been normal.

In the first months of life *syphilis* can result in metaphyseal and periosteal lesions similar to those under discussion. However, the bone lesions of syphilis tend to be symmetrical and are usually accompanied by other stigmata of the disease. Serological tests should be obtained in questionable cases.

Osteogenesis imperfecta also has bony changes which may be confused with those due to trauma, but it too is a generalized disease, and evidence of the disorder should be present in the bones which are not involved in the disruptive-productive reaction. Even when skull fractures are present, the mosaic ossification pattern of the cranial vault, characteristic of osteogenesis imperfecta, is not seen in the battered-child syndrome. Fractures in osteogenesis imperfecta are commonly of the shafts; they usually occur in the metaphyseal regions in the battered-child syndrome. Blue sclerae, skeletal deformities, and a family history of similar abnormalities were absent in reported instances of children with unrecognized trauma.

Productive diaphyseal lesions may occur in *infantile cortical hyperostosis*, but the metaphyseal lesions of unrecognized trauma easily serve to differentiate the 2 conditions. The characteristic mandibular involvement of infantile cortical hyperostosis does not occur following trauma although obvious mandibular fracture may be produced.

Evidence that repetitive unrecognized trauma is the cause of the bony changes found in the battered-child syndrome is, in part, derived from the finding that similar roentgenographic findings are present in *paraplegic patients with sensory deficit* and in patients with *congenital indifference to pain*; in both of whom similar pathogenic mechanisms operate. In paraplegic children unappreciated injuries have resulted in radiologic pictures with irregular metaphyseal rarefactions, exaggerated subperiosteal new bone formation, and ultimate healing with residual external cortical thickening comparable to those in the battered-child sydrome. In paraplegic adults, excessive callus may form as a consequence of the lack of immobilization, and the lesion may be erroneously diagnosed as osteogenic sarcoma. In children with congenital indifference (or insensitivity) to pain, identical radiologic manifestations may be found.

To summarize, the radiologic manifestations of trauma are specific, and the metaphyseal lesions in particular occur in no other disease of which we are aware. The findings permit a radiologic diagnosis even when the clinical history seems to refute the possibility of trauma. Under such circumstances, the history must be reviewed, and the child's environment, carefully investigated.

Management

The principal concern of the physician should be to make the correct diagnosis so that he can institute proper therapy and make certain that a similar event will not occur again. He should report possible willful trauma to the police department or any special children's protective service that operates in his community. The report that he makes should be restricted to the objective findings which can be verified and, where possible, should be supported by photographs and roentgenograms. For hospitalized patients, the hospital director and the social service department should be notified. In many states the hospital is also required to report any case of possible unexplained injury to the proper authorities. The physician should acquaint himself with the facilities available in private and public agencies that provide protective services for children. These include children's humane societies, divisions of welfare departments, and societies for the prevention of cruelty to children. These, as well as the police department, maintain a close association with the juvenile court. Any of these agencies may be of assistance in bringing the case before the court which alone has the legal power to sustain a dependency petition for temporary or permanent separation of the child from the parents' custody. In addition to the legal investigation, it is usually helpful to have an evaluation of the psychological and social factors in the case; this should be started while the child is still in the hospital. If necessary, a court order should be obtained so that such investigation may be performed.

In many instances the prompt return of the child to the home is contraindicated because of the threat that additional trauma offers to the child's health and life.

Temporary placement with relatives or in a well-supervised foster home is often indicated in order to prevent further tragic injury or death to a child who is returned too soon to the original dangerous environment. All too often, despite the apparent cooperativeness of the parents and their apparent desire to have the child with them, the child returns to his home only to be assaulted again and suffer permanent brain damage or death. Therefore, the bias should be in favor of the child's safety; everything should be done to prevent repeated trauma, and the physician should not be satisfied to return the child to an environment where even a moderate risk of repetition exists.

Summary

The battered-child syndrome, a clinical condition in young children who have received serious physical abuse, is a frequent cause of permanent injury or death. Although the findings are quite variable, the syndrome should be considered in any child exhibiting evidence of possible trauma or neglect (fracture of any bone, subdural hematoma, multiple soft tissue injuries, poor skin hygiene, or malnutrition) or where there is a marked discrepancy between the clinical findings and the historical data as supplied by the parents. In cases where a history of specific injury is not available, or in any child who dies suddenly, roentgenograms of the entire skeleton should still be obtained in order to ascertain the presence of characteristic multiple bony lesions in various stages of healing.

Psychiatric factors are probably of prime importance in the pathogenesis of the disorder, but our knowledge of these factors is limited. Parents who inflict abuse on their children do not necessarily have psychopathic or sociopathic personalities or come from borderline socioeconomic groups, although most published cases have been in these categories. In most cases some defect in character structure is probably present; often parents may be repeating the type of child care practiced on them in their childhood.

Physicians, because of their own feelings and their difficulty in playing a role that they find hard to assume, may have great reluctance in believing that parents were guilty of abuse. They may also find it difficult to initiate proper investigation so as to assure adequate management of the case. Above all, the physician's duty and responsibility to the child requires a full evaluation of the problem and a guarantee that the expected repetition of trauma will not be permitted to occur.

REFERENCES

1.   SNEDECOR, S. T.; KNAPP, R. E.; and WILSON, H. B.: "Traumatic Ossifying Periostitis of Newborn," *Surg Gynec Obstet* 61:385-387, 1935.

2.   CAFFEY, J.: "Multiple Fractures in Long Bones of Infants Suffering from Chronic Subdural Hematoma," *Amer J Roentgenol* 56:163-173 (Aug.) 1946.

3.   SNEDECOR, S. T., and WILSON, H. B.: "Some Obstetrical Injuries to Long Bones," *J Bone Joint Surg* 31A:378-384 (April) 1949.

4.   SMITH, M. J.: "Subdural Hematoma with Multiple Fractures," *Amer J Roentgenol* 63:342-344 (March) 1950.

5.   FRAUENBERGER, G. S., and LIS, E. F.: "Multiple Fractures Associated with Subdural Hematoma in Infancy," *Pediatrics* 6:890-892 (Dec.) 1950.

6.   BARMEYER, G. H.; ALDERSON, L. R.; and COX, W. B.: "Traumatic Periostitis in Young Children," *J Pediat* 38:184-190 (Feb.) 1951.

7.   SILVERMAN, F.: "Roentgen Manifestations of Unrecognized Skeletal Trauma in Infants," *Amer J Roentgenol* 69:413-426 (March) 1953.

8.   WOOLLEY, P. V., Jr., and EVANS, W. A., Jr.: "Significance of Skeletal Lesions in Infants Resembling Those of Traumatic Origin," *JAMA* 158:539-543 (June) 1955.

9.   BAKWIN, H.: "Multiple Skeletal Lesions in Young Children Due to Trauma," *J Pediat* 49:7-15 (July) 1956.

10.   CAFFEY, J.: "Some Traumatic Lesions in Growing Bones Other Than Fractures and Dislocations: Clinical and Radiological Features," *Brit J Radiol* 30:225-238 (May) 1957.

11.   WESTON, W. J.: "Metaphyseal Fractures in Infancy." *J Bone Joint Surg (Brit)* (no. 4) 39B:694-700 (Nov.) 1957.

12.   FISHER, S. H.: "Skeletal Manifestations of Parent-Induced Trauma in Infants and Children," *Southern Med J* 51:956-960 (Aug.) 1958.

13.   MILLER, D. S.: "Fractures Among Children," *Minnesota Med* 42:1209-1213 (Sept.) 1959; 42:1414-1425 (Oct.) 1959.

14.   SILVER, H. K., and KEMPE, C. H.: "Problem of Parental Criminal Neglect and Severe Physical Abuse of Children," *J Dis Child* 95:528, 1959.

15.   ALTMAN, D. H., and SMITH, R. L.: "Unrecognized Trauma in Infants and Children," *J Bone Joint Surg (Amer)* 42A:407-413 (April) 1960.

16.   ELMER, E.: "Abused Young Children Seen in Hospitals," *Soc Work* (no. 4) 5:98-102 (Oct.) 1960.

17.   GWINN, J. L.; LEWIN, K. W.; and PETERSON, H. G., Jr.: "Roentgenographic Manifestations of Unsuspected Trauma in Infancy," *JAMA* 176:926-929 (June 17) 1961.

18.   BOARDMAN, H. E.: "Project to Rescue Children from Inflicted Injuries," *Soc Work* (no. 1) 7:43 (Jan.) 1962.

4

History and Demography of Child Abuse *

Theo Solomon, Ph.D.

A historic and demographic discourse at a gathering of this nature is usually provided for three purposes:

1. To offer an informational background to those who are not aware of or are not up to date about a particular phenomenon.

2. To ring the alarm of crisis pointing to the seriousness and pervasiveness of the phenomenon discussed.

3. To provide a perspective from which to initiate discussion.

As to the first two purposes your attendance demonstrates your concern and your alarm. Moreover, other speakers shall provide particulars on these points.

I shall attempt to provide the perspective for subsequent discussion.

History

In order to provide this perspective, I wish to define some basic terminology regarding acts performed in concert and/or individually upon children.

Infanticide has been practiced in almost every nation, both civilized and uncivilized since recorded time. This act has been responsible for more child deaths than any other single cause in history, other than possibly bubonic plague.

Its two characteristics have been the tacit acceptance or active participation by elements in the society in which it was found, and a rationale for its existence, which is generally woven into the fabric and culture of that society. In most cases infanticide has involved the infliction of body trauma upon a newborn child so as to willfully and knowingly cause death. This does not exclude the less common practices of intentional neglect at birth, or the ritual killing of older children. The rationales for this practice have generally been (1) religious appeasement and reactions to prophecies of doom; (2) collective or individual acts of faith and proofs of worthiness; (3) Darwinian survival and Malthusian population control.

Characteristically, the onus of individual responsibility for the act is transferred to a higher institution, leaving the individual psyche undamaged in the process. Parenthetically, our system of capital punishment functions in a similar manner.

Biblical and mythological examples are readily available. It will suffice to recall the stories of Abraham and Isaac, Moses and Medea, and to recount the lesser known story of King Nimrod of Babylon. King Nimrod, upon being informed by his astrologer that a boy would be born in Mesopotamia who would declare war upon the king, slew every first-born in his kingdom. Historic calculation places the number slain at 70,000. The New Testament begins with the "slaughter of the innocents" from which Jesus was saved.

In classic times, Seneca, Plato, and Aristotle maintained that killing defective children was a wise custom. In early Scandinavia a ceremony called *Wasser weihe* was the occasion for a father's decision to kill or not kill a newborn child. Infanticide had been reported as a regular feature of numerous cultures including Eskimo, Polynesian, Egyptian, African, American Indian, and Australian aborigine. As late as 1837 female infanticide was permitted in China and until the early nineteenth century Hindu women in Bengal cast newborn children into the Ganges River.

With the arrival of urbanization, industrialization, and technological change, insofar as they altered the value of children and parents to each other, a new phenomenon developed—that of *child abuse*. By definition, this practice differed in some respects from infanticide in that the motives for the abuse might generally be classified as exploitation or profit, or punishment or salvation.

Moreover, the abused were generally not newly born but children of working age, that is, 5 years and older.

The writings of Charles Dickens about the hard lot of children in a growing industrial society are indicative of the conditions in which he lived. "The Dickens" remains as a euphemism in our language for the beating of children. In the eighteenth century, parents sometimes maimed their children so they could be used to beg or be sold to circuses. Victor Hugo's novel *The Boy Who Laughed* concerned a boy whose face was mutilated by surgery so as to appear to be continually smiling. Kempe and Helfer in their book, *The Battered Child*, cited the inhumanity occasioned by the factory system. "Children from 5 years of age upward worked sixteen hours at a time sometimes with irons riveted around their ankles to keep them from running away. They were starved, beaten, and in many other ways maltreated. Many succumbed to occupational diseases, and some committed suicide; few survived for any length of time."

The Encyclopaedia Britannica of 1890 states: "It is difficult to say to what extent infanticide prevailed in the United Kingdom. At one time a large number of children were murdered in England for the mere purpose of obtaining burial money from a benefit club.'' In 1871 the House of Commons found it necessary to appoint a select committee "to inquire as to the best means of preventing the destruction of the lives of infants put out to hire by their parents.''

Not until the last half of the nineteenth century was the first Society for the Prevention of Cruelty to Children (SPCC) organized in the United States. It came about as the result of New York City's infamous Mary Ellen case in 1874, which brought out that the American Society for the Prevention of Cruelty to *Animals* was the only agency willing and able to intervene to protect a child suffering from abuse. It is from this case that recognition of the existence of child abuse may be dated. Medical recognition of this phenomenon was first introduced in 1888 by Dr. S. West in a paper on acute periosteal swelling in infants. However, it was not until work done by Drs. W. A. and F. N. Silverman and Dr. John Caffey in the last 20 years that we arrive at the recognition of the specific syndrome we have come to know as *child battering*. Child abuse, and child battering, may be described as the infliction of bodily trauma upon a child so as to willfully and knowingly cause injury—or death. Within this definition, we must add that the infliction of injury often follows a quite regular, even ritualistic, pattern, as though to inflict cumulative injuries on the child.

Originally, the focus of the SPCC was on removal of the child from the abusive environment and punishment of the parents for cruel treatment. Norris Class points out that early practitioners in the field of child welfare proceeded on the assumption that physical abuse was associated almost exclusively with poverty, slums, ignorance, industrial exploitation, and immigration. Physical mistreatment was quite open in these sectors, and it was not difficult to introduce admissible evidence to the courts in the prosecution of abusive parents.

With America's whirlwind courtship of psychoanalysis in the 1920s and 1930s, more concern was placed upon emotional factors and treatment. As the family system came to be seen as the diagnostic and eventually the treatment unit of reference, greater attention was paid to the possibility of treating the parents and attempting to maintain the structural integrity of the family. In child welfare today, the basic problem still exists: at what point does the harm of leaving a child in an abusive environment override the negative consequences of splintering the family by use of placement facilities?

Despite the historical trend toward increased children's rights and protection including the SPCC, child labor laws, the day care movement, Head Start, and the Gault Decision of the Supreme Court, it seems clear that the perception of children as property or chattels has strong roots in our society. Parental rights are still rated high on the scale of values.

Dimensions of Problem

What, then, are the dimensions of child abuse? Some of the numbers are somewhat impressionistic. Some hard statistics are available, but due to the nature of the phenomenon, we must view these in the same perspective as statistics on drug abuse, alcoholism, homosexuality, and other socially unacceptable behavior.

There are further difficulties that arise in attempting to assess the number of children being physically abused or battered. Even the number of abuse cases that actually are reported is not known. Figures reported by individual protective agencies or hospitals may be typical only for their geographic locality. Reported statistics on referrals to protective agencies often include cases of both abuse and neglect; there is no nationwide consistency. Some statistics are reported in terms of number of children needing protective services.

On a nationwide basis, the American Humane Society has estimated that 10,000 cases of child abuse were reported in 1969. One-quarter (2,600) of these cases were from New York City alone. Of these 2,600 cases, only *11* were reported by private physicians—and *none* by dentists. It is frightening to note that since the inception of a central registry in New York in 1966, the local rate of abused children reported has increased 549%.

Data from California and Colorado—when extrapolated—yield a conservative estimate of 200,000 to 250,000 children in the United States annually in need of protective services, of which 30,000 to 37,500 may have been badly injured.

A composite demographic picture of the abused as well as the abusive appears as follows:

A. The Abused Child

1. Average age: under 4 years, most under 2.
2. Average death rate: 5% to 25%. (Regional figures: highest reported rate from California; New York City; substantiated, 5.4%, unsubstantiated, 17%.)
3. Average age at death: slightly under 3 years.
4. Average duration of exposure to battering: 1 to 3 years.
5. Sex differentiation: none.

B. The Abusive Parent

1. Marital status: overwhelming majority were married and living together at the time of the abuse.
2. Average age of abusive mother: 26 years.
3. Average age of abusive father: 30 years.
4. Abusive parent: father slightly more often than mother.
5. Most serious abuse: mother more often than father.
6. Most common instrument for abuse: hairbrush.

C. Family Dynamics

1. Thirty to sixty percent of abusing parents claim to have been abused as children themselves.
2. High proportion of premarital conception.
3. Youthful marriage.
4. Unwanted pregnancies.

5. Illegitimacies.
6. Forced marriages.
7. Social and kinship isolation.
8. Emotional problems in marriage.
9. Financial difficulty.

There is uncertainty concerning socioeconomic status. The American Humane Society states: "The problem of the battered child is a phenomenon common to every community. It knows no bounds in relation to economic or educational levels of parents. Cases of abuse are reported from the seemingly well-regulated home and from the obviously disorganized and broken home." Findings by David Gil, however, indicate a higher incidence of child abuse at the lower end of the socioeconomic ladder, especially among broken homes and in large families. Private and public institutions are more likely to intervene in the lives of the more visible and vulnerable lower class than they would in the lives of the affluent.

Practitioners argue that the abused child in the affluent family will in most cases come to the attention of a private physician, who upon making arrangements to hospitalize the child *will not report the source of injury*. A poor family in a hospital setting would not be privy to such treatment.

Related Problems

Though they are not specifically related to the battered child syndrome, and are somewhat far afield, the following three observations should be included in a discussion of abuse to children:

1. Severe or gross child neglect, while not having the dramatic impact of abuse among the news media and general public, is more widespread and potentially more dangerous than child abuse in many cases. It has been estimated that neglected children coming to public attention during 1970 in New York City alone numbered 10,000. However, nationwide statistics on this phenomenon do not exist. Cases of neglect may be potentially more dangerous in that they are more difficult to identify, *i.e.,* once identified, the damage done to a child *over time* (by definition, a pattern of noncare must be established) may be more difficult to reverse therapeutically than some abuse cases. Concerning emotional neglect, never has there been a problem so well understood in terms of its dynamics and prognosis and yet so little corrected by using available knowledge.

2. It is not generally appreciated that juveniles are subject to stricter laws and to more severe penalties for noncriminal acts than many adults who commit felonies. The Second United Nations Congress on the Prevention of Crime and Treatment of Offenders recommended that juveniles should not be prosecuted as delinquents for behavior which, if exhibited by adults, would not be a matter of legal concern. New York, adhering to this recommendation, developed a juvenile status category distinct from Juvenile Delinquency. It is called PINS (Person in Need of Supervision).

As Paul Lerman states: ". . . it is difficult to read the historical record and not conclude that many juvenile status actions could have been defined as cultural differences and play fads, as well as childhood troubles with home, school, and sex." It further states that statistics compiled by the Children's Bureau indicate, ". . . about one out of every five boys' delinquency petitions and over one half of all girls' cases are based on charges for which an adult would not be legally liable even to appear in court."

Meanwhile, PINS children can still be mixed up in detention facilities with delinquents; transfers to reformatories are technically possible, and subsequent commitments to delinquency institutions apparently are permitted. In addition, it is doubtful whether the public distinguishes between children in need of supervision and those adjudicated as delinquents.

3. A report made this year by the Federal Trade Commission indicates a certain attitude toward children. The report said that 700,000 children were injured in this country due to defective or dangerous children's toys.

In conclusion, for those with no identification personally with child-battering, how many have tenderly sung to their children the Western world's most popular lullaby. "Rock-a-bye, Baby," or recounted "Snow White," "Hansel and Gretel," or "Rumpelstiltskin?"

5

*The Diagnosis of the Maltreatment Syndrome in Children**

Vincent J. Fontana, M.D.

The maltreatment of children is a disease affecting the child and the parents. It is difficult to accept the fact that in our society today inhuman cruelty to children appears to be rapidly increasing. The perpetrators of these crimes are, for the most part, not strangers but the parents themselves. In 1968, in New York City, there were 956 cases of abuse reported. In 1969, there were 1,600 and in 1970, the incidence rose to approximately 3,000 cases. The number of neglected children during this time has been noted to be approximately 35,000. Within the period 1966 to 1970, there has been a total percent increase of 549 in reported cases of child abuse to New York's Central Registry.

It is most important for all of mandated sources under the present child abuse law—especially the physician in the hospital—to be able to recognize situations in which abuse or neglect may exist. It is not necessary for a physician to be absolutely sure about any abuse or neglect, as the law clearly states that cases of suspicion must also be reported. This disease, if not properly managed, leads to critical consequences. It is estimated that one out of every two battered children dies after being returned to his parents. Many of these battered children, if they survive and approach adolescence, begin to show signs of pyschological and emotional disturbances reported as irreversible in most cases. There has been expressed concern that the probable future tendency of abused children is to become the future battering parent or the hard-core criminal responsibile for crimes and violence in our society.

* Vincent J. Fontana, "The Diagnosis of the Maltreatment Syndrome in Children," *Pediatrics,* Vol. 51, No. 4, Part II: 780-782, April, 1973. Copyright © American Academy of Pediatrics 1973. Reproduced by permission.

The neglect and abuse of children denotes a situation ranging from the deprivation of food, clothing, shelter, and parental love to instances in which children are physically abused and mistreated by an adult, resulting in obvious physical trauma to the child and often leading to death. Kempe, in 1962, described repeated physical abuse to children and called it the "battered child syndrome." Other reports in the medical literature have referred to this disease over the years as "unrecognized trauma," a term limited to a description of the bone lesions found in the maltreatment of children. Unfortunately, both these terms do not fully describe the true picture of this often life-threatening condition. The more precise descriptive term that could be applied to this clinical entity is that of the "maltreatment syndrome" in children. A maltreated child often presents with no obvious signs of being battered and has multiple, minor physical evidences of emotional and, at times, nutritional deprivation, neglect, and abuse. In these cases, the diagnostic ability of the physician can prevent the more severe injuries of inflicted trauma that are significant causes of childhood deaths.

The maltreated child is often taken to the hospital or private physician with a history of "failure to thrive," poor skin hygiene, malnutrition, irritability, a repressed personality, and other signs of obvious neglect. The more severely abused children are seen in the emergency rooms of hospitals with external evidences of body trauma, bruises, abrasions, cuts, lacerations, burns, soft-tissue swellings, and hematomas. Some are seen with an unexplained ruptured stomach, bowel, or liver, or the maternal deprivation syndrome, wherein a mother allows a child to suffer the ill effects of deprivations, leading to physical and mental retardation. Most recently, hypernatremic dehydration, following periodic water deprivation by psychotic mothers, has been reported as a form of child abuse by other investigators. Inability to move certain extremities because of dislocations and fractures associated with neurological signs of intracranial damage are additional signs of inflicted trauma. Children manifesting maltreatment give evidence of one or more of these complaints. Those with the most severe maltreatment injuries arrive at the hospital or the physician's office in coma, convulsions, or even dead. The signs and symptoms indicating the maltreatment of children, therefore, range from the simple undernourished infant reported as "failure to thrive" to the "battered child" which is often the last phase of the spectrum of the maltreatment syndrome.

Many of these children are not taken to the physician or hospital for medical care because parents fear legal entanglements unless the child is in acute distress and the parents fear impending death. If the infant or child is taken to a physician or hospital, the history related by the parents is often at variance with the clinical picture and the physical findings noted on examination of the child. The physician often discovers that the mother has taken the child to various hospitals and physicians in an effort to negate any suspicion of parental abuse. Difficulty in obtaining any type of history is often encountered and diagnosis is dependent on the physical examination, x-ray findings, and a high index of suspicion on the part of the physician. The Table indicates the physician's index of suspicion as related to the history, physical examination, differential diagnosis, and radiologic manifestations of child abuse.

X-rays of the infant's fractures may present in various stages of reparative changes. On the other hand, if no fractures or dislocations are apparent on examination, bone injury may remain obscure during the first few days after inflicting

TABLE

Physician's Index of Suspicion

History

1. Parents often relate story that is at variance with clinical findings
2. Multiple visits to various hospitals
3. Familial discord or financial stress, alcoholism, psychosis, perversion, drug addiction, etc.
4. Reluctance of parents to give information
5. Admittance to hospital during evening hours
6. Child brought to hospital for complaint other than one associated with abuse and/or neglect, e.g, cold, headache, stomach ache, etc.
7. Date of injury prior to admission
8. Parent's inappropriate reaction to severity of injury
9. Inconsistent social histories

Physical Examination

1. Signs of general neglect, poor skin hygiene, malnutrition, withdrawal, irritability, repressed personality
2. Bruises, abrasions, burns, soft-tissue swellings, hematomas, old healed lesions
3. Evidence of dislocation and/or fractures of the extremities
4. Coma, convulsions, death
5. Symptoms of drug withdrawal

Differential Diagnosis

1. Scurvy and rickets
2. Infantile cortical hyperostosis
3. Syphilis of infancy
4. Accidental trauma

Radiologic Manifestations

1. Subperiosteal hemorrhages
2. Epiphyseal separations
3. Periosteal shearing
4. Metaphyseal fragmentation
5. Previously healed periosteal calcifications
6. "Squaring" of the metaphysis

trauma. In these cases, bone repair may become evident weeks after the specific bone trauma. For this reason, x-rays should be repeated approximately five to seven days after the suspected inflicted trauma in order to evaluate the presence of diagnostic radiologic findings.

The unusual bone changes have been described previously by the leaders in the field of x-rays as "unrecognized trauma" (see Table).

The diagnosis of the maltreatment syndrome in children must encompass the physical examination of the child, the questionable history as to the cause of the physical condition of the child on examination, and the diagnostic x-ray findings that oftentimes speak for the child. A precise differential diagnosis to rule out other organic causes of the x-ray findings must be undertaken by the physician. In addition to his diagnosis, a social service investigation will confirm the diagnosis of maltreatment in a specific patient. Colored photographs of the child, particularly in the areas of injury should be taken on admission and should become a part of the permanent record of the child. This will assist the physician and social worker if it becomes necessary that court action be taken to protect the child from further abuse.

Those individuals mandated to report cases of child abuse and neglect may also be guided in making a diagnosis by indicators of a child's need for protection. A child's aggressive, disruptive, destructive behavior may be an acting out to secure attention and may be a form of shouting for help. This type of behavior may be a reflection of the hostile climate at home, or the child may be imitating destructive parental behavior at home. Is the child an habitual truant, chronically late or tardy? This type of school performance may point to problems at home, within the child, or both.

The child's appearance often tells a story of neglect. If the child is inadequately dressed for the weather; is wearing clothing that is torn, tattered, or unwashed; or if the child is not clean and unbathed, and has body odor—all these are signs of neglect that relate to poor household conditions and no concern for the child's welfare. The parental attitudes may also justify suspicion. The parents may be aggressive and abusive when approached about problems concerning the child. They may be apathetic or unresponsive. The parents may relate to the child in a bizarre and strange manner. They may show little or no concern about the child's activities either in or outside the school.

6

Failure to Thrive and Fatal Injury as a Continuum*

Bertram S. Koel, M.D.

The infant who is hospitalized for failure to thrive, and in whom, after extensive investigation, no pathologic diagnosis can be made, is a familiar phenomenon in pediatric practice.[1-6] The sequence of diagnostic procedures frequently involves a protracted hospital stay. This interval also permits observation of emotional and motor development as well as parent-child interaction.

The infant usually improves in the hospital setting, but may not. If the studies yield no evidence of organic disease, emotional or nutritional deprivation may be suspected. Appropriate psychosocial remediation is initiated, and the patient is discharged to be followed as an outpatient. It is the purpose of this communication to point out that these babies may be at risk of serious injury or violent death within the ensuing months.

The three cases reported were admitted to the Kaiser Foundation Hospital in San Francisco.

Report of Cases

Case 1.—A 13-month girl weighing 5,104 gm (11 lb 4 ounces) was admitted for failure to thrive. The infant was emaciated and anxious with superficial ulcers and some healing lacerations. Findings from laboratory examinations were within normal limits, except for evidence of a urinary tract infection. Roentgen examinations revealed a periosteal double line of one of

* Bertram S. Koel, "Failure to Thrive and Fatal Injury as a Continuum," *American Journal of the Diseases of Children*, Vol. 118, 1969:565-567. Copyright © 1969 American Medical Association. Reproduced by permission.

the phalanges. The infant was discharged after one month, having gained 2,268 gm (5 lb). There was one visit to the outpatient clinic.

At age 17 months, the child was admitted cachectic, with numerous lacerations, contusions, and infected burns of the face, mouth, head, trunk, labiae, and extremities. She was critically ill and in coma. Roentgen examinations revealed a fractured skull, as well as periosteal new bone formation of the long bones. The mother had entered the hospital earlier that day in labor; the child was brought by an uncle. The child was discharged six weeks later to a foster home.

Case 2.—A 5-month-old female infant was admitted for failure to thrive, weighing 4,678 gm (10 lb 5 ounces). There had been two previous admissions at another hospital; the first for pneumonia, and the second for fracture of the humerus.

The baby, on admission, was listless and did not smile. She was emaciated and had small bilateral, congenital cataracts. Findings from laboratory examinations were within normal limits. Roentgen examination revealed new bone formation of the humeri. Subdural taps were nonproductive. The infant was discharged in three weeks, alert and smiling but having gained only 227 gm (8 ounces). Thereafter, there were regular home nursing visits and outpatient clinic visits but no significant weight gain. There was a one week hospitalization at age 7 months for pneumonia. Final admission occurred at age 9 months. The baby entered in status epilepticus, having been asphyxiated in her crib at home. Death occurred on the third hospital day.

Case 3.—A 2½-month-old girl was admitted for failure to thrive, weighing 3,913 gm (8 lb 10 ounces). Physical examination showed an emaciated infant quietly sucking her fingers. Findings from laboratory examinations were within normal limits. The baby was discharged after ten days, having gained 454 gm (1 lb). Second admission was at age 1 year for fever and failure to thrive. Weight was 5,160 gm (11 lb 6 ounces). She could turn over but could not sit alone. Physical examination revealed an emaciated, apathetic infant with protuberant abdomen. Findings from laboratory examinations were within normal limits. Roentgen examinations were within normal limits except for distension of the colon. Rectal biopsy was normal. The infant became "voracious" and "enthusiastic". She was discharged after 17 days, having gained 1,361 gm (3 lb).

Third admission was at age 14 months for dehydration and failure to thrive. She was apathetic and appeared acutely and chronically ill. Laboratory findings and roentgen examinations were within normal limits. She became "playful," gained 2,268 gm (5 lb) and was discharged in one month. Thereafter, she was seen on several occasions in the outpatient clinic, and gained another 907 gm (2 lb) in three months.

Final admission was at age 20 months for second and third degree burns over 55% of the body. She had been scalded in the bathtub. Death occurred on the 23rd hospital day.

Comment

The literature contains references to 13 cases of coexisting failure to thrive and trauma,[2, 6-8] and one case of a sequence of failure to thrive followed by trauma.[9] In an epidemiologic study of all reported cases of child abuse in New York City for one year, it was shown that there was a spectrum of maltreatment patterns including neglect, abuse, and accidental injury.[10]

Though the admission diagnosis was "failure to thrive" in all three of the cases here reported, patients 1 and 2 had evidences of trauma. Patients 1 and 3 made significant gains in weight during hospitalization. Patients 2 and 3 were seen on numerous occasions as outpatients after discharge. However, in all three cases there appears to have been a sequence starting with deprivation and ending with violent death or near-death.

Therapeutic success, then, cannot be measured in pounds of weight gained, since in none of these instances did the pediatric care suffice to prevent the final result. Indeed, this may have been anticipated in terms of the psychodynamics of abusing or neglectful parents.[5,8] Nutritional and developmental improvement in the hospital setting cannot but reinforce parental feelings of inadequacy and guilt and further erode an already low self-esteem. Definitive therapy would also have been directed at the underlying problem: the strengthening of an insufficient relationship.

It has been pointed out that most of these parents are basically dependent persons,[11] and many have experienced abuse or neglect during their own childhood.[8, 11-13] However, they are not always identifiable as having symptoms of emotional illness.[8, 9, 11] The implication is, that if not challenged by the role of parent, this person may have functioned either marginally or adequately in most life situations.

The concept of mother-child role reversal, where the infant's demands are perceived as threats, and his crying as judgmental, has been developed by other authors.[5, 13] In this distorted schema, the infant's responses must satisfy the needs of the parents.

There is general agreement that interrogation, confrontation, and explicit or implicit criticism are counter-productive.[5, 6, 8] Fragments of deeper feelings may be perceived, following expressions of concern for the family's problems or praise for seeking medical attention. Maximal inclusion of the parents in the hospital caring routines give them a share in the child's improvement.[4-6] After discharge, continuation of nurturing behavior depends on initiating and sustaining a long term program of providing the mother with medical and social services and emotional "supplies."[8, 12]

If deemed necessary, some form of protective intervention should also be sought.

Summary

Three cases of failure to thrive in infancy were investigated but no pathologic diagnosis was made. Within months after discharge, each was readmitted, critically ill from trauma. Two infants died. Fattening a puny infant is satisfying to the staff, but the child remains at risk of subsequent violence if he is sent back to untreated parents.

REFERENCES

1.   ELMER, E.: "Failure to Thrive, Role of the Mother," *Pediatrics* 25:717-725 (April) 1960.

2.   BULLARD, D. M., Jr., et al.: "Failure to Thrive in the 'Neglected' Child," *Amer J Orthopsychiat* 37:680-690 (July) 1967.

3.   RILEY, R. L., et al.: "Failure to Thrive: An Analysis of 83 Cases," *Calif Med* 108:32-38 (Jan.) 1968.

4.   LEONARD, M. F.; RHYMES, J. P.; and SOLNIT, A. J.: "Failure to Thrive in Infants: A Family Problem," *Amer J Dis Child* 111:600-612 (June) 1966.

5.   BARBERO, G. J.; MORRIS, M. G.; and REFORD, M. T.: "Malidentification of Mother-Baby-Father Relationships Expressed in Infant Failure to Thrive," in *The Neglected Battered-Child Syndrome: Role Reversal in Parents*, New York: Child Welfare League of America, Inc., 1963.

6.   BARBERO, G. J., and SHAHEEN, E.: "Environmental Failure to Thrive: A Clinical View," *J Pediat* 71:639-644 (Nov.) 1967.

7.   GLASER, H. H., et al.: "Physical and Psychological Development of Children With Early Failure to Thrive," *J Pediat* 73:690-698 (Nov.) 1968.

8.   HELFER, R. E., and KEMPE, C. H.: *The Battered Child*, Chicago: University of Chicago Press, 1968.

9.   FONTANA, V. J.; DONOVAN, D.; and WONG, R. J.: "The 'Maltreatment Syndrome' in Children," *New Eng J Med* 269:1389-1394 (Dec. 26) 1963.

10.   SIMONS, B., et al.: "Child Abuse: Epidemiologic Study of Medically Reported Cases," *New York J Med* 66:2783-2788 (Nov.) 1966.

11.   COHEN, M. I.; RAPHLING, D. L.; and GREEN, P. E.: "Psychologic Aspects of the Maltreatment Syndrome of Childhood," *J Pediat* 69:279-284 (Aug.) 1966.

12.   HOLTER, J. C., and FRIEDMAN, S. B.: "Principles of Management in Child Abuse Cases," *Amer J Orthopsychiat* 38:127-136 (Jan.) 1968.

13.   MORRIS, M. G., and GOULD, R. W.: "Role Reversal: A Concept in Dealing With the Neglected/Battered Child Syndrome," in *The Neglected Battered-Child Syndrome: Role Reversal in Parents*, New York: Child Welfare League of America, Inc., 1963.

7

Professional Abuse of Children: Responsibility for the Delivery of Services*

Hon. Justine Wise Polier

Examination of professional responsibility for delivery of services within the larger framework of professional abuse of children is based on the acceptance of an important premise—that professionals are responsible for what they fail to do as well as for what they actually do. The purpose of this paper is, therefore, to present questions that professionals must face as they decide what services will or will not be provided.

Roughly the questions fall within four areas: 1) the responsibility of the individual professional; 2) the responsibility of social agencies empowered to deliver services; 3) the rights of children to receive services in accordance with law and social morality; and 4) professional responsibility in resolving larger social issues which determine the rights and entitlements of children.

The Individual Professional

Members of many different professions exercise decision making powers over the lives of children when they determine whether services are to be withheld or granted, and what services are to be delivered. Intake workers in welfare departments make decisions on eligibility for benefits and refer or fail to refer persons for special services. Workers in welfare or child welfare divisions (where they still exist) accept or

---

* Hon. Justine Wise Polier, "Professional Abuse of Children: Responsibility for the Delivery of Services," *American Journal of Orthopsychiatry*, 45(3)357-362. Copyright © 1975, the American Orthopsychiatric Association, Inc. Reproduced by permission.

reject children for placement when requested by parents or referred by other agencies. Protective service workers determine whether services should be granted to a family when neglect or abuse is reported, whether "voluntary" commitments for placements shall be taken, or whether court actions should be initiated charging parents with neglect or abuse.

Workers in voluntary agencies have even broader discrimination in deciding whether they will accept a child or family for direct services or for placement in foster care. In making such decisions, members of the social work profession, psychologists, psychiatrists, and administrative personnel may become involved. If referral for placement is recommended, the outcome may depend on professional workers in other agencies who determine whether to accept or reject a child.

When mental health clinics and hospitals become involved, one again finds professional personnel whose review of histories, and whose evaluations of need and their ability or readiness to provide treatment, will determine the outcome of a referral.

Finally, there is the personnel within the orbit of the law: intake workers, prosecuting attorney, counsel for the child, counsel for parents, probation, and finally the judge. At each step in the process, individuals serving in professional capacities participate in what will ultimately be presented to the court at trial and subsequently in determining the court disposition.

In each of these areas and countless others, including day care centers, schools, special services of many kinds, medical services, housing, and manpower, individual professionals exercise all but unchecked discretion in determining to whom services shall be given and from whom they shall be withheld. The fragmentation of professional authority is all too likely to make the determinations easier for each decision-maker by obscuring the consequences of rejection for the child in need of services.

It is not only fragmentation, but lack of standards and the absence of monitoring which leave unchecked power in the hands of decision-makers and reduce those in need to a state of powerlessness. The mushrooming of commercial child care facilities now confronts professionals with added responsibility, if more children are not to be abused.

In these day of growing concern over invasion of privacy through computerization and dissemination of records, it is important to question whether the concept of privacy as now used is not archaic, and a contributing factor to the denial of service delivery. While privacy of records may have been initiated to prevent the village gossip from unwarranted information, it is now necessary to ask whether privacy has not become a cloak that prevents the subject of the records, his parent, counsel, and the courts from knowing, questioning, and evaluating their content. A recent study of records of "hard to place" children reported that the records focused almost entirely on negative reports from third persons, or agencies, and that the children had not been seen prior to the classification. Disposal of human beings by professional classification based on scraps of paper is symptomatic of the all too common alienation of professionals that spells abuse.

Tragically, this is reflected in casework reports, in mental health reports, in probation reports, and in dispositions by judges made on the basis of superficial presentence reports. Courts have been too prone to regard conformity with the requirements of due process as more worthy of scrutiny and concern than what happens to a convicted defendant when he is shuffled of to prison. In recent months this same attitude has become evident both on the part of would-be reformers and members of the juvenile court judiciary, for far different reasons. The would-be reformers have given up hope that the juvenile justice system can be made a constructive force in American society. Some would return to mini-criminal courts with penalties fixed for various offenses, on the premise that we really want to punish deviant children and should put aside the hypocrisy that belies commitment to rehabilitation. For entirely different reasons some judges in the juvenile court are convinced that if they are relieved of responsibility for seeking the most appropriate care and treatment of children, they will then be regarded as real judges and no longer be seen as part of a lower order of the judiciary, namely, persons concerned with social problems. They want to streamline the court procedures in the name of efficiency without regard to what is needed to become effective on behalf of individual children.

Both such "reformers" and such judges have thus accepted positions that reflect alienation from professional responsibility for the delivery of services, and become party to the abuse of children.

Social Agencies

To a large extent, sweeping powers are given to professional persons for determination of services to be provided for or withheld from children or their families. The wide disparity in who is accepted and who is rejected by professionals in agencies theoretically prepared to meet similar populations suggests there may be greater differences among those exercising the power of selection than among those children who are accepted or rejected. When certain agencies explained denial of services on the ground that the children rejected were older or more disturbed, an analysis of a random number of case records has shown that the information in the records did not sustain the explanation.

While it is generally, too generally, asserted that boards make policy and staff implements policy, this alleged dichotomy cannot justify the forswearing of professional responsibility to a single client when intervention and delivery of services is in the child's best interest according to the best judgment of the professional. Professionals surely see themselves as more than employees restricted to doing the bidding of an agency if it violates their sense of responsibility. There are many ways of being coopted which professionals may have to challenge. Among them is the seductive lure of focusing increasingly on discrete ways for improving the quality of professional services to a smaller and smaller segment of those most in need. The rationale is constantly presented for providing limited professional services to those most accessible, those most likely to make fullest use of what agencies regard as their superior services. Such explanations or excuses leave many questions of professional responsibility unanswered, even when they are not used as cloaks for discriminatory practices or as a creaming process that separates out all but those children whose success is most promising.

How far has this position fed into increasing specialization and fragmentation of services that, in turn, narrow access to help for those most in need, or add to the labyrinth of endless by-paths and dead-end referrals through which they must grope?

How far have professionals come to feel that they achieve hierarchical status by becoming participant observers, consultants whose focus is more on observing than participating in the rendering of services?

How far does such status carry with it a position immunized from responsibility except for the rendering of a final verdict that sanctifies or sanitizes the decision not to provide services?

Does the price exacted for achieving such status include non-identification with the powerless and over-identification with the establishment that represents power?

To what extent has a new professionalism developed which, like foster homes required to provide "neutral settings," is drained of vital life-giving warmth to children whose well-being is the agency's justification for being? In other words, has the institutionalization of professional services within agencies created procedures for self-protection against what is seen as over-involvement, and created a *cordon sanitaire* against any sense of urgency to provide services when they are needed? Can such "cool" and remoteness be compatible with professional responsibility for the welfare of children?

It would seem that agencies organized to provide professional services have a responsibility to their professional staff, themselves, and to the larger community to be concerned with not only the children they accept and the quality of service they render to these children. As with individual members of the professions, the search for status or success by agencies narrows vision, and leads to failure or denial of services to which children are entitled. Overemphasis on compiling of records, on paper records, and on referrals elsewhere without concern for the outcome for the children, and satisfaction with islands of service in a sea of neglect run counter to the requirements of social and professional responsibility.

Although the medical model is in ill-repute these days, it is relevant that professional medical responsibility demands acceptance of patients who are ill, even if there is no known cure. There remains the responsibility for treatment and easing of pain. It would seem that such values should be accepted by a far greater proportion of our child caring agencies, and not denigrated as beneath their talents or concern.

Children's Right to Services

It is true that the rights of a child as a person have only begun to be articulated by the federal courts in recent years. However, each federal decision in this field only expresses obligations to children that should long ago have been recognized by professionals responsible for the delivery of services.

In deciding that children have constitutional rights, including the right to counsel and a fair hearing, the Supreme Court laid down ground rules that still require implementation in most parts of this country. The right to counsel becomes a mockery when a public defender gives a child five minutes, when a judge appoints counsel who will not make trouble, or when a court official tells the parents of a child charged with delinquency that he will do better before this judge if they waive the right to counsel. Likewise, one must question social agencies which employ high-priced expert counsel in their business affairs, but are unready to spend funds or time to provide competent legal services for children in their care, when questions of custody arise.

The protection by the federal courts of the rights of children has been invoked where social agencies are charged with cruel and unusual punishment, with interference with the first amendment rights of children, such as refusing to let them write in Spanish to parents. In situations such as those found in the Texas Training Schools *(Morales* v. *Turman)*, one must ask, what was the professional responsibility of teachers, social workers, and mental health personnel who tolerated the cruel, barbaric treatment condemned by Federal Court Judge Wayne Justice?

The concept of the right to appropriate treatment when a person is denied freedom in the name of treatment has now been extended to children in schools for the retarded and the mentally ill in Alabama by Judge Johnson. After a lengthy trial and the taking of extended testimony on minimum standards, his decision in *Wyatt* v. *Stickney* underlined the trailblazing in this field by Judge David Bazelon. And, happily, this decision has been affirmed recently by the Circuit Court of Appeals. It becomes necessary to ask not only what the courts are deciding, but where the professionals were while children were subjected to mistreatment and where they will stand in regard to the implementation of these decisions.

New issues raised in federal cases to assert the rights of all children to equal protection by tax exempt agencies licensed to provide care to children raise challenging questions for professionals engaged in the delivery of services. Where have they stood, where will they stand when they know that children are suffering denial of services by agencies they serve in violation of constitutional rights by reason of race, color, national origin, or religion? Surely, they are aware of such discrimination where it is practiced in overt fashion, as in Alabama where none of the major group residences accepted non-white children. They are also among the first to be aware of discriminatory practices where they are covert. Can professional responsibility for the delivery of services become meaningful so long as those engaged in rendering professional services are party to the denials of constitutional rights by tacit consent or by the pretense of not knowing?

Professional Responsibility for Larger Social Issues

Self-examination and ongoing scrutiny of agency practices, as necessary elements for determining one's professional role in fulfilling responsibility for the delivery of services to children, inevitably lead to further questions. The day-to-day experience of witnessing unmet needs of children, the barriers that prevent delivery of appropriate services, impel the facing of larger social issues.

The lawyer sees vast differences in the quality of service available to those who can and cannot pay. The physician recognizes the cause of lead poisoning in children, and the dangers to child development that result from malnutrition of pregnant women. The welfare worker is confronted with neglect of young children that cannot be isolated from the sub-poverty level AFDC grants on which eight million children and their mothers must subsist. Availability of public funds for foster care, but the absence of such funds for preventive services present social workers with a vast gap between rhetoric and practice concerning the value of the family. Lack of mental health services and appropriate care for children and parents confront all professional workers who seek to deliver services. And, cutting across and underlying all these denials are the added burdens and discriminatory practices imposed on minority groups. These are but illustrations of societal abuse of children witnessed by professionals in their daily work.

Is it too much to ask that, where special knowledge, special skills, and expertise sensitize one to conditions that constitute societal abuse, professionals accept responsibility to identify and seek to end such abuses? Each professional cannot be expected to undertake such tasks alone, although some individuals can give significant leadership. The question is rather how professionals within their own fields and in concert with other professional groups can join to challenge the societal abuses that undermine and defeat efforts to provide essential services for all children.

During these last years, all concerned with human services have suffered repeated defeats and engaged in necessary rearguard actions. The times now call for a new stance: the positive insistence on what is needed to deliver services to children. There must be an end to the nightmarish apathy, alienation, and hostility toward children who suffer from societal abuse. This, too, is our common professional responsibility. The urgency for change, the changing political climate, and the decisions of the federal courts on the rights of children provide new opportunities and a new challenge to professionals for the delivery of services to children.

8

Abuse of the Child Abuse Law*

Abraham B. Bergman

In the belief that public officials potentially can affect health more than physicians, for the past 15 years I have engaged in the part-time practice of "political medicine." When I started as a starry-eyed rookie, I viewed successful passage of some legislation as a big deal. As a scarred, and perhaps burned-out, veteran I now know that getting a law enacted by Congress is simple compared to seeing that it is implemented in the manner intended by its original sponsors. The reason is as much due to the fraility of human nature as to the constitutional separation of powers among the three branches of government. If an official of the executive branch, from the President on down, is handed a program to administer that he did not ask for in the first place, nothing short of thumb screws will cause him to consult with the authors on what they had in mind.

Rather than recount old political war stories, however, these comments concern a piece of legislation in which I was not involved: *The Child Abuse Prevention and Treatment Act* (PL93-247). My perspective is from worm's eye. I am the pediatrician for the child abuse team at my hospital. We see most of the physically abused children who require hospitalization in our population area of approximately 1 million. We average about 50 cases per year.

Treatment Resources Lacking

Our greatest frustration is the pitiful lack of treatment resources in the community after the child leaves the hospital. The pioneer studies of Kempe, Helfer, Fontana,

* Abraham B. Bergman, "Abuse of the Child Abuse Law," *Pediatrics*, Vol. 62, No. 2: 266-267, August, 1978. Copyright © American Academy of Pediatrics 1978. Reproduced by permission.

De Francis, Steele, Pollack, and others have provided us with information both on the origins of child abuse as well as the means of dealing with it. Denver has shown us an effective community model; replication is needed.[1]

The shock troops in any community's campaign against child abuse are Children's Protective Services (CPS) workers. They provide the vital surveillance lifeline for the children. Yet because of universal lack of support, both moral and financial for CPS, the "burn-out" rate among these valiant souls exceeds 100% per year in most areas. As far as I am concerned, failure to provide treatment services for child abuse victims and their families falls into the same category as withholding steroids from children with nephrosis. Like many others involved with child abuse, I naively viewed PL93-247 as the vehicle whereby funds for needed treatment would become available. It was not to be. Instead, the bulk of the money provided under *The Child Abuse Prevention and Treatment Act* has been frittered away on "research" attempts to reinvent the wheel and "educational" programs designed to enhance the incomes of public relations firms and the travel industry.

Where the Money Went

Last summer a mega-course was held in Seattle on the relationship of juvenile delinquency and child abuse. It was well advertised with multicolored brochures. A big feature was the presence of no less than 21 out-of-state "experts" flown in especially for the occasion. Each received a $200 honorarium along with travel expenses direct from the trough of John Q. Public. For those not fortunate enough to attend, a transcript of the proceedings has been promised. Similar publications emanating from the National Center of Child Abuse and Neglect (NCCAN) could probably fill the New Orleans Superdome.

A veteran in child abuse work, Vincent Fontana, says,

> progress in attacking the root causes of child maltreatment in this country does not lie in our public relations firms or in model legislation or media commercialism. Inadequacy of effort and insufficient expertise at the [Child Abuse] Center and in the Office of Child Development have allowed expenditures of limited dollars to carry out needless research, collect information through additional unnecessary surveys and support conference and education programs through so-called federally funded demonstration projects.[2]

The law requires that at least 50% of appropriated funds be used for demonstration grants. Information dissemination, including operation of the Child Abuse and Neglect Clearinghouse, is performed by contract. Training and technical assistance are funded by competitive contracts and grants. State grants to improve services are made directly to "eligible" states. No less than 5% nor more than 20% of the appropriations can be used to fund state grants.

A total of $59.1 million has been spent in the four years since enactment of the law. As a tribute to the American free-enterprise system, *all* of the contract money, $8,759,461, has gone to for-profit corporations. Space does not allow a listing of the titles and amounts of money for the individual contracts and research grants. The information can be obtained by writing one's congressman. One can be assured of some fascinating reading as well as demonstrating interest. If few abused children benefited, one can hope that at least the Dow-Jones averages gained a few points.

How about research? Sixteen projects have been funded to the tune of $5.2 million, not in itself an extravagant amount. While new vistas are undoubtedly being opened by some of them, perusal of the titles does not overpower me with a sense of originality.

A consequence of all the "attention" given to child abuse is that politicians at the local, state, and national levels feel that they have actually accomplished something. Why bother funding expensive child protective services, foster homes, and mental health treatment when "media messages" provide the illusion of meaningful activity? Mandatory reporting laws are cheap. Doing something about the cases that are reported is not.

A Modest Proposal

So what can be done? Make me HEW Secretary for a day, and the following regulations would be issued without preliminary notice.

A moratorium would be placed on all conferences and publications on child abuse. The pages of established journals are available to authors with anything new to say. No more research proposals would be entertained unless the investigator submitted a term paper demonstrating familiarity with previous studies of child abuse and made a convincing case on how the proposed research would lead to improved treatment or prevention.

By far my most important move would be to require that all NCCAN administrators spend at least half of their time in the trenches as CPS workers. I doubt that many have even seen abused children, let alone worked with them. I am sure there are enough vacancies within commuting distance of D.C. If the paperwork piles up on their desks while they are away, less mischief will be perpetrated.

Precious few pediatric disorders lend themselves as readily to prevention as child abuse. A lot of young lives and souls will continue to be sacrificed until bureaucratic tail-chasing and public indifference are overcome.

REFERENCES

1. KEMPE, C. H., HELFER, R. E.: *Helping the Battered Child and His Family.* Philadelphia, J. B. Lippincott Co, 1972.

2. FONTANA, V. J.: Testimony before the U.S. House of Representatives, Subcommittee on Select Education of the Committee on Education and Labor, Feb. 25, 1977.

9

Child Abuse and Neglect: The Myth of Classlessness*

Leroy H. Pelton, Ph.D.

Child abuse is not a black problem, a brown problem, or a white problem. Child abusers are found in the ranks of the unemployed, the blue-collar worker, the white-collar worker and the professional. They are Protestant, Catholic, Jewish, Baptist and atheist.[7]

. . . [C]hild abuse and neglect occur among families from all socioeconomic levels, religious groups, races and nationalities.[16]

The problem of child abuse is not limited to any particular economic, social, or intellectual level, race or religion.[6]

[C]hild abuse and child neglect afflict all communities, regardless of race, religion or economic status.[4]

While such oft-repeated statements are true, they are often half-true. Child abuse and neglect have indeed been found among all socioeconomic classes, and within all of the other groupings mentioned. But these statements seem to imply that child abuse and neglect occur without regard to socioeconomic class, or are distributed proportionately among the total population. The impression that these problems are democratically distributed throughout society is increasingly being conveyed by professionals writing in academic journals, and to the public through the news media, despite clear evidence to the contrary.

This paper will be concerned primarily with three issues: 1) the extent and nature of the evidence associating child abuse and neglect with social class; 2) the reasons

* Leroy H. Pelton, "Child Abuse and Neglect: The Myth of Classlessness," *American Journal of Orthopsychiatry*, 48(4):608-617. Copyright © 1978 the American Orthopsychiatric Association, Inc. Reproduced by permission.

why the myth of classlessness continues to be promulgated; and 3) the damaging effects of the myth on our ability to understand and deal with the problems.

What the Studies Show

Substantial evidence of a strong relationship between poverty and child abuse and neglect currently exists. Every national survey of officially reported child neglect and abuse incidents has indicated that the preponderance of the reports involves families from the lowest socioeconomic levels.

In the first of these studies, a nationwide survey of child abuse reports made to central registries, Gil[8] found that nearly 60% of the families involved in the abuse incidents had been on welfare during or prior to the study year of 1967, and 37.2% of the abusive families had been receiving public assistance at the time of the incident. Furthermore, 48.4% of the reported families had incomes below $5000 in 1967, as compared with 25.3% of all American families who had such low incomes. Only 52.5% of the fathers had been employed throughout the year, and at least 65% of the mothers and 55.5% of the fathers did not graduate from high school. On the other side of the coin, only three percent of the families had incomes of $10,000 or over (as compared with 34.4% of all American families for the same year), and only 0.4% of the mothers and 2.2% of the fathers had college degrees.

More recent data have been collected by the American Humane Association (AHA) through its national study of official child abuse and neglect reporting. For the year 1975,[2] family income information was provided by twenty states and territories on a total of 12,766 validated reports. For 53.2% of these reports, the yearly income was under $5000, and 69.2% of the families had incomes of less than $7000. In fact, less than eleven percent of the families had incomes of $11,000 or over.

The AHA 1976 data[1] on 19,923 validated reports, from a greater number of states and territories, show that 49.6% of the families had incomes under $5000, and 65.4% under $7000. Forty-two percent of the families were receiving public assistance, mostly Aid to Families with Dependent Children (AFDC). Only 14.9% of the reports indicated family incomes of $11,000 or over, and only nine percent of the families had incomes of $13,000 or above. The median family income was $5051 (which is at the 1976 poverty level for a family of four), as compared with about $13,900 for all American families in 1976. For reports of neglect only, the median income dipped slightly to $4250, and it rose slightly to $6882 for abuse only.

More geographically limited but indepth studies substantiate this poverty picture. In her classic study of child abuse and neglect in the early 1960s, Young[20] examined the case records of 300 families, taken from the active files of child protection agencies in several different urban, suburban, and rural areas of the country. She found that: "Most of the families studied were poor, many of them very poor." Her data indicate that 42.7% of the families had been on public assistance at some time, and that only 10.7% of all of the families "were financially comfortable and able to meet their physical needs." In 58% of the families, the wage earner had not held one job continuously for as long as two years; in 71% of the families, the wage earner was an unskilled laborer. Furthermore, few of the families lived in adequate housing: "Poorly heated, vermin-ridden, in various states of disrepair, much of the housing was a hazard to health."

A recent study[14] in which a random sample of active cases from the state child protection agency caseload in Mercer County, New Jersey, was carefully screened for abuse and neglect, and the case records thoroughly analyzed, revealed that 81% of the families had received public welfare benefits at some time. Seventy-nine percent of the families had an income of $7000 or less at the time of case acceptance. Two-thirds of the mothers had left school by the end of the tenth grade.

Many more statistics are available that lead to the same unmistakable conclusion: The lower socioeconomic classes are disproportionately represented among all child abuse and neglect cases known to public agencies, to the extent that an overwhelming percentage—indeed, the vast majority—of the families in these cases live in poverty or near-poverty circumstances.

Those who uphold the myth of classlessness do not generally dispute such findings. Rather, they offer several disclaimers. Poor people, it is suggested, are more available to public scrutiny, more likely to be known to social agencies and law enforcement agencies, whose workers have had the opportunity to enter their households. The family lives of middle-class and upperclass people, on the other hand, are less open to inspection by public officials; they are less likely than people in poor neighborhoods to turn to public agencies when help is needed. Thus, injuries to children of the middle and upper classes are less likely to arouse outside suspicion of abuse and neglect; even when they do, the private physicians whom the parents consult, and with whom they may have a rather personal relationship, will be reluctant to report their suspicions to public authorities.

Therefore, it is claimed, the socioeconomic distribution of *reported* child abuse and neglect cases does not reflect that of *all* cases. It is further implied that there are proportionately more *unreported* cases among the middle and upper classes than among lower-class families, to such extent that child abuse and neglect are more or less proportionately distributed among all socioeconomic classes.

While the premises are valid—poor people *are* more subject to public scrutiny—the conclusions do not follow logically from them. We have no grounds for proclaiming that if middle-class and upper-class households were more open to public scrutiny, we would find proportionately as many abuse and neglect cases among them. Undiscovered evidence is no evidence at all.

Although poor people are more susceptible to public scrutiny, there is substantial evidence that the relationship between poverty and child abuse and neglect is not just an anomaly of reporting systems. The public scrutiny argument cannot explain away the real relationship that exists.

First, while it is generally acknowledged that greater public awareness and new reporting laws have led to a significant increase in reporting over the past few years, the socioeconomic pattern of these reports has not changed appreciably. The findings already reviewed here indicate that an expanded and more vigilant public watch has failed, over the years, to produce an increased proportion of reports from above the lower class.

Second, the public scrutiny argument cannot explain why child abuse and neglect are related to *degrees* of poverty, even *within* that same lower class that is acknowledged to be more open to public scrutiny. In studying only poor families, Giovannoni and Billingsley[9] found the highest incidence of child neglect to have occurred in families living in the most extreme poverty. A large, more recent study[19] in northern New Jersey compared AFDC recipient families known to the state child protection agency and identified as having abused or neglected their children, with AFDC families not known to that agency. The maltreating families were found to be living in more crowded and dilapidated households, to have been more likely to have gone hungry, and, in general, to be existing at a lower material level than the other AFDC families. The mothers in the maltreating families had fewer years of education than the mothers in the other families. The investigators concluded that the abusing and neglecting families are the poorest of the poor.

Third, the public scrutiny argument cannot explain why, among the reported cases, the most severe injuries have occurred within the poorest families. In his study of child abuse reports, cited earlier, Gil[8] found that injuries were more likely to be fatal or serious among families whose annual income was below $3500.

Severity certainly seems an important factor in this regard. If definitions of child abuse and neglect are viewed on a long continuum, and stretched to their most innocuous limits, it may indeed be concluded that, by "definition," child abuse and neglect are rampant throughout society. Moreover, the myth itself conveys the impression that severity, as well as frequency, of abuse is distributed proportionately among the classes. But, as Gil[8] pointed out, officially reported incidents are more likely than unreported incidents to involve severe injury, since severity is an important criterion of reporting; as we have seen, the relationship between poverty and severity of injury obtains even among the reported incidents.

A British study[15] of 134 battered infants and children under five years of age, most of whom had been admitted to hospitals, found that the parents were predominantly from the lower social classes. The investigators concluded that "battering is mainly a lower class phenomenon." They further stated that,

> . . . as the criteria for referral of cases were medical we are reasonably confident that if more children from high social class families had been admitted with unexpected injuries then consultant paediatricians would have referred them.

The most severe and least easily hidden maltreatment of children is that which results in death. As a forensic pathologist associated with the Office of the Medical Examiner in Philadelphia, Weston[17] reviewed the mortality of all children under sixteen years of age in that city from 1961 through 1965. During this five-year period, 60 deaths due to child abuse and neglect were found. Among the 24 deaths due to neglect, Weston noted that more than 80% of the families had received some form of public assistance. The investigator divided the abuse victims into two categories, according to prior trauma. Of the thirteen children with no previous injury (36% of the abuse victims), he reported that "more than half" came from middle-class homes. As for the 23 children with a history of repetitive trauma (64% of the abuse victims), he noted that, with few exceptions, most came from "homes of extremely low socioeconomic level," and none came from upper-middle or upper-class families.

Kaplun and Reich[11] studied 112 of the 140 apparent homicides of children under fifteen years of age, recorded by New York City's Chief Medical Examiner, which occurred in that city during 1968 and 1969. Over two-thirds of the assailants in these homicides were parents or paramours. The authors found:

> Most of the families of the murdered children (70%) lived in areas of severe poverty, and almost all were known to the city's public welfare agency.

Thus, we can conclude from these studies that the vast majority of the fatal victims of child abuse and neglect are from poor families.

Unlike certain other injuries to children, in only rare instances can death be hidden. Because of its greater severity and openness to public scrutiny than other injuries, its true causes, too, are less likely to go undetected. Death will prompt an investigation. However, it is probable that some child homicides have been successfully passed off as accidents by the parents, and some people will argue that investigative authorities have been more readily deceived by middle-class and upper-class parents than by lower-class parents.

Yet there is simply a massive amount of evidence, from our country and many others, that

> . . . the overwhelming majority of homicides and other assaultive crimes are committed by persons from the lowest stratum of a social organization.[18]

As Magura[12] noted, the source of such evidence is not limited to official statistics and, moreover, any presumed bias in the detection of offenses cannot explain the fact that official crime rate differences between social classes are substantially greater for physically aggressive crimes than for property offenses. If anything, as Magura pointed out, since the seriousness of an offense is known to be related to the probability of police intervention, the role of a bias in police recognition of offenses would be expected to be least influential in the detection of the most serious offenses. The rate differentials can only mean that, in actuality, crimes of violence are far more prevalent among the lowest socioeconomic classes. There is little reason to believe that child abuse (leaving aside, for the moment, child neglect, which is an act of a different nature than most violent crimes) conforms to any different socioeconomic pattern than that of violent crimes in general. In fact, the available evidence, including that pertaining to fatal child abuse, indicates that it does not.

Why the Myth Persists

That belief in the classlessness of child abuse and neglect has taken hold with such tenacity among professionals and the public, despite evidence and logic to the contrary, suggests that it serves important functions for those who accept it. Maintenance of the myth permits many professionals to view child abuse and neglect as psychodynamic problems, in the context of a medical model of "disease," "treatment," and "cure," rather than as predominantly sociological and poverty-related problems. Moreover, like the popular conception of an epidemic disease, afflicting families without regard to social or economic standing, the myth allows the problems of abuse and neglect to be portrayed as broader than they actually are; indeed, as occurring in "epidemic" proportions.

Boehm[5] has pointed out that the strong psychodynamic orientation in the field of social work has led to the assumption that neglect is a classless phenomenon. Conversely, it can be said that the assumption of classlessness plays a key role in upholding the psychodynamic orientation, as well as the medical model of treatment.

The mystique of psychodynamic theories has captivated many helping professionals, who seem to view the espousal and practice of such theories as conferring status and prestige upon themselves. Unfortunately, the mundane problems of poverty and poverty-related hazards hold less fascination for them; direct, concrete approaches to these problems appear to be less glamorous professionally than psychologizing about the poor and prescribing the latest fashions in psychotherapy. Although concrete services are the ones most attractive to prospective lower-class consumers, they are the services that are least appealing to the middle-class helping professionals immersed in the "psychological society."[10]

Thus the myth serves several functions. It supports the prestigious and fascinating psychodynamic medical-model approach and, by disassociating the problems from poverty, accords distinct and separate status to child abuse and neglect specialists. The myth holds that child abuse and neglect are not, for the most part, mere aspects of the poverty problem. Ultimately, by encouraging the view that abuse and neglect are widespread throughout society, the myth presumably aids in prying loose additional federal funds for dealing with these problems.

Politicians, for their part, have been amenable to the myth of classlessness because it serves certain functions for them. The questioning of David Gil by then-Senator Walter Mondale at the 1973 Senate hearings on the Child Abuse Prevention and Treatment Act was most revealing of this preference. Invoking the public scrutiny argument, Mondale pressed hard to establish that child abuse "is not a poverty problem." As Patti[13] noted,

> . . . it seems that the Senator wished to avoid treating child abuse as another manifestation of poverty out of a concern that the poverty issue had lost its political appeal.

Berleman[3] commented on the same hearings:

> Some legislators wished to be reassured that abuse was not disproportionately distributed according to socioeconomic class; they were particularly anxious not to have the problem become identified with the lower class. Many witnesses also gave the impression that the problem was not class-related.

Thus, both professional and politician, each for his own reasons, is disinclined to see the problems as poverty-related: the former to increase his chances of gaining funding for a medical-model approach, the latter to increase his own chances of getting a bill passed and thus being seen as aggressively dealing with the phenomenon of child "battering," which the public already perceives as a "sickness."

But the ends (obtaining increased funding) cannot justify the means (presenting a picture of child abuse and neglect not supported by the evidence) even on tactical grounds. When certain claims are made in order to secure funding, these claims will determine the disposition of the funds. If it is asserted that there are millions of undiscovered abuse and neglect cases among the middle classes, then legislators must reasonably conclude that money should be earmarked for finding them. And if it is claimed that the problems are unrelated to poverty, then money and attention will be diverted from poverty-oriented services.

Well-meaning mental health professionals may be drawn to the myth of classlessness, believing that the association of child abuse and neglect with poverty constitutes one more insulting and discriminatory act toward poor people, one more way to "stigmatize" them unjustly. In fact, the myth does a disservice to poor people and to the victims of child abuse and neglect; it undermines development of effective approaches to dealing with their real and difficult problems, and directs us toward remedies more oriented to the middle classes.

To say that child abuse and neglect are strongly related to poverty is not to say that poor people in general abuse and neglect their children. On the contrary, only a tiny minority of lower-class parents do so.[14] But the myth of classlessness diverts our attention from the "subculture of violence,"[18] the stresses of poverty that can provoke abuse and neglect, and the hazardous poverty environment that heightens the dangerousness of child neglect.

How The Myth Serves As A Smokescreen

In the face of the evidence that child abuse and neglect, especially in their most severe forms, occur disproportionately among the lower socioeconomic classes, proponents of the myth of classlessness have provided little substance for their beliefs. Nonetheless, as suggested above, the myth is persistent and powerful enough to blind many of us to the real poverty-related problems of most abuse and neglect cases. For poverty is not merely "associated" with child abuse and neglect; there is good reason to believe that the problems of poverty are causative agents in parents' abusive and negligent behaviors and in the resultant harm to children.

As Gil[8] has pointed out, the living conditions of poverty generate stressful experiences that may become precipitating factors of child abuse, and the poor have little means by which to escape from such stress. Under these circumstances, even minor misbehaviors and annoyances presented by powerless children may trigger abuse. Such poverty-related factors as unemployment, dilapidated and overcrowded housing, and insufficient money, food, recreation, or hope can provide the stressful context for abuse. This is not to say that middle-class parents never experience stresses that might lead to child abuse, or that abuse is always contributed to by environmental stress. Nor does it mean that the additional stresses of poverty cause most impoverished families to maltreat their children. But, given the established fact that poverty is strongly related to child maltreatment, we find that there are sensible explanations as to why poverty might be a partial determinant of it.

Child neglect is a far more pervasive social problem than is abuse, occurring in more than twice as many cases.[1, 14] Moreover, when harm to the child severe enough to have required hospitalization or medical attention has occurred, it is from one-and-a-half to two times as likely to have been due to neglect than to abuse. In addition, neglect is somewhat more strongly related to poverty than is abuse.[1, 14]

Like abuse, neglect may partially result from poverty-related stresses. In leading to neglect, these stresses may produce the mediating factor of despair rather than anger when, for example, a single parent attempts to raise a large family in cramped and unsafe living quarters with no help and little money. The relationship can be seen most clearly in those cases in which a terrible incident, such as a fire devastating the home, also destroys the mother's capacity to cope with poverty any longer.

However, no matter what the origins of neglectful behavior, there is a more immediate way in which poverty causes harm to neglected children. Poverty itself directly presents dangers for children, and very often neglect merely increases the likelihood that those dangers will result in harm.

Neglectful irresponsibility more readily leads to dire consequences when it occurs in the context of poverty than when that same behavior is engaged in by middle-class parents.[14] In middle-class families there is some *leeway* for irresponsibility, a luxury that poverty does not afford. A middle-class mother can be careless with her money and squander some of it, but still have enough so that her children will not be deprived of basic necessities. Identical lapses in responsibility on the part of an impoverished mother might cause her children to go hungry during the last few days of the month. The less money one has, the better manager of money one has to be.

Leaving a child alone or unattended is the most prevalent form of child neglect, occurring in 50% of all neglect cases.[14] A middle-class parent's inadequate supervision will not put the children in as great danger as will that of the impoverished parent, because the middle-class home is not as drastically beset with health and safety hazards. The context of poverty multiplies the hazards of a mother's neglect. Thus, poor people have very little margin for irresponsibility or mismanagement of either time or money.

In some cases, the mother does not have much choice but to leave her children alone. A welfare mother with many children cannot easily obtain or pay for a babysitter every time she must leave the house to do her chores; in addition, she may find it more difficult to do her shopping than would a middle-class mother. If she leaves her children alone, she is taking a gamble with their safety; if she stays with them, it may mean being unable to provide proper food or other immediate necessities. Thus, some mothers are caught up in difficult and dangerous situations that have less to do with their adequacy and responsibility as parents than with the hard circumstances of their lives.

The myth of classlessness diverts attention from the environmental problems of poor households that make neglect so much more dangerous to children than it would be in middle-class homes. Recognition of the impoverished context of child neglect points us to the need for concrete services directed at the dangers of poverty, services such as house-finding, rat control, in-home babysitter services, installation of window guard-rails, and emergency cash for the repair of boilers or plumbing, the payment of gas and electric bills, a security deposit on a new apartment, or the purchase of food, crib, playpen, etc. Such measures will often directly prevent harm to children in protective services cases, and obviate the need for immediate child placement. In addition, reducing the immediate stresses of poverty may have a rapid and positive impact upon the parents' behavior.

Although the stresses of poverty certainly have psychological effects, the strong relationship between poverty and child abuse and neglect suggests that remediation of situational defects should take precedence over psychological treatments. These parents' behavior problems are less likely to be symptoms of unconscious or intrapsychic conflicts than of concrete antecedent environmental conditions, crises, and catastrophes. It is these root causes that must be addressed.

Child welfare agencies can neither enter the housing industry nor raise clients' welfare benefits. But they can seek to remedy many of the health and safety hazards that attend poverty and inadequate housing and that, in combination with parental factors produced in part by those very hazards, place children in danger of harm and abuse.

Conclusion

Both evidence and reason lead to the unmistakable conclusion that, contrary to the myth of classlessness, child abuse and neglect are strongly related to poverty, in terms of prevalence and of severity of consequences. This is not to say that abuse and neglect do not occur among other socioeconomic classes, or that, when they do occur, they never have severe consequences. However, widespread reports suggesting that abuse and neglect are classless phenomena are unfounded and misleading. The myth of classlessness persists not on the basis of evidence or logic, but because it serves certain professional and political interests. These interests do not further the task of dealing with the real problems underlying abuse and neglect; adherence to the myth diverts attention from the nature of the problems and diverts resources from their solution.

REFERENCES

1.   AMERICAN HUMANE ASSOCIATION. 1978. *National Analysis of Official Child Neglect and Abuse Reporting.* American Humane Association, Denver.

2.   AMERICAN HUMANE ASSOCIATION. *Statistics for 1975.* American Humane Association, Denver.

3.   BERLEMAN, W. 1976. *An analysis of issues related to child abuse and neglect as reflected in Congressional hearings prior to the enactment of the Child Abuse Prevention and Treatment Act of 1974.* Center for Social Welfare Research, School of Social Work, University of Washington.

4.   BESHAROV, D. AND BESHAROV, S. 1977. "Why do parents harm their children?" *National Council of Jewish Women* (Winter):6-8.

5.   BOEHM, B. 1964. "The community and the social agency define neglect." *Child Welfare* 43:453-464.

6.   FONTANA, V. 1977. In statement printed in Senate hearings on extension of the Child Abuse Prevention and Treatment Act, April 6-7:505.

7.   FRASER, B. 1976-77. "Independent representation for the abused and neglected child: the guardian ad litem." *Calif. Western Law Rev.* 13.

8.   GIL, D. 1970. *Violence Against Children.* Harvard University Press, Cambridge, Mass.

9.   GIOVANNONI, J. AND BILLINGSLEY, A. 1970. "Child neglect among the poor: a study of parental inadequacy in families of three ethnic groups." *Child Welfare* 49:196-204.

10.   GROSS, M. 1978. *The Psychological Society.* Random House, New York.

11.   KAPLUN, D. AND REICH, R. 1976. "The murdered child and his killers." *Amer. J. Psychiat.* 133:809-813.

12.   MAGURA, S. 1975. "Is there a subculture of violence?" *Amer. Sociol. Rev.* 40:831-836.

13.   PATTI, R. 1976. *An analysis of issues related to child abuse and neglect as reflected in Congressional hearings prior to the enactment of the Child Abuse Prevention and Treatment Act of 1974.* Center for Social Welfare Research, School of Social Work, University of Washington.

14. PELTON, L. 1977. *Child abuse and neglect and protective intervention in Mercer County, New Jersey: a parent interview and case record study.* Bureau of Research, New Jersey Division of Youth and Family Services.

15. SMITH, S., HANSON, R. AND NOBLE, S. 1975. "Parents of battered children: a controlled study." In *Concerning Child Abuse,* A. Franklin, ed. Churchill Livingstone, Edinburgh.

16. STEELE, B. 1975. "Working with abusive parents: a psychiatrist's view." *Children Today* 4:3.

17. WESTON, J. 1974. "The pathology of child abuse." In *The Battered Child* (2nd ed.), R. Helfer and C. Kempe, eds. University of Chicago Press, Chicago.

18. WOLFGANG, M. 1967. "Criminal homicide and the subculture of violence." In *Studies in Homicide,* M. Wolfgang, ed. Harper and Row, New York.

19. WOLOCK, I. AND HOROWITZ, B. 1977. "Factors relating to levels of child care among families receiving public assistance in New Jersey." *Final Report,* Vol. 1, June 30, 1977 (grant No. 90-c-418). Submitted to the National Center on Child Abuse and Neglect, DHEW.

20. YOUNG, L. 1971. *Wednesday's Children.* McGraw-Hill, New York.

10

Sexual Abuse, Another Hidden Pediatric Problem: The 1977 C. Anderson Aldrich Lecture*

C. Henry Kempe, M.D.

Pediatrics started, about a hundred years ago, around the single critical issue of deaths due to diarrhea, caused by unsafe milk. Pediatrics has progressed to a comprehensive approach to child health, with intermittent episodes of acute illness and the skilled management of chronic illnesses. The modern pediatrician, modeling himself after Dr. Aldrich, will attempt to return the child to his normal and optimal state of health as soon as possible and to try to minimize the deleterious effects of illness on the normal growth and development of the child, from both the emotional and the physical point of view.

I have chosen to speak on the subject of sexual abuse of children and adolescents as another hidden pediatric problem and a neglected area. More and more clinical problems related to sexual abuse come to our attention every year. In our training and in our practice, we pediatricians are insufficiently aware of the frequency of sexual abuse; it is, I believe, just as common as physical abuse and the failure-to-thrive syndrome.

Just as the "battered child syndrome" rang a responsive chord among pediatricans 20 years ago, it is my hope that with this brief discussion I might stimulate a broader awareness among pediatricians of the problems of sexual abuse.

---

* C. Henry Kempe, "Sexual Abuse, Another Hidden Pediatric Problem: The 1977 C. Andersen Aldrich Lecture," *Pediatrics*, Vol. 62, No. 3:382-389, September, 1978. Copyright © American Academy of Pediatrics 1978. Reproduced by permission.

I shall try to do so from a developmental point of view, since the child's stage of development profoundly influences the evaluation and treatment we give.

During last year's influenza vaccination campaign, a 10-year-old girl was seen in consultation with the possible diagnosis of Guillain-Barré syndrome. She was, in fact, suffering from hysterical paralysis. Everyone was relieved by what she did not have, but not so impressed with the discovery that her hysterical paralysis stemmed from the fact that she had been the subject of an incestuous relationship with her father. This had become increasingly intolerable to her, with the resulting symptoms. Physicians and, surprisingly, nurses generally shunned her and were not very sympathetic. She was somehow in the wrong. There was some discussion that she was "seductive," and that she "might have been asking for it." Another group didn't believe the diagnosis in the first place. I found her to be a lonely and almost suicidal youngster in need of immediate rescue through active intervention. Her masked depression was characterized by inability to eat or sleep.

Sexual abuse is defined as the involvement of dependent, developmentally immature children and adolescents in sexual activities that they do not fully comprehend, to which they are unable to give informed consent, or that violate the social taboos of family roles.

Sexual abuse includes pedophilia (an adult's preference or addiction for sexual relations with children), rape, and all forms of incest. "Sexual exploitation" is another term frequently used, and it is true that these children are "exploited," because sexual abuse robs the child and adolescent of their developmentally determined control over their own bodies, and they are further robbed of their own preference, with increasing maturity, for sexual partners on an equal basis. This is so regardless of whether the child has to deal with a single overt, and perhaps violent, act, often committed by a stranger, or with incestuous acts, often continued for many years, which may be carried out under actual or threatened violence or may be nonviolent or even tender, insidious, collusive, and secretive.

Scientific studies of incidence are even rarer in the field of sexual abuse than in the field of physical abuse. Data collection has been impaired by what has been euphemistically referred to as a "family affair." In discovered acts of pedophilia, such as occurs in fondling or exhibitionism, the child complains to his parents, the police are involved, and an incidence report is made. The same holds true of child rape. In these situations, incidence data are at least minimally correct. As far as the child is concerned, family and professional support for the victim is strong, and criminal conviction rates are relatively high. Pediatricians here are often informed early on, and they do participate in the diagnosis and even the early treatment of victims. In instances of nonviolent pedophilia, particularly a single act involving a stranger, simple reassurance of the child and more massive reassurance of the parents are all that is required. Forcible sexual abuse and child rape involving strangers, aside from the management of the sexual injuries, often call for long-term supportive therapy to each member of the family.

The discovery of incest, on the other hand, finds the family and the community reacting in a different way. If reports are made by the victim, they rarely result in family support, nor do they often result in successful criminal prosecution. Moreover, it is common for children, who are regularly cared for by their pediatrician, to be involved in incest for many years without their physician knowing. Incest makes pediatricians and everyone else very uncomfortable.

Some physicians routinely ascribe specific complaints of incest, and even incestuous pregnancy, to adolescent fantasy. Often, pediatricians will simply not even consider the diagnosis of incest in making an assessment of an emotionally disturbed child or adolescent of either sex. Still, a history of incest is so commonly found among adults coming to the attention of psychiatrists, marriage counselors, mental health clinics, the police, and the courts—10 or 15 years after the events—that the failure to consider the diagnosis early on is somewhat surprising. Most of the youngsters we now see are under the care of a pediatrician in private practice or a clinic setting. With remarkable regularity they represent the children of professionals, white- and blue-collar workers, as well as of the poor, in a way that reflects a cross section of our community. And so it is with the racial distribution, which, contrary to published reports from welfare departments and the police, reflects that no race in Denver is overrepresented in sexual abuse, provided one considers all levels of society who come to our attention.

Underreporting is massive. In incest there is often long-standing active or passive family collusion and support. Disruption of the ongoing set relationships is generally resisted, and understandably so; disclosure will result in public retribution, with the firm expectation of total family disruption, unemployment and economic disaster, loss of family and friends for the victim, and likely incarceration for the perpetrator, at least until bail is posted. There is also the public shame of failure for each person involved in their own role as father, mother, and child, with resulting further loss of self-esteem by all. The Children's Division of the American Humane Society reported 5,000 cases of sexual abuse for the United States in 1972. Since only a small fraction of instances of sexual abuse are reported at the time of occurrence, as opposed to those that come to light ten or more years later, it is our view that the true incidence must be at least ten times higher. In the first six months of this year, the Denver General Hospital alone saw 89 cases. We are increasingly seeing younger and younger children who require urgent care. The group of children from birth to age 5 years has increased in recent years from 5% to 25% of the total, while the incidence during the latency age period from 5 to 10 has remained stable at 25%. Between 1967 and 1972 the number of sexually abused children increased tenfold in our hospital.

Incest is usually hidden for years, and comes to public attention only as a result of a dramatic change in the family situation, such as adolescent rebellion or delinquent acts, pregnancy, venereal disease, a great variety of psychiatric illnesses, or something as trivial as a sudden family quarrel. One half of our adolescent runaway girls were involved in sexual abuse, and many of them experienced physical abuse as well.

Nature of Sexual Abuse

Pedophilia. Pedophilia often involves nonviolent sexual contact by an adult with a child, and it may consist of genital fondling, orogenital contact, or genital viewing.

Case 1.—A brilliant young lawyer, father of two children, on several occasions engaged in genital fondling of 6- to 8-year-old girls who were friends of his children. The neighbors contacted us with a view toward stopping this behavior, while at the same time wanting to prevent the ruin of this attractive family and to get psychiatric help for the patient. Much of this compassionate and nonpunitive view was the result of their affection for the patient's young wife, whom they greatly liked. They insisted, however, that the family promptly leave the neighborhood. The patient moved to a distant city, where he entered psychotherapy and has had a long-term cure of his addictive pedophilia. His professional and family life has remained stable.

Case 2.—A 53-year-old physician was accused of fondling the genitalia of his preadolescent male patients. A hearing before the medical board confirmed that he regularly measured the penis of all his male patients, much as he would examine their weight. His defense was that measurements such as these are part of comprehensive care, but the board held that the procedure was not routine anywhere, except when the specific medical problem concerned the size of the penis, as is the case in some hormonal disorders. He voluntarily resigned his license to practice but refused offers of help.

Violent Molestation and Rape. While all sexual exploitation of minors is illegal, society is particularly concerned with retribution to prevent repetition when rape or other forcible molestation occurs. It is not necessary for hymenal rupture or vaginal entry to occur to have the rape statute apply; frequently, vaginal tears and/or evidence of sperm or a type-specific gonococcal infection can be the ultimate proof. However, perineal masturbatory action often leads to emission of sperm outside the vagina, on the skin or the anus. Many molestors experience premature ejaculation, and others are impotent. We find sperm less than 50% of the time. Orogenital molestation may leave no evidence, except the child's story. This must be believed! Children do not fabricate stories of detailed sexual activities unless they have witnessed them, and they have, indeed, been eyewitnesses to their abuse.

Case 3.—The 23-year-old unemployed boyfriend of a divorced middle-class woman was babysitting for the woman's two daughters, aged 6 and 14. He first began to sexually assault the 14-year-old girl and raped her, despite her efforts to resist by screaming, hitting, and biting. While she ran for help to distant neighbors, he raped the 6-year-old and fled. When captured, he told the police that he had had two beers and remembered nothing of the events. The children both required hospital care for emotional as well as medical reasons. The 6-year-old had a 2.5-cm vaginal tear that was repaired. The older child had a hymenal tear and many bruises. Both had semen in the vagina, and both required antibiotics to prevent gonorrhea with which the attacker was afflicted. Loving and supportive nursing and, later, psychiatric care were given to both victims, who seemed to view the event as "a bad accident." The mother had much reason to feel guilt, since she had known of her friend's inability to handle alcohol without becoming violent. The psychiatric diagnosis of the perpetrator was "violent and sociopathic personality, not likely to change at any time." He remains in prison for an indeterminate sentence, but he is a model prisoner to date, and will eventually be paroled.

Incest. Father-daughter incest accounts for approximately three fourths of cases of incest, while mother-son, father-son, mother-daughter, and brother-sister account for the remaining one fourth. It is our belief that incest has been increasing in the United States in recent years, perhaps because of the great changes in family life: increasing divorce rates, birth control, abortion, and an increasingly more tolerant view of sexual acts between blood-related household members who come from divorced or previously separated homes. This is particularly true as it affects brother-sister incest between stepchildren, who are living as a family but are not related. We believe that cultural attitudes in regard to this latter group of adolescents are rapidly changing to a less concerned stance.

Father-daughter incest tends to be nonviolent, but in the preadolescent and early adolescent, the coexisting relationship between physical abuse and sexual exploitation is often striking, but rarely discussed. It is not uncommon for acting-out adolescent girls to be suffering from both physical and sexual abuse. We find men with psychopathic personalities and indiscriminate sexuality who view children as objects, and these men are often violent. Some nonviolent abuse is seen in pedophiles who seduce both their own and other children. Most fathers involved incestuously with their daughters have introverted personalities, tend to be socially isolated, and have an intrafamily orientation. Many are gradually sliding toward incestuous behavior, with the extra push given, often, by a wife who either abets or arranges situations likely to make privacy between father and daughter easier. She may, for example, arrange her work schedule to take her away from home in the evenings and tell her daughter to "take care of Dad" or to "settle him down." It is not hard to see how a very loving and dependent relationship between father and daughter might result, first in acceptable degrees of caressing and later in increasingly intimate forms of physical contact. The silent agreement between husband, wife, and daughter is a triad in which each plays a role and which is generally free of marked guilt or anger unless a crisis occurs. One of these crises is public discovery. A daughter is, of course, robbed of her developmentally appropriate sexuality and is often caught in the dilemma of forcing an end to a now embarrassing affair in order to live a more usual life with her peers and of losing her family security which, she believes, her compliance has assured her, her mother, and her siblings. It is a terrible burden to carry for these immature women, and relief may not come until they leave home and try to build a new life.

Writers have, for the most part, stressed unduly the seductive nature of young girls involved sexually with fathers or brothers as opposed to the more important participatory role played by mothers. Our experience suggests that the seduction that some young girls tend to experiment with to a certain degree and usually safely, within the family, is usually normal and does not explain incest, which is not initiated by the child but by the adult male, with the mother's complicity. Stories by mothers that they "could not be more surprised" can generally be discounted; we have simply not seen an innocent mother in cases of long-standing incest. Still, the mother escapes the punishment her husband will likely suffer.

Why do mothers play such an important role in incest between father and daughter? Often, a very dependent mother is frantic to hold her man to the family for her needs and the financial support he provides. The sexual role of the daughter is seen as one way of providing him a younger, more attractive bond within the family than she can provide. This is especially true if she is frigid, rejected sexually, or is herself promiscuous. Rationalizations for incest abound and must be dealt with in a direct manner. The "I only wanted to show her how to do it" school is often talked about but rarely encountered. The same is true for "he just needs a lot of sex" attitude. The vast majority of incest situations find people literally caught up in a life-style from which they find no easy way out and in which discovery must at all cost be avoided. In order to preserve the family, even after discovery has occurred, admission is often followed by denial, and the immediate family tends to condemn the victim if she is the cause of discovery. She is then bereft of all support and has few choices. Far more often, of course, there is no immediate discovery and only after some time does the victim's emotional need bring about an understanding of her difficult past.

Case 4.—An 18-year-old college student with many minor physical complaints and episodes of insomnia told freely of her anger at her father who, on her leaving for college, was having an incestuous affair with her younger sister. She maintained that she was not jealous but rather wanted him stopped: as she said, "I have given my best years to him to keep us together."

Her father, a judge, had begun to sexually stimulate her at bedtime when she was 12 and commenced regular intercourse when she was 14, often six times each week. Her mother knew of these acts from the start, encouraged them subtly at first, and then simply would not discuss the matter. Whenever the patient threatened to leave home, she was told by her mother that she kept the family together and that her two younger siblings would be forever grateful to her for preventing a divorce. The patient had had no boyfriends and few girlfriends, and was anxious until she left home to "have things stay the same." On discussion with the mother, it appeared that she was frightened and angry, denied that her husband, "an important man in this community," could be so ungratefully accused, asked that he not be contacted, and disowned her daughter as a chronic liar. Her father admitted, in medical confidence, that his daughter was totally correct and that he was, indeed, involved with his second daughter. He entered therapy with an experienced psychiatrist and has, over the past years, been able to desist from all incestuous relationships. His eldest daughter will not see him, and he accepts this. He blames himself fully, is puzzled by his craving for love from his daughters, and finally blames himself for his wife's frigidity. He is chronically depressed, and takes medication, and he has been a borderline alcoholic in recent years.

Case 5.—A 14-year-old girl was seen on request by the police because her 16-year-old brother, when arrested as a runaway, had told them that his father had an incestuous relationship with his sister. The parents denied the allegation and, initially, so did the patient. But on the second interview, she began to discuss her fears about pregnancy and venereal diseases and, with reassurance, described her four-year involvement with her father, a 35-year-old computer programmer with a college education. The patient was placed in foster care but repeatedly ran away. The father lost his job when he was first arrested and, while awaiting trial, attempted suicide. Subsequently, criminal prosecution was deferred, and both parents received joint treatment around their failing marriage and their relationship with both children. Both children elected to remain in different foster homes until graduation from high school. Criminal charges were eventually dropped, and employment was resumed. The marriage was stabilized. Both children, who are in college now, seem to be on friendly terms with both parents, although they never visit overnight.

Case 6.—A 14-year-old girl was seen with a history of marked weight loss and a diagnosis of anorexia nervosa. Her 16 year-old brother was extremely worried about her deteriorating condition, and confessed to his father that he had carried on a brief incestuous relationship with her for four months and that he wondered if he had caused her illness. The patient recovered promptly, and both youngsters received individual therapy. Each requested a therapist of his/her own sex. Both remained in the household, and both have done well personally and professionally.

Case 7.—A 16-year-old girl was seen because an unrelated household member, a boy of 16, had been treated for gonorrhea and listed her as one of his sexual contacts. She was asymptomatic, but her vaginal and rectal cultures were also positive, although for a distinctly different strain of the gonococcus organism. The remaining members of the large family were then cultured. Her stepfather was positive for gonorrhea with the same strain as were her 14-year-old and 18-year-old stepsisters. Throat cultures for the gonococcus were positive in her 9-year-old stepbrother, as was his anal culture. Her mother was culture-negative, as were two cousins and another, younger stepbrother. It is likely, but was not admitted, that the stepfather, who had a criminal record, and not the 16-year-old boy had infected by sodomy and vaginal intercourse the index patient, who was not clinically ill. The stepfather had further, through fellatio by his stepson on himself and by sodomy, infected the 9-year-old boy, and caused vaginal infections in the 14- and 18-year-old girls. The health department administered curative doses of penicillin to all members found to be infected. They noted, wryly, that the initial report of the 16-year-old boy was not related to the family infection, and ignored all other implications of this family's chaotic incestuous life.

Age of Partners

In pedophilia or child rape, the age of the child tends to be between 2 years and early adolescence, while incestuous relationships may begin at the toddler age and continue into adult life. The median age for incestuous behavior in recent years has been between 9 and 10 years, well within the age group routinely seen by pediatricians, including those pediatricians who shun the care of the adolescent patient.

Society tends to be more concerned with fathers sleeping with or genitally manipulating daughters or sons than mothers doing the same to sons or, rarely, daughters. This double standard is most likely based on the belief that the sheltering mother is simply prolonging, perhaps unusually but not criminally, her previous nurturing role. That mothers who regularly sleep with their school-age sons, referring to them as "lovers" and sexually stimulating them, are very seriously mentally ill, as are their children, is quite clear to us, but intervention is difficult because mothers are given an enormous leeway in their actions, while fathers and brothers are not.

Violent acts of sexual exploitation or rape are usually perpetrated by males under the age of 30, while father-daughter incest tends to involve middle-aged men between 30 and 50. Other incestuous relationships, such as those between siblings, can vary from mutual genital play in early childhood and during the school-age years to attempted and, sometimes successful, intercourse in adolescence. A grandson-grandmother relationship involved a boy, age 18, and an exceedingly wealthy woman, aged 70. At least three physicians dealt with the emotional problems of the delinquent grandson, but none of them was prepared to accept the diagnosis readily admitted to by both patients.

Girls involved with father or stepfathers are often the first daughters in preadolescence or early adolescence.

Subtle Clinical Findings

In cases in which the parents report a single episode caused by either a stranger, a babysitter, a relative, or a household member other than the parents, the diagnosis is made before the physician is ever involved. More troubling are those subtle manifestations that are not ordinarily thought to relate to the diagnosis and that call forth the pediatrician's best diagnostic acumen.

In the child under 5 years of age, aggressive sexual abuse, that is, any forced sexual act, often results in fear states and night terrors, clinging behavior, and some form of developmental regression. The pediatrician's role is to provide reassurance. In a stable family setting, it is the parents rather than the child who need repeated help. It may be that from time to time the event will have to be worked through with the child once again, but this can often be done in a nursery school setting with active support from loving teachers and parents, and again in adolescence, if needed.

In the school-age child, subtle clinical manifestations may include sudden onset of anxiety, fear, depression, insomnia, conversion hysteria, sudden massive weight loss or weight gain, sudden school failure, truancy, or running away.

In adolescence, serious rebellion, particularly against the mother, is often the presenting finding. The physician who is aware of a specific estrangement between the mother and daughter should consider this diagnosis. Girls involved in incest often will eventually forgive their fathers, but rarely will they forgive their mothers who failed to protect them. Further, if the pediatrician notices that the daughter has suddenly been assigned virtually all the functions ordinarily taken by a mother within the family group, by looking after the house and siblings, the diagnosis is often made. Parents have reassigned to the daughter the mother's function both in the kitchen and in bed. These youngsters must be given an opportunity to share their secret with a sympathetic person.

As children get older, we often find more serious delinquency, including massive loss of self-esteem ("I am a whore," "I am a slut"). We see prostitution, along with chronic depression, social isolation, and increasing rebellion and runaways. There are, on the other hand, some very compliant and patient youngsters who carry the load of the family on their frail shoulders, at great sacrifice to their personal development and happiness. These adolescents are in a terrible dilemma. They are in no way assured of ready help from anyone, but they risk losing their family and feel guilty and responsible for bringing it harm if they share their secret. Youngsters may come to the attention of the health care system or the law only through pregnancy, prostitution, venereal disease, drug abuse, or antisocial behavior.

Treatment of Sexual Abuse

There is a chance, particularly when dealing with nonviolent sexual exploitation, to use the criminal justice system to initiate treatment, when the condition is treatable. Filing of criminal charges and a deferred prosecution to await evaluation and treatment are possible, provided certain requirements are met:

1. Exploitation must assuredly be stopped and for good.
2. Law enforcement officials must be involved in planning and must agree to the proposed treatment plan.
3. The prosecuting attorney and the court must feel that the criminal system is not being thwarted but that rehabilitation is an acceptable course, if it is under the supervision, even if remote, of the probation department or law enforcement.
4. Treatment failure, including nonparticipation in an agreed-to program, should bring the criminal process back at once, because, while the bypass process is recognized as an option for the legal system, it is strictly limited to effecting a better outcome than can be foreseen by incarceration following conviction.

Pedophilia may never be cured, but it is often possible to bring all illegal acts under control (case 1). There is no certain cure for the aggressive sociopath who engages in violent sexual molestation and rape. Until we know what to do for such people we must be certain that they never have control of a child, who is always defenseless in their presence. Moreover, they are often a menace to all, and, in many cases, nothing but prison is left for their management if they are convicted or psychiatric commitment to a secure setting if they are judged to be legally insane and unable to stand trial.

The treatment of incest, on the other hand, is far more likely to be successful and to result in the three desired goals: (1) stopping the incest; (2) providing individual and, later, group treatment to victim and each parent; and (3) healing the victim's wounds so that he/she grows up as a whole person, with the ability to enjoy normal sexuality.

In our experience, it has not been possible to reunite families after incest has been stopped through either placing the child or removing the offender unless two conditions have been met: (1) the mother must be shown to be willing and able to protect her children, and (2) both parents must admit to the problem and have a shared desire to remedy it, while at the same time either improving their failing marriage or divorcing. Ultimately, treatment can be judged to be successful only many years later, when the child has grown up and made a success of life.

Projective psychological tests reveal that incest victims see themselves as defenseless, worthless, guilty, at risk, and threatened from all sides, particularly from their father and mother who would be expected to be their protectors. Improvement in these projective tests is a useful aid to progress of therapy. Projective tests also clearly differentiate the angry, wrongful accuser from the rather depressed incestuous victim, and are therefore most useful in early family evaluation when the facts of incest are denied. Questions to be answered early on are these: Can the child forgive the perpetrators? Can the child regain self-confidence and self-esteem, and have a better self-image?

In a report from Santa Clara County, California, 90% of the marriages were saved, 95% of the incestuous daughters returned home, and there was no recidivism in families receiving a minimum of ten hours of treatment. Regrettably, we have been far less successful! In my experience, between 20% and 30% of the families have not been reunited, no matter what we have attempted, and I have come to feel that they should not be reunited. Reuniting families should not be the overriding goal. Rather, the best interests of the child should be served. Many adolescent girls do far better as emancipated minors, in group homes or in carefully selected foster home settings. Once they have broken the bond of incest, society must not condemn these victims to an additional sentence, but it must provide loving protection and supportive adults who are better models than their fathers and mothers can ever hope to be. They will, of course, still have ties of affection to their family, but they will see them in a more mature, compassionate way. In any case, the dependency on the family is over somewhat sooner than it would normally be.

Much less is known about the treatment of mother-son or homosexual incest between a parent and child, but these general observations can be made. The gray area of incest in the preadolescent cuddly behavior is not without danger. Even quite early, children receive cues about their role vis-à-vis each parent, and sexual models can be normal or highly distorted. After adolescence has begun, guilt, fear of discovery, low self-esteem, isolation, all extract a frightful toll. These problems must always be faced, either sooner or later, and later is generally much worse.

Prognosis of Sexual Exploitation

A one-time sexual molestation by a stranger, particularly of a nonviolent kind, such as a pedophilic encounter, appears to be harmless to normal children living with secure and reassuring parents. The event still needs to be talked out and explained at an age-appropriate level, and all questions need to be answered. Fierce admonishment such as "Don't let anyone touch you there!" or "All men are beasts" is, at most, not helpful.

All victims of violent molestation and rape need a great deal of care. For many reasons, a brief, joint hospital stay with the mother may help to take care of injuries, such as a vaginal tear, and to satisfy the legal requirements for criminal evidence in a setting that is sympathetic and supportive. During examination, the presence of the mother, sister, or grandmother is essential. A female phsycian-gynecologist who is gentle and who explains the examination is equally important. With her help, a vaginal specimen can be obtained for possible identification of semen (which can be typed and compared to the accused offender's) and for cultures for venereal diseases. The culture findings can be of use in understanding the chain of transmission within the family and in influencing treatment. At times, children are so afraid and in such pain that an almost equally violent form of rape occurs in the emergency room on the part of inexperienced and rough physicians and nurses. It is far better to take time and try to do all that is needed under gentle guidance and among faces that are familiar to and beloved by the frightened child than to attempt force. It is best, at times, to give the child a brief anesthetic to allow for examination and obtaining samples while she is asleep. In any event, a terrifying experience must not be made even worse by those providing treatment. We have tended to resist the request for physical examination in nonviolent abuse cases. In children under 12, the story given or the acts demonstrated by children are to be believed because of the very nature of their detail and clarity of description. This is not fantasy!

Incest occurring before adolescence and then stopped appears to cause less havoc than incest continuing into or throughout adolescence. The principal and major exception to this is the not uncommon situation in which a very young girl is trained to be a sexual object and to give and receive sexual pleasure as the one way to receive approval. These girls make each contact with any adult male an overt sexual event, with genital stimulation sought, supplied, and rewarded. They have, in short, been trained for the profession of prostitution. Nothing is more pathetic and more difficult to manage, because these girls are far too knowing and provocative to be acceptable in most foster or adoptive homes. They are socially disabled until cared for, at length, by a mature and understanding couple. We have found that fathers involved in this form of early "training incest" are not curable. The outlook for the children also is not good, even with treatment, because of the timing and prolonged imprinting nature of their exploitation.

Incest during adolescence is especially traumatic because of the heightened awareness of the adolescent and the active involvement in identity formation and peer group standards. Frigidity, conversion hysteria, promiscuity, phobias, suicide attempts, and psychotic behavior are some of the chronic disabilities one sees in some women who experienced adolescent incest without receiving help. It is only in retrospect that these histories are obtained many years later, and, generally the affair never came to the notice of anyone outside the family.

Boys do much worse than girls! Either mother-son (or grandmother-grandson) or father-son incest leaves a boy with such severe emotional insult that it blocks normal emotional growth. They tend to be severely restricted and may be unable to handle any stress without becoming frankly psychotic. Incest is ruinous for the male, but can be overcome with or without help by many girls. In general, workers agree that early and humane working through of the complex emotions and distorted relationships is curative and that late discovery after serious symptoms have appeared is far less satisfactory. The focus of treatment is the family, but sometimes there really is no functional family, and the youngster must try to build an independent life with sympathetic help from others.

In contemporary society, many explain the incest taboos as having no function other than the prevention of close inbreeding, with its deleterious genetic effects. Where this explanation has been accepted as sufficient, it has meant a weakening of the sanctions that, in the past, protected the relation between adults and children, including stepchildren. Mead feels that where the more broadly based sanctioning system has broken down, the household may become the setting for cross-generational reciprocal seduction and exploitation, rather than fulfilling its historic role of protecting the immature and permitting the safe development of the strong affectional ties in a context where sex relationships within the family are limited to spouses. Home must be a safe place!

We believe that *all* sexual exploitation is harmful and that it must be stopped!

This does not imply that criminal sanctions must always follow, though they are often an expression of public fury and demand for retribution. What is clear is that the child may need weeks and months of individual or group psychotherapy to come to terms with the event and to integrate the sometimes puzzling, sometimes frightening, and sometimes guilt-laden occurrence back into a normally progressing and safe environment. The growing child and adolescent increasingly assumes charge of his or her control over body and mind. Failure to treat the victim is a far more serious societal act than failure to punish the perpetrator.

Conclusion

Each week we find among our pediatric-adolescent patients, among youngsters at the Kennedy Child Development Center, and among the children seen at our child psychiatric service, increasing numbers of sexually abused children whose presenting chief complaint is nonspecific.

The nonspecific symptoms I have described may be the only clues we physicians have that we may be dealing with sexual abuse. One requires sensitive attention to the patient, good listening, taking time, and always going beyond the presenting "chief complaint."

The runaway who is simply asked "Why did you run away?" will say, "I had a fight with my folks." The next question is "What was your fight about?" The answer, "I was out late." Most professionals stop right there, but that's where we should all start. We simply have to know more. One needs to lead up to the relationships with the child's mother and father, and then one finally has to ask some direct questions, in as kind a way as possible, in order to give the child permission to relate his/her loneliness, shame, and fears.

Sexual abuse should always be viewed from a developmental point of view, and it is the point of each child's development which determines the ultimate impact that sexual abuse has. Early and decisive intervention, rescue, and supportive therapy work well, even if the family is not reunited. The child deserves a chance at therapy just as much as if there were any other insult to development.

Pediatricians routinely try to find children who have hearing and speech problems. Should we not be equally open and ready, intellectually and emotionally, for the condition of incest, which is the last taboo?

Thank you for allowing me to share with you this hour honoring the late Dr. Aldrich. I hope that I have done him honor.

ACKNOWLEDGMENT

I gratefully acknowledge support received by the William T. Grant Foundation and the Robert Wood Johnson Foundation.

11

Incest: Review and Clinical Experience*

Ida I. Nakashima, M.D., and
Gloria E. Zakus, M.S.W.

Information about incest has been little emphasized in medical journals. There is a need to become more aware of this problem, its magnitude, its characteristics, and its ramifications in order to identify and intervene in such cases.

The Adolescent Clinic at the University of Colorado Medical Center is a multidisciplinary facility providing comprehensive health care for teenagers. Incest is rarely seen as a presenting complaint. However, in the past 15 years, diagnoses of incestuous situations, occurring either currently or in the past, have been made on 23 cases. Information has been available from the medical and psychosocial evaluations. In reviewing the literature and the case material, some specific characteristics of involved individuals and families were identified, and these will be described in this article.

Incidence

Incest has remained one of the strongest and most consistent taboos of both primitive and highly developed societies. Accurate reporting of incest has been hampered by cultural inhibitions, the shame and guilt associated with disclosure, and the failure of professionals to recognize it. Estimates of incest in the United States have ranged from approximately one case per million population per year

* Ida I. Nakashima, and Gloria E. Zakus, "Incest: Review and Clinical Experience," *Pediatrics*, Vol. 60, No. 5:696-701, November, 1977. Copyright © American Academy of Pediatrics 1977. Reproduced by permission.

from 1910 to 1930[1] to 5,000 cases per million per year from 1948 to 1965.[2-4] Accurate statistics are difficult to obtain, and there is general agreement that the figures available are underestimates.

The recent strengthening of child abuse laws in many states has increased the reporting of all forms of child maltreatment, including incest. In 1969, in New York, DeFrancis[5] reported 3,000 cases a year of sexual molestation of children. In 72% of these cases, parents were involved in perpetrating or condoning the offense. In 1974, in Connecticut, 8.8% of all reported child abuse was categorized as sexual abuse, with a parent or guardian involved in 80% of such cases.[6]

Categories

The laws dealing with incest are confusing, as some states only recognize sexual intercourse among blood relatives, and are based on the hypothesis of harmful biological effects on the offspring of such unions. Other states recognize as incest any sexual relations between various combinations of "legal" relatives, e.g., adoptive parents or stepparents and their children. These laws are based on current sociological and psychological thinking that sexual relations between parent and child interfere with family functioning and prevent the healthy development of the child.

Descriptive categories of incest include relations between brother and sister, father and daughter, mother and son, father and son, and other relatives, e.g., uncles and grandparents. Data compiled by Kinsey et al.[2, 3] and Gebhard et al.[4] indicate that brother-sister incest occurs most often, probably five times as often as father-daughter incest. Because of its relative transience, and perhaps lack of social and behavioral sequelae, it appears in statistics less often. Father-daughter and stepfather-stepdaughter incest appears to be reported with the greatest frequency. Incest between mother and son is extremely rare and usually involves severely disturbed participants. Father-son incest is the rarest of all.

Types of Families

In reviewing 23 Adolescent Clinic cases, social service evaluations of the families were available in 19 cases of father-daughter or stepfather-stepdaughter incest. There were four other cases with insufficient information. Most of the data had been obtained from interviews with the mothers and from collaborative social agency sources.

The complex cultural, social, and psychiatric factors involved in the occurrence of incest have been summarized.[7] Some studies reported major mental illness in individual family members, others did not. Family interactions have been described by a number of authors.[8, 9]

The typical father-mother-daughter triad involved a domineering and patriarchal father, a passive and ineffectual mother, and a daughter who may have actively encouraged the father's sexual advances or at least not resisted them. The mother colluded by pushing the daughter into becoming the central female figure in the household. The incestuous interaction often continued over a period of years and in some instances eventually included younger female siblings.

Incest offenders are reported from two types of family backgrounds.[1] In the first, the family was so ingrown that the developing child found it difficult to cultivate social relationships outside the home and subsequently was unable to direct sexual desires to members outside the family. In the second, the family was so loosely organized and sexual impulses so ineffectively suppressed that the developing child did not learn adequately the prohibitions pertaining to sexual behavior among family members. These attitudes from the family of orientation were then carried over and repeated in the next generation's family system.

The families from the Adolescent Clinic have been classified into two groups: (1) the classic incest family and (2) the multiproblem incest family.

Classic Incest Family

In these cases, the pathology was primarily confined within the family and within the home. On a superficial level the family appeared to be quite stable and individual family members were functioning fairly well. Problems were well concealed from outsiders. There was little or no acting-out in the community, and these families were usually not known to social agencies.

Tormes[10] listed some of the following characteristics of incest families: an early marriage of long duration, with many children; the absence of acting-out behavior by the children; the absence of extramarital affairs by the parents; a pattern of rigid, restrictive control by the father of the social life of his female children; and limited contacts with the outside world by the family as a whole and by its individual members. These descriptions seemed valid in our classic incest families.

Two of our 19 families belonged in this classic incest category. One family was a striking example of being regarded as "healthy" by the community. A local child welfare department had placed a foster child in this home after evaluating it as a satisfactory placement. The incestuous activity had been occurring for several years, both before and after the placement of the foster child. The incestuous activity was uncovered only after the girl developed severe psychosomatic problems and was seen for a comprehensive evaluation.

With only two cases falling into this category, it is interesting to speculate about the reasons for the disproportionate distribution in our study. It may be that these kinds of families tend to be seen more frequently in other settings, or perhaps they are so well defended against exposure that our clinic staff failed to identify them.

Multiproblem Incest Family

In these cases, the incest appeared to be only one small aspect of the total family disorganization. These families had multiple problems. Their pathology (but not the incest) was recognized by outsiders. There was much acting-out in the community, and these families were often known to many different social agencies. In the Adolescent Clinic group there were 17 families that matched the above description.

Within the families, parenting problems appeared to be typical. Available information about the incest victim and the siblings revealed nine families with indications of possible child abuse and three others with questions of neglect. In the community, acting-out behaviors by parents and children were common. Parents had been involved in murder, assault, drug dependency, attempted kidnapping, and drunk driving. Children had been involved in school truancy, arson, dealing in heroin, thefts, sexual promiscuity, and illegitimate pregnancies.

All of these families had had contact with at least one or more social agencies in the community around issues other than the incest. They had been seen in the adult and juvenile courts, in child welfare departments, and in psychiatric inpatient and outpatient facilities. This information does tend to support the concept that the incest in some situations may be only a minor theme in the pathological chaos of the multiproblem family.

Weinberg's description[1] of different kinds of incestuous fathers included one where the incest was a part of the man's pattern of indiscriminate promiscuity, and another where the father had an intense craving for young children (pedophilia) and included the daughter as a sexual object. Four of the fathers in our group were reported as being sexually promiscuous, and another two fathers had been involved in sexual molestation of neighborhood children.

Chaneles[11] studied the families of sexually abused children and included incest cases. He emphasized that the reported incident of sexual molestation was only the latest in a long series of victimization of the child, reflecting the family's broad pattern of crises, disorganization, maladjustment, and separation from the established values of the community. This seemed typical of the 17 cases in our multiproblem incest group.

Family Characteristics

The Adolescent Clinic case material revealed three characteristics of family life that occurred in the majority of our cases, and in both the classic incest family and in the multiproblem incest family: (1) sexual difficulties between the parents, (2) mothers condoning the incest, and (3) shared fears of family disintegration by all individual members.

Parents' Sexual Problems

Sexual incompatibility in the marital relationship was seldom presented as a problem by the mother or by the father in incest situations. Consequently, this required specific questioning by the professional staff involved in assessing the case.

In our study group there were 11 families (out of 19 from whom information was elicited) indicating problems in the parents' sexual relationship. Most often this consisted of infrequent or no sexual contact. One mother found intercourse painful following her hysterectomy three years previously; another couple arranged to have their 6-year-old son sleep between them in their double bed; one father feared he would "catch" cancer from his wife. Avoidance of sexual intercourse between the parents was usually a well-established pattern of some years' duration. Many of the parents displayed remarkably little conflict in discussing this aspect of their sexual life, appearing to be comfortable with it.

Mothers Condoning the Incest

The conscious or unconscious sanction of the nonparticipant mother in condoning the incestuous activity and its perpetuation has been described in the literature. The mother's role is seen as critical in the pathological family system.

In our study group, this was specifically mentioned in most cases and alluded to in the remainder. It appeared to be a universal finding. Frequently, the need to deny the incest was so great that the mothers could not take any action to protect the child, unless forced to do so by outside sources. Comments such as, "I thought I was just imagining things—it didn't happen—I felt I was losing my mind" were typical. Even in those situations in which the incest was reported as part of the history, the mothers retrospectively still described these types of reactions.

Shared Fears of Family Disintegration

Lustig et al.[9] found that fathers involved in incest typically came from a background of emotional deprivation with resultant strong desertion anxiety. The mothers had also suffered from physical or psychological desertions in their childhood, and, as described by Kaufman et al.[12] they too displayed signs of pervasive desertion anxiety. For these parents, the threat of a family breakup created extreme stress.

All family members shared fears of family disintegration. These fears were associated with the revelation of the incest, the reactions of the community, and the possible consequences. The threat was perceived as changing family equilibrium and possibly altering family composition. In some cases, whoever had revealed the incest (most often the daughter) was under intense pressure from other family members to retract and deny the original statement.

The Girls

In reviewing the Adolescent Clinic cases, adequate information was available on 23 girls. Four of them were less than 11 years old at the time the incest first occurred, while the remainder were 12 years or older. Medical problems, with particular emphasis on the genitourinary tract, were first examined since it seemed logical that incest should be suspected in any child with repeated bouts of vaginitis or vaginal discharge. While urinary tract infections commonly occur in childhood, particularly in girls, sexual molestation or incest should at least be considered as a possible cause.

Prior to the disclosure of incest, however, our data revealed only one girl with chronic vaginitis and two with enuresis. One girl presented with encopresis presumably related to her father's attempts at rectal intercourse.

Of the psychological diagnoses available from hospital charts, only two of 23 girls were considered normal at the time they were evaluated through the pediatric psychiatry and psychology services. Twelve were seen within a few months of the disclosure of incest. Five evaluations were done one to five years afterward due to further psychiatric difficulties. No information was available on four girls.

Behavior problems were manifested by six of the girls in our group at the time of incest (lying, stealing, running away). School problems (truancy, absenteeism, failing grades) were reported in 12. Depression was noted in five.

Adolescence appears to be a time when incest can inflict the greatest damage. The girls are at an age when they are acutely aware of social disapproval and sensitive to community attitudes. They may see themselves as "dirty, different," contaminated because of this aberrant kind of early sexual experience. As summarized by Sarles,[13] there are contradictory findings concerning guilt feelings in these girls. Kaufmann et al.[12] in their study of 11 girls, ages 10 to 17, showed that all manifested depression and guilt. They appeared anxious, confused as to sexual identity, and afraid of their own sexuality, using repression and denial to defend against their feelings. Their guilt appeared related to the disintegration of the home following discovery of incest.

Data on the personality of these girls are sparse. The majority are of normal intelligence, and in our study group 21 of 23 had normal IQs. In other studies, Rorschach responses were variable, not too different from normal adolescent girls,[13] and there is little consensus as to the role incest itself plays in the development of the subsequent psychopathology seen in these daughters.

Lukianowicz[14] followed up 26 girls to adulthood and classified them in four groups. Eleven girls became promiscuous with disorganized antisocial behavior; five became frigid, showing symptoms of hysterical personality with attention-seeking behavior; four developed neurotic reactions characterized by depression and suicide attempts. Six girls showed no apparent ill effects. They married and made adequate sexual and social adjustments, viewing the sexual experience with the father as a pleasant interlude, indicative of his affection for them.

In the follow-up data available on our cases, 1 to 12 years after the reported incest, poor adjustment as manifested by depression (four girls, three of whom made suicide gestures) and other psychiatric problems was seen in 13 out of 23. Only four girls seemed to have a reasonable adjustment (in school or in marriage), while no information was available on the remaining six.

Children of Incest

The offspring of incestuous unions (i.e., those children resulting from biologically related parents) suffer a high incidence of mental retardation and congenital defects.[15-17] Adams and Neel[15] reported on a group of 18 such children using as matched controls unwed mothers under the care of the same agencies from which the incest cases were derived. Twelve of the children were results of brother-sister incest, six of father-daughter incest. By 6 months of age, seven of the children appeared normal. Three were dead, three others had major defects (cleft palate in one, the others severely retarded with seizures and cerebral palsy), and five were mildly retarded (IQs 50 to 70 on repeated testing). Of the control group, while some had IQs lower than 80, all were living and none was institutionalized. The authors point out that an extrapolation of studies on the effects of inbreeding in first cousins to the outcome of incestuous unions would call for no more than a 16% increase in death and major defect in the child, whereas the observed increase is 28%.

In the article by Roberts,[16] Carter's study of 13 children of incest showed that five were normal. Three died before age 9, one of cystic fibrosis, one of progressive cerebral degeneration with blindness, and one of congenital heart disease. Of the living children, one was severely retarded and four were mildly retarded.

In an extensive report from Czechoslovakia, Seemanova[17] reports on 161 children, 88 from father-daughter incest, 72 from brother-sister, and 1 from mother-son. The control group was composed of 95 children of the same mothers by unrelated fathers. Of the 141 mothers who had produced these children, 116 had normal IQs, while 20 were "subnormal," 2 were deaf-mutes, and 3 were schizophrenic. Among the 138 related fathers, eight were retarded. The peak age of women who bore children from father-daughter and brother-sister unions was 14 to 15 years; for offspring from unrelated partners the mean maternal age appeared to be 20 years. Of the incest children, 12 males and 9 females died, 10 of them from known congenital malformations. Of the control group of 95 children, there was a total of five deaths (four boys, one girl), only one of which was attributed to a congenital defect (hydrocephalus).

These studies clearly demonstrate that the children of incest suffer from higher infant mortality, severe congenital malformations, and lowered intelligence levels. Some of these results undoubtedly can be attributed to the genetic risks of such close inbreeding. But the mothers of these children often came from chaotic families with disturbed members and distorted relationships. Many of them were only teenagers, adding the risks of extreme maternal youth. When poor prenatal care and a minimally nurturing environment are added to the genetic disadvantage of the children of incest, it is not surprising that they frequently emerge as such a physically and mentally handicapped group.

Evaluation in a Pediatric Setting

In some cases the disclosure of the incest first takes place in a medical setting. A crisis develops, and it must be dealt with immediately. Family defenses are lowered, and it is an opportune time to obtain a beginning evaluation of the problem and of the family. If there is a delay even of a few days, the opportunity for intervention may be lost. A daughter who reveals the incest situation may retract her original statements later. Daughter, mother, and father should be seen for individual interviews.

At the time of disclosure, professional personnel in a clinic have three responsibilities in dealing with this situation. They should help the family deal with their reactions to the stress of this crisis, begin to evaluate the need and kind of treatment services that will be ultimately required, and prepare the family for the next steps in the process, including mandatory reporting, court involvement, and child welfare referral.

The documentation of incest is almost totally dependent on the history. Of the greatest importance then is a relaxed, kindly, tactful approach in eliciting such a history from a frightened and apprehensive young girl. She should be encouraged to reveal all details concerning the incidents, including, if possible, times, place, and persons involved. The sites of abuse should also be documented (mouth, breasts, genitalia, anus) since this kind of information is critical for legal documentation and reporting. In particular, the use of threats or force should be noted.

The patient should have a general physical examination with the mouth, anus, and external genitals receiving special scrutiny for signs of trauma. The hymenal ring should be examined for intactness and cultures for gonorrhea should be taken. Often there may be other evidence of abuse or injury such as bruises or lacerations. Depending on state law, once incest is definitely documented, an official written report of the sexual abuse is completed by the examining physician and brought to the attention of the appropriate state agency.

Psychiatric evaluation of the girl is very helpful at this stage of initial discovery. It can help delineate the girl's strengths and weaknesses, define her ability to function, and give some idea of ultimate prognosis regarding emotional stability. Such an evaluation may be a valuable tool when the case is brought to court in helping to determine the kind of placement and therapy that would be most beneficial to her.

Treatment

Because incest is a complicated diagnosis covering a broad range of individual and family pathology, intervention must be planned according to the needs of each individual case. Agencies most commonly involved in treatment planning include the courts, child welfare services, and the mental health clinics. A variety of approaches may be used, including physical separation, treatment of individuals involved, marital counseling, and family therapy. These may occur separately and/or conjointly and/or sequentially.

Physical separation may take place when the father moves out of the home, is jailed, or perhaps hospitalized in a psychiatric setting. Treatment of individual family members will involve father, mother, and daughter recognizing that each of them participated in an active or passive way in the perpetuation of the incest. Therapy for one member of the triad will not be helpful if the other two remain unchanged. Marital counseling may help the parents improve their sexual relationship. Family therapy, as described by Machotka,[18] is felt by some to be the most appropriate treatment modality. It will focus on pathological family dynamics rather than the sexual activity that is seen as a symptom of the underlying skewed family relationship problems.

Conclusion

In diagnosing incest, a high index of suspicion is of the greatest importance. Given the reluctance of professionals to consider this possibility and the unwillingness of the family to reveal its pathology, incest becomes doubly difficult to identify.

In a pediatric setting the victim of incest may be the young girl who presents with a variety of physical or psychosomatic or behavioral complaints. Her family may appear to be stable and well functioning, or they may have many problems obvious to the community because of their acting-out. In either situation, family dynamics may reveal an inadequate sexual relationship between the parents, condoning of the incest by the mother, and denial of this behavior by all individual members who fear exposure and resultant family disintegration.

Incest arises as a symptom of severely distorted family relationships and can inflict considerable psychological damage on the child involved in this pathological triangle. This is particularly true when the girl is an adolescent. For these reasons, professionals who deal with children need to have a heightened awareness of the possibility of incest so it can be identified and reported to the appropriate authorities, and intervention instituted.

REFERENCES

1. WEINBERG, S. K.: *Incest Behavior*. New York, Citadel Press, 1955.

2. KINSEY, A. C., POMEROY, W. B., MARTIN, C. E.: *Sexual Behavior in the Human Male*. Philadelphia, W. B. Saunders Co., 1948.

3. KINSEY, A. C., POMEROY, W. B., MARTIN, C. E., GEBHARD, P. H: *Sexual Behavior in the Human Female*. Philadelphia, W. B. Saunders Co.,1953.

4. GEBHARD, P. H., GAGNON J. H., POMEROY, W. B., CHRISTENSON, C. V.: *Sex Offenders: An Analysis of Types*. New York, Harper & Row, 1965.

5. DEFRANCIS, V: *Protecting the Child Victim of Sex Crimes Committed by Adults*. Denver, American Humane Association, 1969.

6. SGROI, S. M.: "Sexual molestation of children," *Child Today* 18:19, 1975.

7. HENDERSON, D. J.: "Incest: A synthesis of data". *Can. Psychiatr. Assoc. J.* 17:299, 1972.

8. CORMIER, B. M., KENNEDY, M., SANGOWICZ, J: "Psychodynamics of father-daughter incest." *Can. Psychiatr. Assoc. J.* 7:203, 1962.

9. LUSTIG, N., DRESSER, J. W., SPELLMAN, S. W., MURRAY, T. B.: "Incest: A family group survival pattern." *Arch. Gen. Psychiatry* 14:31, 1966.

10. TORMES, Y. M. *Child Victims of Incest*. Denver, American Humane Association, 1968.

11. CHANELES S.: *Sexual Abuse of Children*. Denver, American Humane Association, 1967.

12. KAUFMAN, I., PECK. A. L., TAGIURI, C. K.: "The family constellation and overt incestuous relations between father and daughter." *Am. J. Orthopsychiatry* 24:266, 1954.

13. SARLES, R. M.: "Incest: Symposium on behavioral pediatrics." *Pediatr. Clin. North Am.* 22:108, 1975.

14. LUKIANOWICZ, N.: "Incest: I. Paternal incest: II. Other types of incest." *Br. J. Psychiatry* 120:301, 1972.

15. ADAMS, M. S.: NEEL, J. V.: "Children of incest." *Pediatrics* 40:55, 1967.

16. ROBERTS, D. F.: "Incest, inbreeding and mental abilities." *Br. Med. J.* 4:336, 1967.

17. SEEMANOVA, E.: "A study of children of incestuous matings." *Hum Hered* 21:108, 1971.

18. MACHOTKA, P., PITTMAN, F. S., FLOMENHAFT, K.: "Incest as a family affair." *Family Process* 6:98, 1967.

12

Unraveling Child Abuse*

David G. Gil, D.S.W.

This paper is an attempt to clarify the sources and dynamics of child abuse and to suggest approaches to its primary prevention. To gain understanding of any social problem one needs to view it in the total societal context within which it evolves, rather than, as is so often done, as an isolated, fragmented phenomenon. Furthermore, one needs to avoid the fallacious tendency of interpreting its dynamics along single causal dimensions such as biological, psychological, social, economic, etc., a tendency which in our society is usually weighted in favor of individual interpretations and which thus leads to ameliorative programs designed to change individuals rather than pathogenic aspects of the social order.

A Value-based Definition of Child Abuse

Understanding and overcoming the dynamics of social problems also requires specification of, and a societal commitment to, certain value premises, and a definition logically linked to such premises. I have suggested such a value-based definition of child abuse at hearings on the *Child Abuse Prevention Act* (S. 1191 of 1973) before the Sub-Committee on Children and Youth of the U. S. Senate. This definition views child abuse as inflicted gaps or deficits between circumstances of living which would facilitate the optimal development of children, to which they should be entitled, and their actual circumstances, irrespective of the sources or agents of the deficit:

---

* David G. Gil, "Unraveling Child Abuse," *American Journal of Orthopsychiatry,* 45(3):346-356. Copyright © 1975 the American Orthopsychiatric Association, Inc. Reproduced by permission.

Every child, despite his individual differences and uniqueness is to be considered of equal intrinsic worth, and hence should be entitled to equal social, economic, civil, and political rights, so that he may fully realize his inherent potential and share equally in life, liberty, and happiness. Obviously, these value premises are rooted in the humanistic philosophy of our Declaration of Independence.

In accordance with these value premises then, any act of commission or omission by individuals, institutions, or society as a whole, and any conditions resulting from such acts or inaction, which deprive children of equal rights and liberties, and/or interfere with their optimal development, constitute, by definition, abusive or neglectful acts or conditions.

Analytic Concepts

The definition of child abuse presented above suggests the use of two related analytic concepts for studying the nature of child abuse and for developing effective policies and programs for its prevention. These concepts will be referred to here as "levels of manifestation" and "levels of causation" or "causal dimensions." The levels of manifestation identify the agents and the settings in which children may experience abuse. The levels of causation unravel the several causal dimensions, the interactions of which result in abusive acts and abusive conditions at the levels of manifestation. The distinction implicit in these analytic concepts, between the levels at which abuse occurs and the forces that underlie the occurrences, is important, for these levels and forces are not the same. They do, however, complement each other and interact with each other in multiple ways. Moreover, interaction also takes place among the levels themselves, and among the forces. Clarifying the nature of child abuse means, essentially, tracing these multiple interactions among the levels of manifestation and the causal dimensions.

Levels of Manifestation

Three levels of manifestation of child abuse may be distinguished. The most familiar one is abusive conditions in the home, and abusive interaction between children and their caretakers. Abuse on this level consists of acts of commission or omission by individuals which inhibit a child's development. The perpetrators are parents, permanent or temporary parent substitutes, or others living in a child's home regularly or temporarily. Abuse in the home may be intentional and conscious or unintentional and also unconscious. Abuse may result from supposedly constructive, disciplinary, educational attitudes and measures, or from negative and hostile feelings toward children. Abusive acts in the home may be one-time events, occasional incidents, or regular patterns. So far, child abuse at this level of manifestation has been the dominant focus of scholarly, professional, and public concern with this destructive phenomenon.

A second level at which child abuse occurs is the institutional level. This includes such settings as day care centers, schools, courts, child care agencies, welfare departments, and correctional and other residential child care settings. In such settings, acts and policies of commission or omission that inhibit, or insufficiently promote, the development of children, or that deprive children of, or fail to provide them with, material, emotional, and symbolic means needed for their optimal development, constitute abusive acts or conditions. Such acts or policies may originate with an individual employee of an institution, such as a teacher, child care worker, judge, probation officer, or social worker, or they may be implicit in the standard practices and policies of given agencies and institutions. In the same way as in the home, abusive acts and conditions in institutional settings may also result from supposedly constructive, or from negative and hostile attitudes toward children, and they may be one-time or occasional events or regular patterns.

Institutional child care settings such as schools are often perceived by parents as bearers of cultural norms concerning child rearing practices and discipline. Hence, when schools and other child care settings employ practices that are not conducive to optimal child development, *e.g.*, corporal punishment and other demeaning and threatening, negative disciplinary measures, they convey a subtle message to parents —namely, that such measures are appropriate, as they are sanctioned by educational authorities and "experts." Influence also flows in the other direction, from the home to the institutional level. Teachers and child care personnel will frequently adopt child rearing practices and disciplinary measures similar to those practiced in the homes of children in their care, on the assumption that this is what the children are used to, what they expect, and to what they respond. In this way, methods conducive or not conducive to optimal child development tend to be transmitted back and forth, and reinforced, through interaction between the home and the institution.

When child abuse is viewed as inflicted deficits between a child's actual circumstances and circumstances that would assure his optimal development, it seems to be endemic in most existing institutional settings for the care and education of children, since these settings usually do not facilitate the full actualization of the human potential of all children in their care. Analysis of institutional child abuse reveals that this form of abuse is not distributed randomly throughout the population. Schools and institutions serving children of minority groups, children from deprived socioeconomic backgrounds, handicapped children, and socially deviant children are less likely to facilitate optimal development of children's inherent potential than are schools and institutions serving children of majority groups, "normal" children, and children from affluent families and neighborhoods. However, even settings serving children from privileged backgrounds rarely encourage the optimal development of all children in their care. They, too, tend to inhibit the children's spontaneity and creativity, and to promote conformity rather than critical, independent thought. Only rarely will children in these settings develop all their inherent faculties and their unique individuality.

Worse, though, than the educational system, with its mind-stifling practices and its widespread use of corporal punishment and other demeaning and threatening forms of discipline, is the legally sanctioned, massive abuse of children under the policies and practices of the public welfare system, especially the "Aid to Families with Dependent Children" (AFDC) program. This system of grossly inadequate income maintenance—inadequate even by measures of minimal needs as published by the US Bureau of Labor Statistics—virtually condemns millions of children to conditions of existence under which physical, social, emotional, and intellectual development are likely to be severely handicapped.

Similarly destructive versions of legally sanctioned abuse on the institutional level are experienced by several hundred thousands of children living in foster care, in training and correctional institutions, and in institutions for children defined as mentally retarded. That these settings of substitute child care usually fail to assure optimum development for the children entrusted to them has been amply demonstrated,[1, 5] and does not require further documentation here.

The massive manifestations of institutional child abuse tend to arouse much less public concern and indignation than child abuse in the home, although the abusive conditions and practices of public education, public welfare, and child placement are endemic to these systems, and are visible to all who care to see. Perhaps the enormity of institutional abuse dulls our sensibilities in the same way in which the fate of inmates of concentration camps tends to arouse a lesser response than does the killing of a single individual with whom we are able to identify.

Institutional child abuse is linked, intimately, to the third level at which child abuse is manifested, namely, the societal level. On this level originate social policies which sanction, or cause, severe deficits between the actual circumstances of children and conditions needed for their optimal development. As direct or indirect consequences of such social policies, millions of children in our society live in poverty and are inadequately nourished, clothed, housed, and educated; their health is not assured because of substandard medical care; their neighborhoods decay; meaningful occupational opportunities are not available to them; and alienation is widespread among them. No doubt, these destructive conditions which result, inevitably, from the normal workings of the prevailing social, economic, and political order, and from the value premises which shape that order and its human dynamics, cannot fail to inhibit severely the development of children exposed to them.

Of the three levels of child abuse sketched here, the societal level is certainly the most severe. For what happens at this level determines not only how children fare on the institutional level, but also, by way of complex interactions, how they fare in their own homes.

Levels of Causation

Before discussing the causal dimensions of child abuse, it should be reiterated that the conventional dichotomy between individual and societal causation of social problems distorts the multidimensional reality of human phenomena. We know that psychological forces which shape individual behavior evolve out of the totality of life experiences in specific historical, cultural, social, economic, and political contexts. Individual motivation and behavior are thus always rooted in a societal force field. Yet societal forces are always expressed, or mediated, through the behavior of individuals, for societies cannot act except through their individual members. Clearly, then, any human phenomenon, at any moment, involves both social and individual elements. In real life, these elements are inseparable. Their separation in theory is merely a product of scholarly, or rather pseudoscholarly, abstraction.

Based on this reasoning, child abuse, at any level of manifestation, may be understood as acts or inactions of individuals, on their own or as institutional agents, whose behavior reflects societal forces mediated through their unique personalities.

The most fundamental causal level of child abuse consists of a cluster of interacting elements, to wit, a society's basic social philosophy, its dominant value premises, its concept of humans; the nature of its social, economic, and political institutions, which are shaped by its philosophy and value premises, and which in turn reinforce that philosophy and these values; and, finally, the particular quality of human relations prevailing in the society, which derives from its philosophy, values, and institutions. For, in the final analysis, it is the philosophy and value premises of a society, the nature of its major institutions, and the quality of its human relations that determine whether or not individual members of that society will develop freely and fully in accordance with their inherent potentialities.

To discern a society's basic social philosophy and values and its concept of humans, one needs to ascertain whether it considers everyone to be intrinsically of equal worth in spite of his or her uniqueness and, hence, entitled to the same social, economic, and political rights; or whether everyone in the society considers himself, and those close to himself, of greater worth than anyone else, and hence entitled to more desirable or privileged circumstances. The former, egalitarian philosophy would be reflected in institutional arrangements involving cooperative actions in pursuit of common existential interests. Every individual, and that includes every child, would be considered an equally entitled subject, who could not be exploited and dominated by any other individual or group, and whose right to fully and freely develop his individuality would be assured and respected, subject to the same right of all others. The latter, non-egalitarian philosophy, on the other hand, as we know so well from our own existence, is reflected in institutional structures which encourage competitive behavior in pursuit of narrowly perceived, egotistical interests. Everyone strives to get ahead of others, considers himself entitled to privileged conditions and positions, and views and treats others as potential means to be used, exploited, and dominated in pursuit of his egotistical goals.

Analysis of these contrasting social philosophies, societal institutions, and modes of human relations suggests that full and free development of every child's inherent potential may be possible only in a society organized consistently around egalitarian and cooperative value premises, since the equal right to self-actualization is implicit in an egalitarian philosophy, while such a right is incompatible with a non-egalitarian philosophy. In a society organized on non-egalitarian and competitive principles, full and free development for all children is simply impossible, as, by definition, there must always be losers in such societies, whose chances to realize their inherent potential will be severely limited. Hence, significant developmental deficits for large segments of the population or high levels of socially structured and sanctioned abuse of children, are endemic in such societies.

A second, more specific, level of causation of child abuse may be intrinsic to the social construction, or definition, of childhood prevalent in a society. Obviously, this level is closely related to the first level. How does a society view its children, all its children, and how does it define their rights? How much obedience, submission, and conformity does it expect of children? Does it process children through caste-like channels of socialization into relatively closed and inflexible social and occupational structures, or does it encourage them, within limits of reason, to discover and develop their individuality and uniqueness, and to shape their lives accordingly? Obviously, optimal development of the inherent potential of all children is a function of the extent to which a society's processes of socialization are permeated with a commitment to such self-actualization for all. When this commitment is lacking altogether, or when it varies with such factors as sex, race, and social and economic position of a family, then different children will experience varying deficits in realizing their potential. Presently, in our society, social policies that sustain different levels of rights for children from different social and economic backgrounds are a major, direct cause of many forms of child abuse on the societal and institutional levels, and an indirect cause of abuse on the family level.

A further causal dimension of child abuse is a society's attitude toward the use of force as a legitimate means for attaining ends, especially in imbalanced, interpersonal relations such as master-slave, male-female, guard-prisoner, and adult-child. The tendency to resort to the use of force for dealing with conflicts in our society seems to require no documentation here, nor does it seem necessary to document the specific readiness to use force, or the threat of it, as a means to maintain authority and discipline in adult-child relations in the public domain, such as schools and other child care settings, and in the private domain of the family. The readiness to use physical force for disciplinary objectives is certainly endemic in our society.

It should be noted that the readiness to use force in general, and in adult-child relations in particular, is intimately linked to a society's basic philosophy and value premises, and to its concept of humans and their rights. A non-egalitarian philosophy is much more likely to sanction the use of force than is an egalitarian one, since the use of force against other humans constitutes the strongest possible negation of equality. The use of force toward children is also related to the manner in which childhood, and the rights of children are defined by a society, and in turn tends to reinforce that definition.

As mentioned earlier, the use of force toward children is widespread in our society on the institutional and family levels. Attempts to limit and outlaw it in public institutions have had only limited success so far. It may be noted, in this context, that because of the compatibility between the use of physical force on the one hand, and an inegalitarian philosophy and competitive social, economic, and political institutions on the other, corporal punishment and the threat of it may actually be highly functional in preparing children for adult roles in an inegalitarian and competitive social order. For, were our children reared in a harmonious fashion without threats, insults, and physical force, they might not be adequately prepared and conditioned for adult roles in our inegalitarian, competitive reality.

Whenever corporal punishment in child rearing is sanctioned, and even subtly encouraged by a society, incidents of serious physical abuse and injury are bound to happen, either as a result of deliberate, systematic, and conscious action on the part of perpetrators, or under conditions of loss of self-control. In either case, but especially in the latter, physical attacks on children tend to relieve tensions and frustrations experienced by the perpetrators. Clearly, then, these attacks are carried out to meet emotional needs of the perpetrators rather than educational needs of the victims, as is often claimed by advocates of corporal punishment.

The next causal dimension may be referred to as "triggering contexts." These contexts operate jointly with the societal sanction of the use of physical force in adult-child relations. Adults who use force toward children do not do so all the time, but only under specific circumstances which serve as triggers for their abusive behavior. In general, abusive attacks tend to be triggered by stress and frustration which may cause reduction or loss of self-control. Stress and frustration may facilitate abusive attacks even without causing a reduction or loss of self-control, as long as the appropriateness of the use of force in child rearing is accepted.

One major source of stress and frustration for adults in our society are the multi-faceted deprivations of poverty and its correlates, high density in over-crowded, dilapidated, inadequately served neighborhoods; large numbers of children, especially in one-parent, mainly female-headed households; and the absence of child care alternatives. Having identified poverty and its correlates as an important triggering context of child abuse in the home, we may now note that social policies which sanction and perpetuate the existence of poverty among large segments of the population, including millions of children, are thus indirect sources of child abuse in the home. It should be emphasized, though, that poverty, per se, is not a direct cause of child abuse in the home, but operates through an intervening variable, namely, concrete and psychological stress and frustration experienced by individuals in the context of culturally sanctioned use of physical force in child rearing.

Poverty is not the only source of stress and frustration triggering child abuse in the home. Such abuse is known to occur frequently in many homes in adequate, and even affluent, economic circumstances. One other, important source of stress and frustration in our society is the alienating circumstances in most workplaces, be the work manual labor, skilled and unskilled occupations, or administrative, managerial, and professional work through all levels and sectors of business, academic, and government bureaucracies. A recent report by a task force of the U.S. Department of Health, Education, and Welfare[6] documented the seriousness of work alienation experienced by constantly growing segments of the working population. This government report reached conclusions similar to those voiced by many severe critics of our economic system in recent years—that the prevailing competitive and exploitative human relations in the work place, and its hierarchical and authoritarian structures, tend to cause psychological stress and alienation for nearly every working person. These pressures may lead to various forms of deviant behavior, such as alcoholism, drug addiction, mental illness, white collar crime, etc. Perhaps the most frequent locus for discharging feelings of stress and frustration originating in the formal world of work is the informal world of primary relations, the home and the family. Conflicts between spouses are one form this discharge may take. Child abuse in the form of violent physical outbursts is another.

Here, then, we identify once again a triggering context for child abuse on the interpersonal level, which is rooted deeply in societal forces, namely, the alienating quality of our society's economic and productive system complemented by the culturally sanctioned use of physical force in child rearing.

The final causal dimension of child abuse on the interpersonal level in the home and in child care settings is made up of intrapsychic conflicts and various forms of psychopathology on the part of perpetrators. Child abuse literature is largely focused on this dimension and thus little needs to be said here to document it. What needs to be stressed, however, is that psychological disturbances and their manner of expression are not independent factors but are deeply rooted in, and constantly interact with, forces in the social environment of the disturbed individual. To the extent that psychopathology is not rooted in genetic and biochemical processes, it derives from the totality of the life experiences of the individual, which are shaped by continuous interactions between the person and his social setting, his informal and formal relations in primary and secondary contexts. However, it is not only the etiology of intrapsychic conflicts and disturbances that is conditioned, in part, by social forces, but also the manner in which these conflicts and disturbances are expressed in social relations. The symptoms of emotional disturbance and mental illness are not randomly generated phenomena, but derive from normal behavioral traits in a culture. These normal traits appear in exaggerated or negated forms in behavior which is considered deviant, neurotic, and psychotic. Hence, one may assume that in a society in which the use of physical force in general, and toward children in particular, is not sanctioned, intrapsychic conflicts and psychopathology would less often be expressed through violence against children. It follows from these considerations that the "battered baby" syndrome,[3,4] and other forms of child abuse associated with psychological disturbance of one kind or another, are not independent of societal forces, although the perpetrators of these acts may be emotionally ill individuals. We are thus again led to the conclusion that abusive acts and conditions, irrespective of the level of manifestation, cannot be understood in terms of one specific causal dimension, but only in terms of complex interactions among the several causal dimensions sketched here.

Primary Prevention

According to a general conceptual model, primary prevention proceeds from identification toward elimination of the causal context from which specified, undesired phenomena derive. It needs to be realized that the prevention of undesired phenomena may also result in the elimination of other phenomena whenever such other phenomena derive from, or are part of, the same causal context. The likelihood of simultaneous prevention of several phenomena could lead to serious dilemmas if some of the phenomena are desired, while others are considered undesirable, or when groups in a society differ in their respective evaluation of the desirability of the several phenomena. Decisions concerning primary prevention of social phenomena and of "social problems" are thus essentially political choices.[2]

Turning now to the primary prevention of child abuse, we may begin by summarizing our conclusions so far. Child abuse, conceived of as inflicted deficits on a child's right to develop freely and fully, irrespective of the source and agents of the deficit, was found to occur on several related levels: on the interpersonal level in the home and in child-care settings; on the institutional level through the policies and practices of a broad array of child care, educational, welfare, and correctional institutions and agencies; and on the societal level, where the interplay of values and social, economic, and political institutions and processes shapes the social policies by which the rights and lives of all children, and of specific groups of children, are determined. The causal dimensions of child abuse are, first of all, the dominant social philosophy and value premises of a society, its social, economic, and political institutions, and the quality of human relations to which these institutions, philosophy, and values give rise; other causal dimensions are the social construction of childhood and the social definition of children's rights, the extent to which a society sanctions the use of force in general and, more specifically, in the child rearing context, stress and frustration resulting from poverty and from alienation in the workplace which may trigger abusive acts, and expressions of intrapsychic conflicts and psychopathology which, in turn, are rooted in the social fabric. While child abuse, at any particular level, may be more closely related to one rather than another causal dimension, none of these dimensions are independent, and they exert their influence through multiple interactions with each other.

This analysis suggests that primary prevention of child abuse, on all levels, would require fundamental changes in social philosophy and value premises, in societal institutions, and in human relations. It would also require a reconceptualization of childhood, of children's rights, and of child rearing. It would necessitate rejecting the use of force as a means for achieving societal ends, especially in dealing with children. It would require the elimination of poverty and of alienating conditions of production, major sources of stress and frustration which tend to trigger abusive acts toward children in adult-child interaction. And, finally, it would necessitate the elimination of psychological illness. Because of the multiple interactions among the several causal dimensions, progress in overcoming the more fundamental dimensions would also reduce the force of other dimensions. Thus, transforming the prevailing inegalitarian social philosophy, value premises, and institutions, and the kind of human relations they generate, into egalitarian ones would also result in corresponding modifications of children's rights, elimination of poverty and alienation of work, and rejection of the use of force. It would indirectly influence psychological well-being, and would thus eliminate the processes that now trigger child abuse in interpersonal relations.

Effective primary prevention requires working simultaneously toward the transformation of all the causal dimensions. Fragmented approaches focused on one or the other causal dimension may bring some amelioration, but one should entertain no illusions as to the effectiveness of such piecemeal efforts. Even such important and necessary steps as outlawing corporal punishment in schools and other child care settings would have only limited, though highly desirable, results. There simply is no way of escaping the conclusion that the complete elimination of child abuse on all levels of manifestation requires a radical transformation of the prevailing unjust, inegalitarian, irrational, competitive, alienating, and hierarchical social order into a just, egalitarian, rational, cooperative, humane, and truly democratic, decentralized one. Obviously, this realization implies that primary prevention of child abuse is a political issue which cannot be resolved through professional and administrative measures.

Primary prevention of child abuse would bring with it the prevention of other equally undersirable and inevitable consequences or symptoms of the same causal context, including many manifestations of social deviance. However, it would also result in the complete transformation of the prevailing social, economic, and political order with which large segments of our society are either identified or drifting along, because this order conforms to their accustomed mental sets, and because they seem reluctant, due to inertia, to search actively for alternative social, economic, and political institutions that might be more conducive to human fulfillment for all. Some or many members of our society may even be consciously committed to the perpetuation of the existing order, not realizing how destructive that order may be to their own real interests.

Whatever one's attitude may be toward these funadmental political issues, one needs to recognize and face the dilemmas implicit in them and, hence, in primary prevention of child abuse. If one's priority is to prevent all child abuse, one must be ready to part with its many causes, even when one is attached to some of them, such as the apparent blessings, advantages, and privileges of inequality. If, on the other hand, one is reluctant to give up all aspects of the causal context of child abuse, one must be content to continue living with this social problem. In that latter case, one ought to stop talking about primary prevention and face the fact that all one may be ready for is some measure of amelioration.

REFERENCES

1.   GIL, D. 1970. *Violence Against Children.* Harvard University Press, Cambridge, Mass.

2.   GIL, D. 1973. *Unraveling Social Policy.* Schenkman Publishing Co., Cambridge, Mass.

3.   HELFER, R. AND KEMPE, C., eds. 1968. *The Battered Child,* University of Chicago Press, Chicago.

4.   KEMPE, C. AND HELFER, R., eds. 1972. *Helping the Battered Child and His Family.* Lippincott, Philadelphia.

5.   SCHORR, A., ed. 1974. *Children and Decent People.* Basic Books, New York.

6.   TASK FORCE TO THE SECRETARY OF HEW. 1973. *Work in America.* MIT Press, Cambridge, Mass.

Part Two

Sources of Abuse

The assembled theoretical and research studies on causation are not sufficiently consistent nor conclusive to warrant the use of the term "explanations". In spite of the fact that the link between postulated relationships and supporting research is very limited, generalizations tend to be repeated until they assume the nature of "truth". In order to emphasize the tentative nature of the research findings, the articles in this part are arranged according to the four major hypothesized "sources" of abuse:

a) those within the parent—the predisposing personality characteristics of abusers.

b) those within the child—the characteristics of the abused child which may act as precipitators of abuse.

c) those within the family and its socioeconomic environment—the role played by interpersonal relationships and the influence of social class and cultural factors in producing stress which stimulates abusive behavior.

d) those within society—the way in which cultural, social and legal institutions may contribute to the prevalence of abuse.

A. Within the Parent

J. J. Spinetta and D. Rigler   In this review of the literature on the psychological characteristics of parents who physically abuse their children the authors note that few studies have carefully tested hypotheses about child abuse. As a consequence, most observations about causes consist of professional opinion rather than conclusions based on research. The generalizations commonly proposed are: 1) that abusers were most likely mistreated as children; 2) that abusing parents have inappropriate expectations of their young and hence, mistaken notions of child rearing; 3) that such parents exhibit a general character disorder; 4) that socioeconomic factors may place added stress on basic personality deficits. They include an extensive critique of David Gil's thesis that socioeconomic factors are crucial variables in the etiology of abuse.

J. Fischhoff et al.   In contrast to Spinetta and Rigler who reviewed the physical assault literature, these authors examine the personalities of mothers who deprive their children. On the basis of previous clinical observations they formulate the hypothesis that a character disorder underlies neglect. To test this hypothesis twelve depriving mothers were evaluated. Ten were diagnosed as having character disorders. While the authors acknowledge that social and economic factors can play a role in neglect, the personality component may explain why some parents physically abuse and neglect their children while most parents do not, even in those contexts where demographic predictors indicate the greatest probability. They note that traditional psychotherapeutic approaches have limited utility in changing basic character structure. Therefore, intervention involving supportive teaching by a homemaker or social worker is more likely to be successful. In any event, they state, foster care may eventually be necessary.

L. Wright   The "sick but slick syndrome" refers to the ability of psychopathically disturbed parents to present a "distorted picture of themselves as healthy and unlikely to abuse their children." Wright examines that particular aspect of character disorder which might be easily overlooked if the clinician is not sensitive to it. Using a psychological test battery, he compared the personalities of battering and non-battering parents. His analysis shows significant differences between the two groups on five of the twenty-one variables assessed. In summary, "battering parents were able to appear significantly healthier on those instruments . . . in which the social desirability of each item is more obvious. However, for items . . . where the socially desirable response is more ambiguous, they appeared significantly more disturbed." These findings raise two important considerations for those dealing with abusers: to be aware of the potential disturbance in "reasonable-appearing" parents, and to be cognizant of the unlikelihood of success with traditional psychotherapy.

J. Vesterdal   Stating that whenever a child is maltreated, the non-active abuser acts as a tacit accessory, Vesterdal posits the mother-child symbiosis as the crucial component in explanations of abuse. Any disturbance in this reciprocal relationship may precipitate violent behavior. The disorder in the symbiosis may be triggered by the mother, who may act and react inadequately, or by the child, whose responses to parenting may not meet the mother's expectations, or by the separation of the child from the mother after birth because of prematurity or illness. Agreeing that such a disturbance may be exacerbated by environmental stress, Vesterdal states that such stress is not a necessary condition for abuse to occur.

B. *Within The Child*

W. N. Friedrich and
J. A. Boriskin

While a significant portion of the child abuse literature maintains a parental depravity or parental inadequacy explanation of child abuse, Friedrich and Boriskin challenge this hypothesis by arguing that "a certain amount of child abuse is a function of child-produced stress." They note two major ways in which an infant's behavior may create stress. First, the child may, because of its own characteristics, place extra heavy demands on the parent. Second, the child may behave in such a way that the expectations about child behavior (for example, responsiveness) which the parent has acquired from the culture, are not met. Friedrich and Boriskin review forty-six sources seeking to identify those types of children most likely to provoke maltreatment. The factors they consider most significant are prematurity, mental retardation, physical handicaps, genetically determined temperamental patterns and parental perceptions of the child as different. They describe how the behavior of infants in these five categories might stimulate aggressive responses or make a child vulnerable to scapegoating. The authors conclude that these types of children are over-represented in abuse populations.

R. S. Hunter et al.

As indicated in the previous paper, retrospective studies have shown a relationship between neonatal problems and subsequent abuse. Dr. Hunter and her colleagues designed a project to gather data prospectively on the families of infants who were admitted to a newborn intensive care unit. Infants within the study sample were classified as being at high or low risk according to the scores on a set of indices previously assumed to be associated with abuse. All the parents were encouraged to make use of counselling and other social services. Thus, those supports which are often suggested to be a factor in the prevention of maltreatment were provided. Nevertheless, of the 255 infants returned to their parent's care, 10 of the children classified as at high risk were, within one year, reported to be maltreated. This incidence was approximately eight times as high as the incidence of first year abuse among all newborns in the state. The authors systematically review several factors associated with abuse and the particular characteristics of premature neonates which might be related to subsequent abuse. They conclude that three unique components acting in combination increase the risk of maltreatment; 1) vulnerable, unsupported families; 2) biologically impaired infants; and 3) limited parent-infant contact during the nursery stay. The multiplicity of factors leads the authors to be reserved about causal connections. They find it encouraging, however, that many of the families who were judged as high risk did not maltreat their children. Therefore, they suggest that greater research emphasis should be given to accounting for successful parenting by those families with socio-economic and health problems.

C. *Within the Family and its Socio-economic Environment.*

M. A. Kerr et al.

Some of the foregoing articles have noted that abuse is often associated with poor socio-economic conditions, social isolation and disturbances in family relationships. Kerr et al. examine those caretakers who abuse children by neglecting their nutritional needs. A review of the literature on the psycho-social characteristics of mothers whose children fail to thrive led them to hypothesize that "similar factors are operating in families of malnourished children." They compare mothers of healthy children with mothers of malnourished children, all of whom live in similar economically deprived conditions. The specific variables examined are housing, employment, interpersonal relationships (with men, with children, with family and friends), childhood experiences and personality patterns. Although no single factor was statistically significant, the profile from all indicators confirms their hypothesis that the lives of malnourishing mothers "are characterized by disruption and isolation." They do not believe the indicators are sufficiently reliable to predict the likelihood of neglect. Their suggestions for alleviating risk point out the importance of continuing personal contact and support from community institutions.

S. Smith et al.

Using extensive psychiatric, psychological and social interview data, Smith and his associates compare battering and non-battering parents. Data are presented in the form of statistical association between battering and sixteen socio-economic and personality characteristics. The conclusion reached by the authors is that "baby battering occurs alongside a constellation of other social inadequacies or failure of adaptation rather than in isolation." The predominant social factors associated with abuse were: lack of family cohesiveness, marriage before age twenty, pre-marital conception and short acquaintance before marriage, social isolation, and a reluctance to utilize available social support. The authors assert that many of the generalizations made associating poverty and battering are in error and the implication that socio-economic support would be ameliorative is not convincing. They contend that "constitutional personality differences are more fundamental than financial factors in the causation of baby battering." They are pessimistic about the success of treatment programmes for abusers. Prevention ". . . must lie in the effective education of the next generation and in changes in child care legislation."

L. L. Geismar

Examining the relationship between social class and abuse, Geismar contends that while the criteria for defining neglect are culturally determined, all societies value adequate child care and thus abuse and neglect are "the most virulent kinds of faulty socialization." He describes the disorganized family as one in which "the functions necessary for the survival and well-being of its members are not being performed." Citing the lack of empirical research on the relationship between family disorganization and deficient child care, he examines some of the relevant literature. He agrees with the contention that modification of the socio-economic conditions that are associated with family disorganization and consequent neglect will be the most effective policy of prevention of abuse. Geismar's paper is particularly interesting for the discussion of faulty socialization. This conception lends support to the two-victim theory of abuse which proposes that those who were abused as children tend to abuse their own offspring.

S. M. Smith and R. Hanson   Further consideration of the relevance of socialization on child rearing practices is included in this paper. As in their previous study, the authors compare batterers and a control group on several variables hypothesized to be associated with abuse. Many of the hypothesized relationships were not upheld. For example, although it is popularly maintained that abusing parents are dependent on their children in periods of distress the authors find no confirmation of this. They present substantial evidence to support the argument that "it seems likely that baby battering is provoked less by the child itself than by unhappiness due to unsatisfactory marital and other social relationships; such interpersonal difficulties having begun in childhood." The authors note the significance of the inconsistency between parents' demanding and punitive behaviour on the one hand, and lack of concern for, and supervision of the child on the other. Their conclusions support the argument that child abuse is a reflection of a general pattern of family disorganization.

R. C. Conger et al.   This paper expands on the previous three by relating abuse to previous life experience and present life changes. This is a matched control study, but the authors are cautious about conclusions because their sample is small. A social learning explanation of child abuse is advanced; that the combination of a life crisis and a previous punitive upbringing appear to enhance the potential for abusive behaviour.

D. Finkelhor   Finkelhor examines some of the variables associated with sexual abuse. He frankly acknowledges that theoretical work on the sexual exploitation of children is currently in a crude brainstorming stage. He discusses six factors relevant to the development of incestuous patterns in families. In general, his argument is that incest is more likely to occur in the disorganized family. (Further explanations of the etiology of sexual abuse are furnished by Kempe and Nakashima in their articles in Part One).

A. H. Green et al.   After studying a sample of abusing mothers, the authors propose a three-factor model of the etiology of abuse: 1) the personality characteristics of the parents which contribute to "abuse proneness", 2) the characteristics of the child which enhance scapegoating, and 3) the current environment stress which increases demand for care. Interactions between these variables are discussed. The authors conclude that abuse can be regarded as a "dysfunction of parenting in which the parent misperceives the child due to the parent's own frustrating childhood experiences."

R. Gaines et al.

This article describes an attempt to test the multi-factor hypothesis proposed in the previous study.

The authors compare abusing, neglecting, and control mothers on twelve variables. Environmental stress was one of the few which proved to discriminate between samples. The scores for neglecting mothers on this variable were significantly higher than those of either the abusing or control mothers. The authors conclude that their research results do not confirm the multi-factor explanation of child abuse. In fact, the evidence is so weak that Gaines and his associates caution against use of these factors in any attempt to identify potential abusers.

R. D. Parke

Parke argues that "abuse . . . is an orderly outcome of a network of cultural and community forces that, in turn, affect the development of family interaction patterns leading to abusive incidents." He states that much abuse occurs as a result of a learned pattern, and therefore, alternate behaviour can be learned. In support of his thesis he reviews several of the proposed hypotheses and explanations which appear in the previous papers. The influence of such factors as labelling, cultural sanctioning of violence, lack of community support systems, and family roles in abuse patterns are considered in terms of the socialization process. Parke goes on to discuss the changes or interventions in the cultural, legal, community and family systems through which resocialization can be accomplished. He concludes with an argument for wider recognition of children's rights.

13

The Child-abusing Parent:
A Psychological Review*

John J. Spinetta and David Rigler

Why does a parent physically abuse his or her own child? During the past 10 years, many attempts have been made to answer this question. An extensive litera- ture has emerged on the medical and legal aspects of the problem of child abuse since the publication of an article by Kempe, Silverman, Steel, Droegemueller, and Silver (1962) and the pursuit of child-protective laws in California by Boardman (1962, 1963). Sociologists and social workers have contributed their share of in- sights, and a few psychiatrists have published their findings, but surprisingly little attention has been devoted to the problem of child abuse by the psychologist. One seeks with little success for well-designed studies of personality characteristics of abusing parents. What appears is a literature composed of professional opinions on the subject.

The aim of this review is to bring together professional opinions of this decade on the psychological characteristics of the abusing parent in order to determine from the most commonly held opinions what generalizations can be induced and thus to lay the ground-work for systematic testing of hypotheses.

* The authors wish to thank James Kent, of the Division of Psychiatry, Childrens Hospital of Los Angeles, for his critical reading of earlier versions and for his helpful suggestions and support during the research.

John J. Spinetta and David Rigler, "The Child-abusing Parent: A Psychological Review," *Psychological Bulletin* (1972), 77(4):296-304. Copyright © 1972 by the American Psychological Association. Reproduced by permission.

Definition

What is child abuse? Kempe et al. (1962) limited their study to children who had received serious physical injury, in circumstances which indicated that the injury was caused willfully rather than by accident. They coined the term "battered child" to encompass their definition. Zalba (1966), after a brief review of definitions, likewise addressed himself primarily to those cases in which physical injury was willfully inflicted on a child by a parent or parent substitute.

Because of the difficulty of pinpointing what is emotional or psychological or social neglect and abuse, and because of the extent of the literature on physical abuse alone, this review, following Kempe's and Zalba's lead, limits the term "child abuse" to the concept of physical injury to the child, willfully inflicted. The review omits studies of parents who neglect their children—emotionally, socially, or psychologically—and adults who sexually molest them.

Medical and Legal History

Literature on the medical and legal aspects of the problem of child abuse is extensive. The edited volume of Helfer and Kempe (1968) contains a general overview, as do the articles by Paulson and Blake (1967), Silver (1968), and Zalba (1966). Legal aspects are delineated in De Francis (1970), McCoid (1965), and the various articles by Paulsen (1966a, 1966b, 1967, 1968a, 1968b). Simons and Downs (1968) gave an overview of patterns, problems, and accomplishments of the child-abuse reporting laws. A thorough bibliography on child abuse was published by the United States Department of Health, Education and Welfare (1969).

This review is not concerned with the medical and legal aspects of the problem and refers only to those articles that gave more than a passing mention to the psychological and social determinants of parental abuse of children.

Review of the Literature

Most of the studies of child abuse are subject to the same general criticism. First, the studies that set out to test specific hypotheses are few. Many start and end as broad studies with relatively untested common-sense assumptions. Second, in most studies in this area, the researchers used samples easily available from ready-at-hand local populations, and thus the samples were not truly representative. We shall have to rely on the convergence of conclusions from various types of sampling to establish generalizations. Third, practically all of the research in child abuse is ex post facto. What is left unanswered and still to be tested is whether one can determine prior to the onset of abuse which parents are most likely to abuse their children, or whether high-risk groups can only be defined after at least one incident of abuse has occurred.

In spite of these criticisms, the studies of child abuse do give general data that can furnish hypotheses for more rigorous research design, and for a more differentiated approach to the question of why parents abuse their children.

Demographic Characteristics

In an attempt to discover whether or not various social or economic stresses make abuse more likely, many of the studies have described demographic characteristics of abusing families. Kempe et al. (1962) found in the abusing families a high incidence of divorce, separation, and unstable marriages, as well as of minor criminal offenses. The children who were abused were very young, often under one year of age. In many of the families, children were born in very close succession. Often one child would be singled out for injury, the child that was the victim of an unwanted pregnancy.

Various other studies enter figures from their own samples, generally repeating Kempe's findings (Birrell & Birrell, 1968; Cameron, Johnson, & Camps, 1966; Ebbin, Gollub, Stein, & Wilson, 1969; Elmer & Gregg, 1967; Gregg & Elmer, 1969; Helfer & Pollock, 1967; Johnson & Morse, 1968; Nurse, 1964; Schloesser, 1964; Skinner & Castle, 1969).

Elmer (1967) and Young (1964) add to Kempe's findings the factors of social and economic stress, lack of family roots in the community, lack of immediate support from extended families, social isolation, high mobility, and unemployment.

While pointing to the role that economic and social stresses play in bringing out underlying personality weaknesses, the majority of the foregoing authors caution that economic and social stresses alone are neither sufficient nor necessary causes for child abuse. They point out that, although in the socially and economically deprived segments of the population there is generally a higher degree of the kinds of stress factors found in abusing families, the great majority of deprived families do not abuse their children. Why is it that most deprived families do not engage in child abuse, though subject to the same economic and social stresses as those families who do abuse their children?

A study that sheds light on the fact that social and economic factors have been overstressed as etiological factors in cases of child abuse is that of Steele and Pollock (1968), whose sample of abusers consisted mainly of middle-class and upper-middle-class families. Though social and economic difficulties may have added stress to the lives of the parents, Steele and Pollock considered these stresses as only incidental intensifiers of personality-rooted etiological factors.

Simons, Downs, Hurster, and Archer (1966) conducted a thorough study delineating abusing families as multiproblem families in which, not the socioeconomic factors alone, but the interplay of mental, physical, and emotional stresses underlay the abuse.

Allowing that child abuse in many cases may well be the expression of family stress, Adelson (1961), Allen, Ten Bensel, and Raile (1969), Fontana (1968), Holter and Friedman (1968), and Kempe et al. (1962) considered psychological factors as of prime importance in the etiology of child abuse. There is a defect in character structure which, in the presence of added stresses, gives way to uncontrolled physical expression.

Paulson and Blake (1969) referred to the deceptiveness of upper- and middle-class abusers, and cautioned against viewing abuse and neglect as completely a function of educationally, occupationally, economically, or socially disadvantaged parents, or as due to physical or health impoverishment within a family.

If it is true that the majority of parents in the socially and economically deprived segments of the population do not batter their children, while some well-to-do parents engage in child abuse, then one must look for the causes of child abuse beyond socioeconomic stresses. One of the factors to which one may look is parental history.

Parental History

One basic factor in the etiology of child abuse draws unanimity: Abusing parents were themselves abused or neglected, physically or emotionally, as children. Steele and Pollock (1968) have shown a history of parents having been raised in the same style that they have recreated in the pattern of rearing their own children. As infants and children, all of the parents in the groups were deprived both of basic mothering and of the deep sense of being cared for and cared about from the beginning of their lives.

Fontana (1968) also viewed the parents as emotionally crippled because of unfortunate circumstances in their own childhood. The parents reacted to their children in keeping with their own personal experiential history of loneliness, lack of protection, and lack of love. Many authors corroborated the hypotheses of Steele and Pollock and of Fontana.

In a study surveying 32 men and 7 women imprisoned for cruelty to their children, Gibbins and Walker (1956) concluded that it was rejection, indifference, and hostility in their own childhood that produced the cruel parents.

Ten years later, Tuteur and Glotzer (1966) studied 10 mothers who were hospitalized for murdering their children and found that all had grown up in an emotionally cold and often overtly rejecting family environment, in which parental figures were either absent or offered little opportunity for wholesome identification when present.

Komisaruk (1966) found as the most striking statistic in his study of abusing families the emotional loss of a significant parental figure in the early life of the abusive parent.

Perhaps the most systematic and well-controlled study in the area of child abuse, that of Melnick and Hurley (1969), compared two small, socioeconomically and racially matched groups on 18 personality variables. Melnick and Hurley found, among other things, a probable history of emotional deprivation in the mothers' own upbringing.

Further support for the hypothesis that the abusing parent was once an abused or neglected child is found in Bleiberg (1965), Blue (1965), Corbett (1964), Curtis (1963), Easson and Steinhilber (1961), Fairburn and Hunt (1964), Fleming (1967), Green (1965), Harper (1963), Kempe et al. (1962), McHenry, Girdany, and Elmer (1963), Morris, Gould, and Matthews (1964), Nurse (1964), Paulson and Blake (1969), Silver, Dublin, and Lourie (1969b), and Wasserman (1967).

In a summary statement, Gluckman (1968), repeating the findings of earlier observers, set up a 10-point differential diagnosis category. His main point, and the point of this section of the review, is that the child is the father of the man. The capacity to love is not inherent; it must be taught to the child. Character development depends on love, tolerance, and example. Many abusing parents were raised without this love and tolerance.

Parental Attitudes toward Child Rearing

In addition to concurring on the fact that many abusing parents were themselves raised with some degree of abuse or neglect, the authors agreed that the abusing parents share common misunderstandings with regard to the nature of child rearing, and look to the child for satisfaction of their own parental emotional needs.

Steele and Pollock (1968) found that the parents in their study group expected and demanded a great deal from their infants and children, and did so prematurely. The parents dealt with their children as if older than they really were. The parents felt insecure and unsure of being loved, and looked to their children as sources of reassurance, comfort, and loving response, as if the children were adults capable of providing grown-up comfort and love.

Melnick and Hurley (1969), in their well-controlled study of personality variables, also found in the mothers severely frustrated dependency needs, and an inability to empathize with their children.

Galdston (1965) concurred that abusing parents treated their children as adults, and he added that the parents were incapable of understanding the particular stages of development of their children.

Bain (1963), Gregg (1968), Helfer and Pollock (1967), Hiller (1969), Johnson and Morse (1968), Korsch, Christian, Gozzi, and Carlson (1965), and Morris and Gould (1963) also reported that abusing parents have a high expectation and demand for the infant's or child's performance, and a corresponding disregard for the infant's or child's own needs, limited abilities, and helplessness. Wasserman (1967) found that the parents not only considered punishment a proper disciplinary measure but strongly defended their right to use physical force.

In a 1969 study, Gregg and Elmer, comparing children accidentally injured with those abused, judged that the mother's ability to keep up the personal appearance of the child when well, and her ability to provide medical care when the child was moderately ill, sharply differentiated the abusive from the nonabusive mothers.

The authors seem to agree that abusing parents lack appropriate knowledge of child rearing, and that their attitudes, expectations, and child-rearing techniques set them apart from nonabusive parents. The abusing parents implement culturally accepted norms for raising children with an exaggerated intensity and at an inappropriately early age.

Presence of Severe Personality Disorders

There has been an evolution in thinking regarding the presence of a frank psychosis in the abusing parent. Woolley and Evans (1955) and Miller (1959) posited a high incidence of neurotic or psychotic behavior as a strong etiological factor in child abuse. Cochrane (1965), Greengard (1964), Platou, Lennox, and Beasley (1964) and Simpson (1967, 1968) concurred. Adelson (1961) and Kaufman (1962) considered only the most violent and abusive parent as having schizophrenic personalities. Kempe et al. (1962), allowing that direct murder of children betrayed a frank psychosis on the part of the parent, found that most of the abusing parents, though lacking in impulse control, were not severely psychotic. By the end of the decade, the literature seemed to support the view that only a few of the abusing parents showed severe psychotic tendencies (Fleming, 1967; Laupus, 1966; Steele & Pollock, 1968; Wasserman, 1967).

Motivational and Personality Variables: A Typology

A review of opinions on parental personality and motivational variables leads to a conglomerate picture. While the authors generally agree that there is a defect in the abusing parent's personality that allows aggressive impulses to be expressed too freely (Kempe et al., 1962; Steele & Pollock, 1968; Wasserman, 1967), disagreement comes in describing the source of the aggressive impulses.

Some authors claim that abuse is a final outburst at the end of a long period of tension (Nomura, 1966; Ten Have, 1965), or that abuse stems from an inability to face life's daily stresses (Heins, 1969). Some claim that abuse stems from deep feelings of inadequacy or from parental inability to fulfill the roles expected of parenthood (Cohen, Raphling, & Green, 1966; Court, 1969; Fontana, 1964; Johnson & Morse, 1968; Komisaruk, 1966; Silver, 1968; Steel & Pollock, 1968). Others described the parents as immature, self-centered, and impulse-ridden (Cochrane, 1965; Delaney, 1966; Jacobziner, 1964; Ten Bensel, 1963).

Some authors consider a role reversal between the spouses as a prime factor in the etiology of child abuse. A home in which the father is unemployed and the mother has taken over the financial responsibility of the family is considered a breeding ground for abuse (Galdston, 1965; Greengard, 1964; Nathan, 1965; Nurse, 1964).

Finally, there are those authors who considered low intelligence as a prime factor in the etiology of child abuse (Fisher, 1958; Simpson, 1967, 1968), although this point is disputed in the findings of Cameron et al. (1966), Holter and Friedman (1968), Kempe et al. (1962), and Ounsted (1968).

Is there a common motivational factor behind child abuse? Is there only one "type" of abusing parent? Realization that each of the above described characteristics was found to exist at least in some individual circumstances has led some authors to group together certain characteristics in clusters, and to evolve a psychodynamic within each cluster. The first major attempt at a typology was made by Merrill (1962). Because Merrill's typology is the most often quoted it is summarized in some detail.

Merrill identified three distinct clusters of personality characteristics that he found to be true both of abusing mothers and fathers, and a fourth that he found true of the abusing fathers alone. The first group of parents seemed to Merrill to be beset with a continual and pervasive hostility and aggressiveness, sometimes focused, sometimes directed at the world in general. This was not a controlled anger, and was continually with the parents, with the only stimulation needed for direct expression being normal daily difficulties. This angry feeling stemmed from conflicts within the parents and was often rooted in their early childhood experiences.

The second group Merrill identified by personality characteristics of rigidity, compulsiveness, lack of warmth, lack of reasonableness, and lack of pliability in thinking and in belief. These parents defended their right to act as they had in abusing their child. Mothers in this group had marked child-rejection attitudes, evidenced by their primary concern with their own pleasures, inability to feel love and protectiveness toward their children, and in feelings that the children were responsible for much of the trouble being experienced by themselves as parents. These fathers and mothers were extremely compulsive in their behavior, demanding excessive cleanliness of their children. Many of these parents had great difficulty in relaxing, in expressing themselves verbally, and in exhibiting warmth and friendliness.

Merrill's third group of parents showed strong feelings of passivity and dependence. Many of these parents were people who were unassuming, reticent about expressing their feelings and desires, and very unaggressive. They were individuals who manifested strong needs to depend on others for decisions. These mothers and fathers often competed with their own children for the love and attention of their spouses. Generally depressed, moody, unresponsive, and unhappy, many of these parents showed considerable immaturity.

Merrill's fourth grouping or cluster of personality characteristics included a significant number of abusing fathers. These fathers were generally young, intelligent men with acquired skills who, because of some physical disability, were now fully or partially unable to support their families. In most of these situations, the mothers were working, and the fathers stayed at home, caring for the children. Their frustrations led to swift and severe punishment, to angry, rigid discipline.

Two further attempts at classification, Delsordo (1963) and Zalba (1967), with slight modifications, can be reduced to Merrill's categories.

The use of categories seems simple, unifying, and time saving. If further work can be done in refining the categories, validating them in field research, perhaps they or similar clusters shown to be empirically valid can be used as an aid in the determination of high-risk parents.

In this section, we have seen a conglomerate picture of parental motivational and personality variables, with one author's attempt to cluster the characteristics into a workable unity. One basic fact of agreement emerges from the studies in this section. The authors feel that a general defect in character—from whatever source—is present in the abusing parent allowing aggressive impulses to be expressed too freely. During times of additional stress and tension, the impulses express themselves on the helpless child.

Critique of a Survey

Of the studies surveying the demographic characteristics of families in which child abuse has occurred, the most extensive in scope was the national survey undertaken by Gil (1968a, 1968b, 1969).[1] In 1969, Gil reported that the phenomenon of child abuse was highly concentrated among the socioeconomically deprived segments of the population. Concluding that "physical abuse is by and large not very serious as

---

[1]Gil's book reporting his national findings (*Violence against children: Physical child abuse in the United States.* Cambridge, Mass.: Harvard University Press, 1970) appeared after the present review was accepted for publication. Although the book has greater detail, the findings and conclusions are identical to those in the cited references.

reflected by the data on the extent and types of injury suffered by the children in the study cohort [p. 862]," Gill placed his intervention strategy in the general betterment of society. For Gil, the cultural attitude permitting the use of physical force in child rearing is the common core of all physical abuse of children in American society. Since he found the socioeconomically deprived relying more heavily on physical force in rearing children, he recommended systematic educational efforts aimed at gradually changing this cultural attitude, and the establishment of clear-cut cultural prohibitions against the use of physical force as a means of rearing children. He viewed this educational effort as likely to produce the strongest possible reduction in the incidence and prevalence of physical abuse of children.

For Gil, child abuse is ultimately the result of chance environmental factors. While admitting to various forms of physical, social, intellectual, and emotional deviance and pathology in caretakers, and in the family units to which they belong, Gil stressed a global control of environmental factors as the solution to the problem of child abuse. He suggested: (*a*) the elimination of poverty from the midst of America's affluent society; (*b*) the availability in every community of resources aimed at the pervention and alleviation of deviance and pathology; (*c*) the availability of comprehensive family planning programs and liberalized legislation concerning medical abortions, to reduce the number of unwanted children; (*d*) family-life education and counseling programs for adolescents and adults in preparation for and after marriage, to be offered within the public school system; (*e*) a comprehensive, high-quality, neighborhood-based national health service, to promote and assure maximum feasible physical and mental health for every citizen; (*f*) a range of social services geared to the reduction of environmental stresses of family life; and (*g*) a community-based system of social services geared to assisting families and children who cannot live together because of severe relationship problems. Gil's ultimate objective is "the reduction of the general level of violence, and the raising of the general level of human well-being throughout our entire society [p. 863]."

While one must praise the efforts of the Gil study in data collection, and the ultimate objective of reducing the general level of violence and raising the general level of human well-being in our entire society, one cannot help but feel that Gil did not address himself to the question of child abuse. If there really does exist as strong a link as Gil suggests between poverty and physical abuse of children, why is it that all poor parents do not batter their children, while some well-to-do parents engage in child abuse? Eliminating environmental stress factors and bettering the level of society at all stages may reduce a myriad of social ills and may even prove effective, indirectly, in reducing the amount of child abuse. But there still remains the problem, insoluble at the demographic level, of why some parents abuse their children, while others under the same stress factors do not.

Other authors throughout the decade have allowed for the types of services outlined by Gil, but less globally and in a manner less disregarding of parental personality factors. That raising the general educational and financial level of families that are socioeconomically deprived is of long-range value in the lessening of the prevalence of child abuse is generally agreed upon, and finds support throughout the literature. However, most of the authors explicitly caution against considering abuse, as does Gil, as a function solely of educational, occupational, economic, or social stresses. This point is made by Adelson (1961), Allen et al. (1969), Elmer (1967), Fontana (1968), Helfer and Pollock (1967), Holter and Friedman (1968),

Kempe (1968), Kempe et al. (1962), Paulson and Blake (1967), Silver et al. (1969a, 1969b), and Steele and Pollock (1968).

The great majority of the authors cited in this review have pointed to psychological factors within the parents themselves as of prime importance in the etiology of child abuse. They see abuse as stemming from a defect in character leading to a lack of inhibition in expressing frustration and other impulsive behavior. Socioeconomic factors sometimes place added stress on the basic weakness in personality structure, but these factors are not of themselves sufficient or necessary causes of abuse.

Conclusion

The purpose of this review has been to bring together the published professional opinions on the psychological characteristics of the abusing parent, in order to determine from the most commonly held opinions what generalizations can be induced, and thus to lay the groundwork for more systematic testing of hypotheses.

The psychologist, both as a specialist in the functioning of the human as an individual, and as a scientist trained in research methodology, is in a unique position to test the hypotheses raised by professionals in the fields of medicine and social work, in the study of the personality characteristics of the abusing parent.

Certainly, one would hope that research can eventually develop criteria to distinguish those inadequate parents who, with professional help, can meet the needs of their children, from those who cannot. We need eventually to be able to identify the high-risk families prior to the onset of abuse, but should be satisfied for the time being if we can help determine after the fact of abuse which families must receive the most attention to assure the further safety of their child.

REFERENCES

ADELSON, L "Slaughter of the innocents: A study of forty-six homicides in which the victims were children." *New England Journal of Medicine,* 1961, 264, 1345-1349.

ALLEN, H. D., TEN BENSEL, R. W., & RAILE, R. B. "The battered child syndrome." *Minnesota Medicine,* 1969, 52, 155-156.

BAIN, K. "Commentary: The physically abused child." *Pediatrics,* 1963, 31, 895-898.

BIRRELL, R. G., & BIRRELL, J. H. W. "The maltreatment syndrome in children." *Medical Journal of Australia,* 1968, 2, 1023-1029.

BLEIBERG, N. "The neglected child and the child health conference." *New York State Journal of Medicine,* 1965, 65, 1880-1885.

BLUE, M. T. "The battered child syndrome from a social work viewpoint." *Canadian Journal of Public Health,* 1965, 56, 197-198.

BOARDMAN, H. E. "A project to rescue children from inflicted injuries." *Social Work,* 1962, 7, 43-51.

BOARDMAN, H. E. "Who insures the child's right to health?" *Child Welfare,* 1963, 42, 120-124.

CAMERON, J. M., JOHNSON, H. R. M., & CAMPS, F. E. "The battered child syndrome." *Medicine, Science, and the Law,* 1966, 6, 2-21.

COCHRANE, W. "The battered child syndrome." *Canadian Journal of Public Health,* 1965, 56, 193-196.

COHEN, M. I., RAPHLING, D. L., & GREEN, P. E. "Psychologic aspects of the maltreatment syndrome of childhood." *Journal of Pediatrics,* 1966, 69, 279-284.

CORBETT, J. T. "A psychiatrist reviews the battered child syndrome and mandatory reporting legislation." *Northwest Medicine*, 1964, 63, 920-922.

COURT, J. "The battered child: Historical and diagnostic reflections, reflections on treatment." *Medical Social Work,* 1969, 22(1), 11-20.

CURTIS, G. "Violence breeds violence—perhaps." *American Journal of Psychiatry,* 1963, 120, 386-387.

DE FRANCIS, V. *Child abuse legislation in the 1970's.* Denver, Colo.: American Humane Association, 1970.

DELANEY, D. W. "The physically abused child." *World Medical Journal*, 1966, 13, 145-147.

DELSORDO, J. D. "Protective casework for abused children." *Children*, 1963, 10, 213-218.

EASSON, W. M., & STEINHILBER, R. M. "Murderous aggression by children and adolescents." *Archives of General Psychiatry*, 1961, 4, 1-10.

EBBIN, A. J., GOLLUB, M. H., STEIN, A. M., & WILSON, M. G. "Battered child syndrome at the Los Angeles County General Hospital." *American Journal of the Diseases of Children*, 1969, 118, 660-667.

ELMER, E. *Children in jeopardy: A study of abused minors and their families.* Pittsburgh: University of Pittsburgh Press, 1967.

ELMER, E., & GREGG, G. S. "Developmental Characteristics of Abused Children." *Pediatrics*, 1967, 40, 596-602.

FAIRBURN, A. C., & HUNT, A. C. "Caffey's 'third syndrome': A critical evaluation." *Medicine, Science, and the Law*, 1964, 4, 123-126.

FISHER, S. H. "Skeletal manifestations of parent-induced trauma in infants and children." *Southern Medical Journal*, 1958, 51, 956-960.

FLEMING, G. M. "Cruelty to children." *British Medical Journal*, 1967, 2, 421-422.

FONTANA, V. J. *The maltreated child: The maltreatment syndrome in children.* Springfield, Ill.: Charles C. Thomas, 1964.

FONTANA, V. J. "Further reflections on maltreatment of children." *New York State Journal of Medicine*, 1968, 68, 2214-2215.

GALDSTON, R. "Observations on children who have been physically abused and their parents." *American Journal of Psychiatry*, 1965, 122, 440-443.

GIBBINS, T. C. N., & WALKER, A. *Cruel parents.* London: Institute for the Study and Treatment of Delinquency, 1956.

GIL, D. G. "California pilot study." In R. E. Helfer & C. H. Kempe (Eds.), *The battered child*. Chicago: University of Chicago Press, 1968. (a)

GIL, D. G. "Incidence of child abuse and demographic characteristics of persons involved." In R. E. Helfer & C. H. Kempe (Eds.), *The battered child*. Chicago: University of Chicago Press, 1968. (b)

GIL, D. G. "Physical abuse of children: Findings and implications of a nationwide survey." *Pediatrics*, 1969, 44(5, Supplement), 857-864.

GLUCKMAN, L. K. "Cruelty to children." *New Zealand Medical Journal*, 1968, 67, 155-159.

GREEN, K. "Diagnosing the battered child syndrome." *Maryland State Medical Journal*, 1965, 14(9), 83-84.

GREENGARD, J. "The battered-child syndrome." *American Journal of Nursing*, 1964, 64(6), 98-100.

GREGG, G. S. "Physicians, child-abuse reporting laws, and injured child: Psychosocial anatomy of childhood trauma." *Clinical Pediatrics*, 1968, 7, 720-725.

GREGG, G. S., & ELMER, E. "Infant injuries: Accident or abuse?" *Pediatrics*, 1969, 44, 434-439.

HARPER, F. V. "The physician, the battered child and the law." *Pediatrics*, 1963, 31, 899-902.

HEINS, M. "Child abuse: Analysis of a current epidemic." *Michigan Medicine*, 1969, 68, 887-891.

HELFER, R. E., & KEMPE, C. H. (Eds.) *The battered child*. Chicago: University of Chicago Press, 1968.

HELFER, R. E., & POLLOCK, C. B. "The battered child syndrome." *Advances in Pediatrics*, 1967, 15, 9-27.

HILLER, R. B. "The battered child: A health visitor's point of view." *Nursing Times*, 1969, 65, 1265-1266.

HOLTER, J. C., & FRIEDMAN, S. B. "Principles of management in child abuse cases." *American Journal of Orthopsychiatry*, 1968, 38, 127-136.

JAFOBZINER, H. "Rescuing the battered child." *American Journal of Nursing*, 1964, 64(6), 92-97.

JOHNSON, B., & MORSE, H. A. "Injured children and their parents." *Children*, 1968, 15, 147-152.

KAUFMAN, I. "Psychiatric implications of physical abuse of children." In V. De Francis (Ed.), *Protecting the battered child*. Denver, Colo.: American Humane Association, 1962.

KEMPE, C. H. "Some problems encountered by welfare departments in the management of the battered child syndrome." In R. E. Helfer & C. H. Kempe (Eds.), *The battered child*. Chicago: University of Chicago Press, 1968.

KEMPE, C. H., SILVERMAN, F. N., STEELE, B. F., DROEGEMUELLER, W., & SILVER, H. K. "The battered-child syndrome." *Journal of the American Medical Association*, 1962, 181, 17-24.

KOMISARUK, R. "Clinical evaluation of child abuse: Scarred families, a preliminary report." *Juvenile Court Judges Journal* (Wayne County, Michigan), 1966, 17(2), 66-70.

KORSCH, B. M., CHRISTIAN, J. B., GOZZI, E. K., & CARLSON, P. V. "Infant care and punishment: A pilot study." *American Journal of Public Health*, 1965, 55, 1880-1888.

LAUPUS, W. E. "Child abuse and the physician." *The Virginia Medical Monthly*, 1966, 93(1), 1-2.

McCOID, A. H. "The battered child and other assaults upon the family." *Minnesota Law Review*, 1965, 50, 1-58.

McHENRY, T., GIRDANY, B. R., & ELMER, E. "Unsuspected trauma with multiple skeletal injuries during infancy and childhood." *Pediatrics*, 1963, 31, 903-908.

MELNICK, B., & HURLEY, J. R. "Distinctive personality attributes of child-abusing mothers." *Journal of Consulting and Clinical Psychology*, 1969, 33, 746-749.

MERRILL, E. J. "Physical abuse of children: An agency study." In V. De Francis (Ed.), *Protecting the battered child*. Denver, Colo.: American Humane Association, 1962.

MILLER, D. S. "Fractures among children: Parental assault as causative agent." *Minnesota Medicine*, 1959, 42, 1209-1213.

MORRIS, M. G., & GOULD, R. W. "Role reversal: A concept in dealing with the neglected/battered child syndrome." In, *The neglected battered-child syndrome: Role reversal in parents*. New York: Child Welfare League of America, 1963.

MORRIS, M. G., GOULD, R. W., & MATTHEWS, P. J. "Toward prevention of child abuse." *Children*, 1964, 11, 55-60.

NATHAN, H. "Abused children." *American Journal of Psychiatry*, 1965, 122, 443.

NOMURA, F. M. "The battered child 'syndrome': A review." *Hawaii Medical Journal*, 1966, 25, 387-394.

NURSE, S. "Familial patterns of parents who abuse their children." *Smith College Studies in Social Work*, 1964, 35, 11-25.

OUNSTED, C. "Review of K. Simpson, Battered baby syndrome." *Developmental Medicine and Child Neurology*, 1968, 10, 133-134.

PAULSEN, M. G. "Legal protection against child abuse." *Children*, 1966, 13, 43-48.(a)

PAULSEN, M. G. "The legal framework for child protection." *Columbia Law Review*, 1966, 66, 679-717.(b)

PAULSEN, M. G. "Child abuse reporting laws: The shape of the legislation." *Columbia Law Review*, 1967, 67, 1-49.

PAULSEN, M. G. "A summary of child-abuse legislation." In R. E. Helfer & C. H. Kempe (Eds.), *The battered child*. Chicago: University of Chicago Press, 1968.(a)

PAULSEN, M. G. "The law and abused children." In R. E. Helfer & C. H. Kempe (Eds.), *The battered child*. Chicago: University of Chicago Press, 1968.(b)

PAULSON, M. J., & BLAKE, P. R. "The abused, battered and maltreated child: A review." *Trauma*, 1967, 9(4), 3-136.

PAULSON, M. J., & BLAKE, P. R. "The physically abused child: A focus on prevention." *Child Welfare*, 1969, 48, 86-95.

PLATOU, R. V., LENNOX, R., & BEASLEY, J. D. "Battering." *Bulletin of the Tulane Medical Faculty*, 1964, 23, 157-165.

SCHLOESSER, P. T. "The abused child." *Bulletin of the Menninger Clinic*, 1964, 28, 260-268.

SILVER, L. B. "Child abuse syndrome: A review." *Medical Times*, 1968, 96, 803-820.

SILVER, L. B., DUBLIN, C. C., & LOURIE, R. S. "Child abuse syndrome: The 'gray areas' in establishing a diagnosis." *Pediatrics*, 1969, 44, 594-600.(a)

SILVER, L. B., DUBLIN, C. C., & LOURIE, R. S. "Does violence breed violence? Contributions from a study of the child abuse syndrome." *American Journal of Psychiatry*, 1969, 126, 404-407.(b)

SIMONS, B., & DOWNS, E. F. "Medical reporting of child abuse: Patterns, problems and accomplishments." *New York State Journal of Medicine*, 1968, 68, 2324-2330.

SIMONS, B., DOWNS, E. F., HURSTER, M. M., & ARCHER, M. "Child abuse: Epidemiologic study of medically reported cases." *New York State Journal of Medicine*, 1966, 66, 2783-2788.

SIMPSON, K. "The battered baby problem." *Royal Society of Health Journal*, 1967, 87, 168-170.

SIMPSON, K. "The battered baby problem." *South African Medical Journal*, 1968, 42, 661-663.

SKINNER, A. E., & CASTLE, R. L. *78 battered children: A retrospective study*. London: National Society for the Prevention of Cruelty to Children, 1969.

STEELE, B. F., & POLLOCK, C. B. "A psychiatric study of parents who abuse infants and small children." In R. E. Helfer & C. H. Kempe (Eds.), *The battered child*. Chicago: University of Chicago Press, 1968.

TEN BENSEL, R. W. "The battered child syndrome." *Minnesota Medicine*, 1963, 46, 977-982.

TEN HAVE, R. "A preventive approach to problems of child abuse and neglect." *Michigan Medicine,* 1965, 64, 645-649.

TUTEUR, W., & GLOTZER, J. "Further observations on murdering mothers." *Journal of Forensic Sciences*, 1966, 11, 373-383.

UNITED STATES DEPARTMENT OF HEALTH, EDUCATION AND WELFARE. *Bibliography on the battered child*. Washington, D. C.: United States Government Printing Office, 1969.

WASSERMAN, S. "The abused parent of the abused child." *Children*, 1967, 14, 175-179.

WOOLLEY, P. V., & EVANS, W. A. "Significance of skeletal lesions in infants resembling those of traumatic origin." *Journal of the American Medical Association*, 1955, 158, 539-543.

YOUNG, L. *Wednesday's children: A study of child neglect and abuse*. New York: McGraw-Hill, 1964.

ZALBA, S. R. "The abused child: A survey of the problem." *Social Work*, 1966, 11(4), 3-16.

ZALBA, S. R. "The abused child: A typology for classification and treatment." *Social Work*, 1967, 12(1), 70-79.

14

A Psychiatric Study of Mothers of Infants with Growth Failure Secondary to Maternal Deprivation*

Joseph Fischhoff, M.D.,
Charles F. Whitten, M.D., and
Marvin G. Pettit, M.S.W.

The syndrome of maternal deprivation was first recognized in institutionalized infants. A combination of insufficient personnel to provide sensory and social stimulation and a lack of awareness of the devastating effect of environmental deprivation on the development of the infant appear to be the reasons for the deprivation. Only recently has it been recognized that infants living with their mothers may sustain maternal deprivation. Little has been published concerning the reasons these mothers have inadequately cared for their infants,[1-6] and virtually no data are available on the mothers' personality structures.

In 16 infants we have tested the hypothesis that growth failure in the maternal deprivation syndrome is secondary to the infant's psychological state. Our data suggest that maternally deprived infants are underweight because of undereating which is secondary to not being offered adequate food or not accepting it, and not because of some psychologically induced defect in absorption or metabolism.[7]

---

* Supported by a grant (RR-74) from the General Clinic Research Centers Program of the Division of Research Resources, National Institutes of Health.

Joseph Fischoff, et al., "A Psychiatric Study of Mothers of Infants with Growth Failure Secondary to Maternal Deprivation" *Journal of Pediatrics*, 79:209-215, 1971. Copyright © The C. V. Mosby Co., St. Louis, Missouri, U.S.A. Reproduced by permission.

TABLE I

Highlights of Psychiatric Assessment of the Mothers

Psychiatric diagnosis	Inappropriate affect	Evidence of depression	Fantasies reflect hope	Predisposition toward acting out	Behavior on initial contact indicative of psychopathology
1 Character disorder	Yes	No	No	Yes	Yes
2 Character disorder	Yes	Yes	No	Yes	Yes
3 Character disorder	Yes	No	Unknown	No	No
4 Psychoneurotic	No	Yes	Yes	Yes	No
5 Character disorder	Yes	Yes	Unknown	Yes	Yes
6 Character disorder	Yes	Yes	No	Yes	Yes
7 Character disorder	No	Yes	No	Yes	No
8 Character disorder	Yes	No	No	No	No
10 Character disorder	Yes	Yes	No	Yes	Yes
11 Character disorder	Yes	Yes	No	Yes	No
12 Character disorder	Yes	Yes	No-yes	Yes	Yes
16 Psychoneurotic	No	Yes	Yes	No	No

Criteria for admission to the study were: (1) age, 3 to 24 months; (2) gestation, at least 9 months; (3) birth weight, more than the premature level of 5 pounds 8 ounces or 2,500 Gm.; (4) current height and weight, below the third percentile on the Stuart growth grids; (5) no evidence of an organic cause for the failure to thrive by history, physical examination, or routine laboratory analysis; (6) presence of at least one of the following: autoerotic behavior, watchfulness, apathy, or development lags; and (7) historical data that indicated the infant had had little physical handling by, and social contact with, the mother. In all, the diagnosis of maternal deprivation syndrome was subsequently established by the demonstration of marked improvement following a period of adequate mothering (which includes provision of adequate food).

This paper reports a psychiatric study of 12 of the mothers of 13 of these infants (1 mother had 2 maternally deprived infants). Each mother was seen for 2 extensive psychiatric interviews. Information from these interviews was supplemented by briefer contacts with the mother during ward visits, an unstructured interview with all of the available fathers (8), pertinent data obtained by the psychiatric social worker, and observations of the pediatrician and nurses.

We wish to stress that our paper will not deal with other factors which undoubtedly play a role in the pathogenesis of the maternal deprivation syndrome; such as the role of the father, mother-father interaction, and social, economic, and environmental conditions. Our clinical experience had suggested that the vast majority of depriving mothers had a character disorder; the purpose of this study was to ascertain by systematic investigation the validity of this observation.

A dynamic and genetic assessment of the mothers' personalities, in addition to a cross-sectional study, were the goals of the psychiatric evaluation. This emphasized how each mother developed into the individual she is, and how she came to express herself both verbally and nonverbally in relation to her infant and in relation to her total environment. We were interested in identifying the forces that entered into the

TABLE I

Highlights of Psychiatric Assessment of the Mothers

Abnormal past history	Concrete thinking patterns	Poor self-image	Poor performance in day to day activities	Poor object relationships	Significant use of isolation for defense	Significant use of denial for defense
Yes	Yes	Yes	Yes	Yes	No	Yes
Yes	Yes	Yes	Yes	Yes	No	Yes
No	Yes	Yes	Yes	Yes	Yes	Yes
Yes	No	No	No	No	Yes	No
No	Yes	Yes	Yes	Yes	Yes	Yes
Yes	Yes	Yes	Yes	Yes	Yes	Yes
Yes	Yes	Yes	Yes	Yes	Yes	Yes
Yes	Yes	Yes	Yes	Yes	No	Yes
Yes	Yes	Yes	Yes	Yes	Yes	Yes
Yes	Yes	Yes	Yes	Yes	Yes	Yes
Yes	Yes	Yes	Yes	Yes	No	Yes
Yes	No	No	No	No	No	No

organization of her particular personality, and in determining how these forces influenced the child-rearing function of the mother. What the mother was able to relate about her past and present was important. However, equally important was her nonverbal behavior.

The psychiatric interviews were unstructured, but we attempted to explore as many facets of the mother's personality development as possible. Her early childhood development and significant personal relationships were discussed. We attempted to elicit important experiences at any time during her life, to discover areas of conflict and how they were handled, and to determine what defense mechanisms appeared to be most important. Since the mother might not recognize the significance of her own past history, the significance of her interaction with her infants, or the importance of the infant's nonverbal behavior, the psychiatric evaluation included assessments of the mother's emotional and social development. Her comments about her children and observations, if possible, of her interaction with her children were noted. An attempt was made to summarize the material for each mother under the following headings: age and marital status, initial appearance and manner, affect and mood, past history, past memories, self-image and ego functions, present mode of behavior, object relationships, defenses, and fantasies, hopes, and day dreams.

The following 3 cases illustrate the method of analysis (Cases 1, 2, and 7). (The numbers for the mothers correspond with the numbers used to identify the infants in the previous report of this study.[7]) Highlights of the psychiatric assessment of the mothers are listed in Table I.

Case Reports

Case 1.—This mother was 21 years of age. She was 18 years old at the time of her first pregnancy. She was pregnant when she married.

Initial appearance and manner. She had a little girl manner, was overly compliant, eager to please, and wore very tight-fitting clothes. She wore an excessive amount of makeup. Her tension was apparent as she smoked rapidly and constantly. She spoke about everything with ease, except she was somewhat tearful about her father's death.

Affect and mood. There was an air of forced gaiety, with laughter and euphoria initially. At other times she seemed almost bland and expressionless.

Past history. Her father was very strict, but she felt she was his favorite. Her mother allowed her to date without her father's knowledge, but she felt that her mother favored her sister. She left school at age 15 in the ninth grade, and she worked until she was 18. Her father died when she was 17; her mother became suicidal and was hospitalized. Her mother has had recurrent depression since that time. At 18 she married a man who has been diagnosed as a chronic paranoid schizophrenic and has been hospitalized several times.

Highlights of free association to questions about the past. At first she said "I had a pleasant childhood." Then she spoke about her father's rigidity and her need to hide from him what she was doing. She thought she was discriminated against by other children in school because she was from a minority. She has been "bothered since my marriage." She could only say that she was more anxious since her marriage.

Self-image and ego functions. She saw herself as a "good little girl," and she was unable to alter her present circumstances. Her perception of her environment was very limited, and she had no insight into her relationships to adults or her children. She thought in a very concrete manner, had poor judgment, and her concepts were very primitive. She expressed herself through action rather than through thought.

Present mode of behavior. She was consistent in her behavior, but it was highly constricted and repetitious. She felt she had no future, and "it doesn't look like we are going to have anything, life will continue as it is." She stays in her house and never goes out. Eight months after our initial contact she was content because her mother was living with her and helping her. She denied the severity of her infant's illness.

Object relationships. Her object relationships were of the anaclitic type, and she had a little girl relationship to others. She never felt equal but always dependent and never felt herself to be in a mothering role.

Predominant defenses. Denial was a predominant defense. She denied any difficulties before she was married and denied that her children had any difficulties, yet one of the other children had retarded growth and displayed a very flat affect. She also used isolation as a major defense.

Fantasies. She said that she always knew she would marry at 18 but did not know why. She had hoped to be a singer with a band but made no efforts in this direction. There were no conscious hopes or fantasies about the future.

Case 2.—The second mother was 23 and married. She had 2 illegitimate children and was first pregnant at age 18.

Initial appearance and manner. She appeared very disorganized, harassed, and was under extreme tension. Pressure of speech was very marked.

Affect and mood. She was chronically anxious and depressed.

Past history. This mother's own father had married 6 times, and her mother married 3 times. She said that her mother and father "ran around," and left her with other relatives. She left school at 16 and went to work. Her mother called her a "street walker," and she attempted to hide her illegitimate pregnancies from her mother. Her first child was given up for adoption, and her own parents were divorced when she was 8 years old. In her teens she was in a boarding school for a time and considered becoming a nun.

Highlights of free association to questions about the past. She thought she was close to her father and longed to see him even now. She thought that her mother was critical and degraded her. In addition, she thought her mother neglected her and left her with relatives impulsively. At the time of her parent's divorce she went to live with her father.

Self-image and ego functions. She saw herself as a nervous helpless isolated person. She attempted to rationalize her difficulties and discharged her anxiety by excessive talking. Her perception was poor, and she was unable to perceive the needs of her children. Judgment was poor regarding what others could do to her. There was limited or no insight into her relationships to others, children or adults. At times she acted out her difficulties, and her ego functions appeared very fragile.

Present mode of behavior. Appointments were cancelled frequently and her behavior was variable. She appeared harassed and was overly dramatic. At times she even appeared disheveled. She spoke about her suffering with a sense of pleasure, and she had a need to "believe everybody." She believed herself helpless so that others could do what they wished with her.

Object relationships. Her relationships to others were anaclitic but very tenuous. She felt alone and neglected but wished to be cared for. She did marry but said her husband neglected her.

Predominant defenses. Denial was striking in that she still believed that her father cared for her. Under stress there was marked regression with free-flowing anxiety, helplessness, and immobility.

Fantasies. She imagined that her husband had rescued her and that she was worthless. He knew about her pregnancies and disorganized home before the marriage. She feared abandonment because of her worthlessness. She saw one of her children as a replacement for the child given out for adoption.

Case 7.—This mother was 20 years of age. At age 19 she had an illegitimate pregnancy.

Initial appearance and manner. She was well dressed, lacked spontaneity, but did respond to questions.

Affect and mood. She expressed hopelessness and anger in addition to bitterness and a feeling of depression.

Past history. She was illegitimate and in early adolescence was placed in a girl's training school because of her uncontrollable behavior. There she was said to be "belligerent" and the psychiatric report noted that "the prognosis is not good." She was reared by her grandparents until she was 11 years old and from 17 years of age she lived with one man but was not married to him.

Highlights of free association to questions about the past. She was furious with her mother and believed her mother did not want her. She said her mother was "selfish" and "I never had a mother." She felt "betrayed by my mother."

Self-image in ego functions. She consciously distorted factual material and prevaricated. At times she acted out to avoid thinking and impulsively left her infant with others. Anxiety was felt and impulsively discharged through action. At other times she felt lonely, abandoned, and "no good." She had very poor judgment and insight into her difficulties.

Present mode of behavior. Present behavior was highly variable and often concealed by prevarication or confabulation. She leaned on an older man who she hoped would care for her financially. Her infant was shifted from one group to another so that they would care for him and she blamed others for her difficulties. With case work intervention she continued to act out.

Object relationships. She wanted others to care for her, and she wanted them to gratify her needs. However, she did not feel close to anyone though she wanted to be cared for.

Predominant defenses. We observed conscious distortion, acting out, projection, isolation, and denial as defenses.

Fantasies. She "wanted 3 children so someone would belong to me." She hoped that an older man would care for her and give her security.

Comments

Ten of the mothers (all but Mothers 4 and 16) had a sufficient number of the following characteristics to be diagnosed as character disorders: (a) disturbed early childhood histories, (b) poor performance in current day-to-day activities, (c) behavior on initial contact indicative of fairly severe psychopathology, (d) desire for an anaclitic relationship with an intense need to be taken care of, (e) literal, concrete thinking patterns, with a limited capacity for abstraction or planning for the future, (f) the use of denial, isolation, and projection as major mechanisms of defense, and (g) a predisposition toward action or acting out as opposed to thought.

Engle[8] states that character structure defines a more or less consistent, habitual way of thinking, feeling, and behaving. A set of attitudes and mechanisms are habitually adopted by the ego to deal with instinctual forces, assure satisfaction, reconcile conflicts, and achieve adjustment within a particular environment. The term character disorder implies rigidity and inflexibility of mental mechanisms, and also less over-all effectiveness in maintaining an adjustment and assuring development.

Frequently, the mothers with character disorders dealt with conflicts as if they were localized only in the environment. Their capacity for successful adaptation to changing environmental circumstances or stresses was limited because of inflexible personalities. Their ability to adapt was further compromised by their inability to assess the stresses or changes in their environment, their internal needs, or the needs of their children. As a result, the adverse social factors that were frequently present could be caused by, as well as contribute to, their inadequate behavior.

The mothers also demonstrated defects in the quality of their object relationships. They had a need to be taken care of and a poor "sense of personal identity." As a corollary their capacities for perceiving and caring for the needs of their infants were deficient.

The personality structure of 2 mothers (4 and 16) was very different from the 10 mothers diagnosed as having character disorders. Daily activities were performed well with the obvious exception of the handling of the infant who failed to thrive. Appearance and behavior on initial contact was not indicative of severe psychopathology. Desire for an anaclitic relationship with an intense need to be taken care of was not present. The capacities for abstraction, *introspection*, and planning for the future were good. The use of denial, isolation, and projection were minimal and repression was the predominant defense. A predisposition to acting out was not present, and the capacity for thinking and ideation was good. There was an attempt to speculate and form cause and effect relationships in behavior.

We believe that the significantly greater frequency of character disorders over psychoneurotic personalities in the depriving mothers is the result of character disorders having a constellation of features which are more conducive to inadequate mothering, i.e., limited ability to accurately perceive and assess the environment, their own needs or the needs of their children, limited ability to adapt to changes in the environment, adverse affective state, defective object relationships, and limited capacity for concern.

Although the vast majority of the mothers in our study have a character disorder whether this is true of depriving mothers in general is unknown. Our sample is small and there are no comparable studies in the literature. With one exception,[6] the few investigators[1-6] who have reported on the psychological features of mothers whose infants were maternally deprived have not provided a psychiatric diagnosis or comprehensive data. However, in most instances there is evidence to suggest the subjects had a defective character structure.

Barbero and associates,[3] state that mothers of infants who fail to thrive are in general, depressed, angry, helpless and desperate, and had problems in maintaining self-esteem. In their generalizations about the mothers in their study it is stated, "In those instances where the malidentification is part of a more pervasive and structured pathology, it becomes obvious to all concerned that these parents should be referred to the appropriate psychiatric and social agencies.'' This statement suggests that some of the mothers may have had character disorders.

Barbero and Shaheen[5] state that depriving mothers have lived under significant environmental psychosocial disruption, such as alcoholism, childhood deprivation, physical abuse between parents, and considerable strain of the parents with their own families. One mother felt isolated from early childhood, had very little relationship with her mother, constantly felt criticized by her mother, and never felt competent. Another mother was severely deprived and abused in her childhood. She disliked her child from the time of his birth and was angry with him. Sometimes after his first admission he again was losing weight and was found to be a ''battered child.'' These excerpts indicate that the mothers may have character disorders though, again, adequate data are not available in the report.

Leonard and associates[4] describe some characteristics of 13 mothers of infants who failed to thrive. Tension, anger, anxiety, depression, and inappropriate behavior were present. They found the mothers lacking in self-esteem, unable to assess their baby's needs and their own worth realistically. ''Not a single mother reported sustained supportive nurturing in her own childhood,'' and the mothers were lonely and isolated. The type of psychopathology described by these authors suggests severe disturbances in the character structure of the mothers.

Elmer[2] describes 5 cases of failure to thrive and presents highlights of the mothers' emotional psychological state. One mother had ''excessively strong needs to be cared for,'' and appeared to dislike males. Another mother appeared anxious and depressed. In another case the mother had been ''nervous,'' since age 10. She had not wanted her pregnancy. She was very depressed and remote from her infant. In these cases there is reference to severe personality difficulties, anxiety, and depression, but not sufficient data to draw conclusions about personality structure. With the exception of one mother, it is stated that there were many difficulties growing out of the immature and neurotic personalities of the parents.

Bullard and associates[6] report some aspects of mothers' personality and behavior in 3 cases. One mother resented her 2 children and was ''openly abusive with the boy during the interview.'' Ultimately, she left her child with a neighbor and moved to another city. In the second case when the child was ready to be discharged the psychiatrist noted, ''Child to be discharged home, recognizing that mother has not recognized the cause of Linda's trouble and is not willing to be under psychiatric care.'' In the third case the mother had many neurasthenic complaints. ''She was hyperactive, overtalkative, and extremely anxious. Her thoughts shifted from topic to topic, her feelings varied quickly from forced gaiety, and thence to emotions clearly depressive in nature.'' Her history and confirmation from other sources confirmed a long standing condition. The ''impression was of a severe and chronic disorder of character in which depressive, compensatory euphoric, and hysterical elements were prominent.'' The data for the first mother is suggestive and for the second indicative of character disorder. The authors considered that the third mother had a character disorder.

Coleman and Provence[1] give some pertinent information about 2 mothers of infants who failed to thrive. In one case when the infant was 7 months old the mother was 3 months pregnant, and the father committed suicide. She developed a prolonged period of grief, depression, and anger. The second mother was isolated and detached from her infant. She stopped breast-feeding on the fourth day because she was afraid she would smother it and spanked the infant because the crying drove her "wild." She alternated between depression and hopelessness over the baby's developmental lag and wondered whether or not she should "start over with a new baby." Later she denied that she was concerned; the observations suggest that she had a character disorder.

The probability of a high incidence of character disorders in the depriving mothers is important because of its implications for the usual choice of intervention strategy. A verbal, problem-solving, psychotherapeutic approach is appropriate for a mother with a psychoneurosis. She has the capacity for introspection and abstraction. She is also capable of self-awareness and has the ability to perceive and assess the environment and the needs of her children under conditions of great stress. A mother with a character disorder has a limited capacity to perceive and assess the environment, the needs of her children, and their adverse affective state. She also has primitive or defective object relationships and a limited capacity for concern, and she desires an anaclitic relationship. Her patterns of thought are literal and concrete. It is unlikely that a problem-solving, psychotherapeutic approach to help the mother understand her difficulties would be successful. Therefore one could not hope for character change in a period of months, and it is possible that the basic personality structure will not change even over an extended period of time; the infant is at risk all of this time. Though verbal discussion should not be neglected or avoided, the mother is more likely to respond to intervention involving action. She needs to be provided with someone to "lean on." She should be shown how to feed, play with, interact with, and care for her infant in a benign, direct, tutorial relationship (usually with a homemaker or social worker). She needs help in all phases of her life, since she may not be able to perceive and assess the requirements of her child or herself. The program should extend over a long period of time because the mother may or may not learn to comprehend and conceptualize how she functions as a person.

It should be recognized that with certain mothers suffering from a character disorder, these procedures will not be successful and placement of the child in a foster home may be necessary.

REFERENCES

1. COLEMAN, R. W., and PROVENCE, S.: "Environmental retardation (hospitalism) in infants living in families." *Pediatrics* 19:285, 1957.

2. ELMER, E.: "Failure to thrive. Role of the mother," *Pediatrics* 25:717, 1960.

3. BARBERO, G. J., MORRIS, M. G., and REFORD, M. T.: "Malidentification of mother-baby-father relationships expressed in infant failure to thrive," *Child Welfare* 42:13, 1963.

4. LEONARD, M. F., RHYMES, J. P., and SOLNIT, A. J.: "Failure to thrive in infants. A family problem," *Amer. J. Dis. Child.* 3:600, 1966.

5. BARBERO, G. J., and SHAHEEN, E.: "Environmental failure to thrive," *J. Pediat.* 71:639, 1967.

6.   BULLARD, D. M., Jr., GLASSER, H. H., HEAGARTY, M. C., and PIVCHIK, E. C.: "Failure to thrive in the neglected child," *Amer. J. Orthopsychiat.* 37:680, 1967.

7.   WHITTEN, C. F., PETTIT, M. G., and FISCHHOFF, J.: "Evidence that growth failure from maternal deprivation is secondary to undereating," *J.A.M.A.* 209:1675, 1969.

8.   ENGEL, G. L.: *Psychological development in health and disease*, Philadelphia, 1962, W. B. Saunders Company.

15

The "Sick but Slick" Syndrome as a Personality Component of Parents of Battered Children*

Logan Wright

Problem

The battered child represents a very important developmental and social as well as mental health problem and very appropriately has become the object of widespread interest by clinicians and researchers alike. Discovery of any existing personality profile, or description of any personality characteristics common to battering parents, is a prerequisite to identifying and treating suspected or potential child abusers. Researchers[1-4, 6, 9, 11, 12] have reported a variety of characteristics of battering parents. One is they are emotionally immature, poorly prepared for the problems of parenthood, and maintain unrealistic fantasies and expectations for their child's rate of development and his ability to take care of himself:

> Henry J., in speaking of his sixteen month old son, Johnny, said, "He knows what I mean and understands it when I say 'come here.' If he doesn't come immediately, I go and give him a gentle tug on the ear to remind him of what he's supposed to do." In the hospital it was found that Johnny's ear was lacerated and partially torn away from his head.[6, p. 110]

These parents also seem to see their children as agents for providing emotional support to mother rather than *vice versa*:

* Logan Wright, "The 'Sick but Slick' Syndrome as a Personality Component of Parents of Battered Children," *Journal of Clinical Psychology*, Vol. 32, No. 1 (January, 1976):41-45. Reproduced by permission of the Clinical Psychology Publishing Co. and the author.

"I have never felt really loved all my life. When the baby was born, I thought he would love me; but when he cried all the time, it meant he didn't love me, so I hit him." Kenny, age three weeks, was hospitalized with bilateral subdural hematomas.[6, p. 110]

Many battering parents are found to have a history of deprivation of love and affection from their parents and often have been battered themselves. As a result, they are presumed to have many unmet dependency needs. Economic and social difficulties (such as having too many babies over a short period of time, inability to meet economic demands, or separation from supportive relatives) also are felt to contribute to battering.

Wright[13] has described a picture of battering parents as disturbed, but capable of presenting an outwardly convincing picture of being normal and highly unlikely to abuse their children. This cluster of traits was termed the "sick but slick syndrome." Similarly, Smith, Honigsberger, and Smith[10] and Lund[8] have stressed the combined schizoid and psychopathic nature of disturbance in parents of battered children. Also, Steele[12], as well as Isaacs[7], has described child abusers as normal-appearing and overly conscientious parents.

The logistics of research on child abuse sometimes can be overwhelming, and Ss may have valid reasons to be evasive and uncooperative. These problems, combined with the primitive level of theory and research in this area, have produced a body of literature comprised primarily of impressionistic articles rather than more vigorously conducted studies. With the exception of Melnick and Hurley[9] and Lund[8], the research cited above is based on clinical observations rather than quantifiable data that utilized control groups, *etc.* The purpose of the present study was to explore the personalities of battering parents by obtaining quantifiable data about them from standard personality measures. This was not an experimental study in the sense that an independent variable is manipulated, with the predicted effect on a dependent variable determined on an *ad hoc* basis. Rather, the investigation was an inductive search for any consistencies in the personalities of child abusers.

Method

Ss were 13 parents convicted in court, but not incarcerated, for battering their children (experimental group) and 13 nonbattering, control parents of children hospitalized with infections, bone fractures, *etc.* in which the parents were not felt to be negligent. Each was selected because he represented a matched pairs partner for a given experimental S on the basis of age, sex, race, number of children, marital and educational status, family income and the fact that his child had been hospitalized. Each group consisted of 5 males and 8 females. Age differences between the matched pairs did not exceed 1 year. Total family income differences between the matched pairs of each group were less than $1000 per year. Parents were matched on years of schooling to within 2 years, and differences in number of children did not exceed one. The Peabody Picture Vocabulary Test (PPVT) also was administered to both groups in an attempt to control for the effects of intelligence.

Each parent received a battery of personality tests between 2 and 6 months after the battering episode. The battery consisted of the Rorschach, Minnesota Multiphasic Personality Inventory (MMPI), and Rosenzweig Picture Frustration

Study (PF). The 13 validity and clinical scales of the MMPI were selected to measure overall level of psychopathology as well as to indicate specifics with regard to affect, character and other symptoms. The Rosenzweig was employed because intropunitiveness, extrapunitiveness and impunitiveness seemed highly relevant to child abuse. Also, the group conformity rating supposedly is related to psychopathic tendencies. The Rorschach was used in order to balance the battery with a less structured, projective task. It was scored for overall psychopathology, negative affect, psychopathic deviancy and bizarre content. The latter rating was an attempt to assess "craziness" in an overt sense. All four variables on the Rorschach were scored by an experienced clinician who was naive with regard to which group, experimental or control, given Ss belonged.

Results

Since *ad hoc* predictions were not made, two-tailed, match-pair t-tests were performed on each of the study variables between experimental and control Ss. These results are shown in Table 1. Battering parents received scores significantly lower than nonbattering parents on the Rorschach variable of bizarre content ($t = 2.35$, $df = 12$, $p < .05$). Battering parents obtained scores significantly higher than nonbattering parents on the Rosenzweig group conformity rating ($t = 2.41$, $df = 12$, $p < .05$), the Rosenzweig intropunitiveness scale ($t = 3.17$, $df = 12$, $p < .01$), the MMPI lie scale ($t = 2.86$, $df = 12$, $p < .05$), and the MMPI K scale ($t = 2.37$, $df = 12$, $p < .05$). Thus, statistically significant differences were found for 5 of the 21 variables, while fewer than 2 would be expected by chance if the variables are assumed to be uncorrelated. The difference between experimental and control Ss on the psychopathic deviancy (PD) scale of the MMPI approached significance ($t = 2.10$, $t .05 = 2.18$); battering parents appeared more psychopathic. Battering parents also scored significantly lower than nonbatterers on the intelligence control measure (PPVT) ($t = 2.95$, $df = 12$, $p = < .05$).

Discussion

The fact that battering parents differed from their control Ss on IQ is difficult to explain. It seems unlikely that this could be accounted for by an emotional disturbance that affected cognitive functioning on a simple task such as the PPVT. On the other hand, the possibility that true differences in IQ exist between two populations matched so closely on the number of years of education and income is hard to accept. One possible explanation is a characterological one, wherein the energies of psychopathic individuals tend to be vested in atypical or "divergent" thinking[5] rather than in typical or "convergent" tasks such as measured by IQ tests. Smith, *et al.*[10] previously have reported battering parents to be both psychopathic and of low intelligence. In any event, this variable was not controlled successfully in the selection of the two study groups. The obtained differences on personality measures, however, do not seem attributable to IQ.

This study was not structured in such a manner as to make its results definitive. The sample is small, the number of comparisons relatively large and the number of

TABLE 1

Performance of Experimental and Control Parents on 25 Study Variables

Measure	X_E	X_C	df	t
Rorschach				
Level, Overall Pathology	28.0	27.7	12	.11
Negative Affect	30.0	28.5	12	.57
Psychopathic Deviancy	30.5	26.9	12	1.11
Bizarre Content	24.0	29.6	12	2.35*
Rosenzweig Picture Frustration				
Group Conformity Rating	64.3	57.3	12	2.41*
Extrapunitive	31.3	43.5	12	2.06
Intropunitive	35.6	25.0	12	3.17**
Impunitive	32.0	31.4	12	.14
MMPI				
L	54.7	46.7	12	2.86*
F	61.0	54.7	12	1.52
K	56.2	49.5	12	2.37*
H_S	56.5	54.9	12	.38
D	61.5	53.2	12	1.74
H_Y	60.2	57.3	12	.81
P_D	67.6	57.5	12	2.10
M_F	52.2	54.9	12	1.05
P_A	60.2	55.8	12	1.35
P_T	61.3	52.5	12	1.84
S_C	64.2	56.9	12	1.10
M_A	57.9	59.1	12	.23
S_I	55.2	53.7	12	.50
PPVT				
IQ	97.0	111.2	12	2.95*

* $p < .05$;
** $p < .01$

significant findings somewhat meager. By design, the data are interpreted on a *post hoc* rather than an *ad hoc* basis. Such studies are not so much of value to test hypotheses, but rather to generate them. Hopefully, such new hypotheses serve a heuristic function and are tested in future investigations. More importantly, it is hoped that they may be tried and tested in the clinical work of practitioners.

Within the framework of this inductive search for relevant data on battering parents, the study data are internally consistent. Their most interesting characteristic is that experimental parents appear significantly less like batterers on test items that are logically derived (low bizarre content on the Rorschach, high *intro*-punitiveness and group conformity on the Rosenzweig). They appeared *more* psychopathic on the L, K and P_D scales of the MMPI, whose items were derived empirically. In other words, the battering parents were able to appear significantly healthier on those instruments based on content or face validity, in which the social desirability of each item is more obvious. However, for items based on concurrent or statistical validity, where the socially desirable response is more ambiguous, they appeared significantly more disturbed. This, combined with the fact that the nature of the revealed disturbance on the MMPI is a near-classic profile for psychopathy, suggests that battering parents do possess such tendencies, but will portray themselves inversely whenever possible. This latter tendency is apparently the manifestation of defense mechanisms such as compensation and/or reaction formation.

These data support a "slick but sick" (particularly "slick") component in the personality characteristics of parents of battered children. Yet the fact that these data do not portray battering parents as severely disturbed is more open to conjecture. Possible *S*s are a biased sample due to the fact that only convicted parents were studied. More obviously disturbed parents might have been dealt with differently by physicians, the police or the courts and thus prevented from entering the study. On the other hand, most earlier conclusions, that battered parents are highly disturbed, are based on the clinical impressions of experienced psychodiagnosticians. Possibly their intuition was biased by the fact that they knew the parents had battered their children. Or, possibly the clinicians are right, and such parents *are* disturbed, in spite of the fact they can successfully appear healthy on psychometric items that possess rather obvious social desirability.

The psychopathic character of battering parents, which is suggested here, irrespective of the severity of any accompanying disturbance, carries implications for those who deal with suspected child abusers. One is that we should be careful not to be lulled or conned into underestimating the potential of certain reasonable-appearing adults for disturbance and violence. The "sick but slick" syndrome also suggests potential deterrents to success with traditional psychotherapeutic intervention, namely denial and misrepresentation of self.

Summary

Thirteen parents convicted in court of battering their children and 13 matched controls were administered a battery of personality tests, with significant differences obtained on 5 of 21 study variables. Battering parents appeared healthier on those instruments based on content validity, where the social desirability of the items is more obvious. They appeared more disturbed (*i.e.*, psychopathic) on items based on concurrent or statistical validity. It was concluded that battering parents were psychopathically disturbed, but whenever possible presented a distorted picture of themselves as healthy and unlikely to abuse their children. This tendency has been labeled the "sick but slick syndrome."

REFERENCES

1.   BISHOP, F. I. "Children at risk." *Med. J. Austral.*, 1971, *1,* 623-628.

2.   BUGLASS, R. "Parents with emotional problems." *Nursing Times*, 1971, *67*, 1000-1001.

3.   CALLAGHAN, K. A. and FOTHERINGHAM, B. J. "Practical management of the battered baby syndrome." *Med. H. Austral*, 1970, *1*, 1282-1284.

4.   COURT, J. and KERR, A. "The battered child syndrome. 2. A preventable disease?" *Nursing Times*, 1971, *67*, 695-597.

5.   GUILFORD, J. "Three faces of intellect." *Amer. Psychol.*, 1959, *14*, 469-479.

6.   HELFER, R. E. and KEMPE, C. H. *The Battered Child*. Chicago: University of Chicago Press, 1968.

7.   ISSACS, S. "Neglect, cruelty and battering." *Brit. med. J.*, 1972, *3*, 224-226.

8.   LUND, S. N. "Personality and personal history factors in child abusing parents." Paper presented for preliminary oral examination, University of Minnesota, May 8, 1973.

9.   MELNICK, G. and HURLEY, J. R. "Distinctive personality attributes of child-abusing mothers." *J. consult. clin. Psychol.*, 1969, *33*, 746-749.

10. SMITH, S. M., HONIGSBERGER, L. and SMITH, C. A. "E.E.G. and personality factors in baby batterers." *Brit. med. J.*, 1973, *3*, 20-22.

11. SPINETTA, J. J. and RIGLER, D. "The child-abusing parent: A psychological review." *Psychol. Bull.*, 1972, *77*, 296-304.

12. STEELE, B. F. "Violence in our society." *Pharos Alpha Omega Alpha Honor Med. Soc.*, 1970, *33*, 42-48.

13. WRIGHT, L. "Psychologic aspects of the battered child syndrome." *South. Med. Bull.*, 1970, *58*, 14-18.

16

Psychological Mechanisms in Child Abusing Parents*

J. Vesterdal

This chapter considers rather briefly what sort of people child abusers are. What are the psychological mechanisms involved, how and when do these abnormal ways of thinking and feeling arise, and how early can we detect them? I must emphasize that the term 'child abuse' is used only for the sake of brevity, as we cannot clearly separate it from psychological maltreatment or neglect.

This topic is a rather new field of scientific investigation, and it is only in the last few years that we have gained some insight into the psychological disorders which cause these patterns of behavior. This is due to the work of Kempe, Helfer, Klaus, Franklin, Margaret Lynch, their co-workers, and others.

Who in the Family Maltreats the Child?

There are no good statistics about this; some of the published figures are based on court findings of guilt and this mainly represents cases of the most severe physical abuse. In a Swedish government report (*Barn som far illa[1]*) the mother alone was found guilty or suspect of physical injury in 30 percent of the cases, and it was the mother together with the father or stepfather in 11 percent. It was the biolgoical father alone in 34 percent, and a stepfather in 11 percent. In other words: the mother

---

* J. Vesterdal, "Psychological Mechanisms in Child Abusing Parents," in *Family Violence: An International and Interdisciplinary Study*, John M. Eekelaar, Sanford N. Katz (eds.), Butterworths, Toronto, Canada, 1978.

was involved in 41 percent and the biological father in 40 percent of the cases. But that concerned only physical injury. When psychological maltreatment and neglect are included there is no doubt that the mother plays a predominant role.

In practical work with these cases it seems, however, more appropriate just to say that there is violence in the family making it dangerous for the child. It is less important to identify the offender, particularly because even if only one of the parents maltreats the child, the other one will know about it and will cover it up and thus acts as an accessory.

Only a few of the abusers have a manifest psychosis, such as schizophrenia or depressive psychosis. Much more common are various types of psychoneurosis and character disorders. The abusing parents frequently have psychosomatic illnesses and very often a slight degree of depression. There is no single psychiatric diagnosis that is characteristic of child abusers, and we must say that child abuse is a disorder of the parent-child relationship which can exist in combination with practically any other psychological state (Lee).[4] Smith & al.[6] found that 76 percent of the mothers had an abnormal personality and 48 percent were neurotic. Their mean IQ was significantly lower than in a control group, and the same was true about the fathers. Among these, 29 percent had a criminal record, and one-third were psychopaths. But that a variety of other factors may be present is made clear by the description which follows of how disturbances might arise in the mother-child relationship.

In studies done in recent years of the psychological disorders that cause abnormal parent-child relationships, the interest has mainly been focused on the mothers because they are most often involved, and also because the symptoms of the disorders are more easily observed in the mothers than in the fathers. The following therefore mainly concerns the mothers, but it should be remembered that similar factors may play a role in the male.

The Mother-Child Symbiosis

It is now becoming clear that the ability of the female to act as a mother is something which is deeply influenced by the events around her own birth and of the way in which her own mother took care of her in infancy. This has been observed in both animal and human mothers, but I shall deal only with the latter.

If the start has been wrong, the ability of the female later in life to bond herself to her own child will be impaired, and she may not be able to live up to the task of taking care of her child in an appropriate way.

Normally the birth of the child will elicit a specific behavior in the mother, and this works with great force. We must remember, without being too lyrical, that the normal pattern of reactions of the mother is that she feels that her newborn baby is the most wonderful thing in the world, and she will love the baby to such an extent that she devotes her life completely to it. She takes care of it all around the clock, feeds it, shifts its diapers, strokes it, talks to it, soothes it and treats it with infinite tender loving care. As Klaus *et al.*[2] pointed out, when the mother sees the child for the first time immediately after its birth, she will react in a certain way. All normal mothers will look at the baby, touch it, stroke it, *etc.*, in practically the same way.

It must, however, be emphasized that in the normal relationship between mother and child there is a reciprocity such that the sequence of actions which the mother performs will influence the infant, generally so that it will be calmed and soothed, which in turn will have a satisfying effect on the mother. In other words, it is necessary for an optimal interaction that the infant also reacts in a certain way. Under normal circumstances the result is a development of a symbiosis between mother and child which is extremely important.

Under primitive conditions in developing countries this symbiosis is necessary simply for keeping the child alive. In developed countries it cannot be said to be absolutely necessary for the survival of the infant, although severe disturbances of it ultimately may result in the death of the child by maltreatment or neglect. This symbiosis is nevertheless very important for the happiness and thriving of the child, and also for the happiness of the mother. And it has a deep influence on the behavior of the child later in life, particularly on its ability to act as a parent when it grows up and becomes fertile.

Disturbances in the Mother-Child Relationship

This symbiosis between mother and infant can be disturbed or inhibited by inadequate reactions from both sides. *The mother* can react inadequately in several ways. First, it may happen that the mother does not like the newborn baby; she may even hate it from its birth or even from before its birth. She may not want the baby and may feel that the child has brought disaster into her life. Some of the mothers in Klaus' series did not like the look of the baby when it was shown to them by the nurse just after birth. They did not want to touch it and asked the nurse to take it away. Such an unwanted child will not be exposed to normal warm and gentle care, and as a result it may become an unhappy, unruly, crying baby, and this may again increase the mother's aversion against it, thus starting a vicious circle. Another inadequate reaction by the mother is caused by false expectations about the child. Perhaps because she is very young and inexperienced, she may not understand how little such a small infant can comprehend and do. If the baby cries, she will tell it to stop, and if it does not obey this order, she will interpret it as naughtiness and feel that the baby has deserved to be punished for this insubordination.

In some cases the mother has very much wanted to have a child, and she expects that it can bring her happiness and comfort. There is here an inversion of the parent-child roles in such a way that the mother, instead of devoting her life to the child, expects that the child should take care of her and her problems. When she feels tired, unhappy and lonely, she wants the baby to smile at her and comfort her and if the baby does not do that but cries, burps and soils it diapers, she will get disappointed and angry with it. This abnormality of the parent-child relationship is seen very frequently in families with child abuse and neglect. The origin of it apparently lies in the infancy of the mother. If she as an infant has been treated harshly by her mother instead of being comforted, she has not learned the normal parent-child relationship. The mother will then seek in her own child the comforting parent she did not know in her infancy. When the child grows up, it in turn will lack the ability to take adequate care of its own child and thus this disorder will 'infect' successive generations.

Normally the mother is the only, or at least the most important, person with whom the infant can find safety and protection. But if the mother is unkind to the baby every time it turns to her for comfort, this will of course have a very frustrating effect on the baby, and one consequence of this is that the child later in life will have great difficulty in trusting other persons and establishing durable friendships. The deleterious effect will be even worse if the mother is very inconsistent in the care of the child in such a way that she is sometimes kind, hugging and kissing the baby, and at other times treats it coldly and harshly.

These psychological disturbances in the mothers may of course appear in varying degrees of seriousness. There are mothers who are quite unable to take care of their children under any circumstances and there are others who can act reasonably well under optimal conditions, but who will prove inadequate under conditions that are less than optimal. Thus we may see that the abnormal behavior may be elicited under situations of stress such as unemployment, poverty, bad housing conditions, marital problems, or single parenthood.

The stress situation may also be caused by *the child*. This may happen if the child is a difficult baby. We must admit that babies are born with different temperaments. Some are placid and quiet, they cry only rarely and are easy to soothe. Others are restless and fidgety. They cry night and day and are difficult to handle. A child of the latter group does not respond well when the mother tries to calm and soothe it, and one may say that it does not play its role in the symbiosis well. Only a particularly patient mother can cope with such a baby. A somewhat inadequate mother may be able to take care of an easy child reasonably well, but it may be beyond her powers to handle a difficult child. This may in turn make the child still more difficult so that the problems will increase. If the child has congenital defects, such as malformation or mental deficiency, the result may be that the mother rejects the child, and she may feel frustrated or have a sense of guilt because she has not been able to give birth to a normal child.

Finally we come to a very important point: the mother-child interaction may be stopped at the very beginning by separation of the child from the mother. This will happen if the baby has to be taken to a special care unit of the hospital immediately after birth because of prematurity or some serious illness. Also in these cases the mother may feel disappointed with the baby or with herself, and there will of course be enormous difficulties in establishing contact between mother and child, with the result that she may feel alienated towards it and a normal bonding cannot develop. It is a general experience that there is a much higher proportion of prematurity and neonatal disease in abused children than in the normal population.[5]

From all this it can be seen that factors both in the mother and in the child can have an adverse effect on the symbiosis between mother and child, and this effect may be enhanced by environmental factors. It is therefore easy to understand that under bad social conditions the risk of child abuse is much greater than in the upper levels of society. It is, however, well known that it also occurs there. There was a case in Denmark where the father was a psychiatrist, head of a hospital department, and the mother a nurse. They adopted 10 children, mainly from Korea and other places overseas, and maltreated six of them. Three children died, probably from maltreatment or neglect, but this was rather obscure because the father, being a doctor, wrote the death certificate himself.

Child abuse in the upper classes may in some cases be due to stress, perhaps financial or marital, but in other cases, where there apparently are no such problems, it may be due to religious or other strong moral convictions where the parents believe in very severe methods of upbringing to counteract the sinful tendencies of the child. Certain ethnic groups in our society may have similar customs.

The importance of identifying psychological factors tending to abuse is illustrated by the predictive and follow-up studies such as those of Margaret Lynch. Much work is currently in progress in this field. In the investigation by Gray *et al.*,[2] which is still in progress at the time of writing this article, a large number of mothers were examined by interviews and questionnaires before the birth of the child and by observation during and after delivery, and a group of 100 mothers were identified as high risks for abnormal parenting practices. Fifty of these mothers were treated in the ordinary way and the other 50 were given special care, *e.g.*, by a health visitor or nurse in the home. During the first year after delivery child abuse occurred in both groups, but the number of severe cases was significantly lower in the group treated with special care. Thus it is to some extent possible to identify a risk group of mothers and to do something to prevent the maltreatment of the children, but the intensity at which such services can be offered depends on the resources available and the precision with which such identification can be made. The question how far intervention may be imposed on the basis of risk prediction also raises important legal and policy issues.

NOTES

1.   *Barn som far illa. Nya Lagerblads Tryckeri A B*, Karlshamn, Sweden, 1975.

2.   GRAY, J. D.; CUTLER, C. A.; DEAN, J., and KEMPS, C. H., "Prediction and Prevention of Child Abuse", trans. of 1st Int. Congr. of Child Abuse and Neglect, Geneva 1976, p. 15.

3.   KENNEL, J.; VOSS, D., and KLAUS, M., "Parent-infant Bonding", in Helfer, R. E., and Kempe, C. H., *Child Abuse and Neglect*. Cambridge, Mass.: Ballinger, 1976, p. 25-53.

4.   LEE, H. S., "The Psychological Aspects of Abusing Parents," trans. of 1st Int. Congr. on Child Abuse and Neglect, Geneva 1976, p. 110.

5.   LYNCH, M., and ROBERTS, J., "Child Abuse—Early Identification in the Maternity Hospital," *ibid.*, p. 13.

6.   SMITH, S. M.; HANSON, R., and NOBLE, S., "Parents of Battered Children: a Controlled Study", in Franklin, A. W. (ed.), *Concerning Child Abuse*. London, Eng.: Livingstone Churchill, 1974, p. 41-55.

17

The Role of the Child in Abuse:
A Review of the Literature*

William N. Friedrich, M.P.H., and
Jerry A. Boriskin, B.A.

A number of current theories concerning the etiology of child abuse place heavy emphasis on the role of parental psychopathology. Spinetta and Rigler[43] concluded their review of the child-abusing parent by stating that

> . . . the great majority of the authors cited . . . have pointed to psychological factors within the parents themselves as of prime importance in the etiology of child abuse. They see abuse as stemming from a defect in character . . . (p. 302)

Socioeconomic factors were not felt to contribute significantly to abuse.

However, Kempe and Helfer[22] stated that only a small number (less than ten percent) of the parents of abused children are seriously mentally ill. In addition, Steele and Pollock[44] maintained that psychopaths and sociopaths make up only a small portion of abusers, and that their sample of abusers would not seem much different than a random sample of people on a downtown street. More important to Steele and Pollock than severe psychopathology was the disruption of the "mothering function" in the development of children who later became abusers.

Increasingly, research on abused and neglected children suggests that the child plays more than a passive role in abuse. Gelles's[15] social-psychological model of the causes of child abuse, which admirably demonstrated the complexity and interrelatedness of the factors leading to abuse, assumes that a certain amount of child

---

* William N. Friedrich and Jerry A. Boriskin, "The Role of The Child in Abuse: A Review of the Literature," *American Journal of Orthopsychiatry* 46(4):580-590. Copyright © 1976 the American Orthopsychiatric Association, Inc. Reproduced by permission.

abuse is a function of child-produced stress. Helfer's psychodynamic model of abuse[20] holds that, for abuse to occur, three conditions are required: 1) a very special kind of child, 2) a crisis or series of crises, and 3) the potential (in the parent) for abuse. Although the potential may be composed of many characteristics the parent has acquired as he moves through his "world of abnormal rearing,"[20] it is triggered by a "special" child, a crisis, or both. Helfer took great pains to state that the child is either viewed by the parent as being special, or actually is a special, different child. Green[17] offered a four-factor explanation of the etiology of child abuse, similar to Helfer's, but adding as the fourth factor "a cultural tolerance for severe corporal punishment."

Sandgrund, Gaines, and Green[39] stated that child abuse appears to result from the interaction of three factors: immediate environmental stress, personality traits of the parent, and actual characteristics of the child that make him vulnerable to scapegoating. In this view, theories that focus on only the first two etiological factors would fail to present the complete picture.

An early theory on the role of the child in abuse was offered by Milowe and Lourie,[32] who suggested four possible causal factors of abuse, two of which dealt specifically with characteristics of the child. One category included those cases in which the precipitating factor was a defect in the child (especially a defect that contributed to a lack of responsiveness, resulting in parental frustration). The second category included physical damage resulting from parental neglect or mishandling. Their third category covered a little-researched area of abuse—abuse resulting from assaultive behavior by unsupervised siblings. The final category included abuse resulting from characteristics in the child's personality that served to invite others to hurt him. As far as can be determined, these categories are the result of clinical experience, not controlled empirical investigation.

It is uncomfortable to think that a child can play a role in his own abuse. Furthermore,

> . . . despite the contributions which infants make toward the disappointments and burdens of their parents, they can hardly be used as an excuse or adequate cause for child abuse.[44] (p. 115)

Nevertheless, the fact remains that the child is not always a benign stimulus to the parent. For example, although it is not necessarily the fault of the child or the mother that a birth is premature, this characteristic of the child has an effect on its caregiver.

The paper will survey evidence that particular types of children produce parental stress reactions, some of which might stimulate abuse. It will consider the following points, in turn: 1) prematurity and children at risk for abuse, 2) mental retardation and children at risk for abuse, 3) physically handicapped and sickly children at risk for abuse, 4) genetic contributions to the child at risk for abuse, and 5) parents' perceptions of the abused child as different.

Prematurity

Although one can only speculate as to cause and effect, the recently revealed association of child abuse and prematurity cannot be ignored. Elmer and Gregg,[10] in a sample of twenty battered children in the Chicago area, found 33% to have been premature. Klein and Stern[24] studied 88 battered children at the Winnipeg Children's Hospital, of whom eleven (12.5%) were premature. In addition, Klein and Stern reviewed the records of 51 battered children in the Montreal area, and found twelve (23.5%) to have been low-birth-weight infants; the rate of premature birth in Montreal is between nine and ten percent. It was suggested that multiple factors (pre-existing mental retardation, maternal deprivation, isolation from mother in the early post-partum period, etc.) may increase the risk for these infants. Conversely, it was suggested that certain social characteristics of the mother (poverty, lack of prenatal care) may result in the delivery of low-birth-weight infants.

In an unpublished retrospective study of 292 suspected abuse cases in England from 1970, referred to by Martin *et al.*,[31] it was noted that 14.5% of the children, or twice the national average, had had a low birth-weight. However, it was not specified whether the children were born prematurely or were of adequate gestation with poor prenatal growth.

Fomufod, Sinkford and Louy,[12] in a retrospective analysis of child abuse in the District of Columbia, found ten of 36 (27.8%) abused children to be of low birth-weight; the incidence of low birth-weight in the D.C. area is 13.2%. A larger scale prospective study is underway to compare low-birth-weight infants with and without prolonged maternal separation.

Martin *et al.*[31] found that eleven (19%) of their sample of 58 abused children weighed less than 2500 grams at birth. This was in comparison to an incidence rate of only 9.2% of all babies born in 1971 in Colorado. They feel that the normal mean IQs of even their smallest prematurely-born children do not support the hypothesis that mental retardation or brain damage stemming from prematurity elicits abuse by parents. In this study, Martin *et al.* took special pains to include children with soft tissue damage, in addition to those who had incurred fractures, so that their sample would be as typical as possible of abused children, since only a small proportion of abused children receive fractures.

Bishop[4] supports the view that premature babies are particularly vulnerable. It is suggested that some premature babies are hypersensitive to all stimuli, and may even object to gentle handling. What proportion of abused premature babies fit this hypersensitive handling pattern is still unknown. Mussen, Conger and Kagan[35] also stated that the premature child is more likely to be restless, distractible, and difficult to care for than a full-term baby, especially during the first year of life. A reason for this is that prematures are more prone to anoxia and colic, and irritability in the newborn period can result from these conditions. In addition, Dreyfus-Brisac[7] has pointed out that disturbances in sleep organization are very common among premature infants. Ounsted, Oppenheimer and Lindsay[37] reported that the colicky child syndrome was a prominent feature during infancy of most of the abused children in their sample.

Maternal attitudes toward premature infants must certainly play a role. Elmer and Gregg[10] suggested that the mother may perceive a child as being abnormal simply because it is premature. Leiderman[28] has found significant differences in both attitudes and behavior between mothers of premature infants and mothers of full-term infants. He stated that the

. . . attenuated relationship of mothers of prematures with their infants is consistent with reports in the literature that premature infants are more likely the victims of battering by their parents and are more likely to have behavior problems as children. (p. 154)

Klaus and Kennell[23] also raised the question of whether the battered child syndrome is in part related to hospital care practices that frequently separate mothers from their premature infants for prolonged periods of time.

Fanaroff, Kennell and Klaus[11] analyzed the frequency of visits of 146 mothers of low-birth-weight infants. Thirty-eight mothers visited their babies less than three times in a two week period. Follow-up data from six to 23 months after release show that, in the eleven cases of abuse or failure to thrive, nine mothers were in the infrequent visiting group. Thus, problems may be identified early, simply by monitoring the frequency of visits to the premature child.

Pasamanick[38] noted a significant linear relationship between maternal tension and signs of brain dysfunction in a longitudinal study of premature infants. Mothers of neurologically normal premature infants were no more tense than were mothers of neurologically normal, full-term infants.

> It was the neurologically abnormal child, whether full-term or premature, who had a significantly tense mother. (p. 550)

Knobloch and Pasamanick[25] contended that these abnormal children are disorganized, unstable, and more sensitive to stress. Pasamanick[38] speculated that these abnormalities precipitate parental distress, thereby reinforcing abnormal behavior in the child, which may ultimately result in abuse.

Whereas maternal perceptions of abnormality, socioeconomic status, prenatal care, and hypersensitivity in the premature infant are interacting variables of as yet unknown significance, current data do indicate significant association of prematurity and child abuse. Unraveling the complex interactions involved has only begun, but the basic point to be noted is that premature infants should be considered "children at risk" within the battered child syndrome.

Mental Retardation

Several researchers have reported a high incidence of mental retardation among battered and neglected children. However, the complexity of the phenomenon and the large number of interacting variables make any position as to cause and effect most tenuous. Elmer[9] reported 55% of the children in her sample had an IQ of less than 80; Morse, Sahler and Friedman[34] found 43% of their sample of abused children were similarly classified—all but one of the nine retarded children in this study were thought to have been retarded prior to abuse.

Brandwein,[5] noting the association of abuse and mental retardation, suggested that brain damage resulting from child abuse was the primary factor in the increased frequency of mental retardation. One cannot ignore socioeconomic factors, stress, prenatal care or lack of it, parental depravity, differences in learning and reinforcement contingencies, physical damage to the CNS from abuse, genetic variables, as well as the inherent flaw of intelligence measures in accounting for any of the above variables, when evaluating this relationship. Considering what is known to date, and the difficulties inherent in this area of research, the factors contributing the most weight to the disproportionate retardation associated with abuse will not be readily apparent for some time. But we should not now overlook the distinct possibility that the child born with mental deficiencies may be more "abuse prone;" his unfortunate state may make him highly vulnerable to scapegoating.

In a recent study by Sandgrund, Gaines and Green,[39] children from the same socioeconomic level were divided into three groups: confirmed abuse, confirmed neglect, and nonabused controls; the neglected group was included to control for the impact of neglect upon the abused children. They found that 25% of the abused sample were classified as retarded, 20% of the neglected children were deemed retarded, and only three percent of the nonabused controls were categorized as retarded. Whereas the relative weights of neglect and abuse are indeterminable from this study, a more careful examination of these variables is warranted. It is in fact impossible to make any statements as to what factors differentiate a neglected and abused child. It is precisely this lack of clarity that highlights current methodological problems and investigational gaps. Sandgrund, Gaines and Green excluded subjects known to have suffered any serious head trauma; on this basis, their findings seriously challenge Brandwein's[5] organic damage hypothesis.

Sandgrund, Gaines and Green's[39] hypothesis is supported by Martin et al.'s[31] determination that 43% of a sample of 37 abused children with no history of head trauma manifested slight to severe neurologic dysfunctions. However, only 29% of their sample of 21 abused children with a history of skull fracture did not manifest any neurologic dysfunction.

Nichamin[36] presented some reasons why the child with neurologic dysfunction can be very difficult to tolerate. He mentioned that these babies appear to be unhappy throughout infancy, and are very difficult to appease. Their crying consists to a great extent of highpitched, disagreeable screaming.

While the association of retardation and abuse is clear-cut, etiological factors remain muddled, and there is a dearth of experimental data. Whereas the parental depravity hypothesis is well known and widely accepted, further experimental and clinical attention should be given to the "abuse prone" hypothesis.

Physical Handicaps

Johnson and Morse[21] reported on a study the Denver Department of Welfare carried out with 97 abused children. Based on child welfare worker reports, it was noted that nearly 70% of the children exhibited either a mental or physical deviation prior to the reported abuse. In addition, twenty percent were considered unmanageable due to severe temper tantrums, nineteen percent had retarded speech development, and seventeen percent demonstrated either a learning disability or mental retardation. However, the data in this study do not thoroughly substantiate that these behaviors were congenital or had occurred prior to abuse. Freidman,[13] on the basis of a retrospective study of 25 cases of abused children, hypothesized that some abused children are hyperactive or intellectually precocious. He reported several instances in which the inquisitive behavior of a child who was intellectually more capable than his parents caused the child to be more vulnerable to abuse.

Green[17] found that 23% of 70 school-age schizophrenic children had suffered abuse. It was suggested that because schizophrenic children are generally unrewarding to the parents and are emotionally deviant, there is an increased risk of physical abuse. However, not enough information was provided to choose between this hypothesis, or the alternate possibility that schizophrenic behavior may result *from* abuse.

Gil,[16] from data garnered in a two-year nationwide study, discovered that 29% of the abused children in his sample of 12,000 children had demonstrated abnormal social interactions in the year preceding the abusive act. He also noted that approximately 22% were suffering from either a deviation in physical or intellectual function. Among those children of school age, approximately thirteen percent were in special classes or were in grades below their age level; however, at least half of these children had incurred abuse prior to the study year.

Ounsted, Oppenheimer and Lindsay[37] cited the case of an abused child who was found to be blind. Upon hearing this, the parents broke down, the mother saying that "he cried and cried and he never looked at me." (p. 448)

Birrell and Birrell,[3] in an analysis of 42 cases of abuse, found congenital physical abnormalities (cleft lip, fibrocystic disease, talipes, etc.) in eleven cases (approximately 25%). However, this finding has not been substantiated by other studies; in a study of 58 abused children,[31] no children with major abnormalities, or with more than one or two minor abnormalities (clinodactyly, hermis, etc.), were found.

Baron, Bejar and Sheaff[1] presented the case of an infant with no signs of abuse but with a presenting problem very similar to organic brain disease. The child was treated for a number of months before it was noticed that she had been battered. When the child was admitted to the hospital, her symptoms of organic brain disease cleared up within a week. The point made is that only adequate follow-up can show how often seemingly congenital neurologic abnormalities are the result of physical abuse.

In unpublished material from the National Clearing House on Child Abuse and Neglect at the American Humane Association in Denver, Soeffing[42] reported on preliminary incidence data from 1974. Of 14,083 abused and neglected children, 1680 had one or more "special" characteristics. For example, 288 were classified as mentally retarded, 195 had been born prematurely, 250 had a chronic illness (*e.g.*, multiple sclerosis, diabetes), 234 were physically handicapped, 130 were either twins or triplets, 180 had a congenital defect, 669 were reported as being emotionally disturbed, and 267 had "other special characteristics." It was also noted that the number of reported handicaps could increase as social workers learned how to better diagnose a handicap.

Lynch[29] found a significantly greater frequency of serious illness in the first year of life among abused children. It has been suggested by Morris[33] that sickly infants and premature infants, by virtue of their extended hospital stay, make it difficult for "claiming behavior" on the part of the mother to occur, and if this "claiming behavior" (attachment) does not occur, the child is at greater risk for abuse.

Genetic Contributions

Although not as clearly related as are physical abnormalities, individual differences and behavioral styles present in infants from birth may also contribute to abuse. Thomas, Chess and Birch,[45] on the basis of data gathered in their New York

Longitudinal Project, were able to demonstrate that, seemingly from birth, children display nine different temperament styles. These temperaments tend to be present in clearly defined clusters, giving rise to a minimum of three "types" of children. "Slow-to-warm-up" children have as a significant core of their pattern of activity quiet withdrawal from, and then slow adaptation to, the new. The "difficult" child shows irregularity in biological functions, nonadaptability, predominantly negative (withdrawal) responses to new stimuli, high intensity, and frequent negative mood expressions. At the opposite end of the temperament spectrum from the "difficult" child is the "easy" child, who exhibits regularity in biological functions, approach responses to new stimuli, easy adaptability to change, and predominately positive mood of mild or moderate intensity. In this study, roughly 70% of the "difficult" children developed behavior problems; although they comprised only ten percent of the sample, these children accounted for 23% of the group of children who later developed behavior problems.

Milowe and Lourie[32] made reference to children who seem to fall into the category of "difficult" children. At first, the researchers thought the irritable characteristics of the abused children they came in contact with were a result of their being battered. But after nurses found it difficult to take some of these infants for an eight-hour tour of duty, the researchers began to have second thoughts. The nurses commented on the irritable cry, the difficulty in managing, and the unappealing nature of some of these children. In this study, reference was also made to two children who each received battering in two different homes, presumably because of their "difficult" natures. Silver[41] also cited a case of an abused child who was admitted to the hospital, was subsequently removed to a foster home, and was battered in the foster home.

In a vein similar to Thomas, Chess and Birch's[45] temperament clusters, Schaffer and Emerson[40] isolated two groups of infants—those who actively resisted close physical contact under all conditions (noncuddlers), and those who accepted close physical contact under all conditions (cuddlers). It was determined that this behavior was not peculiar to the relationship of the child with the mother. Shaffer and Emerson felt that a noncuddling pattern is not clinically a bad sign. Only if the mother is too rigid to attempt alternate methods of relating to the child, or if she feels the noncuddling behavior is a sign of rejection, is there risk of a pathological mother-child relationship. Ounsted, Oppenheimer and Lindsay[37] have pointed out the implications of this risk for abused children. In their study of 24 children, about two-thirds of the mothers complained that the child could not be cuddled, although it was not reported whether this feature of the child's interactional pattern was present from birth.

In the area of individual differences in infants, Korner[26] has found differences in crying patterns among infants, and differences in soothability once they begin to cry. She pointed out the implications this could have for a young and inexperienced mother with a difficult to soothe child. These differences can directly affect the mother's feelings of competence as a caregiver.

In addition, Benjamin[2] has suggested that infants with low sensory thresholds are very prone to develop colic during the first few postnatal weeks, thus aggravating a developing mother-child relationship.

Woolf[46] described seven normal infant states: regular sleep, irregular sleep, periodic sleep, drowsiness, alert inactivity, waking activity, and crying. Korner[27] has suggested a concept of state-immaturity, in which infants exhibit only a limited range of states (*e.g.* two or three). These children have been shown to be very difficult to care for and will often develop subsequent psychopathological symptoms. For example, Brazelton[6] described a case in which an infant, capable of only two extreme states, so demoralized his mother, a young professional woman, that she became totally ineffectual and depressed. From the start, the mother felt "rejected" by the child.

Korner[26] concluded her paper by saying

> . . . the finding that infants differ significantly from each other right from the very start suggests that there is more than one way of providing good child care; . . . the only way to do so is to respond flexibly to . . . each and every child. (p. 617)

However, parents are trained in the "right" way to raise kids, rather than focusing on each child's particular needs. Consequently, mothers are prone to feel a lot of guilt over deviant behavior in their children.[6] Some of this might be reflected in battered children.

Parents' Perceptions of The Child As Different

A number of studies[8, 14, 16] have shown that generally, even in multi-child families, only one child is abused. This has given rise to suggestions that the abused child is selected as a scapegoat, either because he is truly different from his siblings, or for some other, inexplicable reason. For example, Lynch's[29] study of 25 abused children and their nonabused siblings reported the non-abused siblings

> . . . to have been exceptionally healthy, and, where population figures are available, show a lower than expected incidence of adverse factors. (p. 319)

However, Johnson and Morse[21] noted that, while 36% of the abused children were illegitimate, 40% of the non-abused siblings were also illegitimate. In addition, there were similarities among the siblings in terms of personality and intellectual performance.

Morse, Sahler and Friedman[34] noted that the mothers of six abused children who were progressing normally at the time of follow-up saw the parent-child relationship as good. However, the mothers of seven abused children who were quite disturbed at follow-up described the parent-child relationship as poor. Originally, of the 25 children observed in this study, fifteen were considered different by their parents. Nine of the children were retarded, and three of these were thought by their parents to be sickly. Six others were thought by their parents to be bad, selfish, spoiled rotten, or defiant in comparison to siblings. This suggests that, in addition to the child's abnormalities, the parents' perception of the child can also be critical.

Bishop[4] cited four cases of young children overdosed with sedatives by disorganized and depressed mothers who had perceived their child as "damaged." Physical examinations of the children provided no support of this perceptual bias. Consequently, Bishop claimed that when the parental perception of a "damaged" child is counter to objective evidence, the risk may be even greater.

In a similar vein, Martin and Beezley[30] have hypothesized that it is the children with mild or borderline abnormalities who are at greatest risk, while severely handicapped children are at lower risk for abuse. The basis for this hypothesis is unclear. Perhaps it is the ambiguity that introduces the greatest stress to the parent. Whatever the case, more data on parental perception of abnormalities in their abused children is needed.

Conclusion

On the basis of the evidence presented, it would be fanciful to conclude that the special child is the sole contributor to abuse. But the opposite extreme, the all too prevalent notion that abuse is exclusively a function of a parental defect, seems equally specious. Abuse is the product of a complex set of interactions, and assigning weights to any of its components is premature. A conceivable expansion upon Green's[17] four-factor equation of the causes of abuse may help to illustrate the problem:

a) special child + special parent + crisis + cultural tolerance = abuse
b) special child + normal parent + crisis + cultural tolerance = abuse
c) special child + normal parent + cultural tolerance = abuse

Each equation is feasible and has been clinically demonstrated. While the factors making up the first have been noted by Green and others, the implications of the other two equations have all too often been ignored. Emphasis upon a single factor in abuse (psychopathology of the parent, environmental stresses, etc.) may obscure the importance of relevant variables, and lessen the effectiveness of therapeutic and prevention programs. Popular emphasis on the depraved-parent model of abuse may make other parents more reluctant to seek counseling (for fear of labeling). A broader dissemination of the fact that there are "difficult" children who can induce stress, and that relatively normal mothers can experience severe anxiety with respect to child rearing, could reduce this reluctance and the guilt attached to it.

Furthermore, it must be shown that it is not necessary for a special child to be present, but that the parent's perception of the child as different can be sufficient to instigate abuse.

Current research does demonstrate that prematurity, mental retardation, physical handicaps, congenital malformations, and similar conditions are overrepresented in abused populations. Even Martin *et al.*,[31] who stress the role of the parent and deemphasize the role of the child, stated that the proportion of premature infants in their population was significantly different from the norms.

Obviously, a great deal of research is required before the multifaceted aspects of the etiology of child abuse are determined. However, particularly within the realm of present knowledge, we must take into account a relatively consistent correlation—the special child is at greater risk for abuse. In planning prevention and treatment programs, those who deal with child abuse must keep this postulate in mind.

REFERENCES

1.   BARON, M., BEJAR, R. AND SHEAFF, P. 1970. "Neurologic manifestations of the battered child syndrome." *Pediatrics* 45:1003-1007.

2.   BENJAMIN, J. 1961. "The innate and the experiential in development." In *Lectures on Experimental Psychiatry*, H. Brosin, ed. University of Pittsburgh Press, Pittsburgh.

3.   BIRRELL, R. AND BIRRELL, J. 1968. "The maltreatment syndrome in children: a hospital survey." *Med. J. Austral.* 2:1023-1029.

4.   BISHOP, F. 1971. "Children at risk." *Med. J. Austral.* 1:623-628.

5.   BRANDWEIN, H. 1973. "The battered child: a definite and significant factor in mental retardation." *Ment. Retard.* 11:50-51.

6.   BRAZELTON, T. 1961. "Psychophysiologic reactions in the neonate: I. the value of observation of the neonate." *J. Pediat.* 58:508-512.

7.   DREYFUS-BRISAC, C. 1974. "Organization of sleep in prematures: implications for caregiving." In *The Effect of the Infant on Its Caregiver*, M. Lewis and L. Rosenblum, eds. John Wiley, New York.

8.   EBBIN, J. ET AL. 1969. "Battered child syndrome at the Los Angeles County General Hospital." *Amer. J. Dis. Childhd* 118:660-667.

9.   ELMER, E. 1965. *The fifty families study: summary of phase—I. neglected and abused children and their families*. Children's Hospital of Pittsburgh, Pittsburgh.

10.   ELMER, E. AND GREGG, G. 1967. "Developmental characteristics of abused children." *Pediatrics* 40:596-602.

11.   FANAROFF, A., KENNELL, J. AND KLAUS, M. 1972. "Follow-up of low birth weight infants—the predictive value of maternal visiting patterns." *Pediatrics* 49:287-290.

12.   FOMUFOD, A., SINKFORD, S. AND LOUY, V. 1975. "Mother-child separation at birth: a contributing factor in child abuse." *Lancet* 2:549-550.

13.   FRIEDMAN, S. 1972. "The need for intensive follow-up of abused children." In *Helping the Battered Child and his Family*. C. Kempe and R. Helfer, eds. Lippincott, Philadelphia.

14.   FRIEDRICH, W. 1975. "A survey of reported physical child abuse in Harris County, Texas." Unpublished Master's thesis, University of Texas School of Public Health, Houston.

15.   GELLES, R. 1973. "Child abuse and psychopathology: a sociological critique and reformulation." *Amer. J. Orthopsychiat.* 43:611-621.

16.   GIL, D. 1970. *Violence against children: physical child abuse in the U.S.* Harvard University Press, Cambridge, Mass.

17.   GREEN, A. 1968. "Self-destruction in physically abused schizophrenic children: report of cases." *Arch. Gen. Psychiat.* 19:171-197.

18.   GREEN, F. 1975. "Child abuse and neglect: a priority problem for the private physician." *Pediat. Clin. N. A.* 22:329-339.

19.   HELFER, R. 1973. "The etiology of child abuse." *Pediatrics* 51:777-779.

20.   HELFER, R. 1975. *The diagnostic process and treatment programs*. Office of Child Development, Washington, D.C.

21.   JOHNSON, B. AND MORSE, H. 1968. "Injured children and their parents." *Children* 15:147-152.

22. KEMPE, C. AND HELFER, R., eds. 1972. *Helping the battered child and his family.* University of Chicago Press, Chicago.

23. KLAUS, M. AND KENNELL, J. 1970. "Mothers separated from their newborn infants." *Pediat. Clin. N.A.* 17:1015-1037.

24. KLEIN, M. AND STERN, L. 1971. "Low birth weight and the battered child syndrome." *Amer. J. Dis. Childhd* 122:15-18.

25. KNOBLOCH, H. AND PASAMANICK, B. 1966. "Prospective studies on the epidemiology of reproductive causality: methods, findings, and some implications." *Merrill-Palmer Quart.* 12:27-43.

26. KORNER, A. 1971. "Individual differences at birth: implications for early experience and later development." *Amer. J. Orthopsychiat.* 41:608-619.

27. KORNER, A. 1974. "Individual differences at birth: implications for child care practices." In *The Infant at Risk*, D. Bergsma, ed. Stratton Intercontinental, New York.

28. LEIDERMAN, P. 1974. "Mothers at risk: a potential consequence of the hospital care of the premature infant." In *The Child in His Family: Children at Psychiatric Risk*, E. Anthony and C. Koupernik, eds. John Wiley, New York.

29. LYNCH, M. 1975. "Ill-health and child abuse." *Lancet* 2:317-319.

30. MARTIN, H. AND BEEZLEY, P. 1974. "Prevention and the consequences of child abuse." *J. Operational Psychiat.* 6:68-77.

31. MARTIN, H. ET AL. 1974. "The development of abused children: a review of the literature and physical, neurologic, and intellectual findings." *Advances in Pediat.* 21:25-73.

32. MILOWE, I. AND LOURIE, R. 1964. "The child's role in the battered child syndrome. *J. Pediat.* 65:1079-1081.

33. MORRIS, M. *Detection of High Risk Parents.* (unpublished)

34. MORSE, C., SAHLER, O. AND FRIEDMAN, S. 1970. "A three-year follow-up of abused and neglected children." *Amer. J. Dis. Childhd* 120:439-446.

35. MUSSEN, P., CONGER, J. AND KAGAN, J. 1974. *Child Development and Personality, 4th ed.* Harper and Row, New York.

36. NICHAMIN, S. 1973. "Battered child syndrome and brain dysfunction." *JAMA.* 223:1390.

37. OUNSTED, C., OPPENHEIMER, R. AND LINDSAY, J. 1974. "Aspects of bonding failure: the psychopathology and psychotherapeutic treatment of families of battered children. *Developmental Med. Child Neurol.* 16:447-456.

38. PASAMANICK, B. 1975. "Ill-health and child abuse." *Lancet* 2:550.

39. SANDGRUND, A. GAINES, R. AND GREEN, A. 1974. "Child abuse and mental retardation: a problem of cause and effect." *Amerc. J. Ment. Defic.* 79:327-330.

40. SCHAFFER, H. AND EMERSON, P. 1964. "Patterns of response to physical contact in early human development." *J. Child Psychol. Psychiat.* 5:1-13.

41. SILVER, L. 1968. "The psychological aspects of the battered child and his parents." *Clinical Proceedings of the Children's Hospital.* Washington, D.C. 24:355-364.

42. SOEFFING, M. 1975. "Abused children are exceptional children." *Exceptional Children* 42:126-133.

43. SPINETTA, J. AND RIGLER, D. 1972. "The child-abusing parent: a psychological review." *Psychol. Bull.* 77:296-304.

44.   STEELE, B. AND POLLOCK, C. 1974. "A psychiatric study of parents who abuse infants and small children." In *The Battered Child*, R. Helfer and C. Kempe, eds. University of Chicago Press, Chicago.

45.   THOMAS, A., CHESS, S. AND BIRCH, H. 1968. *Temperament and behavior disorders in children*. New York University Press, New York.

46.   WOOLF, P. 1966. "The causes, controls and organization of behavior in the neonate." *Psychol. Issues* 5 (monogr. 17).

18

Antecedents of Child Abuse and Neglect in Premature Infants: A Prospective Study in a Newborn Intensive Care Unit*

Rosemary S. Hunter, M.D.,
Nancy Kilstrom, A.C.S.W.,
Ernest N. Kraybill, M.D., and
Frank Loda, M.D.

Retrospective studies of abused and neglected children have shown that a disproportionately large number were premature or had other neonatal problems.[1-3] Prospective studies of the relationship between major neonatal illness and subsequent child abuse have not been reported, so information regarding the etiologic factors remains speculative. This lack of knowledge has prevented an accurate assessment of the relative significance of infant, parental, and environmental factors in subsequent abuse and it has severely hampered the development of effective intervention.

This report describes a clinical experience with a large group of infants and their families studied from the time of admission into a neonatal intensive care unit. It is an initial effort to understand the complex relationships between neonatal illness and subsequent maltreatment.

* Supported by grant 90-C-408 from the National Center on Child Abuse and Neglect, Children's Bureau, Office of Child Development, Department of Health, Education and Welfare.

Rosemary S. Hunter et al., "Antecedents of Child Abuse and Neglect in Premature Infants: A Prospective Study in a Newborn Intensive Care Unit," *Pediatrics*, Vol. 61, No. 4 (April 1978); 629-635. Copyright © American Academy of Pediatrics, 1978.

Methods .

The babies in this study were all hospitalized in the newborn intensive care unit of North Carolina Memorial Hospital, a regional intensive care nursery in a state-supported university facility. Newborns transported from outlying hospitals constitute half of the patient population. The study population included families from 45 of the state's 100 counties. The nursery fosters family-infant interaction through a policy of unlimited visiting by parents and grandparents, who are encouraged to touch and handle their infants; however, family contact is often impeded by distance.

There were 422 infants admitted to the newborn intensive care unit from May 1975 through June 1976. The study did not include 130 of these infants who were in the unit less than a week either because of death or rapid recovery. An additional 21 families whose infants were in the nursery for a period greater than one week were excluded because the project staff did not have sufficient contact with them for adequate assessment. The remaining 271 families with their 282 newborns are the subject of this report.

Data on each child were obtained from family interviews, medical chart audit, newborn intensive care unit visiting records, outpatient clinic follow-up, contact with local care providers, and a search of state death records and of the central registry of abused and neglected children.

An initial, semistructured interview by the nursery social worker (N.K.) or child psychiatrist (R.S.H.), held as soon as possible after admission, provided information on family characteristics early in the course of the hospitalization. A family psychosocial risk inventory (Table I) was developed from the current literature on the etiology of child abuse and neglect, with special attention to maternal personality characteristics described in studies of rural families from the southeastern United States.[4] This 24-item inventory was used to record the interviewer's impressions and was scored immediately after the admission assessment. Items were scored as absent (0), present to some degree (1), or strongly present (2). Summation of item scores provided a total risk score for each family. Since all items were negatively stated, high scores indicated potential high risk for maltreatment. A pattern of distribution of scores emerged during the first two months of study that allowed the provisional assignment of families to high- and low-risk groups, using a total risk score of 10 as the dividing point.

Forty families were assessed and rated independently by both interviewers with high inter-rater agreement on total risk scores. The greatest difference between total risk scores for any family was 3 points. In all cases, the examiners agreed in the assignment of families to either the high- or low-risk group. For purposes of item analysis (Table I), all items rated as present to some degree (1) or strongly present (2) by either interviewer were considered present.

All parents, regardless of scores, were encouraged to take advantage of the nursery's unlimited visiting policy. All parents were also provided with crisis counseling, assistance with financial arrangements, access to overnight accommodations, public health nurse referrals, and follow-up in a multidisciplinary clinic. When an infant was thought to be at high risk of subsequent abuse or neglect on the basis of the family inventory score, an effort was made to involve local agencies in planning supportive services for the family during and after the baby's hospitaliza-

TABLE I

Association of Reported Abuse and Neglect With Percent of Families Possessing Characteristics Assessed by Family Psychosocial Risk Inventory

Inventory Item	% Reported Group (No. = 10)	% Nonreported Group (No. = 245)	P
Adolescent or inexperienced in child care	30	61	NS
Prior neonatal morbidity or mortality	30	25	NS
Inadequate child spacing	60	11	<.0005
Abortion of this pregnancy seriously considered	40	7	<.05
Failure to accept pregnancy after first trimester	30	9	NS
Failure to obtain needed infant equipment	30	11	NS
Poor utilization of medical care	40	9	<.05
Socially isolated with poor support system	80	9	<.0005
Major life stress during pregnancy	80	49	NS
Marital maladjustment, separation, divorce*	60	14	<.005
Precarious financial situation	80	37	<.05
Inadequate child care arrangements	80	11	<.0005
Family history of abuse or neglect	90	17	<.0005
Lack confidence in parenting skills	10	9	NS
Unrealistic expectations of infant	20	9	NS
Disappointment over sex of infant	30	6	<.05
Impulsive personality style	40	9	<.05
Apathetic-futile personality style	40	5	<.005
Childish-dependent personality style	60	12	<.005
Verbally inaccessible	10	6	NS
Retarded or illiterate	20	3	<.05
Major psychiatric diagnosis*	0	4	NS
Alcohol or drug abuse*	20	3	NS
Police or imprisonment record*	20	2	NS

*Data on these items available on the families of 163 infants.

tion. In this group, particular attention was given to facilitating family visiting to the intensive care unit. The local department of social services was also asked to support these families with appropriate services.

Outcome parameters were assessed in December 1976 when study infants reached a mean age of 12 months (range, 6 to 19 months). The criteria for maltreatment in this assessment were that the child had been reported to the local department of social services under the Child Abuse and Neglect Reporting Law of North Carolina and that the local agency had confirmed the presence of maltreatment.

The null hypothesis used in the statistical analysis was that there was no difference between the children and their families who were reported for maltreatment and the nonreported infants and their families. The categorical variables in contingency tables were tested by the Fisher exact test. This test was appropriate because of the small number of abused children. Means were computed for continuous variables and differences between means were tested by the t test.

Results

Of 282 study infants admitted to the newborn intensive care unit, 255 were eventually discharged home to their parents. Ten of these 255 babies (3.9%) were subsequently reported for abuse and neglect during the first year of life. All ten reports were confirmed as instances of maltreatment following an investigation by the county department of social services.

Serious physical abuse occurred in two of the ten cases of maltreatment. One abused child suffered multiple long bone and skull fractures with cerebral contusion and subsequent severe neurological impairment. The other victim of physical abuse had extensive superficial injuries. Neglect was the primary basis for the other eight reports. In most cases there were multiple reasons for the neglect complaint. Most frequent (five cases) was a failure to provide needed medical care for significant chronic or acute illnesses including hydrocephalus, disseminated scabies, and meningitis. Failure to comply with minimal well child care, including routine immunizations, was also frequently noted (five cases). In two infants, failure to provide adequate nutrition was cited in neglect reports. Inadequate parental supervision was also frequently cited in the neglect reports. Three infants were reported after being found unattended at home. At the time of reported abuse or neglect, the children ranged in age from 2 to 11 months (mean age of 6.5 months). Currently, there have been no reports of abuse or neglect in study children more than 12 months of age. Reports of maltreatment were initiated by several sources, including a local physician, a law enforcement officer, a neighbor, public health nurses, and social workers. In two cases the report was initiated solely by physicians in the North Carolina Memorial Hospital.

The family psychosocial risk inventory was useful as an initial step in identifying families who might maltreat their children. There were 52 infants who were initially considered at high risk for maltreatment due to inventory scores greater than 10. Four of these infants (7.7%) died in the nursery, a rate comparable to that for the 230 low-risk babies of whom 16 (6.9%) died in the nursery. In addition, seven high-risk infants were relinquished by their parents or voluntarily placed in foster care prior to discharge from the nursery. Such custody changes did not occur in the low-risk group. As a result of these deaths and placements, only 41 high-risk and 214 low-risk babies were eventually discharged home to their parents. These 255 infants comprised the population studied for the occurrence of abuse. All ten cases of subsequently reported maltreatment came from the group of 41 infants discharged home who were considered at high risk (Table II).

Although additional cases of maltreatment may eventually be found in the high-risk group, to be precise the remainder of this report will focus on reported and confirmed cases only. The ten known cases of maltreatment (reported group) will be compared with the other 245 children in both the high-risk and low-risk groups

TABLE II

Association of Psychosocial Risk Group With Subsequent Outcome* in 255 Infants Discharged Home

Outcome	High-Risk Group (No. = 41), No. (%)	Low-Risk Group (No. = 214), No. (%)
Reported for abuse or neglect	10 (24.4)	0
Custody change after discharge	7 (17.1)	0
Deaths after discharge	3 (7.3)	11 (5.1)
Remaining at home	31 (75.6)	203 (94.9)

*Mean follow-up period was one year (range, 6 to 19 months).

discharged home who have not been reported for abuse or neglect (nonreported group).

Item analysis revealed significant differences between reported and nonreported infants on 13 of the 24 family characteristics studied (Table I). At the time of initial assessment, families subsequently reported for abuse and neglect differed from nonreported families in several ways. The social setting of reported families revealed severe isolation without adequate social support systems and frequently was characterized by marital maladjustment, financial problems, poor use of medical services, and inadequate child care arrangements. In terms of personality factors, the parents were more likely to be rated by the interviewer as impulsive, apathetic-futile, childish-dependent, or retarded or illiterate. Characteristically, the reported families revealed a family history of abuse or neglect on the initial interview. With respect to the index pregnancy, the reported families were more likely to have inadequate child spacing, to have seriously considered abortion, and to have expressed disappointment over the sex of the baby.

Analysis of maternal sociodemographic and medical factors (Table III) showed mothers of reported and nonreported infants to have no significant differences in terms of age, marital status, or in the incidence of medical problems predating or involving the current pregnancy and delivery. Mothers of reported infants were more likely to be living in situations other than with maternal families or the father of the child and less likely to have completed high school. They frequently failed to obtain minimal prenatal care.

The reported infants themselves differed from other babies admitted during the same time period to the intensive care nursery (Table IV). At birth they were significantly less mature (mean gestational age, 31.5 weeks) than the infants who were not reported (mean gestational age, 35.3 weeks). Mean birth weights were considerably less for the reported group (1,477 gm) compared with their nursery mates (2,224 gm). All ten reported infants had birth weights of less than 2,200 gm. In addition, congenital defects were noted in six of the ten infants later reported for maltreatment, a significantly higher incidence than in babies not reported. Three reported infants had more than one congenital defect, and three infants required surgery for the repair of defects during their nursery stay. No significant differences were found between the reported and nonreported groups in terms of the infant's sex or race or whether the baby was born at our hospital or transported from an outlying hospital.

TABLE III

Association of Maternal Sociodemographic and Medical Factors With Subsequently Reported Child Abuse and Neglect

Factor	Reported Group (No. = 10)	Nonreported Group (No. = 245)	P
Age of mother, mean ± SD (yr)	21.40 ± 3.31	22.87 ± 6.26	NS
Years of completed education, mean ± SD	10.20 ± 1.75	11.65 ± 2.20	<.05
Mother married (%)	60.0	73.5	NS
Mother not living with her mother or father of child (%)	40.0	5.8	<.005
Primigravida (%)	10.0	41.8	NS
Fewer than 3 prenatal visits (%)	50.0	17.3	<.05
Preexisting maternal medical problems (%)	10.0	8.6	NS
Medical problems during current pregnancy (%)	30.0	37.1	NS
Complications of labor & delivery other than premature labor (%)	50.0	57.1	NS

Differences were also seen in the hospital course followed by the two groups (Table IV). Those reported for abuse or neglect were more likely than their nursery mates to have remained in the intensive care nursery for longer than 40 days. During their longer hospital stays, reported infants tended to require oxygen and isolettes for longer periods of time, although these differences failed to reach statistical significance.

Analysis of visiting records revealed that reported babies received less frequent visits than other babies in the nursery, even though the percentage of families living more than 80 km (50 miles) from the nursery was similar in both groups (Table V). Despite efforts to encourage and facilitate contact, visiting rates of mothers, fathers, and extended family remained significantly lower in the group which was subsequently reported for maltreatment.

Discussion

This prospective study confirmed that there was a high rate of reported abuse and neglect in infants discharged from a newborn intensive care unit. Retrospective investigations[1-3] suggest incidence rates of maltreatment in premature infants of three to five times the expected rate. The best available North Carolina data for reports for child abuse and neglect during the infant's first year of life indicate a rate of 0.5%.[5] Data are not available on the statewide incidence of confirmed cases of maltreatment in this age group, but it would be less than the 0.5% incidence of reported cases. The overall rate of confirmation of abuse and neglect in reported cases in North Carolina has ranged from 40% to 60% in recent years. Thus the incidence rate of confirmed cases found in this study (3.9%) represents at least an

TABLE IV

Birth and Hospital Stay Characteristics of Reported and Nonreported Infants

Characteristic	Reported Group (No. = 10)	Nonreported Group (No. = 245)	P
Gestational age, mean ± SD (wk)	31.50 ± 3.75	35.26 ± 4.10	<.005
Birth weight			
Mean ± SD (gm)	1,477.00 ± 369.21	2,224.39 ± 831.75	<.0005
<1,500 gm (%)	60	19.3	<.05
Sex (% male)	60	53.0	NS
Race (% white)	70	55.1	NS
Born at N.C. Memorial Hospital (%)	30	50.2	NS
Congenital defects (%)	60	20.9	<.05
Infants with residual problems at discharge (%)	50	23.7	NS
Duration of hospitalization, mean ± SD (days)	47.00 ± 36.89	23.47 ± 22.58	NS
Infants who remained in hospital more than 40 days (%)	60.0	15.9	<.005
Day of life when infant's condition was stable in room air, mean ± SD	21.25 ± 33.50	3.97 ± 6.08	NS
Day of life when infant was removed from isolette, mean ± SD	33.00 ± 26.13	17.23 ± 15.41	NS

eightfold increase in risk for premature and ill newborns. The risk in families with high scores on the family psychosocial risk inventory was even higher. Ten of the 41 infants (24.4%) in the high-risk category who were discharged home subsequently were reported and confirmed as victims of maltreatment.

Families of infants reported for abuse and neglect characteristically lacked social support from family, friends, and community at the time of the baby's birth. Their failure to derive support from a potential array of sources was apparent in most aspects of their lives—marriage, schooling, living and child care arrangements, finances, and medical care. This study cannot answer the question of whether the failure to relate to these supports indicated the differential nonavailability of services or was a reflection of the family's inability to utilize available help. The poor response of these families to services offered to assist in visiting their infants in the nursery would tend to favor the latter possibility.

The parents in reported families had impressive histories of abuse and neglect in their own childhoods. It has been observed[6] that adults who were abused or

TABLE V

Association of Visiting by Family to the Intensive Care Nursery With Subsequently Reported Child Abuse and Neglect

Visiting Data	Reported Group (No. = 10)	Nonreported Group (No. = 245)	P
No. of visits per day of hospital stay, mean ± SD			
By mother	0.152 ± 0.065	0.406 ± 0.444	<.005
By father	0.076 ± 0.058	0.308 ± 0.490	<.005
By other relatives	0.015 ± 0.036	0.188 ± 0.481	<.005
By all visitors	0.243 ± 0.108	0.902 ± 1.224	<.005
Families living more than 80 km from Chapel Hill (%)	50	54.9	NS

neglected as children do not possess the sense of trust needed for effective utilization of social support systems. The life experience of parents, however, can explain only partially why certain children are maltreated. Four times as many study parents were abused and neglected as children as were actually reported for the maltreatment of their own newborns. Inadequate social support systems characterized all of the families of the 41 high-risk infants discharged to their homes, yet not all of these infants were reported for maltreatment. It is likely that characteristics of individual children played an important role in determining which of the vulnerable parents became abusers. The reported infants were different at birth, not only from average full-term babies, but also from other babies in the intensive care unit. On the average, they were smaller, less mature, and less perfect in appearance. Several writers[7-9] have stressed the concept that adaptation to the birth of a premature or deformed child requires great emotional effort by the parents as well as assistance from support systems. When such infants are born to parents who have few social and emotional reserve strengths, it seems reasonable than an optimal resolution with positive attachment to the infant will be difficult.

Several authors have emphasized that early separation of mother and child, often a consequence of neonatal illness, may be a major contributing factor to subsequent child abuse.[10-12] In support of this, differences in the nursery-visiting behaviors of subsequently abusive parents have been seen in other studies.[12-14] The question of whether these differences are causal remains unanswered. In this prospective study, parents who subsequently abused or neglected their infants did visit their babies in the nursery less frequently. This difference in visiting rates appeared unrelated to distance from the nursery or the incidence of maternal medical complications. The latter finding differs from recently reported results[12] in which mothers subsequently reported for abuse were more likely to have suffered gestational illness. In our experience, infrequent parental visiting appeared to be one of the many reflections of the preexisting, pervasive social isolation of the most vulnerable parents. The infants who were subsequently abused also tended to be the least mature and sickest infants in the nursery, and it is probable that these neonates provided very few positive responses to their parents to encourage repeated visiting.

Unique factors appear to act in combination to increase the rate of maltreatment of infants discharged from a newborn intensive care unit. This study suggests three essential components that contribute to this risk: (1) vulnerable, unsupported families, (2) biologically impaired infants, and (3) limited parent-infant contact during the nursery period. A systematic plan to minimize this risk would need to address all three areas. Developing families need improved access to social supports. There must also be continued attention to the physical and psychosocial factors that lead to poor reproductive performance and perinatal morbidity. The study further suggests that imaginative ways of supporting early parent-infant rapport must go beyond the current receptive stance of opening the nursery door to families. Further work is needed concerning the most effective ways to achieve these goals of intervention.

Although this report has stressed the high rate of abuse and neglect in premature infants, this clinical experience was not without encouraging aspects. The babies of very young adolescent mothers, for example, did not appear to be at added risk, as is frequently assumed. Many other families who were judged as high risk did not maltreat their children. Increased emphasis should be placed on the mechanisms by which some families faced with great social, economic, and health problems successfully meet the demands of parenting.

REFERENCES

1. ELMER, E., GREGG, G. S.: "Developmental characteristics of abused children." *Pediatrics* 40:596, 1967.

2. KLEIN, M., STERN, L.: "Low birth weight and the battered child syndrome." *Am J Dis Child* 122:15. 1971.

3. LYNCH, M. A., ROBERTS, J.: "Predicting child abuse: Signs of bonding failure in the maternity hospital." *Br Med J* 1:624, 1977.

4. POLANSKY, N. A., DeSAIX, C., SHARLIN, S. A.: *Child Neglect: Understanding and Reaching the Parent: A Guide for Child Welfare Workers.* New York, Child Welfare League of America Inc, 1972.

5. *Neglect and Abuse of Children in North Carolina*, special report 30. North Carolina Department of Human Resources, Division of Social Services, 1975, pp. 5-6.

6. POLLOCK, C., STEELE, B.: "A therapeutic approach to the parents," in Kempe, C. H., Helfer, R. E. (eds): *Helping the Battered Child and His Family.* Philadelphia, J. B. Lippincott Co, 1972, p. 9.

7. KAPLAN, D. M., MASON, E. A.: "Maternal reactions to premature birth viewed as an acute emotional disorder." *Am J Orthopsychiatry* 30:539, 1960.

8. SOLNIT, A. J., STARK, M. H.: "Mourning and the birth of a defective child." *Psychoanal Study Child* 16:523, 1961.

9. DROTAR, D., BASKIEWICZ, B. A., IRVIN, N., et al.: "The adaptation of parents to the birth of an infant with a congenital malformation: A hypothetical model." *Pediatrics* 56:710, 1975.

10. FOMUFOD, A. K., SINKFORD, S. M., LOUY, V. E.: "Mother-child separation at birth: A contributing factor in child abuse." *Lancet* 2:549, 1975.

11. KLAUS, M. H., KENNELL, J. H.: "Mothers separated from their newborn infants." *Pediatr Clin North Am* 17:1015, 1970.

12   TEN BENSEL, R. W., PAXSON, C. L.: "Child abuse following early postpartum separation." *J Pediatr* 90:490, 1977.

13.   FANAROFF, A. A., KENNELL, J. H., KLAUS, M. H.: "Follow-up of low-birth-weight infants: The predictive value of maternal visiting patterns." *Pediatrics* 49:287, 1972.

14.   MINDE, K., FORD L., CELHOFFER, B., BOUKYDIS, C.: "Interactions of mothers and nurses with premature infants." *Can Med Assoc J* 113: 741, 1975.

ACKNOWLEDGEMENT

We thank Beverley Hulbert, M.A., and Diane Makuc, M.S.P.II., for statistical analysis of the data.

19

Psychosocial Functioning of Mothers of Malnourished Children*

Mary Ann D. Kerr, M.S.W.,
Jacqueline Landman Bogues, M.Sc., and
Douglas S. Kerr, M.D., Ph.D.

Infant malnutrition among impoverished populations and "failure-to-thrive" in more affluent societies are frequently assumed to be separate entities with different origins. It is well known that malnourished infants usually come from families who lack jobs, education, health and sanitary facilities, and whose only abundance is children.[1-4] However, those features have not been adequately described that distinguish families of malnourished children from the majority who live under the same desperate conditions but manage to produce relatively healthy children.

Where it has been difficult to attribute "failure-to-thrive" to food scarcity, attention has focused on psychosocial functioning. Mothers of these babies have been observed to be depressed and isolated from any supportive system, including husbands and extended families.[5-12] Many have been severely deprived themselves and show an excessive need to be cared for as children.[5, 6, 8-11, 13, 14] This limits their capacity to provide their youngsters with intellectual and emotional stimulation or even to see them as separate individuals.[6-10, 12-14]

There have been observations that similar psychosocial factors are operating in families of malnourished children. Previous investigators have observed a sparcity of any supportive contacts, including community services.[1, 15] Often fathers are absent,[1, 2, 4, 15, 16] and mothers have been described as lacking motivation and

* Mary Ann D. Kerr, et al., "Psychosocial Functioning of Mothers of Malnourished Children," *Pediatrics*, Vol. 62, No. 5 (November, 1978):778-784. Copyright © American Academy of Pediatrics 1978. Reproduced by permission.

resourcefulness.[1, 15-17] There is a higher incidence of antisocial behavior in these families.[4] Understimulation and rejection also have been considered as important factors.[18-21] These can be documented as early as 6 months of age, that is, before the children become malnourished.[21]

This project was undertaken to examine the role of maternal psychosocial functioning in the development of infant malnutrition. It was hypothesized that the lives of mothers of malnourished children, as those of mothers whose children have "failed to thrive," are characterized by disruption and isolation. This was measured by the mothers' descriptions of their relationships. Interview responses of mothers of malnourished children were compared with those of mothers whose children maintained normal growth in spite of equally extreme poverty conditions.

Methods

All mothers who participated in this study lived in one or two rooms, usually without electricity and with water provided by a community tap. Toilet facilities ranged from a pit latrine, shared by as many as 60 people, to an indoor toilet used by several families. Cooking was done in a common kitchen or on a coal pot in the yard.

Two populations of mothers were studied. Within each group mothers of malnourished children (MMC) were compared with matched controls. Group 1 included mothers of six children who had been admitted to University Hospital for severe malnutrition and six controls whose children had been hospitalized for another illness. The diagnosis of primary malnutrition was made on the basis of lack of evidence of other causes of growth failure and rapid weight gain after dietary therapy in the hospital. The malnourished children in group 1 were all less than 70% of expected weight for age (four were less than 60% of expected weight for age). Children whose weights were more than the third percentile for age were selected as controls. Four had been admitted for gastroenteritis, one for meningitis, and one for heart disease.

The mothers in group 2 were selected from an independent prospective study of feeding practices and growth of 82 babies born at University Hospital (West Indies, Kingston, Jamaica) who lived in the same area.[22] In spite of normal birth weights and frequent home visits emphasizing proper nutrition, two children required hospitalization at 12 months of age weighing 66% and 60% of expected weight for age; three others were 72%, 80%, and 85% of expected weight for age.

Groups 1 and 2 differed in that (1) all of the children of group 1 mothers were inpatients and more were severely malnourished; (2) the families of group 1 children were less affluent; and (3) the mothers in group 2 had been required to register at the antenatal clinic by the third month of pregnancy and maintain regular appointments before delivery.

MMC and controls were selected to be pair-matched for family income and approximate age of the children by an individual unfamiliar with the subjects. None of the controls had a history of malnutrition among their children. When it was not possible to select controls whose children were of equal age, controls were selected whose children were older so as to increase the probability that they had grown normally (Table). The MMC did not have more social or educational disadvantages than their controls (Table).

Socioeconomic Comparison of Families of Malnourished and Control Children

		Group 1							Group 2				Average
Mother	MMC*	A	B	C	D	E	F	G	H	I	J	K	. . .
	Controls	L	M	N	O	P	Q	R	S	T	U	V	. . .
Age of child	MMC	10	10	9	3	11	14	9	9	9	9	9	9.3
(mo)	Controls	8	18	19	8	13	22	9	9	9	9	9	12.1
Relative income (subsistence• = 1.0)	MMC	1.5	1.0	2.0	1.5	1.5	<1.0	1.0	2.5	2.0	2.0	<1.0	1.2
	Controls	1.5	1.0	2.0	1.5	1.5	1.0	1.5	2.5	2.0	1.5	1.0	1.5
Age of mother	MMC	27	19	34	17	23	20	28	20	29	30	19	24.2
(yr)	Controls	20	30	21	30	32	27	34	17	23	38	17	26.3
Age of mother at first pregnancy (yr)	MMC	17	17	22	16	17	14	19	18	20	19	17	17.8
	Controls	17	21	16	19	20	14	20	16	21	22	16	18.4
No. of children in family	MMC	5	2	6	1	3	4	5	2	5	7	2	3.8
	Controls	2	4	4	5	7	4	5	1	2	12	1	4.3
Education of	MMC	P‡, T§	P	P	P	P,T	P	HS‖,T	P	P,T	P	P	. . .
mother	Controls	P	P	P	HS	. . .	. . .	P	P	P	P	P	. . .

* MMC = mothers of malnourished children.

• Subsistence is based on 1973 Board of Supervision estimate of $3.60 for head of household, $1.80 for spouse, and 84 cents per child per week.

‡P = primary grades.

§T = technical school.

‖HS = high school.

After mothers had been identified as possible participants in the study, the nature of the project was described to them and consent obtained. Subsequently, they were interviewed in their homes for a total of two to four hours. The interviewer was not aware of the classification of the mothers. The interviews were open-ended, and the replies were recorded on a form according to the mothers' own description of the way they felt about the significant people they had encountered. This information was later categorized according to specific issues (Fig. 1 to 6). In evaluating the data the χ^2 test was used to determine the significance of all the information except that given in the table for which the matched t test was used.

Results

Housing

The controls made better use of their tiny plots for gardens and fowl (Fig. 1). Inside even the poorest of homes were curtains, plants, and figurines. Many control mothers had saved toward owning their own homes. Some had constructed their

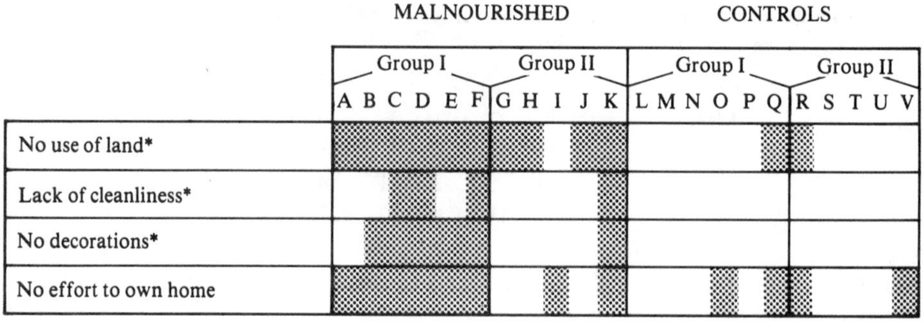

	MALNOURISHED				CONTROLS			
	Group I		Group II		Group I		Group II	
	A B C D E F	G H I J K			L M N O P Q	R S T U V		
No use of land*	▓▓▓▓▓▓	▓▓ ▓▓			▓	▓		
Lack of cleanliness*	▓▓▓ ▓	▓						
No decorations*	▓▓▓▓							
No effort to own home	▓▓▓▓▓▓	▓ ▓▓			▓▓▓	▓▓		

* p < .05

Fig. 1. Housing conditions. Shaded areas indicate positive response. For explanation of groups 1 and 2 refer to text.

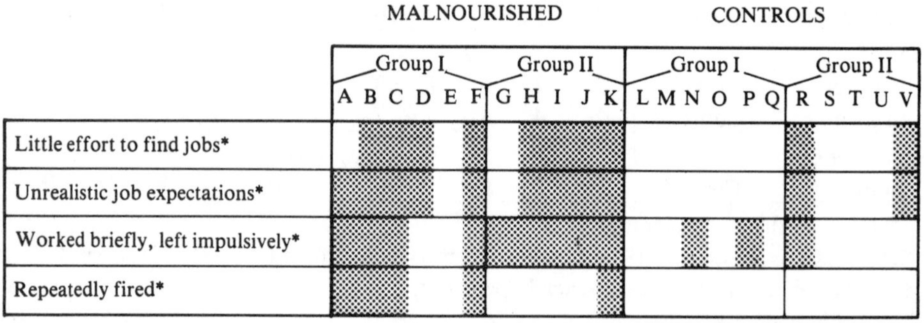

	MALNOURISHED				CONTROLS			
	Group I		Group II		Group I		Group II	
	A B C D E F	G H I J K			L M N O P Q	R S T U V		
Little effort to find jobs*	▓▓▓ ▓	▓▓▓			▓	▓		
Unrealistic job expectations*	▓▓▓	▓			▓	▓		
Worked briefly, left impulsively*	▓▓▓▓▓	▓▓▓			▓ ▓	▓		
Repeatedly fired*	▓▓▓	▓						

* p < .05

Fig. 2. Employment history.

dwellings out of boards they had collected from gulleys and roadsides. In contrast, many homes of the MMC were barren of attempts to enhance their surroundings and were exceedingly unkempt.

Employment

In spite of the slight educational advantage of the MMC, their work histories were poor (Fig. 2). Of the ten MMC who claimed they wanted to work, eight were waiting passively for "someone" to find it for them. Child care was never mentioned as a factor in obtaining a job. Their previous job failures were blamed on unreasonable employers.

Eight of the ten control mothers who wanted to work were employed. They tended to choose sewing or selling because of the opportunity to use skills creatively and to be near their children while working. For example, control mother U, while managing her 12 children, also cultivated and sold produce, vended charcoal, and babysat for three neighborhood children.

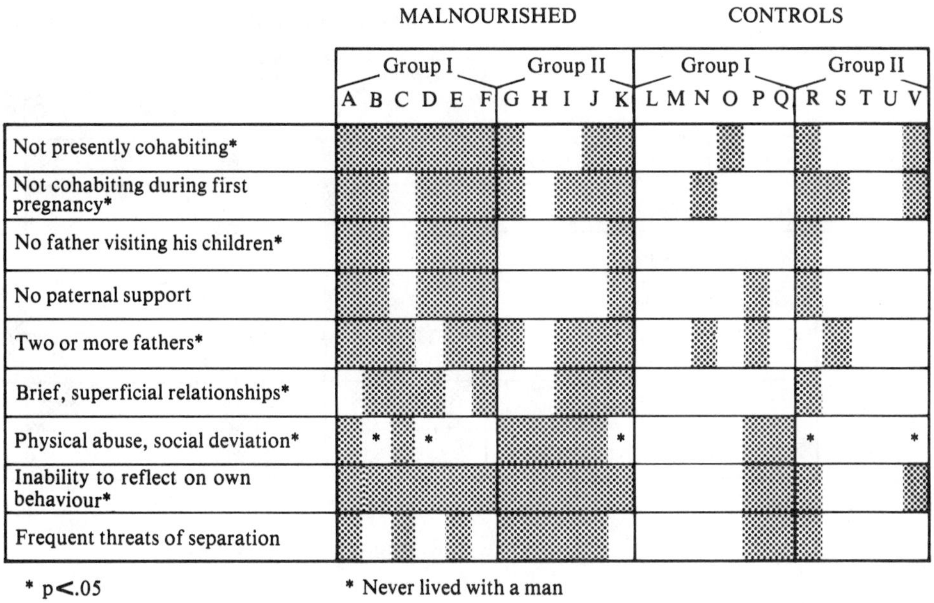

	MALNOURISHED		CONTROLS	
	Group I	Group II	Group I	Group II
	A B C D E F	G H I J K	L M N O P Q	R S T U V
Not presently cohabiting*				
Not cohabiting during first pregnancy*				
No father visiting his children*				
No paternal support				
Two or more fathers*				
Brief, superficial relationships*				
Physical abuse, social deviation*	* *	*	*	* *
Inability to reflect on own behaviour*				
Frequent threats of separation				

* p<.05   * Never lived with a man

Fig. 3. Relationships with men.

Relationships With Men

A high incidence of common-law relationships has previously been described in this population.[23, 24] Only two women in this study were legally married. Nevertheless, the control mothers' relationships with men were more stable, with mothers seeing themselves as active participants (Fig. 3). Four MMC reported never having a relationship with a man lasting more than six months. For many pregnancy was repeatedly the unfortunate result of casual meetings. They saw sexual favors as sources of money, cuddling, or other immediate compensations and spoke of men as objects to be manipulated but not trusted. In families where the fathers were present, there was often intense parental conflict and physical abuse.

Relationships With Children

Both groups in this study population followed the previously described custom of passing on children to grandparents, relatives, or other adults.[23, 24] However, the MMC were often aware of poor treatment in day care or other homes but did nothing about it (Fig. 4). Three malnourished babies were hospitalized after such experiences and on recovery were returned to the same situations. Seven MMC described encountering malnutrition in other offspring and apparently had not been able to change feeding patterns. The MMC showed a lack of anxiety about their children's health. Resentment was expressed about children becoming ill and "causing too much trouble." They found little enjoyment in the development of their youngsters, whose value was determined by their ability to fill their mothers' needs. For example, mother J had left her six children, ages 2 through 9, and their father several times to live with her mother. She indicated that she need not worry about the children because their father knew how to cook and wash. However, he worked

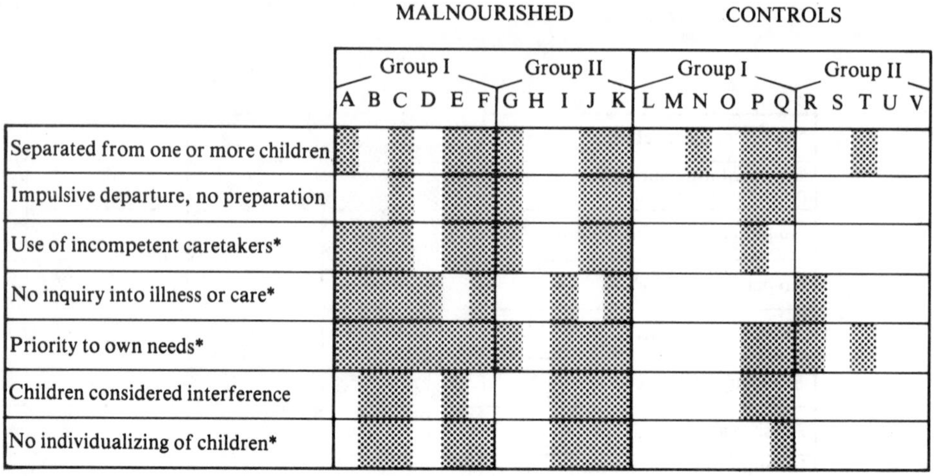

MALNOURISHED   CONTROLS

	Group I						Group II					Group I						Group II				
	A	B	C	D	E	F	G	H	I	J	K	L	M	N	O	P	Q	R	S	T	U	V
Separated from one or more children																						
Impulsive departure, no preparation																						
Use of incompetent caretakers*																						
No inquiry into illness or care*																						
Priority to own needs*																						
Children considered interference																						
No individualizing of children*																						

* $p < .05$

Fig. 4. Relationships with children.

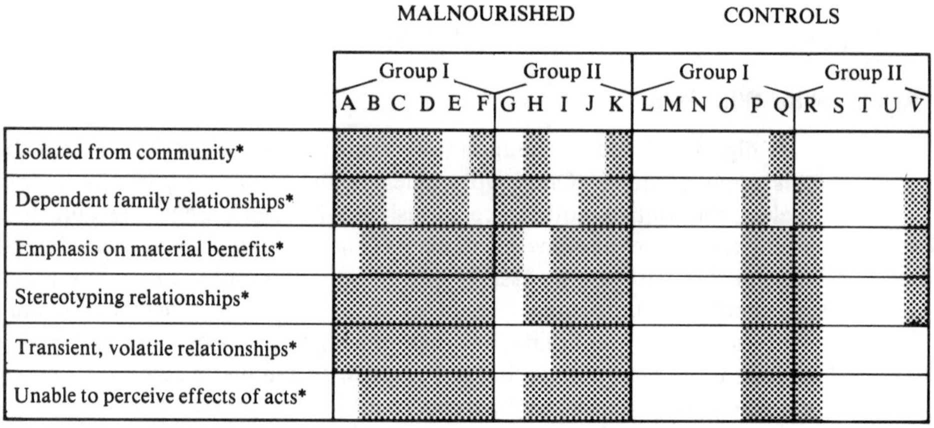

MALNOURISHED   CONTROLS

	Group I						Group II					Group I						Group II				
	A	B	C	D	E	F	G	H	I	J	K	L	M	N	O	P	Q	R	S	T	U	V
Isolated from community*																						
Dependent family relationships*																						
Emphasis on material benefits*																						
Stereotyping relationships*																						
Transient, volatile relationships*																						
Unable to perceive effects of acts*																						

* $p < .05$

Fig. 5. Relationships with family and friends.

all day and spent every evening in a bar. She saw the children only when they sought her out. With her approval, the older ones had taken money from their father's pocket when he was drunk and brought it to her. She disliked one of the children who "favored his father." Another child was her favorite because he tried to please her.

Relationships With Family and Friends

Most of the control mothers had mutually supportive associations with churches, neighborhoods, and extended families (Fig. 5). Such contacts were effective in overcoming environmental hardships. By contrast, most MMC had never been able to

	MALNOURISHED											CONTROLS										
	Group I						Group II					Group I						Group II				
	A	B	C	D	E	F	G	H	I	J	K	L	M	N	O	P	Q	R	S	T	U	V
Vague history		X	X	X		X		X	X		X				X			X				X
Early traumatic separation	X			X	X	X				X			X	X		X	X	X			X	
Separation seen as desertion*	X			X	X	X				X							X					
Felt rejected criticized	X	X		X	X	X	X	X	X	X	X		X	X		X	X	X	X			X
Severe maternal abuse				X	X	X			X		X			X		X	X	X	X			
Severe paternal abuse*	X		X	X	X	X			X	X							X					
Pregnancy seen as self-assertion*	X	X		X	X	X	X	X	X	X	X			X				X				X

* p<.05

Fig. 6. Childhood experiences.

depart from close family supervision that served as their sole relationships outside of the home. These extended family ties were fraught with dependency and ambivalence. Relationships in general often involved intense attachment followed by accusations of having been exploited.

Childhood Experiences

Only one of the 22 mothers in the study (L) grew up in a warm family situation with a father and mother. Early traumatic separations had occurred with similar frequency among the MMC and controls (Fig. 6). Most of the control mothers thought that these had resulted from major upheavals that were out of control of their families and maintained positive feelings toward their natural parents. On the other hand, all of the MMC who had been separated perceived that they had been deliberately deserted or sent away as a matter of convenience. Both MMC and controls who had been separated described feelings of rejection by their subsequent caretakers.

Although severe abuse from mother figures was encountered equally by MMC and controls, there was a difference in experiences with paternal figures. Of the nine MMC who had fathers or father substitutes, seven had encountered severe beatings and four had suffered sexual abuse from these men. Most control mothers had positive memories of their paternal figures. By the time they had reached late adolescence, most of the controls had left home and were independent. However, the MMC were still living in hostile family situations. For them, pregnancy became a means of escape or self-assertion, an often futile attempt to establish a separate identity.

Personality Patterns

Two personality patterns became apparent within the MMC group. One set (B, D, F, H, K) were apathetic, dependent, passive, and isolated. They gave histories that were vague, remembering few details before adolescence. Their families were their only contacts, which alternated between intrusion and rejection. Their relationships with men were superficial and lacked discretion. With their babies they seemed absent-minded and, at times, hostile. They were essentially unemployable.

Another set of MMC (A, C, E, G, I, J) seemed more vigorous and self-confident. The content of their histories was richer, characterized by exaggeration, inconsistencies, and omissions. Their family ties were strong but sporadic. Because it was important to them to be seen as functioning independently, help from family and others was either avoided or obtained through manipulation. Employment was meaningful but also sporadic. Relations with men were marked by the need to control. Fearing rejection, they seemed uninvolved, preferring to terminate relationships before being deserted themselves. Children were ignored or over-stimulated as the occasion suited.

Three control mothers (P, Q, R) had personalities similar to those of the MMC. However, each was receiving considerable outside support. The church played an active role with one (P) by providing milk and guidance. The children's father was supportive of another (Q). In the third case (R), a great-grandmother was doing much of the caretaking.

Discussion

In spite of an equally deprived environment, the psychosocial functioning of the MMC and controls was significantly different. Although no single indicator completely distinguished the MMC from the controls, together they form a profile of the MMC group that bears a strong resemblance to that of parents of children who are neglected or who "fail to thrive."

The miserable surroundings of the MMC reflected their poor self-esteem and low energy level. They had unrealistically high expectations for achievement in monetary matters and personal relationships but were unable to plan for fulfillment. All-consuming ties to their extended families trapped them in situations that fostered inadequacy and isolation. They lacked trust and stereotyped others according to their own needs. Their difficulty in delaying gratification and tendency to repeat experiences of rejection severely impaired appropriate behavior. In childlike ways, concrete services and material goods replaced emotional attachment.

Preoccupation with their chaotic environment prevented their taking responsibility and profiting from mistakes. Misfortunes were relentlessly attributed to the maleficence of others. Their problems did not result from isolated crises but from long-standing upheaval that affected all the areas studied. This pervasive quality has contributed to the frustration sensed by many professionals who treat malnutrition.

The observation that some MMC are apathetic whereas others are aggressive and manipulative is consistent with Polansky and co-workers' description of mothers who neglect their children.[25] They described "apathetic-futile mothers" as being those who respond to severe deprivation by becoming numb, refusing to experience emotions at all, and having little energy or purpose. On the other hand, the "impulse-ridden mothers" have periods of relative maturity and do allow themselves to feel, but their feelings get out of hand. They are restless, manipulative, and unable to tolerate frustration because of their sense of helplessness in the face of their own overpowering impulses and fears of loss of love.

It was not anticipated that both the MMC and control mothers would describe severe early deprivation. However, this brief retrospective analysis suffers from limitations of recollection. By analogy to previous studies of personality functioning of mothers whose children "fail to thrive," it seems probable that the behavior of the MMC was related to more damaging childhood experiences. It is also possible that intervening factors could have helped the control mothers overcome severe deprivation. The control mothers were observed to have remarkable personal strength and ability to generate support. Perhaps feeling valued by an adult, even though absent, had given these mothers confidence in overcoming subsequent hardships. Their ability to benefit from male support may have derived from healthier early relationships with paternal figures.

Ideally, one would like to establish predictive measures to identify mothers at risk. None of the specific measures used in this project seems to be sufficiently reliable for this purpose. For the present, it is more relevant to identify the modifying circumstances which might help support mothers of malnourished children.

The implications for intervention are not simple, especially in those areas where malnutrition is prevalent and resources limited. An important first step is to establish a firm, nonblaming approach. Because of the tendency of the MMC to displace blame and anxiety, it is necessary to explicitly identify the mothers' responsibilities for maintaining the health of their children, to help them understand exactly what procedures they must undertake to achieve this end, and to enumerate the consequences of failure to follow through. Continued support should be planned.

Professionals have tended to underestimate the contributions of existing community institutions. How these resources can be used and fostered requires further investigation. Many control mothers found them supportive. The strict expectations espoused by many churches and subcultures often supply the structure and security needed by some of the most desperate members of the community. Similarly, Mothercraft Centers and other programs provide food in settings that also offer families support and education.[26, 27] Limited intervention approaches such as food distribution programs without personal contact for mothers can be expected to have little impact. The goal of intervention should be not only to give attention to the nutritional needs of the children but also to provide the family with emotional supports that might prevent perpetuation of another generation of deprived parents.

REFERENCES

1.   BALLWEG, J. A.: "Family characteristics and nutrition problems of preschool children in Fond Parisien, Haiti," *J Trop Pediatr* 18:230, 1972.

2.   DESAI, P., STANDARD, K. L., MIALL, W. E.: "Socioeconomic and cultural influences on child growth in rural Jamaica." *J Biosoc Sci* 2:133, 1970.

3.   POLLITT, E.: "Ecology, malnutrition, and mental development." *Psychosom Med* 31:193, 1969.

4.   STOCH, M. B., SMYTHE, P. M.: "The effect of undernutrition during infancy on subsequent growth and intellectual development." *S Afr Med J* 41:1027, 1967.

5. BARBERO, G. J., SHAHEEN, E.: "Environmental failure to thrive: A clinical view." *J Pediatr* 71:639, 1967.

6. ELMER, E.: "Failure to thrive—The role of the mother." *Pediatrics* 25:717, 1960.

7. FABIAN, A. A., DONAHUE, J. F.: "Maternal depression: A challenging child guidance problem." *Am J Orthopsychiatry* 26:400, 1956.

8. KRIEGER, I.: "Food restriction as a form of child abuse in ten cases of psychosocial deprivational dwarfism." *Clin Pediatr* 13:217, 1974.

9. LEONARD, M. F., RHYMES, J. P., SOLNIT, A. J.: "Failure to thrive in infants—A family problem." *Am J Dis Child* 111:600, 1966.

10. PATTON, R. G., GARDNER, L. I.: "Influence of family environment on growth." *Pediatrics* 30:957, 1962.

11. SILVER, H., FINKELSTEIN, M.: "Deprivation dwarfism." *J Pediatr* 70:317, 1967.

12. TALBOT, N. B., SOBEL, E. H., BURKE, B. S., et al.: "Dwarfism in healthy children: Possible relationship to emotional, nutritional, endocrine disturbances." *N Engl J Med* 236:783, 1947.

13. FISCHHOFF, J., WHITTEN, C. F., PETTIT, M. G.: "A psychiatric study of 12 mothers of infants with growth failure secondary to maternal deprivation." *J Pediatr* 79:209, 1971.

14. KOEL, B. S.: "Failure to thrive and fatal injury as a continuum." *Am J Dis Child* 118:565, 1969.

15. MORLEY, D., BICKNELL, J., WOODLAND, M.: "Factors influencing the growth and nutritional states of infants and young children in a Nigerian village." *Trans R Soc Trop Med Hyg* 62:164, 1968.

16. GREWAL, T., GOPALDAS, T., GADRE, V. J.: "Etiology of malnutrition in rural Indian preschool schildren (Madhya Pradesh)." *J Trop Pediatr* 19:265, 1973.

17. HEPNER, R., MAIDEN, N. C.: "Growth rate, nutrient intake and "mothering" as determined in malnutrition of disadvantaged children." *Nutr Rev* 29:219, 1971.

18. WIDDOWSON, E. M.: "Mental contentment and physical growth." *Lancet* 260:1316, 1951.

19. GEBER, M., DEAN, R. F. A.: "Psychological factors in the etiology of kwashiorkor." *WHO Bull* 12:471, 1955.

20. MORA, J. O., AMESQUITA, A., CASTRO, L., et al.: "Nutrition, health and social factors related to intellectual performance." *World Rev Nutr Diet* 19:205, 1974.

21. CRAVIOTO, J., DELICARDIE, E.: "Environmental correlates of severe clinical malnutrition and language development in survivors from kwashiorkor or marasmus," in *Nutrition, the Nervous System, and Behavior: Proceedings of the Seminar on Malnutrition and Subsequent Mental Development*, publication 251. Washington, DC, Pan American Health Organization 1972, pp. 73-94.

22. LANDMAN, J. SHAW-LYON, V.: "Breast-feeding in decline in Kingston, Jamaica, 1973." *West Indian Med J* 25:43, 1976.

23. SCHLESINGER, B.: "Family patterns in Jamaica: Review and commentary." *J Marriage Family* 30:136, 1968.

24. CLARKE, E.: *My Mother Who Fathered Me.* London, George Allen and Unwin, 1966, pp. *i-xliv.*

25. POLANSKY, N. A., DeSAIX, C., SHARLIN, S. A.: *Child Neglect: Understanding and Reaching the Parent.* New York Child Welfare League of America Inc, 1973.

26.   BEGHIN, I., VITERI, E. F. E.: "Nutritional rehabilitation centers: An evaluation of their performance." *J Trop Pediatr* 19:404, 1973.

27.   JELLIFFE, D. B.: "Combatting malnutrition," in Jeliffe D. B. (ed): *Child Nutrition in Developing Countries: A Handbook for Fieldworkers*. Office on War on Hunger Agency for International Development, US Department of State, 1969, p. 115.

ACKNOWLEDGMENT

We thank Professor Colin Miller, director of the Department of Pediatrics, University of the West Indies, for his cooperation in making this study possible. We also thank Mrs. Una Tapper, director of the Social Service Department, and her staff for their assistance in devising interview questions and techniques, Hilda Williams for her patience and secretarial skills, and Shelley Gabor for typing the manuscript.

20

Social Aspects of the Battered Baby Syndrome*

Selwyn M. Smith,
Ruth Hanson and
Sheila Noble

In spite of increasing interest, the problem of the battered child remains controversial. Some see the problem as a response to stressful social circumstances and society's permissive attitude to violence[23], others view it as primarily a manifestation of parental maladjustment.[64]

A vast array of environmental stresses have been regarded as contributory. Some have commented on the frequency of out-of-wedlock pregnancies.[2, 58] A high incidence of divorce, separation and unstable marriages has also been reported.[30] Social isolation, unemployment and lack of immediate support from other relatives are thought to be important.[18, 72] Other factors thought to be predisposing include promiscuity,[72] larger than average family size,[23] poverty, insufficient education,[20] geographical mobility[21, 56] and inadequate housing.[2] Paulsen and Blake[44] have cautioned against viewing battering parents as a function of educational, occupational and social disadvantage and have pointed out that most people in deprived sections of the community do not batter their children. In fact some regard social, education, economic and demographic factors as irrelevant;[64] instead emphasis is laid on maladjustment resulting from harsh childhood experiences. Baby batterers are not, however, unique in this respect, for the same is said to apply to murderers[16, 35] and other criminals.[36]

---

* Selwyn N. Smith, et al., "Social Aspects of The Battered Baby Syndrome," *British Journal of Psychiatry*, Vol. 125, 1974, pp. 568-82. Copyright © the Royal College of Psychiatrists. Reproduced by permission.

Previous studies have not considered the issue that some factors may be typical of low social class populations and not particularly characteristic of baby batterers. Nor has the relative importance of the various social stresses been adequately assessed. This paper attempts to reconcile diverging opinions by examining a wide variety of social characteristics and the role of social class.

Subjects and Methods

Index cases. Over a two-year period the parents of 134 battered children under 5 years were studied in detail. Most of the children had been admitted to hospital. All their parents had either confessed to battering or could give no adequate explanation of their child's injuries.

Control group. The controls consisted of 53 children under 5 years of age who were emergency admissions and where there was no question of battering. Mother's age, area of residence, and consultants refering cases were also held constant.[61]

All parents were seen both at the hospital as soon as possible after the child's admission and at home, and were given standardized psychiatric, psychological and social interviews. In the social interview, questions initially covered child-rearing practices, and subsequently family constitution, occupation, ethnic and religious background, financial circumstances and mother's attitude to the pregnancy and the child, in this order. Accommodation, social life and marriage were covered next, and finally enquiry was made into satisfaction with life in general and into significant worries. Results have been presented comparing index and control samples without controlling for class. (The Appendix gives questions and response categories which are not self-evident.)

The problem of finding a control sample of equally low social class to match the index cases was insuperable. However, it was possible to weight the index sample results equating them for social class of the controls.[39] This made it possible to determine whether abnormalities in the index sample were as significant when class was held constant. Details of statistical work on the class control will be published elsewhere, but the results are summarized in the text of this paper.

Results

Classification

For 59 index cases (44 per cent) there was a confession of battering from a parent. In 43 (32 per cent) cases the index mother was identified as the perpetrator.

Marital status

Of the index mothers 36 (29 per cent) were unmarried, compared with 3 control mothers (6 per cent) $\chi^2 = 10 \cdot 19$; d.f. $= 1$; $p < \cdot 01$. In 44 index (35 per cent) compared with 2 control cases (4 per cent) the biological father was absent ($\chi^2 = 17 \cdot 17$; d.f. $= 1$; $p < \cdot 001$). Table I shows the situation at time of interview. More than half

TABLE I

Family situation of index mothers

(n = 124)

	No.	(%)
Single and living alone........	19	15
Single and cohabiting.........	4	3
Separated and living alone........	6	5
Separated and cohabiting.........	7	6
Separated and married..........	7	6
Total..............	43	35%

the index mothers (54 per cent) had given birth to their first child before the age of 20, compared with 10·6 per cent in the population at large.[49] Twelve index parents (15 per cent) compared with none of the controls ($\chi^2 = 6·62$; d.f. = 1; p < ·01) had known each other for less than six months before marriage. Among the index group 36 mothers (30 per cent) and 11 fathers (13 per cent) described their marriage or liaison as unsatisfactory. No control parent reported this. This was significant ($\chi^2 = 17·43$; d.f. = 1; p < ·001) for index mothers only. All these findings held after controlling for class.

Pre-marital conception and illegitimacy

Eighty-seven index mothers (71 per cent) compared with 17 controls (33 per cent) had conceived pre-maritally ($\chi^2 = 19·44$; d.f. = 1; p < ·001). Forty-five battered children (36 per cent) compared with 3 controls (6 per cent) were illegitimate ($\chi^2 = 15·48$; d.f. = 1; p < ·001). Table II shows the occurrence of pre-marital conception and illegitimacy broken down by age, and compares both with national norms.[49] In every age group index mothers have pre-marital pregnancies and illegitimate babies much more frequently. Social class adjustments did not affect these findings.

Attitude to pregnancy and abortion

Twenty-three index mothers (20 per cent) were displeased, compared with 3 controls (6 per cent) $(\chi)^2 = 4·32$; d.f. = 1; p < ·05). Fifteen index (13 per cent) compared with none of the controls claimed that their partners were displeased over the pregnancy ($\chi^2 = 6·14$; d.f. = 1; p < ·05). This finding was not significant when class was taken into account. Fifty-seven index (49 per cent) compared with 19 control mothers (37 per cent) had reservations about the pregnancy, but this was not a significant finding. Fifteen index mothers (12 per cent) and only one control mother

TABLE II

Pre-marital conception and illegitimacy rates of index and census mothers by age

Mother's age	Pre-marital pregnancy (%)		Illegitimacy (%)	
	Index	Census	Index	Census
15-19	94·1	69·7	33·3	25·8
20-24	48·2	20·6	25·9	7·7
25-29	52·9	7·1	50·0	4·6
30-34	25·0	6·4	50·0	5·5

(2 per cent) had considered an abortion during the relevant pregnancy, but this difference was not significant (Table III).

Contraception

Forty-two index mothers (35 per cent) were using contraceptives, but those who did not expressed a negative attitude significantly more often than did the control mothers towards the future taking of contraceptives (Table III). This remained true after adjustments for social class.

Family size

The mean number of children in the index families was 2·3 and for controls 2·0 ($\chi^2 = 6·62$; d.f. = 1; p < ·01). Forty-three battered babies (32 per cent) were first-born or only children in the family, and 91 (68 per cent) were second or subsequent born children. When family size is taken into account, battered babies were observed to be randomly distributed among the different birth orders (Table IV). In families of two children the observed proportion of second born was higher than expected ($\chi^2 = 5·76$; d.f. = 1; p < ·05). For the controls it was also the younger child who was admitted to hospital.

Parents' family size of origin

The parents' mean family size of origin was 5·6 for index mothers, 4·3 for controls, 4·7 for index fathers and 5·3 for controls. (Statistically not significant, as the apparently larger differences are due to a few very large families).

Family disharmony

Fifteen index mothers (13 per cent) had low opinions of their partners, as compared with none of the controls ($\chi^2 = 5·76$; d.f. = 1; p < ·05). Seventeen (15 per

TABLE III

Use of and attitude towards contraception and abortion among index and control mothers

	Index mothers		Control mothers		Significance (d.f. = 1)	
	No.	(%)	No.	(%)	χ^2	p
Using contraceptives...........	42/121	(35)	13/51	(26)	1·01	N.S.
Not using contraceptives and negative attitude............	43/ 79	(54)	8/38	(21)	10·32	<·01
Abortion considered...........	15/121	(12)	1/51	(2)	3·48	N.S.

TABLE IV

Position in family of index and control children

		Index child								Control child							
		1	2	3	4	5	6	7	8	1	2	3	4	5	6	7	8
	1	43								28							
	2	13	37							0	11						
	3	1	6	10						0	1	6					
Family	4	0	1	6	3					0	0	1	3				
Size	5	0	3	3	2	4				0	0	0	0	0			
	6	0	0	0	0	0	2			0	0	0	0	0	0		
	7	0	0	0	0	0	0	0		0	0	0	0	0	0	1	
	8	0	0	0	0	0	0	0	0	0	0	0	0	0	0	0	1
Totals		57	47	19	5	4	2	0	0	28	12	7	3	1	0	0	1

cent) admitted that their partners rejected the child, as compared with none of the controls ($\chi^2 = 5·87$; d.f. = 1; p < ·01). Thirty-one index (27 per cent) as compared with 3 control mothers (6 per cent) reported that they did not participate in child rearing discussions ($\chi^2 = 19·39$; d.f. = 1; p < ·01). Rejection and non-participation remained significant after class control. Forty-seven (41 per cent) reported disagreement over child rearing (χ^2 19·39; d.f. = 1; p< ·001) but this particular contrast disappeared when social class was held constant.

On direct questioning about strained relationships within the family a smaller proportion of index, 79 (72 per cent), than control parents 44 (92 per cent), admitted marriage problems ($\chi^2 = 6·53$; d.f. = 1; p < ·05). Twenty-one index (18 per cent) and one control mother (2 per cent) reported that it was they who took the important family decisions ($\chi^2 = 6·81$; d.f. = 1; p < ·01), and this held after adjustments for social class. Twenty-three index mothers (22 per cent), as compared with 5 controls (10 per cent), reported quarrels not long before their child's admission to hospital (difference not significant).

TABLE V

Characteristics of West Indian group. Index cases only

	West Indian		White		Significance (d.f. = 1)	
	No.	(%)	No.	(%)	χ^2	p
Biological father absent..........	17/19	(90)	26/94	(28)	23·06	<·001
Rare contact with parents.........	13/19	(68)	35/93	(38)	4·91	<·05
Frequent use of physical punishment...................	14/19	(74)	42/88	(48)	3·24	N.S.

Ethnic characteristics

One hundred and two index cases (76 per cent) were White, 19 were West Indian (14 per cent) and 13 were Asian (10 per cent).

Table V shows that three characteristics differentiated the West Indians from the White index sample. These were absence of biological father, frequent use of physical punishment and rare contact with parents. Biological fathers were absent in only two Asian homes (17 per cent). When compared with the White sample the difference was not significant. Nine of the Asians (90 per cent) had rare contact with their parents, and when compared with the White sample this was a significant difference ($\chi^2 = 8·09$; d.f. = 1; p < ·01).

Religion

Among the index mothers 71 were Church of England (57 per cent), 23 were Roman Catholic (18 per cent), 15 Nonconformist (12 per cent), 11 (9 per cent) belonged to various Asian religions (2 Sikhs, 2 Hindus, 4 Moslems, and 3 unidentified). There were no Jewish mothers, and 5 (4 per cent) declared that they had no religion. Among the index fathers 44 were Church of England (51 per cent), 20 were Roman Catholic (23 per cent), 2 Nonconformist (2 per cent), 13 belonged to Asian religions (3 Sikhs, 2 Hindus, 5 Moslem, and 3 unidentified). There were no Jewish fathers, and 7 (8 per cent) declared that they had no religion.

Affiliation was nominal for 71 index mothers (58 per cent) and 46 index fathers (61 per cent).

Among the index group 40 mothers (33 per cent) and 19 fathers (26 per cent) reported a personal faith. For the controls the proportions were 21 mothers (40 per cent) and 5 fathers (25 per cent) but when compared with the index group these were not significantly different. Forty-seven (39 per cent) index mothers and 39 (54 per cent) index fathers reported that at least one of their parents had a personal faith. For the controls the proportions were 15 (29 per cent) mothers and 6 (30 per cent) fathers but when compared with the index group these also were not significantly different.

TABLE VI

Types of accommodation occupied by index and control families

	House		Maisonette or flat in small block		Flat in tall block		Sharing house		Other*		Total
	No.	(%)	No.	(%)	No.	(%)	No.	(%)	No.	(%)	
Index.........	46	(37)	24	(19)	8	(6)	18	(14)	29	(23)	125
Control.......	24	(46)	9	(17)	6	(12)	7	(14)	6	(12)	52

* Other includes room in multi-occupied house, lodgings or 'halfway house'.

Accommodation

The various types of accommodation occupied by index and control families are shown in Table VI. Most index families were living in houses, maisonettes, or flats in small blocks. Only 8 index (6 per cent) and 6 control families (12 per cent) were living in tower block flats. Forty-three index (37 per cent), compared with 13 (25 per cent) of the control homes, were rated as being dilapidated (difference not significant). However, 54 index (43 per cent) compared with 8 controls (15 per cent) had homes lacking in one or more essential amenities ($\chi^2 = 11 \cdot 29$; d.f. = 1; p < $\cdot 001$), and class control did not affect this result. Twenty-five index (28 per cent) compared with 3 control homes (6 per cent) were rated as dirty and untidy ($\chi^2 = 8 \cdot 22$; d.f. = 1; p < $\cdot 01$). Seventy-three index (60 per cent), compared with 16 control parents (31 per cent), had moved house on more than two occasions in the three year period prior to interview ($\chi^2 = 70$; d.f. = 1; p < $\cdot 01$). One hundred and six index (87 per cent), compared with 32 control children (63 per cent), shared a bedroom with another member of the family ($\chi^2 = 11 \cdot 53$; d.f. = 1; p < $\cdot 01$). Eighty-seven index (71 per cent) compared with 22 control homes (43 per cent) had cramped sleeping accommodation ($\chi^2 = 11 \cdot 07$; d.f. = 1; p < $\cdot 001$). All these findings, except child's possession of his own room, became insignificant when class was held constant.

Social isolation

A sizeable proportion of index mothers reported having infrequent or no contact with their parents, relatives, neighbours or friends (Table VII). Fifty-three (54 per cent) as compared with 16 control mothers (31 per cent) described themselves as lonely ($\chi^2 = 6 \cdot 80$; d.f. = 1; p < $\cdot 01$). Thirty-nine index (32 per cent) compared with 5 (10 per cent) control mothers, had no social activities ($\chi^2 = 8 \cdot 65$; d.f. = 1; p < $\cdot 01$). Fifty-seven index (49 per cent), compared with 13 controls (26 per cent), reported that they had no opportunities of having a break from the child ($\chi^2 = 7 \cdot 19$; d.f. = 1; p < $\cdot 01$). When the social class distribution of the two samples was held constant, loneliness and contact with neighbours and friends became insignificant, but on other measures the contrast remained. Boredom was reported by slightly though not significantly more control than index mothers, 29 (57 per cent) as against 51 (44 per cent).

TABLE VII

Indices of social isolation among index and control mothers

	Index		Control		Significance (d.f. = 1)	
	No.	(%)	No.	(%)	χ^2	p
Rare contact with parents......57/122		(47)	12/52	(23)	7·56	<·01
Rare contact with relatives......60/122		(49)	9/52	(17)	14·17	<·001
Rare contact with neighbours...62/121		(51)	17/52	(33)	4·32	<·05
Rare contact with friends.......68/122		(56)	15/52	(29)	9·52	<·01

Only 3 index (4 per cent) and 2 control fathers (10 per cent) reported having no social activities. This contrasts sharply with the marked difference between index and control mothers ($x^2 = 8·19$; d.f. = 1; p < ·01). The difference between index mothers and index fathers is also highly significant ($\chi^2 = 18·22$; d.f. = 1; p < ·001) in this same respect.

Of those index mothers who rarely saw their parents, 25 (81 per cent) said they had an unhappy childhood, as compared with 15 (52 per cent) of those who saw their parents frequently ($\chi^2 = 4·42$; d.f. = 1; p < ·05).

Income

The average weekly income of index fathers was £21.50 with a range of £8-40 and a median bracket of £21 to £25. For the controls the mean was £31. Forty-nine index fathers (71 per cent) compared with 9 controls (41 per cent) earned less than £25 per week ($\chi^2 = 5·29$; d.f. = 1; p < ·05). Twenty-two index fathers (31 per cent) regarded their income as 'inadequate', but the difference was not significant when compared with 7 controls (35 per cent).

Index fathers were mainly manual workers, whereas control fathers were normally distributed among the different occupational levels.[61] In 1972 the average weekly earnings for manual workers (aged 21-65) for Great Britain was £30.90 and for all workers it was £37.[62] Though both index and control fathers earned less than the national average, this is a reflection of their lower age group (17-46 years). However, when their mean earnings are related to their respective national class populations, the disparity is only £3.40 greater for control than for index fathers. Furthermore, when social class is held constant there is no longer a significant contrast between the two groups.

Mothers' assessment of allowance and food expenditure

Forty-four index (26 per cent), compared with 9 control mothers (18 per cent), regarded their housekeeping allowance as inadequate ($\chi^2 = 5·05$; d.f. = 1; p < ·05). Sixty index (54 per cent) spent less than £2 per head on food per week, compared with 14 control mothers (28 per cent). This difference was significant ($\chi^2 = 8 \cdot 92$; d.f. = 1; p < $\cdot 01$), but not after social class had been taken into account.

Unemployment and stability of employment

Fifteen of the index fathers (14 per cent) were unemployed at the time of the battering incident. Seven of the control fathers (13 per cent) were unemployed (difference was not significant). Slightly more, though not significantly more, index than control fathers had changed their jobs on more than five occasions, 55 (64 per cent) as against 10 (42 per cent).

Dissatisfaction

Thirty-two index (26 per cent), compared with 2 control mothers (4 per cent), reported that they were generally dissatisfied with their total situation ($\chi^2 = 10 \cdot 24$; d.f. = 1; p < $\cdot 01$), and this result held with social class control. Thirteen (20 per cent) index compared with none of the control fathers described themselves as being generally dissatisfied.

Worries

Ninety-three index (74 per cent), compared with 25 control mothers (48 per cent), reported that they had two or more significant worries ($\chi^2 = 7 \cdot 79$; d.f. = 1; p. < $\cdot 01$). The most frequent worries described were health of others 70 (56 per cent), money 70 (56 per cent), housing 62 (49 per cent), domestic friction 34 (27 per cent), unemployment 33 (26 per cent), own health 31 (25 per cent) and marital status 20 (25 per cent). The rank order was the same for the controls, but the proportions having money and housing problems were lower. Domestic friction, marital status and unemployment were seldom mentioned by the control mothers.

Fifty index (70 per cent) and 8 controls (40 per cent) reported two or more significant worries ($\chi^2 = 5 \cdot 9$; d.f. = 1; p < $\cdot 05$). Among the index fathers the worries described were approximately in the same rank order as the index mothers.

The proportion of index parents having worries was no higher than for the control sample when equated for social class.

Characteristics of identified perpetrators

Table VIII compares the percentages of those cases where a perpetrator was identified with the percentages for the total sample on each variable found to be significant for the index sample. The proportions on almost every variable tended to be a little higher than those reported for the total sample. Some differences between cases with an identified perpetrator and the remainder were significant. These are indicated on the Table.

TABLE VIII

Characteristics of identified perpetrators compared with total sample

Data from index mothers	Total sample		Identified perpetrators		χ^{2}*	p*
	N	%	N	%		
Marital status................	36/124	29	18/55	33	N.S.	
Absent father.................	44/125	35	27/55	49	7·26	<·01
Age at 1st child..............	(mean = 19·8 years for 131 cases)		(mean = 20·0 for 58 cases)		N.S.	
6 mths. acq. before marriage...................	12/ 81	15	6/36	17	N.S.	
Unsatisfactory marriage.........	36/121	30	26/53	49	15·21	<·001
Pre-marital conception.........	87/123	71	44/55	80	3·36	= ·07
Illegitimacy	45/125	36	24/55	44	N.S.	
Reservations about pregnancy...................	57/117	49	31/55	56	N.S.	
Partner had reservations.........	44/112	39	23/54	43	N.S.	
Abortion considered...........	15/121	12	7/54	13	N.S.	
Low opinion of partner........	15/118	13	13/54	21	9·77	<·01
Partner rejects child...........	17/117	15	12/54	22	3·70	≃05
Lack of agreement over child rearing.................	47/115	41	32/52	62	15·25	<·001
Strained relationships...........	79/110	72	43/54	80	N.S.	
Mother head of house..........	21/117	15	16/54	30	7·88	<·01
Non-white case...............	32/134	24	9/55	30	N.S.	
Lack of amenities.............	54/125	43	23/55	42	N.S.	
House dirty and untidy.........	25/ 90	28	12/34	35	N.S.	
Two plus moves in 3 years.......	(mean = 2·0 for 122 cases)		(mean = 2·3 for 55 cases)		(t = 2·66)	<·01
Cramped sleeping.............	87/122	71	35/55	64	N.S.	
Rare contact with parents.......	57/122	47	27/55	49	N.S.	
Rare contact with relatives......	60/122	49	27/55	49	N.S.	
Rare contact with neighbours....	62/121	51	31/54	57	N.S.	
Rare contact with friends.....................	68/122	56	33/55	60	N.S.	
Loneliness	63/117	54	15/55	27	13·49	<·001
Father's income...............	(mean = £21.5 for 69 cases)		(mean = £21.9 for 26 cases)		N.S.	
Housekeeping allowance inadequate.................	44/121	36	29/55	53	10·41	<·01
Dissatisfaction with situation...................	32/122	26	26/55	47	20·98	<·001
Father dissatisfied with his situation†................	13/ 64	20	8/24	33	N.S.	
Worries......................	109/123	87	53/55	96	4·61	<·05
Father has worries†...........	61/ 70	87	23/24	96	N.S.	

* These values are for the comparison between cases for whom a parent was identified as a perpetrator and those without such identification.
† Rating by father, not mother.

Discussion

All these findings suggest that lack of family cohesiveness is an important factor underlying baby battering. In over one third of cases the biological father was absent from the home, and in half the mothers were living with some other man. These findings closely agree with those of several other authors[19, 23, 58] and are at variance with the view that battering parents have stable personal relationships.[64]

Half the mothers in the index sample had married before the age of 20 years, and three-quarters had conceived pre-maritally. Among the population at large such a combination is particularly likely to be associated with marital breakdown.[25, 53] Though fewer index than control parents directly admitted marriage problems, a significant proportion reported disharmony in child-rearing and dissatisfaction with the partner's handling of the child. These characteristics may be taken as indices of disagreement between husband and wife over their respective roles; such indices are also predictors of divorce.[25] Short acquaintance before marriage is another predictor of divorce also found in our sample. Half the mothers were neurotic and two-thirds of the fathers had a personality disorder.[61] Neurotic and personality disorders are factors also associated with marital breakdown.[4, 33] In contrast, in early marriages the kinship support has been shown to be an important contributory force in stabilizing the marriage.[15] However, the parents in our sample had little contact with their own parents and other relatives. Considering, therefore, that a significant proportion suffered all these marital adversities and that one-third of battered babies were already living with one natural parent only, it may be predicted that a substantial number will eventually grow up in broken homes.

Broken homes, unhappy homes and one-parent families are associated with delinquency,[22, 24] deviant behaviour,[52] and social and educational deprivation[10] respectively. Our sample has a very large share of such predictors of maldevelopment in the child. Fatal battering has been shown to occur where young, unstable, deserted and unhappy women associate with young, psychopathic and criminal men.[57] Such parents were over-represented in our sample,[61] suggesting that battered children are at risk not only of social maldevelopment but also of fatal injury.

A high proportion of index mothers conceived premaritally, and more than one third of battered children were illegitimate. This finding is in close agreement with that of other investigations both in the United States[1, 37, 58] and in the United Kingdom.[21, 34] Our findings are also particularly striking in the light of those studies[10, 68] which showed that premarital pregnancy and illegitimacy are not directly related to social class. This was also borne out by our observation that equating index and control samples for class did not reduce the contrast between them. Among the population at large the highest proportion of premaritally conceived and illegitimate births is found between 15-19 years and then decreases with maternal age.[10, 49] Our mothers, however, differed in this respect, the highest proportions of such births occurring in those between 25-34 years. Furthermore, in all age groups studied our mothers have strikingly more premarital pregnancies and illegitimate births than occur in the general population.[49] The highest proportion of all were aged 20-24 years,[61] the rate of occurrence of pre-marital pregnancy and illegitimacy among them being two and three times respectively higher than the general population rates. Our findings, therefore, strongly suggest that pre-marital conception and illegitimacy are important precursors of baby battering. It is disconcerting also to observe that illegitimacy was present in 60 per cent of Weston's fatal battered baby cases,[70] and that the inconvenience of an unwanted illegitimate child was the most common motive responsible for child murder.[50]

Though displeasure at pregnancy was reported by one fifth of index mothers, they were not atypical of their social class in this respect. A smaller but nevertheless significant proportion described their partners as currently rejecting of the child, and this was not class linked. Several authors[18, 34, 40, 66] have postulated an association between unwanted conception and baby battering but there have been no previous controlled investigations of this suggestion. Attempts to do so may, therefore, appear to document the obvious. Nevertheless, research into feelings of unwantedness is fraught with difficulties.[46] It may be argued that parents who have confessed to battering a child will rationalize their behaviour by recalling that conception was unwanted. In the index sample those parents who confessed to battering reported as much displeasure at the pregnancy as those parents who denied it.

A degree of ambivalence about pregnancy is common in the population at large[12] and was also observed in our control sample. Harsh childhood experiences have been assumed to be responsible for lack of maternal feelings among baby batterers.[64] Our findings suggest that while failure to adjust to the parental role also occurs among the population at large[29] it happens more frequently among baby batterers and can be more simply understood in the context of pre-marital conception, illegitimacy and marital disharmony rather than by linking it directly to harsh childhood experiences.

A high proportion of out-of-wedlock pregnancies are unwanted.[28, 42, 46] Kempe and Helfer[32] have asserted that the most effective way to prevent battering of children is to prevent unwanted births. Several authors[5, 6, 23] have suggested that pre-natal training for motherhood, ready availability of contraceptives, abortion on demand and encouragement of sterilization after the birth of the third child can be important factors in the prevention of child abuse. However, there have been no controlled studies demonstrating that early and complete sex education, including contraceptive information, has led to any decline in unwanted conceptions.[27] Indeed, in Sweden the illegitimacy rates actually increased following the introduction of such a programme. The evidence also suggests that knowledge about the availability of contraceptives also offers no ready solution,[27] for in fact the recent increases in illegitimacy rates in England, the United States and Jamaica have occurred despite such increasing knowledge and availability.

The proportion of illegitimate births rose sharply over the 1950's and 1960's,[69] and the younger the mother's age group the greater the rise in proportion.[51] Child abuse is associated with both illegitimacy and prematurity of parenthood,[61] and these findings cannot be accounted for by social class. Although it cannot be proved that child abuse has increased over the last two decades, its clear association with both illegitimacy and teen-age parenthood suggest that a real increase in child abuse may have occurred. The simplest explanation of the rise in illegitimacy rates, especially among teen-agers, is that society's changing attitude had encouraged extra-marital sexual activity. An effective reversal, therefore, of those attitudes to sex and family which are responsible for increasing rates of illegitimacy might possibly lead to a decline in the numbers of battered babies.

Although society may facilitate or impede the availability of abortion of unwanted conceptions, the evidence suggests[13, 28] that abortion will only produce a reduction in unwanted births if the motivation for limiting family size already exists. The same argument holds for sterilization.[46] Our findings that a significant proportion of battering parents expressed a negative attitude towards contraception, and that only 12 per cent of mothers might have even considered an abortion during the study child pregnancy, suggest that the preventative methods outlined by Gil[23] and Caffey,[5] admirable though some of them may be, will have very little impact in preventing baby battering. Indeed, considering that quite as many of the index as of the control parents were in fact using some form of contraceptive, it is perhaps somewhat unrealistic to expect battering parents to become enthusiastic about birth control. Our pessimistic view that such parents are ineffective in and distrustful of birth control is shared by Oliver and Taylor[41] and is also supported by our own findings that the battering sample, unlike the controls, were well on the way to perpetuating the large size of their family of origin.

Among our sample, one third of the battered babies were first-born and only children, and two thirds were second and subsequent born children. Lukianowicz[34] and others[1, 23] have suggested that it is usually the only or youngest child in a family who is battered. Our index sample bears out this trend. This, however, may be reconciled with the general tendency for infants to be admitted to hospital more frequently than older children.[11] Indeed, when birth order is properly related to family size the suggestion that a child's particular ordinal position carries more risk of battering does not hold. Furthermore the finding, reported elsewhere,[61] that 19 per cent of the child's siblings had also been battered are at variance with Zalba's assertion[73] and Merrill's result[37] that only one particular child in a family is abused.

Several American authors[9, 54, 72] have regarded sub-standard living accommodation as a particularly important stress that contributes to baby battering. Cherry and Kuby[9] vividly describe their apartments 'as drab, dark and frequently foul-smelling', and most of Young's[72] families were living in cold vermin-infested and overcrowded rooms that lacked modern conveniences. In the United Kingdom several authors[21, 57, 59] have also mentioned that accommodation problems are important stress factors operating within these families. In our sample dilapidation was not a significant feature. Dirty and untidy homes and cramped sleeping accommodation were more common than in the control group, but when adjustments were made for social class the contrast was no longer significant. Lack of one or more essential amenities and possession by a child of its own room were, however, still significant findings when the comparison was class-comparable. Nevertheless, our families are not the most handicapped even in this respect, for in a sample of 'inadequate' families[45] who had not battered their children 96 per cent lacked one or more basic amenities; a considerably higher proportion than in our sample. Our results should therefore caution against the optimistic belief,[23] that re-housing will reduce the prevalence of baby battering, since, on the whole, families in our sample were no worse off than others of low social class. This argument is also supported by the observation[21, 59] that re-housing, although providing temporary relief from external pressures, may actually precipitate battering incidents. Our findings suggest, therefore, that personality disorders frequently observed among such parents[57, 61] are more important than environmental factors in contributing to child abuse.

Our findings support those of others who have suggested that baby battering is not related to any particular religious affiliation.[3, 34] No support, however, was found for Steele's statement[64] that proportionately more baby batterers belong to strong, rigid, authoritarian and 'fundamentalist' types of religions. Indeed most of our parents were of nominal religion only. However, although both they and a similar proportion of control parents lacked a personal faith it was nevertheless interesting to observe that proportionately fewer battering parents retained the personal faith of their parents. In the context of hypotheses about a battering parent's own deprived childhood experiences, lack of a persisting religious influence may be a factor worthy of further exploration.

One fifth of the battered children were non-White, compared with 15 per cent non-White children aged 5 years and under in the Birmingham population at large.[8] Owing to communication difficulties our sample did not include all Asian battered babies, and our numbers on this are probably an underestimate. Nevertheless, Schloesser[56] and Kempe[31] have asserted that baby battering is not related to ethnic or cultural factors, in contrast to several other American studies[17, 58] which have demonstrated that proportionately more battered children are coloured. However, information on the ethnic background of battered children in the United Kingdom has been limited, and for this reason a comparison with the United States may not be valid. Skinner and Castle[59] observed that 6.5 per cent of their sample were West Indian and Asian, while Scott[57] in a study of fatal battered baby cases observed that 10 per cent of the fathers were coloured and a high proportion were Irish, but neither author reported control figures. The slight over-representation of non-White battered children in our sample may reflect a higher morbidity of non-White groups. It may also be a reflection of the particular characteristics of the ethnic group concerned.[48] We found no support for Gil's suggestion[23] that the over-representation of non-White children indicates discriminating attitudes and practices on the part of the referring agency. We also found no support for suggestions that Asians and West Indians are younger, have more children and live in poorer conditions than parents of White battered babies.

Battering among West Indians may be a reflection of the higher incidence of broken homes (absence of natural father) and excessive use of physical punishment. Although few Asians had broken homes they more frequently lacked the support of contact with their parents. Thus lack of support was common to both Asian and West Indian groups.

Ebbin[17] has suggested that the type of injury inflicted is not related to ethnic factors. Our findings concur with this statement. Of our battering group 4 mothers were psychotic, 2 being paranoid schizophrenics. Both were West Indians who inflicted bizarre injuries. Although the preference for male children in Moslem cultures is strong,[63] we did not find more Moslem girls than boys in our sample.

Financial problems have been regarded as an important precipitant of baby battering.[2, 23] However, when compared with samples of similar age and social class the income and expenditure on food of the battering group was not low. Unemployment was a characteristic of index fathers, but was no less frequent in the controls and does not therefore have the significance attributed to it by others.[59] It is thus erroneous to conclude that the provision of economic security to battering families by such mechanisms as 'mother's wages', 'children's allowances', 'negative income tax',[23] and of 'homemaker services',[32] will markedly reduce the prevalence of baby battering. In this and other related fields[67] considerable emphasis has been placed upon the relief of material hardships to the exclusion of less easily eradicated handicaps. The Children and Young Persons Act[7] makes provision for 'giving assistance in kind or in exceptional circumstances in cash' to deserving families. However, even when aid is granted from public assistance agencies it does not prevent baby battering, for in Gil's series[23] nearly two-thirds of the parents had received financial assistance during or prior to the year of the battering incident. It is our contention, therefore, that constitutional personality differences are more fundamental than financial factors in the caustion of baby battering.

Though loneliness was reported by many index mothers, it was also reported by many controls, especially in the low social classes. More than half the index mothers lacked social contacts with neighbours and friends. Among the population at large this is also a feature that characterizes working class families, who, in contrast to middle class families, compensate for this deficiency by maintaining contact with their parents and other relatives.[71] However, a significant proportion of our sample did not compensate in this respect and were devoid of all forms of social contact. Although social isolation may be dependent upon geographical mobility,[55] a more significant association occurred in our sample between lack of social contact with parents and an unhappy childhood, and this may also be a reflection of the poor relationship such mothers had with their own parents. Unlike other socially isolated populations,[55] our index parents did not avail themselves of social support at crises times even though two-thirds had previous contact with social agencies. Social isolation and a reluctance to avail themselves of social support has also been observed in other battered baby studies.[14, 40, 72] Nurse[40] has asserted that because battering parents do not turn to society for help society must seek out and help battering parents. This would seem to be true, but it is unrealistic to expect such parents to take the initiative and avail themselves of 24-hour life-line services[32] operating on the lines of the Samaritans.[65]

Working class populations have fewer social activities.[26, 38, 71] The proportion of our mothers who were devoid of social activity is even higher than expected for their social class, and this concurs with the findings of those authors[14, 40] who have maintained that community contacts of battering parents are minimal. However, the contrast between mothers and their spouses in this respect is striking, for only 3 fathers did not manage to occupy their leisure time. Considering that nearly half the mothers lacked baby-sitting arrangements and that this result was not affected by controlling for class, it could be argued that this was the prime reason for their failure to occupy themselves socially in the community. It is more probable, however, that this failure to participate in recreational activities is a reflection of the incompatability between parents themselves. This in itself may be partially explained by the high frequency of psychopathy in the fathers and neuroticism and subnormality in the mothers.[61] In the course of our research we have found a semantic differential technique[43] to be a useful means of communicating with battering parents. Psychotherapy which concentrates on the parents' perception of themselves in relation to others, taking into account their low intelligence, should be explored further as a method of relieving the mother's loneliness and possibly preventing baby battering.

Our results also showed that when only those cases for whom a perpetrator had been identified were considered, all the characteristics described above, with the exception of loneliness, applied to at least the same proportion. Marital disharmony emerged as particularly characteristic of the known perpetrators and this finding merits further explorations.

Conclusion

Our results show that when a variety of social and economic factors are carefully examined baby batterers are observed to be far less handicapped than previous studies have indicated. Furthermore, when placed alongside the high incidence of personality disorders, anomalies of status and youthfulness of the parents, socio-economic support to such families will only be meaningful if included in a programme of adaptation to such handicaps.

The similarities between baby battering and other forms of deviant behaviour are striking. Like delinquency and crime in general, baby battering occurs alongside a constellation of other social inadequacies or failure of adaptation rather than in isolation. Such consideration might save some disappointment and wasted effort. Innumerable studies of deviant behaviour have been remarkably unrewarding in establishing either causes or treatment. Battering parents must first be properly classified and the natural history of the condition closely observed before we can be confident about treatment measures other than emergency action. Indeed, no study has convincingly shown that any treatment of battering parents is effective.

We have previously cautioned against supporting the parents to the detriment of the safety of the child.[60] In the light of our findings we would agree with Polansky's[47] view that this is 'an area in which social, medical and legal action must be authoritative, intrusive and insistent'. As with crime and delinquency, treatment is only likely to be a supporting exercise. True prevention must lie in the effective education of the next generation and in changes in child care legislation.

Summary

A controlled investigation of 214 parents of battered babies shows that pre-marital pregnancy and illegitimacy, absence of the child's father, marital disharmony and rejecting attitude towards the child are precursors of baby battering. Battered babies are likely to be reared in broken homes and are at risk of social maldevelopment and death. Ineffectiveness and distrust of contraception by these parents suggests that various birth control measures are unlikely to be effective in reducing the prevalence of battered babies.

Battering parents compare reasonably with other low social class groups, in their standards of income, and weekly food expenditure. Housing is in some respects worse. Improvement in material benefits without regard to the parents' personality deficiencies is therefore unlikely to affect the increase in the number of battered babies. Social isolation is a characteristic of these parents and reflects their unhappy childhood. Lack of kinship support was particularly important among the non-White parents. Treatment can be supportive only, and true prevention must lie in effective education of the next generation and in possible changes in the law relating to child care.

ACKNOWLEDGEMENTS

We are grateful to Mrs. Carol Smith, Mrs. Irene Brown and the staff of the Hospital Statistics Department, who helped with the statistical analysis. Professor W. H. Trethowan provided valuable criticism throughout the course of the study. The study was supported by a grant from the Barrow and Geraldine Cadbury Trust.

REFERENCES

1. BENNIE, E. H. & SCLARE, A. B. (1969) "The battered child syndrome." *American Journal of Psychiatry*, 125, 975-9.

2. BIRRELL, R. G. & BIRRELL, J. H. W. (1968) " The maltreatment syndrome in children: a hospital survey." *Medical Journal of Australia, ii*, 1023-9.

3. BOARDMAN, H. E. (1962) "A project to rescue children from inflicted injuries." *Social Work*, 7, 43-51.

4. BURGESS, E. W. & WALLIN, P. (1953) *Engagement and Marriage*. New York: Lippincott.

5. CAFFEY, J. (1972) "The parent-infant traumatic stress syndrome." *American Journal of Roentgenology, Radium Therapy and Nuclear Medicine*, 114, 218-29.

6. CALEF, V. (1972) "The hostility of parents to children: some notes on infertility, child abuse and abortion." *International Journal of Psychoanalytic Psychotherapy*, 1, 79-96.

7. *Children and Young Persons Act 1963*. Part I, Section 1. London: H.M.S.O.

8. CITY OF BIRMINGHAM (1972) *Abstracts of Statistics* (1970-71). City of Birmingham: Central Statistics Office.

9. CHERRY, B. J. & KUBY, A. M. (1971) "Obstacles to the delivery of medical care to children of neglecting parents." *American Journal of Public Health*, 61, 568-73.

10. CRELLIN, E., PRINGLE, M. L., KELLMER & WEST, P. (1971) *Born Illegitimate: Social and Educational Implications*. National Foundation for Educational Research in England and Wales.

11. CROSS, K. W. (1973) Personal communication.

12. COLMAN, A. D. & COLMAN, L. L. (1971) *Pregnancy: The Psychological Experience*. New York: Herder and Herder.

13. DAVIS, K. (1973) "The theory of change and response in modern demographic history." *Population Index*, 29, 345-66.

14. DAVOREN, E. (1968) "The role of the social worker." In *The Battered Child* (eds. R. E. Helfer and C. H. Kempe), pp. 153-68. Chicago: Chicago University Press.

15. DE LISSOVOY, V. (1973) "High-school marriages: a longitudinal study." *Journal of Marriage and the Family*, 35, 245-55.

16. DUNCAN, G. M., FRAZIER, S. H., LITIN, E. M., JOHNSON, A. M. & BARRON, A. J. (1958) "Etiological factors in first degree murder." *Journal of the American Medical Association*, 168, 1755-8.

17. EBBIN, A. J., GOLLUB, M. H., STEIN, A. M. and WILSON, M. G. (1969) "Battered child syndrome at the Los Angeles County General Hospital." *American Journal of Diseases of Children*, 118, 660-667.

18. ELMER, E. (1967) *Children in Jeopardy: A Study of Abused Minors and their Families*. Pittsburgh: Pittsburgh University Press.

19. FONTANA, V. J. (1971) *The Maltreated Child: The Maltreatment Syndrome in Children*. Springfield, Illinois: Charles C. Thomas.

20. GALDSTON, R. (1965) "Observations on children who have been physically abused and their parents." *American Journal of Psychiatry*, 122, 440-443.

21. GIBBENS, T. C. N. & WALKER, A. (1956) *Cruel Parents*. London: Institute for the Study and Treatment of Delinquency.

22.   GIBSON, H. B. (1969) "Early delinquency in relation to broken homes." *Journal of Child Psychology and Psychiatry*, 10, 195-204.

23.   GIL, D. G. (1970) *Violence against Children: Physical Child Abuse in the United States*. Cambridge, Massachusetts: Harvard University Press.

24.   GLUECK, S. & GLUECK, E. (1962) *Delinquents and Non-Delinquents in Perspective*. Cambridge, Massachusetts: Harvard University Press.

25.   GOODE, W. J. (1966) "A sociological perspective on marital dissolution." In *Sociology of the Family* (ed. M. Anderson), pp. 301-320. Harmondsworth, Middlesex: Penguin Books.

26.   GORER, G. (1955) *Exploring English Character*. London: The Cresset Press.

27.   HARTLEY, S. F. (1971) "Contributions of illegitimate and pre-maritally conceived births to total fertility." *Social Biology*. 18, 178-87.

28.   HOROBIN, G. (Editor) (1973) *Experience with Abortion: A Case Study of North East Scotland*. Cambridge University Press.

29.   JENKINS, R. L. (1954) "The significance of maternal rejection of pregnancy for future development of the child." In *Therapeutic Abortion* (ed. H. Rosen), pp. 269-75. New York: Julian.

30.   KEMPE, C. H., SILVERMAN, F. N., STEELE, B. F., DROEGEMUELLER, N. & SILVER, H. K. (1962) "The battered child syndrome." *Journal of the American Medical Association*, 181, 17-24.

31.   ____ (1969) "The battered child and the hospital." *Hospital Practice*, 4, 44-57.

32.   ____ & HELFER, R. E. (1972) In *Helping the Battered Child and His Family* (eds. C. H. Kempe & R. E. Helfer). Oxford: Lippincott.

33.   KREITMAN, N., JOYCE, C., BARBARA, N. & JANE, J. (1970) "Neurosis and marital interaction II." *British Journal of Psychiatry*, 117, 47-58.

34.   LUKIANOWICZ, N. (1971) "Battered children." *Psychiatrica Clinica*, 4, 257-80.

35.   MACDONALD, J. (1963) "The threat to kill." *American Journal of Psychiatry*, 120, 125-30.

36.   MENNINGER, K. (1942) *Love Against Hate*. New York: Harcourt, Brace.

37.   MERRILL, E. J. (1962) "Physical abuse of children: an agency study." In *Protecting the Battered Child* (ed. V. de Francis), pp. 1-15. Denver, Colorado: The American Humane Association, Children's Division.

38.   NEWSON, J. & NEWSON, E. (1963) *Patterns of Infant Care in an Urban Community*. London: Allen and Unwin (Penguin Books, 1972).

39.   NEWSON, J. (1973) Personal communication.

40.   NURSE, S. M. (1966) "Familial patterns of parents who abuse their children." *Smith College Studies in Social Work*, 35, 11-25.

41.   OLIVER, J. E. & TAYLOR, A. (1971) "Five generations of ill-treated children in one family pedigree." *British Journal of Psychiatry*, 119, 473-80.

42.   OSBORN, F. (1963) "Excess and unwanted fertility." *Eugenics Quarterly*, 10, 59-72.

43.   OSGOOD, C. E., SUCI, G. J. & TANNENBAUM, P. H. (1957) *The Measurement of Meaning*. Urbana, Illinois: University of Illinois Press.

44.   PAULSON, M. J. & BLAKE, P. R. (1969) "The physically abused child: a focus on prevention." *Child Welfare*, 48, 86-95.

45.   PHILLIPS, C. J., WILSON, H. & HERBERT, G. W. (1972) *Child Development Study (Birmingham 1968-71): A Study of Inadequate Families, Part 1*. Centre for Child Study, School of Education, University of Birmingham.

46. POHLMAN, E. (1973) *The Psychology of Birth Planning*. Cambridge, Massachusetts: Schenkman Publishing Company Incorporated.

47. POLANSKY, N. & POLANSKY, N. (1968) "The current status of child abuse and child neglect in this country." Report to the Joint Commission on Mental Health for Children (cited by Gil, p. 43).

48. POLLAK, M. (1972) *Today's Three Years Olds in London*. William Heinemann, Spastics International Medical Publications.

49. REGISTRAR GENERAL (1973) *Statistical Review of England and Wales for the year 1971. Part 2*. London: H.M.S.O.

50. RESNICK, P. J. (1969) "Murder of the newborn: a psychiatric review of neonaticide." *American Journal of Psychiatry*, 126, 1414-20.

51. RUSSELL, J. K. (1970) "Pregnancy in the young teenager." *Practitioner*, 204, 401-405.

52. RUTTER, M. (1971) "Parent-child separation: psychological effects on the children." *Journal of Child Psychology and Psychiatry*, 12, 233-60.

53. ROWNTREE, G. (1964) "Some aspects of marriage breakdown in Britain during the last 30 years." *Population Studies*, 18, 147-63.

54. SATTIN, D. B. & MILLER, J. K. (1971) "The ecology of child abuse in a military community." *American Journal of Orthopsychiatry*, 41, 675-8.

55. SCHAFFER, H. R. & SCHAFFER, E. B. (1968) "Child care and the family: a study of short term admission to care." Occasional Papers on Social Administration. No. 25. London: Bell and Sons Limited.

56. SCHLOESSER, P. T. (1964) "The abused child." *Bulletin of the Menninger Clinic*, 28, 260-68.

57. SCOTT, P. D. (1973) "Fatal battered baby cases." *Medicine, Science and the Law*, 13, 197-206.

58. SIMONS, B., DOWNS, E. F., HURSTER, M. F. & ARCHER, M. (1966) "Child abuse: epidemiologic study of medically reported cases." *New York State Journal of Medicine*, 66, 2783-8.

59. SKINNER, A. E. & CASTLE, R. L. (1969) *78 Battered Children: a Retrospective Study*. London: National Society for the Prevention of Cruelty to Children.

60. SMITH, S. M., HONIGSBERGER, L. & SMITH, C. (1973) "EEG and personality factors in baby batterers." *British Medical Journal, iii*, 20-22.

61. ____ HANSON, R. & NOBLE, S. (1973) "Parents of battered babies: a controlled study." *British Medical Journal, iv*, 388-91.

62. *Social Trends (1972) No. 3*, Central Statistics Office, H.M.S.O.

63. SODDY, K. (1964) "The unwanted child." *Journal of Family Welfare*, 11, 39-52.

64. STEELE, B. F. & POLLOCK, C. B. (1968) "A psychiatric study of parents who abuse infants and small children." In *The Battered Child* (eds. R. E. Helfer & C. H. Kempe), pp. 103-147. Chicago: University Press, Chicago.

65. STENGEL, E. (1964) *Suicide and Attempted Suicide*. Harmondsworth, Middlesex: Penguin Books.

66. VESTERDAL, J. (1972) "The battered child syndrome." *Annales Nestlé*, 27, 5-11.

67. WEDGE, P. & PROSSER, H. (1973) *Born to Fail*. Arrow Books.

68. WEIR, S. (1970) "A study of unmarried mothers and their children in Scotland." *Scottish Health Service Studies, No. 13*. Scottish Home and Health Department.

69.   WEISS, R. S. (1970) "Marriage and the family in the near future." In *The Family and its Future* (ed. K. Elliott), p. 51-67. Ciba Foundation Symposium. London: Churchill.

70.   WESTON, J. T. (1968) "The pathology of child abuse." In *The Battered Child* (eds. R. E. Helfer & C. H. Kempe), pp. 77-100. Chicago: Chicago University Press, Chicago.

71.   WILLMOTT, P. & YOUNG, M. (1960) *Family Class in a London Suburb*. Routledge and Kegan Paul.

72.   YOUNG, L. (1964) *Wednesday's Children: A Study of Child Neglect and Abuse*. New York: McGraw Hill.

73.   ZALBA, S. R. (1966). "The abused child: I. A survey of the problem." *Social Work*, 11, 3-16.

APPENDIX

Questions and response categories	Category combinations for χ^2 test	Questions and response categories	Category combinations for χ^2 test
Social class was based on the Registrar General's Classification of Occupations, 1966. * Pre-marital pregnancy was questioned and checked on the basis of dates of marriage and birth of first child.		* *Contraception* 'Do you want any more children? Are you doing anything about contraception?' No/Yes.	
Attitude to pregnancy 'Did you feel when you were expecting . . . that it was a good time to have a baby? Or would it have been better to wait?' (a) delighted; (b) pleased on the whole, some reservations; (c) displeased.	a and b *vs.* c also a *vs.* b and c	*Husband's reaction to relevant pregnancy* 'How did your husband feel about your pregnancy with . . .?' OR if not the biological father 'How did your husband take to . . .?' (a) delighted; (b) pleased on the whole; (c) generally displeased.	a *vs.* b and c (= ambivalent) also b and b *vs.* c
* *Abortion* 'Would you have liked an abortion when pregnant with . . .?' No/Yes.		*Evaluation of partner* 'How much alike do you think you and your husband are? Would you rather have . . . to grow up to be like you or like your husband?' (a) thinks highly of; (b) appreciates on the whole, dislikes some things; (c) thinks poorly of.	a and b *vs.* c
Partner's relationship with child 'Will you tell me how . . .'s father gets on with him? Does he like to help with him?' (a) very fond of child, enjoys playing, etc.; (b) quite fond of child, takes interest; (c) rejects or is not interested in the child.	a and b *vs.* c	*M.S.W.'s assessment of housing* (a) good; (b) reasonable condition; (c) dilapidated	a and b *vs.* c

Questions and response categories	Category combinations for χ^2 test	Questions and response categories	Category combinations for χ^2 test
Agreement on child rearing practices 'In general, how well would you say you and your husband agree about the best way to handle . . .?' (a) discuss and/or usually agree; (b) disagree frequently; (c) partner doesn't participate.	a *vs.* b and c also a and b *vs.* c	*M.S.W.'s assessment of care of home* (a) obsessionally clean and tidy; (b) reasonable; (c) dirty and untidy	a and b *vs.* c
Head of household 'Who makes the important decisions for the family?' (a) father; (b) share; (c) mother.	a and b *vs.* c	*Contact with (i) parents; (ii) other relatives; (iii) neighbours; (iv) friends.* (a) almost daily; (b) approx. weekly; (c) monthly; (d) infrequently; (e) never.	a, b and c *vs.* d and e
Personal significance of religion 'Does religion mean anything to you?' (a) nothing; (b) goes to or nominally attached to place of worship; (c) personal faith.	a and b *vs.* c	*Regular social activities* (a) sports; (b) other clubs; (c) evening classes; (d) public house; (e) church; (f) visiting friends; (g) others.	any *vs.* none
Religious background (a) none; (b) one or both parents nominally religious; (c) one or both parents had personal faith.	a *vs.* b and c	*Opportunity for breaks from care of child* 'Can . . . play (or be in pram) out of doors without you being with him all the time? Can baby sitting be arranged?'	Yes to one or both *vs.* no to both and including cases where baby sitting 'available' but not desired
Amenities (a) fixed bath (own or shared); (b) running water inside own accommodation; (c) W.C. indoors; (d) own kitchen.	all present *vs.* 1 or more missing	*Assessment of allowance* (a) generous; (b) adequate; (c) inadequate.	a and b *vs.* c
Child's sleeping arrangements (a) own room; (b) shares room with sibs; (c) shares bed with sibs; (d) shares room with parents; (e) shares bed with parents.	a *vs.* others for 'lacks own room' also a and b *vs.* others for 'cramped sleeping accommodation'	*Any significant worries* 'Are any of the following worries for you?' (a) money; (b) domestic friction; (c) own health; (d) health of others; (e) housing; (f) employment; (g) marital status; (h) moral or personal.	none or one *vs.* two or more
		Reaction to total situation 'How satisfied are you with your present life?' (a) very; (b) fairly; (c) not at all.	a *vs.* b and c

Items marked * are from psychiatric interview.

21

Family Disorganization:
A Sociological Perspective*

Ludwig L. Geismar, Ph.D.

More than two decades ago in the New City of Jerusalem, an immigrant woman from Kurdistan had burst, unannounced, into the home of a next door neighbor. The reason for this intrusion was the unrestrained crying of a baby, lying in a crib in the bedroom. The child's mother had gone out to hang up the laundry, and she arrived just in time to see the intruder, hair bound in rags with long skirts billowing, rush toward the infant and lift him into her arms. Seeing the surprised expression on the mother's face, the immigrant abandoned her effort to quiet the child and, in the absence of a common language between the two women, began to gesticulate intensely, admonishing the mother to put the baby to her breast and stop him from crying. It was clear that the Kurdish immigrant had viewed the child's condition with great alarm and had taken urgent steps to remedy it. A crying, unattended baby, the mother quickly learned, was considered by Kurdish women as a product of neglect and such a situation was not to be tolerated. Clearly, this view was not shared by the mother, also an immigrant but from a Western society, nor was it shared by the local public health nurses who had told this young mother that because her baby seemed to cry all the time, it was best to ignore the crying when tasks had to be done. These nurses also disapproved of the Kurdish habit of placing babies in swinging hammocks which the mother could push every few minutes as a means of keeping the child placated and quiet while the mother was busy doing daily chores. The position of the Western immigrant and the professional nurse in contrast to that of the rural,

* Ludwig L. Geismar, "Family Disorganization: A Sociological Perspective," *Social Casework*, Vol. 59, No. 9 (November 1978): 545-550. Copyright © Family Service Association of America. Reproduced by permission.

nonindustrialized Kurds, could be characterized as tolerating a measure of benign neglect in order to condition the child to a schedule, to accomplish the necessary work at hand, and to develop within the child a measure of frustration tolerance and autonomy.

The foregoing anecdote makes two points: (1) definitions of child neglect clearly differ from culture to culture, and (2) certain cultural norms represent safeguards against behavior that is accepted or tolerated elsewhere. The fact that the Kurds cannot or do not tolerate crying babies denotes a standard of nurturing behavior that limits the occurrence of neglect due to inattention by adults. This form of neglect, however, is more prevalent where mothers are expected to stress scheduling and training for independence.

A contrasting situation was once described by a child care supervisor who had worked on an Indian reservation in the American Southwest. The supervisor was attempting to correct what she regarded as child neglect, which here took the form of leaving children alone at night while parents went out. The Indians, however, did not view this as neglectful behavior, claiming that they were in the habit of having friends or neighbors look in on their children to make sure they were asleep. In this situation, the professional child care worker with more restrictive standards was clearly at odds with a culture that had a more relaxed attitude toward child care.

Faulty Socialization of Children and Child Neglect

Criteria for defining child neglect are then, to some extent, culturally determined. Some cultural norms are more attuned than others to the prevention of abuse and neglect of children. But, in a broader sense (and to validate it, it would be necessary to consider not only two or three cultures, but two or three dozen cultures), societies generally make adequate provisions for the care and socialization of their young. In fact, the very survival and vitality of a society is greatly dependent on its ability to provide effective conditions and means for child rearing and mobility into adult society. The neglect and abuse of children in any culture represents a breakdown in child socialization. If socialization of children is a process encompassing learning—by way of parental care and instruction—of behavior in accordance with cultural norms, abuse and neglect can be viewed as prime indices of faulty socialization in the form of the omission or commission of acts resulting in physical, emotional, or social harm to the child. Deficiencies in the socializing process do not inevitably lead to abuse and neglect, for they may result in other forms of behavior not quite so intolerable. Instead, abuse and neglect are the most virulent kinds of faulty socialization and, therefore, of focal interest to all societies.

Family Malfunctioning and the Socialization of Children

Faulty socialization of children is considered the root of family malfunctioning or disorganization. This is because of the contention in Western society that the nuclear family bears the main responsibility for rearing and educating the young. Although other institutions such as the schools, churches, neighborhoods, youth centers and groups, and so on, share these functions, the converging evidence of research in the fields of education and child development points to the family as the central socializing agent.

The concept of family disorganization implies that the family is unable to act as a socializing agent. The term, however, is actually broader in meaning because it implies that there is a state of disorder in the family's pattern of functioning. Family disorganization can also be defined as a system-dissolution in the sense that disorganization is the opposite of organization or system-maintenance.[1] However, a nonevaluative definition is largely devoid of meaning because it treats disorder and dissolution as structural attributes that bear no relationship to the roles of family members. A more tenable definition is failure on the part of family members to fulfill basic, socially expected tasks or functions. Accordingly, a family is disorganized if the functions necessary for the survival and well-being of its members are not being performed.

This definition recognizes the existence of numerous family functions such as the marital relationship, sibling relations, the provision of food and shelter, maintaining relations with the community, and so forth, but it puts child socialization tasks at the center of family concerns. The relationship between family disorganization and deficient socialization of children is conceptual. They are related by definition, although the concepts do not represent a tautology. Instead, inadequate child-rearing practices, including a high prevalence of neglect, are a central component of family disorganization.[2]

As a starting point, two questions should be posed when addressing the problems of child neglect and abuse: (1) In family situations characterized by social disorganization in general and inadequate child care in particular, how prevalent is child neglect and abuse? (2) If the assumption is accepted that deficient child care is closely associated with family disorganization, how common is family disorganization in our society?

Because there has been little empirical research on the first issue and the studies that have been done used divergent definitions of all three concepts, it is virtually impossible to say anything beyond the common, but unsystematic, observation that serious family disorganization tends to have a deleterious effect on the growth and development of children, and this effect is often best described as physical or emotional abuse.[3] The second question cannot be answered on the basis of solid research evidence either. However, some cross-cultural research being carried out by the author may chart the direction for accumulating knowledge on this subject.

Research Efforts

The majority of the research efforts on the subject of family disorganization have relied on readily available criteria such as divorce, separation, placement of children; and statistics of deviant behavior from incarceration, probation, parole, and institutionalization for mental illness and addiction reports. The shortcomings in such indices are clear. They denote either a structural condition reflecting the separation of the marriage partners or the deviant behavior of one or more family members that has come to the attention of the community. Neither is a good indicator of the manner in which the family performs its socially expected tasks. Separation and divorce, although generally the result of a poor marital relationship in the past, are not a reliable index of family problems today. The deviant behavior of a family member, on the other hand, may or may not be a reflection of problems affecting the entire family system. There are many more family situations, characterized by mental illness, addiction, or delinquency of one or more family members, than there are cases of genuine social disorganization. Empirical evidence for this statement could only be derived by citing a vast amount of census as well as special survey statistics, many of which are of questionable reliability.

Research efforts to obtain estimates of the number of socially disorganized families have been conducted by two methods: communitywide checklist surveys based on officially reported data, and sample studies of subpopulations with the aid of interviews conducted with family members.

Checklist Surveys

In the late 1950s and early 1960s two communitywide surveys were conducted to identify socially disorganized families using information from the major health and welfare agencies in their communities. The Family Centered Project of St. Paul, Minnesota, and the Area Development Project of Vancouver, British Columbia, both used the same procedure for identifying socially disorganized or multiproblem families.[4] The method was as follows: for both studies, an unduplicated account of families was obtained. These families had been served by one of the local public health and welfare agencies, had one or more children aged eighteen or under, and at least one parent or parent-surrogate in the home. Out of this group cases were selected in which one or more family members manifested some form of behavior disorder, a term which was defined as both socially and psychologically deviant behavior. The final criterion for being characterized socially disorganized was evidence of serious malfunctioning in the economic or the health areas, or in both.

The decision to attach the label socially disorganized or multiproblem was based on the assumption that the prevalence of behavior disorders coupled with major problems in two other areas of family functioning (the term problem was not defined simply as economic need or as ill health but as a condition associated with an inability to cope) is generally indicative of a general failure to carry out socially expected roles and tasks. This assumption, of course, took the place of a clinical case-by-case analysis seeking to determine whether each family was indeed disorganized by the terms of the definition.

The results of this checklist survey showed the percentage of disorganized families in the total number of families to be 2.2 percent in the St. Paul community and 2.3 percent in the Vancouver community. The figures for each Vancouver census tract ranged from a high of 13.4 to a low of 0 percent, according to this estimate. Out of a total of forty-nine tracts in Vancouver, two had rates over 10 percent and seven had fewer than 0.5 percent.[5]

Undoubtedly, these percentages underestimate the prevalence of family disorganization in the community because they are based solely on disorganization cases known to an agency, public or private. The survey data do not include families —generally those in the upper-income group—that do not come to the attention of social agencies because they use private psychiatrists and clinical psychologists in private practice. Other disorganized families may escape community notice because they do not utilize any professional resources. Such families also are more likely to be in the higher social status groups whose lifestyle shields them from community attention. Moreover, higher-income families tend to fall outside the socially disorganized category more often than low-income families because by definition the category includes economic malfunctioning.

Sample studies using interviews

A study to determine the prevalence of family disorganization in a poverty area was carried out in New Haven, Connecticut, in 1961.[6] Using the definition of family disorganization applied in the St. Paul and Vancouver studies, all households in a three-hundred unit, low-income housing project were studied. The study used housing authority and other agency records in stage one, and personal contacts, by way of a network of community activities extended to all age groups, in stage two. The estimate of thirty-five families as being socially disorganized relied on the observations of the project's community workers who were personally acquainted with nearly every family in the project. The thirty-five families represented about 12 percent of all families and approximately 18 percent of families with dependent children. The category of child care and socialization was found to be the third most problematic area (after individual role performance and relationship among family members) in the disorganized families studied.

Another study, which involved interviewing probability samples of female heads of households in their homes in three New Jersey communities—Newark, New Brunswick and Plainfield—estimated the prevalence of family disorganization as ranging from 5 and 7 percent in young families with a first child under one year of age to 18 percent in families with children in middle school.[7] The populations from which the samples were drawn are disproportionately of lower occupational status and minority group in character than the state as a whole. The extent of disorganization may have been understated in the New Brunswick and Plainfield samples where data relied on one-time interviews in contrast to the multiple-interview contacts made in the study of the Newark families. The overall estimates grounded on an actual assessment of the family situation with the aid of a home interview range between 5 and 20 percent of families with children, depending on social status (lower status families have higher disorganization rates) and age of family (families with teenage children experience more disorganization).

The lower figures attained in the St. Paul and Vancouver surveys, which utilized available agency data, undoubtedly understated the scope of the problem because they failed to furnish information about higher-income families whose problems do not come to the attention of the community to the same extent as those of the economically deprived households.

Family Malfunctioning and Social Class

The relationship between family malfunctioning and social status spotlights the connection between social disorganization and poverty. Statistics from the New

Jersey study clearly indicate that the lower the socioeconomic status of a family, the greater the likelihood of its manifesting social malfunctioning.[8] This finding might be dismissed as another commonsensical conclusion that adds little to real knowledge of the subject. However, the presumed association between social class and family functioning is neither commonsensical nor theoretically compelling.

The evidence challenging the notion that family malfunctioning is inevitably a function of social class comes from a recent Australian study which sought to replicate the New Jersey research. The Australian study, aimed at identifying social and economic factors that mediate between social status and family life, reached the tentative conclusion that in Australia the social functioning and the occupational status of urban families are not significantly related.[9]

It is beyond the mandate of the present article to explore the reasons for the differences between the American and the Australian findings. The results of the two studies challenge the commonsense notion of an irrevocable inverse relationship between social status and family function and offer instead the hypothesis that the relationship between them is mediated by a variety of sociocultural factors. The preliminary evidence emanating from the data, which has not been fully analyzed, suggests that two factors account for the different relationship between social status and family functioning in Australia: (1) greater economic equality, which expresses itself mainly in a lesser relative deprivation of the lower socioeconomic strata, and (2) a strong family tradition among Australia's predominantly lower-class new immigrants from Europe and the Middle East.

Conclusion

Available data permit the inference that family disorganization, although not randomly distributed throughout society, is not a universal class phenomenon and its prevalence is affected by the economic and cultural factors that shape family life. This does not rule out psychological and biological determinants as contributing to family malfunctioning. If the above argument is valid, however, it requires an examination of the effect of such variables as personality, health, intelligence, and so on, within the context of sociocultural differences.

Although tentative at this stage, research findings point toward possible strategies for dealing with family disorganization and its correlate, child neglect and abuse. If family malfunctioning is to a large extent affected by cultural traditions, or their absence, and the manner in which society deals with its lower-status population, intervention by means of individual and family treatment is going to be of limited utility. Such service will, in fact, seek to remedy on a case-by-case basis the ill effects of the more powerful forces operating at the community, state, or national levels. Case-focused treatment as the chief program of intervention will mean giving preference to the remedial rather than the preventive approach in dealing with the problem. A preventive policy must address itself to modifying those socioeconomic conditions that are significantly associated with family disorganization and child neglect.

Although social planners are rarely faced with a clean choice between these two approaches and must realistically give top priority to dealing with emergencies at the time they occur, social policy on behalf of the child and the family must take a long-range perspective that ties programs to comprehensive knowledge about causation.

REFERENCES

1. These concepts were first defined several years ago. See Jetsey Sprey, "Family Disorganization: Toward a Conceptual Clarification," and John Scanzoni, "Family Organization and the Probability of Disorganization," *Journal of Marriage and the Family* 28 (November 1966):398-411.

2. LUDWIG L. GEISMAR, MICHAEL A. LASORTE, and BEVERLY AYRES, "Measuring Family Disorganization," *Marriage and Family Living* 24 (February 1962):51-56.

3. The National Survey of the Incidence and Severity of Child Abuse and Neglect, a study in progress, conducted by Westat, Inc., of Rockville, Maryland, is looking at the relationship between abuse and neglect on the one hand and family organization or disorganization on the other. See Westat, Inc., "National Survey of the Incidence and Severity of Child Abuse and Neglect—Pretest Plan and Operational Definition Report," Rockville, Maryland, 1 November 1976.

4. For reports of these projects, see Ludwig L. Geismar and Michael A. LaSorte, *Understanding the Multiproblem Family* (New York: Association Press, 1964), pp. 52-64; and Beverly Ayres and Joseph C. Lagey, "Checklist Survey of Multiproblem Families in Vancouver City" (Vancouver, B.C.: Community Chest and Councils of the Vancouver Area, 1961).

5. AYRES and LAGEY, "Checklist Survey," pp. 38-39.

6. LUDWIG L. GEISMAR and JANE KRISBERG, *The Forgotten Neighborhood* (Metuchen, N.J.: Scarecrow Press, 1967).

7. LUDWIG L. GEISMAR, *555 Families—A Social Psychological Study of Young Families in Transition* (New Brunswick, N.J.: Transaction Books, 1973), pp. 37-53; and Ludwig L. Geismar, *Preventive Intervention in Social Work* (Metuchen, N.J.: Scarecrow Press, 1969).

8. GEISMAR, *555 Families*, p. 59; and Geismar, *Preventive Intervention in Social Work*, pp. 36-37.

9. LUDWIG L. GEISMAR, "Family Structure and Social Roles in Two Melbourne Suburbs" (Melbourne, Australia: Department of Social Studies, Melbourne University, 1976); and Ludwig and Shirley Geismar, *Families in an Urban Mold: Policy Implications of an Australian-U.S. Comparison* (Elmsford, N.Y.: Pergamon Press, forthcoming).

22

Interpersonal Relationships and Child-Rearing Practices in 214 Parents of Battered Children*

Selwyn M. Smith and
Ruth Hanson

Introduction

Baby batterers have been regarded as exhibiting a specific pattern of child-rearing, characterized by demands for premature high performance and a disregard for the child's limited abilities.[1, 14, 17, 36] Such parents, being deprived of mothering in childhood,[9, 24] and having had harsh childhood experiences,[36] consider punishment a proper disciplinary measure[38, 41] and look to the child for satisfaction of their own emotional needs; such characteristics being independent of age and social class.[36] By way of contrast, punitiveness and non-permissiveness are more common among working class than middle class parents,[25, 28, 32] and intolerance in child-rearing is prevalent among very young parents.[4]

Previous studies have not considered the issue that some child-rearing practices may be typical of low social class populations and not particularly characteristic of baby batterers. Nor has the relative importance of various background factors been adequately assessed. This paper examines a wide variety of child-rearing methods, background factors and personality characteristics among 214 parents of battered children and the role of social class. These variables are also examined for those parents who confessed to battering and differences with the remainder of the sample are highlighted.

* Selwyn M. Smith and Ruth Hanson, "Interpersonal Relationships and Child-Rearing Practices in 214 Parents of Battered Children," *British Journal of Psychiatry*, Vol. 127 (1975): 513-25. Copyright © Royal College of Psychiatrists. Reproduced by permission.

Subjects and Methods

Over two years 134 battered infants and children aged under 5 years and their parents were studied in detail. Fifty-three children who were admitted to hospital as emergencies other than on account of accident or trauma provided a control group. The distribution of mother's age, area of origin, and consultants referring were the same in both groups.

Up-to-date relevant norms were thus obtained on child-rearing, personal relationships and social circumstances and on the various tests of personality, attitude and intelligence, any of which may have been affected by anxiety due to the child's admission to hospital. The only closer match in this respect would have been a sample of 'accident' cases, but these might well have included non-accidental injuries.

A further control on matters most likely to be distorted by fear of 'being found out' was provided by the distinction within the index sample between the 44 per cent of cases where a parent admitted and the 56 per cent where both denied responsibility for the child's injuries. Differences between these two sections of the index sample were no greater for hard than for soft variables, suggesting that the 'softest' parts of the interviews prompted valid responses. (Results of these analyses will be reported elsewhere.)

All parents were seen both at hospital as soon as possible after the child's admission and at home, and were given standardized psychiatric, psychological and social interviews. Questions requiring self-reports on sensitive or threatening matters were carefully worded and embedded in acceptable parts of the various interviews. Response categories were provided for the interviewers. (These are available to interested readers from the authors.)

Parents were told that they were among a large number helping to supply confidential background material for research on problems similar to those of their children. Parents who asked for further help at the end of research interviews were given this where possible, the research data being frozen before such additional supportive intervention began. Although many questions touched on the circumstances surrounding the incident, giving the opportunity to describe it fully if they wished, at no point was it necessary for parents to 'tell the whole truth' about the reason for the child's injuries.

The problem of finding a control sample of equally low social class to match the index cases was insoluble. However, it was possible to weight the index sample results equating them for the social class of the controls.[26] This made it possible to determine whether abnormalities in the index sample were as significant when class was held constant. Results have been presented comparing index and control samples both before and after controlling for social class. Details of statistical work on the class control have been reported elsewhere,[34] but the results are summarized in the text of this paper.

Details of personality diagnoses, neuroticism and the classifications adopted have been previously described.[33, 34] Hostility was measured by Foulds' Hostility and Direction of Hostility Questionnaire.[2] Psychomotor performance was measured by the Gibson Spiral Maze.[12]

A variety of difficulties the parents experienced with the child were explored by a specifically designed 'Difficult Times' test. The emotional reactions experienced by the parents when difficulties arose were measured by a semantic differential technique. Details of these measures are available to interested readers and will be reported elsewhere.

The child's social maturation was measured by the Vineland Social Maturity Scale.[5] The subscales on the Griffiths' Mental Developmental Scale[15] were measured in all children whose physical condition did not obviously entail brain damage. The child's social precocity was ascertained by calculating the discrepancy between the standard scores on these two tests.[29]

Results

Child-Rearing Practices

Mothers

Demands upon the child: The self-reported child-rearing methods of index and control mothers are shown in Table I. Index mothers were characterized in several respects by demanding behaviour which exceeded that to be expected in relation to their social class.

Methods of control: Table I also compares the disciplinary methods used by index and control mothers. Significantly more index than controls frequently smacked the child. A smaller but nevertheless significant proportion withheld love as a method of discipline. Good behaviour was materially rewarded more often by index than by controls. Both samples seldom used deprivation of privileges or praise for good behaviour.

Social maturity of the child: The scores of 11 index children (15 per cent) compared with 3 controls (8 per cent) were one or more standard deviations higher on the Vineland Social Maturity Scale than on the Griffiths' General Development Quotient (difference not significant). Twelve index (16 per cent) and 4 control (11 per cent) children were one or more standard deviations lower on the Vineland than on the Griffith's, and this difference was also not significant.

Problems with the child: A variety of problems index and control mothers experienced with the child are shown in Table II. Significant proportions of index mothers reported that the child's demanding and clinging behaviour and failure of their spouse in helping to care for the baby were problems.

Reactions to problem behaviour: Among the mothers there was no difference between index and controls in the degree to which they were upset by the child's difficult behaviour. Mean scores on all negative self-ratings combined of the Semantic Differential (underlined adjectives in Fig. 1) were $43 \cdot 87$ and $42 \cdot 32$ respectively (difference not significant). Fig. 1 illustrates the profile obtained and demonstrates that index and controls differed appreciably on only one rating scale; weepy—unshaken. The difference between index mothers and index fathers on overall self-rating (mean score $36 \cdot 62$) was significant ($t = 2 \cdot 62$; $p < 0 \cdot 01$) and Fig. 2 demonstrates that the profile obtained was rather dissimilar.

Affection towards the child: Significant proportions of index mothers were not very demonstrative towards the child (see Table II). Significantly more control mothers reported they enjoyed the child but were glad to get away at times. More index than controls reported having little time to play with the child, but this difference became insignificant when adjusted for social class.

BY SELWYN M. SMITH AND RUTH HANSON

TABLE I

Comparison of child-rearing methods and methods of control among index and control mothers

	Index		Controls		Significance (df = 1)	
	No.	(%)	No.	(%)	χ^2	p
Child-rearing methods						
Allows to cry unless something obviously wrong	68	(59)	41	(79)	5·59	<0·05
Punishment for screaming	22	(29)	1	(4)	5·00	<0·05*
Isolation for screaming	29	(28)	7	(29)	7·26	<0·01*
Breast feeding	35	(30)	13	(25)	N.S.	
Rigid feeding schedules	25	(22)	9	(18)	N.S.	
Emotional overinvolvement when food refused	28	(29)	3	(6)	9·32	<0·01
Potty training before 12 months	38	(36)	9	(56)	N.S.	
Severe in training methods	60	(74)	7	(44)	4·42	<0·05*
Non-permissive regarding aggressive behaviour	54	(81)	10	(59)	N.S.	
Punishes aggressive behaviour ...	58	(85)	11	(61)	3·82	<0·05*
Restrictions re access to household items	59	(55)	13	(65)	N.S.	
Close surveillance	72	(65)	47	(96)	15·61	<0·001
Obedience demanded	86	(84)	19	(49)	16·98	<0·001
Instant obedience expected	31	(30)	4	(10)	5·10	<0·05*
Methods of control						
Frequent use of smacking	58	(50)	6	(13)	17·92	<0·001
Withholds love	18	(17)	1	(3)	4·18	<0·05
Rarely deprives	11	(11)	1	(4)	N.S.	N.S.
Rarely praises	11	(10)	1	(2)	N.S.	N.S.
Gives tangible rewards for good behaviour	53	(51)	6	(20)	8·08	<0·01

* Difference became insignificant after adjustments made for social class.

Fathers

More index (24, 37 per cent) than control fathers (2, 10 per cent) reported that they used physical punishment frequently in disciplining their child ($\chi^2 = 4·03$; df = 1; p <0·05). This difference held after social class adjustment. On all other child-rearing methods index fathers did not differ significantly from the controls.

TABLE II

Mothers' reports of problems with the child and affection towards the child

	Index		Controls		Significance (df = 1)	
	No. (%)		No. (%)		χ^2	p
Problems						
Demanding and clinging behaviour	39	(36)	4	(8)	11·49	<0·001
Screaming in temper	17	(16)	8	(17)	N.S.	
Messy or destructive behaviour	9	(8)	2	(4)	N.S.	
Disobedience	10	(8)	6	(13)	N.S.	
Partner fails to help	22	(21)	2	(4)	5·52	<0·05
Recent quarrels with the spouse	23	(21)	5	(10)	N.S.	
Affection						
Little time to play	58	(49)	14	(27)	6·19	<0·05*
Not very demonstrative........	59	(51)	7	(13)	18·40	<0·001
Enjoyed child, but glad to get away at times	60	(50)	38	(73)	5·88	<0·05

* Difference became insignificant after adjustments made for social class.

Both parents

On self-ratings related to difficulties with the spouse, mean scores for index mothers were 52·51 and 56·43 for control mothers (difference not significant). For index fathers the mean score was 49·14. There were too few control fathers with these problems to yield reliable means. The difference between means for ratings on difficulties with the child (43·87) and difficulties with the spouse (52·51) was significant for index mothers. It was also significant for control mothers (means 42·32 and 56·43).

Recollections of Childhood

Mothers

Neurotic symptoms in childhood

Significant proportions of index mothers reported being unhappy in childhood and having two or more neurotic symptoms (see Table III). The types of individual neurotic symptoms were nail-biting 50 (50 per cent), 'nervous' child 24 (24 per cent), nightmares 10 (10 per cent), thumb-sucking 9 (9 per cent), enuresis 8 (8 per cent), and fear of the dark 3 (3 per cent). Other miscellaneous neurotic symptoms were reported by 23 (23 per cent) index mothers. Seventeen (17 per cent) index and none of the controls reported that they were emotionally handicapped as a result of these symptoms.

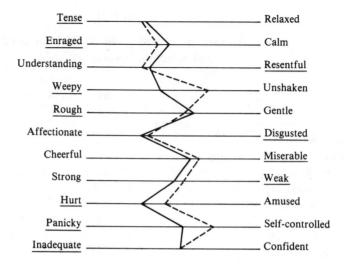

Key   (-) Index Mother
       (---) Control Mother

Fig. 1.—Profile of mean scores on problems with the child. Index and control mothers. (Semantic Differential.)

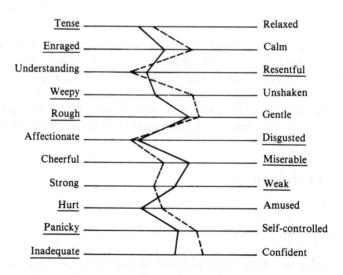

Key   (-) Index Mothers
       (---) Index Fathers

Fig. 2.—Profile of mean scores on problems with the child. Index mothers and fathers. (Semantic Differential.)

TABLE III

Recollections of childhood among index and control mothers

	Index	Controls	Significance (df = 1)	
	No. (%)	No. (%)	χ^2	p
Unhappy childhood.............	42 (34)	2 (4)	15·87	<0·001
Two or more neurotic symptoms	62 (51)	4 (8)	26·84	<0·001
Serious accidental head injury	15 (12)	1 (2)	N.S.	
Poor scholars	41 (34)	0 (0)	20·64	<0·001
Unhappy at school.............	43 (35)	8 (16)	5·71	<0·05*
Close relatives hospitalized for psychiatric illness.........	33 (27)	6 (12)	4·08	<0·05*
Relatives suffered from 'nerves'	38 (31)	10 (20)	N.S.	
Own mothers warm and affectionate	80 (70)	47 (90)	7·42	<0·01*
Own fathers warm and affectionate	69 (73)	45 (88)	N.S.	

* Difference became insignificant after adjustments made for social class.

Physical health and head injury

Three index (2 per cent) and two controls (4 per cent) had convulsions in childhood. Ten index (8 per cent) had had some degree of physical handicap. Accidental head injury was not a significant finding among index mothers.

Interpersonal relationships in child and adulthood

Parents: Forty-three index (36 per cent) and 4 controls (8 per cent) had impaired relationships with their parents ($\chi^2 = 11·93$; d.f. = 1; p < 0·001). In childhood the proportions were 39 (32 per cent) and 4 (8 per cent) respectively ($\chi^2 = 9·63$; d.f. = 1; p < 0·01). Both these differences remained significant after class control.

Siblings: Twenty-two index (19 per cent) and 1 control (2 per cent) had impaired relationships with their siblings ($\chi^2 = 6·77$; d.f. = 1; p < 0·01). In childhood the proportions were 39 (32 per cent) and 4 (8 per cent) respectively ($\chi^2 = 9·63$; d.f. = 1; p < 0·01). Both these differences remained significant after class control.

Friends: Fifty-six index (46 per cent) compared with 8 controls (16 per cent) had no friends ($\chi^2 = 12·55$; d.f. = 1; p < 0·01). This finding held after class control. In childhood the proportions were 24 (20 per cent) and 10 (20 per cent) respectively and this difference was not significant.

Upbringing: The chief technique of discipline employed by their own mothers was scolding. This was reported by 63 index mothers (57 per cent) and 39 controls (80 per

TABLE IV

Types of discipline experienced by index and control mothers in childhood

	Index		Controls		Significance (df = 1)	
	No. (%)		No. (%)		χ^2	p
Mothers' upbringing by own mother						
Reasonable	65	(55)	50	(100)	*30·76	<0·001
Strict	26	(22)	0	(0)		
Rejecting....................	19	(16)	0	(0)	**11·99	<0·001
Harsh	8	(7)	0	(0)		
Mothers' upbringing by own father						
Reasonable..................	54	(40)	45	(92)	*24·56	<0·001
Strict	20	(18)	0	(0)		
Rejecting....................	18	(16)	3	(6)	** 9·59	<0·01
Harsh	18	(16)	1	(2)		

* Reasonable versus strict, rejecting and harsh.
** Reasonable and strict versus rejecting and harsh.

cent). This difference was significant ($\chi^2 = 6·71$; d.f. = 1; $p < 0·01$) and remained so after class control.

Table IV describes the types of discipline experienced by both index and control mothers during their childhoods. A significant proportion of index mothers described their parents as harsh and rejecting. The significant differences shown in the table remained after adjusting for social class.

Eighty index mothers (70 per cent) compared with 47 controls (90 per cent) described their own mothers as warm and affectionate ($\chi^2 = 7·42$; d.f. = 1; $p < 0·01$). This finding became insignificant after adjustments were made for social class. Sixty-nine index (73 per cent) compared with 45 controls (88 per cent) described their own fathers as warm and affectionate. This difference did not reach statistical significance.

Fathers.

Head injury

Thirty-six fathers (40 per cent) compared with 3 controls (13 per cent) had suffered serious accidental head injuries ($\chi^2 = 5·36$; d.f. = 1; $p < 0·05$). This difference became insignificant after adjustments were made for social class.

Upbringing

Twenty-six fathers (32 per cent) and none of the controls described their mothers as unreasonable in their discipline ($\chi^2 = 7·69$; d.f. = 1; $p < 0·01$). This difference remained significant after class control. Thirty-five index (44 per cent) and 2 controls (10 per cent) described their fathers as unreasonable ($\chi^2 = 6\cdot97$; d.f. = 1; $p < 0\cdot01$). This difference also remained significant after class control.

On all other recollections of childhood index fathers did not differ significantly from the controls.

Personality Characteristics

Psychiatric interview

Among the index group 60 mothers (48 per cent) and 9 fathers (10·1 per cent) were neurotic.[40] Compared with the controls neurosis was a significant finding among index mothers only ($\chi^2 = 12\cdot08$; d.f. = 1; $p < 0\cdot001$). The types of neurotic disturbance have been described elsewhere.[33, 34] The mean scores on the General Health Questionnaire[13] (see Table V) support the validity of clinical diagnosis of neurosis found among index mothers.

Eysenck Personality Inventory

Fig. 3 compares Neuroticism scores of index and control mothers with the normal female population.[6] The mean scores are shown in Table V. When those mothers who scored 4 plus on the lie scale were excluded (48 index and 10 controls), the means were 14·9 and 13·0 respectively, and this difference was statistically significant (t = 2·04; $p < 0\cdot05$). For fathers none of these differences were statistically significant.

Hostility and Direction of Hostility Questionnaire

Fig. 4 shows the mean scores on the various types of hostility for index and control mothers and compares them with normal females.[2] The mean Total Hostility scores and significant differences on the various types of hostility are shown in Table V. When those with 4 plus Lie scores on the Eysenck Personality Inventory were excluded from the index sample, index mothers also scored higher than controls on Acting-Out Hostility (means (5·1 and 4·3 respectively, $p < 0\cdot05$) and Self-Criticism (means 5·9 and 5·1 respectively, $p < 0\cdot05$). The Direction of Hostility score was not found to be a useful discriminator between index and controls.

The only significant difference found between index and control fathers among the types of hostility was on Guilt. Differences on Paranoid Hostility approached significance.

The Spiral Maze

Mean time and error scores for index and control mothers are shown in Table V. On the 'quick and careless' dimension the difference between index and control mothers was not significant. Index mothers were significantly more 'slow and clumsy' than control mothers ($\chi^2 = 12\cdot17$; d.f = 1; $p < 0\cdot001$). Index and control fathers did not differ significantly on Time and Error scores.

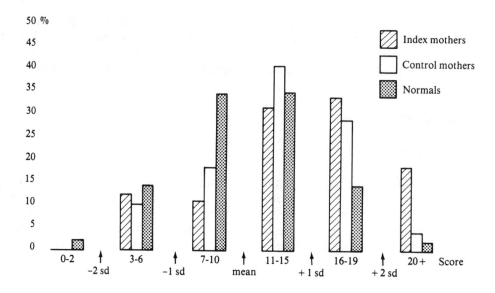

Fig. 3.—Comparison of Neuroticism scores of index and control mothers with the normal female population using the Eysenck Personality Inventory.

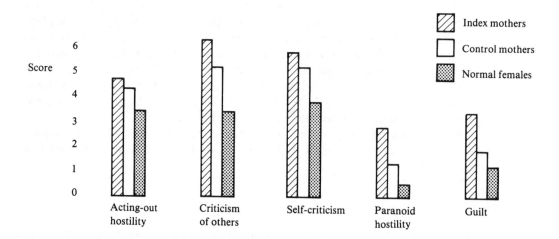

Fig. 4.—Comparison of mean Hostility scores (H.D.H.Q.) among index and control mothers and normal females.

TABLE V

Comparison of personality characteristics among index and control parents— mean scores

	Mothers		t	p	Fathers		t	p
	Index	Controls			Index	Controls		
General Health Questionnaire (Goldberg)	19·2	7·2	5·27	<0·001	11·0	6·1	1·93	<0·57
E.P.I.								
Extraversion	13·3	13·8	N.S.		15·1	16·1	N.S.	
Lie score	3·2	2·3	3·51	<0·001	2·5	2·0	N.S.	
Neuroticism	14·4	12·9	1·92	<0·57	9·6	9·9	N.S.	
H.D.H.Q. (Foulds)								
Total hostility	22·8	17·6	4·01	<0·001	18·6	16·9	N.S.	
Criticism of others	4·7	5·1	2·61	<0·01	5·9	5·3	N.S.	
Paranoid hostility	2·7	1·3	4·75	<0·001	2·1	1·4	N.S.	
Guilt	3·3	1·8	4·63	<0·001	2·2	1·4	2·06	<0·05
Spiral maze								
Time scores (secs.)	43·0	37·5	3·57	<0·001	—	—	—	
Error scores..........	20·2	14·0	2·19	<0·5	—	—	—	

Characteristics of Identified Perpetrators

Sixty parents confessed to battering their child; 43 were mothers and 17 were fathers. There were 74 cases where neither parent was identified as a perpetrator.

Tables VI and VII compare findings for those parents who were identified as perpetrators with the total index sample and contrasts them with those parents who were not so identified. Where there was no significant difference between those parents who were identified as perpetrators and the remainder of the index sample the variable has been omitted from the tables.

Discussion

Having controlled for age, the results showed that battering parents did not practise early toilet training, restrictivensss over property, rigid feeding schedules or strictness with regard to aggressive behaviour. After making further allowances for their predominantly low social class our results showed that severity of toilet training, intolerance of screaming, and punishment of aggression had also—as characteristics peculiar to battering parents—to be dismissed.

However, battering parents were found to use physical punishment far more than was to be expected for their age and class. This suggests that they are 'uncontrolled' rather than 'overcontrolled aggressors'.[22] Mothers were also characterized

TABLE VI

Characteristics of identified mother perpetrators compared with total sample and with those unidentified as perpetrators

Data from index mothers	Total sample		Identified		Unidentified		Significance*	
	No.	(%)	No.	(%)	No.	(%)	χ^2	p
Recollections of childhood								
Unhappy childhood	42	(66)	25	(81)	17	(52)	4·72	<0·05
Two or more neurotic symptoms	63	(51)	29	(69)	34	(42)	7·07	<0·01
Impaired relationships with parents............	43	(36)	23	(56)	20	(25)	9·82	<0.01
Impaired relationships as a child	39	(32)	22	(51)	17	(21)	10·50	<0·01
Impaired relationships with siblings	22	(19)	14	(37)	8	(10)	9·86	<0·01
Physical maltreatment	31	(25)	22	(51)	9	(11)	22·32	<0·001
Own father rejecting or harsh	36	(32)	18	(50)	18	(24)	6·13	<0·05
Own father warm and affectionate............	69	(73)	18	(54)	51	(84)	7·84	<0·01
Child-rearing practices								
Frequent use of physical punishment	58	(50)	28	(67)	30	(41)	6·31	<0·05
Praises for good behaviour	11	(10)	8	(19)	3	(4)	4·69	<0·05
Severe potty training	12	(15)	8	(27)	4	(8)	3·92	<0·05
Demands for instant obedience..............	31	(30)	17	(49)	14	(21)	7·07	<0·01
Demands for obedience	86	(84)	32	(91)	44	(81)	5·73	<0·05
Crying and clinging not necessarily a problem	69	(64)	33	(80)	36	(54)	6·78	0·01
Partner not necessarily a problem	47	(44)	26	(63)	21	(32)	8·64	<0·01
Punishment for screaming...	22	(29)	17	(57)	5	(11)	16·36	<0·001
Isolation for screaming	29	(28)	6	(20)	23	(50)	5·71	<0·05
Aggressive behaviour punished	20	(29)	12	(48)	8	(19)	5·24	<0·05
Rigid feeding schedule	25	(22)	14	(33)	11	(15)	4·37	<0·05
Emotional overinvolvement when child refuses food ...	28	(29)	19	(51)	9	(15)	13·01	<0·001

* This comparison is between identified and unidentified perpetrators.

TABLE VII

Personality characteristics of identified perpetrators compared with total sample and with those unidentified as perpetrators

	Total sample		Identified		Unidentified		Significance*	
Index mothers	No.	(%)	No.	(%)	No.	(%)	χ^2	p
Abnormal personality	95	(76)	38	(88)	57	(70)	4·51	$<0·05$
Neurosis.................	60	(48)	33	(77)	27	(33)	19·6	$<0·001$
Criminal record	14	(11)	2	(5)	12	(14)	Nos. too small for χ^2	

	No.	Mean	No.	Mean	No.	Mean	t	p
Social class	119	3·9	34	4·2	85	3·8	2·09	$<0·05$
Neuroticism (EPI)	112	14·4	41	17·8	71	12·5	5·98	$<0·001$
G.H.Q. (Goldberg)	83	19·2	34	31·4	49	10·8	6·14	$<0·001$
H.D.H.Q. (Foulds)								
Total hostility	105	22·5	39	26·9	66	20·3	4·44	$<0·001$
Acting-out hostility		4·7		5·6		4·2	2·94	$<0·01$
Self criticism		5·7		6·5		5·2	2·60	$=0.01$
Projected hostility		2·7		3·6		2·3	2·64	$<0·01$
Guilt..................		3·3		4·5		2·6	4·33	$<0·001$

	No.	(%)	No.	(%)	No.	(%)	χ^2	p
Index fathers								
Abnormal personality	57	(64)	13	(87)	44	(60)	10·72	$<0·01$
Criminal record	26	(29)	5	(42)	21	(2)	Nos. too small for χ^2	

	No.	Mean	No.	Mean	No.	Mean	t	p
Age.....................	105	27·0	15	23·2	90	27·6	5·39	$<0·001$
Wife's age	131	23·5	16	21·1	115	23·9	4·09	$<0·001$
Neuroticism (EPI)	66	9·6	13	13·4	55	8·7	2·40	$<0·05$
H.D.H.Q. (Foulds)								
Total hostility	65	18·6	14	24·9	51	16·8	2·79	$=0·01$
Acting-out hostility		4·4		5·6		4·1	1·97	$=0·07$
Self-criticism		3·9		5·4		3·5	2·07	$=0·05$
Paranoid hostility		2·1		3·8		1·7	2·85	$=0·01$
Guilt..................		2·2		4·1		1·7	3·05	$<0·01$

* This comparison is between identified and unidentified perpetrators.

by being punitive on other indices; in their tendency to use love-withdrawal as a sanction against misbehaviour, in their use of material rewards (pacifiers) and in their demands for obedience. At the same time they were relatively careless over the whereabouts or well-being of their child. Similar inconsistent attitudes are repeatedly found in the histories of other types of deviants.[21, 30, 39] It is also instructive to note—considering the likelihood that baby batterers are transmitting their childhood experiences to their own children—that Farrington and West[7] found under-vigilance to be an even more important predictor of violent delinquency than of delinquency in general. Inconsistency towards the child on the part of the mother has not previously received comment in battered baby studies, but should perhaps be considered as providing a clue to their failure in child management.

Malone[18] has observed that children living in dangerous environments have certain 'areas of hypertrophied ego functioning'—precocious ability. The child makes decisions for the parents and takes care of them and younger siblings. This precocious behaviour is reinforced by parental demands. Others[3, 19] have noted that some battered children are bright, precocious and capable of responding in a mature fashion to their parents' needs. Our results, however, showed that battered children were no more likely to be socially precocious in relation to their general development level than were the control children.

Morris and Gould[24] have remarked that 'the concept of role reversal is necessary' for an understanding of the parents' behaviour. These authors suggest that such parents are provoked into battering because they feel unloved, unhappy and anxious when the child cries or misbehaves. To date there has been only one replicable investigation of this hypothesis,[23] which suggested that mothers who batter babies have severely frustrated dependency needs and an inability to empathize with their children. This conclusion was, however, based upon only ten cases of suspected child abuse, eight of whom were Negro. We have explored Morris and Gould's concept by a semantic differential technique constructed specifically to enable parents to articulate their reactions to difficult behaviour in the child. The results showed that although their children exhibited dependent behaviour which upset the mothers more frequently, the control mothers felt equally unhappy on the occasions when such behaviour occurred. Frequency of occurrence of dependent behaviour in the child was significant, however, and was associated with maternal neuroticism in the index sample.

The differences between index mothers and index fathers and between types of problems for both index and control mothers showed that the Semantic Differential test was capable of discriminating between groups of subjects and groups of problems. (Detailed results will be reported elsewhere.) However, the differences the test was designed to explore were based on suggestions in the literature relating to battered children; these did not emerge. Furthermore index and control parents did not differ in their patterns of reactions to problems with the child.

It was most interesting and important to discover that index mothers (in common with the control mothers) reacted more negatively to difficulties with their marriage than to difficulties with the child. This finding is reminiscent of the discussion in a previous paper[35] that marital problems and an inability to get on with adults were more significant than most material and economic problems. Inter-personal difficulties re-emerged when problems with the spouse were discussed in the context of child-rearing. It may be argued, considering also that baby batterers assumed their parental roles prematurely, that their hostility is based not on rejection of the child as such but rather on a rejection of their unsatisfactory social, marital and parental roles. The finding that index mothers had problems with their partners, especially those concerned with their lack of support in child-rearing, more frequently than the controls deserves further study. They—as indeed did the controls—reacted more negatively to spouse than to child problems. The results suggest, therefore, that it would be more fruitful to concentrate on a battering parent's general dissatisfaction, neuroticism and hostility towards other adults than on such phenomena as a need to be nurtured by the child.

The results also showed that battering parents were deficient in realistic attitudes towards the child—for example, in the sentiment that a child is enjoyable on the whole but that relief is welcome at times. Instead they tended to say that either they did not enjoy the child or (more commonly) that the child meant everything to them. They were also deficient in the normal practice of allowing the child to cry for a while unless something is obviously wrong; instead they were either unresponsive or excessively responsive to crying.

As well as having problems with the child's clinging behaviour, battering mothers became emotionally over-involved when their child refused food. Despite their emotional over-involvement there was a lack of demonstrativeness in the sample. On the whole, perpetrators did not differ from the total battered baby sample of parents in their child-rearing practices. However, some already significant findings were intensified, and some differences which were insignificant for the group as a whole emerged as significant when identified perpetrators were selected for comparison. These were for the latter group—severe potty training and rigid feeding schedules.

Steele and Pollock[36] have suggested that baby batterers were deprived both of basic mothering and of the deep sense of being cared for from the beginning of their lives. Some of our findings are at variance with this suggestion. Significant proportions of index mothers said they were physically maltreated in childhood and that their parents were unreasonable, rejecting and harsh. High proportions of index fathers also experienced punitiveness from their own parents, and significant proportions said their parents were unreasonable in their disciplinary methods, supporting those authors[8, 10, 36, 37] who have suggested that such child-rearing practices reflected childhood experiences. On the other hand the sample did not report lack of affection to any greater extent than others of low social class. Considering that our parents were willing to report unreasonable discipline, there is no reason to assume that lack of affection was not reliably reported. Such inconsistencies may be realistic illustrations of the backgrounds of baby batterers.

Neuroticism was found to be an important characteristic of mothers of battered children. Among the fathers who were identified as perpetrators, the mean scores on both the Eysenck Personality Inventory and the General Health Questionnaire were also abnormally high.

Foulds has shown that as a general rule the hostility of neurotics is of the introverted kind.[2] Our results, however, showed that our sample of rather neurotic parents were not predominantly intropunitive but were characterized equally by extrapunitiveness. The most clear-cut for both mothers and fathers were the bizarre forms of hostility hitherto found only in psychiatric populations,[27] namely projected hostility and guilt. While guilt and remorse have often been dismissed as symptoms unrelated to actual circumstances in psychiatric populations and as glib sophistication among psychopaths[16] there is no reason to suppose that the guilt experienced by our sample is not reality-orientated or genuine, considering recent events. Considering their impaired relationships, their high level of paranoid hostility is perhaps also understandable.

The need for these parents to act out their hostility was not detected for the sample as a whole but emerged when only those who confessed to battering were singled out. This is not surprising, as items on this scale would be particularly revealing when put to a battering parent. For example, 'when I'm angry I feel like smashing things'. Self-criticism was also not detected for the sample as a whole, so that on first inspection of the results the pattern of significant types of hostility was most reminiscent of psychopaths who 'may regard themselves as hot-tempered, cynical, interestingly mad or diabolically wicked; but . . . draw the line at appearing faintly inferior or incompetent'.[27] However, those who confessed to battering did not draw this line in their self-descriptions. This group of baby batterers may possibly, as we have suggested before,[33] be more amenable to treatment.

Thus our results depict baby batterers as neurotic—chiefly depressed—and characterized by all kinds of hostility directed by the subjects, against both others and themselves. This description resembles that of the depressive psychopath.[31] Indeed, in the backgrounds of our sample there was considerable evidence of psychiatric disturbance; childhood neurotic symptoms, childhood unhappiness, a family history of psychiatric illness, physical handicaps, head injuries and lack of school success. Despite such adversities, very few baby batterers had received any formal psychiatric treatment.

The Gibson Spiral Maze—a test of risk-taking while under pressure—has demonstrated that delinquents have relatively fast and careless performances, while behaviour-disordered children are likely to be either fast and careless or slow and careless.[11] West and Farrington[39] have pointed out that clumsiness, although significantly predictive of both juvenile delinquency and recidivism, seems to be 'of importance only because of its association with low intelligence'. We found that index and control mothers did not differ on the 'quick and careless (to slow and accurate)' dimension, but that index mothers were more slow and clumsy. The prevalence of depression in this sample probably contributed something to the slow tempo,[20] but the clumsiness may be regarded as a reflection of low intelligence. The relative effects of personality and intelligence on the psychomotor behaviour of baby batterers deserves more attention. However, risk-taking when under pressure does not appear, from the results of the Spiral Maze Test, to be a characteristic of battering parents.

Considering all the variables outlined in this paper, battering mothers were most clearly characterized by punitiveness, carelessness in supervision, emotional overinvolvement, neuroticism, hostility, marital unhappiness and adverse childhood experiences. For fathers, punitiveness, hostility and neuroticism were important characteristics.

Conclusion

A fairly comprehensive inquiry about child-rearing practices demonstrated that the demanding behaviour of battering parents did not exceed that which generally characterizes low social class populations. In a few specific respects it was excessive; maternal over-involvement, demands for obedience and use of physical punishment. Of greater explanatory value was the finding of inconsistency and unreasonableness in child management. In their childhood recollections there was also some evidence of inconsistent attitudes on the part of their own parents, and this may underlie the development of their violent behaviour. Role reversal between battering parents and their children was found to be no greater than in a normal sample.

It seems likely that baby battering is provoked less by the child itself than by unhappiness due to unsatisfactory marital and other social relationships; such interpersonal difficulties having begun in childhood. If early detection and prevention in at-risk populations are to be successful, these particular features should be taken into account.

ACKNOWLEDGEMENTS

We are grateful to Mrs. Sheila Noble, who carried out the social interviews, and to the staff of the Hospital Statistics Department, who helped with the statistical analysis. Professor W. H. Trethowan provided valuable criticism throughout the course of study. The study was supported by a grant from the Barrow and Geraldine Cadbury Trust.

REFERENCES

1. BAIN, K. (1963) "The physically abused child." *Pediatrics*, 31, 895-7.

2. CAINE, T. M., FOULDS, G. A. & HOPE, K (1967) *Manual of the Hostility and Direction of Hostility Questionnaire*. London: University of London Press.

3. DAVOREN, E. (1968) "The role of the social worker". In *The Battered Child* (eds. R. E. Helfer and C. H. Kempe). Chicago: University of Chicago Press.

4. DE LISSOVOY, V. (1973) "High school marriages: a longitudinal study." *Journal of Marriage and the Family*, 35, 245-55.

5. DOLL, E. A. (1947) *Vineland Social Maturity Scale, Manual of Directions*. Minneapolis: Minnesota Educational Test Bureau.

6. EYSENCK, H. J. & EYSENCK, S. B. G. (1964) *Manual of the Eysenck Personality Inventory*. London: University of London Press Limited.

7. FARRINGTON, D. P. & WEST, D. J. (1971) "A comparison between early delinquents and young aggressives." *British Journal of Criminology*, 11, 341-58.

8. FONTANA, V. J. (1968) "Further reflections on maltreatment of children." *New York State Journal of Medicine*, 68, 2214-15.

9. GALDSTON, R. (1965) "Observations on children who have been physically abused and their parents." *American Journal of Psychiatry*, 122, 440-3.

10. GIBBENS, T. C. N. & WALKER, A. (1956) *Cruel Parents*. London: Institute for the Study and Treatment of Delinquency.

11. GIBSON, H. B. (1964) "The Spiral Maze: a psychomotor test with implications for the study of delinquency" *British Journal of Psychology*, 55, 219-25.

12. ____ (1965) *Manual of the Gibson Spiral Maze*. London: University of London Press Limited.

13. GOLDBERG, D. P. (1972) *The Detection of Psychiatric Illness by Questionnaire: a Technique for the Identification and Assessment of Non-Psychotic Psychiatric Illness*. London: Oxford University Press.

14. GREGG, G. S. (1968) "Physicians, child abuse, reporting laws and injured child: phychosocial anatomy of childhood trauma." *Clinical Pediatrics*, 7, 720-5.

15. GRIFFITHS, R. (1954) *The Abilities of Babies: a Study in Mental Measurement*. University of London Press.

16. HARE, R. D. (1972) "Depression." In *Encyclopaedia of Psychology* (eds. H. J. Eysenck, W. A. Arnold and R. Meili). London: Research Press.

17. KORSCII, B. M., CHRISTIAN, J. B., GOZZI, E. K. & CAROLSON, P. V. (1965) "Infant care and punishment: a pilot study." *American Journal of Public Health*, 55, 1880-8.

18. MALONE, C. A. (1966) "Safety first: comments on the influence of external danger in the lives of children of disorganized families." *American Journal of Orthopsychiatry*, 36, 3-12.

19. MARTIN, H. (1972) "The child and his development." In *Helping the Battered Child and His Family* (eds. C. H. Kempe and R. E. Helfer). Oxford: J. P. Lippincott Company.

20. MAYO, P. R. (1966) "Speed and accuracy of depression on a Spiral Maze test." *Perceptual and Motor Skills*, 23, 1034.

21. McCORD, W., McCORD, J. & ZOLA, I. K. (1959) *Origins of Crime*. New York: Columbia University Press.

22. MEGARGEE, E. I. (1966) "Undercontrolled and overcontrolled personality types in extreme antisocial aggression." *Psychological Monographs: General and Applied*, 80, no. 611.

23. MELNICK, R. & HURLEY, J. R. (1969) "Distinctive personality attributes of child abusing mothers." *Journal of Consulting Clinical Psychology*, 33, 746-9.

24. MORRIS, M. G. & GOULD, R. W. (1963) "Role reversal: a necessary concept in dealing with the 'battered child syndrome'." *American Journal of Orthopsychiatry*. 33, 298-9.

25. NEWSON, J. & NEWSON, E. (1968) *Four Years Old in an Urban Community*. London: George Allen and Unwin. (Pelican Books, 1970.)

26. _____ (1973) Personal communication.

27. PHILIP, A. E. (1969) "The development and use of hostility and direction of hostility questionnaire." *Journal of Psychosomatic Research*, 13, 283-7.

28. PHILLIPS, C. J., WILSON, H. & HERBERT, G. W. (1972) *Child Development Study (Birmingham 1968-71): a Study of Inadequate Families, Part 1*. Centre for Child Study, School of Education, University of Birmingham.

29. PRINGLE, M. L., KELMER (1969) *Social Learning and its Measurement*. London: Longman Green and Company Limited.

30. ROBINS, L. N. (1966) *Deviant Children Grown Up: a Sociological and Psychiatric Study of Sociopathic Personality*. Baltimore: Williams and Wilkins Company.

31. SATTES, H. (1972) "Psychopathy." In *Encyclopaedia of Psychology* (eds. H. J. Eysenck, W. A. Arnold and R. Meili). London: Research Press.

32. SEARS, R. R., MACCOBY, E. E. & LEVIN, H. H. (1957) *Patterns of Child Rearing*. New York: Evanston; London: Harper and Row.

33. SMITH, S. M., HANSON, R. & NOBLE, S. (1973) "Parents of battered babies: a controlled study." *British Medical Journal, iv,* 388-91.

34. _____ (1975) *The Battered Child Syndrome*. London: Butterworths.

35. _____ HANSON, R. & NOBLE, S. (1974) "Social aspects of the battered baby syndrome." *British Journal of Psychiatry*, 125, 568-82.

36. STEELE, B. F. & POLLOCK, S. B. (1968) "A psychiatric study of parents who abuse infants and small children." In *The Battered Child* (eds. R. E. Helfer and C. H. Kempe). Chicago: University of Chicago Press.

37. TUTEUR, W. & GLOTZER (1966) "Further observations on murdering mothers." *Journal of Forensic Science*, 11, 373-83.

38. WASSERMAN, S. (1967) "The abused parent of the abused child." *Children*, 14, 175-9.

39. WEST, D. J. & FARRINGTON, D. P. (1973) *Who Becomes Delinquent? Second Report of the Cambridge Study in Delinquent Development*. London: Heinemann Educational Books Limited.

40. WORLD HEALTH ORGANIZATION (1968) *International Classification of Diseases*. Geneva: W.H.O.

41. YOUNG, L. (1964) *Wednesday's Children: a Study of Child Neglect and Abuse*. New York: McGraw-Hill.

23

Child Abuse Related to Life Change
And Perceptions of Illness:
Some Preliminary Findings*

Rand D. Conger,
Robert L. Burgess, and
Carol Barrett

In recent years there has been an increasing interest in the physical mistreatment of children. Estimates concerning the extent of child abuse vary dramatically ranging from a low figure of 6,000 per year (Gil, 1970) to a high of well over one million annually (Fontana, 1973). While earlier estimates have relied primarily on official statistics derived from limited populations, Gelles (Note 1) has just completed a self-report survey on childrearing practices using a national probability sample. These findings suggest that even the high estimate of one million abused children annually may be too conservative and that a figure of one and one-half to two million may be a better reflection of reality.

The various explanations for this high rate of caretaker violence include such factors as psychological disturbance, learning history, social stress, and situational inducements (Parke & Collmer, 1975). In the research reported here, we examine the first three of these variables, touching only tangentially on those conditions in the immediate environment which might spark an instance of child abuse.

* We wish to thank Professor Thomas Holmes for his help in applying the life change concept to behavioral problems. Support for this research was provided by grant number 90-c-445 from the Office of Child Development, Department of Health, Education and Welfare.

Rand D. Conger, et al., "Child Abuse Related to Life Change and Perceptions of Illness: Some Preliminary Findings," *Family Coordinator*, January 1979, pp. 73-78. Copyright © 1979 National Council on Family Relations. Reproduced by permission.

In order to examine the issue of personal stress, the concept of life change will be borrowed from work done in psychosomatic medicine. A review by Holmes and Holmes (1975) has shown that psychological and social changes in the life of an individual appear to have a direct impact on a person's physical health. That is, the more rapidly life changes occur, the more likely it is that a person will develop symptoms of poor health. This finding has been demonstrated with a multitude of dissimilar illnesses.

More interesting here, however, are recent studies which have focused not only on the relationship between life change and the onset of physical health problems, but also on the degree to which life change can negatively influence ongoing behavior. For example, both college students (Harris, 1972) and high school teachers (Carranza, 1972) have shown decreased behavioral competence apparently resulting from increasing magnitudes of life change. Another study by Rahe, Biersner, Ryman and Arthur (1972) showed that trainees with high life change scores were more likely to drop out of a stressful navy training program than were those with lower scores. They also found that reports of psychological disturbance were positively related to drop out. The measures used by these researchers are employed in the study reported here in which we assume that adequate childrearing involves a complex of skills as do the activities studied in these earlier reports.

A specific test of the relationship between life change and child abuse has been conducted by Justice and Duncan (1976). As predicted, they found a significant difference between life change scores for abusing parents and a matched control group. These authors explain their findings in terms of Selye's (1956) theory of stress. According to Selye, when life events change too rapidly, people become so exhausted by the strain of coping that they eventually lose control over their situation. When controls weaken, Justice and Duncan suggest, the chance increases that a parent will act out in an inappropriate manner, e.g., by abusing a child. However, Bandura (1973) has noted that one can learn a variety of responses to stressful, or frustrating, situations. That is, it is possible for a person to learn to withdraw passively when coping becomes difficult rather than to strike out at others.

In this research, then, life change will be examined within the context of a personal history which might influence one's reaction to stress and the effects that reaction may have on the treatment of children. In addition, the degree of emotional disturbance experienced by parents will also be explored both separately and in combination with the life change variable.

Method

Subjects: Forty parents, 20 abuse and 20 controls, were recruited in Central Pennsylvania. Abuse families were obtained through the cooperation of county child welfare agencies while matched controls from the same counties were recruited by interviewers. The abuse and control families were matched in terms of (a) income, (b) education, (c) age of parents and children, and (d) number of children. Compared to county norms, parents in both samples were poorer, had more children, and were less educated than their peers. All parents and children were Caucasian.

Measures: Two questionnaires are used in this study. The first, the *Schedule of Recent Experience (SRE)*, also known as the *Social Readjustment Rating Scale*

(Holmes & Rahe, 1967), is used for scoring recent life changes. The second, the *Cornell Medical Index (CMI)*, is used to assess perceptions of physical and emotional well-being (Brodman & Erdmann, 1956). Each measure was administered as part of a larger study which involved observing these families in their homes (Conger, 1976). Research assistants gave the forms to each parent independently and remained in the room to answer any questions which arose. The *SRE* scores reported here represent the period of time before the last reported incident of abuse, usually encompassing two or more years. The scores for each matched control over the same time span.

The SRE is used to quantify life change where items are weighted according to their empirically derived influences on future health. Mild life crisis is usually defined as 150-199 *Life Change Units (LCU)*, moderate life crisis as 200-299 *LCU* and major life crisis as 300 or more *LCU*. The two-year period following a cluster of life changes is the time when a subject is "at risk" for negative health or behavior influences (Holmes & Masuda, 1973). Standard scoring is used for the *CMI* which involves negative or affirmative responses to 185 items descriptive of physical or emotional health problems.

In addition to the *CMI* and *SRE*, one item was used from the "Survey on Bringing Up Children" developed by Helfer and Schneider (Note 2). This survey was another measure used in the larger project from which these materials originated. It was administered to parents in the same fashion as the *CMI* and *SRE*. The particular question used from this instrument helps to specify childhood experiences which might influence whether life change or illness result in severly distorted childrearing practices. The question asked whether the respondent, or his or her siblings had been severely punished as children. Subjects answered on a seven point scale with strongly agree scored 1, neither agree nor disagree scored 4, and strongly disagree scored 7.

Results

The findings show that the abuse parents differ from their respective controls in terms of average number of life change units (*LCU*). The abuse (*M* = 340) control (*M* = 244) difference is statistically significant (*p* < .025) using the Wilcoxon matched-pairs, signed-ranks test.

Subdivisions of the data by parental sex or by perpetrator produced no significant differences. Evidently, life change experienced by either spouse has ramifications for the other.

Given the small sample to date, only one specific item on the life change schedule was significantly different, i.e., personal injury or illness (*p* < .05). While 40% of the abusive parents report health change or injury, only 15% of the controls respond similarly. While none of the other individual life change items were significantly different, there is some evidence that controls are more likely to experience positive life changes, e.g., "outstanding personal achievement," while abusive parents are more likely to encounter negative life events, e.g., becoming injured or ill. As our sample size increases, the examination of each individual item will become more meaningful.

In order to test the interaction between current life crisis and learning history, the data for abuse parents and their controls were cross-tabulated by life crisis, dichotomized as mild or none and moderate or severe, and agreement or disagreement on the question, *"When I was a child my parents used severe physical punishmet on me or at least one of my siblings."* Abuse parents reported higher agreement with this latter test item than controls (mean difference $= 1.65$, $p < .025$, Wilcoxon test). Respondents who neither agreed nor disagreed with the statement were removed from the analysis leaving 17 subjects in the abuse group, 18 in the control. Of the abuse parents who remained in the sample after dichotomizing the punishment question, 47% agreed that they were or a sibling was severely punished as a child. Only 6% of the controls responded similarly. In addition, 41% of the abuse parents both agreed that severe punishment occurred in their family of origin and also reported experiencing moderate to severe life change at the time of the abuse incident. None of the control parents reported both moderate to severe life change and punitive parents.

Also interesting is the fact that life change appears to have its greatest impact on those abusive parents who had severely punitive parents. While an almost equal number of abusive parents who did not experience such a background fall into each of the life crisis categories (24% and 29% respectively), only 6% of the abusive parents who agreed their parents were punitive experienced low life crisis compared to 41% who experience moderate or severe crisis. Apparently, life crisis has its most significant impact on those respondents with a punitive history. These findings are consistent with a social learning interpretation that those abusers who had punitive parents probably experienced higher levels of punishment when their parents were faced with stressful situations.

Clearly, the data suggest that a combination of particular childhood experiences together with rapid life change may be an influence on the occurrence of child abuse. Indeed, these abuse parents or their siblings may have been most severely punished when their caretakers were under stress and this experience seemingly has acted as a model for their own reaction to life crisis. Also clear, however, is the fact that over one-half (53%) of the abusive parents do not report a history of being abused. Moreover, life crisis does not discriminate well within this group. We will return to these findings in the discussion.

Table 1 provides similar findings for scores on the *Cornell Medical Index*. The mean score for abusive parents is higher for each category in the table than for controls. By their higher score in the total "yes" column, abusive parents show a greater number of both physical and emotional health problems than controls ($p < .01$). While abusive parents also score higher on items descriptive on fatigue and illness frequency, the difference is not statistically significant. The last page of the *CMI* is devoted to symptoms of emotional illness, e.g., anxiety and depression. Here, the difference between abusive and control parents approaches statistical significance ($p < .10$). When the last page of the questionnaire is dropped from the analysis, the resultant score pertains primarily to physical health problems. Consistent with the findings on the *SRE*, the abusive parents seem to suffer more physical ill-health than controls ($p < .025$).

While the *CMI* scores are significantly higher for abusive parents than their controls, the entire population of this study has an extremely large number of "yes" responses. For example, Rahe, et al., (1972) report an average total *CMI* score of only 10.8 for a general Navy population which is considerably lower than the mean of 24.2 for our control group. Apparently, the poor life circumstances of all the

TABLE 1

Mean Scores on the Cornell Medical Index for Abuse and Control Families

	Total Yes Responses	Yes Responses for Fatigue/Illness Frequency	Yes Responses for Emotional Health Problems	Total Minus the last page	N
Families					
Abuse	37.9*	2.6	9.3***	28.6**	16[a]
Abuse Control	24.2	1.9	6.7	17.5	20

[a] The lower n for the abuse group occurred because questionnaire forms arrived after the first 4 families were interviewed.

 * $p < .01$.

 ** $p < .025$.

 *** $p < .10$.

Note: Significance figures were computed using the Wilcoxon matched-pairs, signed-ranks test.

parents in this study are partially reflected in these scores. Should these data be compared with those produced by parents more representative of the general population, we would expect the abuse parents would be even more remarkable in their deviation from the norm.

Additional analysis showed that affirmative responses on the *CMI* interact with learning experiences to distinguish further abuse from control parents. While this latter interaction is not nearly so dramatic as in the case of life crisis, fully 27% of the abusive parents score thirty or more "yes" responses on the *CMI* and agree their parents were severely punitive while none of the controls fits into the same combined category.

Discussion

While *post hoc* explanations for previously occurring events are less satisfactory than the prediction of particular phenomena, the findings in the present analysis grew logically from previous research and theory. Indeed, prospective studies as well have shown the predictive validity of *CMI* and life change scores (Holmes & Masuda, 1973; Rahe, et al., 1972). The extension of the life change paradigm from physical to social deviations offers an interesting new tool for the study of social behavior and its correlates with physical and emotional health. The data contained herein suggest that those interested in predicting the occurrence of a child abuse event would do well to investigate not only the childhood experiences of parents and their current perceptions of their children, but also the interaction between those two factors and current life change. Moreover, the parent's perception of his or her physical or emotional well-being must be considered.

The results from this study are limited by the small number of parents involved. However, given the statistically significant differences found with such a small number of cases, it seems safe to conclude that life change, perceptions of physical or emotional ill-health and a punitive family of origin are factors much more characteristic of this sample of abusive than of control parents. Importantly, we have added to the findings of Justice and Duncan (1976) by showing a direct interaction between life crisis and learning experiences rather than seeing them only as independently related to child abuse.

Also clear from the present results is the conclusion that only part of the abuse problem appears to hinge on the factors studied here. While 47% of the abusive parents felt their own caretakers were severe disciplinarians, 53% did not. In addition, while 70% of the abusive parents were experiencing moderate or severe life crisis at the time of the abuse incident, 30% of them were not. However, almost all of those abusive parents who report extreme life crisis also experienced a punitive childhood. On the other hand, those not reporting such a punitive background divide about equally on the life crisis variable. It appears then that life crisis is most critical for parents with a punitive history—consistent with a learning perspective.

Rather than conclude that these factors either singly or in combination determine an abuse incident, they should be seen as two of several possible variables which influence harsh treatment of children. Untouched by the current research are many situational events which may precipitate an abuse incident. For example, misbehavior of children and the heat of the day may provide the immediate grist which determines whether a parent will physically injure a child. Life crisis, physical and emotional health plus childhood experiences of a particular type of predisposing events which may turn the similar situations which all parents face into an abusive encounter in one instance while not in another.

In attempting to generalize these findings, another cautionary note must be considered. The victims of mistreatment here were generally older than those found in the usual analyses of the "battered-child syndrome." In fact, they were all beyond infancy, some of them entering the early adolescent period. It is likely, therefore, that most parents included in this sample had functioned well enough as caretakers to rear their children through the first few years of life. Unlike some other parents who have been similarly labeled for much more severe offenses, e.g., situations where children have been removed from the home or died from their injuries, parents of the type reported in this study would seem to be particularly well-suited for intervention efforts. If our somewhat tentative interpretation of these data is correct, i.e., that many abusive parents have learned from models who are particularly punitive to their children during stressful periods, then a treatment program should involve opportunities to react to children in less violent ways when stress occurs. Therapies which involve the learning of alternative responses to such conditions, then, may be particularly appropriate to the problem of many abusive parents.

REFERENCE NOTES

1.   GELLES, R. J. *Violence towards children in the United States*. A paper presented to the American Association for the Advancement of Science, Denver, February, 1977.

2.   HELFER, R., & SCHNEIDER, C. *Survey on bringing up children*. Unpublished paper, Michigan State University, College of Human Medicine, 1974.

REFERENCES

BANDURA, A. *Aggression: A social learning analysis*. New Jersey: Prentice-Hall, 1973.

BLALOCK, H. M. *Social statistics* (2nd ed.). New York: McGraw-Hill, 1972.

BRODMAN, K., ERDMANN, A. J., & WOLFF, H. G. *Cornell Medical Index Health Questionnaire (Rev. ed.).* New York: Cornell University Medical College, 1956.

CARRANZA, E. *A study of the impact of life changes on high-school teacher performance in the Lansing School District as measured by the Holmes and Rahe Schedule of Recent Experience.* Unpublished doctoral dissertation, Michigan State University, 1972.

CONGER, R. D. *A comparative study of interaction patterns between deviant and non-deviant families.* Unpublished doctoral dissertation, University of Washington, 1976.

GIL, D. G. *Violence against children: Physical child abuse in the United States.* Cambridge, Mass.: Harvard University Press, 1970.

HARRIS, P. W. *The relationship of life change to academic performance among selected college freshmen at varying levels of college readiness.* Unpublished doctoral dissertation, East Texas State University, 1972.

HOLMES, T. S., & HOLMES, T. H. "Risk of illness." *Continuing Education.* 1975, 18, 48-51.

HOLMES, T. H., & MASUDA, M. "Life change and illness susceptibility." *AAAS' separation and depression*, 1973, 161-186.

HOLMES, T. H., & RAHE, R. H. "The social readjustment rating scale." *Journal of Psychosomatic Research*, 1967, 11, 213-218.

JUSTICE, B., & DUNCAN, D. F. "Life crisis as a precursor to child abuse." *Public Health Reports*, 1976, 91, 110-115.

PARKE, R. D., & COLLMER, C. W. "Child abuse: An interdisciplinary analysis." In E. M. Hetherington (Ed.), *Review of child development research* (Vol. 5). Chicago: University of Chicago Press, 1975.

RAHE, R. H., BIERSNER, R. J., RYMAN, D. H., & ARTHUR, R. J. "Psychosocial predictors of illness behavior and failure in stressful training." *Journal of Health and Social Behavior*, 1972, 13, 393-397.

SELYE, H. *The stress of life.* New York: McGraw-Hill, 1956.

24

Psychological, Cultural and Family Factors in Incest and Family Sexual Abuse*

David Finkelhor

The National Center for Child Abuse and Neglect estimates that between 40,000 and 60,000 children are sexually abused by their parents or caretakers each year (My husband, 1977). My own estimates, based on the results of an in-progress survey of college students, are that about 90 women out of every 1000 have been sexually victimized by a family member and that between five and ten women out of every 1000 have had an incestuous experience with their father (Finkelhor, 1979). Other surveys confirm the more impressionistic evidence of recent clinical reports from all over the country that incest occurs in a substantial number of families (Benward and Densen-Gerber, 1975; Hunt, 1974.

This paper is a review of clinical and sociological descriptions of incestuous families. The reports on which it is based leave much to be desired. They are mostly reports of small numbers of incest cases that have come to professional attention either through the police or through mental health agencies. As such, they may not reflect at all the vast number of families where incest occurs, but is never reported. Still, they represent the only evidence we have and may at least give an accurate portrayal of the kinds of families clinicians and social workers can expect to see.

First, some clarifications are in order. I am going to use incest to mean more than sexual intercourse. In terms of this discussion, incest will mean any kind of intentionally arousing contact to the sexual organs by a family member.

* The writing of this paper has been assisted by NIMH grants T32-MH15161 and R01-MH30939. It has also benefitted greatly from the comments of Murray Straus. A version of it appeared in the *Journal of Marriage and Family Counseling*, October, 1978.

David Finkelhor, "Psychological, Cultural and Family Factors in Incest and Family Sexual Abuse," Publication VS-2. Reproduced by permission of the author.

Secondly, I am going to limit the discusion almost exclusively to father-daughter sexual experiences. This is because it is the main kind of incest to have received clinical attention.

Popular Misconceptions

Rape and Incest

Many people today realize that father-daughter incest is substantially different from rape. But because they both connote sexual exploitation of women, a strong association of the two often exists. Susan Brownmiller in her recently popular *Against Our Will* (1975), which drew much public attention to the problem of sexual exploitation of women, argued that incest, in fact, should be called "father rape".

But the analogy of rape with incest is largely misleading. Most incest, as it has been reported, does not involve single acts of sexual violation. Most of the incestuous relationships that have been examined last quite a long time, anywhere from six months to seven or eight years (Gebhard et al., 1965; Maisch, 1972).

The coercion involved in incest, moreover, is different from that involved in rape. Few incestuous relationships start as the result of physical force and violence. In most instances, children appear to passively submit to or co-operate in the sex (Gebhard et al., 1965). That the offender is an extremely powerful and often emotionally essential person in the child's life makes this understandable. Physical and psychological coercion are more apparent in the continuation of the relationship. Incest is prolonged in many instances through threats the offender makes of the dire consequences that will ensue if the victim should reveal the incest to any third party.

Incestuous relationships generally start around the time a daughter has reached puberty or before. The average age of onset was found to be between 13 and 15 according to one study (Maisch, 1972), and one or two years earlier according to others (De Francis, 1969; Landis, 1956). What is remarkable, however, is how much sexual abuse occurs to children before puberty, even starting as early as 3 and 4 years of age (Gagnon, 1965; Gebhard et al., 1965), or earlier (Sgroi, 1975). These prepubertal experiences involve less intercourse and more other kinds of sexual stimulation, but often they continue into adolescence (Gebhard et al., 1965).

Socioeconomic Status and Incest

Incest may be more common in rural areas, but the evidence from which to judge is scanty. Rural states like Maine and West Virginia have developed reputations for having pockets of incest, but a study that compared the regional distribution of its incest victims could find no bias toward more rural segments of the country (Benward and Densen-Gerber, 1975).

Certainly studies done in urban court settings have had no difficulty discovering cases (De Francis, 1969; Szabo, 1958; Weinberg, 1955). As we will argue later, there is a particular kind of incest that flourishes in a rural environment. Its particular visibility is responsible for the stereotype.

Up until quite recently, there was a general consensus that incestuous families came almost entirely from the low end of the socio-economic scale.

But as organized treatment programs for sexual abusers and physical abusers have been established, middle-class incest families have "come out of the closet" (My husband, 1977; Giaretto, 1976). Apparently, these families have managed in the past to handle their incest through other means without bringing it to the attention of courts and social agencies. Data from sexual surveys would indicate that there is a large amount of middle-class incest that has not yet come to public awareness (Finkelhor, 1977).

Causes of Incest: Six Factors

I am going to discuss six factors which appear to be important in creating an incestuous family situation: 1) personality of father, 2) role of the mother, 3) milieu of abandonment, 4) isolation, 5) poor family sexual boundaries and 6) opportunity factors.

I. Incestuous Personality

Many investigators have noticed a group of incestuous fathers who appear to be very tyrannical (Lustig et al., 1966; Maisch, 1972; Weinberg, 1955; Weiner, 1962). They dominate their wives and families, they behave without regard for the feelings of family members, they intimidate them and are often violent. As part of the pattern, they foist themselves sexually on their daughters.

But not all incestuous fathers are such tyrants. A second group, probably a minority to judge by its visibility in the literature, appears to be quite a bit more restrained, in fact inhibited. These men are described as shy, ineffectual types, who had difficulty in their social relations prior to marriage. They are often quite dependent on their wives for emotional and even financial support (Cormier, 1962). They have poor employment records and are often out of work, a condition which sometimes provides the opportunity for the initiation of incest with a daughter. They may share with their tyrannical equivalents a sense of masculine inadequacy and anger toward women. For them incest appears to take the place of an extramarital affair which they feel too inhibited to pursue (Gebhard et al., 1965).

Both of these personality types have something important in common: alcohol. Almost all researchers have been struck by the presence of a high degree of alcoholism among incest offenders and have tried to measure its incidence in their surveys. The studies reveal an average of from 30% to 50% of the incest offenders to be chronic alcoholics (Maisch, 1972).

II. Family Role Confusion

One of the most consistent findings over the years of clinical experience with incest is that it usually occurs after the cessation of sexual relations between husband

and wife (Henderson, 1972; Maisch, 1972; Molnar and Cameron, 1975). Sometimes this cessation is the result of pregnancy or physical incapacitation of the wife, but more often than not, it is the result of severely strained husband-wife relations. These marital problems are part of a system of role confusion that involves at least father, mother and daughter, if not other family members. The basic configuration in such families is a father and daughter who constitute the main emotional axis of the family, and a mother who is peripheral.

In many incestuous families, it has been noted that the mothers are particularly withdrawn and depressed or incapacitated (Browning and Boatman, 1977; Weinberg, 1955). Often they retreat from family involvement to seek refuge with other relatives or in non-family activities. Their relationships with their daughters are often as disturbed as their relationships with their husbands, and they leave the daughters in charge of family responsibilities and the younger children. Under encouragement from the father, such daughters may take over the mother's sexual functions along with her other responsibilities.

The defect in the mother-daughter relationship also contributes to the daughter's vulnerability. The mother lacks willingness or ability to ally with her daughter, to protect her, or to motivate her to resist the father. One could imagine this stemming from many sources including jealousy of the daughter, low self-image, and perhaps most likely, subservience to the father.

It is important not to conclude on the basis of such evidence as some apparently have, that it is the mother who is the real culprit (Rush, 1974). There is a complex system at work in these families, and mothers are often as much victims as daughters. Such mothers often lack social and economic resources to defend themselves and have been conditioned into a state of helplessness. The tyrannical character of many of the husbands also helps explain the passivity seen in these women.

In sum, a common situation in incestuous families is essentially the following: The husband-wife relationship has broken down and often so has the mother-daughter relationship. Powerless, and perhaps unwilling, to defend her own position, the mother withdraws from the family, as a new father-daughter coalition forms. Deprived of a partner, his sexuality perhaps in question, the father may be very eager to sexualize this coalition. Unprotected by her mother and lacking another parent to turn to, the daughter is in a highly vulnerable position. Under such conditions or variants of these, incest may be very likely to occur.

III. The Milieu of Abandonment

Incest may also occur in response to a pervasive kind of family emotional climate, one dominated by the fear of abandonment. In families dominated by an anxiety that each member may be abandoned by all others, sexuality may be the final resource used by family members to stave off this loss. Fathers may seek out their daughters and daughters accept their fathers' overtures, when the specter of abandonment looms large (Henderson, 1972; Kaufman et al., 1954).

Such families seem to have a history of abandonment that dominates family history. Grandfathers had abandoned grandmothers; parents had abandoned their children.

Secondly, the cast of characters in many such families seems to be constantly changing. Step-parents and foster children have moved in and out of the family circle, and the family boundary seems to be diffuse and poorly maintained.

In trying to explain why daughters tolerate and in some cases encourage incestuous relationships that extend over periods of months and years, one frequently cited factor is that daughters may be receiving a kind of attention and affection which was otherwise unavailable to them. Besides the affection and attention, daughters may also harbor the accurate notion that without the incestuous relationship there would be no family at all (Lustig et al., 1966). Of course, once the incest begins this fantasy becomes all the more realistic, since revelation and termination of the relationship are virtually certain to bring about the crisis of family dissolution that was feared all along.

IV. The Isolated Incestuous Subculture

There appear to be some very poor, very rural subcultures where incest is quite conspicuous. Such families live in isolated regions, such as the hollows of West Virginia, or in rural reaches of New England, often in extended family groups. Cousins intermarry; women become pregnant early; illegitimacy is widespread.

The level of apparent pathology in many of these families is often so great that it is hard to distinguish which of the many factors is most directly responsible for the incest.

1) Such subcultures may take a less restrictive view of incestuous behavior. 2) Incest may result from the family disorganization connected to the poverty in which these families live. And also 3) the isolation of these families may insulate them from the scrutiny of public view which acts to enforce incest taboos in less isolated communities. Isolation would also mean that there were fewer alternative places offenders could go for sex, and victims for help. A self-contained subculture more favorable to incest might be more likely to evolve under such conditions (Bagley, 1969; Riemer, 1940).

V. The Sexualized Family

Some families sexualize family relationships because they fail to recognize privacy and personal boundaries.

In highly sexualized families, members use one another as objects to their sexual role-playing. Each member tests out powers of attraction and adequacy on one another.

With poorly demarcated personal boundaries, family members do not respect privacy, they intrude upon one another, and adult sexual behavior is not clearly distinguished from child sexual behavior.

This pattern has been very often associated with large families and overcrowding, situations where the physical environment itself did not permit healthy personal boundaries. But it can appear in conventional family situations, too.

VI. Opportunity Factors

Finally we should not overlook factors in family life which directly affect whether the opportunity for sexual abuse arises. In some studies sexually abusive fathers are often unemployed (Weinberg, 1955). In addition to whatever personal turmoil this may create, it also provides the fathers the time and opportunity to initiate incest. Mothers who are working or absent may create similar opportunities. Much incest appears to arise when a situation allows a father and daughter to spend a great deal of time alone. Although this does not inevitably lead to incest, it probably is one of the opportunity factors that permits a family configuration such as one of those described earlier to develop from a potential to an actual incest relationship.

Summary

The serious study of any social phenomenon goes through two phases. The first is the period of brainstorming, as new possible hypotheses about the causes of the phenomenon are added to the debate. The second is a period of refinement, when the wealth of theories challenges the scientist to find out which ones can really be empircally verified. Incest is still in its brainstorming phase, but pressure is building toward refinement. Perhaps soon we will have some systematic data about incest from which to begin the culling and weeding.

REFERENCES

BAGLEY, C. 1969. "Incest behavior and incest taboo." *Social Problems*. 16:505-519.

BENWARD, J. AND DENSEN-GERBER, J. 1975. "Incest as a causative factor in anti-social behavior: an exploratory study." Paper presented at the American Academy of Forensic Sciences.

BROWNING, D. AND BOATMAN, B. 1977. "Incest: children at risk." *A. J. Psychiatry*. 134:69-72.

BROWNMILLER, S. 1975. *Against Our Will: Men, Women and Rape*. Simon and Schuster, New York.

CORMIER, B. ET AL. 1962. "Psychodynamics of Father-Daughter Incest." *Canadian Psychiatric Association Journal*. 7:203-217.

DE FRANCIS, V. 1969. *Protecting the Child Victim of Sex Crimes Committed By Adults*. American Humane Association, Denver Colo.

GAGNON, J. 1965. "Female child victims of sex offenses." *Social Problems*. 13:176-192.

FINKELHOR, D. 1979. *Sexually Victimized Children*. Free Press, New York.

GEBHARD, P. ET AL. 1965. *Sex Offenders: An Analysis of Types*. Harper and Row, New York.

GIARETTO, H. 1976. "Humanistic treatment of father daughter incest." In R. E. Helfer and C. H. Kempe (Eds.), *Child Abuse and Neglect: The Family and The Community*. Ballinger, Cambridge.

HENDERSON, J. 1972. "Incest: a synthesis of data." *Canadian Psychiatric Association Journal*. 17:299-313.

HUNT, M. 1974. *Sexual Behavior in the 1970's*. Playboy Press, Chicago.

KAUFMAN, I. ET AL. 1954. "The family constellation and overt incestuous relations between father and daughter." *A. J. Ortho*. 24:266-79.

LANDIS, J. 1956. "Experiences of 500 children with adult sexual deviants."*Psychiatric Quarterly Supplement*. 30:91-109.

LUSTIG, N. ET AL. 1966. "Incest: a family group survival pattern." *Arch. Gen. Psychiat*. 14:31-40.

MAISCH, H. 1972. *Incest*. Stein and Day, New York.

MOLNAR, B. AND CAMERON, P. 1975 "Incest syndromes: observations in a general hospital psychiatric unit." *Canadian Psychiatric Association Journal*. 20:1-24.

"My husband broke the ultimate taboo." *Family Circle*. March 8, 1977.

RIEMER, S. 1940. "A research note on incest." *Amer J. Sociol*. 45:566-572.

RUSH, F. 1974. "The sexual abuse of children: a feminist point of view." In N. Connell and C. Wilson, ed. *Rape: The First Sourcebook For Women*. NAL Plume, New York.

SGROI, S. 1975. "Sexual Molestation of children: the last frontier of child abuse." *Children Today*. May-June 18-21:44.

SZABO, D. 1958. "L'inceste en milieu urbain." *L'annee Sociologique*.

WEINBERG, S. K. 1955. *Incest Behavior*. Citadel, New York.

25

Child Abuse: Pathological Syndrome of Family Interaction*

Arthur H. Green, M.D.,
Richard W. Gaines, and
Alice Sandgrund, Ph.D.

Within the decade since the pioneering description of the battered child syndrome by Kempe and associates,[1] a great variety of behavioral characteristics and psychopathology have been attributed to abusive parents. They have been described as immature,[2] impulsive,[3] isolated from family and friends,[4] rigid and domineering,[5] dependent and narcissistic,[6] chronically aggressive,[5] and prone toward marital difficulties[1] One observer noted that abusive mothers were "masculine" while their husbands were "passive".[7] Role reversal[8, 9] has also been described, by which the abusive parent seeks love and approval from the child. Some investigators[10, 11] have regarded child abuse as a syndrome that appears primarily in families in the lowest socioeconomic levels, while others[4] have cited its occurrence in the middle and upper classes. Other workers[12, 13] maintained that child abuse is psychodynamically determined and is independent of education, race, and socioeconomic level. Some abused children manifest signs of physical neglect, while others are said to receive adequate material and physical care.

* This work was supported by Public Health Service grant MH-188897 from the Center for Studies of Suicide Prevention, National Institute of Mental Health.

The authors gratefully acknowledge the assistance of the Bureau of Child Welfare and the Family Court of the City of New York. They also wish to thank Dr. Lillian Gross, Dr. Bernardo Scheimberg, and Ms. Colette Brousal for their help as interviewers.

Arthur Green, et al., "Child Abuse: Pathological Syndrome of Family Interaction," *American Journal of Psychiatry*, Vol. 131, No. 8 (August 1974):882-886. Copyright © 1974 the American Psychiatric Association. Reproduced by permission.

More incisive descriptions of the psychopathology of abusing parents and their interaction with their children have been revealed during the course of psychiatric treatment. Steele[13] described a clinical syndrome of parental dysfunction with rather specific key psychodynamics in which he stressed the importance of the parent's closely linked identifications with a harsh, rejecting mother and with a "bad" childhood self-image. These are reenacted in the current child-rearing situation. The abusive parents submit their children to the same traumatic experiences that they themselves had endured, using such defense mechanisms as denial, projection, role reversal, and identification with the aggressor. Galdston[14] reported the treatment of parents of abused preschool children who attended a therapeutic day care center. He emphasized the parents' unresolved oedipal conflicts and phobias in attempting to explain their current difficulties. Feinstein and associates[15] explored in group therapy the behavior of women with infanticidal impulses. These women were characterized by the resentment they showed toward their parents for not satisfying their dependency needs and by their affinity for "maternal" husbands. Many had witnessed or had been subjected to excessive parental violence.

The widely varying behavioral characteristics, personality traits, and psychiatric symptoms described in parents who physically abuse their children suggest that a specific "abusive" personality does not exist. The personality attributes of these parents do not seem to be sufficient to cause child abuse in the absence of potentiating factors within the family. The behavior of the child and the quality of the relationship of the child-abusing parent with the spouse and family must also be weighed as possible contributors to a context in which abuse might occur.

It is the purpose of this study to: 1) describe the most common personality characteristics of the mothers or maternal caretakers of abused children, including the manner in which they perceive themselves and their children; 2) explore the contribution of the child in the abuse process; 3) determine patterns of parent-child interaction in which abuse typically occurs; 4) construct a psychodynamic framework for understanding the phenomenon of child abuse in a disadvantaged population; and 5) assess the environmental factors associated with child abuse.

Method

The sample consisted of mothers or maternal caretakers of 60 abused children referred by the Bureau of Child Welfare and the Family Court of New York City. Almost all of the families resided in inner-city ghetto areas and represented the lowest socioeconomic group, with a majority receiving public assistance. All of the children were between their fifth and 13th birthdays. The ethnic composition was primarily black and Hispanic. (see table 1). The mothers or maternal caretakers were under the supervision of protective service units of the Bureau of Child Welfare or on probation with the Family Court. The criteria for identifying abuse specified that it be of an ongoing or recurrent nature and be confirmed by investigation.

A child psychiatry staff member conducted a structured interview, requiring approximately one and a half hours, with each mother or maternal caretaker to obtain the following information: obstetrical, birth, and perinatal history; family background and early experience; interaction with parents, siblings, and peers; dating, courtship, and marital history; maternal behavioral assessment of the child,

TABLE 1

Sex and Ethnic Background of Abused Children

Ethnic Background	Male (N = 32)		Female (N = 28)	
	Number	Percent	Number	Percent
Black	22	68	17	63
White	5	16	3	11
Hispanic	5	16	8	26

including symptoms, school performance and behavior, and peer and family relationships; maternal attitudes toward the abused child and siblings; maternal attitudes toward child rearing and punishment; presence of outstanding maternal psychopathology: psychosis, addiction, alcoholism, etc.; relationships with men (husbands, boyfriends, etc.).

These data were augmented by agency records, which included reports by protective caseworkers and probation officers. Additional information on family psychodynamics and patterns of interaction was obtained from follow-up interviews with approximately 20 percent of the mothers and children who were interested in receiving outpatient treatment. Over half of this group participated in the psychotherapy program, which became a valuable source of information regarding unconscious determinants in the parent-child relationship. The abused children served as subjects in additional studies in which their ego functions, behavior, intelligence, and neurological status were determined.[16] These data provided valuable impressions regarding the impact of each child's personality, ego capacity, and developmental status on the mothering process.

Results

The mothers or maternal caretakers of the abused children frequently reported difficulties with their parents. These relationships were marred by criticism, rejection, and physical punishment. They also described current marital discord and stressed the emotional unavailability and physical brutality of their spouses. They complained of an inability to secure help with the burdens of child rearing, which was a consequence of their alienation from their spouses and families. The failure to find support from the environment facilitated turning toward their children for dependency gratification. Their long-term experience of criticism and punishment reinforced their feelings of having been burdensome children and promoted their identification with a hostile, rejecting parental figure.

These women characteristically reported the abused children as aggressive and unmanageable at home and in school. The abused children usually required more attention than their siblings. The mother's perception of the abused child as the most aggressive and demanding of her offspring contributed to the child's scapegoating.

The in-depth exploration of the personality structure of the mothers and their abused children during psychotherapy provided a better understanding of the etiology and psychodynamics of the child abuse syndrome. The focus of the interviews and treatment on patterns of family interaction spanning three generations added a longitudinal perspective to the study.

Child abuse may be construed as the end result of an interaction among three major factors: parents' personality attributes that contribute to their "abuse proneness" and are incompatible with adequate child rearing; characteristics of the child that increase the likelihood of his being abused; and immediate environmental stresses that maximize the burden of child rearing.

Personality Characteristics of Abuse-Prone Parents

1. The parents rely on the child to gratify dependency needs that are unsatisfied in their relationships with their spouses and families. This constitutes role reversal.

2. The parents manifest impaired impulse control based on childhood experience with harsh punishment and identification with violent adult models.

3. The parents are handicapped by a poor self-concept. They feel worthless and devalued, which reflects the rejection and criticism accorded them by adults during their own childhood.

4. They display disturbances in identity formation. Identifications are shifting and unstable and are dominated by hostile introjects derived from the internalization of "bad" self and object representations of early childhood.

5. They respond to assaults on their fragile self-esteem with a compensatory adaptation. Because of their need to maintain a positive facade, they must desperately defend themselves against the awareness of underlying feelings of worthlessness by the frequent use of projection and externalization as defense mechanisms.

6. The projection of negative parental attributes onto the child causes him to be misperceived and used as a scapegoat in order to bear the brunt of the parent's aggression.

Case 1.—Sonia, a six-year-old Puerto Rican girl, was severely beaten by her mother when she was four, resulting in a fractured femur. Sonia was the daughter of Ms. G.'s first husband, who, after frequent quarreling, drinking, and "running around," left her when Sonia was one year old. Ms. G. subsequently entered into a common-law relationship with a man who fathered her two young boys.

Ms. G. initially married in order to escape from her brutal godparents, who had raised her since the age of 18 months after her mother had abandoned her. They had been extremely punitive and restrictive. Ms. G. remembered one occasion in which her godfather had broken a flowerpot over her head. Ms. G.'s marriage was arranged by the godparents. She went to work in a factory and was virtually ignored by her husband. She soon became pregnant but did not want a child since her husband spent no time with her. He deserted a first time when she was six weeks pregnant, and Ms. G. moved in with her sister-in-law to have the baby. She hoped for a boy, stating, "I don't like girls. Boys are more interesting."

In addition to displacing her rage toward her ex-husband and godparents onto Sonia, Ms. G. obviously identified with her little girl and brutalized her in the same manner as her own experience with her godparents. She described the following feelings toward Sonia: "Since she was born, I let out all the anger and frustration that I had in myself on her. Whenever she came to me, I sent her away with a beating." It is worth noting that Ms. G.'s relationship with her male children is better.

Characteristics of the Child

1. Pathological traits that might constitute an additional stress for "average" nonabusive parents include extreme physical or psychological deviance of the child. Children with major physical defects and congenital anomalies, as well as psychotic, retarded, or brain-damaged youngsters, are tolerated poorly by narcissistic parents, who regard them as new editions of their own defective self-image. These children are also extremely burdensome and increase the task of child rearing.

Case 2.—Martin, a seven-year-old white boy, was referred to the Bureau of Child Welfare by school personnel, who noticed numerous marks on his body. Ms. C., his mother, admitted hitting him daily, often with a broomstick, because of his disruptive behavior, which included restlessness, excessive demands for attention, silliness, and his failure to learn. She felt that Martin's misbehavior was an effort to punish her. Ms. C. complained about her alcoholic husband's failure to involve himself with Martin and her three other young children.

Ms. C. reported an unhappy childhood marked by a frustrating relationship with her mother, who consistently criticized and punished her while showing affection to her four brothers. Her mother forced her out of the house when she was 16 years old.

Psychiatric examination of Martin revealed a clumsy, awkward child who was agitated and hyperactive. His speech was grossly impaired, and he was preoccupied with uncontrollable aggressive and destructive fantasies. There was a pronounced lag in his acquisition of speech and motor functions. The neurological examination indicated impaired motor coordination and perceptual motor deficits, with an abnormal EEG. Full-scale IQ on the Wechsler Intelligence Scale for Children (WISC) was 72. Ms. C. admitted disliking Martin from birth because he was "difficult" and demanded so much attention.

Another group of children with pathological traits that might constitute additional stress are those who respond poorly to nurturance. These may be colicky, irritable, and hypertonic infants who are difficult to satisfy and comfort. The mothers perceive their unresponsiveness as a rejection reminiscent of experiences with their own parents and intensifying their sense of inadequacy.

Older children who display difficulties with impulse control also comprise part of this group. They manifest such behavior problems as lying, stealing, and assaultiveness and are often disruptive in school. They relate to significant objects in a provocative, sado-masochistic fashion. They clearly find some gratification in their ability to elicit punishment from the abusive parent.

2. Normal or "accidental" traits, which are misperceived by, or only attain special significance for, abuse-prone parents, include the child who is identified with a hated person or situation. For example, a mother will beat a child whose conception forced her into a premature and unhappy marriage. Another mother will abuse a child who resembles a despised ex-husband or boyfriend.

Case 3.—Sam, a nine-year-old Jamaican boy, was severely beaten with a broomstick by his mother for distributing the family's food stamps at school. This event occurred shortly after his return from Jamaica where he had been cared for by several "babysitters" since the age of two when his mother left him and his year-old brother in order to go to New York. Ms. R. had beaten Sam frequently as an infant before she left him, and he and his brother were given regular severe beatings by the woman who was responsible for most of their care. Ms. R. subsequently had three children out of wedlock in New York. She readily agreed to allow Sam to live with her own mother after she was reported to the Bureau of Child Welfare.

Ms. R. had conceived Sam when she was 16 and had broken off with her boyfriend before she was aware of the pregnancy. Her mother became enraged, subjected her to beatings, and put her out of the house before she had the baby. Another son was born 16 months later, and Ms. R. left for New York shortly thereafter. Ms. R. recently married the father of her youngest child and has not visited Sam since he was placed with the grandmother. Ms. R. could cope with this unfortunate child, whom she unconsciously blamed for her mother's abuse and abandonment of her, only by subjecting him to the same punishment.

Also included in the group of children with misperceived normal traits is the child whose parent remarries and who is subsequently regarded by the stepparent as an unwelcome and burdensome stepchild. The stepchild is often treated as a sibling rival who threatens the stepparent's dependency on the mate. The stepchild also becomes a convenient target for the stepparent's hostility directed originally toward the spouse.

Case 4.—Don, an 11-year-old black child, was severely beaten by his stepfather, resulting in multiple contusions and lacerations of his back and buttocks that necessitated his hospitalization. Don is an only child who had lived with his mother and maternal grandparents on a farm in the South. Don remained with his grandparents when his mother came to New York to find employment. When his mother married Mr. P., Don, then seven, came to New York to live with them. Since his arrival, Don has been a source of constant friction between his mother and stepfather. The latter accused his wife of spoiling Don and failing to curb his "meanness." Mr. P. complained that Don was a financial burden and subjected him to frequent and excessive beatings. When Don's mother would intervene to protect him, Mr. P. threatened to leave if the boy was not sent back to the grandparents.

A young child who exhibits age-appropriate sexual or aggressive behavior that is considered to be abnormal is also included in this group of abused children. This behavior cannot be tolerated because it evokes the parent's own unacceptable impulses that are excluded from consciousness and ascribed to the child by means of denial and projection. Sexual acting out in older children will often elicit physical abuse from a parent who identifies with these unacceptable impulses.

Case 5.—Debby P., a seven-year-old black girl, had been subjected to recurrent abuse by her mother for alleged mutual masturbation with her five-year-old sister. Ms. P. habitually examined Debby's panties for stains or some other evidence of masturbation. She would then accuse her and punish her with a beating. The abuse was accompanied by threats of abandonment.

Ms. P.'s childhood had been marred by her mother's abandonment and a punitive relationship with her grandmother, who used to beat Ms. P. and her twin sister while they slept. At the age of 14, Ms. P. was placed in a training school, where she had engaged in some homosexual activity. Debby's masturbation undoubtedly evoked her mother's long-standing guilt and anxiety over homosexuality, which she managed by attacking Debby with the full fury of her punitive superego.

Current Environmental Stress

Environmental stress includes current events that widen the discrepancy between the limited capacity of the parents and increased child-rearing pressures. The stress may consist of a diminishing of child-rearing resources, which might be due to a spouse's illness or desertion or to the unavailability of an earlier caretaker, such as a neighbor or some other family member.

Case 6.—Calvin, a 10-year-old black boy, was referred to the Bureau of Child Welfare by the school guidance counselor because bruises, scars, and cuts were observed all over his body. These resulted from beatings inflicted by his father, Mr. A. An alcoholic, Mr. A. began to beat Calvin and his two younger children regularly with a knotted ironing cord two years before, after he had assumed full-time child-care responsibility when his wife became incapacitated following a stroke. Mr. A. decided to leave his job and seek public assistance in order to take care of the three children. These arrangements broke down, however, when the pressures of child care caused an increase in Mr. A.'s drinking, which was accompanied by a progressive loss of impulse control.

Another environmental stress is the actual or threatened loss of a key relationship that provides the parent with emotional security and dependency gratification. This may occur when the spouse becomes physically or emotionally unavailable or when ties with parents or important relatives are severed due to estrangement, illness, or death. Additional child-rearing pressures, such as the birth of another child, children becoming ill, or assuming the temporary care of other children occasioned by illness or death of friends or relatives, create environmental stress that might lead to child abuse.

Discussion

One might summarize the typical psychodynamic pattern operant in the abusive mother or maternal caretaker during interaction with the scapegoated child as follows:

The increased demand for nurturing by the child intensifies the mother's own unsatisfied dependency longings. Since the mother is usually unable to receive gratification and support from her spouse and family, she turns to the child for the satisfaction of these needs. These claims on the child are inevitably frustrated, since they are incompatible with the satisfaction of the child's own urgent demands. At this point the mother unconsciously equates the child with her own critical, rejecting mother who never could satisfy her.

The mother passively reenacts with the abused child the rejection and humiliation she originally experienced with her own mother. The resulting anxiety, guilt, and loss of self-esteem threaten the mother's fragile, narcissistic equilibrium. Her "bad" self-image and unacceptable feelings become intolerable and are displaced onto the child with the aid of such defense mechanisms as denial, projection, and externalization. With this shift, the mother assumes the identification with her "bad" mother, representing her punitive superego, and attacks her child, who now symbolizes her past and current inadequacies. This identification with the aggressive mother allows her to actively master the traumatic rejection she had passively experienced as a child at the hands of her own mother. Signs of poor responsiveness, failure to thrive, or deviancy on the child's part may increase the mother's feelings of inadequacy and the transfer of unacceptable maternal traits onto the child.

In addition to representing the "bad mother" and "bad childhood self" in the mother's unconscious, the abused child may become linked to other individuals who have been associated with ambivalence and/or rejection. The child may symbolize a despised former mate or lover, a hated sibling rival, or a disappointing parental substitute; but all of these additional objects retain a tie to the original "bad," rejecting mother.

Nonabusive mothers whose children have been battered by husbands or boyfriends exhibit a slight variation in the psychodynamic pattern. The interaction between mother and child begins in a similar fashion as the mother endows the child with the attributes of her own rejecting mother. However, the resulting "bad" childhood self-image derived from her mother is partly maintained and partly transferred to the child, while the internalized "bad mother" is projected onto the abusive mate. The mother identifies primarily with the "child victim" rather than with the "mother aggressor."

These women submit to the physical cruelty of their mates as a masochistic repetition of their childhood victimization by rejecting, hostile parents. The pain-dependent attachment to the spouse serves as a defense against their hostility toward the child. This is confirmed by the tenacity with which these women cling to such brutal and humiliating partners and by their tendency to assume the abusive role if the spouse leaves.

Conclusion

Child abuse may be regarded as a dysfunction of parenting in which the parent misperceives the child due to the parent's own frustrating childhood experiences. In beating the child, the parent attempts to actively master the trauma he passively endured during his early life. The etiology of child abuse is based upon an interaction among three factors: the personality traits of the parents that contribute to "abuse proneness"; the child's characteristics that enhance his scapegoating; and the increased demand for child care exerted by the environment.

Any logical plan for the prevention or treatment of child abuse must be designed to modify these crucial variables and to acknowledge the intrusion of the past into the parent's current relationship with the abused child.

REFERENCES

1. KEMPE, C. H., SILVERMAN, F. N., STEELE, B. F., et al.: "The battered child syndrome." *JAMA* 181:17-24, 1962.

2. COHEN, M., RAPHLING, D., GREEN, P.: "Psychological aspects of the maltreatment syndrome of childhood." *J Pediatr* 69:279-284, 1966.

3. ELMER, E.: *The Fifty Families Study: Summary of Phase 1, Neglected and Abused Children and Their Families*, Pittsburgh, Children's Hospital of Pittsburgh, July 26, 1965.

4. STEELE, B. F., POLLOCK, C. B.: "A psychiatric study of parents who abuse infants and small children." In *The Battered Child*. Edited by Helfer R. E. Kempe, C. H. Chicago, University of Chicago Press, 1968, pp. 103-147.

5. MERRILL, E. J.: "Physical abuse of children: an agency study," in *Protecting the Battered Child*. Edited by De Francis V. Denver, American Humane Association, 1962, pp. 1-15.

6. YOUNG, L.: *Wednesday's Children: A Study of Child Neglect and Abuse*, New York, McGraw-Hill Book Co. 1964.

7. GALDSTON, R.: "Observations on children who have been physically abused and their parents." *Am J Psychiatry* 122:440-443, 1965.

8. SIMONS, B., DOWNS, E., HURSTER, M. et al.: "Child abuse." *NY State J Med* 66:2783-2788, 1966.

9. MORRIS, M., GOULD, R.: "Role reversal: a necessary concept in dealing with the battered-child syndrome." *Am J Orthopsychiatry* 33:298-299, 1963.

10. JOHNSON, B., MORSE, H.: "Injured children and their parents." *Children* 15:147-152, 1968.

11. GIL, D. G.: *Violence Against Children.* Cambridge, Mass. Harvard University Press, 1970.

12. HELFER, R. E., POLLOCK, C. B.: "The battered child syndrome." *Adv Pediatr* 15:9-27, 1968.

13. STEELE, B. F.: "Parental abuse of infants and small children." in *Parenthood: Its Psychology and Psychopathology.* Edited by Anthony E. J., Benedek T. Boston, Little, Brown and Co., 1970, pp. 449-477.

14. GALDSTON, R.: "Violence begins at home." *J Am Acad Child Psychiatry* 10:336-350, 1971.

15. FEINSTEIN, H. M., PAUL N., PETTISON, E.: "Group therapy for mothers with infanticidal impulses." *Am J Psychiatry* 120:882-886, 1964.

16. GREEN, A. H., SANDGRUND, A., GAINES, R. W., et al.: "Psychological sequelae of child abuse and neglect." Read at the 127th annual meeting of the American Psychiatric Association, Detroit, Mich, May 6-10, 1974.

26

Etiological Factors in Child Maltreatment: A Multivariate Study of Abusing, Neglecting, and Normal Mothers*

Richard Gaines,
Alice Sandgrund,
Arthur H. Green, and
Ernest Power

Numerous single-factor theories have been advanced to explain the maltreatment of children by their parents. Early investigations of the "battered child syndrome" (Cohen, Raphling, & Green, 1966; Steele & Pollock, 1968) focused on life histories and personalities of abusing parents, and penetrating psychodynamic impressions emerged from their psychiatric treatment (Steele, 1970) and observations of mother-child interactions (Galdston, 1971). Morris and Gould (1963) and Steele (1970) were the first to describe the "role reversal" phenomenon, in which the abusing parent turns toward the child for an inordinate amount of dependency gratification. There

* This project was supported by Grant 90-C-421 from the National Center on Child Abuse and Neglect, Office of Child Development, U.S. Department of Health, Education, and Welfare. The authors would like to thank Janet Graber, Joanne Douglas, Howard Grohman, and Leifur Magnusson for their assistance. The cooperation of the Department of Obstetrics and Gynecology, Kings County Hospital, the Bureau of Child Welfare, New York City Special Services for Children, and the Scientific Computing Center, Downstate Medical Center is gratefully acknowledged.

have been few rigorous studies of child abusers and, to date, the preponderance of personality characteristics ascribed to them has been generated from clinical practice. A common critical assumption is that severe dysfunctions of parenting can be explained by an intrapsychic model. Some have sought to identify character types or diagnostic categories prevalent among child abusers, whereas others have focused on traits or needs. The greatest consensus centers on negative childhood experiences thought to antecede aberrant child rearing. Green, Gaines, and Sandgrund (1974) have described childhood rejection, criticism, and punishment experienced by abusing mothers, who typically perceive their offspring the way they were regarded by their own parents.

The few controlled typological studies of this population have relied heavily on self-administered personality inventories. Paulson, Afifi, Thomason, and Chaleff (1974) and Griswold and Billingsley (Note 1) reported Minnesota Multiphasic Personality Inventory profile differences between abusing parents and normal controls. In Griswold and Billingsley's study, female abusers obtained high scores on subscales suggestive of psychosis. Paulson et al.'s female subjects suffered from authority-related conflicts and excessive aggression, whereas male abuser profiles were significantly more psychotic. Smith, Hanson, and Noble (1973) found a high incidence of "abnormal personality features" and neuroses among abusive mothers, whereas abusive fathers were reportedly psychopathic. Thus, the few controlled studies have found abusive parents to suffer from moderate to severe psychopathology, but the disorder specified varies across sexes and from study to study.

The child's role in the abuse process is a subject of controversy. No studies have been designed explicitly to assess the child's functioning prior to abuse, although this would represent a potentially important independent variable for any context in which abuse ultimately ensues. Retrospective studies (Elmer & Gregg, 1967; Klein & Stern, 1971) have found that the incidence of premature births among children subsequently abused is considerably higher than regional averages. Others have reported the prevalence of unrecognized physical handicaps (Ounsted, Oppenheimer, & Lindsay, 1974) and congenital anomalies (Birrell & Birrell, 1968). A direct causal inference is that abused children may be management problems and prone to scapegoating. Alternatively, difficult infant temperaments may impede the establishment of maternal-infant bonding. Fanaroff, Kennell, and Klaus (1972) found that mothers who later maltreated their children visited their low-birth-weight infants less frequently than normal controls. Ounsted et al. (1974) observed "high-risk" mother-infant dyads characterized by puerperal depression among the mothers and colic, irritableness, and incessant crying among the children.

Child characteristics predisposing a parent with limited child-rearing capacities to commit abuse aroused our interest in a study of 120 children from known-abused, neglected, and control populations (Green, Sandgrund, Gaines, & Haberfeld, 1974; Sandgrund, Gaines, & Green, 1974). Both maltreated groups displayed severely impaired ego functions with an alarming incidence of mental retardation difficult to attribute to abuse because of the exclusion of known brain-injured children. Although some may have sustained cognitive damage as a direct result of maltreatment, it appeared likely that many exhibited prior developmental lags. Whether cognitive impairment observed in abused children antedates or results from maltreatment remains inconclusive; however, the abuse-prone parent-deviant child hypothesis seems a more powerful theoretical formulation than the strictly intrapsychic model originally proposed.

In addition to parental personality characteristics and possible preexisting deviancy in abused children, environmental stress has often been implicated in the etiology of child maltreatment. Gil (1970) has attributed abuse almost entirely to socioeconomic determinants. A single study (Justice & Justice, 1976) has shown a relation between life change and child abuse, and economic pressures have been associated in other investigations (Johnson & Morse, 1968; Kempe, Silverman, Steele, Droegemueller, & Silver, 1962). The occurrence of maltreatment in advantaged populations has been noted as well; and the stress argument may be, in part, a spurious inference from the number of poor families in child abuse registers throughout the country. When maltreatment is suspected, deprived persons served by municipal agencies are more likely to be reported. In their 1972 review, Spinetta and Rigler concluded that environmental stress had not been shown to be either necessary or sufficient for child abuse. It may, in some instances, interact with personality and child variables to potentiate maltreatment by widening the discrepancy between limited parental capacities and demanding offspring.

The current study attempted to consolidate previous findings into a multifactor theory that could be corroborated by multivariate methodology. On this basis, maltreatment would result from (a) personality characteristics of parents, (b) children "at risk" due to preexisting deviancy, and (c) environmental stress. A model incorporating all of these agents has received greater attention recently (Green, Gaines, & Sandgrund, 1974; Kempe & Helfer, 1972) but has yet to be tested. Moreover, little is known about the relative contributions of each factor to the maltreatment syndrome.

Method

Subjects

Subjects were 80 mothers, each from known-abuse, neglect, and normal control populations. All had at least one child between 1 and 11 years of age. In the maltreatment groups, a target child was in this age range. All of the families resided in Brooklyn, New York, either at the time of testing (1976-1977) or between 1973 and 1976 when the maltreatment first became known. In the abuse sample, the time between the approximate date of abuse and testing ranged between 4 and 68 months ($M = 22.53$, $SD = 15.29$). Criteria for abuse specified that it be physical abuse confirmed by the Brooklyn Bureau of Child Welfare or Brooklyn Family Court (New York City). Cases of exclusively sexual abuse or in which a finding of neglect had been made in addition were not acceptable. Families engaged in litigation were also excluded. It was required that the mother be the definite perpetrator. The neglect sample also consisted of cases confirmed by a Bureau of Child Welfare or Family Court investigation. Criteria specified failure of the mother to provide adequate physical care (e.g., food, clothing, medical care, and supervision). Evidence of physical or sexual abuse in addition excluded some cases from the final neglect sample. Prospective normal control subjects were selected from the records of the past 11 years of the Department of Obstetrics and Gynecology, Kings County Hospital, Brooklyn, New York.

TABLE 1

Characteristics of Subjects

Characteristic	Group Abuse	Neglect	Control	Characteristic	Group Abuse	Neglect	Control
Age (in years)				Number of			
M	27.19	27.50	27.85	children (%)			
SD	5.70	6.83	6.00	1	17.5	16.3	25.0
				2	23.8	18.7	37.5
				3	30.0	21.3	20.0
				4	16.2	13.7	8.8
Race (%)				5	7.5	10.0	2.5
White	22.5	25.0	8.7	>6	5.0	20.0	6.2
Black	68.8	66.3	88.8				
Other	8.7	8.7	2.5	Age of youngest			
				child (%)			
				<2 mo.	1.2	2.5	5.0
Religion (%)				2-12 mo.	13.7	13.8	6.3
Protestant	31.2	37.5	48.8	13-30 mo.	26.3	40.0	33.7
Catholic	31.2	36.2	17.5	31-47 mo.	12.5	21.2	15.0
Jewish	3.8	2.5	1.2	4-6 yr.	21.3	15.0	22.5
Other	22.5	17.5	30.0	6-12 yr.	25.0	7.5	17.5
None	11.3	6.3	2.5				
				Age of oldest			
				child (%)			
Annual				13-30 mo.	7.5	13.7	16.2
income (%)				31-47 mo.	10.0	7.5	11.2
<$4,000	66.3	70.0	54.4	4-6 yr.	16.2	20.0	18.8
$4,000-$6,000	21.2	11.2	21.5	6-8 yr.	16.2	12.5	17.5
>$6,000	12.5	18.8	24.1	9-12 yr.	30.0	20.0	18.8
				13-18 yr.	16.2	15.0	10.0
				>18	3.8	11.3	7.5
				Marital status (%)			
Education—				Married	21.2	21.2	25.0
highest grade (%)				Divorced	3.8	10.0	8.7
<8th	13.7	12.5	3.7	Separated	30.0	25.0	15.0
8th	13.7	13.7	5.0	Never married	41.2	41.2	50.0
10th	30.0	33.7	36.2	Widowed	3.8	2.5	1.3
12th	27.5	31.3	35.0				
College				Having a			
incomplete	13.7	8.8	18.8	telephone (%)			
College				Yes	66.3	58.8	82.5
completed	1.3	0.0	1.3	No.	33.7	41.2	17.5

Note. For each of the three groups, $n = 80$.

All eligible abuse subjects and a random selection of neglect and control subjects received letters inviting them to participate in a study of child-rearing attitudes. Approximately 20% across all groups were positive respondents, with the highest percentage in the abuse sample, attributable to a more intense effort to obtain current addresses. Final study participants were transported to and from the hospital for testing and compensated $15.00. The project was explained as a study of child-rearing attitudes, and informed consents were obtained.

The three groups were comparable with respect to important demographics, although there were some significant differences (see Table 1). The abuse and neglect groups were 68.8% and 66.3% black, respectively, whereas the control group was 88.8%, $\chi^2(4) = 12.91$, $p < .05$. The maltreating parents tended to have more children, $\chi^2(10) = 25.42$, $p < .01$, and were less likely to own a telephone, $\chi^2(2) = 11.07$, $p < .01$, suggesting social isolation. There were relatively more Catholics in the maltreating groups, $\chi^2(8) = 16.88$, $p < .05$. And 93% of all subjects were classified as Class IV-V on the Hollingshead two-factor index (Hollingshead, Note 2).

Measures

The multivariate analysis included 12 variables. Figure 1 shows each variable name, its relation to factors theorized, and the source. Four self-report instruments were administered, including the Michigan Screening Profile of Parenting (MSPP; Helfer, Schneider, & Hoffmeister, 1977), the Schedule of Recent Experience (SRE; Holmes & Rahe, 1967), the Downstate Childrearing Questionnaire, and the Family Life Form.

The MSPP is a 50-item questionnaire developed to measure child-rearing attitudes and to identify parents at risk for a range of problems including maltreatment. Items are scored on 7-point scales, and five cluster scores are generated—Relationship with Parents, Emotional Needs Met, Dealing with Others, Expectations of Children, and Coping. Parents are scored "at risk" on the basis of high scores on a particular cluster or inconsistency within a cluster (nonconvergence). In an initial reliability trial, the percentage of subjects with stable scores ranged from a low of 62% on Dealing with Others and Expectations of Children to a high of 85% on Emotional Needs Met (Helfer et al., 1977). These percentages obtained high, middle, low, or inconsistent scores on both test and retest. Parents can be designated *at risk* on any or all clusters. Helfer (et al., 1977) reported a sensitivity of 85.7% (ability to identify accurately mothers with known problems) and a specificity of 79.8% (ability to identify accurately parents with no apparent problems). In addition, a factor analysis of scores from subjects in the current study yielded three interpretable factors: Relationship with Parents—Feelings about One's Childhood; Self-Concept—Adequacy; and Perfectionism—Denial of Problems.

The SRE is a schedule of 42 life-change events that have been weighted according to the amount of readjustment or adaptation that each requires. The survey covers the 3-year period prior to the evaluation and yields a total score expressed as "life-change units." Items include such areas as marriage, occupation, health and finance. The instrument has been shown to predict changes in physical health (Rahe, 1972); and Justice and Justice (1976) have used a variant of the SRE to associate

THEORETICAL   VARIABLE   MEASURE
   FACTOR

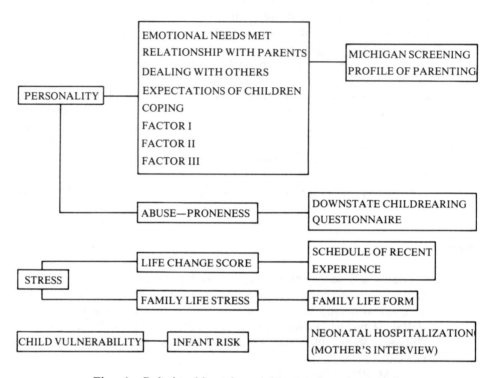

Fig. 1. Relationship of variables and measures to theorized causal factors.

stress with child abuse. Test-retest reliabilities have ranged from .64 to .74 (Casey, Masuda, & Holmes, 1967).

Two newly developed instruments, the Downstate Childrearing Questionnaire and the Family Life Form, were administered to supplement the MSPP and SRE. The child-rearing questionnaire was developed from interviewing and piloting to generate a total abuse proneness score from 42 attitude statements scored on 6-point Likert-type scales. Co-efficient alpha (Cronbach, 1951) was .80 for the study sample. The Family Life Form is an inventory of 32 negative life experiences typically encountered by ghetto families (e.g., evictions, muggings, unemployment, arrests). A total score is obtained from the number of years out of the last 5 in which these events have occurred.

Finally, target children were rated for postnatal risk or deviancy on the basis of the number of days each infant spent in the hospital following birth. These data were supplied by mothers in an interview, and corroboration was sought from actual hospital records. Neonates hospitalized more than 1 week were designated "at risk" and scored + 1; those not at risk were coded –1. Of 115 birth records received, the mother's report was confirmed for 108. Hobel, Hyvarienen, Okada, and Oh (1973) have reported a significant relation between postnatal hospitalization and other prenatal, intrapartum, and neonatal risk indices.

Procedure

Subjects were tested and monitored individually, with Spanish and French translations available for those few who required them. The MSPP was recorded on tape and the other questionnaires read to nonreaders. Assistance was often necessary to insure that the SRE was completed according to instructions.

Data Analysis

A stepwise multiple discriminant analysis was performed on the 12 variables (a) to find the linear combination(s) that would maximally discriminate the abusing, neglecting, and normal control mothers, and (b) to determine how accurately the optimal set of variables could reclassify subjects with known group membership. A Statistical Package for the Social Sciences (Nie, Hull, Jenkins, Steinbrenner, & Brent, 1975) program was used. The stepwise procedure employed selects an initial variable that by itself has the greatest amount of discriminatory power. A second variable is then selected that, in combination with the first, yields the best criterion value, and so forth until additional variable entries fail to produce a significant increment. The minimization of Wilks' lambda with partial multi-variate F to enter greater than unity was the criterion that determined variable selection. Therefore, two discriminant functions could possibly be derived from an optimal set of variables. Functions were interpreted with reference to group centroids, the means for each group on respective functions, standardized discriminant function coefficients, and preliminary data including univariate F tests for each of the 12 variables and correlation matrices.

Results

Univariate F tests (see Table 2) revealed significant between-population differences on MSPP Emotional Needs Met, $F(2, 237) = 3.10$, $p < .05$, MSPP Coping, $F(2, 237) = 3.59$, $p < .05$, and the Family Life Form stress variable, $F(2, 237) = 6.21$, $p < .01$. The SRE total life-change score and the Downstate abuse proneness score were marginal ($.05 < p < .10$), whereas there were no significant differences on the remaining MSPP variables and infant risk. The combined sample and within-groups correlation matrices (see Table 3) showed substantial common variance among the personality and child-rearing attitude variables, which was expected insofar as the MSPP served as the data base for eight of these.

Six variables were entered into the discriminant analysis, after which additional entries failed to produce a significant increment. In order of entry, these were Family Life Form stress, MSPP Coping, MSPP Factor III (Perfectionism-Denial of Problems), SRE total life changes, MSPP Factor I (Relationship with

TABLE 2

Means and Standard Deviations of Abuse, Neglect, and Control Mothers

	Group					
	Abuse		Neglect		Control	
Variable	*M*	*SD*	*M*	*SD*	*M*	*SD*
Emotional needs met	.42	.91	.62	.79	.27	.90
Relationship with parents	-.37	.93	-.40	.92	-.47	.89
Dealing with others	-.75	.67	-.75	.67	-.70	.72
Expectations of children	.00	1.01	.02	1.01	.05	1.01
Coping	-.37	.93	-.25	.97	-.62	.79
MSPP Factor I[a]	-.07	.97	-.03	.91	.10	.92
MSPP Factor II[a]	.00	1.00	-.13	.89	.12	.76
MSPP Factor III[a]	-.01	.86	-.07	.92	.07	.83
DCQ abuse proneness	129.69	26.32	129.94	26.83	122.07	20.78
SRE life changes	820.30	643.66	1121.30	1114.00	968.79	799.00
Family Life Form stress	10.64	5.87	14.65	9.71	11.66	6.26
Infant risk	-.60	.80	-.45	.90	-.42	.91

Note. For each of the three groups, $n = 80$. MSPP = Michigan Screening Profile of Parenting; DCQ = Downstate Childrearing Questionnaire; SRE = Schedule of Recent Experience.
[a] Missing data on one neglect subject.

Parents—Feelings about One's Childhood), and MSPP Emotional Needs Met. A first and statistically significant discriminant function was derived, A = .8759, $\chi^2(12) = 30.934$, $p < .005$. The second function was not significant. Eigenvalues revealed that the first function accounted for 76.81% of the total discriminatory power of the variables, whereas the second function accounted for only 23.19%. Canonical correlations, the relation between each function and the final set of variables, were .310 and .176, respectively. The total variability in discriminant space attributable to group differences was approximately 12%, as determined by Tatsuoka's (1970, p. 48) formula.

Group centroids (see Table 4) for the three criterion groups suggested that the neglecting mothers differed from the abusing and control mothers on the first function; on the second, all three groups were approximately equally separated, with the abuse and control groups farthest apart. Standardized discriminant function coefficients (see Table 5) for the first function showed Family Life Form stress to predominate, with MSPP Emotional Needs Met and Coping entering in the same direction. These variables had significantly distinguished the three groups on univariate *F* tests, and Scheffé contrasts were consistent with differences observed on group centroids, separating the neglect group from abusers and controls. MSPP Factors I and III, which fell short of significance on univariate tests and load in opposite directions on the first function, appear to enter as suppressor variables, whereas MSPP Coping seems to absorb some variation due Emotional Needs Met. The second function appears to be defined primarily by Coping and the two stress variables, entering in the opposite direction.

TABLE 3

Combined Sample Correlation Matrix (above diagonal) and Within-Groups Correlation Matrix (below diagonal)

Variable	1	2	3	4	5	6	7	8	9	10	11	12
1. Emotional needs met	—	.26	.08	.10	.28	-.48	-.48	-.06	.44	.14	.16	.04
2. Relationship with parents	.26	—	.13	.04	.21	-.71	-.04	.18	.36	.06	.24	-.06
3. Dealing with others	.08	.14	—	-.06	.10	-.07	-.11	.23	.11	-.11	-.02	.08
4. Expectations of children	.10	.04	-.05	—	.06	-.03	-.21	-.38	.10	.03	.00	-.06
5. Coping	.26	.21	.09	.07	—	-.24	-.50	.16	.41	.16	.10	-.02
6. MSPP Factor I	-.48	-.70	-.07	-.03	-.23	—	.07	-.07	-.51	-.13	-.28	.06
7. MSPP Factor II	-.47	-.03	-.11	-.22	-.49	.07	—	.08	-.48	-.12	-.04	-.04
8. MSPP Factor III	-.05	.19	.22	-.38	.17	-.07	.07	—	.01	.08	.24	.09
9. DCQ abuse proneness	.44	.36	.13	.11	.40	-.51	-.47	.02	—	.09	.18	-.06
10. SRE life change units	.14	.06	-.10	.02	.16	-.14	-.11	.08	.09	—	.23	.05
11. Family Life Form stress	.14	.24	.00	-.01	.09	-.28	-.02	.26	.17	.20	—	.11
12. Infant risk	.05	-.06	.09	-.07	-.01	.05	-.04	.09	-.05	.04	.10	—

Note. All correlation coefficients were based on a total N of 240, with the exception of those involving MSPP Factors I, II, and III ($N = 239$); MSPP = Michigan Screening Profile of Parenting; DCQ = Downstate Childrearing Questionnaire; SRE = Schedule of Recent Experience.

TABLE 4
Centroids of Groups in Reduced Space

	Function	
Group	1	2
Abuse[a]	−.23	.21
Neglect[b]	.44	.01
Control[a]	−.20	−.22

[a] N = 80.
[b] N = 79.

TABLE 5
Standardized Discriminant Function Coefficients

	Function	
Variable	1	2
Family Life Form stress	.80	−.29
SRE total	.22	−.46
MSPP Factor 1	.41	−.37
MSPP Factor 3	−.39	−.27
Emotional needs met	.38	.15
Coping	.31	.69

Note. SRE = Schedule of Recent Experience, and MSPP = Michigan Screening Profile of Parenting.

The discriminant analysis as a whole, therefore, revealed (a) a clear dimension separating the neglecting mothers from abusers and controls on the basis of Family Life Form stress and MSPP Emotional Needs Met, and (b) a more dubious dimension ($p < .20$) related to coping and stress. The most important discriminating variable was family stress, followed by selected personality features. Infant risk, determined on the basis of neonatal hospitalization, was not a successful discriminator-predictor.

To assess the value of the discriminant analysis, classification functions based on the optimal set of six variables were used to reclassify the 240 known cases. A total of 48.75% of all cases from the three samples were reclassified correctly.

Discussion

The results of this study indicated that 6 variables from the original set of 12 discriminated the abusing, neglecting, and normal mothers at the .005 level of significance; however, only 12% of the discriminant space was accounted for. Although MSPP factors implicated coping and meeting emotional needs in the etiology of maltreatment, stress contributed more to the overall analysis than did any of these personality variables. Infant risk, determined on the basis of neonatal complications requiring hospitalization, was not a successful discriminator; therefore, the hypothesized relationship between mother-neonate bonding and maltreatment was not supported. Similarly, the theory that defective children are likely targets for abuse (Green, Gaines, & Sandgrund, 1974; Sandgrund et al., 1974) was not corroborated, if one accepts Hobel et al.s's (1973) finding that neonatal hospitalization correlates with other infant risk indices.

Although as expected the abusing mothers scored high on stress, it is not altogether surprising that the neglecting mothers exceeded them. Unemployment, illness, eviction, and arrest are representative of the life events inventoried by the Family Life Form. These poverty-related experiences are particularly common in neglecting families. That stress was appreciably lower in the abuse group, however, casts doubt on the three-factor theory that posits environmental pressure as a child abuse precipitant or catalyst. The retrospective nature of the study may account, in part, for this finding. Conceivably, stressful life events accumulate and peak prior to abuse, dissipating as aggression is displaced onto the child. Such scapegoating (Green, 1976) can temporarily stabilize the family until the pathological equilibrium is disturbed by the removal of the target child from the home. Among chronically disorganized, neglecting families, however, stress may be an omnipresent phenomenon more easily detected by questionnaires.

That maltreatment can be primarily attributed to child-rearing attitudes or an "abuse-prone personality" is seriously challenged by the results, because of the relatively trivial contribution of these variables. More pronounced personality differences in the domains surveyed might have been apparent when maltreatment was imminent or in progress; and it is possible to speculate that parents who had been involved in investigations and court actions might suppress or deny feelings and attitudes associated with these experiences. Additional confounding factors may arise from the use of paper-and-pencil instruments with these populations. With the exception of the Family Life Form, all of the questionnaires demanded some ability to introspect and to make fine discriminations. Many subjects expressed difficulty with the scales despite the availability of monitor assistance. Helfer et al. (1977) have noted the tendency of maltreating parents to render inconsistent or nonconvergent responses. Subsequent studies might profit from greatly simplified instruments. Controls for intelligence and social desirability or denial would also appear warranted, since these represent potentially important moderator or suppressor influences on the outcome variables of interest.

Despite these measurement problems, however, the results show that the maltreating groups have more difficulty meeting emotional needs (neglecters, primarily) and have retained a sense of coping failure (abusers). Stress, although relatively ubiquitous, was highest in the neglect group, distinguishing these women from abusers or controls. Although the first discriminant function was significant, strong confirmation was not found for the multifactor hypothesis, as shown by the percentage of the discriminant space accounted for. It may be concluded that although stress and personality variables are indeed relevant to the maltreatment syndrome, they leave 88% of the phenomenon unexplained and predict parent category only 15% better than chance. Furthermore, the extent of capitalization on chance due to particular samples is indeterminate; any claims for accuracy must be qualified in the absence of cross-validation. This would certainly militate against the use of these instruments for screening a socially stigmatizing phenomenon whose incidence in the general population is low. The "hit" percentage was not improved by using all 12 variables for classification. This is both perplexing and discouraging because policies and programs might be directed toward early identification of parents at risk for maltreatment and toward preventive intervention.

A number of factors may limit the generalizability of the results and serve as a guide to further research. In the current study, the abuse and neglect samples were compiled from a list of cases confirmed by the Bureau of Child Welfare on whom recent addresses were available. From this sizable list, a smaller percentage of subjects responded to our invitation to participate, and still fewer actually came in. The control mothers were volunteers matched on relevant variables who had visited an obstetrics and gynecology clinic at a municipal hospital. Sampling from the Bureau of Child Welfare records of confirmed cases is contingent both on the agency definition of what constitutes maltreatment and on its application of the definition to individual cases. Gelles (Note 3) has highlighted the diverse and, at times, capricious definitions of different social agencies, or "gatekeepers." In New York State, for example, the official definition of *maltreatment* is itself very broad and applied somewhat arbitrarily by workers overwhelmed by large case loads. Plea bargaining is common. From this, one can assume that the 80 abusers and 80 neglecters in this study fall on a continuum of maltreatment severity, ranging from mild cases, which probably overlap with subcultural norms, to very severe cases, which would be classified as child maltreatment in most jurisdictions. Because the actual participants were voluntary respondents, it is likely that the sample is somewhat biased toward those less severe cases, the assumption being that more deviant mothers would opt not to participate. Some nonrespondents were institutionalized, in jail, or had left the state to avoid prosecution. The ultimate consequence of such sampling is that although the control group is probably representative of the subculture from which it was drawn, the matched maltreatment samples may not be sufficiently extreme on this critical variable. Although it is a poor alternative to compare known abusers with "best moms," dramatic results will not be forthcoming if a walk-in group is contrasted with matched groups other than the most severe abusers and neglecters.

This investigation has shown that the three-factor theory proposed to explain child abuse and neglect has limited applicability ex post facto in closely matched samples. Rather than abandon or drastically modify the theory as yet, large-scale prospective and longitudinal investigations would ultimately subject these formulations to a stronger test with potentially more compelling conclusions. An unavoidable weakness in this retrospective study was the infant risk measure, on which the three groups were not found to differ. Despite evidence that neonatal hospitalization generally indicates high risk, such a gross marker variable may mask information germane to maltreatment vulnerability. More revealing, perhaps, would be a prospective investigation at a large hospital in which detailed birth histories of the children to be followed could be recorded in a consistent fashion. The state of the art in child abuse research is predicated almost entirely on retrospective studies that have found partial support for the parent personality—infant deviancy—environmental stress model. Although a major longitudinal study would be a considerable undertaking, the implications of the results for programs affecting children appear to warrant such an effort.

REFERENCE NOTES

1.   GRISWOLD, B. B., & BILLINGSLEY, A. *Personality and social characteristics of low-income mothers who neglect or abuse their children* (In, Final Report, Grant No. PR1100[R]). Washington, D.C.: Children's Bureau, Welfare Administration, U.S. Department of Health, Education, and Welfare, 1969.

2.   HOLLINGSHEAD, A. B. *Two-factor index of social position.* Unpublished manuscript, 1957. (Available from the author, 1965 Yale Station, New Haven, Connecticut 06515.)

3.   GELLES, R. J. *Community agencies and child abuse: Labeling and gatekeeping.* Paper presented to the Study Group on Research and the Family, October 1975. (Available from the author, Department of Sociology, University of Rhode Island, Kingston, Rhode Island 02881.)

REFERENCES

BIRRELL, R., & BIRRELL, J. "The maltreatment syndrome in children: A hospital survey." *Medical Journal of Australia*, 1968, *2*, 1023-1029.

CASEY, R., MASUDA, M., & HOLMES, T. "Quantitative study of recall of life events." *Journal of Psychosomatic Research*, 1967, *11*, 239-247.

COHEN, M., RAPHLING, D., & GREEN, P. "Psychological aspects of the maltreatment syndrome of childhood." *Journal of Pediatrics*, 1966, *69*, 279-284.

CRONBACH, L. J. "Coefficient alpha and the internal structure of tests." *Psychometrika*, 1951, *16*, 297-334.

ELMER, E., & GREGG, G. "Developmental characteristics of abused children." *Pediatrics*, 1967, *40*, 596-602.

FANAROFF, A., KENNELL, J., & KLAUS, M. "Follow-up of low birth weight infants—The predictive value of maternal visiting patterns." *Pediatrics*, 1972, *49*, 287-290.

GALDSTON, R. "Violence begins at home." *Journal of the American Academy of Child Psychiatry*, 1971, *10*, 336-350.

GIL, D. G. *Violence against children: Physical child abuse in the United States.* Cambridge, Mass.: Harvard University Press, 1970.

GREEN, A. H. "A psychodynamic approach to the study and treatment of child-abusing parents." *Journal of the American Academy of Child Psychiatry*, 1976, *15*, 414-429.

GREEN, A. H., GAINES, R. W., & SANDGRUND, A. "Child abuse: Pathological syndrome of family interaction." *American Journal of Psychiatry*, 1974, *131*, 882-886.

GREEN, A. H., SANDGRUND, A., GAINES, R. W., & HABERFELD, H. "Psychological sequelae of child abuse and neglect." *Scientific Proceedings in Summary Form, the 127th Annual Meeting of the American Psychiatric Association.* Washington, D.C.: American Psychiatric Association, 1974.

HELFER, R., SCHNEIDER, C., & HOFFMEISTER, J. *Manual for the use of the Michigan Screening Profile of Parenting.* East Lansing, Mich.: Department of Human Development, Michigan State University, 1977.

HOBEL, C. J., HYVARIENEN, M. A., & OKADA, D. M., & OH, W. "Prenatal and intrapartum high risk screening." *American Journal of Obstetrics and Gynecology*, 1973, *117*, 1-9.

HOLMES, T. H., & RAHE, R. *Schedule of recent experience (SRE).* Seattle, Wash.: School of Medicine, University of Washington, 1967.

JOHNSON, B., & MORSE, H. "Injured children and their parents." *Children*, 1968, *15*, 147-152.

JUSTICE, B., & JUSTICE, R. *The abusing family.* New York: Human Sciences Press, 1976.

KEMPE, C. H., & HELFER, R. E. (Eds.). *Helping the battered child and his family.* Philadelphia, Pa.: Lippincott, 1972.

KEMPE, C., SILVERMAN, F., STEELE, B., DROEGEMUELLER, W., & SILVER, H. "The battered-child syndrome." *Journal of the American Medical Association*, 1962, *181*, 17-24.

KLEIN, M., & STERN, L. "Low birth weight and the battered child syndrome." *American Journal of Diseases of Childhood*, 1971, *122*, 15-18.

MORRIS, M., & GOULD, R. "Role reversal: A necessary concept in dealing with the battered-child syndrome." *American Journal of Orthopsychiatry*, 1963, *33*, 298-299.

NIE, N. H., HULL, C. H., JENKINS, J. G., STEINBRENNER, K., & BRENT, D. H. *Statistical package for the social sciences* (2nd ed.). New York: McGraw-Hill, 1975.

OUNSTED, C., OPPENHEIMER, R., & LINDSAY, J. "Aspects of bonding failure; the psychopathology and psychotherapeutic treatment of families of battered children." *Developmental Medicine in Child Neurology*, 1974, *16*, 447-456.

PAULSON, M. AFIFI, A., THOMASON, M. & CHALEFF, A. "The MMPI: A descriptive measure of psychopathology in abusive parents." *Journal of Clinical Psychology*, 1974, *30*, 387-390.

RAHE, R. "Subject's recent life changes and their near-future illness reports." *Annals of Clinical Research*, 1972, *4*, 1-16.

SANDGRUND, A., GAINES, R. W., & GREEN, A. H. "Child abuse and mental retardation: A problem of cause and effect." *American Journal of Mental Deficiency*, 1974, *79*, 327-330.

SMITH, S., HANSON, R., & NOBLE, S. "Parents of battered babies: A controlled study." *British Medical Journal*, 1973, *4*, 388-391.

SPINETTA, J., & RIGLER, D. "The child-abusing parent: A psychological review." *Psychological Bulletin*, 1972, *77*, 296-304.

STEELE, B. "Parental abuse of infants and small children." In E. Anthony & T. Benedek (Eds.), *Parenthood, its psychology and psychopathology*. Boston: Little, Brown, 1970.

STEELE, B., & POLLOCK, C. "A psychiatric study of parents who abuse infants and small children." In R. Helfer & C. H. Kempe (Eds.), *The battered child*. Chicago: University of Chicago Press, 1968.

TATSUOKA, M. M. *Selected topics in advanced statistics (No. 6): Discriminant analysis*. Champaign, Ill.: Institute for Personality and Ability Testing, 1970.

27

Socialization into Child Abuse:
A Social Interactional Perspective*

Ross D. Parke

Child abuse has received much recent attention due in part to a reported rise in child abuse and in part to a societal reawakening to the rights and treatment of children. The purpose of this chapter is to advance a social interactional analysis of child abuse as an alternative to the traditional personality-psychiatric approach. The model presented here builds on the view that the family is one rule system within a structure of multiple, interactive, and overlapping rule systems (for this approach, see Fuller, 1969b; Tapp, 1971a; Tapp & Levine, 1974). Abuse, it will be argued, is an orderly outcome of a network of cultural and community forces that, in turn, affect the development of family interaction patterns leading to abusive incidents. Furthermore, by reducing isolation and enhancing educative experiences, family exposure to and interaction with other rule systems can modify and/or deter abuse. In contrast to an emphasis on blame/responsibility or health/disease, this approach suggests that social problems can be managed more effectively by using the link with other "legal" systems as "complementary, yet diverse . . . alternatives to redress

* The chapter was prepared with the support of the National Science Foundation grant GS-31885X to the author. Parts of this chapter are derived from an earlier review by Parke & Collmer (1975). Thanks to M. Gillian Parke and June Louin Tapp for comments on earlier drafts of this chapter. Finally, a special note of appreciation to Frances Hall and Cathy Prinslow for their able assistance in the preparation of the manuscript.

grievances, accommodate interests, or secure rights [Levine & Tapp, Chap. 15]," whether for children or adults.

Definition of Abuse

Definitions shape theory and research; the area of child abuse is no exception. Most definitions have been largely asocial, focusing on the parent as the sole agent inflicting injury on a passive child-victim. Kempe and Helfer, medical experts on child abuse, defined the phenomenon as "any child who received nonaccidental physical injury (or injuries) as a result of acts (or omissions) on the part of his parents or guardians [1972, p. 1]." The same perspective is revealed in the nonmedical definition offered in Gil's influential volume *Violence against Children*: "Physical abuse of children is the intentional, nonaccidental use of force, on the part of a parent or other caretaker interacting with a child in his care aimed at hurting, injuring or destroying that child [Gil, 1970, p. 6]."

While these two definitions recognize the need to exclude accidental occurrences of physical harm, serious conceptual problems remain. They imply that child abuse can be clearly identified as a set of behaviors imposed on a child by an adult. Ignoring the obvious inferential difficulties of attributing intentionality accurately (Kelley, 1973), these definitions are too narrow. First, they direct attention to only one side of the parent-child dyad, namely the adult. No recognition is paid to the child's role in eliciting abuse from his caretakers. Second, the sociocultural context of behaviors is not recognized, in part stemming from the assumption that an absolute standard for judging the occurrence of abuse is obtainable. Such a definition is neither empirically possible nor logically valid.

The Role of Contexts in Definitions

Child abuse is not merely a set of behaviors but is rather a culturally determined label applied to injury patterns as an outcome of a judgment process by an observer. According to a social judgment approach (Bandura & Walters, 1963; Parke & Sawin, 1975a; Walters & Parke, 1964), an observer takes into account various factors in deciding whether a particular injury is an instance of child abuse. Intention is merely one criterion. Other variables include the antecedents, form, and intensity of the response, the extent of the injury, and the role and status of agent and victim. For example, the same injury labeled abuse in one situation, for one child, or in one social class may not be judged abuse in another situation, for another child, or in another social class. Even a simple definition in terms of injuries must include estimates of severity based on culturally defined standards.

In short, child abuse is a phenomenon that must be viewed in the context of community norms. To date, insufficient attention has been paid to developing an empirically derived set of standards based on community consensus concerning the rights of children and parents. For purposes of this chapter, a modification of the Kempe-Helfer definition of the abused child is used: any child who during the course of parent-child interaction receives nonaccidental physical injury (or injuries) resulting from acts on the part of his or her caretakers that violate the community standards concerning the treatment of children.

The Implications of Being Labeled Abusive

Labeling a family as abusive has important implications for treatment both informally by friends, neighbors, and relatives and from formal agencies such as social welfare and law-enforcement groups, school authorities, and employers. Once an agency within an interrelated services structure labels a parent as abusive, other agencies tend to accept this label and treat the family accordingly. Consistency across agencies occurs even though initially a second agency may not have labeled the family as abusive by its own criteria. Similarly, informal communication of the label through the family's court appearances or social worker's visits may promote adoption of the abuse tag by friends and relatives in the informal social network.

Once a family has been labeled "abusive," treatment may vary. For example, the adequacy of the home may be assessed; legal machinery may be activated with ensuing public exposure; a child's subsequent bruises may be more readily defined as abuse by school officials. Friends and relatives may avoid the "accused" family from fear of guilt by association or the embarrassment of interacting with a "deviant" individual. The alterations at informal and formal levels can significantly affect a parent's attitudes and behaviors. As Gelles (1975, p. 365) wisely argued, "being labeled an abuser may have produced the personality characteristics— anxiety, depression, etc.—which were later called the causes of the abuse!" Nor should this argument be restricted to personality charcteristics. The social isolation characteristics of the abusive family (Elmer, 1967) may also result from community rejection of the labeled family.

This exploration of labeling effects may challenge the oft-made claim that child abuse is a lower-class phenomenon (Gil, 1970). The social network used by middle-class families in crisis importantly differs from that available to lower-class families. Middle-class families are likely to use private agencies, while lower-class families rely on public agencies, clinics, and hospitals. Private physicians and social agencies are less likely to report and publicly label child-abuse incidents. For example, in one national survey hospitals, police, and public social agencies accounted for 80 percent of reported incidents, while private sources contributed only 3 percent of the cases (Gil, 1970). In short, lower-class individuals are probably overrepresented in child-abuse estimates and thus more likely to suffer the consequences of being officially designated as abusive.

The implications of labeling errors merit attention. Although labeling permits institutionalized response in the form of state-sponsored intervention and support, mistaken labeling can have harmful effects for the mislabeled family. Recent suggestions (see Kempe, cited in Light, 1973) for programs to improve detection of abused children increase the probability of misidentification. Even with such a low base-rate event, small margins of error can result in high levels of false positive predictions. For example, when an abused child is detected 90 percent of the time and nonabuse is correctly identified 95 percent, only 15.4 percent of the children are actually abused—estimating the abuse incidence rate at .010. Thus, 85 percent of the parents accused of abuse would be mistakenly labeled (Light, 1973, p. 570-571)! Given such an error rate, the justification for massive screening programs is questionable. Further, the public labeling of families as abusive by the legal or welfare systems may interfere with the resocialization process. Recidivism rates of labeled and nonlabeled families would provide an important index of the consequences of labeling.

Socialization into Child Abuse

How do families become socialized into abusive patterns of child treatment? The most influential and popular model, derived from psychiatric analyses, focuses on the parent as the principal cause: Abusive parents are assumed to have personality characteristics distinct from other parents. There is also the implicit assumption that abusive parents are abnormal or "sick," therefore requiring extensive psychiatric treatment to overcome their "illness." Recently the utility of this approach has been questioned (e.g., Gelles, 1973; Parke & Collmer, 1975). An alternative model of child abuse shifts the causal focus from an analysis of the individual parent to the social environment.

To understand this socialization process, three levels of social-environmental influence require attention. In contrast to a traditional psychiatric emphasis on abnormality, I assume that normal parents are socialized into abusive child-care patterns through the interaction of cultural, community, and familial influences. Child abuse is viewed not as an isolated social phenomenon but as a manifestation of a general cultural attitude to violence. Accordingly, I first explore the cultural sanctioning of violence and aggression, then examine the familial context in which abuse is executed, and, third, analyze the community rule systems in which the family system operates.

Cultural Sanction of Violence as a Contributor to Child Abuse

Some commentators have argued that the level of child abuse in U.S. society is partly due to cultural sanctioning of physically violent tactics for resolving social conflict (Gil, 1970; see also Palmer, 1972; Pinkney, 1972). For example, in the United States in 1972 there were nearly 20,000 murders known to the police, a rate of 8.9 per 100,000 inhabitants (Kelley, 1973); yet, the rate was only one-tenth as high in England (Geis & Monahan, 1976). Similarly, the assault and battery rate for Canada in 1968 was 28.6 per 100,000, while the U.S. rate was 141 per 100,000 (Steinmetz, 1974a). Nor are law-enforcement officers exempt from violent tactics. Stark (1972) has estimated that there are three million instances of unnecessary physical abuse by police officers (see also Black & Reiss, 1967).*

---

* There are other forms of institutionalized violence commonly executed by corporate and government officials such as failing to enforce pollution standards and permitting dangerous drugs to be profitably marketed (Geis & Monahan, 1976).

The level of television violence is also higher in the U.S. than in countries such as Sweden, Israel, or Britain (Liebert, Neale, & Davidson, 1973). Gerbner's careful analysis (1972) of the content of TV programs over five years revealed that over 75 percent contained violence. Stein and Freidrich (1975) summarized these effects: Both behaviors and attitudes are shaped by TV programming. In fact, children and adults are repeatedly and consistently exposed to the moral lesson that violence is an appropriate means for resolving conflict.

Other evidence suggests that levels of violence in a society are reflected in levels of violence within the family. In a comparison of German, Italian, and Danish cities, Bellak and Antell (1974) found that higher suicide and homicide rates corresponded to higher levels of both parental and child aggression. Similarly, Steinmetz (1974a) in a U.S.-Canadian comparison found lower levels of intrafamilial aggression in Canada, where criminal aggressive activity is also lower. In a U.S. study, Steinmetz (1974b) reported that parents who used verbal and physical aggression to resolve husband-wife disputes tended to use similar techniques in disciplining children— with children duplicating these tactics with siblings.

Given these repeated patterns of violence, it is not surprising that physical punishment is a widely used disciplinary and child-rearing technique. Stark and McEvoy (1970) reported that 93 percent of all parents employed physical punishment, although some only rarely and only on young children. In fact, one investigation by Korsch, Christian, Gozzi, and Carlson (1965) revealed that of a sample of 100 Los Angeles mothers, a quarter spanked infants in the first six months of life, and nearly half spanked infants by the end of the first year. However, later studies (Steinmetz, 1974c; Straus, 1971) showed that physical punishment was not restricted to young children. Straus found that 52.3 percent of his adolescent sample experienced actual or threatened physical punishment during their last year of high school. Erlanger's recent study (1974) indicated that physical punishment as a disciplinary technique was used at all social levels—contrary to earlier reports (Bronfenbrenner, 1958). Professional groups also have advocated the use of physical punishment in child-rearing. Viano (1974) found that of the educators, police, and clergy questioned, two-thirds condoned spanking children for disciplinary purposes with belts, straps, and brushes!

Is physical punishment as a child-rearing technique in U.S. society a factor in the level of child abuse? Gil argued:

> A key element to understanding child abuse . . . seems to be that the context of child rearing does not exclude the use of physical force. . . . Rather, American culture encourages in subtle and at times not so subtle ways the use of "a certain measure" of physical force in rearing children . . . [1970, p. 134].

Support for this assertion comes from other cultures where physical punishment is not sanctioned. Recent reporters on China (Sidel, 1972; Stevenson, 1974) described only rare use of physical punishment, little aggression among children, and no incidents of child abuse. Data from Taiwan and the U.S. (Niem & Collard, 1971) indicated that physical punishment in any form was used less than half as often by Taiwanese families and spankings were only a quarter as frequent (see also Freedmam & Freedman, 1969). Goode (1971) noted a similar situation in Japan, where physical punishment is not a common disciplinary tactic and child abuse is infrequent. Also this pattern is evident in other cultures such as the Arapesh (Mead, 1935) and the Tahitians (Levy, 1969).

These examples suggest that variations in the cultural level of violence are reflected in family violence, particularly in the use of physical punishment in child rearing. Whether these variations are responsible for different levels of child abuse is left unanswered. However, in the next section the processes by which physical punitiveness *can* lead to child abuse are analyzed in detail.

The Family as the Context of Child Abuse

To understand how abuse develops within a family, a variety of factors must be examined. First, parents' histories define the guidelines for child rearing. Second, the nature of parent-child interaction helps explain the development of abusive tactics. As noted earlier, it is not enough to view child abuse as unidirectional, with the main cause located in the parent; husband, wife, and child-victim each may play a role. Finally, the social and community support available to the family for providing alternative "rule" guidelines or assistance in times of crises must be considered.

Transmission of cultural attitudes to parents: The impact of punitive child-rearing. Although child-rearing information, norms, and rules are transmitted in a variety of ways, such as through schools and the news media, the most powerful vehicle within a culture is the family. Steele & Pollock (1968) have documented that abusive parents were themselves abused as children. There is a clear parallel between this finding and the more general relation between exposure to physical punishment during childhood and the high rate of aggression of both children and adults (Erlanger, 1974). Physically punitive tactics are probably learned through imitation of parents. Bandura (1967) summarized how parental modeling may account for the physical discipline-aggression relation:

> When a parent punishes his child physically for having aggressed toward peers, for example, the intended outcome of this training is that the child should refrain from hitting others. The child, however, is also learning from parental demonstration how to aggress physically. And the imitative learning may provide the direction for the child's behavior when he is similarly frustrated in subsequent social interactions [p. 43].

In essence, one's history of treatment conveys a set of rules about appropriate child-rearing practices. Consistent exposure to physically punitive disciplinary patterns may serve to sanction such behaviors so that they are viewed as normative for child-rearing. Likewise, due to the legitimacy accorded to physical punishment, inhibitions against using physical force generally are lessened. A recent experiment confirmed the relation between type of training and type of tactics used in a subsequent supervisory role (Gelfand, Hartmann, Lamb, Smith, Mahan, & Paul, 1974). Investigators found that a child disciplined by an adult with punitive tactics was more likely to use such tactics when given the chance to train another child.

This legitimation of violence in the form of physically punitive child-rearing may aid in understanding child abuse. Physical punishment (in severe forms, abuse) may be a deliberate and rational execution of well-ingrained patterns of behavior viewed by the parent as a reasonable and necessary aspect of appropriate child-rearing. Parents not only learn to use physically punitive tactics but also come to view these tactics as morally right and justified. In fact, they may say that physical punishment and even abuse are *necessary* to instill appropriate social and moral conduct (Steele & Pollock, 1968).

For these abusive families, physically punitive control tactics are legitimate techniques for preserving the family rule system. Often cooperation with authorities is minimal; law-enforcement agents and social service workers are viewed as interfering with parental rights to elect their own methods of discipline. There is limited sharing of values between the abusive family and the institutions of law or other community rule systems. Often guilt, remorse, or even recognition of social deviance, which may serve as inhibitors for future abusive attacks (Berkowitz, 1962), are lacking, thus increasing the probability of future abuse. In fact, adults may invoke the justification of a higher moral cause as a means of reducing dissonance for their norm violation.

Abuse is not always rational, deliberate, preplanned, or executed in the service of upholding a family moral code and "legal" control system. As Berkowitz argued regarding murder, "These violent outbursts are often too impulsive, too quick and involuntary to be greatly affected by the aggressor's belief as to what will be the outcome of their behavior, beyond the simple idea they will hurt their victim [1974, p. 65]." Prior child-rearing contributes to this scenario by providing the parent with a limited repertoire of child-care tactics. To the extent that physical punishment is the main control tactic, the general class of physically violent responses such as hitting will be well-rehearsed and highly available. A number of studies (e.g., Davitz, 1952) have shown that, under conditions of stress and frustration, predominant responses are likely to be emitted. Just as the availability of and prior experience with a gun make murder more likely under stress and anger, so previously experiencing and using violent child-rearing tactics make child abuse more likely.

On the misuse of punishment. But to restrict the focus to child-rearing histories is too limited. Current situations must be studied to reveal the conditions that accelerate physical punishment to abusive levels. Classic studies on the antecedents of delinquency are instructive. Glueck and Glueck (1950) found that parents of delinquent boys were more "erratic" in their disciplinary practices than parents of nondelinquent boys. Other investigators (e.g., McCord, McCord, & Howard, 1961) noted that erratic disciplinary procedures correlated with high degrees of criminality. A strikingly similar pattern of inconsistent discipline is typical of abusive parents. Young (1964) reported that almost all abusive families (91-100%) were inconsistent in disciplining their children. By analyzing the consequences of such inconsistencies, the transformation of physical punishment into abuse becomes clear.

Laboratory studies of the effects of inconsistent punishment on children's aggression indicate that intermittent punishment administered by a single agent is less effective than consistent punishment (e.g., Parke & Deur, 1972). Nor is it simply intra-agent inconsistency that produced poor control. Stouwie (1972) and Parke and Sawin (1975b) found that inconsistency between two socializing agents leads to ineffective control of children's behavior. Inconsistent discipline also has long-term implications for social control. Deur and Parke (1970) found that boys who were inconsistently disciplined by occasionally being rewarded and at other times punished persisted in aggressive behavior longer than did boys who were treated consistently. The implication is clear: The socializing agent using inconsistent punishment meets resistance to future attempts to either extinguish deviant behavior or suppress it by consistently administered punishment.

Consideration of another outcome of inconsistent punishment may aid in understanding the punishment-abuse relationship: namely, the acceleration of low-intensity punitive responses into more intense and therefore potentially abusive responses. Since high-intensity punishment is more effective than low-intensity punishment (Parke, 1969), in the face of inconsistent handling socializing agents may accelerate the intensity of their punitive tactics. But if the punishment is erratic, only momentary control will be achieved, and a parent may resort to even more intense punishment on some future occasion. Abusive levels of punishment could develop out of such a parent-child interaction in a disciplinary context.

Patterson and colleagues have conceptualized a related type of interaction pattern wherein participants accelerate the exchange of aversive stimuli in the coercion process (Patterson & Cobb, 1971, 1973; Patterson & Reid, 1970). According to this paradigm, when one person presents an aversive stimulus, the second is likely to respond with an aversive stimulus, if the initial aversive stimulus appears alterable. The aversive interchange continues escalating in intensity until one person withdraws the aversive stimulus; at this point, the other person withdraws as well. Although their work focused on peers and siblings as shapers of aggression, Patterson and Cobb spelled out the possible implications of their model for abuse:

> In the case of mothers, it is hypothesized that there are many grown women with no past history of hitting, who are shaped by interactions with infants and children to initiate physical assaults. Presumably the shaping process is analogous to that provided by children, for children. The mother learns that hits terminate aversive child behavior. She may then be trained to display behavior of increasingly high amplitude as a function of contingencies supplied by children. We also suspect that many of the child homicides reported are in fact the outcome of such training programs. A young woman, unskilled in mothering, is trained by her own children to carry out assaults that result in bodily injury to her trainers [1971, p. 124].

Similarly Parke, Sawin, and Kreling (1974) found that responding to discipline by defying or ignoring an adult may accelerate the severity of adult treatment. A parent's success in inhibiting highly disruptive behaviors through the use of high-intensity tactics may serve to maintain these tactics.

Aggressive families base interaction on the exchange of aversive and noxious stimuli; their rates of exchange for positive events are much lower than those of nonaggressive families (Patterson, 1975). The rules governing family interaction in aggressive and abusive families are such that the probability of acceleration of aversive tactics to abusive levels is heightened. This evidence is strong support for the position that child abuse must be viewed from an interactive perspective. Clearly abuse develops not only as a result of parents' own prior experience but also through the interaction patterns parents evolve with their children.

The child's role in abuse. To understand child abuse, both the child and the parent need to be considered. With few exceptions (Milowe & Lourie, 1964; Parke & Collmer, 1975; Sameroff & Chandler, 1975), the child's role in eliciting abuse has received little attention, although investigators have pointed to the selectivity of abuse: Not all children are abused; even within a family usually only a single child is selected.

The child may contribute to abuse in a variety of ways. First, the child may have physical and behavioral characteristics that make abuse more likely. For example, hyperactivity may elicit abuse—of particular interest because of the relations between prematurity and later activity level patterns, and prematurity and abuse (Parke & Collmer, 1975; see also Steven-Long, 1973). Or, the child may develop behaviors through interaction with parents and peers that target him or her for abuse. Or, as a result of physical abuse, the child may develop behavior patterns that elicit more abuse even from those who may not have originally maltreated the child. As Bakan (1971, p. 109) noted, "the well taken care of child attracts positive reactions. The child who is abused and neglected becomes ugly in appearance and behavior and invites further abuse and neglect." In support of this speculation, Dion (1974) recently experimentally demonstrated that the degree of adult punitiveness is determined by the physical attractiveness of the child: An unattractive child receives more severe punishment than an attractive child.

While all children can contribute to their own abuse, the infant is often a target. The birth of an infant may be a stressful event affecting the relations of family members. Many tasks must be mastered including routine caretaking; also schedules and activities must be modified to accommodate another person (Bakan, 1971). In a unique longitudinal study Ryder (1973) found that women with a child, compared to those without, were less satisfied with their marriage and specifically reported that their husbands were paying insufficient attention to them. Special circumstances may make abusive reactions to the newborn more likely. For example, dissatisfactions are probably exaggerated when a child is the product of an unwanted pregnancy (see, e.g., Birrell & Birrell, 1968; Kempe, Silverman, Steele, Droegemueller, & Silver, 1962; Nurse, 1964).

Abusive patterns may also result from a mismatch in the modes of interaction preferred by the mother and her infant. For example, some babies resist being embraced, hugged, and held tight (Schaffer & Emerson, 1964). This apparent genetic predisposition may be disruptive for mothers who prefer cuddly infants. Also, as Steele and Pollock (1968, p. 129) noted, "Some parents are disappointed when they have a placid child instead of a hoped-for more reactive, responsive baby. Other parents are equally distressed by having an active, somewhat aggressive baby who makes up his own mind about things when they had hoped for a very placid compliant infant." Current research aimed at isolating adaptations in parent-infant dyads should prove fruitful in the early identification of potential breakdowns in parent-infant interaction (Osofsky & Danzger, 1974; Parke & O'Leary, 1976; Parke & Sawin, 1975c).

The role for the partner in child abuse. Child abuse may be the outcome of parent-parent interaction. Particularly where strong norms limit husband-wife violence, the child may become a victim. Aggression may be directed toward the child too when extreme dominant-submissive patterns between the parents prevent a passive parent from directly expressing aggression toward the spouse (see Terr, 1970). Fenigstein and Buss (1974) recently provided evidence supporting the hypothesis of selective aggression against a weak victim: Angered adults were given the opportunity to deliver a mildly noxious stimulus to a confederate associated with an insulting experimenter *or* to aggress in a more intense manner against a non-associated individual. Subjects preferred to display intense aggression rather than aggress against the victim most similar to the anger inducer. Analogously, a child as a weak victim sometimes serves as the target for anger elicited by a spouse.

The reaction of a partner or spouse may also contribute to abuse. Milgram (1974) found that in a situation in which adults made increasingly harmful aggressive responses to a victim, the presence of two supportive peers increased the subject's level of aggressiveness. But the presence of partners who refused to escalate aggressiveness served to lower the subject's aggressive behavior. Although abuse may seem more likely in single-parent homes because there is no partner to prevent serious acceleration of punishment, no simple prediction is possible without exploring the partner's attitudes. Nonreaction from a partner in situations involving serious harm may function as positive reinforcement or approval (Bandura, 1965). Clearly, the interaction patterns among all family members merit consideration.

The Role of Community Support Systems in Child Abuse

If abuse is the outcome of mounting stress (Gil, 1970; Parke & Collmer, 1975), then the availability of supportive arrangements to provide periodic alleviations of sharing of responsibility for children may be important. This is particularly true where the extended family has been replaced by a self-contained nuclear family, often removed from its original community and established family ties (Bronfenbrenner, 1974). In times past, the extended family may have functioned in various ways to reduce the level of child abuse. The stresses of child care were often alleviated by other family members. The novice mother had an experienced model from whom to acquire mothering skills. At the same time an older caretaker could modify "inappropriate" tactics before escalation to abusive levels. With the demise of the extended family, these roles may be played by the informal network in the neighborhood and community or by formal support systems in law, health, and welfare. But members of a family isolated from both extended family and community contacts—informal and formal—have little opportunity to learn alternative resocialization strategies. Instead, they must rely on their own histories, untempered by the education and elaboration that stem from diverse experiences.

Using U.S. census data across 58 counties in New York State, Garbarino (1976) hypothesized that the rate of child abuse/maltreatment is inversely related to the socioeconomic support system for the family in each county. Based on a multiple regression approach, which controlled for the intercorrelation among socioeconomic and demographic indices, Garbarino found that five indices, including employment and income levels for mothers and educational opportunities for both mothers and pre-school children, accounted for 36 percent of the variance in child abuse across counties. His findings support a social-situational analysis of child abuse. While the data were derived from public agency sources that potentially overrepresent lower socioeconomic classes, the study nevertheless does suggest that environmental stress exacerbated by the unavailability of resources—even within lower-class groups—is related to child abuse.

While informal and formal support systems can be used in time of crisis, unfortunately abusive families generally make poor use of such resources. Considerable data suggest that abusive parents are social isolates. Young (1964) reported that 95 percent of severe-abuse families and 83 percent of moderate-abuse families had no continuing relations outside the family. Friendships usually ended after a few weeks or months in a violent quarrel and bitterness; moreover, 85 percent of the abusive families did not participate in any organized groups. In Merrill's research (1962), 50 percent of the abusive families had no formal group association; 28 percent had only one group association—most frequently church. Using an anomie scale that measured distrust of society, retreat from it, and resulting isolation, Elmer (1967) found a difference between abusive and nonabusive mothers. Likewise, Lenoski (1974) detected self-imposed isolation; 89 percent of the abusive parents had unlisted telephone numbers in contrast to only 12 percent of the nonabusive parents. In addition, almost twice as many of the abusive families (81% versus 43%) preferred to resolve crises alone. Other evidence indicates that such isolation may not be entirely voluntary. Merrill (1962) reported that abusive families were accepted only moderately (36%) and minimally (47%) well by their communities. Schloesser (1964) too found that some families were actively rebuffed by the community.

The lack of social integration of abusive families may be a function of their high mobility. Few have nearby relatives or other roots in the community (Gil, 1970; Scholesser, 1964). The special point of mobility is the loss of the extended family, with a probable increase in psychosocial isolation (see also Giovannoni & Billingsley, 1970). Basically the extended family is just one more support system missing from abusive parents' lives: "Although certain natural forces may be conducive to making parents care for their children, nonetheless there must be adequate contextual supports for the parents in this enterprise. In the relative absence of social support, one may expect that contrary impulses arise, even if they are not always acted out [Bakan, 1971, pp. 89-90]."

Resocialization of Abusive Families

Control of child abuse through the resocialization of abusive families can be viewed in short- and long-term perspectives. Short-term control involves crisis intervention to prevent imminent cases of abuse. Telephone hot-lines, police intervention, crisis nurseries, and day-care dropoff centers are examples of short-term control. Temporary removal of the abused child from the home by the courts is yet another form of short-term control. But given the large number of abused children reported annually, neither removal nor foster-care placement is an economically feasible solution. Long-term control aims to restructure the family's interaction patterns that may cause abuse or modify the child's or the parent's attitudes, values, personality, and/or behaviors that are viewed as causative. The particular forms of long-term intervention and control vary with the theoretical orientation of the intervention agent. While some control tactics focus on changing the individual, other control programs aim to alter abuse rates by modifying social institutions and social conditions.

In this section, I examine strategies for controlling child abuse: (1) the role of the legal system, specifically the police and the courts; (2) changes in social structure and community support systems; (3) the potential of alternative family models; and (4) modification of interaction patterns of abusive families. My underlying assumption is that abusive patterns are learned and therefore can be modified.

The Role of the Legal System: Police and Court Intervention

Child abuse is not only a sociopsychological problem but a legal one as well. "Every state now has criminal child neglect, abuse, or cruelty statutes [Mnookin,

1973, p. 629]," and legal machinery is often invoked in handling such cases. Police, prosecutors, and courts traditionally have been oriented to imposing criminal sanctions and intervening coercively in dealing with child abuse (Kempe & Helfer, 1972). Recently, however, there has been a marked skepticism among legal authorities and scholars (Delaney, 1972; Pitcher, 1972) about the utility of treating child abuse as a criminal offense. Revised goals as well as roles for professionals within the legal systems are evolving. In part, this shift is a multiply determined outcome of several factors: changing legal philosophy (Worsfold, 1974); limited success of the traditional adversary system in child-abuse cases (Mesch, 1971); and the potential benefits of alternative therapeutic resocialization programs.

The police. Although police are often the first formal authority to intervene in intra-family conflict, little attention has been paid to their role in the prevention and control of child abuse and family violence. Parnas (1967) estimated that more police calls involve family conflict than all other types of criminal incidents. Police intervention often occurs before conflict has escalated to the abusive level, while medical authorities typically encounter the family only *after* the abusive incident. Unfortunately, police intervention itself frequently exaggerates rather than limits both individual violence (Toch, 1969) and collective aggression (Marx, 1970), perhaps due to serious differences in values between police and their clientele (Rokeach, Miller & Synder, Chap. 13) or to lack of specific training in handling familial violence (Bandura, 1973; Bard, 1971).

Bard's work provides evidence that police can function effectively in settling intrafamily disputes and thereby may prevent the escalation of violence to abusive levels. A special "Family Crisis Unit" was trained to handle family disputes through such techniques as modeling, role playing, lectures, and discussion groups. Bard (1971, p. 152) noted that, although "40% of injuries sustained by police occur when they are intervening in family disputes . . . the 18-man unit, exposed for more than would ordinarily be the case to this dangerous event, sustained only one minor injury" during the two-year project. The use of nonphysical tactics in interventions in family disputes, such as advice and mediation, not only defuses a short-term problem but also serves as a model of alternative ways of settling conflict.

The police officer's initial handling of the dispute affects later events. If an arrest is made, charging and labeling processes are activated that, in turn, may end up in a court hearing.* But if an arrest is not made, costly legal procedures can be avoided, and social service agency assistance can be invoked. Bard (1971) found that in the non-trained unit, family court was the referral choice in 95 percent of the cases, with no referrals to social and mental health agencies. In the trained (experimental) unit, 45 percent of the referrals are made to family court and 55 percent to social and mental health agencies. In addition, there were about 22 percent fewer arrests in the experimental unit. Bard concluded:

> The lower rate of arrests in the experimental precinct is suggestive of the greater use of referral resources and of mediation. . . . It is well known that upon reaching the courts, and long after the heated dispute has cooled, most complaints of this type are dropped anyway. Sophisticated police intervention can provide immediate mediation service but

---

* A court hearing involves public disclosure of the family's mishandling of their child-care responsibilities. "Moreover, once the arrest has been made and criminal charges are pending, the parents are usually very uncooperative [Helfer & Kempe, 1974, p. 187]."

can also serve as a preliminary screening mechanism for final resolution of family disharmony [1971, p. 160].

In sum, Bard's project shows that professionals within the legal system can effectively serve as facilitators of more constructive family functioning rather than
merely as agents of law enforcement.

The courts. Most cases of child abuse fall within the jurisdiction of juvenile or
family courts. The typical judicial solution has been removal of the child from the
home and/or the imposition of criminal sanctions on the parent, but neither solution helps correct the abusive situation. Basically treating child abuse as criminal is
aimed at punitive rather than rehabilitative goals, with generally poor results. For
example, Pitcher reports:

> Incarceration of a convicted abusive parent achieves only a temporary period of safety
> for a child-victim, at best, and prisons cannot be expected to improve parental caretaking
> abilities. At worst, this respite for the child is gained at the cost of the family's means of
> support or the potential for adequate future child care in the same family [1972, p. 244].

Courts can play a constructive role, however. Multiple alternatives that do not
sacrifice due process guarantees and protections of the adversary system are
available. The adversary system "must yield to or at least share with another system
in which other disciplines also join in the fact finding and decision-making
[Delaney, 1972, p. 193]." Specifically, the legal system can function as an
authoritative partner in resocializing child abusers by (1) making parents aware of
available social services and (2) facilitating and enforcing parental participation in
therapeutic programs established by other community agencies.

Increased sharing of decision-making responsibility will not alone improve the
judicial treatment of child abusers. As noted earlier, child abuse is community defined. To the extent that judgments of abuse reflect middle-class community values
of appropriate child-rearing, lower-class defendants may be unable to get an un-
biased hearing (see also Mnookin, 1973). To protect against such unfairness,
Rodham suggests:

> One way to answer that complaint is to entrust the discretion . . . for evaluating a child's
> needs to persons representing the milieu in which a family lives. Boards composed of
> citizens . . . could make the initial decision regarding intervention or review judicial deci-
> sions. . . . Providing a check on judicial and bureaucratic discretion, this form of com-
> munity involvement also might broaden the constituency of adults actively concerned
> about services for children. Without an increase in community involvement, the best
> drafted laws and most eloquent judicial opinions will merely recycle past disappointments
> [1973, p. 514].

Nor should participation in court decision making be limited to adults. Children
need representation of their rights in legal contexts. Child advocates, such as the law
guardian concept, which involves appointing an attorney to represent the interests of
the child (Mesch, 1971), are important in gaining children's participation and in
socializing both children and community to the elements of choice and competence,
need and interest [cf. Tapp & Levine, 1974]. Children deserve a larger role in
deciding among alternative solutions in child-abuse cases. In many court-
adjudicated cases, the abused child is placed in a state-sponsored foster home—with

little opportunity to express a preference. Although foster care is often justified in terms of a "best interests" argument, Mnookin (1973) argued that this solution is generally not in the child's best interests given the long-term negative effects of foster care on the developing child (Eisenberg, 1962; Parfit, 1967). Instead, he held that removal was appropriate only when the child could not be protected in the home. Increasing both community and child participation in the disposition of child-abuse cases should contribute to ensuring the integrity of the family unit and the rights of children and their parents. Such reforms would also curb the wide discretionary power of the court—a fundamental problem in the U.S. legal system (Mnookin, 1973, p. 630).

Societal and Community Control of Child Abuse

The most consistent advocate of social changes as a solution to child abuse is Gil (1970, 1975), who emphasizes the importance of social support systems. He recommends comprehensive family planning programs and legal medical abortions—suggested by the finding that child abuse is more frequent in large families and with unwanted children. He also supports family-life education and counseling programs for both teenagers and adults to provide realistic information about the tasks and demands of marriage and child-rearing and to avoid the unrealistic expectations that abusive parents often have of children (see Steele & Pollock, 1968). Another of his suggestions has been incorporated into many child-abuse control programs: support services for mothers to relieve the stress of child care. Gil's underlying assumption is that "no mother should be expected to care for her children around the clock 365 days a year [1970, p. 147]." His recommendations offer considerable promise for the control of child abuse. They not only may serve to relieve the stress of child-care responsibilities but also may provide an opportunity for the child to learn new rules of social interaction from peers and other adults.

But more social services may not be sufficient. Publicity about institutional social support may be necessary as well. Often those most in need of social services do not know that government agencies are available. In a recent national survey of federal services, Kahn, Gutek, Barton, and Katz reported: "American bureaucracy apparently faces problems not only in helping people once they come in for service, but in getting them to come in at all. Among those who reported specific problems that the government might solve, many never found their way to the right agency and some had no idea an agency could help them [1975, p. 68]."

At the neighborhood level, various strategies can increase contacts among families. Groups such as Parents Anonymous can reduce the social isolation of abusive families. Hot-lines, modeled after the suicide emergency telephone lines, provide a valuable immediate resource. Other efforts include the Block Mothers' Program of St. Louis, Virginia Beach, and Des Moines, which are concerned about child abuse and runaways (*Parade*, June 22, 1975). Such programs could incorporate behavioral techniques aimed at modification of social isolation behavior through modeling of social skills (see Rimm & Masters, 1974). Further, programs within the community can implicitly and explicitly present rules for child care that offer alternatives for family governance and facilitate understanding the needs and rights of parents and child.

Alternative Family Arrangements

New family life-styles may contribute to abuse reduction. Whitehurst (1974) has argued that alternative family structures (i.e., families with more members than the traditional nuclear family), such as communes and group marriages, might reduce the potential for family violence. In addition to increased solidarity and the availability of others in crisis situations, Whitehurst asserted that most alternative families share norms of nonviolence. All these features should lead to lessened potential for violence. Although this nonviolence hypothesis remains untested, some support comes from earlier studies of the kibbutz (Rabin, 1965) and a recent study by Minturn, Gunnery, Holloway, and Peterson, which reported that commune residents in contrast to college students viewed their situations as "less competitive, more cooperative and less aggressive [1974, p. 494-495]."

Whitehurst offers the following warning: "[I]f we continue in conventional families to attempt to use outmoded legal and moral a priori answers to problems of life instead of rationally looking at the disparity of ends and means, we may well find more violence as a predicted outcome of family life [1974, p. 319]." To avoid such consequences, the rule structure and social control strategies within the nuclear family system need to be evaluated. Alternative family models may be instructive in that regard.

Modification of Family Interaction Patterns

Intervention need not be restricted to changes at the cultural, legal, and community levels; techniques for modifying family interaction styles are needed as well. The basic assumption of this type of intervention program is that attitudes about physical punishment can change as a result of providing parents with alternative disciplinary techniques. Such intervention can be viewed as a resocialization process whereby parents acquire new child-rearing skills. The aim is to alter the rules governing interaction from a negative, coercive basis to a more consensual model in which the rights and responsibilities of all participants are recognized.

Programs for altering family interaction patterns have a two-level focus. First, the parents themselves who are using physically punitive tactics need a new repertoire of training strategies that are effective in child control and, therefore, can replace punitive methods. Second, through the use of new techniques, child behaviors that may be eliciting highly punitive parental reactions will be altered.

A variety of social control techniques avoid the negative consequences of physical punishment. Risley and Baer (1973) have reviewed these behavior modification techniques in detail. Extinction (Williams, 1959), reinforcement of incompatible responses (Brown & Elliott, 1965), time-out (Hawkins, Peterson, Schweid, & Bijou, 1966), and verbal reasoning (Parke, 1970, 1974) are effective for improving parental control of children's behavior. For example, a number of investigators have demonstrated the usefulness of the "time-out" procedure for modifying deviant child behaviors in home situations, and they have trained mothers to use these procedures (Hawkins, Peterson, Schweid, & Bijou, 1966).

All these techniques may be used by a therapist or change agent to reduce the child's deviant behavior that may be eliciting the punitive treatment. However, abusive behavior of parents may be more adequately modified through a program of parental retraining, perhaps using the same procedures in conjunction with modeling techniques (Bandura, 1969).

Patterson (1974) has developed a comprehensive program for the retraining of parents of aggressive children based on social learning principles, particularly operant conditioning concepts, in which the relation between parental reactions and deviant behavior is the focus. By making parents aware of such a relationship and by providing the opportunity to learn and rehearse alternative techniques for dealing with their children, the deviant behavior can be modified.

In this program parents are first required to study a programmed text on social learning-based child management techniques. They next are taught to carefully define, track, and record a series of targeted deviant and/or prosocial child behaviors. Then the parents work in a training group with two or three other sets of parents, where modeling and role playing are used as instructional techniques, usually for 8 to 12 weekly sessions. Where needed, training sessions are held in the home with the experimenters modeling the appropriate parenting skills. Finally, parents learn to build contracts that spell out what to do with particular behaviors at home and/or at school. Patterson combines these procedures with a set of classroom interventions.

Effectiveness of the program is assessed through careful observations by trained observers of the interaction patterns between the parents and the deviant child in the home situation. Study of 27 families in the program indicated that there was a significant decrease in deviant behavior across the treatment phase. Follow-up assessments revealed that noxious behavior increased for half the families during the month after the end of treatment; but the deviant behavior was reduced by providing families with a "booster shot" of about two hours of extra treatment. Most important, the results suggest that the effects induced by the training were relatively stable over one year. Finally, in contrast to long-term psychiatric therapy, this type of intervention program was relatively economical: Therapist contact time was 31.4 hours.

The success of this program clearly documents the feasibility of retraining parents to use nonpunitive techniques for effective child control. Part of the reason for the long-term stability of the changes is that as the child's behavior changes, the child may become a more attractive and valued family member and thus a less likely target for abuse. Patterson's work should serve as a model for future intervention attempts in terms of the careful assessment, programmatic intervention and detailed documentation of outcomes. Further, this program illustrates the value of voluntary rehabilitation and nonpunitive procedures—in this case, for socializing children's deviant behaviors and resocializing abusive parent "offenders."

Epilogue: The Rights of Children

In the final analysis, child abuse must be viewed as inevitably intertwined with the broader issue of children's rights. Some (e.g., Zalba, 1971) have argued that the historical view of children as property has set the stage for child abuse. If so, control and decline of child abuse as a cultural phenomenon can only come about as rapidly as individuals in society reconceptualize and redefine the status and rights of children.

Overall, there has been a failure to appreciate the wide range of individual competence among children and the vast differences in the 18- or 20-year span of childhood (Rodham, 1973). Both the use of physical disciplinary tactics in controlling children and the limitations on children's rights are often justified in terms of children's limited cognitive abilities. But research over the past two decades has clearly shown that children can understand the sociolegal and moral basis of social rights at a much earlier age than generally had been assumed (Tapp & Kohlberg, Chap. 9; Tapp & Levine, 1974). Evidence also suggests that young children are responsive to nonphysical control tactics in the form of rationales (Parke, 1974). For example, 5-year-olds were effectively controlled by a prohibitory rationale based on property rights. In short, children can both understand and effectively use rationally based social rules to govern their own behavior well before adulthood or even before adolescence.

Justifying physical punishment as a control tactic in terms of the child's limited capacity for appreciating more humane cognitively derived procedures is simply not tenable. A shift on the part of parents and other caretakers toward nonpunitive child-rearing tactics has implications beyond the possible reduction of child abuse. It is consistent with a more profound shift in thought and action concerning the rights of children, which suggests that the rights of children as individuals are not limited by their status but only by their capacity to participate competently in the formulation of social rules (Rawls, 1971; Worsfold, 1974). From this perspective, parents may not arbitrarily impose regulations and restrictions on children. Basically "children have a right to make just claims and adults must be responsive to these claims [Worsfold, 1974, p. 157]."

Moreover, children's rights should not be limited solely to family settings. Their rights within the legal system need to be recognized and guaranteed as well. As is evident from the discussion and research presented in this chapter, the child should be an active participant in the judicial process and in decision making. Further, children and adults both should be accorded the rights and responsibilities—benefits and burdens—that result from interaction between individuals and within institutions.

Too often it is easy to dismiss parental responsibility in the name of children's rights. Socialization involves a responsibility on the part of parents to give children a chance to learn the rules and norms of their society and culture and at the same time to realize their full social and cognitive potential. While it is most unlikely that physical punishment is either necessary or useful in this process, a shift away from physically punitive control tactics (wherever the setting) does not imply a shift to unsupervised freedom. Socialization implies control, but a view of the child as a self-respecting and self-determining human needs to be given primary recognition in evaluating the goals and types of regulation.

REFERENCES

BAKAN, D. *Slaughter of the innocents.* San Francisco: Jossey-Bass, 1971.

BANDURA, A. "Influence of model's reinforcement contingencies on the acquisition of imitative responses." *Journal of Personality and Social Psychology*, 1965, 1, 589-595.

BANDURA, A. "The role of modeling processes in personality development." In W. W. Hartup & L. Smothergill (Eds.), *The young child: Reviews of research.* Washington: National Association for the Education of Young Children, 1967.

BANDURA, A. *Principles of behavioral modification.* New York: Holt, Rinehart & Winston, 1969.

BANDURA, A. *Aggression: A social learning analysis.* New York: Prentice Hall, 1973.

BANDURA, A., & WALTERS, R. H. *Social learning and personality development.* New York: Holt, Rinehart & Winston, 1963.

BARD, M. "The study and modification of intra-familial violence." In J. L. Singer (Eds.), *The control of aggression and violence.* New York: Academic Press, 1971.

BELLAK, L., & ANTELL, M. "An intercultural study of aggressive behavior on children's playground." *American Journal of Orthopsychiatry*, 1974, 44, 503-511.

BERKOWITZ, L. *Aggression: A social psychological analysis.* New York: McGraw Hill, 1962.

BLACK, D. J., and REISS, A. J., JR. "Patterns of behavior in police and citizen transactions." *Studies of crime and law enforcement in major metropolitan areas.* Washington, D.C.: United States Government Printing Office, 1967.

BIRRELL, R. G., and BIRRELL, J. H. W. "The maltreatment syndrome in children: A hospital survey." *Medical Journal of Australia*, 1968, 2, 1023-1029.

BRONFENBRENNER, U. "The origins of alienation." *Scientific American*, 1974, 231 (2), 53-57, 60-61.

BRONFENBRENNER, U. "Socialization and social class through time and space." In E. E. Maccoby, T. M. Newcomb, and E. L. Hartley (Eds.), *Readings in social psychology.* New York: Holt, 1958.

BROWN, P., and ELLIOTT, R. "The control of aggression in a nursery school class." *Journal of Experimental Child Psychology*, 1965, 2, 103-107.

DAVITZ, J. R. "The effects of previous training on postfrustration behavior." *Journal of Abnormal and Social Psychology*, 1952, 47, 309-315.

DELANEY, J. J. "The battered child and the law." In C. H. Kempe and R. E. Helfer (Eds.), *Helping the battered child and his family.* New York: Lippincott, 1972.

DEUR, J. L., and PARKE, R. D. "The effects of inconsistent punishment on aggression in children." *Developmental Psychology*, 1970, 2, 403-411.

DION, K. K. "Children's physical attractiveness and sex as determinants of adult punitiveness." *Developmental Psychology*, 1974, 10, 772-778.

EISENBERG, L. "The sins of the fathers: Urban decay and social pathology." *American Journal of Orthopsychiatry*, 1962, 32, 14.

ELMER, E. *Children in jeopardy: A study of abused minors and their families.* Pittsburgh: University of Pittsburgh Press, 1967.

ERLANGER, H. S. "Social class differences in parents' use of physical punishment." In S. K. Steinmetz and M. S. Straus (Eds.), *Violence in the family.* New York: Dodd, Mead and Co., 1974.

FENIGSTEIN, A., & BUSS, A. H. "Association and affect as determinants of displaced aggression." *Journal of Research in Personality,* 1974, 7, 306-313.

FREEDMAN, D. A., & FREEDMAN, N. "Behavioral differences between Chinese-American and European-American newborns." *Nature*, 1969, 224, 1227.

FULLER, L. L. *The morality of law.* (Rev. ed.) New Haven: Yale University Press, 1969.

GARBARINO, J. "Some ecological correlates of child abuse: The impact of socioeconomic stress on mothers." *Child Development*, 1975.

GEIS, G., & MONAHAN, J. "The social ecology of violence." In T. Lickona (Ed.), *Man and morality*. New York: Holt, Rinehart & Winston, 1975.

GELFAND, D. M., HARTMANN, D. P., LAMB, A. K., SMITH, C. L., MAHAN, M. A., & PAUL, S. C. "The effects of adult models and described alternatives on children's choice of behavior management techniques." *Child Development*, 1974, 45, 585-593.

GELLES, R. J. "Child abuse as psychopathology: A sociological critique and reformulation." *American Journal of Orthopsychiatry*, 1973, 43, 611-621.

GELLES, R. J. "The social construction of child abuse." *American Journal of Orthopsychiatry*, 1975, 45, 363-371.

GERBNER, G. "The violence profile: Some indicators of the trends in and the symbolic structure of network television drama 1967-1970." Unpublished manuscript, University of Pennsylvania, 1972.

GIL, D. G. *Violence against children: Physical child abuse in the United States*. Cambridge, Mass.: Harvard University Press, 1970.

GIL, D. G. "Unraveling child abuse." *American Journal of Orthopsychiatry*, 1975, 45, 346-356.

GIOVANNONI, J. M., & BILLINGSLEY, A. "Child neglect among the poor: A study of parental adequacy in families of three ethnic groups." *Child Welfare*, 1970, 49, 196-204.

GLUECK, S., & GLUECK, E. *Unraveling juvenile delinquency*. Cambridge, Mass.: Harvard University Press, 1950.

GOODE, W. J. "Force and violence in the family." *Journal of Marriage and the Family*, 1971, 33, 624-636.

HAWKINS, R. P., PETERSON, R. F., SCHWEID, E., & BIJOU, S. W. "Behavior therapy in the home: Amelioration of problem parent-child relations with the parent in the therapeutic role." *Journal of Experimental Child Psychology*, 1966, 4, 99-107.

HELFER, R. E., & KEMPE, C. H. *The battered child*. (2nd ed.) Chicago: University of Chicago Press, 1974.

KAHN, R. L., GUTEK, B. A., BARTON, E., & KATZ, D. "Americans love their bureaucrats." *Psychology Today*, 1975, 9 (1), 66-71.

KELLEY, H. H. "The process of causal attribution." *American Psychologist*, 1973, 28, 107-128.

KELLEY, C. *Crime in the United States—1972*. Washington, D.C.: United States Government Printing Office, 1973.

KEMPE, C. H., & HELFER, R. E. *Helping the battered child and his family*. Philadelphia: J. B. Lippincott, 1972.

KEMPE, C. H., SILVERMAN, F. N., STEELE, B. B., DROEGEMUELLER, W., & SILVER, H. K. "The battered child syndrome." *Journal of the American Medical Association*, 1962, 181, 17-24.

KORSCH, B., CHRISTIAN, J., GOZZI, E., & CARLSON, P. "Infant care and punishment: A pilot study." *American Journal of Public Health*, 1965, 55, 1880-1888.

LENOSKI, E. F. "Translating injury data into preventive and health care services—physical child abuse." Unpublished manuscript, University of South California, 1974.

LEVY, R. I. "On getting angry in the Society Islands." In W. Caudill and T. Y. Lin (Eds.), *Mental health research in Asia and the Pacific*. Honolulu: East-West Center Press, 1969.

LIEBERT, R. M., NEALE, J. M. and DAVIDSON, E. S. *The early window: Effects of television on children and youth*. New York: Pergamon, 1973.

LIGHT, R. "Abuse and neglected children in America: A study of alternative policies." *Harvard Educational Review*, 1973, 43, 556-598.

MARX, G. T. "Civil disorders and the agents of social control." *Journal of Social Issues*, 1970, 26 (1), 19-58.

McCORD, W., McCORD, J., and HOWARD, A. "Familial correlates of aggression in non-delinquent male children." *Journal of Abnormal and Social Psychology*, 1961, 62, 79-93.

MEAD, M. *Sex and temperament in three savage tribes*. New York: Morrow, 1935.

MERRILL, E. J. *Protecting the battered child*. Denver, Colo.: American Humane Association, 1962.

MESCH, M. "The role of the attorney." In A. Glazier (Ed.), *Child abuse: A community challenge*. Buffalo: Henry Stewart, 1971.

MILGRAM, S. *Obedience to authority*. New York: Harper and Row, 1974.

MILOWE, I., and LOURIE, R. "The child's role in the battered child syndrome." *Society for Pediatric Research*, 1964, 65, 1079-1081.

MINTURN, L., GUNNERY, K., HOLLOWAY, M., and PETERSON, C. "The peaceful communities." In J. de Wit and W. W. Hartup (Eds.), *Determinants and origins of aggressive behavior*. The Hague: Mouton, 1974.

MNOOKIN, R. H. "Foster care: In whose best interests?" *Harvard Educational Review*, 1973, 43, 599-638.

NIEM, T. C., & COLLARD, R. "Parental discipline of aggressive behaviors in four-year old Chinese and American children." Paper presented at the Annual Meeting of the American Psychological Association, Washington, D.C., 1971.

NURSE, S. M. "Familial patterns of parents who abuse their children." *Smith College Studies in Social Work*, 1964, 35, 11-25.

OSOFSKY, J. D., & DANZGER, B. "Relationships between neonatal characteristics and mother-infant interaction." *Developmental Psychology*, 1974, 10, 124-130.

PALMER, S. *The Violent Society*. New Haven: College & University Press, 1972.

PARFIT, J. (Ed.) *The community's children: Longterm substitute care: A guide for the intelligent layman*. New York: Humanities Press, 1967.

PARKE, R. D. "Effectiveness of punishment as an interaction of intensity, timing, agent nurturance, and cognitive structuring." *Child Development*, 1969, 40, 213-235.

PARKE, R. D. "The role of punishment in the socialization process." In R. A. Hoppe, G. A. Milton, & E. C. Simmel (Eds.), *Early experiences and the process of socialization*. New York: Academic Press, 1970.

PARKE, R. D. "Rules, roles and resistance to deviation in children: Explorations in punishment, discipline and self control." In A. Pick (Ed.), *Minnesota symposia on child psychology*. Vol. 8. Minneapolis: University of Minnesota Press, 1974.

PARKE, R. D., & COLLMER, C. W. "Child abuse: An interdisciplinary analysis." In E. M. Hetherington (Ed.), *Review of child development research*. Vol. 5. Chicago: University of Chicago Press, 1975.

PARKE, R. D., & DEUR, J. L. "Schedule of punishment and inhibition of aggression in children." *Developmental Psychology*, 1972, 7, 266-269.

PARKE, R. D., & O'LEARY, S. "Family interaction in the newborn period: Some findings, some observations, and some unresolved issues." In K. Riegel & J. Meacham (Eds.), *The developing individual in a changing world*. Vol. 2. *Social and environmental issues*. The Hague: Mouton, 1976.

PARKE, R. D., & SAWIN, D. B. "Infant characteristics and behavior as elicitors of maternal and paternal responsivity in the newborn period." Paper presented at the Biennial Meeting of the Society for Research in Child Development, Denver, Colorado, 1975. (a)

PARKE, R. D., & SAWIN, D. B. *Aggression: Causes and controls.* Homewood, Ill.: Learning Systems Co., 1975. (b)

PARKE, R. D., & SAWIN, D. B. "The effects of inter-agent inconsistent discipline on aggression in children." Unpublished manuscript, Fels Research Institute, 1975.

PARKE, R. D., SAWIN, D. B., & KRELING, B. "The effect of child feedback on adult disciplinary choices." Unpublished manuscript, Fels Research Institute, 1974.

PARNAS, R. I. "The police response to the domestic disturbance." *Wisconsin Law Review*, 1967, 914-960.

PATTERSON, G. R. "Interventions for boys with conduct problems: Multiple settings, treatments and criteria." *Journal of Consulting and Clinical Psychology*, 1974, 42, 471-481.

PATTERSON, G. R. "The aggressive child: Victim and architect of a coercive system" In L. A. Hamerlynck, E. J. Mash, & L. C. Handy (Eds.), *Behavior modification and families.* New York: Brunner & Mazell, 1975.

PATTERSON, G. R., and COBB, J. A. "A dyadic analysis of "aggressive" behavior." In J. P. Hill (Ed.), *Minnesota symposia on child psychology.* Vol. 5. Minneapolis: University of Minnesota Press, 1971.

PATTERSON, G. R. and COBB, J. A. "Stimulus control for classes of noxious behavior." In J. F. Knutson (Ed.), *The control of aggression: Implications from basic research.* Chicago: Aldine, 1973.

PATTERSON, G. R., and REID, J. B. "Reciprocity and coercion: Two facets of social systems." In C. Newunger and J. Michael (Eds.), *Behavior modification in clinical psychology.* New York: Appleton-Century-Crofts, 1970.

PINKNEY, A. *The American way of violence.* New York: Random House, 1972.

PITCHER, R. A. "The police." In C. H. Kempe and R. E. Helfer (Eds.), *Helping the battered child and his family.* Philadelphia: J. B. Lippincott 1972.

RABIN, A. I. *Growing up in the kibbutz,* New York: Springer, 1965.

RAWLS, J. *A theory of justice.* Cambridge, Mass.: Belknap Press of Harvard University Press, 1971.

RIMM, D. C., and MASTERS, J. C. *Behavior therapy: Techniques and empirical findings.* New York: Academic Press, 1974.

RISLEY, T. R., and BAER, D. M. "Operant behavior modification: The deliberate development of behavior." In B. M. Caldwell and H. N. Ricciuti (Eds.), *Review of child development research.* Vol. 3. Chicago: University of Chicago Press, 1973.

RODHAM, H. "Children under the law." *Harvard Educational Review*, 1973, 43, 487-514.

ROKEACH, M., MILLER, M. G., and SNYDER, J. A. "The value gap between police and policed." *Journal of Social Issues*, 1971, 27 (2), 155-171.

RYDER, R. G. "Longitudinal data relating marriage satisfaction and having a child." *Journal of Marriage and the Family*, 1973, 35, 604-606.

SAMEROFF, A. J., and CHANDLER, M. J. "Perinatal risk and the continuum of caretaking casualty." In F. D. Horowitz, E. M. Hetherington, S. Scarr-Salapatek, and G. Siegel (Eds.), *Review of child development research.* Vol. 4. Chicago: University of Chicago Press, 1975.

SCHAFFER, H. R., and EMERSON, P. E. "Patterns of response to physical contact in early human development." *Journal of Child Psychology and Psychiatry*, 1964, 5, 1-13.

SCHLOESSER, P. "The abused child." *Bulletin of Menninger Clinic*, 1964, 28, 260.

SIDEL, R. *Women and child care in China.* New York: Hill and Wang, 1972.

STARK, R. *Police riots: Collective violence and law enforcement.* Belmont, California: Wadsworth, 1972.

STARK, R., and McEVOY, J. "Middle class violence." *Psychology Today.* 1970. 4 (6), 52-54, 110-112.

STEELE, B. F., and POLLOCK, D. "A psychiatric study of parents who abuse infants and small children." In R. E. Helfer and C. H. Kempe (Eds.), *The battered child.* (2nd ed.) Chicago: University of Chicago Press, 1968.

STEIN, A. H., and FREIDRICH, L. K. "Impact of television on children and youth." In E. M. Hetherington (Ed.), *Review of child development research.* Vol. 5. Chicago: University of Chicago Press, 1975.

STEINMETZ, S. K. "Intra-familial patterns of conflict resolution: United States and Canadian comparisons." Paper presented at the Annual Meeting of the Society for the Study of Social Problems, Montreal, Canada, 1974. (a)

STEINMETZ, S. K. "Normal families and family violence: The training ground for abuse." Paper presented at Research NIH Conference on Child Abuse and Neglect, Bethesda, Maryland, 1974. (b)

STEINMETZ, S. K. "Occupational environment in relation to physical punishment and dogmatism." In S. K. Steinmetz & M. A. Straus (Eds.), *Violence in the family.* New York: Dodd, Mead, 1974. (c)

STEVENS-LONG, J. "The effect of behavioral context on some aspects of adult disciplinary practice and affect." *Child Development*, 1973, 44, 476-484.

STEVENSON, H. W. "Reflections on the China visit." *Society for Research in Child Development Newsletter*, Fall, 1974.

STOUWIE, R. J. "An experimental study of adult dominance and warmth, conflicting verbal instructions, and children's moral behavior." *Child Development*, 1972, 43, 959-972.

STRAUS, M. A. "Some social antecedents of physical punishment: A linkage theory interpretation." *Journal of Marriage and the Family*, 1971, 33, 658-663.

TAPP, J. L. "Reflections." *Journal of Social Issues*, 1971, 27(2), 1-16.

TAPP, J. L., & KOHLBERG, L. "Developing senses of law and legal justice." *Journal of Social Issues*, 1971, 27 (2), 65-92.

TAPP, J. L., & LEVINE, F. J. "Legal socialization: Strategies for an ethical legality." *Stanford Law Review*, 1974, 27, 1-72.

TERR, L. C. "A family study of child abuse." *American Journal of Psychiatry*, 1970, 127, 665-671.

TOCH, H. *Violent men: An inquiry into the psychology of violence.* Chicago: Aldine, 1969.

VIANO, E. C. "Attitudes towards child abuse among American professionals." Paper presented at the Biennial Meeting of the International Society for Research on Aggression, Toronto, Canada, 1974.

WALTERS, R. H., & PARKE, R. D. "Social motivation, dependency and susceptibility to social influence." In L. Berkowitz (Ed.), *Advances in experimental social psychology.* New York: Academic Press, 1964.

WHITEHURST, R. N. "Alternative family structures and violence reduction." In S. K. Steinmetz & M. A. Straus (Eds.), *Violence in the family.* New York: Dodd, Mead, 1974.

WILLIAMS, C. D. "The elimination of tantrum behavior by extinction procedures." *Journal of Abnormal and Social Psychology*, 1959, 59, 269.

WORSFOLD, V. L. "A philosophical justification for children's rights." *Harvard Educational Review*, 1974, 44, 142-157.

YOUNG, L. *Wednesday's children: A study of child neglect and abuse.* New York: McGraw-Hill, 1964.

ZALBA, S. "Battered children." *Trans-action*, 1971, 8 (9-10), 58-61.

Part Three

Social Policy Issues

Many of those concerned with eliminating or at least decreasing the incidence of child abuse are advocating check-list inventories for the pre-screening of potentially abusing parents. Their aim is to identify such families and in various ways intervene in the parenting process in order to protect the children. The conflicting theories and lack of consensus in empirical studies evident in the preceding papers must pose problems for such advocates.

The emphasis upon identification, treatment and prevention which runs through most of the literature is tempered by the authors' acknowledgments of the limitations and inadequacies of the research to date.

As the following articles indicate, however, the lack of an explicative base of knowledge is not the only problem for those planning social policy. Questions of definition, of legal rights and the ethics of intervention, of punishment and/or treatment, of professional capabilities and jurisdiction, and of resources and commitment to social change are all complicating factors. Until these issues are successfully confronted it is unlikely that effective programmes will be developed.

S. J. Pfohl   This article provides a history of social policy perspectives and programmes. Pfohl traces the development of attitudes toward abusive behaviour from the 19th century to the present. He places particular emphasis on the cultural values associated with child protection at the time abuse came to be labelled deviant behaviour. He examines the change in philosophy from preventive penology (to protect society) to a concern with protecting the child. Pfohl points out that it was only when certain segments of the medical profession identified the battered child syndrome that a socio-legal reaction against abuse coalesced. He provides an extensive analysis of why the radiology profession was the first to recognize and apply the label of abuse. Pfohl discusses the implication of the "discovery" of abuse as an illness and the adoption of a "sick" label for abusers. He then describes the consequent actions of the medical, legal, media and social welfare systems.

R. Gelles

Using the theoretical framework developed by the labelling school of sociology, Gelles continues the discussion of child abuse as social deviance. He examines the process by which certain individuals and families are identified as "abusers" and the influence of that process on incidence statistics, causal conclusions and intervention strategies. Gelles analyses the ways in which definitions are developed and applied by "gatekeepers" or judges and the resulting consequences. For example, because studies of the correlates of child abuse are most often based on identified cases, the results show the effects of both the characteristics of child abusers and the criteria by which the classification was made. In addition, once labelled, a person is likely to be treated in a different manner which in turn may lead to changes in his behaviour. Thus, the labelling process itself may "cause" certain of the factors associated with abuse. Gelles concludes that the professionals involved with child abusers must be regarded as legitimate objects of inquiry. An understanding of abuse requires an awareness of how various agencies interact and how those labelled flow through these systems.

E. Newberger et al.

This article could appropriately be included in Part Two as it examines the sources of abuse with particular emphasis on the significance of stress factors. However, Newberger and his associates raise several issues which are crucial to social policy decisions. They discuss problems of diagnosis and intervention based upon inadequate information and the ethical issues involved in research of this nature. As well, they note that the assignment of labels which imply parental fault is antithetical to the traditional ethical posture of the helping professions. The study itself was designed to identify the major discriminating characteristics of cases of child abuse, neglect, failure to thrive, accidents and poisonings, and a control group. The method of data collection and analysis are explained in detail. The authors conclude that the basic hypothesis that family stress is associated with the occurrence of abuse is confirmed. They warn, however, that the predictive power of the discriminating features is weak. They elaborate on the danger of misclassification and the implications of selection bias if such research is used as the basis for a screening instrument.

E. H. Newberger

This paper is a reiteration and expansion of the policy problems raised by the research results in the previous paper. Dr. Newberger notes the class bias evident in reporting and labelling child abuse by the medical profession. He believes that the reluctance to report some clients and the ignoring of sexual misuse and institutional abuse has produced narrow, limited research results. He states that at the present time there is no adequate conceptual base for the treatment of abuse and neglect and he is disturbed by the "implications of headlong action." Newberger advocates a better understanding of the type and distribution of family problems and a more accurate accounting of the "relationship of children's symptoms to family dysfunctions." He states that rational clinical practice requires further knowledge of the factors which contribute to family strength and competence.

B. Chisholm

This author notes that the inconsistencies in definition and reporting procedures in Canada result in imprecise data on abuse. The main thrust of Chisholm's paper is a consideration of the management of abuse. The variance of opinion on punishment or treatment of offenders is discused. She points out the implications of the use of treatment terminology to describe what are essentially management procedures. Chisholm assesses the ethical and legal issues of intervention, parental rights and the rights of children. Complicating the prevention of abuse are such factors as the lack of co-operation between service professionals and conflicting opinions on the merits of corporal punishment. Finally, she warns of the danger of overlooking the interests of the child when focusing on helping the abusing parent.

E. H. Newberger and
R. Bourne

In this paper the medical and legal ambiguity concerning child abuse is seen as responsible for theoretical confusion and clinical inadequacy. Dilemmas about social policy result from a conflict between the principle of family autonomy and the strategy of coercive intervention. Like Gelles, the authors use social labelling theory to examine the processes by which child abuse is "medicalized" and "legalized" and the consequences of such conceptualizations for the professionals involved, for the abuser, and for the social system. Concluding that clinical intervention is class and culture based, Newberger and Bourne offer guidelines to "minimize the abuse of power of the definer."

L. S. Crain and
G. K. Millor

This case report shows that social policies designed to benefit one segment of society may have unintended impacts which can be detrimental to another. The authors affirm that there is a lack of data on the "association of parental mental retardation and child abuse." Crain and Millor describe the consequences of the policy of normalization of mentally retarded adults in terms of the children of one such family. The two sons suffered physical abuse and "unintentional neglect". The parents were deemed inherently incapable of providing adequate care. Attempts to protect the children by removal or by provision of special services were thwarted by questions of legal evidence, parental rights and inadequate resources. Crain and Millor's article illustrates the undesirable consequences of social policy decisions taken without ensuring that the resources necessary to their effectiveness will be available.

D. Finkelhor

This brief article concerns the problem of sexual abuse and the ethical questions raised by increasingly liberalized sexual mores. Dr. Finkelhor assesses the traditional arguments against the sexual misuse of children and finds them wanting. He proposes an ethical standard which requires informed consent and equal power relationships. Given the current controversies regarding sexual activity between adults and children, his arguments for ethical clarity can be a valuable contribution to the policies for the protection of children.

28

The "Discovery" of Child Abuse*

Stephen J. Pfohl

Despite documentary evidence of child beating throughout the ages, the "discovery" of child abuse as deviance and its subsequent criminalization are recent phenomena. In a four year period beginning in 1962, the legislatures of all fifty states passed statutes against the caretaker's abuse of children. This paper is a study of the organization of social forces which gave rise to the deviant labeling of child beating and which promoted speedy and universal enactment of criminal legislation. It is an examination of certain organized medical interests, whose concern in the discovery of the "battered child syndrome" manifestly contributed to the advance of humanitarian pursuits while covertly rewarding the groups themselves.

The structure of the present analysis is fourfold: First, an historical survey of social reaction to abusive behavior prior to the formulation of fixed labels during the early sixties, focussing on the impact of three previous reform movements. These include the nineteenth-century "house-of-refuge" movement, early twentieth century crusades by the Society for the Prevention of Cruelty to Children, and the rise of juvenile courts. The second section concentrates on the web of cultural values

---

* The author acknowledges the invaluable collaboration of Judith Dilorio of The Ohio State University in bringing this manuscript to its final form. Also acknowledged are the critical comments of John Conrad, Raymond Michalowski and Dee Roth. Consultation with Simon Dinitz, Gideon Fishman and Andrew Rutherford on an earlier draft of this paper is likewise appreciated. Gratitude is also expressed to Kathy Delgarn for the preparation of the manuscript.

Stephen J. Pfohl, "The Discovery of Child Abuse," *Social Problems*, 24:3 (February, 1977), pp. 310-323.

related to the protection of children at the time of the "discovery" of abuse as deviance. A third section examines factors associated with the organizational structure of the medical profession conducive to the "discovery" of a particular type of deviant label. The fourth segment discusses social reaction. Finally, the paper provides a sociological interpretation of a particular social-legal development. Generically it gives support for a synthesis of conflict and labeling perspectives in the sociology of deviance and law.

The History of Social Reaction: Preventative Penology and "Society Saving."

The purposeful beating of the young has for centuries found legitimacy in beliefs of its necessity for achieving disciplinary, educational or religious obedience (Radbill, 1968). Both the Roman legal code of "Patria Patistas" (Shepard, 1965), and the English common law (Thomas, 1973), gave guardians limitless power over their children who, with chattel-like status, had no legal right to protection.

The common law heritage of America similarly gave rise to a tradition of legitimized violence toward children. Legal guardians had the right to impose any punishment deemed necessary for the child's upbringing. In the seventeenth century, a period dominated by religious values and institutions, severe punishments were considered essential to the "sacred" trust of child-rearing (Earle, 1926:119-126). Even in the late eighteenth and early nineteenth centuries, a period marked by the decline of religious domination and the rise of rationalism and a proliferation of statutes aimed at codifying unacceptable human behavior, there were no attempts to prevent caretaker abuse of children. A major court in the state of North Carolina declared that the parent's judgment of need for a child's punishment was presumed to be correct. Criminal liability was said to exist only in cases resulting in "permanent injury" (*State v. Pendergass*, in Paulsen, 1966b:686).

I am not suggesting that the American legal tradition failed to recognize any abuse of discipline as something to be negatively sanctioned. A few cases resulting in the legal punishment of parents who murdered their children, have been recorded. But prior to the 1960's socio-legal reactions were sporadic, and atypical of sustained reactions against firmly labeled deviance.

Beginning in the early nineteenth century, a series of three reform movements directed attention to the plight of beaten, neglected and delinquent children. These included the nineteenth century "house-of-refuge" movement, the turn of the century crusades by the Society for the Prevention of Cruelty to Children and the early twentieth century rise of juvenile courts. Social response, however, seldom aimed measures at ameliorating abuse or correcting abusive parents. Instead, the child, rather than his or her guardians, became the object of humanitarian reform.

In each case the primary objective was not to save children from cruel or abusive parents, but to save society from future delinquents. Believing that wicked and irresponsible behavior was engendered by the evils of poverty and city life, these movements sought to curb criminal tendencies in poor, urban youths by removing them from corrupt environments and placing them in institutional settings. There they could learn order, regularity and obedience (Rothman, 1970). Thus, it was children, not their abusive guardians, who felt the weight of the moral crusade. They, not their parents, were institutionalized.

The "House of Refuge" Movement

Originating in the reformist dreams of the Jacksonian era, the so-called "House of Refuge Movement" sought to stem the social pathologies of an industrializing nation by removing young people, endangered by "corrupt urban environments," to institutional settings. Neglect statutes providing for the removal of the young from bad home lives were originally enacted to prevent children from mingling freely with society's dregs in alm houses or on the streets. In 1825, the first statute was passed and the first juvenile institution, the New York House of Refuge, was opened. Originally privately endowed, the institution soon received public funds to intervene in neglectful home situations and transplant children to a controlled environment, where they shared a "proper growing up" with other vagrant, abandoned and neglected youths as well as with delinquents who had violated criminal statutes. Similar institutions were established in Philadelphia and Boston a year later, in New Orleans in 1845, and in Rochester and Baltimore in 1849.

The Constitutionality of the neglect statutes, which formed the basis for the House of Refuge Movement, was repeatedly challenged on the grounds that it was really imprisonment without due process. With few exceptions court case after court case upheld the policy of social intervention on the Aristotelian principle of "parens patriae." This principle maintained that the State has the responsibility to defend those who cannot defend themselves, as well as to assert its privilege in compelling infants and their guardians to act in ways most beneficial to the State.

The concept of preventive penology emerged in the wording of these court decisions. A distinction between "delinquency" (the actual violation of criminal codes) and "dependency" (being born into a poor home with neglectful or abusive parents) was considered irrelevant for "child saving." The two were believed to be intertwined in poverty and desolation. If not stopped, both would perpetuate themselves. For the future good of both child and society, "parens patriae" justified the removal of the young before they became irreparably tainted (Thomas, 1972:322-323).

The underlying concept of the House of Refuge Movement was that of preventive penology, not child protection. This crusade registered no real reaction against child beating. The virtue of removing children from their homes was not to point up abuse or neglect and protect its victims, it was to decrease the likelihood that parental inadequacies, the "cause of poverty," would transfer themselves to the child and hence to the next generation of society (Giovannoni, 1971:652). Thus, as indicated by Zalba (1966), the whole nineteenth century movement toward institutionalization actually failed to differentiate between abuse and poverty and therefore registered no social reaction against beating as a form of deviance.

Mary Ellen, the SPCC, and a Short-Lived Social Reaction

The first period when public interest focussed on child abuse occurred in the last quarter of the nineteenth century. In 1875, the Society for the Prevention of Cruelty to Animals intervened in the abuse case of a nine-year old girl named Mary Ellen who had been treated viciously by foster parents. The case of Mary Ellen was splashed across the front pages of the nation's papers with dramatic results. As an outgrowth of the journalistic clamor, the New York Society for the Prevention of Cruelty to Children was formed. Soon incorporated under legislation that required law enforcement and court officials to aid agents of authorized cruelty societies, the NYSPCC and other societies modeled after it undertook to prevent abuse.

Though the police functions of the anti-cruelty societies represented a new reaction to abuse, their activities did not signify a total break with the society-saving emphasis of the House of Refuge Movement. In fact, three lines of evidence suggest that the SPCC enforcement efforts actually withheld a fixed label of deviancy from the perpetrators of abuse, in much the same manner as had the House of Refuge reforms. First, the "saving" of the child actually boosted the number of children placed in institutions, consequently supporting House of Refuge activities (Thomas, 1972:311). Second, according to Falks (1970:176), interorganizational dependency grew between the two reform movements; best evidenced by the success of SPCC efforts in increasing public support to childcare institutions under the auspices of House of Refuge groups. Finally, and perhaps most convincingly, natural parents were not classified as abusers of the great majority of the so-called "rescued children." In fact, the targets of these savings missions were cruel employers and foster or adopted parents (Giovannoni, 1971:653). Rarely did an SPCC intervene against the "natural" balance of power between parents and children. The firmness of the SPCC's alleged social action against abuse appears significantly dampened by its reluctance to shed identification with the refuge house emphasis on the "industrial sins of the city" and to replace it with a reaction against individuals.

The decline of the SPCC movement is often attributed to lack of public interest, funding problems, mergers with other organizations and the assumption of protection services by public agencies (Felder, 1971:187). Its identification with the House of Refuge Movement also contributed to its eventual demise. More specifically, the House of Refuge emphasis on the separation of child from family, a position adopted and reinforced by the SPCC's activities, came into conflict with perspectives advocated by the newly-emerging professions of social work and child psychology (Kadushen, 1967:202f). Instead of removing the child from the home, these new interests emphasized efforts to unite the family (Thomas, 1972). This latter position, backed by the power of professional expertise, eventually undercut the SPCC's policy of preventive policing by emphasizing the protection of the home.

The erosion of the SPCC position was foreshadowed by the 1909 White House Conference on Children. This Conference proclaimed that a child should not be removed from his or her home for reasons of poverty alone, and called for service programs and financial aid to protect the home environment. Yet, the practice of preventive policing and institutionalization did not vanish, due, in part, to the development of the juvenile court system. The philosophy and practice of this system continued to identify abuse and neglect with poverty and social disorganization.

The Juvenile Court and the Continued Shadow of Abuse

The founding of the first juvenile court in Illinois in 1899 was originally heralded as a major landmark in the legal protection of juveniles. By 1920, courts were established in all but three states. Nonetheless, it is debatable that much reform was accomplished by juvenile court legislation. Coalitions of would-be reformers (headed by various female crusaders and the commissioners of several large public reformatories) argued for the removal of youthful offenders from adult institutions and advocated alteration of the punitive, entrepreneurial and sectarian "House of Refuge" institutions (Fox, 1970:1225-29). More institutions and improved conditions were demanded (Thomas, 1972:323). An analysis of the politics of juvenile court legislation suggests, however, that successful maneuvering by influential sectarian entrepreneurs resulted in only a partial achievement of reformist goals (Fox, 1970:1225-26). Legislation did remove juveniles from adult institutions. It did not reduce the House of Refuge Movement's control of juvenile institutions. Instead, legislation philosophically supported and financially reinforced the Movement's "society-saving" operation of sectarian industrial schools (Fox, 1970:1226-27).

The channeling of juvenile court legislation into the "society-saving" mold of the House of Refuge Movement actually withheld a deviant label from abusive parents. Even the reformers, who envisioned it as a revolution in child protection, did not see the court as protection from unfit parents. It was meant instead to prevent the development of "lower class" delinquency (Platt, 1969) and to rescue "those less fortunate in the social order" (Thomas, 1972:326). Again, the victims of child battering were characterized as pre-delinquents, as part of the general "problem" of poverty. These children, not their guardians, were the targets of court action and preventive policies. The courts, like the House of Refuge and SPCC movements before them, constrained any social reaction which would apply the label of deviant to parents who abused their children.

Social Reaction at Mid-Century: The Cultural Setting for the "Discovery" of Abuse

The Decline of Preventative Penology

As noted, preventative penology represented the philosophical basis for various voluntary associations and legislative reform efforts resulting in the institutionalization of neglected or abused children. Its primary emphasis was on the protection of society. The decline of preventive penology is partially attributed to three variables: the perceived failure of "institutionalization," the impact of the "Great Depression" of the 1930's, and a change in the cultural meaning of "adult vices."

In the several decades prior to the discovery of abuse, the failure of institutionalization to "reorder" individuals became increasingly apparent. This realization undermined the juvenile courts' role in administering a pre-delinquency system of crime prevention. Since the rise of juvenile courts historically represented a major structural support for the notion of preventative penology, the lessening of its role removed a significant barrier to concern with abuse as an act of individual victimization. Similarly, the widespread experience of poverty during the Great Depression weakened other beliefs in preventive penology. As impersonal economic factors impoverished a great number of citizens of good moral credentials, the link between poverty and immorality began to weaken.

Another characteristic of the period immediately prior to the discovery of abuse was a changing cultural awareness of the meaning of adult vice as indices of the future character of children. "Parental immoralities that used to be seen as warnings of oncoming criminality in children [became] acceptable factors in a child's homelife" (Fox, 1970:1234). Parental behavior such as drinking, failing to provide a Christian education, and refusing to keep a child busy with useful labor, were no longer classified as unacceptable nor deemed symptoms of immorality transmitted to the young. Hence, the saving of society from the tainted young became less of a mandate, aiding the perception of social harm against children as "beings" in themselves.

Advance of Child Protection

Concurrent with the demise of "social-saving" in the legal sphere, developments in the fields of child welfare and public policy heightened interest in the problems of the child as an individual. The 1909 White House Conference on Children spawned both the "Mother's Aid" Movement and the American Association for the Study and Prevention of Infant Mortality. The former group, from 1910 to 1930, drew attention to the benefits of keeping children in the family while pointing out the detrimental effects of dehumanizing institutions. The latter group then, as now, registered concern over the rate of infant deaths.

During the first half of the twentieth century, the Federal Government also met the issue of child protection with legislation that regulated child labor, called for the removal of delinquent youths from adult institutions, and established, in 1930, a bureaucratic structure whose purpose revolved around child protection. The Children's Bureau of HEW immediately adopted a "Children's Charter" promising every child a home with love and security plus full-time public services for protection from abuse, neglect, exploitation or moral hazard (Radbill, 1968:15).

Despite the growth of cultural and structural dispositions favoring the protection and increased rights of children, there was still no significant attention given to perpetrators of abuse, in the courts (Paulsen, 1966:710), in the legislature (DeFrancis, 1967:3), or by child welfare agencies (Zalba, 1966). While this inactivity may have been partly caused by the lack of effective mechanisms for obtaining data on abuse (Paulsen, 1966:910), these agencies had little social incentive for interfering with an established power set—the parent over the child. As a minority group possessing neither the collective awareness nor the elementary organizational skills necessary to address their grievances to either the courts or to the legislators, abused and neglected children awaited the advocacy of some other organized interest. This outside intervention would not, however, be generated by that sector of "organized helping" most closely associated with the protective needs of children—the growing web of child welfare bureaucracies at State and Federal levels. Social work had identified its professional advance with the adoption of the psychoanalytic model of casework (Zalba, 1966). This perspective, rather than generating a concern with political inequities internal to the family, focused instead on psychic disturbances internal to its members. Rather than challenging the strength of parents, this served to reinforce the role of powerful guardians in the rearing of young.

Nor would advocacy come from the public at large. Without organized labeling interests at mid-century, child abuse had not become an issue publicly regarded as a major social problem. In fact a fairly general tolerance for abuse appeared to exist. This contention is supported by the findings of a nationwide study conducted by NORC during the period in which laws against abuse were actually being adopted (Gil & Nobel, 1969). Despite the wide-scale publicizing of abuse in this "post-discovery" period, public attitudes remained lenient. Data revealed a high degree of empathy with convicted or suspected perpetrators (Gil, 1970:63-67). These findings are understandable in light of cultural views accepting physical force against children as a nearly universally applied precept of intrafamilial organization (Goode, 1971). According to the coordinator of the national survey, "Culturally determined permissive attitudes toward the use of physical force in child rearing seem to constitute the common core of all physical abuse of children in American society" (Gil, 1970:141).

While the first half of the twentieth century is characterized by an increasing concern for child welfare, it developed with neither an organizational nor attitudinal reaction against child battering as a specific form of deviance. The "discovery" of abuse, its definition as a social problem and the socio-legal reaction against it, awaited the coalition of organized interests.

The Organization of Social Reaction against the "Battered Child Syndrome"

What organization of social forces gave rise to the discovery of abuse as deviance? The discovery is not attributable to any escalation of abuse itself. Although some authors have recently suggested that the increasing nuclearization of the family may increase the victimization of its offspring (Skolnick & Skolnick, 1971), there has never been any evidence that, aside from reporting inflation due to the impact of new laws, battering behavior was actually increasing (Eads, 1972). The attention here is on the organizational matrix encouraging a recognition of abuse as a social problem. In addressing this issue I will examine factors associated with the organizational structure of the medical profession leading to the discovery of abuse by pediatric radiologists rather than by other medical practitioners.

The "discovery" of abuse by pediatric radiology has often been described chronologically (Radbill, 1968:15; McCoid, 1965:2-5; Thomas, 1972:330). John Caffey (1946) first linked observed series of long bone fractures in children with what he termed some "unspecific origin." Although his assumption was that some physical disturbance would be discovered as the cause of this pattern of "subdural hematoma," Coffey's work prompted a series of further investigations into various bone injuries, skeletal trauma, and multiple fractures in young children. These research efforts lead pediatric radiology gradually to shift its diagnosis away from an internal medical explication toward the ascription of social cause.

In subsequent years it was suggested that what was showing up on x-rays might be the results of various childhood accidents (Barmeyer, *et al.*, 1951), of "parental carelessness" (Silverman, 1953), of "parental conduct" (Bakwin, 1956), and most dramatically, of the "indifference, immaturity and irresponsibility of parents" (Wooley & Evans, 1955). Surveying the progression of this research and reviewing his own investigations, Caffey (1957) later specified "misconduct and deliberate injury" as the primary etiological factors associated with what he had previously labelled "unspecific trauma." The discovery of abuse was on its way. Both in scholarly research (McCoid, 1966:7) and journalistic outcry (Radbill, 1968:16), the last years of the fifties showed dramatically increased concern for the beaten child.

Why did pediatric radiologists and not some other group "see" abuse first? Legal and social welfare agents were either outside the scene of abusive behavior or inside the constraining vision of psychoanalytically committed casework. But clinicians, particularly hospital physicians and pediatricians, who encountered abused children more immediately, should have discovered "abuse" before the radiologists.

Four factors impeded the recognition of abuse (as it was later labeled). First, some early research maintained that doctors in emergency room settings were simply unaware of the possibilities of "abuse" as a diagnosis (Bain, 1963; Boardman, 1962). While this may be true, the massive symptoms (blood, burns, bruises) emergency room doctors faced far outweighed the lines appearing on the x-ray screens of radiologic specialists. A second line of evidence contends that many doctors were simply psychologically unwilling to believe that parents would inflict such atrocities on their own children (Elmer, 1960; Fontana, Donovan, Wong, 1963; Kempe *et al.*, 1963). This position is consistent with the existing cultural assumptions pairing parental power with parental wisdom and benevolence. Nonetheless, certain normative and structural elements within professional medicine appear of greater significance in reinforcing the physician's reluctance to get involved, even diagnostically. These factors are the "norm of confidentiality between doctor and client" and the goal of professional autonomy.

The "norm of confidentiality" gives rise to the third obstacle to a diagnosis of abuse: the possibility of legal liability for violating the confidentiality of the physician-patient relationship (Boardman, 1962). Interestingly, although some research connotes doctors' concern over erroneous diagnosis (Braun, Braun & Simonds, 1963), physicians primarily view the parent, rather than the child, as their real patient. On a strictly monetary level, of course, it is the parent who contracts with the doctor. Additional research has indicated that, particularly in the case of pediatricians, the whole family is viewed as one's clinical domain (Bucher & Strauss, 1961:329). It is from this vantage point that the impact of possible liability for a diagnostic disclosure is experienced. Although legal liability for a diagnosis of abuse may or may not have been the risk (Paulsen, 1967b:32), the belief in such liability could itself have contributed to the narrowness of a doctor's diagnostic perceptions (McCoid, 1966:37).

A final deterrent to the physician's "seeing" abuse is the reluctance of doctors to become involved in a criminal justice process that would take both their time (Bain, 1963:896) and ability to guide the consequences of a particular diagnosis (Boardman, 1962:46). This deterrent is particularly related to the traditional success of organized medicine in politically controlling the consequences of its own performance, not just for medical practitioners but for all who come in contact with a medical problem (Freidson, 1969:106; Hyde, *et al.*, 1954).

The political control over the consequences of one's profession would be jeopardized by the medical diagnosis of child abuse. Doctors would be drawn into judicial proceedings and subordinated to a role as witnesses. The outcome of this process would be decided by criminal justice standards rather than those set forth by the medical profession. Combining this relatively unattractive alternative with the obvious and unavoidable drain on a doctor's financial earning time, this fourth obstacle to the clinician's discovery of abuse is substantial.

Factors Conducive to the Discovery of Abuse by Pediatric Radiology

Why didn't the above factors inhibit the discovery of abuse by pediatric radiologists as well as by clinicians? First it must be recognized that the radiologists in question (Caffey, Barmeyer, Silverman, Wooley and Evans) were all researchers of children's x-rays. As such, the initial barrier becomes irrelevant. The development of diagnostic categories was a consequence rather than a pre-condition of the medical mission. Regarding the psychological denial of parental responsiblity for atrocities, it must be remembered that the dramatic character of a beating is greatly reduced by the time it reaches an x-ray laboratory. Taken by technicians and developed as black and white prints, the radiologic remnants of abuse carry with them little of the horror of the bloody assault.

With a considerable distance from the patient and his or her family, radiologists are removed from the third obstacle concerning legal liabilities entailed in violating the doctor-patient relationship. Unlike pediatricians, radiologists do not routinely regard the whole family as one's clinical domain. Of primary importance is the individual whose name or number is imprinted on the x-ray frames. As such, fears about legal sanctions instigated by a parent whom one has never seen are less likely to deter the recognition of abuse.

Given the irrelevance of the first three obstacles, what about the last? Pediatric radiologists are physicians, and as such would be expected to participate in the "professional control of consequences" ethos. How is it that they negotiate this obstacle in favor of public recognition and labelling of abuse?

The Discovery: An Opportunity for Advancement Within the Medical Community

To ask why the general norm of "professional control of consequences" does not apply equally to radiologists as to their clinical counterparts is to confuse the reality of organized medicine with its image. Although the medical profession often appears to outsiders as a separate and unified community within a community (Goode, 1957), and although medical professionals generally favor the maintenance of this image (Glaser, 1960), it is nonetheless more adequately described as an organization of internally competing segments, each striving to advance its own historically derived mission and future importance (Bucher & Strauss, 1961). In analyzing pediatric radiology as one such segment, several key variables facilitated its temporary parting with the dominant norms of the larger medical community. This parting promoted the elevation of its overall status within that community.

The first crucial element is that pediatric radiology was a marginal specialty within organized medicine. It was a research-oriented subfield in a profession that emphasized face-to-face clinical interaction. It was a safe intellectual endeavor within an overall organization which placed a premium on risky pragmatic enterprise. Studies of value orientations among medical students at the time of the "discovery" of abuse have suggested that those specialties which stress "helping others," "being of service," "being useful," and "working with people" were ranked above those which work "at medical problems that do not require frequent contact with patients" (Cahalan, 1957). On the other hand, intellectual stimulation afforded very little prestige. Supporting this conclusion was research indicating that although forty-three percent of practicing physicians selected "close patient relations" as a mandate of their profession, only twenty-four percent chose "research" as worthy of such an evaluation (Philips, 1964). Pairing this ranking system with the profession's close-knit, "fraternity-like" communication network (Hall, 1946) one would expect research-oriented radiologists to be quite sensitive about their marginal evaluation by colleagues.

Intramedical organizational rankings extend along the lines of risk-taking as well as patient-encounters. Here, too, pediatric radiologists have traditionally ranked lower than other medical specialties. Becker's (1961) study of medical student culture suggests that the most valued specialties are those which combine wide experiences with risk and responsibility. These are most readily "symbolized by the possibility of killing or disabling patients in the course of making a mistake" (Freidson, 1969:107). From this perspective, it is easy to understand why surgery and internal medicine head the list of the most esteemed specialties. Other research has similarly noted the predominance of surgeons among high elected officials of the American Medical Association (Hall, 1946). Devoid of most risk taking, little involved in life or death decisions, pediatric radiologists are again marginal to this ethos of medical culture.

The "discovery" of child abuse offered pediatric radiologists an alternative to their marginal medical status. By linking themselves to the problem of abuse, radiologists became indirectly tied into the crucial clinical task of patient diagnosis. In addition, they became a direct source of input concerning the risky "life or death" consequences of child beating. This could represent an advance in status, a new basis for recognition within the medical profession. Indeed, after initial documentation of abuse, literature in various journals of radiology, roentgenology and pediatrics, articles on this topic by Wooley and Evans (1955) and Gwinn, deWin and Peterson (1961) appeared in the *Journal of the American Medical Association*. These were among the very few radiologic research reports published by that prestigious journal during the time period. Hence, the first factor conducive to the radiological discovery of abuse was a potential for intraorganizational advance in prestige.

The Discovery: An Opportunity for Coalition Within the Medical Community

A second factor encouraging the discovery of abuse by relatively low-status pediatric radiologists concerns the opportunity for a coalition of interests with other more prestigious segments within organized medicine. The two other segments radiologists joined in alliance were pediatrics and psychodynamically oriented psychiatry. By virtue of face-to-face clinical involvements, these specialties were higher ranking than pediatric radiology. Nevertheless each contained a dimension of marginality. Pediatrics had attained valued organizational status several decades prior to the discovery of abuse. Yet, in an age characterized by preventive drugs and treatments for previously dangerous or deadly infant diseases, it was again sliding toward the margins of the profession (Bucher & Strauss, 1961). Psychodynamic psychiatry (as opposed to its psychosomatic cousin) experienced marginality in dealing with non-physical problems.

For both pediatrics and psychodynamic psychiatry, links with the problem of abuse could partially dissipate the respective marginality of each. Assuming a role in combatting the "deadly" forces of abuse could enlarge the "risky" part of the pediatric mission. A symbolic alliance of psychodynamic psychiatry with other bodily diagnostic and treatment specialties could also function to advance its status. Neither of these specialties was in a position to "see" abuse before the radiologists. Pediatricians were impeded by the obstacles discussed above. Psychiatrists were blocked by the reluctance of abusive parents to admit their behavior as problematic (Steele & Pollock, 1968). Nonetheless, the interests of both could perceivably be advanced by a coalition with the efforts of pediatric radiologists. As such, each represented a source of potential support for pediatric radiologists in their discovery of abuse. The potential for coalition served to reinforce pediatric radiology in its movement toward the discovery of abuse.

The Discovery: An Opportunity for the Application of an Acceptable Label

A crucial impediment to the discovery of abuse by the predominant interests in organized medicine was the norm of controlling the consequences of a particular diagnosis. To diagnose abuse as social deviance might curtail the power of organized medicine. The management of its consequences would fall to the extramedical interests of formal agents of social control. How is it then, that such a diagnosis by pediatric radiology and its endorsement by pediatric and psychiatric specialties, is said to have advanced these specialties within the organization of medicine? Wasn't it more likely that they should have received criticism rather than acclaim from the medical profession?

By employing a rather unique labelling process the coalition of discovery interests were able to convert the possible liability into a discernible advantage. The opportunity of generating a medical, rather than socio-legal label for abuse provided the radiologists and their allies with a situation in which they could both reap the rewards associated with the diagnosis and avoid the infringement of extra-medical controls. What was discovered was no ordinary behavior form but a "syndrome." Instead of departing from the tradition of organized medicine, they were able to idealize its most profound mission. Possessing a repertoire of scientific credibility, they were presented with the opportunity "to label as illness what was not previously labeled at all or what was labeled in some other fashion, under some other institutional jurisdiction" (Freidson, 1971:261).

The symbolic focal point for the acceptable labeling of abuse was the 1962 publication of an article entitled "The Battered Child Syndrome" in the Journal of the American Medical Association (Kempe *et al.*, 1962). This report, representing the joint research efforts of a group of radiologic, pediatric, and psychiatric specialists, labelled abuse as a "clinical condition" existing as an "unrecognized trauma" (Kempe, 1962:17). It defined the deviance of its "psychopathic" perpetrators as a product of "psychiatric factors" representing "some defect in character structure'' (Kempe, 1962:24). As an indicator of prestige within organized medicine, it is interesting to note that the position articulated by these labellers was endorsed by the editorial board of the AMA in that same issue of *JAMA*.

As evidenced by the AMA editorial, the discovery of abuse as a new ''illness'' reduced drastically the intra-organizational constraints on doctors' ''seeing'' abuse. A diagnostic category had been invented and publicized. Psychological obstacles in recognizing parents as capable of abuse were eased by the separation of normatively powerful parents from non-normatively pathological individuals. Problems associated with perceiving parents as patients whose confidentiality must be protected were reconstructed by typifying them as patients who needed help. Moreover, the maintenance of professional autonomy was assured by pairing deviance with sickness. This last statement is testimony to the power of medical nomenclature. It was evidenced by the fact that (prior to its publication) the report which coined the label ''battered child syndrome'' was endorsed by a Children's Bureau conference which included social workers and law enforcement officials as well as doctors (McCoid, 1965:12).

The Generation of the Reporting Movement

The discovery of the ''battered child syndrome'' was facilitated by the opportunities for various pediatric radiologists to advance in medical prestige, form coalitions with other interests, and invent a professionally acceptable deviant label. The application of this label has been called the child abuse reporting movement. This movement was well underway by the time the 1962 Children's Bureau Conference confirmed the radiological diagnosis of abuse. Besides foreshadowing the acceptance of the sickness label, this meeting was also the basis for a series of articles to be published in *Pediatrics* which would further substantiate the diagnosis of abuse. Soon, however, the reporting movement spread beyond intraorganizational medical maneuvering to incorporate contributions from various voluntary associations, governmental agencies, as well as the media.

Extramedical responses to the newly discovered deviance confirmed the recognition of abuse as an illness. These included reports by various social welfare agencies which underscored the medical roots of the problem. For instance, the earliest investigations of the problem by social service agents resulted in a call for cooperation with the findings of radiologists in deciding the fate of abusers (Elmer, 1960:100). Other studies called for ''more comprehensive radiological examinations'' (Boardman, 1962:43). That the problem was medical in its roots as well as consequences was reinforced by the frequent referral of caseworkers to themselves as ''battered child therapists'' whose mission was the ''curing'' of ''patients'' (Davoren, 1968). Social welfare organizations, including the Children's Division of the American Humane Association, the Public Welfare Association, and the Child Welfare League, echoed similar concerns in sponsoring research (Children's Division, 1963; DeFrancis, 1963) and lobbying for ''treatment based'' legislative provisions (McCoid, 1965).

Not all extramedical interests concurred with treatment of abusers as ''sick.'' Various law enforcement voices argued that the abuse of children was a crime and should be prosecuted. On the other hand, a survey of thirty-one publications in major law journals between 1962-1972 revealed that nearly all legal scholars endorsed treatment rather than punishment to manage abusers. Lawyers disagreed, however, as to whether reports should be mandatory and registered concern over who should report to whom. Yet, all concurred that various forms of immunity should be granted reporters (Paulsen, 1967a; DeFrancis, 1967). These are all procedural issues. Neither law enforcers nor legal scholars parted from labelling abuse as a problem to be managed. The impact of the acceptable discovery of abuse by a respected knowledge sector (the medical profession) had generated a stigmatizing scrutiny bypassed in previous eras.

The proliferation of the idea of abuse by the media cannot be underestimated. Though its stories were sensational, its credibility went unchallenged. What was publicized was not some amorphous set of muggings but a "syndrome." Titles such as "Cry rises from beaten babies" (*Life*, June 1963), "Parents who beat children" (*Saturday Evening Post*, October 1962), "The shocking price of parental anger" (*Good Housekeeping*, March 1964), and "Terror struck children" (*New Republic*, May 1964) were all buttressed by an awe of scientific objectivity. The problem had become "real" in the imaginations of professionals and laymen alike. It was rediscovered visually by ABC's "Ben Casey," NBC's "Dr. Kildare," and CBS's "The Nurses," as well as in several other television scripts and documentaries (Paulsen, 1967b:488-89).

Discovered by the radiologists, substantiated by their colleagues, and distributed by the media, the label was becoming widespread. Despite this fact, actual reporting laws were said to be the cooperative accomplishments of zealous individuals and voluntary associations (Paulsen, 1967b:491). Who exactly were these "zealous individuals"?

Data on legislative lobbyists reveal that, in almost every state, the civic committee concerned with abuse legislation was chaired by a doctor who "just happened" to be a pediatrician (Paulsen, 1967b:491). Moreover, "the medical doctors who most influenced the legislation frequently were associated with academic medicine" (Paulsen, 1967b:491). This information provides additional evidence of the collaborative role of pediatricians in guiding social reaction to the deviance discovered by their radiological colleagues.

Lack of Resistance to the Label

In addition to the medical interests discussed above, numerous voluntary associations provided support for the movement against child abuse. These included the League of Women Voters, Veterans of Foreign Wars, the Daughters of the American Republic, the District Attorneys Association, Council of Jewish Women, State Federation of Womens Clubs, Public Health Associations, plus various national chapters of social workers (Paulsen, 1967b, 495). Two characteristics emerge from an examination of these interests. They either have a professional stake in the problem or represent the civic concerns of certain upper-middle class factions. In either case the labelers were socially and politically removed from the abusers, who in all but one early study (Steele and Pollock), were characterized as lower class and minority group members.

The existence of a wide social distance between those who abuse and those who label, facilitates not only the likelihood of labelling but nullifies any organized resistance to the label by the "deviant" group itself. Research findings which describe abusers as belonging to no outside-the-family associations or clubs (Young, 1964) or which portray them as isolates in the community (Giovannoni, 1971) reinforce the conclusion. Labelling was generated by powerful medical interests and perpetuated by organized media, professional and upper-class concerns. Its success was enlarged by the relative powerlessness and isolation of abusers, which prevented the possibility of organized resistance to the labelling.

The Shape of Social Reaction

I have argued that the organizational advantages surrounding the discovery of abuse by pediatric radiology set in motion a process of labelling abuse as deviance and legislating against it. The actual shape of legislative enactments has been discussed elsewhere (DeFrancis, 1967; Paulsen, 1967a). The passage of the reporting laws encountered virtually no opposition. In Kentucky, for example, no one even appeared to testify for or against the measure (Paulsen, 1967b:502). Any potential opposition from the American Medical Association, whose interests in autonomous control of the consequences of a medical diagnosis might have been threatened, had been undercut by the radiologists' success in defining abuse as a new medical problem. The AMA, unlikely to argue against conquering illness, shifted to support reporting legislation which would maximize a physician's diagnostic options.

The consequences of adopting a "sick" label for abusers is mirrored in two findings: the low rate of prosecution afforded offenders and the modification of reporting statutes so as exclusively to channel reporting toward "helping services." Regarding the first factor, Grumet (1970:306) suggests that despite existing laws and reporting statutes, actual prosecution has not increased since the time of abuse's "discovery." In support is Thomas (1972) who contends that the actual percentage of cases processed by family courts has remained constant during the same period. Even when prosecution does occur, convictions are obtained in only five to ten per cent of the cases (Paulsen, 1966b). And even in these cases, sentences are shorter for abusers than for other offenders convicted under the same law of aggravated assault (Grumet, 1970:307).

State statutes have shifted on reporting from an initial adoption of the Children's Bureau model of reporting to law enforcement agents, toward one geared at reporting to child welfare or child protection agencies (DeFrancis, 1970). In fact, the attention to abuse in the early sixties has been attributed as a factor in the development of specialized "protective interests" in states which had none since the days of the SPCC crusades (Eads, 1969). This event, like the emphasis on abuser treatment, is evidence of the impact of labelling of abuse as an "illness."

REFERENCES

BAIN, Katherine. 1963, "The physically abused child." *Pediatrics* 31 (June): 895-897.

BAKWIN, Harry. 1956, "Multiple skeletal lesions in young children due to trauma." *Journal of Pediatrics* 49 (July): 7-15.

BARMEYER, G. H., L. R. ANDERSON and W. B. COX. 1951, "Traumatic periostitis in young children." *Journal of Pediatrics* 38 (Feb): 184-90.

BECKER, Howard S. 1963, *The Outsiders*. New York: The Free Press.

BECKER, Howard S. et al. 1961, *Boys in White*. Chicago: University of Chicago Press.

BOARDMAN, Helen. 1962, "A project to rescue children from inflicted injuries." *Journal of Social Work* 7 (January): 43-51.

BRAUN, Ida G., Edgar J. BRAUN and Charlotte SIMONDS. 1963, "The mistreated child." *California Medicine* 99 (August): 98-103.

BREMNER, R. 1970, *Children and Youth in America: A Documentary History. Vol. I.* Cambridge, Mass: Harvard University Press.

BUCHER, Rue and Anselm STRAUSS, 1961, "Professions in process." *American Journal of Sociology* 66 (January): 325-334.

CAFFEY, John. 1946, "Multiple fractures in the long bones of infants suffering from chronic subdural hematoma." *American Journal of Roentology* 56 (August): 163-173.

_____. 1957, "Traumatic lesions in growing bones other than fractures and lesions: clinical and radiological features." *British Journal of Radiology* 30 (May): 225-238.

CAHALAN, Don. 1957, "Career interests and expectations of U.S. medical students." 32: 557-563.

CHAMBLISS, William J. 1964, "A sociological analysis of the law of vagrancy." *Social Problems* 12 (Summer): 67-77.

CHILDREN'S DIVISION. 1963, *Child Abuse Preview of a Nationwide Survey*. Denver: American Humane Association (Children's Division).

DAVOREN, Elizabeth. 1968, "The role of the social worker." Pp. 153-168 in Ray E. Helfer and Henry C. Kempe (eds.), *The Battered Child*. Chicago: University of Chicago Press.

DeFRANCIS, Vincent. 1963, "Parents who abuse children." *PTA Magazine* 58 (November): 16-18.

_____. 1967, "Child abuse—the legislative response." *Denver Law Journal* 44 (Winter):3-41.

_____. 1970, *Child Abuse Legislation in the 1970's*. Denver: American Humane Association.

EADS, William E. 1969, "Observations on the establishment of child protection services in California." *Stanford Law Review* 21 (May): 1129-1155.

EARLE, Alice Morse. 1926, *Child Life in Colonial Days*. New York: Macmillan.

ELMER, Elizabeth. 1960, "Abused young children seen in hospitals." *Journal of Social Work* 3 (October): 98-102.

FELDER, Samuel. 1971, "A lawyer's view of child abuse." *Public Welfare* 29: 181-188.

FOLKS, Homer. 1902, *The Case of the Destitute, Neglected and Delinquent Children*. New York: MacMillan.

FONTANA, V., D. DONOVAN and R. WONG. 1963, "The maltreatment syndrome in children." *New England Journal of Medicine*. 269 (December): 1389-1394.

FOX, Sanford J. 1970, "Juvenile justice reform: an historical perspective." *Stanford Law Review* 22 (June): 1187-1239.

FREIDSON, Eliot J. 1968, "Medical personnel: physicians." Pp. 105-114 in David L. Sills (ed.), *International Encyclopedia of the Social Sciences*. Vol. 10. New York: Macmillan.

_____. 1971, *The Profession of Medicine: A Study in the Sociology of Applied Knowledge*. New York: Dodd, Mead and Co.

GIL, David. 1970, *Violence Against Children*. Cambridge, Mass.: Harvard University Press.

GIL, David and John H. NOBLE. 1969, "Public knowledge, attitudes and opinions about physical child abuse." *Child Welfare* 49 (July): 395-401.

GIOVANNONI, Jeanne. 1971, "Parental mistreatment." *Journal of Marriage and the Family* 33 (November): 649-657.

GLASER, William A. 1960, "Doctors and politics." *American Journal of Sociology* 66 (November): 230-245.

GOODE, William J. 1957, "Community within a community: the profession." *American Sociological Review* 22 (April): 194-200.

_____. 1971, "Force and violence in the family." *Journal of Marriage and the Family* 33 (November): 424-436.

GRUMET, Barbara R. 1970, "The plaintive plaintiffs: victims of the battered child syndrome," *Family Law Quarterly* 4 (September): 296-317.

GUSFIELD, Joseph R. 1963, *Symbolic Crusades*. Urbana, Ill.: University of Illinois Press.

GWINN, J. J., K. W. LEWIN and H. G. PETERSON. 1961, "Roetenographic manifestations of unsuspected trauma in infancy." *Journal of the American Medical Association* 181 (June): 17-24.

HALL, Jerome. 1952, *Theft, Law and Society*. Indianapolis: Bobbs-Merrill Co.

HALL, Oswald. 1946, "The informal organization of medicine." *Canadian Journal of Economics and Political Science* 12 (February): 30-41.

HYDE, D. R., P. WOLFF, A. GROSS and E. L. HOFFMAN. 1954, "The American Medical Association: power, purpose and politics in organized medicine." *Yale Law Journal* 63 (May): 938-1022.

KADUSHIN, Alfred. 1967, *Child Welfare Services*. New York. Macmillan.

KEMPE. C. H., F. N. SILVERMAN, B. F. STEELE, W. DROEGEMULLER and H. K. SILVER. 1962, "The battered-child syndrome." *Journal of the American Medical Association* 181 (July): 17-24.

LEMERT, Edwin M. 1974, "Beyond Mead: the societal reaction to deviance." *Social Problems* 21 (April): 457-467.

McCOID, A. H. 1965, "The battered child syndrome and other assaults upon the family." *Minnesota Law Review* 50 (November): 1-58.

PAULSEN, Monrad G. 1966, "The legal framework for child protection." *Columbia Law Review* 66 (April): 679-717.

_____. 1967 "Child abuse reporting laws: the shape of the legislation." *Columbia Law Review* 67 (January): 1-49.

PHILIPS, Bernard S. 1964, "Expected value deprivation and occupational preference." *Sociometry* 27 (June): 15-160.

PLATT, Anthony M. 1969, *The Child Savers: The Invention of Juvenile Delinquency*. Chicago: University of Chicago Press.

QUINNEY, Richard. 1970, *The Social Reality of Crime*. Boston: Little Brown.

RADBILL, Samuel X. 1968, "A history of child abuse and infanticide." Pp. 3-17 in Ray E. Helfer and Henry C. Kempe (eds.), *The Battered Child*. Chicago: University of Chicago Press.

ROTHMAN, David J. 1971, *The Discovery of the Asylum: Social Order and Disorder in the New Republic*. Boston: Little Brown.

SHEPARD, Robert E. 1965, "The abused child and the law." *Washington and Lee Law Review* 22 (Spring): 182-195.

SILVERMAN, F. N. 1965, "The roentgen manifestations of unrecognized skeletal trauma in infants." *American Journal of Roentgenology, Radium and Nuclear Medicine* 69 (March): 413-426.

SKOLNICK, Arlene and Jerome H. SKOLNICK. 1971, *The Family in Transition*. Boston: Little Brown.

STEELE, Brandt and Carl F. POLLOCK. 1968, "A psychiatric study of parents who abuse infants and small children." Pp. 103-147 in Ray E. Helfer and Henry C. Kempe (eds.), *The Battered Child*. Chicago: University of Chicago Press.

SUTHERLAND, Edwin H. 1950, "The diffusion of sexual psychopath laws." *American Journal of Sociology* 56 (September): 142-148.

THOMAS, Mason P. 1972, "Child abuse and neglect: historical overview, legal matrix and social perspectives." *North Carolina Law Review* 50 (February): 293-249.

WOOLLEY, P. V. and W. A. EVANS Jr. 1955, "Significance of skeletal lesions in infants resembling those of traumatic origin." *Journal of the American Medical Association* 158 (June): 539-543.

YOUNG, Leontine. 1964, *Wednesday's Children: A Study of Child Neglect and Abuse*. New York: McGraw-Hill.

ZALBA, Serapio R. 1966, "The abused child. I. A survey of the problems." *Social Work* 11 (October): 3-16.

29

The Social Construction of Child Abuse*

Richard J. Gelles, Ph.D.

During the last four years a great deal of attention has been focused on the problem of abused, battered, and murdered children. Numerous newspaper articles, television documentaries, and radio programs have been devoted to this social problem. In addition, the legal area of child abuse has undergone a radical change, with many states updating or instituting new laws on how best to deal with the phenomenon of children abused by their caretakers. The Mondale Bill, or Child Abuse Prevention and Treatment Act of 1973 (PL 93-247), has been implemented to attack the problem of abuse. On another front, the volume of attention received by the topic of child abuse is even more evident. The Department of Health, Education and Welfare[40] published the *Bibliography on the Battered Child* in 1969. Since this bibliography was printed, the number of published articles, research reports, and books on child abuse has multiplied tenfold.** Whereas, Helfer and Kempe's *The Battered Child*[20] was the major source book on child abuse in 1969,† there are now at least eight major works devoted to this topic.[1, 4, 6, 7, 11, 14, 21, 36]

---

* Based on a presentation to the Harvard University Interfaculty Seminar on Child Abuse; submitted to the Journal in August 1974. The project is supported by NIMH grant NH 24002-1.

Richard J. Gelles, "The Social Construction of Child Abuse," *American Journal of Orthopsychiatry*, 45(3), (April, 1975):363-371. Copyright © 1975 The American Orthopsychiatric Association, Inc. Reproduced by permission.

**This is a guess at the increase. The exact number of references listed in the 1974 NIMH bibliography on child abuse is 138.

† Two other major books[8, 41] were also available at this time, but neither was as explicit or detailed.

In June 1973, the Department of Health, Education and Welfare authorized three million dollars for research on child abuse, and the National Institute for Child Development spent an additional $200,000 in 1974. Consequently, we can anticipate a continued rapid growth of the literature and research on child abuse.

We can break down current research on child abuse into three major areas: incidence, etiology, and prevention and treatment. The first major task that faced investigators of child abuse was to determine how extensive the phenomenon was. Estimates ranged from the 6,000 confirmed reported cases found by Gil[14] to a half-million cases estimated by Light,[26] based on Gil's survey data. Other studies[11, 19, 28] attempted to assess the number of cases of child abuse in a given area, such as Boston or New York. At present, we can estimate that perhaps a half-million to a million children are abused by their caretakers each year.

A second phase of research on child abuse was a study of causes of abuse. Early studies using available case data proposed a psychopathological explanation of abuse.[12, 23, 37] However, these unicausal accounts were critically attacked as being too narrow and based on insufficient and inadequate data.[13, 14, 15] However, even these new studies are being criticized through the use of better data and more refined data analysis techniques.[10]

The last facet of work being done on child abuse concerns prevention and treatment of abused children and their parents.[21] In addition to published accounts of treatment programs, we also have learned about other types of treatment and prevention programs, such as a self-help group, Parents Anonymous, formed by Jolly K. The future work in child abuse appears to be in the area of treatment and prevention. The aforementioned National Child Abuse bill authorized 60 million dollars, to be spent over the next three years, for developing programs to prevent and treat cases of child abuse.

Child Abuse as Social Deviance

There is one, as yet unrecognized, theme that runs throughout the study of child abuse, which has not been discussed but which pervades all the work and findings we have to date: child abuse is *social deviance*. Because child abuse is social deviance, all the cases that make up the data on incidence, all the explanatory analyses, and all the prevention and treatment models are influenced by the *social process* by which individuals and groups are labeled and designated as deviants. In other words, there is no objective behavior we can automatically recognize as child abuse.* An example is the definition of child abuse provided by the Child Abuse Prevention and Treatment Act of 1973:

> Child abuse and neglect means the physical or mental injury, sexual abuse, negligent treatment, or maltreatment of a child under the age of eighteen by a person who is responsible for the child's welfare under circumstances which indicate that the child's health or welfare is harmed or threatened thereby . . .

---

* There are *some* cases that so clearly involve abuse that they are indeed automatically recognized. The literature abounds in cases where parents killed or cruelly tortured their children. I argue that there is no objective behavior which can be automatically labeled abuse, because these "outrageous" cases constitute a minor fraction of the overall number of incidents of a caretaker injuring a child.

While some parts of this definition are straightforward, there is a serious problem in determining what constitutes "mental injury," "negligent treatment," "maltreatment," "harm," or "threatened harm." While broken bones can be identified by X-ray, how can we identify a mental injury? Furthermore, if no bones are broken, who is to determine what is an injury and what is the routine use of physical punishment? The judges who develop a definition of child abuse, and the way they apply it, are of critical importance; as yet this phenomenon has not been studied.

Thus, when I speak of the social construction of abuse, I mean the process by which: a) a definition of abuse is constructed; b) certain judges or "gatekeepers" are selected for applying the definition; c) the definition is applied by designating the labels "abuse" and "abuser" to particular individuals and families.

This social process of defining abuse and labeling abusers should be an important facet in the study of child abuse. It should be a central issue because it affects all three main aspects of work in the area of abuse. First, how abuse is defined determines the extent of child abuse in America. If we confine our definition to one that calls abuse only those cases where *observable* physical injury has been *deliberately* caused by a caretaker, then our incidence of abuse will be comparatively small. If, on the other hand, we apply the definition provided by the Child Abuse Prevention and Treatment Act, the incidence of abuse may be as high as tens of millions of children (depending on what we call mental injury). Secondly, *who* gets labeled an abuser will drastically affect our conclusions about the etiology and causes of abuse. One reason the early analyses of the causes of child abuse were so inadequate and inaccurate was that they used only at-hand cases on which to base theories of causation. Thus, the factors which caused patients A, B, C, D, etc. to end up in Colorado Medical Center and then be labeled as cases of abuse were confounded in the causal explanation of abuse (not to mention the fact that being labeled an abuser by the hospital staff may have produced the personality characteristics—anxiety, depression, etc.—which were later called the causes of the abuse!). Lastly, all these factors—defining abuse and selectively labeling certain people abusers—have profound implications on the strategies of intervention designed to prevent and treat abuse. Because of problems of definition and labeling, we may only be treating a very narrow portion of the true population of abusers and our treatment methods may be totally inadequate to deal with the unrecognized population of abusers and abused.

This analysis advances the theme of the social construction of child abuse by presenting a discussion of abuse using a theoretical framework developed by the labeling school of the sociology of deviance.[2, 3, 9, 25, 31] In addition, I shall outline the implications of this focus on socially constructed child abuse for present and future investigations into the area of child abuse.

The Social Construction of Child Abuse

The concept "child abuse" has had a wide variety of definitions applied to it, ranging from an occurrence where a caretaker injures a child, not by accident but in anger or deliberately,[14] to "failure to thrive,"[5, 27] to child theft, abandonment, or emotional mistreatment. Child abuse can be limited to a clinical condition, typically broken bones or physical trauma, which is determined by X-ray (this is the definition that Kempe *et al.*[23] labeled the "battered child syndrome"), or child abuse can be a wide range of activities which include improper clothing, feeding, or caring for a child.[41]

Thus, a major problem in the area of child abuse is that of defining the phenomenon to be investigated. A corrollary problem which arises is that it is impossible to compare the abundant data that have been gathered on abuse because of the idiosyncratic and varying definitions of child abuse.

A fundamental question, therefore, is, how do we deal with the problems of varying definitions of child abuse? One answer is that we make this very problem the subject of empirical investigation by introducing the theoretical perspective developed by the labeling school of social deviance.

Labeling and Social Deviance

The labeling school of deviance focuses its attention on the process by which individuals or groups become designated as deviants. Thus, for labeling theorists, deviance is not a property *inherent* in certain forms of behavior; it is a property *conferred upon* these forms by audiences which directly or indirectly witness the behavior in question.[9] The conferring of a label requires an audience or labeler, and it requires that a label be successfully applied. The successful application of a label of deviance is dependent on circumstances of the situation and place, the social and personal biographies of the labelers and the "deviant," and the bureaucratically organized activities of agencies of social control.[24]

The process of labeling is of critical importance to understanding how deviance is defined and how certain individuals become labeled as deviants. In terms of child abuse, this process or interaction can be seen in the confrontation between accused abusive parents and the accuser, be he neighbor, police, physician, or the court. It involves the accused "accounting"[33] for what happened and the intricate "negotiation of identity" between the accused and the agents of authority.[31]

Rather than struggling for one uniform definition of child abuse, I propose that we investigate *who does the public labeling of abuse, what definitions or standards are employed, under what conditions are labels successfully applied, and what are the consequences of the labeling process.*

Gatekeepers. Of initial interest is the identification of those individuals or agencies that operate as the main "gatekeepers" in the process of labeling and defining a child as abused and a caretaker as an abuser. Research could focus on the flow of people, from the initial suspicion of abuse through the final gate of public labeling of "abuser." It would be important to find out how cases of abuse are typically initiated. Are the parents the ones who report the abuse? Does a neighbor call the police? Where do social work and social service agencies fit in? We need to learn *who the gatekeepers are* who 1) initially attach the label of abuser to a caretaker, and 2) pass this individual through the "gate" and reinforce this label of abuser.

Definitions. Having identified the major labelers or gatekeepers, the next task would be to determine their definitions of abuse. Here it would be interesting to compare definitions of a neighbor, a policeman, a physician or nurse, a lawyer or court, a social worker or welfare worker. The importance of this information is that it provides an insight into why the incidence of reported abuse varies across and within particular social agencies. In addition, as we shall see in the following section, the definition of abuse influences who is labeled an abuser, and this in turn, influences the causal schemes that are developed to explain child abuse.

An examination of the generative sources of the varying definitions held by different gatekeepers would also help explain how and why different labels are attached to suspected abuse cases.

The Successful Labeling of Child Abuse. If we have identified the gatekeepers and their definitions, the next thing we need to know is how the gates operate and how the flow of people through agencies works to label some people abusers and other people non-abusers.

Polsky[30] has pointed out that people who are caught in acts of deviance are systematically different from people who get away with the same acts (*i.e.*, just getting caught indicates that they are ''less'' successful deviants). Thus, in the case of child abuse, our knowledge of who abuses his child, and why, is biased by the fact that the label of ''abuser'' is selectively applied.* The fact that labels are selectively applied mandates the study of the process of successful labeling of abusers and abused.

An important insight into the issue of successful labeling has been offered in the work of Sudnow[38] and Simmons.[34] Sudnow's analysis of public defenders found that defenders' experience with criminal cases causes them to develop an occupational shorthand for ''typing'' crimes. They soon develop a knowledge of the routine grounds of different types of crime—who does them, what time of day, who the victims typically are, etc. Simmons focused on the stereotypes of deviants held by people. These stereotypes were often unrelated to the actual actions considered deviant.

The same phenomenon that Sudnow calls ''normal crime'' is likely to occur in cases of child abuse. Policemen, physicians, nurses, and social workers who have either read literature on child abuse or had experience with child abuse cases, build up a mental inventory of characteristics of people and situations associated with child abuse. They ''know'' that abusers are typically poor and uneducated. Abused children are typically under three years of age. Mothers are more often abusers than are fathers. Thus, when they are presented with a case which is suspected of being abuse, they are likely to apply their previous experience and knowledge to determining whether or not this case is abuse. In short, if the literature states, or the practitioner's experience has been, that a person who has certain personality traits is likely to abuse his children, and a person with those traits then shows up with an injured child, the practitioner would seem likely to label that person an abuser. Conversely, a person who arrives with an injured child, but does not fit the stereotype of abuse, may be more likely to avoid the label.

The previous discussion is only speculative. We need research that provides answers to the hypothesis that the label of abuse is differentially applied to individuals because of certain personal and social characteristics and certain aspects of the situation. Questions that could be answered through investigations which focus on the conditions of successful labeling are: To what degree does educational and occupational status insulate a person from being labeled as an abuser? What are the labelers' conceptions of the ''routine grounds'' of child abuse? Upon what are these

---

* Other methodological problems of child abuse research are noted by Gelles[13] and Spinetta and Rigler.[35]

conceptualizations based? Furthermore, we could begin to learn who abuses their child but does not get labeled an abuser. Information about how many individuals like this there are, and their personal and social characteristics, would go a long way towards refining and making more accurate our estimates of the incidence of child abuse and our causal models of child abuse.

Effects of Labeling. The last facet of studying child abuse by examining labeling and successful labeling is to assess the impact of the label "child abuser" on those individuals who have been successfully labeled abusers. Goffman[17] has extensively analyzed the effects of labeling in his examination of "stigma." Other research has found that the effects of labeling vary, depending on the type of deviance alleged to have occurred and the social characteristics of the suspect.[32]

By investigating the impact of the label "abuser," we would be discovering what the effect of "becoming a child abuser" is on the personal, family, and social life of the accused. Earlier it was noted that the personality disorders commonly held to be the cause of child abuse may well be the *result* of being labeled an abuser.

In addition, the study of the effects of the label "abuser" would be a significant contribution to the creation and implementation of intervention programs designed to prevent and treat abuse. One reason why Parents Anonymous may be so successful is that the individuals involved do not have to suffer the stigma of public labeling. Conversely, the public screening process proposed by C. Henry Kempe, which would have firemen "screen" families for traits of potential abuse, may do more harm than good by subjecting upwards of a million Americans to the stigma of being falsely labeled a potential abuser.[26]

At least it ought to be recognized that the effects of being labeled an abuser may be more damaging to the individual caretaker and his or her child than is the actual instance of abuse. Research that uncovers information about the nature of this effect, and sensitizes us to its existence, would have a major influence on the design and implementation of prevention and treatment programs.

A Systems Approach to the Social Construction of Child Abuse

As a means of summing up these related issues, I propose a general framework within which the study of the social construction of child abuse can take place.

A glaring problem in the area of prevention and treatment of child abuse and other types of social problems is the lack of integration among the various agencies given the charge of dealing with the particular problem. Different agencies often approach the same problem at cross-purposes—many times at odds with each other, more frequently ignorant of what the other is doing. In the case of child abuse, a variety of agencies and agents encounter the problem and are called upon to make decisions. The medical profession is perhaps the most notable agency, because it has produced the majority of research findings and policy suggestions. The medical profession became involved in the area of child abuse when it found that it had a number of cases of physically injured children in which the evidence pointed to caretaker-inflicted injury. When Kempe[23] wrote his breakthrough paper on the "battered child syndrome" in 1962, he was actually pointing out a phenomenon that other pediatricians were aware of but, nevertheless, did not want to recognize. The Kempe article made physicians and medical practitioners aware of the problem of child abuse, but none of this was new to other agencies, which had for years been trying to cope with the problem of abused children. Public and private social work agencies were well aware that many of their clients were either neglecting their children or physically abusing them. Policemen, the most frequent interveners in family disputes, also had firsthand knowledge of the problem. Teachers and guidance counselors also knew of cases of abused children. The courts were perhaps the most shielded from the problem because few of the other agents (policemen included) ever made official legal reports of the cases.

All of these agencies and agents have something to do with some part of the problem of child abuse. Each agency has its own gatekeepers, definitions of child abuse, and criteria for successful labeling; thus, each agency has a different impact on the suspected abuser. One way of beginning to integrate our knowledge about child abuse and our prevention and treatment programs is to take an overall view of the agencies involved in the problem. To do this I propose taking a social systems view of the various agencies, which perspective would employ the "open systems" framework[22, 39] to explore the interactions and interface between the agencies.

At present, I see six systems involved in child abuse: the medical system (doctors, nurses, hospital administrators), the social service system (public and private agencies which provide ameliorative services to families and individuals), the criminal justice system (composed of police and the courts), the school system (teachers and counselors), the neighborhood and friendship system, and the family and kin system. All six social systems are involved in identifying, labeling, treating, and preventing child abuse. Therefore, in order to expand our knowledge of the labelers—what are their definitions, how are their labels successfully applied, and how are we to best implement prevention and treatment programs?—we need to see how the entire system (made up of the six we have identified) operates. What are the interfaces between the various systems? How do people labeled "abusers" flow through the systems (one way, or back and forth)? How are people who abuse their children "lost" in the system, or unidentified, and not given access to treatment programs? These I offer as some of the fundamental questions that need to be answered and that can be answered by taking a social systems view of the problem of child abuse.

Conclusion

The purpose here, and the rationale behind focusing on child abuse as a "socially constructed" phenomenon, has not been to offer a major new approach to child abuse. The issues to which I have addressed myself are not new to those people involved in the area of child abuse. My intention has been to elevate these issues from underlying assumptions into empirically problematic questions. I have offered this commentary as one way of breaking out of the endless definitional hassling about "what really causes abuse," and the shotgun approach to prevention and treatment programs. The issues raised here can serve as a foundation for future research that can and should have important implications for knowledge about child abuse as social behavior.

REFERENCES

1. BAKAN, D. 1971. *Slaughter of the Innocents: A Study of the Battered Child Phenomenon*. Beacon Press, Boston.

2. BECKER, H. 1963. *Outsiders: Studies in the Sociology of Deviance*. Free Press, New York.

3. BECKER, H., ed. 1964. *Perspectives on Deviance—The Other Side*. Free Press, New York.

4. BILLINGSLEY, A. and GIOVANNONI. J. 1972. *Children of the Storm*. Harcourt, New York.

5. BULLARD, D. et al. 1967. "Failure to thrive in the neglected child." *Amer. J. Orthopsychiat*. 37 (July):680-689.

6. DECOURCY, P. and DECOURCY, J. 1973. *A Silent Tragedy*. Alfred Publishing Co., New York.

7. DeFRANCIS, V. and LUCHT, C. 1974. *Child Abuse Legislation in the 1970's*. American Humane Association, Denver.

8. ELMER, E. et al. 1967. *Children in Jeopardy: A Study of Abused Minors and Their Families*. University of Pittsburgh Press, Pittsburgh.

9. ERICKSON, K. 1962. *"Notes on the sociology of deviance."* Social Problems 9 (Spring):307-314.

10. ERLANGER, H. 1974. "Social class and corporal punishment in childrearing: a reassessment." *Amer. Sociol. Rev*. 39 (Feb.):68-85.

11. FONTANA, V. 1971. *The Maltreated Child*. Charles C. Thomas, Springfield, Ill.

12. GALDSTON, R. 1965. "Observations of children who have been physically abused by their parents." *Amer. J. Psychiat*. 122 (4):440-443.

13. GELLES, R. 1973. "Child abuse as psychopathology: a sociological critique and reformulation." *Amer. J. Orthopsychiat*. 43 (July):611-621.

14. GIL, D. 1970. *Violence Against Children: Physical Child Abuse in the United States*. Harvard University Press, Cambridge, Mass.

15. GIL, D. 1971. "Violence against children." *J. Marr. Fam*. 33 (Nov.):637-648.

16. GIOVANNONI, J. 1971. "Parental mistreatment: perpetrators and victims." *J. Marr. Fam*. 33 (Nov.):649-657.

17. GOFFMAN, E. 1963. *Stigma: Notes on the Management of Spoiled Identity*. Prentice-Hall, Englewood Cliffs, N.J.

18. GOODE, W. 1971. "Force and violence in the family." *J. Marr. Fam*. 33 (Nov.):624-636.

19. HEINS, M. 1969. "Child abuse—analysis of a current epidemic." *Michigan Med*. 68 (17):887-891.

20. HELFER, R. and KEMPE, C. eds. 1968. *The Battered Child*. University of Chicago Press, Chicago.

21. HELFER, R. and KEMPE, C. 1972. *Helping the Battered Child and His Family*. Lippincott, Philadelphia.

22. KATZ, D. and KAHN, R. 1966. *The Social Psychology of Organizations*. Wiley, New York.

23. KEMPE, C. et al. 1962. "The battered child syndrome." *JAMA* 181 (July 7):17-24.

24. KITSUSE, J. 1964. "Societal reaction to deviant behavior: problems of theory and method." In *Perspectives on Deviance—The Other Side*, H. Becker ed. Free Press, New York.

25. LEMERT, E. 1951. *Social Pathology*. McGraw Hill, New York.

26. LIGHT, R. 1974. "Abused and neglected children in America: a study of alternative policies." *Harvard Ed. Rev.* 43 (Nov.):556-598.

27. MORRIS, M., GOULD, R. and MATTHEWS, P. 1964. "Toward prevention of child abuse." *Children* 2 (March-April):55-60.

28. NEWBERGER, E., HASS, G. and MULFORD, R. 1973. "Child abuse in Massachusetts." *Massachussetts Physician* 1 (Jan.):31-38.

29. POLANSKY, M., BORGMAN, R. and DESAIX, C. 1972. *Roots of Futility*. Jossey-Bass, San Francisco.

30. POLSKY, N. 1969. *Hustlers, Beats and Others*. Anchor Books, Garden City, N.Y.

31. SCHEFF, T. 1966. "Negotiating reality: notes on power in the assessment of responsibility." *Soc. Problems* 16 (Summer):3-17.

32. SCHWARTZ, R. and SKOLNICK. J. 1964. "Two studies of legal stigma." In *Perspectives on Deviance—The Other Side*, H. Becker, ed. Free Press, New York.

33. SCOTT, M. and LYMAN, S. 1968. "Accounts." *Amer. Sociol. Rev.* 33 (1):46-62.

34. SIMMONS, J. 1965. "Public stereotypes of deviants." *Soc. Problems* 3 (Fall):223-232.

35. SPINETTA, J. and RIGLER, D. 1972. "The child-abusing parent: a psychological review." *Psychol. Bull.* 77 (April):296-304.

36. STEINMETZ, S. and STRAUS, M. 1974. *Violence in the Family*. Dodd Mead, New York.

37. STEELE, B. and POLLOCK, C. 1968. "A psychiatric study of parents who abuse infants and small children." In *The Battered Child*, R. Helfer and C. Kempe, eds. University of Chicago Press, Chicago.

38. SUDNOW, D. 1964. "Normal crimes: sociological features of the penal code in a public defender office." *Soc. Problems* 12(3):255-276.

39. THOMPSON, J. 1966. *Organizations in Action*. McGraw Hill, New York.

40. U.S. DEPARTMENT OF HEALTH, EDUCATION AND WELFARE. 1969. *Bibliography on the Battered Child. Social and Rehabilitation Service*. July.

41. YOUNG, L. 1964. *Wednesday's Children: A Study of Child Neglect and Abuse*. McGraw-Hill, New York.

30

Pediatric Social Illness:
Toward an Etiologic Classification*

Eli H. Newberger, M.D.,
Robert B. Reed, Ph.D.,
Jessica H. Daniel, Ph.D.,
James N. Hyde, Jr., M.S.,
and Milton Kotelchuck, Ph.D.

The "social illnesses" of pediatrics include child abuse and neglect, failure to thrive, accidents, and poisonings. They account for a major share of the mortality of preschool children and often have significant physical and psychological sequelae.[1-4] They are classified partly according to their manifested symptoms and partly on supposed causal factors. But the logic underlying this taxonomy, as can be seen in Table I, provides the clinician with a conceptual framework inadequate to organize the complex data dealt with in practice. These simple formulations can misdirect the approach to the individual patient, and they contribute to the developmental impact of these illnesses on children, for whom clinical practice is of inconsistent organization and quality.[5]

There is, moreover, little reliable observational information to support the notions of cause and effect built into these diagnoses. For example, a child with scat-

* Presented in part before the Society for Research in Child Development, Denver, April 11, 1975.

   Supported by a grant from the Office of Child Development, Department of Health, Education and Welfare (Project OCD-CB-141).

TABLE I

Conceptual Models Implicit in Pediatric Social Diagnoses

Diagnosis	Conceptual Model
Child abuse and neglect	Intentionally motivated parent or caretaker assaults a defenseless child or withholds care from him
Accidents	Isolated, random traumatic events
Failure to thrive	Idiopathic failure of a baby to gain weight

tered bruises on his body might be identified either as an accident victim or as a victim of child abuse.[6] In the latter case, there is a presumption, but rather rarely in practice *knowledge*, of parental fault.[7] Intervention, when it is made available, is often individual-directed psychiatric counseling of the parents while deliberations proceed on whether or not to place the child in foster home care. The criterion of successful management is protection from his parents, the proximal cause of the child's disease, with little regard to the social, familial, environmental, or child developmental determinants of the child's injury. Help in reducing urgent stress on the family is not acknowledged as a treatment vehicle when the diagnostic focus is toward defining the responsibility of the perpetrator for the injuries of the victim.

By contrast, if the child is classified as an accident victim, there may be no implications of familial cause and no treatment. If the presenting lesion is seen as resulting from an act of God, there is hardly any need for diagnosis or therapy from a social worker or psychiatrist. This process of selective classification, based on slim logical and empirical supports, becomes a matter with serious ramifications for clinical practice and social policy given the findings of previous work on the preferential susceptibility of poor and minority children to receive the diagnoses child abuse and neglect, while children of middle and upper class homes may be more often identified as victims of accidents.[8, 9]

Several small clinical studies have suggested common relationships among the various categories of pediatric social illnesses (for example, prior accidents in child abuse cases).[10-14] This report explores underlying common origins among these conditions, with a view to defining a more etiologic (as opposed to manifestational) illness taxonomy.

Stress Theory of Common Etiology

It was posited that this common set of circumstances included elements of historical and contemporaneous stress. Historical stresses were defined as stresses occurring in the life of the maternal care-giver up to the time of the conception of the index child. Contemporaneous stresses refer to environmental, social, familial, and health problems occurring since the conception of the child as well as to stress imposed by unique attributes of the child.

Subjects and Methods

All children under 4 years of age seen in either inpatient or outpatient departments of the Children's Hospital Medical Center in Boston for pediatric social illness were eligible for selection into the study as "cases." Children not bearing pediatric social illness diagnoses were eligible for selection into the control group; children suffering from chronic or terminal illnesses, however, were excluded from the control population. The sample was ascertained between December 1972 and May 1974.

Cases were matched to controls on the basis of age, race, and the most readily available index of socioeconomic status at the time of the family's first contact with the hospital (whether or not the welfare department paid the medical bill).

Because interviews in the emergency room could not be performed after the visit with the physician, cases and controls in that area were sampled on the basis of their presenting symptom (injury or ingestion), not on the basis of a medical diagnostic formulation.

Five hundred sixty children and families were studied, including 303 inpatients and 257 outpatients. Table II summarizes the number of maternal interviews performed for each diagnostic group.

To assure comparability with previous research, child abuse was defined in terms of inflicted injury and a clinical impression of great risk by professionals on the hospital's Trauma X team experienced with such "protective" problems. Child neglect is a rare clinical diagnosis at Children's Hospital; the single case in the present study is included for analytic purposes with the cases of child abuse.

Interview

The principal instrument for the study was a structured interview of the subject's mother, conducted at the hospital. The interview focused on realities of child development, family relationships, health, finances, employment, and housing, as well as on specific life experiences of the mother and her child. Interviews lasted about 45 minutes and were conducted by specially trained interviewers. Although it was not possible to blind the interviewers to the child's clinical diagnosis, careful review of the interview process by a research supervisor and frequent meetings with the interviewers by a staff psychiatrist with no other tie to the project were performed continually to foster interobserver reliability and to minimize observer bias.

Ethical Issues: Confidentiality, Informed Consent, and Advocacy

As information elicited in the course of the interview could serve as a basis for concern about risk to the child, the project developed formal guidelines for sharing access to the data with the hospital professional staff. This was not an easy matter to tackle, for the implications of sharing investigative data in research of this nature are great. On the one hand, we would have preferred to have absolute confidentiality as the operational imperative, because of the potentially deleterious effects of labeling a family as "at risk" for child abuse or neglect. On the other hand, we feared the consequences of not taking any action after obtaining information which suggested danger to the child.

TABLE II

**Number of Interviews
in Each Patient Group**

		No.
Inpatient		
Cases		165
Accidents	73	
Ingestions	34	
Failure to thrive	42	
Abuse	16	
Controls		138
Total		303
Emergency room		
Cases		138
Accidents	112	
Ingestions	26	
Controls		119
Total		257

The written consent form and method for obtaining consent and treating research data attempted to reconcile this ethical dilemma. We scrupulously adhered to the following, multistep procedure for obtaining consent and sharing interview data:

1. Prior to making contact with a mother to ask permission to interview, the physician responsible for the child's hospital care was asked for his or her permission to interview the mother.

2. If a social worker was assigned to the case, he or she was also asked for permission.

3. After permissions 1 and 2 were obtained, contact was made with the mother.

4. After explaining the goals and nature of the study, but before beginning the interview, it was explained to the mother that the information elicited during the conversation was confidential, but that it was possible that information might be shared with the physician and/or social worker if it were felt that it might assist them in caring for the child.

5. In the instances where it was felt necessary to share the information with a professional person responsible for the management of a patient, the interviewer submitted a written abstract of the pertinent portions of the interview to the physician or social worker. The original interview was never released. Each of these abstracts was then stamped: "Not for insertion in the medical record." In only ten of 560 interviews was information shared.

6. Interview schedules were kept in a locked file and referenced only through a coded system designed to prevent linking the names of respondents to the interview form without access to the code.

Because of the emphasis on environmental stress in the interview, we felt an ethical obligation to offer assistance to ameliorate the identified problems. To this end a family advocacy program was developed which was available to all par-

TABLE III

Characteristics of Case and Control Groups

	Matching Variable			Sex (% Male)
	Age (% ≤ 18 mo)	Race (% White)	Medical Payment (% Public Assisted)	
Inpatient				
Case	53.9	66.7	38.2	57.6
Control	62.3	73.2	31.2	58.0
Emergency room				
Case	33.3	53.6	57.2	55.1
Control	48.7	45.4	54.6	53.8

ticipants. Designed initially to help families get such essential, and lacking, supports as adequate housing, child care, legal services, and adult health care, the program evolved into an organized service available to all hospital patients. Personnel with no formal professional training were taught and supervised to help families deal with contemporary life stresses and in gaining access to essential services.[16]

Results

Demographic Characteristics

This study population reflects the differences in demographic composition of the hospital's inpatient and emergency room services. Table III summarizes the demographic characteristics of the case and control groups.

The inpatient study population comes from the greater Boston area and tends to be younger, predominantly white, and more middle class. The emergency room sample more nearly represents the predominantly black and low-income community directly around the hospital. There are slightly more male children in all groups.

The matching of cases and controls on social class, race, and age is satisfactory.

As Table IV illustrates, however, there are marked demographic differences among the case categories. In the present sample, the patients suffering from failure to thrive and child abuse tend to be younger and male, those suffering from failure to thrive are more frequently white, and those suffering from child abuse are poor.

Medical and Family Data

Figure 1 summarizes the weight at admission for the children in the inpatient groups. Implicit in the definition of failure to thrive is the small size of the child.

TABLE IV

Characteristics of Specific Case Groups

	Age (% ≤ 18 mo)	Race (% White)	Medical Payment (% Public Assisted)	Sex (% Male)
Inpatient				
Accident	46.6	68.5	26.0	54.8
Ingestion	29.4	44.1	52.9	44.1
Failure to thrive	81.0	83.3	33.3	69.0
Abuse	68.8	62.5	75.0	68.8
Emergency room				
Accident	32.1	50.0	59.8	53.6
Ingestion	38.5	69.2	46.2	61.5

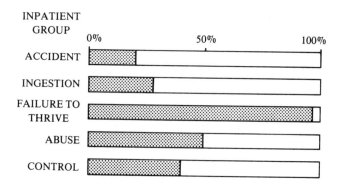

Fig. 1. Proportion of children in inpatient groups who were under tenth percentile for weight.

It is of interest to note that children bearing the child abuse diagnosis in the study sample were also disproportionately small. Inpatient control subjects had acute medical conditions requiring hospitalization, accounting in part for their low weight. Children identified as having had "accidental" traumatic injuries tended to be significantly more robust, as indicated both by their weights and by their mothers' reports of their health, than those in the other study categories.

The results of the maternal interviews were organized into a series of a priori scales developed to integrate and express data bearing on the central hypotheses of the study, the arithmetic means of which are expressed in Table V. (To develop these summative measures, an estimate of the discriminating power of each attribute was made, and a weighted score was devised. The study instruments and details of the analytic method are available on request from the senior author.)

TABLE V

A Priori Stress Scales:
Means for Inpatient Groups Standardized to Mean
and Standard Deviation of Controls

	Stress in Mother's Child- hood	Stress in Current House- hold	Lack of Social Support
Accident	.04	.59°	.19
Ingestion	.46°	.34	.15
Failure to thrive	.47°	.27	.52°
Abuse	1.15°	1.58°	.83°

° $P < .01$ by one-tailed t test.

These scales are based on the sum of positive responses in a given category. Stress in the mother's childhood included frequent family mobility, a broken home, and volunteered information about a personal history of violence and/or neglect. The scale "stress in the current household" was based on recent mobility and change in household composition. The scale "lack of social support" was designed to measure social isolation and included the absence of a telephone and a mother's perception of her neighborhood as unfriendly.

As this table shows, stress was positively associated with all pediatric social illness categories. Accidents were characterized uniquely by a high level of contemporaneous stress. Cases of failure to thrive and of child abuse shared high levels of maternal historical stress and lack of social support. Subjects bearing the diagnosis of child abuse had higher scores in all three stress categories. Particularly of note is the very high level of current household stress in the child abuse cases, suggesting a greater role of ongoing crisis than is commonly acknowledged in the etiology and treatment of child abuse.

Classification Discriminants

Subsequent discriminant function regression analyses were conducted to determine which specific interview variables were predictive of a given category in the conventional taxonomy. (These discriminant functions were determined by defining the category of interest as "1" and defining all other categories, both cases and controls, as "0." A step-wise regression was then calculated on this [1,0] variable.) The results are similar to the stress scale expressions of the findings.

Table VI shows those items, in order of importance, which were significantly predictive of a given inpatient classification. The "control" column summarizes distinctions between cases and controls in the aggregate. Families of children with pediatric social illness contrast sharply with the comparison group. These families have less regular health care, many recent moves, many child-rearing problems, and a history of a broken family in the mother's childhood; they have also experienced mother-initiated separations from the child. These factors suggest several, and somewhat different, patterns of stress on the families of children in the case group. No clear-cut similarities across groups are noted.

The predictors of the specific conditions lead, however, to tentative formulations of etiology which may begin to be translated into a more logical classification scheme. For example, those attributes which are highly predictive of the "child abuse" entity include early and continuing family instability, expressed in mobility, isolation, and early separations of the child from its mother. The familial origins seem prominent, as compared to "failure to thrive," where attributes of the child himself sort out as the more significant descriptors. Although the present data do not define pathogenesis, they describe associations which may help inform practice and guide further research.

Implications of Classification of Social Illness in Pediatric Practice

In present clinical practice, whether or not a child's injuries are characterized as having been "abusively" or "neglectfully" obtained depends on the clinician's ability—or willingness—to attribute the cause of the symptoms to the child's parents. The names "battered child syndrome" and "maltreatment syndrome" have formalized the concept of parental fault in the medical literature.[17, 18]

Making such diagnoses and filing legally mandated case reports have immense value implications which may contradict the traditional ethical posture of medical and behavioral professionals: to help individuals in distress.[19] As it is rare in practice to know with certainty the exact timing, instrument, and circumstances of children's injuries, it is not surprising that many are misclassified as "accident victims," meaning isolated, random events, because of the clinician's understandable reluctance to implicitly condemn the parents of his patients.

Misclassification and Child Abuse Screening

The matter of misclassification is particularly important when one considers current interest in screening for risk of child abuse. Using those items from this study which are most highly discriminating for child abuse (Table VI), it is possible to construct an equation which would allow one to see the extent to which subjects in the pediatric social illness categories and the control group might be identified or misidentified as being at risk for child abuse at different levels of a scale.

Figure 2 expresses as a cumulative percent graph the discriminant function scores for all cases and controls. It is clear that a few characteristics distinguish the child abuse cases from those in other diagnostic categories. High scores mean that families are similar in these discriminating attributes to families where child abuse occurred. The difference in the distribution between child abuse and other cases notwithstanding, it may be noted that were one to develop a "quick and dirty" screening instrument on the basis of these features, one would correctly screen in only 75% of the child abuse cases at the level which would include over 30% of the other categories as well.

Similar equations can be constructed for each diagnostic category. The classification capacity of the set of discriminant functions described in the previous section is

TABLE VI

**Significant Descriptors (*P* < .05) for Inpatient Groups
in Order of Predictive Importance**

Accident	Ingestion	Failure to thrive	Abuse	Control
Good health of child	Child-rearing problems	Poor health of child	Recent moves No telephone	Regular health care
Low household density	Mother-child separations	Younger child	Mother-child separations	Few recent moves
Not welfare dependent	Older child	Male child	Serious child-hood troubles for mother	Few child-rearing problems
Older child	Regular health care	Mother less education than father	Few children	No broken family in mother's childhood
Baby-sitting help			Father older	Child-initiated separations (e.g., for health reasons)
Recent moves	Female child	Neighborhood unfriendly Family physician	Low job status for father	Nobody to care for child when mother goes out

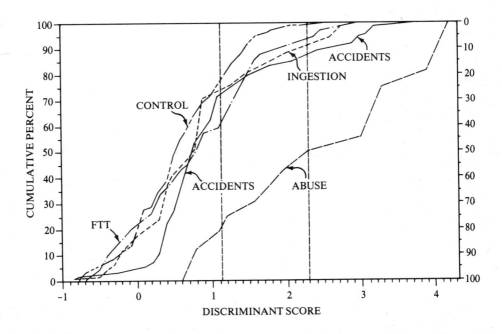

Fig. 2. Discriminant function for inpatient cases of "child abuse."

TABLE VII

. Percent Misclassification Derived from Discriminant Functions for Individual Diagnostic Categories

Classifying Patients in Group	Using Discriminant Function for Patient Category							
	Inpatient (%)					Outpatient (%)		
	Abuse	Failure to Thrive	Accident	Ingestion	Control	Accident	Ingestion	Control
Inpatient								
Abuse	25*	25	62	25	50	62	68	87
Failure to thrive	31	19*	24	31	74	64	64	56
Accident	23	8	12*	55	71	66	68	71
Ingestion	21	17	83	21*	39	81	54	62
Control	16	26	56	39	16*	63	28	78
Outpatient								
Accident	31	5	85	67	61	15*	44	62
Ingestion	42	12	69	75	50	61	19*	61
Control	37	9	74	67	51	71	44	13*

* Percentages marked with asterisks represent "false negative" misclassification; all others are "false positive" misclassification.

summarized in Table VII. (In constructing this table, the cutoff point was set at the means minus one standard deviation for all discriminant scores [roughly comparable to but generally to the left of the dotted lines discussed in Fig. 2]. A column in Table VII refers to the category for which the discriminant function was calculated; a row refers to the group of cases being classified; entries marked with an asterisk show the impressive percentages of false negatives, i.e., the proportion of each category that was not identified by *its own discriminant function*, using the [x-1] cutoff. All other entries are percentages of false positives, i.e., the proportion of a given patient group that would be misclassified by some other discriminant function. Scanning this table indicates that the FTT discriminant function [second column] performs better than the others except on inpatient controls, and that the misclassification is generally large when using the outpatient discriminant functions [last three columns].)

It is well to point out that in the face of rapidly rising numbers of child abuse case reports, protective service institutions across the United States, which even in better economic times were poorly funded and staffed, have had increasingly to resort to rapid clinical screening methods and radical management alternatives to protect victims of child abuse.

Florida's three-year-old central reporting system for cases of suspected child abuse and neglect is still bogged down in an overload of complaints, currently running at 1,500 to 2,000 per month (87,000 complaints have been made since the state-wide hotline started October 1, 1971). . . . In metropolitan areas they are so swamped, workers limit investigations to complaints which "sound the worst," says hotline supervisor Mary Ann Price.[20]

Especially because of known selection bias favoring minority and poor children for the child abuse diagnosis, a phenomenon partly attributable to the public clinical settings in which most of these diagnoses are made and partly to the reluctance of physicians in private practice to make damning value judgments about parents, caution is urged in interpreting these findings to support the value of predictive screening for child abuse. The social policy implications for poor and minority families particularly might be ominous. Other writers have underlined pertinent isues in regard to child abuse screening.[21, 22]

Further study, focusing more specifically and directly on the major discriminating characteristics, is necessary to disentangle the seemingly causal strands associated with symptoms of pediatric social illness. Before more is known about the process of pathogenesis, the extent and nature of what we already know about misclassification should incline us away from child abuse screening.

In the search for a more etiologic taxonomy of pediatric social illness, we shall have to be vigilant neither to blame the victim by focusing on the parent assumed to be responsible for a child's injury nor to fulfill the prophecy of risk by a reflexive application of statistical findings.[23, 24] A focus on the stresses—and the strengths—associated with the victim, his family, and his life setting may enable us more accurately and humanely to identify, to treat, and to prevent these illnesses.

REFERENCES

1. NEWBERGER, E. H., NEWBERGER, C. M., RICHMOND, J. B. "Child health in America: Toward a rational public policy." *Health Society* 54:249, 1976.

2. MORSE, C. W., SAHLER, O. J., FRIEDMAN, S. B. "A three-year follow-up study of abused and neglected children." *Am. J. Dis. Child.* 120:439, 1970.

3. ELMER, E., GREGG, G. S. "Developmental characteristics of abused children." *Pediatrics* 40:596, 1967.

4. MARTIN, H. A., BEEZELY, P., CONWAY, E. F., KEMPE, C. H. "The development of abused children," in Schulman F. (ed.), *Advances in Pediatrics*. Chicago, Year Book Medical Publishers Inc., 1974, pp. 25-73.

5. NAGI, S. Z. *Child Maltreatment in the United States: A Cry for Help and Organizational Response*. Columbus, Ohio, Ohio State University, 1976.

6. GREGG, G. S., ELMER, E. "Infant injuries: Accidents or abuse?" *Pediatrics* 44:434, 1969.

7. NEWBERGER, E. H., HYDE, J. H. "Child Abuse: Principles and implications of current pediatric practice." *Pediatr. Clin. North Am.* 22:695, 1975.

8. GIL, D. G. *Violence Against Children*. Cambridge, Mass., Harvard University Press, 1970.

9. NEWBERGER, E. H. (reviewer), GIL, D. G. "Violence Against Children, book review." *Pediatrics* 48:688, 1971.

10. KOEL, B. S. "Failure to thrive and fatal injury as a continuum." *Am. J. Dis. Child.* 118:51, 1969.

11. HOLTER, J. C., FRIEDMAN, S. B. "Child abuse: Early casefinding in the emergency department." *Pediatrics* 42:128, 1969.

12. MARTIN, H. L. "Antecedents of burns and scalds in children." *Br. J. Med. Psychol.* 43:39, 1970.

13. BULLARD, P. M., GLASER, H. H., HEAGARTY, M. C., PIVCHIK, E. C. "Failure to thrive in the neglected child." *Am. J. Orthopsychiatry* 37:680, 1967.

14. SOBEL, R. "Psychiatric implications of accidental poisonings in childhood." *Pediatr. Clin. North Am.* 17:653, 1971.

15. NEWBERGER, E. H., HAGENBUCH, J. J., EBELING, N. B., et. "Reducing the literal and human cost of child abuse: Impact of a new hospital management system." *Pediatrics* 51:840, 1973.

16. MORSE, A. E., HYDE, J. N., NEWBERGER, E. H., REED, R. B. "Environmental correlates of pediatric social illness: Preventive implications of an advocacy approach." *Am. J. Public Health, to be published.*

17. KEMPE, C. H., SILVERMAN, F. N., STEEL, B. F., et al. "The battered child syndrome." *JAMA* 181:1, 1962.

18. FONTANA, V. J. *The Maltreated Child: The Maltreatment Syndrome in Children,* ed. 2. Springfield, Ill., Charles C. Thomas Publisher, 1971.

19. NEWBERGER, E. H., DANIEL, J. H. "Knowledge and epidemiology of child abuse: A critical review of concepts." *Pediatr. Ann.* 5:140, 1976.

20. *Child Protection Report.* Washington, D.C., March 13, 1975.

21. LIGHT, R. "Abused and neglected children in America: A study of alternative policies." *Harvard Educ. Rev.* 43:556, 1973.

22. FOLTZ, A-M. "The development of ambiguous federal policy: Early and periodic screening, diagnosis, and treatment (EPSDT)." *Health Society* 53:35, 1975.

23. RYAN, W. *Blaming the Victim.* New York, Pantheon, 1971.

24. HOBBS, N. *The Futures of Children.* San Francisco, Jossey-Bass, 1975.

ACKNOWLEDGMENT

We thank the following people for their contributions to this work: S. Block, N. Bloom, G. Farrell, G. Gardner, A. Gordon, T. Holtzman, J. Jameson, E. McAnulty, A. Marshall, P. Moriarty, N. Morse, C. M. Newberger, G. Phillips, H. Reynolds, L. Stein, S. Weiser, N. Williams, and M. C. Winokur. The consistent enthusiasm and interest of Drs. C. A. Janeway, chairman emeritus, and J. B. Richmond, present chairman, of the Departments of Medicine and Psychiatry at the Children's Hospital Medical Center, are also gratefully acknowledged.

31

Child Abuse and Neglect: Toward a Firmer Foundation for Practice and Policy*

Eli H. Newberger, M.D.

Only recently have child abuse and neglect been identified as problems requiring state and federal legislative attention. With the seminal paper in 1962, by Kempe and colleagues[4] on the battered child syndrome, there began an effort to try systematically to identify the victims of child abuse and neglect. This led to the initial development of child abuse and neglect reporting.

But it soon became clear that the children who were being identified were from poor and socially marginal families, with preferential selection of nonwhite children who received their care in public clinics. The illusion is still prevalent that child abuse and neglect are problems of poor people exclusively—even though we now have indirect evidence that the cases are more widespread.

Children of more affluent families, who receive their medical care in private practice settings where the relationship of clinician to family, the payment structure, and the ethics of treating personal information are quite different, are more likely to have their injuries characterized as "accidents." While the term *accident* connotes an isolated, random event, recent research[5, 7] suggests that there are important associations between childhood accidents and child abuse and neglect, having to do with a particular child's innate qualities, developmental level, and behavior; the

* Excerpted from testimony on child abuse and neglect before the US Senate Subcommittee on Child and Human Development, April 1977. Research cited was supported by a DHEW Office of Child Development grant (Project OCD-CB-141).

Eli H. Newberger, "Child Abuse and Neglect: Toward a Firmer Foundation for Practice and Policy," *American Journal of Orthopsychiatry*, 47(3):374-376. Copyright © 1977 the American Orthopsychiatric Association, Inc. Reproduced by permission.

family's ability to protect the child; and the realities of the child's nurturing environment. Accidents at home and in automobiles are the leading cause of childhood morbidity and mortality, and domestic trauma accounts for the greater proportion in preschool children.[6] Thus, many child abuse and neglect cases in richer homes, misdiagnosed as accidents, may not appear on case report rosters.

The very diagnostic terms "abuse" and "neglect" carry important, implicit judgments, which clinicians are understandably reluctant to make. But, regrettably, it's easier to make the diagnosis of child abuse if you are a physician in an inner-city hospital emergency room or in a clinic for the indigent. Calling a poor or black or Indian or Chicano mother a bad parent—that's what the diagnosis means—is acceptable there. It's also less painful to report the case when the family isn't paying you directly, when the family looks very different than your own, and when you may never see them again.

Our concern with child abuse and neglect, and most research on the problems, derives from cases that have come to light through the existing social agencies. In focusing our attention only on those children readily accessible to study, we are working within a very narrow frame and with entirely too limited a population. One of our most important and immediate tasks is to look at the universe of need. I mean this both in the sense of all the children—rich and poor, white and nonwhite—and in the sense of all manifestations of child abuse and neglect. Our research and development efforts largely ignore the sexual misuse of children, the abuse of children in and by institutions, and the relationship between violence among adults and violence toward children. To address these problems would, to be sure, oblige looking at some troubling social realities and facing up to the question of whether we *really* want to deal with the issues beyond the level of individual cases.

Are we willing to look seriously at the values and traditions that shape sexual expression and exploitation? Can we face the widespread cruelty to children in institutions for the retarded and the delinquent—and even in public schools? Do we really want to know what unemployment and public assistance stipends pegged below the subsistence level do to relations between parents and children? How do battered women, the promotion of violence on television, and the coercive, degrading nature of many jobs bear on child abuse?

As Gil[3] and Gelles[1] have pointed out, our preoccupation with sensational violence in individual homes creates a kind of smokescreen. Its effects are felt on two levels. There is a "macro" smokescreen that lets us, as a society, ignore uncomfortable problems such as poverty, and sidestep other basic and related issues of health and mental health. (As child abuse and neglect were being highlighted by the Congress and by the previous administration, resources for children's immunizations and mental health were actually being cut back.) And there is a "micro" smokescreen that allows individual families to take comfort in knowing that those parents over there are the bad ones, the ones who abuse their kids. (What we do in our own home is OK, and we needn't think too much about our easy acceptance of corporal punishment or about the emotional poverty of so many of our lives.)

Administrators of any such federally funded statute as Public Law 93-247 (The Child Abuse Prevention and Treatment Act of 1974) are, of necessity, acutely sensitive politically, and their implementation will inevitably reflect the Administration's and the Congress's values. Reading the Congressional Record of

1973, before this bill first passed, gives one a pretty good idea about what we want to do and find out about child abuse and neglect—and what we don't.

There is no way that this $20 million program can begin to answer the service needs of the million or so children we have reason to believe[2, 3] are abused and neglected each year. At present, we do not have an adequate conceptual base for the treatment of child abuse and neglect, nor have we adequately disseminated technology, even to the extent that we know what good practice is. While this has partly to do with limited resources, it involves as well the need for basic "theory building" in this field.

We have yet to develop a theoretical base that enables us to deal competently with the many kinds of family problems that culminate in the physical symptoms of child abuse and neglect. We clearly need not only better knowledge, in terms of understanding the type and distribution of family problems, but also a much more accurate understanding of the relationship of children's symptoms to family dysfunctions. We need to know what enables parents to cope and, importantly, what realities are associated with family competency and strength. This, in turn, will make for a more informed and rational clinical practice.

Dr. Edward Zigler, addressing the national conference on child abuse in Atlanta early last year, noted that we are, in child abuse and neglect, where we were in mental retardation in the 1950s. This assessment was not received happily by many of the assembled experts. But it made us stop for a moment to consider the implications of our headlong action in this field. A stronger and broader foundation for action is urgently needed.

REFERENCES

1. GELLES, R. 1975. "The social construction of child abuse." *Amer. J. Orthopsychiat.* 45(3):363-371.

2. GELLES, R. 1977. *Violence toward children in the United States.* Presented to AAAS, Denver, February 1977.

3. GIL, D. 1970. *Violence Against Children.* Harvard University Press, Cambridge, Mass.

4. KEMPE, C. ET AL. "The battered-child syndrome." *JAMA* 181(1):17-24.

5. MORSE, A. ET AL. 1977. "Environmental correlates of pediatric social illness: preventive implications of an advocacy approach." *J. Pub. Hlth. Assoc.* (in press).

6. NEWBERGER, E., NEWBERGER, C. and RICHMOND, J. 1976. "Child health in America: toward a rational public policy." *Milbank Mem. Fund Quart./Hlth. and Society* 54(3):249-298.

7. NEWBERGER, E. ET AL. 1977. "Pediatric social illness: toward an etiologic classification." *Pediatrics.* (in press).

32

Questions of Social Policy—
A Canadian Perspective*

Barbara A. Chisholm

1. Introduction—Statistics

There are no accurate figures on the incidence of child abuse in Canada. Reasons for this include:

(1) lack of a standard, useable definition of child abuse;
(2) variation in reporting systems;
(3) lack of consistent procedures in dealing with child abuse;
(4) failure to recognize (or perhaps to acknowledge) child abuse, which thus leads to non-reporting; and
(5) problems of professional and public education.

The types of injuries identified as child abuse vary from province to province. Some provinces provide information on the source of the original complaint report.[1] Some provinces identify emotional and physical neglect, others spell out physical abuse only and still others provide for identification of abuse or neglect without a

* Barbara A. Chisholm, "Questions of Social Policy—A Canadian Perspective," in *Family Violence*, John M. Eekelaar and Sanford N. Katz, eds., Butterworths, Toronto, 1978.

TABLE 1

**Number of Deaths in Ontario
Caused by Child Abuse, 1970-1975**

Chief Coroner's Office Statistics	Central Registry Statistics
50	23

physical injury. At present, nine of the twelve provincial or territorial jurisdictions in Canada have legislation making reporting of abuse or ill-treatment of children mandatory.[2] (The three provinces without such reporting are initiating systematic monitoring programs.) But even within those nine statutes requiring reporting of child abuse, four contain no penalties for failing to report; two have 'general penalties'; one has a penalty which has not yet been proclaimed; and only two provinces have a specific penalty for such failure.[3]

Of the nine jurisdictions in Canada (exclusive of the federal one), only four provinces—Alberta, Manitoba, Quebec, and the Yukon—extend the age of statutory protection against neglect and abuse to the age of majority in that province. This raises a query about adolescent abuse. So much attention is (properly) being directed at infant, toddler and young-child abuse that we may be neglecting another aspect of the problem, but one that is no less urgent. Adolescent suicide is now so serious[4] as to require investigation on its own. Is there a connection? We may be (and probably are) missing many instances of adolescent abuse because it is disguised as teenage behavioral problems or generational conflicts. And, where does the adolescent victim of abuse or incest turn for help and action? The helplessness of the adolescent is just as critical an issue for us.

Many attempts have been made to predict the actual and anticipated incidence of child abuse in Canada,[5] as elsewhere. But we do not yet have consistency in reporting, and therefore, depending upon who is discussing the situation, we may get quite varying pictures. *Table I* illustrates the point regarding the province of Ontario.[6]

Whatever the actual incidence figures, it seems fair to suggest that more physical, sexual, and psychological abuse of minors goes on than is noted and counted and that we appear to tolerate a considerable amount of abuse of children and youth in our society.

2. Punishment and Treatment

Whatever the problems of establishing the incidence, we have the other problems related to response or 'management'. These problems grow out of a significant difference of opinion about the appropriate approach for society and for professionals to take to battering or abusing parents or other adults. Examination of the literature of the past decade[7] reflects the difference of opinion, which in a somewhat oversimplified way may be expressed thus:

a) the 'punish them' approach, with deterrent sentencing as a characteristic; and
b) the 'treat them' approach, which relies on a medical-model.

Polarization to either position is surely not useful. Each merits consideration.

TABLE 2[8]

Number of Child Abuse Reports, Charges Laid, and Convictions, in Ontario, 1970-1975

Number of Reports	Charges Laid	Convictions Obtained
3249	348	78

The Punishment Approach: The Adult Removed From the Child

The use of deterrent sentencing is an old and still (in some circles) honored approach to the problem of serious anti-social behavior. The degree of severity of the punishment is a form of 'weighting', a kind of index of the 'degree of repugnance' society attaches to the event. Thus the Attorney-General of Ontario recently successfully appealed the sentence meted out in a child abuse case, and won a much longer one.

The deterrent point of view may be supported, at least partially, by observing the reality of present society. There *are* adults who are dangerous. We know that. We recognize too, other adults' rights to physical safety and to walk about the city free from fear and potential assault. Therefore, we incarcerate those acknowledged or convicted offenders designated as 'dangerous'. Do we not need to acknowledge that the same situation may pertain to children—that there are adults in their environment who are dangerous to them (or if a child is already dead, potentially dangerous to other children)? Should we retreat from facing the potential necessity of removing from society those adults established as dangerous to children, even if they are their biological parents? Do minors have less defendable rights to physical safety than adults?

Table 2 shows the numbers of charges and convictions relative to reports of child abuse in Ontario 1970-1975. I am not here *advocating* punishment as the way to deal with abusing parents. Rather I am raising a question for consideration: that protection of citizens from dangerous persons may from time to time require that such persons be removed from active society, and this protection applies to children as well as to adults.

The Treatment Approach: The Child is Often Removed From the Adults

Not all adults who have abused a child are dangerous to the community of children at large. This probably constitutes the large bulk of the abusing group; they do not require punitive removal from the community. Indeed, if it is necessary to separate the abused child (or the child at risk of abuse) from the abusing or threatening parent, it is usual for the child to be removed.[9]

Intervention by agents of the community is essential in these instances, to 'catch' the behavior before it becomes even more abusive. Help which involves (or should involve) many years of caring support is indicated; incarceration is not necessary. The prognosis for some parents in this so-called 'treatment' group appears more encouraging than that of the dangerous adult group, largely because we do not seem to know what to do with the dangerous group except incarcerate them. But it seems inexact to suggest that the majority of programs presently in progress in Canada are providing 'treatment', in the narrow medical use of that word. They are, instead, a combination of services more appropriately related to a social work than to a medical model. They may be described as 'environmental manipulation' and 'the provision of support services'.

'Environmental manipulation' means help with the externals of people's lives: decent, spacious-enough housing, for example. A family under stress (indeed, any family) needs housing which provides clean and dry shelter, free of vermin and rodents. A family under stress also requires space sufficient to absorb the realities that come out of inter-personal physical closeness: in other words, a chance to 'get away from each other' from time to time, when pressures and tempers are high. It seems to me that the development of housing policies is one of the issues to which we have failed to pay significant enough attention in Canada. In urban and suburban society we have become a nation of apartment dwellers. Many young families occupy vertical rather than horizontal space. Because we (the planning, building, decision-making administrators of the country) may remember having back-yards and parks to play and roam in our own childhood, we seem to believe that most young families today have the same opportunities. But this is not the case.[10] The present economy makes it impossible for most young families to consider a home like that. The result is that small children, busy toddlers, and active adolescents are cramped in conditions in which they cannot escape one another in moments of stress. Add to this one or two tired adults, and the spark of irritation may feed itself on counter-irritations, flare into out-of-control anger, and someone gets hurt.

Other external needs related to people's lives with which we should be concerned through 'environmental manipulation' in much fuller form that we are at present include:

—day care, and emergency day care services for working parents; sole-support parents; overwhelmed parents;
—homemaker services, short and long term;
—income improvement (basic) and income management assistance (debt counseling);
—help with fighting one's way through the bureaucratic red tape maze of various governmental 'helping' programs; and
—relief for a special child with special needs, at periods of crisis or stress in the family.

Our very hesitant move in the direction of this last item reflects, at least, two current characteristics in much of our thinking: one is the old belief that to help adults (*e.g.*, parents) weakens their capacity to help themselves, which is a preferred societal mode of parental (adult) behavior; and the other is that, in spite of all the evidence of the last two decades, somehow we do not quite believe that the so-called nuclear family is here. We still imagine family members aid one another. This serves to strengthen the anxiety about and resistance to government intervention in the family. While this is a matter of legitimate concern, I suggest that in this context, the state cannot choose to remain out.

'Provision of Support Systems' refers to the sort of practical and emotional assistance required to improve and sustain a person's (or a family's) capacity to deal with day-to-day problems, or with episodes of particular stress. Examples of such help, as related to the managing or prevention of child abuse, would include:

— parents anonymous groups (child battering or potential battering parents who come together for initial help and support, much on the Alcoholics Anonymous pattern);
— 24-hour distress 'hot lines', with well-publicized telephone numbers;
— volunteer befrienders, whose non-judgmental befriending reaches out to the parent(s) in difficulty;
— 'grandmothers-by-informal-adoption' programs; these were originally directed toward helping the separated child without a family but now are seen to be of value to the parent in need of parenting as well;
— self-help groups separate from Parents Anonymous, to assist with the 'post-partum blues', which try to involve husbands and fathers in the attempt to understand what's going on with a depressed new mother, reducing hopefully the buildup of stress which may lead to an assault on the infant, or serious neglect.

Use of the Term 'Treatment'

Intensive social work of one kind or another, then, appears to be the mainstay of our management and/or prevention of child abuse. Of course some parents are referred for treatment by a psychiatrist, and go voluntarily. Such treatment may exist by itself or in cooperation with social work assistance, or parallel to it. Psychiatric consultation can be of use also to social workers and non-professional helpers trying to help the abusing parent.

Common use of treatment terminology, however, instead of the language of 'management', may have harmed our attempts to involve the whole community in dealing with child abuse. Treatment is a process of skill, undertaken by experts, which leads to cure, or at least to a significant reduction in symptoms. Generalized and inexact use of the term, I believe, lulls both professionals and the general public into a feeling that; 1) there are methods more or less readily available to 'cure' the child abuser or significantly to reduce his/her behavior; 2) that if we could only undertake to employ these methods, child abusers could be cured or controlled; and 3) that the skills of such methods are special, and therefore not within the arsenal of tools available to the 'average' social worker or citizen. Such thinking eliminates or excludes the average citizen and may have something to do with the community lethargy reflected in lack of reporting of child abuse cases.

A precedent of a kind exists for this point of view. Insertion of the treatment concept into the area of juvenile delinquency has created a special problem: in trying to make a *quasi*-social agency out of juvenile court we have, in the opinion of some, compromised the court's capacity to be a court. In attempting to 'treat' the youthful offender, we have complicated his need (and some suggest his right) to experience clear and connected consequences to his behavior. In the same sense, I fear we may make the same mistake in child abuse. In focussing exclusively on the concept of treatment, at least in the *language* of our concern, we may (and do, I believe) compromise the functions and the problem. It is probable that some abusing parents (or indeed, other adults in a child's life) are emotionally seriously disturbed or damaged. Victims themselves of too many pathological experiences, they are in danger of failing in life as people, never mind as parents. *These persons are often emotionally sick, and do need treatment.* However, for other abusing or potentially abusing parents, it is possible that the orientation the word 'treatment' creates is a disservice. Not everyone who offends our social codes is 'sick'. Their treatment orientation could lead to these consequences:

a) we may rely on too narrow a conceptual base in our search for viable action-programs directed at child abuse. That is, we may rely too much on the scientific model for the design of programs governments will be willing to fund (*i.e.*, time-limited, research-oriented, control-group restricted projects). Also, our approach may be too 'professional' oriented; and

b) we may continue to exclude from our co-ordinated approach those very programs which are most directly related to 'environmental manipulation' and 'the provision of support systems' mentioned above. Thereby we risk focussing on one aspect (treatment) at the expense of another (those services which are particularly within the scope of social work), and short-circuit the results.

3. Questions of Prevention, Intervention, and Rights

The Government of Canada recently addressed itself to the problem of child abuse in Canada. The Report of the Standing Committee on Health, Welfare and Social Affairs of the Parliament of Canada entitled *Child Abuse and Neglect* was tabled in July 1976.[11] Its findings were many and varied, and a total of fifteen recommendations were made. A significant observation made by the Committee was that the Canadian pattern of response to social problems has been (and is) essentially that of 'waiting till the horse is stolen to lock the barn door'. We wait until a problem is visibly severe before we act; we are not strong on prevention. The Committee made the following statement about prevention:

> The Committee, in noting the lack of support services to families with children, noted also that many services become available to a child once he has been removed from his own home because of family breakdown. The Committee recognizes that there are often no alternatives to the removal of the child. If appropriate support services had been available to the family from the time of the child's birth, it is possible that the child would have remained in his own home.
>
> [The] Committee noted that expensive services are required for emotionally disturbed children, for battered children, for broken families but, unless preventive services are also provided, the cycle becomes self-perpetuating. Services which enable parents to care for their own children can often prevent the need for protection.[12]

Any suggestion of family support raises the spectre of intervention, and this in turn leads to the question of the rights of parents and the rights of children.

(a) *The rights of parents* to the full custody of their children is a traditional manner of thought which is so deeply ingrained in our society that questioning it in any form is guaranteed to raise cautious resistance if not actual hackles. We are reminded that the family is the Basic Unit in Society. As such, it enjoys, and should continue to, a basic right to function with minimum interference, especially from the state.

Of course, this is an over-simplification of the reality. The state is already deeply involved in the affairs and well-being of the family: income tax deduction provisions, the Family Allowance program, housing subsidy policies, education, public health programs, consumer protection legislation, medicare programs, public libraries, public transportation facilities—the list goes on. It is somewhat innocent to argue the case of Parents' Rights on the theme that 'the least government is the best government'. The government is already in.

Nevertheless, there is in our society a general expectation that parents raise their children by themselves. As noted by the Parliamentary Committee, we tend to withhold intervention until a serious problem of incapacity or refusal to parent has emerged. This attitude of public policy reinforces the ancient concept of the 'ownership' rights of parents. Our religious attitudes and our laws have reinforced this position. It has been assumed that the interests of parents and children always coincide, and that the decisions of parents regarding their children will always be made on behalf of the children. Our assumption that every child should be in his own home rationalizes resistance to removing a child or returning a child to his parents. In a large majority of cases that is the right conclusion. But there is another claim which cannot be ignored:

(b) *The competing rights of children* to grow free from fear, capable of trusting others and thus themselves. Our theories of child development—physical, emotional, intellectual, psychological—still view the child as being essentially passive and dependent, however exciting and amusing. His role is to cooperate, obey, and go to school when he's old enough. Although affectionate, this attitude sees the child as having no role to play in adult decision-making about him. Perhaps innocently, but nevertheless effectively, this perception renders the child invisible. But the concept of Children's Rights shifts that perception, to recognition of the child *as a person who happens to be a child*.

This is not just an exercise in word games. If we change our perception of children from that of dependent incompetent possessions, to one of recognizing them as persons in their own right, who happen to be children who are also dependent and in need of protection, then we inevitably shift our weighting of parents' rights, and their burden of parental responsibility.

The Parliamentary Committee referred to earlier took note of this point.

> Among the issues involved in providing preventive services to children and families, the question kept arising. 'What are the rights of the child?' and 'What are the rights of the parent?' It was made clear by a number of witnesses that by tradition and law the rights of the parent have always superseded those of the child unless or until the breakdown of the family necessitates the intervention of a public authority. For this reason, there is often a reluctance on the part of a citizen or even an official agency to intervene in family affairs even if there appears to be some cause for concern on the child's behalf. Established agencies do not usually take any initiative in helping and assisting parents to care for their children until the parent or child directly requests help or someone outside the family complains about the care the child is receiving and by that time it may be too late to help the family.
>
> The Committee believes that it is possible to preserve the integrity, privacy and sanctity of the family and, at the same time offer support services to the family in the raising of their children.[13]

At present the rights of parents and the entitlements of children appear to be on a collision course. Perhaps it will be useful to acknowledge that the claims of parental 'ownership' are neither absolute nor permanent. The dependency of children and youth is reduced with time and maturation. But dependency is not to be equated with subjugation, en route. Perhaps the reluctance to intervene in cases of suspected child abuse reflects an unconscious agreement with the position that children are possessions of their parents. Such an assumption places parents' rights first, even while it may be articulated in phrases of concern for the child.

The philosophical underpinning that states that every child should be in his own family is right and proper, as far as it goes. We have few specific guidelines to assist judgment when situations arise which challenge this moral precept, except listed definitions of neglect which justify action in child welfare cases, or the 1909 White House Conference on Children Credo that no child should be removed from his own home for reasons of poverty alone. Perhaps the statement should now read: "Every child should be in his own home unless to remain there threatens his personal and/or civil rights."

In California recently[14] a Supreme Court decision (June 1975) has brought to the foreground in that state the rights of the child subjected to abuse. Discharge of a 'battered child' back to the battering parent(s) may now constitute malpractice. Thus the role of the professional and the judgments exercised by professionals are coming under scrutiny, with an extension of present accountability for failing to protect the rights of children against their parents.

4. Complicating Factors

Inter-Professional Difficulties

A special problem associated with the management and prevention of child abuse is that related to inter-professional cooperation (or lack of it). Particular attention to the issue is certainly indicated in any serious approach to child abuse. Inter-discipline and inter-agency tensions reduce the effectiveness of any 'team' approach and create resistances which direct the focus of attention away from the problem onto what might be termed 'upmanship' or 'games of control'. Many factors complicate this problem: pressure of work, lack of knowledge (and therefore understanding) of the training of other disciplines; thus a lack of understanding of both the extent and limitation of their skills; ignorance of how the individual agency 'helps'; lack of trust among professionals that the other service or agency will carry out its mandate, leading to the attitude that 'if it's going to get done I'd better do it myself'; lack of reliance on the judgment of other professionals; unresponsiveness of one service or agency to the requests of another for action on behalf of a child, and consequent exasperation and anger; and a simple lack of courtesy toward each other, in terms of information—sharing and joint planning. Medical personnel can inform the child-caring agency early about their concern for a child. Short notice, if avoidable, is a disservice to the child and hinders good planning.

Inter-disciplinary understanding can be fostered in at least two ways: (there are others, of course)

(1) through the development of committees (perhaps called Child Abuse Committees) whose members are professionals and non-professionals and part of whose function it would be to learn about each other and *then* to liaise with each other's organizations and with government; and

(2) through the development of continuing cross-professional education and study programs; some important initiatives have been made between social workers and lawyers, but there is a long way to go.

Corporal Punishment

Concern about the relationship between physical punishment and child abuse is becoming more and more evident. Physical punishment has long been tolerated. The Criminal Code of Canada still allows for it in section 43. Even the Parliamentary Committee Report referred to earlier dealt with the issue briefly:

> Your Committee is pleased to note the reference in the Brief of the Department of Justice to the effect that the question of the necessity and/or desirability of introducing a 'cruelty to children' offense in the Criminal Code is under study by that Department.
>
> Section 43 of the Criminal Code was discussed by several witnesses in the context of child rearing, corporal punishment in the schools, and as a reflection of cultural values. The Committee is aware that some provincial legislation specifically forbids physical punishment of children.
>
> It is felt by many who have experience with the care of children in groups and with the education and training of staff who provide group care, that the elimination of physical punishment encourages staff to develop more creative programs and more sensitive ways of encouraging positive acceptable behavior in children. The result is an improvement in the relations between staff and child.
>
> The Committee considers that the relationship between parent and child needs to be considered separately from the relationship between a child and a teacher, nurse, child care worker or other person standing in the place of the parent.
>
> The Committee recommends further consideration of section 43. . . .
>
> The Committee suggests that alternatives to physical force as a means of discipline be encouraged through studies and programs of public education. . . .[15]

It is to be hoped that exploration of this subject will proceed. Is physical punishment of any constructive educational value? If so, what are its boundaries; if not, how can we replace it with more constructive measures? How should the Criminal Code view the question?

The Difficulties Inherent in Giving Service

Much has been written about the characteristics of abusive parents. This literature tends to focus on their dynamics, or how they became abusive. The literature deals also with another important characteristic, namely, the 'workability' of such adults. It is pointed out that not infrequently they have problems trusting others, and experience great difficulty reaching out for help and in making and sustaining relationships.

Thus, goals in working with abusive adults, or attempting to do so must be practical and realistic. The main responsibility is protection of the child or children, and if hard choices must be made about 'working with parents', the child's claims to emotional and physical integrity must come first. If this means placement, then that will have to be undertaken. If working with the family while the child remains with the parents at home is the undertaking, then very long-term service is subsequently implied. Supervision of a once-abused child in his own home is a very difficult undertaking: one cannot be there all the time. Even the team approach which provides a multiple-person involvement may meet problems of resistance, refusal of access to the home, and differences in judgment and perception about what is going on. The judgments that are demanded in this situation by social workers, public health nurses, physicians and volunteers are of critical importance, and are difficult. In our concern to help parents at risk we must not lose sight of this reality. Otherwise, there is a danger that in concentration on the parents the child may be overlooked.

NOTES

1.   Alberta, Nova Scotia, and Ontario.

2.   Jurisdictions which lack this specific legislation are New Brunswick, the Northwest Territories, and Prince Edward Island. These all have legislation, of course, in company with all other provinces, directed generally to the protection of dependent/neglected children.

3.   (a) British Columbia, Manitoba, Ontario, Saskatchewan; (b) Nova Scotia, Quebec, (c) Alberta; (d) Newfoundland and the Yukon.

4.   See: *Perspective Canada, A Compendium of Social Statistics*, Government of Canada, Ottawa.

5.   See: Stolk, Mary Van, *The Battered Child in Canada* (1972).

6.   Dawson, Ross, "Current Issues in Child Abuse in Ontario" (Nov., 1976), 9 *Journal of the Ontario Association of Children's Aid Societies* No. 19, 3.

7.   See, for example: references contained in *Child Abuse—a Bibliography* by Bakan, Eisner, and Needham, pub. by Canadian Council on Children and Youth, 1976; and Jayaratne, S., "Child Abusers as Parents and Children: A Review" (Jan., 1977), 22 *Social Work* Journal of the National Association of Social Workers (U.S.) No. 1, 5-9.

8.   See: Dawson, Ross, *supra*, p. 3.

9.   This is a topic that requires further separate consideration: removal of children rather than that of the adult further 'victimizes the victim' removing him from siblings, the other parent, *etc.*

10.   See for example: *Perspective Canada, supra,* chapter 10, p. 207.

11.   *Child Abuse and Neglect*—Report to the House of Commons, Standing Committee on Health, Welfare and Social Affairs, First Session, Thirtieth Parliament, 1974-75-76. Ottawa. (Supply and Services Canada).

12.   *Child Abuse and Neglect, supra*, p. 21.

13.   *Ibid.*, pp. 20-21.

14.   *Landeros v. Flood* (1975), 50 Cal. App. 3d. 189. See article on this case entitled "The Battered Child: A Doctor's Civil Liability for Failure to Diagnose and Report", by Clymer, J. N. (1977) 16 *Washburn Law Journal* 543.

15.   *Child Abuse and Neglect, supra*, pp. 18-19.

33

The Medicalization and Legalization of Child Abuse*

Eli H. Newberger,
and Richard Bourne

Child abuse has emerged in the last fifteen years as a visible and important social problem. Although a humane approach to 'help' both victims of child abuse and their families has developed (and in fact is predominantly expressed in the title of one or more influential books on the subject, *Helping the Battered Child and His Family*),[1] a theoretical framework to integrate the diverse origins and expressions of violence toward children and to inform a rational clinical practice does not exist. Furthermore, so inadequate are the 'helping' services in most communities, so low the standard of professional action, and so distressing the consequences of incompetent intervention for the family that we and others have speculated that punishment is being inflicted in the guise of help.[2]

What factors encourage theoretical confusion and clinical inadequacy? We propose that these consequences result, in part, from medical and legal ambiguity concerning child abuse and from two fundamental, and in some ways irreconcilable, dilemmas about social policy and the human and technical response toward families

* Supported in part by a grant from the Office of Child Development, U.S. Department of Health, Education, and Welfare (Project OCD-CB-141).

© E. H. Newberger and R. Bourne, 1978. To be published in *Critical Perspectives on Child Abuse*, Lexington Books, D. C. Heath Co., Lexington, Mass., 1978. Also appeared in *Family Violence*, John Eekelaar and Sanford Katz, eds., Butterworths, Toronto, 1978. A revised version of this article appeared in the *American Journal of Orthopsychiatry*, 48 (4), October, 1978:593-607. Copyright © 1978 the American Orthopsychiatric Association, Inc. Reproduced by permission.

in crisis. We call these dilemmas *Family Autonomy versus Coercive Intervention* and *Compassion versus Control.*

We integrate in this paper a discussion of these dilemmas with a critical sociological perspective on child abuse management. Through the cognitive lens of social labeling theory, we see symptoms of family crisis, and certain manifestations of childhood injury, 'medicalized' and 'legalized', and called 'child abuse', to be diagnosed, reported, treated, and adjudicated by doctors and lawyers, their constituent institutions, and the professionals who depend on them for their social legitimacy and support.

We are mindful, as practitioners, of the need for prompt, effective, and creative professional responses to child abuse. Our critical analysis of the relationship of professional work to the societal context in which it is embedded is meant to stimulate attention to issues which professionals ignore to their and their clients' ultimate disadvantage. We mean not to disparage necessary efforts to help and protect children and their families.

How children's rights—as opposed to parents' rights—may be defined and protected is currently the subject of vigorous, and occasionally rancorous, debate.

The *Family Autonomy v. Coercive Intervention* dilemma defines the conflict central to our ambiguity about *whether* society should intervene in situations of risk to children. The traditional autonomy of the family in rearing its offspring was cited by the majority of the U.S. Supreme Court in its ruling against the severely beaten appellants in the controversial 'corporal punishment' case *(Ingraham v. Wright, et al.)*.[3] The Schools, serving in *loco parentis*, are not, in effect, constrained constitutionally from any punishment, however cruel.

Yet in California, a physician seeing buttock bruises of the kind legally inflicted by the teacher in the Miami public schools risks malpractice action if he fails to report his observations as symptoms of child abuse *(Landeros v. Flood)*.[4] He and his hospital are potentially liable for the cost of the child's subsequent injury and handicap if they do not initiate protective measures.[5]

The dilemma *Family Autonomy v. Coercive Intervention* is highlighted by the recently promulgated draft statute of the American Bar Association's Juvenile Justice Standards Project which, citing the low prevailing quality of protective child welfare services in the U.S., would sharply *restrict* access to such services.[6] The Commission would, for example, make the reporting of child neglect discretionary rather than mandatory, and would narrowly define the bases for court jurisdiction to situations where there is clear harm to a child.

Our interpretation of this standard is that it would make matters worse, not better, for children and their families.[7] So long as we are deeply conflicted about the relation of children to the State as well as to the family, and whether children have rights independent of their parents', we shall never be able to articulate with clarity *how* to enforce them.

The dilemma *Compassion v. Control* has been postulated and reviewed in a previous paper,[8] which discusses the conceptual and practical problems implicit in the expansion of the clinical and legal definitions of child abuse to include practically every physical and emotional risk to children. The dilemma addresses a conflict central to the present ambiguity about *how* to protect the children from their parents.

Parental behavior which might be characterized as destructive or criminal were it directed towards an adult has come to be seen and interpreted by those involved in its identification and treatment in terms of the psycho-social economy of the family. Embracive definitions reflect a change in the orientation of professional practice. To the extent to which we understand abusing parents as sad, deprived, needy human beings (rather than as cold, cruel murderers) we can sympathize with their plight and compassionately proffer supports and services to aid them in their struggle. Only with dread may we contemplate strong intervention (such as court action) on the child's behalf, for want of alienating our clients.

Notwithstanding the humane philosophy of treatment, society cannot, or will not, commit resources nearly commensurate with the exponentially increasing number of case reports which have followed the promulgation of the expanded definitions. The helping language betrays a deep conflict and even ill will toward children and parents in trouble, whom society and professionals might sooner punish and control.

We are forced frequently in practice to identify and choose the 'least detrimental alternative' for the child[9] because the family supports which make it safe to keep children in their homes (homemakers, child care, psychiatric and medical services) are never available in sufficient amounts and quality.

That we should guide our work by a management concept named 'least detrimental alternative' for children suggests at least a skepticism about the utility of these supports, just as the rational foundation for child welfare work is called into question by the title of the influential book from which the concept comes, *Beyond the Best Interests of the Child*. More profoundly, the concept taps a vein of emotional confusion about our progeny, whom we both love and to whom we express kindness with hurt.

Mounting attention to the developmental sequelae of child abuse[10] stimulates an extra urgency not only to insure the physical safety of the identified victims but also to enable their adequate psychological development. The dangers of child abuse, Schmitt and Kempe assert in the latest edition of the Nelson Textbook of Pediatrics,[11] extend beyond harm to the victim:

> If the child who has been physically abused is returned to his parents without intervention, 5 percent are killed and 35 percent are seriously reinjured. Moreover, the untreated families tend to produce children who grow up to be juvenile delinquents and murderers, as well as the child batterers of the next generation.

Despite the speculative nature of such conclusions about the developmental sequelae of child abuse,[12] such warnings support a practice of separating children from their natural homes in the interest of their and society's protection. They focus professional concern and public wrath on 'the untreated families' and may justify punitive action to save us from their children.

This professional response of control rather than of compassion furthermore generalizes mainly to poor and socially marginal families, for it is they who seem preferentially to attract the labels 'abuse' and 'neglect' to their problems in the public setting where they go for most health and social services. Affluent families' childhood injuries appear more likely to be termed 'accidents' by the private practitioners who offer them their services. The conceptual model of cause and effect im-

TABLE ONE

Dilemmas of Social Policy and Professional Response

Response	Family Autonomy	Versus	Coercive Intervention
Compassion ('support')	1 Voluntary child development services		1 Case reporting of family crisis and mandated family intervention
	2 Guaranteed family supports: *e.g.*, income, housing, health services		2 Court-ordered delivery of services
___Versus___			
Control ('punishment')	1 "Laissez-faire": No assured services or supports		1 Court action to separate child from family
	2 Retributive response to family crisis		2 Criminal prosecution of parents

plicit in the name 'accident' is benign: an isolated, random event rather than a consequence of parental commission or omission.[13]

Table One presents a graphic display of the two dilemmas of social policy *(Family Autonomy versus Coercive Intervention)* and professional response *(Compassion versus Control)*. The four-fold table illustrates possible action responses. For purposes of this discussion, it is well to think of 'compassion' as signifying responses of support, such as provision of voluntary counseling and child care services, and 'control' as signifying such punitive responses as 'blaming the victim' for his/her reaction to social realities and as the criminal prosecution of abusing parents.

The Relationship Between Child Abuse and the Professions of Medicine and Law

The importance of a technical discipline's conceptual structure in defining how it approaches a problem is clearly stated by Mercer:[14]

> Each discipline is organized around a core of basic concepts and assumptions which form the frame of reference from which persons trained in that discipline view the world and set about solving problems in their field. The concepts and assumptions which make up the perspective of each discipline give each its distinctive character and are the intellectual tools used by its practitioners. These tools are incorporated in action and problem solving and appear self-evident to persons socialized in the discipline. As a result, little consideration is likely to be given to the social consequence of applying a particular conceptual framework to problem solving.
>
> When the issues to be resolved are clearly in the area of competence of a single discipline, the automatic application of its conceptual tools is likely to go unchallenged. However, when the problems under consideration lie in the interstices between disciplines, the disciplines concerned are likely to define the situation differently and may arrive at differing conclusions which have dissimilar implications for social action.

What we do when children are injured in family crises is shaped also by how our professions respond to the interstitial area called 'child abuse.'

Though cruelty to children has occurred since documentary records of mankind have been kept,[15] it became a salient social problem only after the publication by Kempe and his colleagues describing the 'battered child syndrome'.[16] In the four-year period after this medical article appeared, the legislatures of all fifty states, stimulated partly by a model law developed under the aegis of the Children's Bureau of the U.S. Department of Health, Education, and Welfare, passed statutes mandating the identification and reporting of suspected victims of abuse.

Once the specific diagnostic category "battered child syndrome' was applied to integrate a set of medical symptoms and laws were passed making the syndrome reportable, the problem was made a proper and legitimate concern for the medical profession. Conrad has discussed cogently how 'hyperactivity' came officially to be known and how it became 'medicalized'.[17] Medicalization is defined in this paper as the perception of behavior as a medical problem or illness and the mandating or licensing of the medical profession to provide some type of treatment for it.

Pfohl associates the publicity surrounding the battered child syndrome report with a phenomenon of 'discovery' of child abuse. For radiologists, the potential for increased prestige, role expansion, and coalition formation (with psychodynamic psychiatry and pediatrics) may have encouraged identification and intervention in child abuse. Furthermore,

> . . . [T]he discovery of abuse as a new 'illness' reduced drastically the intraorganizational constraints on doctors' 'seeing' abuse. . . . Problems associated with perceiving parents as patients whose confidentiality must be protected were reconstructed by typifying them as patients who needed help. . . . The maintenance of professional autonomy was assured by pairing deviance with sickness. . .[18]

In some ways, medicine's 'discovery' of abuse has benefited individual physicians and the profession. "One of the greatest ambitions of the physician is to discover or describe a 'new' disease or syndrome."[19] By such involvement the doctor becomes a moral entrepreneur defining what is normal, proper, or desirable: he becomes charged "with inquisitorial powers to discover certain wrongs to be righted."[20] New opportunities for the application of traditional methods are also found as, for example, the systematic screening of suspected victims with a skeletal X-ray survey to detect previous fractures and the recent report in the neurology literature suggesting the utility of diphenylhydantoin* treatment for child abusing parents.[21]

Pfohl's provocative analysis also takes note of some of the normative and structural elements within the medical profession which appear to have reinforced a *reluctance* on the part of some physicians to become involved: the norm of confidentiality between doctor and patient and the goal of professional autonomy.[22]

For many physicians child abuse is a subject to avoid.[23] *First*, it is difficult to distinguish, on a theoretical level, corporal punishment that is 'acceptable' from that which is 'illegitimate'. Abuse may be defined variably even by specialists, the definitions ranging from serious physical injury to non-fulfillment of a child's developmental needs.[24] *Second*, it is frequently hard to diagnose child abuse clinically. What appears on casual physical examination as bruising, for example, may turn out to be a skin manifestation of an organic blood dysfunction, or what appear to be cigarette burns may in reality be infected mosquito bites. A diagnosis of abuse

---

* Dilantin, a commonly-used seizure suppressant.

may require social and psychological information about the family, the acquisition and interpretation of which may be beyond the average clinician's expertise.

It may be easier to characterize the clinical complaint in terms of the child's medical symptom rather than in terms of the social, familial, and psychological forces associated with its etiology. We see daily situations where the exclusive choice of medical taxonomy actively obscures the causes of the child's symptom and restricts the range of possible interventions: examples are 'subdural hematoma' which frequently occurs with severe trauma to babies' heads (the medical name means collection of blood under the *dura mater* of the brain) and 'enuresis' or 'encopresis' in child victims of sexual assault (the medical names mean incontinence of urine or feces).

Third, child abuse arouses strong emotions. To concentrate on the narrow medical issue (the broken bone) instead of the larger familial problem (the etiology of the injury) not only allows one to avoid facing the limits of one's technical adequacy, but to shield oneself from painful feelings of sadness and anger. One can thus maintain professional detachment and avert unpleasant confrontations. The potentially alienating nature of the physician-patient interaction when the diagnosis of child abuse is made may also have a negative economic impact on the doctor, especially the physician in private practice.

'Legalization' and Its Problems

The legal response to child abuse was triggered by its medicalization. Child abuse reporting statutes codified a medical diagnosis into a legal framework which in many states defined official functions for courts. Immunity from civil liability was given to mandated reporters so long as reports were made in good faith, monetary penalties for failure to report were established, and familial and professional-client confidentiality privileges, except those involving attorneys, were abrogated.

Professional autonomy for lawyers was established, and status and power accrued to legal institutions. For example, the growth in the number of Care and Protection cases* before the Boston Juvenile Court "has been phenomenal in recent years . . . four cases in 1968 and 99 in 1974, involving 175 different children."[25] Though these cases have burdened court dockets and personnel, they have also led to acknowledgement of the important work of the court. The need for this institution is enhanced because of its recognized expertise in handling special matters. Care and Protection cases are cited in response to recommendations by a prestigious commission charged with proposing reform and consolidation of the courts in Massachusetts. Child protection work in our own institution would proceed only with difficulty if access to the court were legally or procedurally constrained. Just as for the medical profession, however, there were normative and structural elements within law which urged restraint. Most important among them were the traditional presumptions and practices favoring family autonomy.

If individual lawyers might financially benefit from representing clients in matters pertaining to child abuse, they—like their physician counterparts—were personally uncertain whether or how to become involved.

---

* Care and Protection cases are those juvenile or family court actions which potentially transfer, on a temporary or permanent basis, legal and/or physical custody of a child from his biological parents to the state.

Public concern over the scope and significance of the problem of the battered child is a comparatively new phenomenon. Participation by counsel in any significant numbers in child abuse cases in juvenile or family courts is of even more recent origin. It is small wonder that the lawyer approaches participation in these cases with trepidation.[26]

Lawyers, too, feel handicapped by a need to rely on concepts from social work and psychiatry and data from outside the traditional domain of legal knowledge and expertise. As counsel to parents, lawyers can be torn between advocacy of their clients' positions and that which advances the 'best interest' of their clients' children. As counsel to the petitioner, a lawyer may have to present a case buttressed by little tangible evidence. Risk to a child is often difficult to characterize and impossible to prove.

Further problems for lawyers concerned with child abuse involve the context of intervention: whether courts or legislatures should play the major role in shaping practice and allocating resources; how much formality is desirable in legal proceedings; and the propriety of negotiation as opposed to adversary confrontation when cases come to court.

Conflicts Between Medical and Legal Perspectives

Despite the common reasons for the 'medicalization' and the 'legalization' of child abuse, there are several areas where the two orientations conflict:

(1) The Seriousness of the Risk

To lawyers intervention might be warranted only when abuse results in serious harm to a child. To clinicians, however, *any* inflicted injury might justify a protective legal response, especially if the child is very young. "The trick is to prevent the abusive case from becoming the terminal case."[27] Early intervention may prevent the abuse from being repeated or from becoming more serious.

(2) The Definition of the Abuser

To lawyers the abuser might be defined as a wrongdoer who has injured a child. To clinicians both the abuser and child might be perceived as victims influenced by sociological and psychological factors beyond their control.[28]

(3) The Importance of the Abuser's Mental State

To lawyers whether the abuser intentionally or accidentally inflicted injury on a child is a necessary condition of reporting or judicial action. So-called 'accidents' are less likely to trigger intervention. To clinicians, however, mental state may be less relevant, for it requires a diagnostic formulation frequently difficult or impossible to make on the basis of available data. The family dynamics which are associated with 'accidents' in some children (*e.g.* stress, marital conflict and parental inattention) often resemble those linked with inflicted injury in others. They are addressed with variable clinical sensitivity and precision.

(4) The Role of Law

Attorneys are proudly unwilling to accept conclusions or impressions lacking empirical corroboration. To lawyers the law and legal institutions become involved in child abuse when certain facts fit a standard of review. To clinicians, the law may be seen as an instrument to achieve a particular therapeutic or dispositional objective (*e.g.*, the triggering of services or of social welfare involvement) even if, as is most often the case, the data to legally support such objectives are missing or ambiguous. The clinician's approach to the abuse issue is frequently subjective or intuitive (*e.g., a feeling* that a family is under stress or needs help, or that a child is 'at risk') while the lawyer demands evidence.

Doctoring and Lawyering the Disease

These potential or actual differences in orientation notwithstanding, both medicine and law have accepted in principle the therapeutic approach to child abuse.

To physicians, defining abuse as a disease or medical syndrome makes natural the treatment alternative, since both injured child and abuser are viewed as 'sick'—the one, physically, the other psychologically or socially. Therapy may, however, have retributive aspects, as pointed out with characteristic pungency by Illich:

> The medical label may protect the patient from punishment only to submit him to interminable instruction, treatment, and discrimination, which are inflicted on him for his professional presumed benefit.[29]

Lawyers adopt a therapeutic perspective for the following reasons:

(1) The rehabilitative ideal remains in ascendance in criminal law, especially in the juvenile and family courts which handle most child abuse cases.[30]

(2) The criminal or punitive model may not protect the child. Parents may hesitate to seek help if they are fearful of prosecution. Evidence of abuse is often insufficient to satisfy the standard of conviction beyond a 'reasonable doubt' in criminal proceedings. If an alleged abuser is threatened with punishment and then found not guilty, he/she may feel vindicated, reinforcing the pattern of abuse. In fact, they may well be legally freed from any scrutiny, and badly needed social services will not be able to be provided. Even if found guilty, the perpetrator of abuse is usually given only mild punishment, such as a short jail term or probation. If the abuser is incarcerated, the other family members may equally suffer as, for example, the relationship between spouses is undercut and childrearing falls on one parent, or children are placed in foster home care or with relatives. Upon release from jail, the abuser may be no less violent and even more aggressive and vindictive toward the objects of abuse.

(3) The fact that child abuse was 'discovered' by physicians influenced the model adopted by other professionals. As Friedson notes: "Medical definitions of deviance have come to be adopted even where there is no reliable evidence that biophysical variables 'cause' the deviance or that medical treatment is any more efficacious than any other kind of management."[31] Weber, in addition, contends that 'status' groups (*e.g.*, physicians) generally determine the content of law.[32]

The Selective Implementation of Treatment

Medical intervention is generally encouraged by the Hippocratic ideology of treatment, or the ethic that help, not harm, is given by practitioners, and by what Scheff calls the medical decision rule: it is better to wrongly diagnose illness and 'miss' health than it is to wrongly diagnose health and 'miss' illness.[33]

Physicians, in defining aberrant behavior as a medical problem and in providing treatment, become what sociologists call agents of social control. Though the technical enterprise of the physician claims value-free power, socially marginal individuals are more likely to be defined as deviant than are others.

Characteristics frequently identified with the 'battered child syndrome', such as social isolation, alcoholism, unemployment, childhood handicap, large family size, low level of parental educational achievement, and acceptance of severe physical punishment as a childhood socializing technique, are associated with social marginality and poverty.

Physicians in public settings seem from child abuse reporting statistics to be more likely to see and report child abuse than are those in private practice. As poor people are more likely to frequent hospital emergency wards and clinics, they have much greater social visibility where child abuse is concerned than people of means.

The fact that child abuse is neither theoretically nor clinically well defined increases the likelihood of subjective professional evaluation. In labeling theory it is axiomatic that the greater the social distance between the typer and the person singled out for typing, the broader the type and the more quickly it may be applied.[34]

In the doctor-patient relationship, the physician is always in a superordinate position because of his/her expertise; social distance is inherent to the relationship. This distance necessarily increases once the label of abuser has been applied. Importantly, the label is less likely to be fixed if the diagnostician and possible abuser share similar characteristics, especially socioeconomic status. If the inquiry is serious or manifestly a consequence of maltreatment, however, the less likely would social class influence the labeling process.

Once the label 'abuser' has attached, it is very difficult to remove, so even innocent behavior of a custodian may be viewed with suspicion. The tenacity of a label increases as does the official processing. At our own institution, until quite recently, a red star was stamped on the permanent medical record of any child who might have been abused, a process which encouraged professionals to suspect child abuse (and to act on that assumption) at any future time that the child would present with a medical problem.

Professionals thus engage in an intricate process of selection, finding facts which fit the label which has been applied, responding to a few deviant details set within a panoply of entirely acceptable conduct. (Schur calls this phenomenon 'retrospective reinterpretation'.)[35] In any pathological model "persons are likely to be studied in terms of what is 'wrong' with them", there being a "decided emphasis on identifying the characteristics of abnormality"; in child abuse it may be administratively impossible to return to health, as is shown by the extraordinary durability of case reports in state central registers.

The response of the patient to the agent of social control affects the perceptions and behavior of the controller. If, for example, a child has been injured and the alleged perpetrator is repentant, a consensus can develop between abuser and labeller that a norm has been violated. In this situation, the label of 'abuser' may be less firmly applied than if the abuser defends his/her behavior as proper. Support for this formulation is found in studies by Gusfield,[36] who noted different reactions to repentant, sick and enemy deviants, and by Piliavin and Briar,[37] who showed that juveniles apprehended by the police receive more lenient treatment if they appear contrite and remorseful about their violations.

The Consequences of Treatment for the Abuser

Once abuse is defined as a sickness, it becomes a condition construed to be beyond the actor's control.[38] Though treatment, not punishment, is warranted, the *type* of treatment depends on whether or not the abuser is 'curable', 'improvable' or 'incurable' and on the speed with which such a state can be achieved.[39]

To help the abuser is generally seen as a less important goal than is the need to protect the child. If the abusive behavior cannot quickly be altered, and the child remains 'at risk', the type of intervention will differ accordingly (*e.g.*, the child may be more likely to be placed in a foster home). The less 'curable' is the abuser, the less treatment will be offered and the more punitive will society's response appear. Ironically, even the removal of a child from his parents, a move nearly always perceived as punitive by parents, is often portrayed as helpful by the professionals doing the removing ('It will give you a chance to resolve your own problems', *etc.*). Whatever the treatment, there are predictable consequences for those labelled 'abusers'.

Prior to diagnosis, parents may be afraid of 'getting caught' because of punishment and social stigma. On being told of clinicians' concerns, they may express hostility because of implicit or explicit criticism made of them and their childrearing practices yet feel relief because they love their children and want help in stopping their destructive behavior. The fact that they see themselves as 'sick' may increase their willingness to seek help. This attitude is at least in part due to the lesser social stigma attached to the 'sick', as opposed to the 'criminal', label.

Socially marginal individuals are likely to accept whatever definition more powerful labellers apply. This definition, of course, has already been accepted by much of the larger community because of the definers' power. As Davis writes:

> The chance that a group will get community support for its definition of unacceptable deviance depends on its relative power position. The greater the group's size, resources, efficiency, unity, articulateness, prestige, coordination with other groups, and access to the mass media and to decision-makers, the more likely it is to get its preferred norms legitimated.[40]

Acceptance of definition by the child abusers, however, is not based alone on the power of the labellers. Though some would consider the process 'political castration',[41] in fact as long as he is defined as 'ill' and takes on the sick role the abuser is achieving a more satisfactory label and role. Though afflicted with a stigmatized illness (and thus "gaining few if any privileges and taking on some especially handicapping new obligations")[42] he at least is sick rather than sinful or criminal.

Effective social typing flows down rather than up the social structure. For example, when both parents induct one of their children into the family scapegoat role, this is an effective social typing because the child is unable not to take their definition of him into account even if he so wishes.[43] Sometimes it is difficult to know whether an abusive parent has actually accepted the definition or is merely 'role playing' in order to please the definer. If a person receives conflicting messages from the same control agent (*e.g.*, 'you are sick and criminal') or from different control agents in the treatment network (*e.g.*, from doctors who use the sick label, while lawyers use the criminal), confusion and upset predictably result.[44]

As an example of how social definitions are accepted by the group being defined, it is interesting to examine the basic tenets of Parents Anonymous, which began as a self-help group for abusive mothers:

> A destructive, *disturbed* mother can, and often does, produce through her actions a physically or emotionally abused, or battered child. Present available *help* is limited and/or expensive, usually with a long waiting list before the person requesting help can actually receive *treatment* . . . We must understand that a problem as involved as this cannot be *cured* immediately . . . the problem is *within us* as a parent . . .[45]

To Parents Anonymous child abuse appears to be a medical problem, and abusers are sick persons who must be treated.

The Consequences of Treatment for the Social System

The individual and the social system are interrelated; each influences the other. Thus, if society defines abusive parents as sick there will be few criminal prosecutions for abuse; reports will generally be sent to welfare, as opposed to police departments.

Since victims of child abuse are frequently treated in hospitals, medical personnel become brokers for adult services and definers of children's rights. Once abuse is defined, that is, people may get services (such as counseling, child care, and homemaker services) which would be otherwise unavailable to them, and children might get care and protection impossible without institutional intervention.

If, as is customary, however, resources are in short supply, the preferred treatment of a case may not be feasible. Under this condition, less adequate treatment stratagems, or even clearly punitive alternatives, may be implemented. If day care and competent counseling are unavailable, court action and foster placement can become the only options. As Stoll observes, "(T)he best therapeutic intentions may be led astray when opportunities to implement theoretical guidelines are not available."[46]

Treating child abuse as a sickness has, ironically, made it more difficult to 'cure'. There are not enough therapists to handle all of the diagnosed cases. Nor do most abusive parents have the time, money or disposition for long-term therapeutic involvement. Many, moreover, lack the introspective and conceptual abilities required for successful psychological therapy.

As Parents Anonymous emphasizes, abuse is the *abuser's* problem. Its causes and solutions are widely understood to reside in individuals rather than in the social system.[47] Indeed the strong emphasis on child abuse as an individual problem means that other equally severe problems of childhood can be ignored, and the unequal distribution of social and economic resources in society can be masked.[48] The child abuse phenomenon itself may also increase as parents and professionals are obliged to 'package' their problems and diagnoses in a competitive market where services are in short supply.

As Tannenbaum observed in 1938:

> Societal reactions to deviance can be characterized as a kind of 'dramatization of evil' such that a person's deviance is made a public issue. The stronger the reaction to the evil, the more it seems to grow. The reaction itself seems to generate the very thing it sought to eliminate.[49]

Conclusion: Dispelling the Myth of Child Abuse

As clinicians, we are convinced that with intelligence, humanity, and the application of appropriate interventions, we can help families in crisis. We believe, however, that short of coming to terms with—and changing—certain social, political, and economic aspects of our society, we will never be able adequately to understand and address the origins of child abuse and neglect. Nor will the issues of labeling be adequately resolved unless we deal straightforwardly with the potentially abusive power of the helping professions. If we can bring ourselves to ask such questions as 'Can we legislate child abuse out of existence?' and 'Who benefits from child abuse?' then perhaps we can more rationally choose among the action alternatives displayed in the conceptual model *(Table One)*.

Although we would prefer to avoid coercion and punishment, and to keep families autonomous and services voluntary, we must acknowledge the realities of family life and posit some state role to assure the wellbeing of children. In making explicit the assumptions and values underpinning our professional actions, perhaps we can promote a more informed and humane practice.

Because it is likely that clinical interventions will continue to be class and culture-based, we propose the following five guidelines to minimize the abuse of power of the definer.

(1) Give Physicians, Social Workers, Lawyers and other Intervention Agents Social Science Perspectives and Skills

Critical intellectual tools should help clinicians to understand the implications of their work, and, especially, the functional meaning of the labels they apply in their practices.

Physicians need to be more aware of the complexity of human life, especially its social and psychological dimensions. The 'medical model' is not of itself inappropriate; rather, the conceptual bases of medical practice need to be broadened, and the intellectual and scientific repertory of the practitioner expanded.[50] Diagnostic formulation is an active process and it carries implicitly an anticipation of intervention and outcome. The simple elegance of concepts like 'child abuse' and 'child neglect' militate for simple and radical treatments.

Lawyers might be helped to learn that in child custody cases they are not merely advocates of a particular position. Only the child should 'win' a custody case, where, for example, allegations of 'abuse' or 'neglect', skillfully marshalled, may support the position of the more effectively represented parent, guardian, or social worker.

(2) Acknowledge and Change the Prestige Hierarchy of Helping Professions

The workers who seem best to be able to conceptualize the familial and social context of problems of violence are social workers and nurses. They are least paid, most overworked, and have as a rule minimal access to the decision prerogatives of medicine and law. We would add that social work and nursing are professions largely of and by women, and we believe we must objectively come to terms with the many realities—including sexual dominance and subservience—which make these professions unable to carry forth with appropriate respect and support. (We have made a modest effort in this direction at our own institution, where our interdisciplinary child abuse consultation program is organized under the aegis of the administration rather than of a medical clinical department. This is to foster to the extent possible colleagial status and communication on a coequal footing among the disciplines represented in the Trauma X Group (social work, nursing, law, medicine, and psychiatry).)

(3) Build Theory

We need urgently a commonly understandable dictionary of concepts which will guide and inform a rational practice. A more adequate theory base would include a more etiologic (or causal) classification scheme for children's injuries which would acknowledge and integrate diverse origins and expressions of social, familial, child developmental, and environmental phenomena. It would conceptualize strength in families and children as well as pathology. It would orient intervenors to the promotion of health rather than to the treatment of pathology.

A unified theory would permit coming to terms with the universe of need. At present, socially marginal and poor children are virtually the only ones susceptible to being diagnosed as victims of abuse and neglect. More affluent families' offspring, whose injuries are called 'accidents' and who are often unprotected, are not included in 'risk' populations. We have seen examples of court defense where it was argued (successfully) that because the family was not poor, they did not fit the classic archetypes of abuse or neglect.

The needs and rights of all children need legally to be spelled out in relation to the responsibilities of parents and the state. This is easier said than done. It shall require not only a formidable effort at communication across disciplinary lines but a serious coming to terms with social and political values and realities.

(4) Change Social Inequality

We share Gil's[51] view that inequality is the basic problem underlying the labeling of 'abusive families' and its consequences. Just as children without defined rights are *ipso facto* vulnerable, so too, does unequal access to the resources and goods of society shape a class hierarchy which leads to the individualization of social problems. Broadly-focused efforts for social change should accompany a critical review of the ethical foundations for professional practice. As part of his/her formation as doctor, lawyer, social worker, or police officer, there could be developed for the professional a notion of public service and responsibility. This would enable individuals to see themselves as participants in a social process and to perceive the problems which they address in their work at the social as well as the individual level of action.

(5) Assure Adequate Representation of Class and Ethnic Groups in Decision-Making Forums

Since judgments about family competency can be affected by class and ethnic biases, they should be made in settings where prejudices can be checked and controlled. Culture-bound value judgments in child protection work are not infrequent, and a sufficient participation in case management conferences of professionals of equal rank and status and diverse ethnicity can assure both a more appropriate context for decision making and better decisions for children and their families.

NOTES

1.   KEMPE, C. Henry, and HELFER, Ray E. (eds.), *Helping the Battered Child and His Family*. Phil., Pennsylvania: Lippincott, 1972.

2.   BOURNE, Richard, and NEWBERGER, Eli H., " 'Family Autonomy' or 'Coercive Intervention'? Ambiguity and Conflict in a Proposed Juvenile Justice Standard in Child Protection" (1977), 57 *Boston University Law Review* No. 4 670-706. See also Juvenile Justice Standards Project (1977), *Standards Relating to Abuse and Neglect*.

3.   *Ingraham v. Wright*, 45LW 4364 U.S. Supreme Court, 1977.

4.   *Landeros v. Flood*, 131 Calif. R Ptr 69, 1976.

5.   CURRAN, William J., "Failure to Diagnose Battered Child Syndrome" (1977), 296 *New England Journal of Medicine* 795-796.

6.   Juvenile Justice Standards Project (1977), *Standards Relating to Abuse and Neglect*.

7.   BOURNE, Richard and NEWBERGER, Eli H., *op. cit.*, note 2.

8.   ROSENFELD, Alvin A., and NEWBERGER, Eli H., "Compassion Versus Control: Conceptual and Practical Pitfalls in the Broadened Definition of Child Abuse" 237 *Journal of the American Medical Association* No. 19, 2086-2088.

9.   GOLDSTEIN, Joseph R.; FREUD, A.; and SOLNIT, A., *Beyond the Best Interests of the Child*, New York, New York: Free Press, 1973.

10.   GALDSTON, Richard, "Violence Begins at Home" (1971), 10 *Journal of the American Academy of Child Psychiatry* No. 2, 336-350. See also, Martin, Harold P. (ed.). *The Abused Child: A Multidisciplinary Approach to Developmental Issues and Treatment*, Cambridge, Mass.: Ballinger, 1976.

11.   SCHMITT, B. D., and KEMPE, C. H., "Neglect and Abuse of Children", in Vaughan, V. D., and McKay, R. J. (eds.), *Nelson Textbook of Pediatrics* (10th ed.), Phil., Pennsylvania: Saunders, 1975, pp. 107-111.

12.   ELMER, Elizabeth, "A Follow-up Study of Traumatized Children" (1977), 59 *Pediatrics* No. 2, 273-279; and Elmer, Elizabeth, *Fragile Families, Troubled Children* (1977).

13.   NEWBERGER, Eli H., and DANIEL, Jessica, "Knowledge and Epidemiology of Child Abuse: A critical Review of Concepts" (1976), 5 *Pediatrics Annals* No. 3, 140-144; and Newberger, Eli H.; Reed, R. B.; Daniel, Jessica; Hyde, James N.; and Kotelchuck, M., "Pediatric Social Illness: Toward an Etiologic Classification" (1977), *60 Pediatrics* 178-185.

14. MERCER, Jane R., "Who is Normal? Two Perspectives on Mild Mental Retardation", in Jaco, E. G. (ed.), *Patients, Physicians and Illness* (2nd ed), New York, New York: Free Press, 1972.

15. de MAUSE, Lloyd (ed.), *The History of Childhood*. New York, New York: Psycho-history Press, 1974.

16. KEMPE, C. Henry, *et. al.*, "The Battered Child Syndrome" (July 7, 1962), 181 *Journal of the American Medical Association* 17-24.

17. CONRAD, P., "The Discovery of Hyperkinesis: Notes on the Medicalization of Deviant Behavior" (Oct., 1975), 23 (10) *Social Problems* 12-21.

18. PFOHL, Stephen J., "The Discovery of Child Abuse" (1977), 24(2) *Social Problems* No. 2, 310-323.

19. ILLICH, Ivan, *Medical Nemesis: The Expropriation of Health* (1976).

20. *Ibid.*

21. ROSENBLATT, S.; SCHAEFFER, D.; and ROSENTHAL, J. S., "Effects of Diphenylhydantoin on Child-Abusing Parents: A Preliminary Report" (1976), 19 (3) *Current Therapeutic Research* 332-336.

22. *Op cit.*, note 18.

23. SANDERS, R. W., "Resistance to Dealing With Parents of Battered Children" (1972), 50 *Pediatrics* No. 6, 853-857.

24. *Op. cit.*, note 16., see also Fontana, Vincent J., *The Maltreated Child: the Maltreatment Syndrome in Children* (2nd. ed.) Springfield, Illinois: C. C. Thomas, 1974., Gil, David G., "Unravelling Child Abuse" (1975), 45 (4) *American Journal of Orthopsychiatry* 346-356.

25. POITRAST, Francis G., "The Judicial Dilemma in Child Abuse Cases" (1976), 13 *Psychiatric Opinion* 22-28.

26. ISAACS, Jacob L., "The Role of the Lawyer in Child Abuse Cases", in Helfer, R. E., and Kempe, C. H. (eds.), *Helping the Battered Child and His Family*. Phil., Pennsylvania: Lippincott, 1972.

27. *Op. cit.*, note 6.

28. GELLES, Richard J., "Child Abuse as Psychopathology: A Sociological Critique and Reformulation" (1973), 43(4) *American Journal of Orthopsychiatry* 611-621; see also Newberger, Eli H., "The Myth of the Battered Child Syndrome" (1973), 30 *Current Medical Dialog.* 327-334. Reprinted in, Chess, S., and Thomas A. (eds.) *Annual Progress in Child Psychiatry and Child Development*. New York, New York: Brunner Mazel, 1974.

29. ILLICH, Ivan, *Medical Nemesis: The Expropriation of Health*, New York: Random House, 1976.

30. ALLEN, Francis A., *The Borderland of Criminal Justice*. Chicago, Illinois: University of Chicago Press, 1964.

31. FREIDSON, Eliot, *Profession of Medicine: A Study of the Sociology of Applied Knowledge*. New York, New York: Dodd Mead, 1970.

32. RHEINSTEIN, Max (ed.), *Max Weber on Law in Economy and Society*. Cambridge, Mass.: Harvard University Press, 1954.

33. SCHEFF, Thomas J., "Decision Rules, Types of Error, and Their Consequences in Medical Diagnosis", in Freidson, E., and Lorber, J. (eds.), *Medical Men and Their Work*. Chicago, Illinois: Aldine, 1972.

34. RUBINGTON, Earl and WEINBERG, Martin S., *Deviance: The Interactionist Perspective*. New York, New York: Macmillan, 1973.

35.   SCHUR, Edwin, *Labeling Deviant Behavior*. New York, New York: Harper & Row, 1971.

36.   GUSFIELD, Joseph R., "Moral Passage: the Symbolic Process in Public Designations of Deviance" (Fall, 1967), 15 (2) *Social Problems* 175-188.

37.   PILIAVIN, Irving and BRIAR, Scott, "Police Encounters With Juveniles" (1964), 70 (2) *American Journal of Sociology* No. 9, 206-214.

38.   PARSONS, Talcott, *The Social System*. New York, New York: Free Press, 1951.

39.   *Op. cit.*, note 31.

40.   DAVIS, F. James, "Beliefs, Values, Power and Public Definitions of Deviance", in Davis, F. James and Stivers, R. (ed.), *The Collective Definition of Deviance*. New York, New York: Free Press, 1975.

41.   PITTS, Jesse R., "Social Control: the Concept", in *The International Encyclopedia of the Social Sciences*, Vol. 14, New York, New York: Macmillan, 1968, p. 391.

42.   *Op. cit.*, note 31.

43.   *Op. cit.*, note 34.

44.   STOLL, Clarice S., "Images of Man and Social Control" (1968), 47 (2) *Social Forces* No. 12, 119-127.

45.   *Op. cit.*, note 1.

46.   *Op. cit.*, note 44.

47.   GELLES, Richard J., *op. cit.*, note 28; see also Conrad, P., *op. cit.*, note 17.

48.   GIL, David G., *Violence Against Children*. Cambridge, Mass.: Harvard University Press, 1970.

49.   TANNENBAUM, Frank, *Crime and the Community*. New York, New York: Columbia University Press, 1938.

50.   ENGEL, George L., "The Need for a New Medical Model: A Challenge For Biomedicine" (1977), 196 (4) *Science* 129-136.

51.   *Op. cit.*, note 48.

REFERENCES

BECKER, Howard S., *Outsiders: Studies in the Sociology of Deviance*. New York, New York: Free Press, 1963.

CHAMBLISS, William J., "A Sociological Analysis of the Law of Vagrancy" (Fall, 1964), 12 *Social Problems* 67-77.

CUPOLI, Michael, J., and NEWBERGER, Eli H., "Optimism or Pessimism for the Victim of Child Abuse?" (1977), 59 (2) *Pediatrics* 311-314.

FRASER, Brian, "Legislative Status of Child Abuse Legislation," in Kempe, C. H., and Helfer, R. (eds.), *Child Abuse and Neglect: The Family and the Community*. Cambridge, Mass.: Ballinger, 1976.

GELLES, Richard J., "Violence Towards Children in the United States", paper presented at the annual meeting of the American Association for the Advancement of Science, Denver, Feb., 1977.

HYDE, James N., "Uses and Abuses of Information in Protective Services Contexts", *Fifth National Symposium on Child Abuse and Neglect*, Denver, 1974, pp. 56-62.

JOINT COMMISSION ON THE MENTAL HEALTH OF CHILDREN (1970), *Crisis in Child Mental Health*. New York: Harper & Row.

KITTRIE, Nicholas, *The Right to Be Different*. Baltimore, Maryland: John Hopkins University Press, 1971.

NEWBERGER, Eli H.; NEWBERGER, Carolyn; and RICHMOND, Julius, "Child Health in America: Toward a Rational Public Policy" (1976), 54 (2) *Milbank Memorial Fund Quarterly/Health and Society* No. 3, 249-298.

PAULSEN, Monrad, "Juvenile Courts, Family Courts, and the Poor Man" (1966), 54 *California Law Review* 694-716.

RYAN, W., *Blaming the Victim*. New York, New York: Random House, 1971.

SCHEFF, Thomas J., *Being Mentally Ill: A Sociological Theory*. Chicago, Illinois: Aldine, 1966.

SCHRAG, Peter and DIVOKY, Diane, *The Myth of the Hyperactive Child*. New York, New York: Pantheon, 1975.

WHITING, Leila, "The Central Registry for Child Abuse Cases: Rethinking Basic Assumptions" (1977), 56 (2) *Child Welfare*, 761-767.

34

Forgotten Children: Maltreated Children of Mentally Retarded Parents*

Lucy S. Crain, M.D., M.P.H. and
Georgia K. Millor, R.N., M.S.

It is estimated that at least 1 million developmentally disabled adults, half of whom are mentally retarded, now reside in communities throughout the United States.[1,2] With recent emphasis on increased independence, normalization, and reaffirmation of the civil rights of mentally retarded persons, many are now experiencing nonsheltered adult lives and marriage. As emancipated adults, childbearing and childrearing may follow, but few if any communities have developed adequate supportive services for meeting the needs of these mentally retarded parents and their children.

Although there is a lack of data on the prevalence of parenting problems among mentally retarded adults,[3] abuse and neglect have been repeatedly implicated as etiologic factors in mental retardation. In a computer-assisted search of the

* Lucy S. Crain and Georgia K. Millor, "Forgotten Children: Maltreated Children of Mentally Retarded Parents," *Pediatrics*, Vol. 61, No. 1 (January, 1978):130-132. Copyright © American Academy of Pediatrics, 1978. Reproduced by permission.

literature of the last ten years, we found no publication on the association of parental mental retardation and child abuse. The routine practice of removing children from the care of mentally handicapped parents may have precluded the necessity of addressing this issue in the past.

This is a report of our experience with one family in which one or both of the mentally retarded parents abused their sons. The report illustrates the usual problems of parenting intensified by limited parental intellectual capabilities.

The Family

The family consists of mother, father, and two sons. The parents have been married six years and both children were products of planned pregnancies. They live in a one-bedroom apartment in a low-rent residential section of a cosmopolitan city. Although the family is known to many agencies within the city and the grandparents reside in the community, the parents, because of their mental retardation, have difficulty initiating appropriate contacts and utilizing the assistance of potentially supportive persons in either the extended family or community.

The etiology of the parents' mental retardation is attributed to childhood encephalitis for the father and to cerebral trauma secondary to a childhood automobile accident for the mother. From ages 7 to 27, the father resided in a state hospital from which he was discharged to a local group home, where he lived for two years until his marriage. The mother lived with her family and graduated from a local school program for the educably mentally retarded. The couple met when both participated in a sheltered workshop for developmentally disabled adults.

Following their marriage, the father suspected his wife of marital infidelity. He frequently terminated employment to stay at home and monitor his wife's activities. The group home operator, identified by the father as his "foster father," arranged marital counseling for the couple with a private psychiatrist. Their compliance with the counseling was sporadic.

Their first son was born after two years of marriage. Within a few weeks after his birth, one of the mother's former suitors reported his suspicion of child abuse to Children's Protective Services (CPS) but investigation by CPS produced no evidence to confirm this. The case was reopened after another friend of the parents complained to CPS about parental mistreatment of the child. The medical records document numerous acute-care visits for bruises and minor injuries attributed to accidents. After he was enrolled in a day-care center at the age of 3 years, no "accidental" injuries were reported.

The second son was born after 3-1/2 years of marriage. He seemed "special" to his mother, and there was strong mother-son identification. She consistently reported his personality to be similar to that of his sibling at the same age, but frequently commented that he was "clumsy like his mother." He received preferential treatment in the home and had more toys than his older brother. Additional evidence of inappropriate attachment to his mother was noted in her reinforcement of infantile language and dependency patterns and her preference to carry him or keep him in a stroller rather than permit him to walk independently. When counseled regarding this and the need for limit-setting, she responded that it was easier to "keep him out of trouble" if he was physically confined.

According to the father, he was "responsible" for the first son and his wife was "responsible" for the second son. Clarification of this statement revealed that the parents had deliberately chosen the child to be identified as his or her own parenting "responsibility" in order to enable each parent to then "blame" the responsible parent when "his/her" child misbehaved.

Following the second son's birth, the CPS worker visited the home semiweekly. The family, encouraged to find a consistent source of health care, selected the University of California clinics and emergency department. The pattern of visits for accidental- and non-accidental-related health care was sporadic for three years until 1975, when the family decided to enroll in the Family Care Program. Here, the family was assigned a primary health care team, consisting of a pediatric nurse practitioner, pediatrician, and internist.

Developmental screening of the children at ages 3 and 5 years suggested normal intellectual potentials, despite earlier delays in language and personal-social development which were attributed to the parental inability to provide adequate stimulation. Unfortunately, attempts to obtain formal psychological evaluations were unsuccessful because of failed appointments.

Index Child

The second son became the focus of attention at 23 months of age when he incurred four "accidental" injuries in one week: a first-degree burn of the arm due to spilled coffee, first- and second-degree burns of the buttocks due to bumping into a wall heater, a superficial dog bite on the face, and periorbital contusions and hematoma which were attributed to being "pushed out of the high chair by his older brother." This last injury was discovered by the CPS worker and the clinic health care team who visited the home to change burn dressings and evaluate the family for continued CPS supervision. The child, admitted to the hospital for neurological and ophthalmological assessments, results of which were normal, was discharged home with a diagnosis of suspected abuse. Efforts were made to locate a day-care placement for him, for the purposes of alleviating intrafamilial stress and fostering developmental stimulation. No day-care placement was available because he was not toilet-trained.

The health care team continued to see him frequently in the clinics for otitis media and alternating esotropia, and team members made weekly home visits and phone contact with the mother. The child was hospitalized for an adenoidectomy at the age of 26 months. Two months later, he was seen on four alternate-day visits, three of which were in the audiology and ear, nose and throat clinics. On the fourth visit, his distraught mother brought him to the emergency room because of a large parietal hematoma (8 x 10 cm), but denied any knowledge of how the head injury occurred. Roentgenograms revealed a small linear fracture of the right parietal bone and a six- to eight-week-old previously undetected and untreated but healing right ulnar fracture. The child was hospitalized for five days; there was no apparent neurological disability, but the discharge diagnoses again included suspected abuse. He was discharged to a foster home at the direction of the juvenile court.

Discussion

The health and behavioral data of this family revealed that the parents were marginally able to cope with the first son and the birth of the second one. However, as the younger child began to assert his autonomy the parents were no longer able to anticipate the demands of two energetic children, nor were they able to realistically perceive the developmental needs of their sons. The mother was overwhelmed with the tasks involved in the management of cramped living arrangements and keeping up with two active boys. It is of interest that a review of the family medical charts revealed that the locus of accidental injury visits to the medical center shifted from the mother to the first son (at 16 months) and then to the second son beginning at 8 months.

At the time of the documented abuse, the three criteria under which this is most likely to occur were demonstrated by the family data: (1) parental potential for abuse; (2) social disruptions in living accommodations; and (3) a potentially "special" child.[4]

The developmental disability of the parents contributed a fourth criterion which masked the identification of abuse and added a dimension which, to our knowledge, has not been reported previously in the context of neglect and abuse.

Medical-social dilemmas were encountered in planning and providing health care for this family. Initial attempts to refer the index child to protective custody seven months prior to overt abuse were unsuccessful because of "insufficient evidence" to document abuse at that time. Unintentional neglect was not sufficient cause for removal of the children from their parents, even when covert problems were evident and overt sequelae predictable.

Childhood neglect is defined as "an act of omission on the part of the parent, in contrast to those suffering as the result of physical abuse or "trauma.""[5] Such neglect occurs most often during infancy or a child's early months of total dependence on the parents for adequate nutrition and environmental needs. We use the term "unintentional neglect" to indicate acts of omission by parent or guardian because of inability to recognize their child's needs and/or their unrealistic expectations of the child's self-sufficiency. When does "unintentional neglect" become abuse? The intuitive knowledge of potential hazards which most of us take for granted cannot be assumed to be routine cautions for someone with limited intelligence. For them, this information needs to be taught and reinforced until it becomes part of routine behavior. However, supportive parenting services with persistent and effective staff do not generally exist.

Attempts to remove "at-risk" children from their families as a preventive measure tend to be viewed as violations of parental rights. In addition, a recommendation to remove the children in this family was subject to further criticism as a violation of the civil rights of mentally retarded adults. During the seven months prior to the documented abuse incident, the health care team provided supportive interventions which were directed toward (1) supporting the parents' attempts to control their own lives; (2) keeping the family intact; (3) reducing unintentional neglect via environmental safety measures; and (4) providing language and personal-social stimulation for the two boys. It became apparent in this situation that health visitors and multidisciplinary team interventions were not adequate to prevent unintentional neglect and overt abuse.

A frustrating question introduced by this case is "What services are there for 'normal' children of 'special' parents?" Had these two children been mentally or developmentally disabled, they would have qualified for additional special services, including a nursery or respite program for the second son, homemaker services, and developmental stimulation programs. It is ironic that these potentially normal children were almost forgotten, not only by their parents, but also by our child advocacy system.

REFERENCES

1.   US COMMITTEE ON GOVERNMENT OPERATIONS: *Wagner O'Day Acts*, HR 93-1315, 1974.

2.   DEVELOPMENTAL DISABILITIES COMMITTEE: *San Francisco County Plan Update 1976-77*. San Francisco, Developmental Disabilities Council of San Francisco, June 1976.

3.   DAVID, H. P., SMITH, J. D., FRIEDMAN, E.: Family planning services for persons handicapped by mental retardation. *Am J Public Health* 66:1053, 1976.

4.   KEMPE, C. H., HELFER, R. E.: *Helping the Battered Child and His Family*. Philadelphia, JP Lippincott Co., 1972.

5.   HELFER, R. E., KEMPE, C. H. (eds.): *The Battered Child*. Chicago, University of Chicago Press, 1974.

35

What's Wrong with Sex Between Adults and Children? Ethics and the Problem of Sexual Abuse*

David Finkelhor, Ph.D.

Current research on the subject of sexual abuse indicates that a large number of children have sexual encounters with adults.[2] After a long period of ignoring or denying it, the problem has finally established itself on the agenda of many mental health professionals. There is now a great groundswell of interest in the problem, and of concern for studying it and finding ways to cope with it.

In this rush to treatment, certain ethical issues underlying the definition of the problem have been brushed aside. Although there is a widespread consensus that sex between adults and children is wrong, and therefore requires intervention, there is also a widespread confusion about why it is wrong and why it requires intervention. Essentially, those most concerned about sexually-abused children have not had to think through the moral issues, since the weight of traditional morality supports their point of view.

The intent of this paper is to criticize some of the more complacent arguments against sex between adults and children, and to suggest a sounder line of reasoning in support of such a prohibition.

At the outset, it should be made clear what we are discussing. For purposes of this paper, "sex" refers to activities involving the genitals that are engaged in for the gratification of at least one person involved. Thus "sex" is not limited to intercourse. Second, "adult" refers to a person 18 or over, either related or not to the child; "child" means a pre-pubertal youngster.

---

* David Finkelhor, "What's Wrong with Sex between Adults and Children?" *American Journal of Orthopsychiatry*, 49(2) (October, 1979):692-697. Copyright © 1979 the American Orthopsychiatric Association, Inc. Reproduced by permission.

Inadequate Arguments

There are at least three "intuitive" arguments that are often made against the idea of sex between adults and children, none of which seems really adequate.

The most simple argument says that such sex is intrinsically wrong. It is unnatural from a biological and psychological point of view. For instance, a little girl's vagina is too small to accept a mature male's penis. Further, the thought of such relations inspires an innate disgust in most people. As evidence, almost all societies either forbid or tightly regulate sexual contact between the mature and immature. But as an argument against sex between adults and children, this approach is too categorical. Many assertions of "intrinsic wrong" made about other sexual taboos, such as homosexuality, have been called into question in recent times.

A second argument rejects adult-child sex because it entails a premature sexualization of the child. From this point of view, childhood should be a time of relative immunity from sex, a time when the child enjoys freedom from this rather problematical aspect of life. An adult approaching a child is seen as drawing the youngster into a world the child is not ready for. For adults who find sex problematic, this is an attractive fantasy. But children are sexual; the asexuality of childhood is a myth. Most children are curious about sex. They explore sexuality with one another. In fact, when adults shield children from sex, it probably does more harm than good.

A final, very common argument says that sexual encounters with adults are clearly damaging to children. Children are frightened and disturbed by them. They are the source of sexual problems in later life. There is clinical evidence that this is true, at least in many cases, and this is probably the most popular argument against sex between adults and children. But there are at least two reasons why this is a rather weak argument.

For one thing, it is based on an empirical, not a moral, foundation, and an empirical foundation that is far from absolutely established. It is indisputable that some children are harmed by their childhood sexual encounters with adults, some severely so. But what percentage? From clinical reports, we cannot tell. The number of cases that do not come to clinical attention is very large,[2] and it is possible that a majority of these children are not harmed.[3, 4]

The unreliability of this line of argument will become increasingly apparent, as the ranks of those who claim to have had positive child-adult sex experiences become publicized. Inevitably, they will,[5] since our culture has maintained the unrealistic assumption that such relationships do not exist. Because of some of the inherent difficulties of empirical research into this kind of question, it may be some time before a definitive scientific conclusion is reached. In the meantime, the argument that sex between adults and children is bad solely on the empirical grounds that it harms the children will become more and more controversial.

Further, the idea that an experience causes harm is not sufficient in itself to earn condemnation. Compulsory education, divorce, even going to the doctor causes harm and trauma to an important number of children. If sex between children and adults is wrong, and if it merits serious condemnation in our moral hierarcy, then some additional criteria need to be introduced into the argument beside the possibility that it can cause harm.

The Issue of Consent

As a society, we are moving toward a sexual ethic that holds that sex of all sorts between consenting persons should be permitted, but that in situations where a person does not consent, sex should be considered illegal and taboo. Rape, for example, is an act that is clearly criminal because it is done without the consent of one of the parties.

But don't many children "consent" to sexual acts with adults? Sex between adults and children may often seem much less coercive than rape, because many children appear to consent passively or even to cooperate. If we say that sex is permissible where consent is present, doesn't this legitimize much adult-child sex?

The key argument here is that children, by their nature, are incapable of truly consenting to sex with adults. Because they are children, they cannot consent; they can never consent. For this reason, sex between an adult and a child cannot be sanctioned under our moral standard that requires that consent be present. To make this statement meaningful requires a more detailed discussion of what is meant by consent.

For true consent to occur, two conditions must prevail. A person must know what it is that he or she is consenting to, and a person must be free to say yes or no.

Behavioral scientists have recently had extensive encounters with both of these aspects of the consent issue. The ethics of research now demand that a research subject give "informed consent" to participation. Informed consent requires that a person really understands what is likely to happen to him or her during and as a result of participation in the research. Thus, it has been decided that a researcher must give a complete description of research procedures, and also anticipate in a detailed way some of the possible dangers that participation might entail.

Secondly, the current code in research with human subjects also demands that a research subject have true freedom to say yes or no. For example, it has been decided that such conditions do not prevail in the case of research on prisoners. Because they are not free, because the incentives toward participation are so artifically overwhelming in a prison, prisoners do not really have the freedom to say no to participation.

For children, the problem seems fully analogous. Can children give informed consent to sex with adults? It is fairly evident that they cannot. For one thing, children lack the information that is necessary to make an "informed" decision about the matter. They are ignorant about sex and sexual relationships. It is not only that they may be unfamiliar with the mechanics of sex and reproduction. More importantly, they are generally unaware of the social meanings of sexuality. For example, they are unlikely to be aware of the rules and regulations surrounding sexual intimacy, and what it is supposed to signify. They are probably uninformed and inexperienced about what criteria to use in judging the acceptability of a sexual partner. They probably do not know much about the "natural history" of sexual relationships, what course they will take. And, finally, they have little way of knowing how other people are likely to react to the experience they are about to undertake, what likely consequences it will have for them in the future.

They may know that they like the adult, that the physical sensations feel good, and on this basis may make a choice. But they lack the knowledge the adult has about sex and about what they are undertaking. This is something that stems from the very fact of being a child and being inexperienced. In this sense, a child cannot give informed consent to sex with an adult.

Further, a child does not have the freedom to say yes or no. This is true in a legal sense and also in a psychological sense. In a legal sense, a child is under the authority of an adult and has no free will. But in a more important psychological sense, children have a hard time saying no to adults. Adults control all kinds of resources that are essential to them—food, money, freedom, etc. In this sense, the child is exactly like the prisoner who volunteers to be a research subject. The child has no freedom in which to consider the choice.

This is especially true when the adult propositioning the child (assuming the adult even asks the child's consent, which rarely happens) is a parent, a relative, or another important figure in the child's life, as is so often the case. Most children who cooperate in sex with an adult attest to this very thing. As one of my interviewees said, "He was my uncle. He told me what to do and I obeyed. I was taught to obey adults." Thus a child cannot, in a moral sense, consent to sex with an adult because a child is not truly free to say no.

The basic proposition here is that adult-child sex is wrong because the fundamental conditions of consent cannot prevail in the relationship between an adult and a child. The proposition seems to be a great improvement over other arguments, particularly the argument that such acts are wrong solely because they harm the child. It puts the argument on a moral, rather than an empirical, footing.

Thus, even if someone could demonstrate many cases where children enjoyed such experiences and were not harmed by them, one could still argue that it was wrong because children could not consent. The wrong here is not contingent upon proof of a harmful outcome.[1]

An analogous situation is that of sex between therapists and patients. There may be many instances where patients benefit from sex with their therapist. But the argument that such sex is wrong does not hinge on the positive or negative outcome. Rather, it lies in the fundamental asymmetry of the relationship. A patient, I would argue, cannot freely consent to have sex with a therapist. The main consideration here is that, in the context of a therapeutic relationship, a patient is not really free to say yes or no. Even if the patient liked it, a moral wrong had been committed.

Child-adult sex is morally similar, with the addition that the child not only cannot freely consent, the child also cannot give *informed* consent. An adult patient probably is aware of the social significance of sexuality. A patient probably can foresee some of the consequences of sex with a therapist. A child, however, is likely to be unaware of both these elements, and is thus even less equipped to consent than would be the patient.

Some Caveats

Much as this argument is an improvement over others, some objections might be raised. First, is the consent standard outlined really a good one for determining legitimate and illegitimate sexual relationships for adults and for children? I have said that partners need to be informed of the meaning and consequences of their consent and be able freely to say yes or no. How many adult sexual encounters fully conform to this standard?

The truth is that many adults are quite ignorant about sex. And many adult relationships occur under conditions in which one partner can hardly refuse. An obvious example of this last point is marriage. How many women are free to refuse the advances of their husbands, especially if he is the one earning all the money in the family? How free are prostitutes to refuse the business of their customers? How free is a secretary to refuse the attentions of her boss? There is an element of coercion present in all these situations, yet the only one we outlaw is prostitution, and in that case it is hardly to protect the interest of the prostitute. If implicit coercion is present in many, if not most, sexual encounters in our society, what makes adult-child sex any different?

Secondly, how much knowledge is present in most sexual encounters? Do adults know what they are agreeing to? Do they know what the consequences will be? Judging from the degree of tragedy and pain that seems to accompany so much sexual activity in our culture, I would judge that very imperfect awareness of the consequences exists among most adult consentors.

Finally, doesn't this argument constitute a condemnation of all child sexuality? If children cannot consent to sex because they lack knowledge about it, doesn't this include sex among peers? Although not everyone would agree, many, this author included, approve of sexual experimentation among adolescents. I also approve of sex play among prepubescent children. But these children do not have a very good understanding of what they are getting involved in. If lack of knowledge makes adult-child sex wrong, doesn't it also make child-child sex wrong?

The crucial difference in adult-child sex is the combination of children's lack of knowledge *and* lack of power. Children in relationships with adults are both uninformed and unable freely to say no. By contrast, in relationships with peers, children are uninformed, but at least there is no inherent power differential. While relationships between adults often involve subtle coercion, adults have greater knowledge about the social meanings of sexuality, or at least they have accessibility to that knowledge.

Thus, peer experiences among children and among adults are not morally suspect because participants' level of awareness is relatively mutual. It is where the ability to understand the situation is inherently unequal, and is compounded by a serious difference in power, that we draw the line.

Conclusion

The empirical fact that sex with adults often causes harm to children is widely offered as the most compelling argument against such behavior. This paper has argued that a stonger ethical argument exists against such behavior, involving children's incapacity to give true consent to sex with an adult.

Such a distinction may seem to have an academic pallor to it. Many people engaged in work with sexually abused children may find it hard to see its relevance. Certainly, they do not need to be convinced that sexual abuse is wrong.

There are, however, two important reasons for ethical clarity on this issue. One is to be able to explain convincingly to victims and perpetrators of sexual abuse why drastic interference is being made in their private affairs. Adults who take sexual advantage of children are notorious for the justifications they give and for their stubborn refusal to admit to any wrongdoing. "No harm was caused," they often say. Although argument is unlikely to convince them, both they and their victim may benefit in the long run from being exposed clearly to the moral issue involved.

Secondly, ethical clarity on this issue is important for the benefit of society as a whole. In America today, sexual ethics are increasingly confused. Taboos have fallen by the wayside and new standards have not been articulated to replace the old. A sense of polarization exists; many people have the impression that one is either broadly in favour of sexual expression or broadly opposed. Moral confusion about sex is in part responsible for the occurrence of sexual abuse, as some people interpret the current sexual revolution as an exhortation that "all is permitted."

But concern about sexual abuse of children is not part of a Victorian resurgence. It is compatible with the most progressive attitude toward sexuality currently being voiced, a position that urges that consent be the sole standard by which the legitimacy of sexual acts be evaluated. Ethical clarity may help society move toward a more coherent outlook on sexual matters, and may serve to combat at least one significant source of sexual abuse.

REFERENCES

1.   ARKES, H., 1978. *The question of incest and the properties of a moral argument.* Presented to the Conference on Childhood Sexual Abuse, Chicago.

2.   FINKELHOR, D. 1979. *Sexually Victimized Children.* Free Press, New York.

3.   GAGNON, J. 1965. "Female child victims of sex offenses." *Soc. Prob.* 13:176-192.

4.   LANDIS, J. 1965. "Experiences of 500 children with adult sexual deviates." *Psych. Quart. Supplm.* 30:91-109.

5.   NOBILE, P. 1978, "Incest: the last taboo." *Penthouse* (Jan.).

Part Four

The Victims and the Consequences of Abuse

Compared to the literature on abuse and abusers, the research on the consequences for the victims is very sparse. It is unclear whether this is due to a lack of
professional interest or related to the difficulty of obtaining data. As several of the
previous articles indicated, the children who suffer abuse may be severely damaged:
some children die; others live with permanent brain damage resulting in mental
retardation and/or cerebral palsy; many are of subnormal weight and height, show
language delay, impaired speech, motor dysfunction and personality disorder.

There are very few long-term studies on the subsequent development of abused
children, and not many more short-term follow-up papers. Those presented here are
representative of the limited knowledge available of the sequelae of abuse.

S. B. Friedman and
C. W. Morse

This study illustrates the type of research
necessary to test generally accepted assertions
about the subsequent experiences of abused child-
ren. The authors' specific goals were (1) to evaluate whether the judgments cate-
gorizing children as abused, neglected, or accidently injured held up after five
years, and (2) to discover the nature and incidence of subsequent injuries to these
children and their siblings. Friedman and Morse evaluate the suspected relationship
between the special child, family stress and abuse by examining the behavioural and
developmental characteristics of the children, the stability of the family and the
mother-child relationship. Their previous categorizations were confirmed in 85 per
cent of the cases studied. They conclude that abused and neglected children are more
vulnerable to further injuries, as are their siblings. Behaviour problems and poor
mother-child relationships appear to be more frequent in the suspected abusing and
neglecting families. Although the expected differences between the groups were
found, none reached statistical significance.

E. Elmer   Noting the lack of attention to the subsequent development of abused children, Elmer reviews those few studies which found physical, personality and intellectual disabilities in such children. She feels these earlier findings may be due to uncontrolled variables such as social class. Her own study attempts to assess the effects of abuse on children eight years after incidence. Abused children were compared to matched samples of children who had experienced accidents and those who had experienced no trauma. The author found none of the expected differences in health, language development, intellectual status in school, self-concept or behaviour. Surprisingly, language difficulties and psychological handicaps were prevalent in all samples. Elmer advances hypotheses to explain this lack of difference and the high incidence of difficulty. She concludes that "identification of a family with the lower classes may be as potent a factor as abuse for the development of a child." To test such hypotheses, Elmer suggests further controlled investigations of children from a range of socioeconomic situations.

H. Martin and P. Beezley   This is one of several papers by Dr. Martin and his colleagues on the development of the abused child. The particular focus of this report is an assessment of personality and behavioural characteristics of previously abused children. The findings were correlated with evaluations of the home environments and the type of therapy the parents had received. In discussing the psychological symptoms of the children,the authors emphasize that psychic injury continues even when physical abuse is halted. The ways in which children adapt to the psychological trauma of assault indicate that it is not just the physical abuse itself that is damaging so much as the presence of rejection and instability in family relationships. They point out that treatment of the parents does not solve the child's problem. He too needs extensive services.

D. A. Pemberton and
D. R. Benady   Pemberton and Benady study the effect on a child of conscious rejection by his family. After reviewing the relevant literature, the authors examine a sample of 12 consciously rejected children and their families. They conclude that rejected children have great difficulty in interpersonal relationships and tend to show symptoms of aggression, negativism, stealing, lying and encopresis. The lives of the parents are characterized by instability and reaction to environmental stress unrelated to the child's personality. The reasons for scapegoating these children could not be identified but when the child was removed most of the families maintained a fragile stability. They did not aggress against nor reject any of their other children.

K. Tooley   Tooley raises a relatively ignored aspect of abuse —the child who suffers because of the lack of parental protection against assault by unsupervised siblings. Her concern in this report is the impact of such attacks on the victim. Tooley states that most parents were unwilling to permit psychiatric attention for the "aggressed upon." She presents one detailed case history to illustrate the traumatic effects of sibling assault. She notes that the well-being of the victim is often overlooked because of overriding concern with family privacy and the rehabilitation of the aggressor.

B. Bender

Bender describes the treatment of two boys, both of whom had been physically abused and scapegoated in their respective families. Each child appeared to have developed a pattern of behaviour which perpetuated his scapegoating role both with peers and adults. Each exhibited strong senses of guilt, low self-esteem, feelings of inferiority and behaviour which provoked aggression from others. Placement was considered inappropriate as it seemed likely that the boys' actions might even elicit assault in foster homes. Long-term intensive therapy decreased "the compulsive scapegoating behaviour and masochistic need for punishment." Therefore, Bender states, the personality impairment suffered by victims of abuse may be reversible if intensive therapeutic services are provided.

T. J. Reidy

Reidy proposes a social learning formulation to explain aggression. He hypothesizes that children who "have suffered punishment at the hands of aggressive parental models," will "exhibit more aggressive characteristics then their non-abused counterparts." He compares neglected children, abused children in foster and natural homes, and a control group. Data was collected through psychological tests and observational ratings by teachers and clinicians. The results show that abused children are significantly more aggressive in fantasy, free-play and school situations. There were very few differences between those abused children in foster homes and those in their own homes. Therefore, Reidy states, foster care alone is not an adequate remedy for psychological damage: treatment is necessary because those who are abused learn aggressive behaviour and thus are likely to have the potential for abusing their own offspring. He recommends that treatment intervention should occur as soon as abuse is discovered in order to reduce further severe problems.

A. Green

This paper also reports the results of a matched comparison between abused, neglected, and normal children. Green hypothesizes that self-destructive behaviour is potentiated by a child's experience of repeated physical abuse. The results of his study of children between the ages of 5 and 12 years confirm the hypothesis. Several of the children had attempted suicide or made suicidal gestures, some were self-mutilators and others expressed suicidal thoughts. Green considers his findings noteworthy as these behaviours are rarely seen in preadolescents. He examines those components of the child abuse syndrome which might precipitate self-destructive behaviour. His conclusion is that self-destructive activity is not related to guilt and self-punishment but "rather to a more primitive learned behaviour pattern originating in the earliest painful encounters. . . ."

36

Child Abuse: A Five-Year Follow-up of Early Case Finding in the Emergency Department*

Stanford B. Friedman, M.D.,
and Carol W. Morse

Child abuse continues to be of increasing concern to both laymen and professionals, and recently more attention is being focused on prevention.[1-3] Detection and protection were the primary goals after the initial reports in the early 1960s when Kempe *et al.* coined the phrase, "the battered child syndrome."[4] It is hoped that earlier identification and intervention might prevent subsequent and more damaging abuse.[5]

Holter and Friedman[6] conducted a study at the University of Rochester Medical Center to determine whether cases of child abuse and neglect could be identified in children managed in a routine fashion in an emergency department. In that survey, 10% of the children seen for injuries had findings which led the authors to suspect physical abuse and an additional 10% had injuries judged to be the result of gross neglect. Through such case findings, preventive and early protective services might be employed in the emergency room setting to avert additional, more serious injuries.

---

* This study was supported by U.S. Public Health Service grant K3-MH-18, 542 from the National Institute of Mental Health and Children's Bureau grant # 148.

Standford B. Friedman and Carol W. Morse, "Child Abuse: A Five-Year Follow-up of Early Case Finding in the Emergency Department," *Pediatrics*, Vol. 54, No. 4 (Oct. 1974):404-410. Copyright © The American Academy of Pediatrics 1974. Reproduced by permission.

Five years following the emergency room survey by Holter and Friedman,[6] the current study was conducted to evaluate the outcome of children previously judged to have experienced "abuse," "neglect," or an "accident." The specific goals were to determine (1) whether the judgments made in the early case findings held up after careful reexamination five years later and (2) how the original judgments related to subsequent injuries in the children in question and in their siblings.

Method

Study Population

The original study by Holter and Friedman[6] involved 156 cases of injury seen in children under 6 years of age in the Emergency Department of the University of Rochester during two 2-week periods in 1966 (six months apart). The physician's history and physical findings and the complete medical chart were reviewed in each case by the investigators to determine possible maltreatment in the form of physical abuse or gross neglect.* In the second study period, in addition to the medical review, a public health nurse made a follow-up home visit.

All cases for study in this current investigation were selected from the original study, with the original "accident" and "repeated accidents" groups combined. The present study took 54 children from the original 156 study population, 17 from the suspected abuse category, 10 from the suspected neglect category, and 27 from the accident categories. The 27 suspected abused and neglected children represented all such cases found in the original study. The 27 children originally judged to have experienced accidents were chosen randomly from the larger "accident" group. At the time of follow-up, it was possible to locate and study 15 children from the suspected abuse group (88%), 7 from the suspected neglect group (70%), and 19 from the repeated accident group (70%). This reflected three families declining to participate in the study, and ten families that could not be located. The 41 children studied ranged in age from 5-3/12 to 10-1/2 years at the time of this follow-up investigation, and there were 16 males and 25 females, 24 whites and 17 non-whites. The ages for the "abuse," "neglect," and "accident" groups were 7.6, 7.0, and 8.0 years, respectively. The children in these groups, respectively, had an average 2.4, 3.0, and 2.3 siblings ranging from 1 month to 19 years in age living in the home.

Data Collection

Interviews were conducted by one of the investigators (C.W.M.) during visits to the home of the 41 children and their families over a one-year period (1970 to 1971). The interviewer was not informed of whether the initial injury had been judged to represent "abuse," "neglect," or an "accident," and only the date and nature of the injury were known to her.

---

* "Abuse," for the purposes of both the original and follow-up studies, was defined as any willful or grossly careless act on the part of the parent(s) or caretaker which resulted in overt physical injury to the child in question. "Gross neglect" was defined as omission on the part of the parent(s) or designated caretaker to take minimal precautions for the proper supervision of the child's health and/or welfare.

An interview schedule was utilized which was developed specifically for this purpose. The areas covered in each interview were (1) the child's health status (including all in-and-out-patient hospital visits prior and subsequent to the original emergency department visit, (2) child's social, psychological, emotional, and intellectual development, (3) the parent's recollection of the original injury, and (4) siblings' health status (including any hospital visits). Also, the hospital records of the six area hospitals were surveyed for any contact with the children in question or their siblings. Data were obtained by reading 71 medical records on the 41 patients and 195 medical records of patients' siblings in these area hospitals. The local child protective agency was contacted to determine if any of the 41 children and their families had been reported to them.

Mother-child relationships were assessed by the interviewer from observation of mother-child interaction at the time of the home visit and from verbal reports given by the mother of the child's attitudes and behavior. Emotional and behavioral status of the other family members also was judged by observation and verbal communication.

Following the data collection, the interviewer made independent judgments regarding the original injury, according to the original four categories. This assessment was made without knowledge of the impression of the original injury made five years previously by Holter and Friedman.[6]

Findings

Reevaluation of Diagnoses

Of the 41 children reevaluated, Holter and Friedman originally had judged 15 to have injuries involving "suspected abuse," 7 involving "suspected neglect," and 19 were thought to have experienced "accidents."[6] Only one of the 15 cases of suspected abuse had been reported to the child protective authorities, and this was the only case in which abuse to the child was admitted by the mother in this study.

Solely from the follow-up interviews, an independent judgment was made of the original injury. This comparison may be noted in Table I, and represents an agreement between the original and the present investigators in 85% of the cases studied.

Parents were asked to recall the original injury and the circumstances under which it occurred. Their responses were then compared with the original data, and judgments made as to whether or not the parents could recall the injury, and if so, how accurate they were. In the 15 families originally involved in suspected abuse, 11 parents could recall the injury and 4 could not. Of the 11 who did recall the injury, 7 (64%) did not accurately describe the circumstances or nature of the injury. Five of the seven families in which the children's original injuries were thought to be due to neglect could recall the injuries; two of the five (40%) did so inaccurately. Seventeen of the 19 families in the "accident" category recalled the original injury, and of those, only in one case was the injury described in an inaccurate fashion (6%).

Subsequent Injuries

A major goal of the present investigation was to evaluate subsequent injuries to the study population, examining the children in the different categories from the

TABLE 1

Comparison of Original Impression and at Time of Follow-up Five Years Later*

Group	Original Impression	Follow-up Impression
Suspected abuse	15	11
Suspected neglect	7	7
Accident	19	23
Totals	41	41

* The differences are accounted for by four cases of "suspected abuse" and one case of "suspected neglect" now judged to be in the "accident" category, and one case of "accident" now judged to represent "suspected neglect."

viewpoints of number and type of such injuries. In the "suspected abuse" group, 73% (11 of 15) of the children sustained one or more injuries requiring the attention of either a private physician or an emergency department facility, as did 71% (5 of 7) of children in the "suspected neglect" group. Of the children involved in "accidents," 53% (11 of 19) had subsequent injuries. These percentages are not statistically different by χ^2 analysis.

There was a total of 60 subsequent injuries requiring medical attention in these 27 children.* One child from the "accident" group accounted for 11 of the subsequent injuries. No other child had more than five injuries each. Excluding the child with 11 injuries, 17 of the subsequent injuries occurred in the "suspected abuse" group, or 1.1 injuries per child; 12 in the "suspected neglect" group, or 1.7 injuries per child; and 20 in the "accident" group, or 1.1 injuries per child.

In the initial study by Holter and Friedman, two groups of children were defined according to the type of injury sustained, a "low-risk" group and a "high-risk" group. The "low-risk" group consisted of children seen for lacerations or ingestions, and was so labeled as only one child with such injuries contributed to the "suspected abuse" group. The "high-risk" group included head injuries, fractures and dislocations, limb injuries, burns, and abrasions, contusions and bruises, and 16 of the 17 cases of suspected abuse occurred in this category. Thus, the "high-risk" group contained essentially all the suspected abuse cases.

Subsequent injuries were reviewed in the same manner. However, a category of "other injuries" was added to the "low-risk" heading to include complaints of strains, sprains, animal bites, foreign bodies in the eyes, ears, nose and throat, and a single case of questionable sexual abuse. "Suspected abuse" and "suspected

* All of these injuries were confirmed by examination of medical records, except eight injuries reported by mothers on follow-up interview and said to have been cared for by their private physicians. Another seven injuries were reported by mothers to have been in local hospital emergency rooms, though the hospital medical records did not record such visits. However, the authors were inclined to believe the mothers, suspecting perhaps the hospital records might be incomplete or misplaced.

TABLE II

Injuries by Type Occurring During the Five-Year Follow-up Period

Group	High Risk					Low Risk			Total Number
	Head Injuries	Fractures & Dislocations	Limb Injuries	Burns	Abrasions, Contusions & Bruises	Lacerations	Ingestions	Other Injuries	
	% (n)	% (n)	% (n)	% (n)	% (n)	% (n)	% (n)	% (n)	
Suspected abuse & suspected neglect	50 (8)	67 (2)	0 (0)	100 (4)	57 (4)	31 (4)	40 (2)	46 (5)	(29)
Accident and repeat accident	50 (8)	33 (1)	100 (1)	0 (0)	43 (3)	69 (9)	60 (3)	54 (6)	(31)
Total number	(16)	(3)	(1)	(4)	(7)	(13)	(5)	(11)	(60)

neglect'' categories were condensed, since the small numbers precluded any differences emerging between these two groups (Table II).

Bruises, contusions and abrasions, fractures and dislocations, and burns were more frequent in the combined "suspected abuse" and "neglect" groups. Head injuries* were evenly divided, and the single limb injury occurred in a child from the "accident" group (the child with 11 subsequent injuries). The majority of lacerations and ingestions occurred in the "accident" group. There was essentially an even division of the injuries in the "other" category. Thus, the prediction that the "high-risk" type of injuries would occur more frequently in "suspected abuse" and "neglect" groups was observed in evaluating injuries occurring over the five-year follow-up period. However, the *strong association* between the type of injury and suspected etiology of the injury previously reported[6] was not confirmed by the present data.

Two study children were subsequently involved in suspected abuse as judged by the authors after thoroughly examining the complete history of each patient. No additional cases of gross neglect could be discerned. As in the initial study, unless there was substantial evidence to the contrary, injuries were classified as accidents. Both of the children had been categorized in the initial study as children whose injuries had resulted from "suspected abuse."

The mother of one of these two children accused her husband (not the child's father) of abusing the girl prior to the original injury, these accusations being made both at the time of the original injury and during the follow-up interview. Five months after the original injury, this same child was seen in the emergency department for a fractured clavicle. She allegedly fell and hit her shoulder, but was not brought for medical treatment until one week after the injury. No suspicion of abuse was raised at the time by the medical staff. However, three out of four follow-up clinic appointments were broken. One year after the original injury, this same girl

---

* There were no subdural hematomas or skull fractures.

was brought back to the emergency department for "blood coming from ear canal." Trauma was suspected as a possible cause, but denied by the parents. The other child involved in subsequent suspected abuse was brought by her father to another city hospital two years after the original injury. The father stated that the 2-1/2-year-old girl had been sexually molested 1-1/2 months previously, and was experiencing pain and puffiness of the labia. (There was no mention in the hospital record of who might have been involved in the incident.)

The present authors contacted the local child protective agency to determine if any of the 41 children and/or their siblings were known to them. Only one family had been referred in October 1970, and that by an anonymous letter. The child is included in the "accident" group in this study.

Injuries in Siblings

The authors also tabulated injuries requiring medical attention ever suffered by the 100 siblings of the children in the present study. These included only those siblings currently living in the home. Seventy-two percent (26 of 36) of the siblings of children in the "suspected abuse" category had experienced injuries, 80% (16 of 20) of the siblings in the "suspected neglect" group, and 50% (22 of 44) of the siblings in the "accident" group ($\chi^2 = 7.02$; $p < .05$). However, when family units were examined for whether they included one or more siblings with an injury, no significant differences were noted, with 11, 4, and 13 families in the "abuse," "neglect," and "accident" groups, respectively, having one or more injured siblings. Since the average number of siblings per family was approximately equal (2.4, 3.0, and 2.3 for the "abuse," "neglect," and "accident" groups, respectively), the data would indicate that there were more injuries per sibling from the "abuse" and "neglect" categories.

Two children, siblings of the two patients in the "suspected abuse" category who had suffered subsequent abuse, each had an injury judged by the authors to have also resulted from abuse. One was brought to the University of Rochester Medical Center four years after her sister's original injury with a healing fracture of the right clavicle. The other sibling had a perforated ear drum after having been abused by his father.

Behavioral and Developmental Characteristics

In trying to account for differences among the groups in frequency of subsequent injuries, the authors examined behavioral and developmental characteristics of the children and general family stability. A number of areas of child behavior were explored with the mothers at the time of the follow-up interview; specifically, physical activity, temperament, sibling and peer relationships, obedience, specific bedtime and mealtime problems, school performance, and punishment. There were no notable differences among the groups in these areas. However, it is of interest that the vast majority of parents in all groups relied on physical punishment for disobedience as opposed to removal of privileges or restriction of activity. Generally, they believed this method to be effective. Also, mothers were asked during the follow-up interview these two questions: "Which child in the family is hurt most often?" and "How often is the child in question hurt in comparison to other children?" In no

TABLE III

Evaluation of the Mother-Child Relationships

Group	Good % (n)		Fair % (n)		Poor % (n)		Total % (n)	
Suspected abuse	43	(6)	28	(4)	28	(4)	100	(14*)
Suspected neglect	29	(2)	57	(4)	14	(1)	100	(7)
Accident	66	(12)	28	(5)	6	(1)	100	(18*)
Total number		(20)		(13)		(6)		(39)

* One child from each of these groups was not observed by C.W.M. and assessment was not made.

group did a majority of the parents believe that the child in the study was hurt most often in the family or more than other children.

From previous studies,[5, 7] the abused child has been singled out as being somehow different. These vulnerable children are described as being seen as sickly, spoiled, bad, or problem children. Therefore, an assessment was made at the time of the follow-up interview of the mother-child relationship. As might be expected, more children in the "accident" group (66%) exhibited good relationships with their mothers than in the "suspected abuse" (43%) and "suspected neglect" (29%) groups (Table III). Only one child in the "accident" group (6%) was considered to have a poor mother-child relationship as contrasted with four children (28%) in the "suspected abuse" group and one child in the "suspected neglect" category (14%). These differences did not reach significance by χ^2 analysis.

Expanding on the mother-child relationship, the authors also made observations and assessments of the general emotional and behavioral status of other family members. Sixty-seven percent of the children in the "suspected abuse" category came from families with notable behavioral and/or emotional problems, as compared to 28% and 33% of the "suspected neglect" and "accident" categories, respectively. These differences are not statistically significant. It should be understood that these impressions reflect only those problems which were noted at the time of follow-up interview and are undoubtedly conservative as the questionnaire focused primarily on the previously injured child.

The types of disturbances observed may be seen in Table IV. The most prevalent problems were in the realm of child rearing, with parents not setting and maintaining effective and consistent limits for their children's behavior. Some of the parents themselves suffered from emotional problems, with no single diagnosis prevailing. Depression, "nervousness," marked overprotection of children, chronic medical problems, and mental retardation were among the problems noted.

Discussion

In their original paper on case findings in the emergency department setting, Holter and Friedman[6] concluded: ". . . placing a child in the suspected abuse category is a clinical judgment, and only long-term follow-up will define the accuracy of these judgments." The current study was basically an attempt to see if the original judgments were predictive of relative subsequent risk to the child and his

TABLE IV

Cases in Which Families Had Behavioral and/or Emotional Problems

Case	Group*	Sex	Age at Follow-up (yr)	Child Problems	Family Problems
1	SA	F	7-4/12	None evident	Both parents reported to be alcoholics
2	SA	F	8-4/12	Enuretic	Child rearing problems; mother thinks child has "mean temper"
3	SA	F	5-7/12	Overly active child, manipulates mother	Gross child rearing problems; dull mother totally incapable of setting limits
4	SA	F	7-10/12	None evident	Mother nervous, tense, compulsive, impatient with children
5	SA	F	7-10/12	None evident	Child rearing problems; nervous, overly-concerned mother who cannot set consistent limits
6	SA	F	5-5/12	None evident	Gross child rearing problems; psychiatrically disturbed mother and stepfather
7	SA	M	7-10/12	Question of hyper-activity, mother says "accident prone"	Mother unable to "calm down" child
8	SA	M	8-11/12	Behavior problems	Lack of investment in child by mother; child lives with maternal grandmother even though mother is two blocks away
9	SA	M	10-2/12	"Slow" child, question of brain damage	Major child rearing problems
10	SA	F	7-10/12	Insecure, confused due to mother's ambiva-lent feelings	Severe child rearing problems; mother with major emotional problems
11	SN	M	6-7/12	Enuretic, hyperactive	Child rearing problems; mother unsure of how to handle child
12	SN	F	7-2/12	Manipulative child who totally dominates mother	Severe child rearing problems; mother incapable of setting any limits

Case	Group*	Sex	Age at Follow-up (yr)	Child Problems	Family Problems
13	A	F	8-4/12	Hyperactive, behavioral problems	Child rearing problems; chronically ill father; depressed mother unable to set effective limits for child
14	A	F	7-4/12	Behavioral problems, disobedience to mother	Child rearing problems; mother unable to set limits
15	A	M	6-11/12	Hyperactive, mother says "accident prone"	Child rearing problems; mother unable to set limits
16	A	M	8-2/12	None evident	Child rearing problems; mother shows overt ambivalent feelings
17	A	M	7-10/12	None evident	Nervous, overprotective mother over-identifies with children
18	A	M	9-4/12	None evident	Mother with emotional problems; sibling with anorexia nervosa

* SA, suspected abuse; SN, suspected neglect; A, accident.

siblings. The findings of the study would appear to indicate that young children identified as having experienced abuse or gross neglect are more vulnerable to further injuries, as are their siblings. However, the results are far from definitive, and though in the expected direction, do not reach statistical significance.

In this study, the investigator not previously involved in the case finding survey agreed in 85% of the cases with the original judgment of "suspected abuse," "suspected neglect," or "accident." This degree of agreement is not surprising in that the same criteria for inclusion in any of these three categories were used; and though the judgments were made independently, both studies reflect the same research orientation. However, a significant degree of disagreement would invalidate all other findings in this follow-up study in that the reliability of the judgments themselves would be very much in question.

The fact that over 70% of the children from the "suspected abuse" and "suspected neglect" groups had injuries requiring medical attention during the five-year follow-up period would appear higher than what would be expected in a sample of children from the general population. However, these authors were unable to find a satisfactory comparision group, and unfortunately we did not include in our study children who were seen in the same emergency department setting for reasons other than injuries. Finding that seven out of every ten children might be anticipated to have a subsequent injury during the five-year period would, nevertheless, appear to identify a high risk group, though such an interpretation is tenuous when such a figure is compared to slightly over 50% of the children in the "accident" group also sustaining an injury during a comparable period of time. The lack of a significant difference between the suspected "abuse" and "neglect" groups and those children judged to have sustained an "accident" may reflect the fact that accidents themselves are known to recur in certain children at a higher than expected incidence. [8-17] Childhood injuries may, therefore, be viewed as occurring on an accident child abuse continuum. It also may be that if our sample had been larger, even the relatively minor differences among groups might have reached significance. The siblings of the children judged to have experienced "abuse" or "neglect" had a significantly higher number of injuries requiring medical attention.

The number of children thought to have experienced abuse during the follow-up period was too limited for statistical analysis. However, it is of interest that the two children judged to have been abused during this period both came from the original "suspected abuse" category. Further, they each had a sibling also thought to have sustained abuse during the five-year period. In an assessment of the mother-child relationship, more children in the "accident" group were judged to exhibit good relationships with their mothers than in the "abuse" and "neglect" groups. Also, there was a tendency for the families of children judged to have been abused to have a higher frequency of emotional and behavioral problems. However, none of these differences reached statistical significance.

In the original case finding study,[6] there was an empirical association between the type of injury and whether that injury was judged to reflect "abuse," "neglect," or an "accident." Specifically, with one exception, lacerations and ingestions had all been judged to represent "accidents," and bruises and abrasions, fractures, dislocations, burns, and head injuries judged "abuse" and "neglect" cases. In examining the injuries occurring in the five-year follow-up period in a similar manner, the same association was noted but a sharp distinction of a "high-risk" and "low-risk" group of children definable by the type of injury sustained was not confirmed. However, the relative infrequency of lacerations and ingestions in cases of abuse also has been noted by others.[18]

In summary, young children previously judged to have experienced "abuse" or "gross neglect" did tend to experience a greater number of injuries needing medical attention than those children judged to have experienced an "accident." However, this incidence of approximately 70% was not significantly greater than the 50% rate of repeat injury for the "accident" group. There was a higher incidence of injuries of the siblings of the combined "abuse" and "neglect" groups than in the "accident" group. Though again statistical significance was not reached, except in one instance, there did appear to be a greater number of behavioral problems and poor mother-child relationships in the combined "abuse" and "neglect" groups than in children judged to have sustained "accidents." Two cases of abuse were identified in the follow-up period and in both instances these children came from the group originally categorized as "suspected abuse"; each also had a sibling judged to have suffered from abuse during this same follow-up period.

REFERENCES

1.   GALDSTON, R.: "Violence begins at home: The parents' center for the study and prevention of child abuse." *J. Amer. Acad. Child Psychiat.*, 10:336, 1971.

2. OLIVER, J. E., and TAYLOR, A.: "Five generations of ill-treated children in one family pedigree." *Brit. J. Psychiat.*, 119:473, 1971.

3. KEMPE, C. H., SILVERMAN, F. N., STEELE, B. F., DROEGEMUELLER, W., and SILVER, H. K.: "The battered child syndrome." *JAMA*, 181:17, 1962.

4. KEMPE, C. H., SILVERMAN, F. N., STEELE, B. F., DIOEGEMUELLA, W., and SILVER, H. K.: "The battered child syndrome." *JAMA*, 181:17, 1962.

5. MORSE, C. W., SAHLER, O. J. Z., and FRIEDMAN, S. B.: " A three year follow-up study of abused and neglected children." *Amer. J. Dis. Child.*, 120:439, 1970.

6. HOLTER, J. C., and FRIEDMAN, S. B.: "Child abuse: Early case finding in the emergency department." *Pediatrics*, 42:128, 1968.

7. COURT, J.: "The battered child: I. Historical and diagnostic reflections." *Med. Soc. Work*, 22:11, 1969.

8. HUSBAND, P., and HUNTON, P. E.: "Families of children with repeated accidents." *Arch. Dis. Child.*, 47:396, 1972.

9. KLONOFF, H.: "Head injuries in children: Predisposing factors, accident conditions, accident proneness and sequelae." *Amer. J. Public Health*, 61:2405, 1971.

10. MATHENY, A. P., BROWN, A. M., and WILSON, R. S.: "Behavioral antecedents of accidental injuries in early childhood: A study of twins." *J. Pediat.*, 79:122, 1971.

11. MARTIN, H. L.: "Antecedents of burns and scalds in children." *Brit. J. Med. Psychol.*, 43:39, 1970.

12. BALTIMORE, C., and MEYER, R. J.: "A Study of storage, child behavioral traits, and mother's knowledge of toxicology in 52 poisoned families and 52 comparison families." *Pediatrics*, 44:816, 1969.

13. WIGHT, B. W.: "The control of child-environment interaction: A conceptual approach to accident occurrence." *Pediatrics*, 44:799, 1969.

14. MANHEIMER, D. I., and MELLINGER, G. D.: "Personality characteristics of the child accident repeater." *Child Develop.*, 38:491, 1967.

15. MEYER, R. J., ROELOFS, H. A., BLUESTONE, J., and REDMOND, S.: "Accidental injury to the preschool child." *J. Pediat.*, 63:95, 1963.

16. HAGGERTY, R. J.: "Home accidents in childhood." *New Eng. J. Med.*, 260:1322, 1959.

17. FULLER, E. M.: "Injury-prone children." *Amer. J. Orthopsychiat.*, 18:708, 1948.

18. McRAE, K. N., FERGUSON, C. A., and LEDERMAN, R. S.: "The battered child syndrome." *Canad. Med. Assoc. J.*, 108:859, 1973.

37

*A Follow-up Study of Traumatized Children**

Elizabeth Elmer, M.S.W.

In the last few years the burst of activities related to child abuse has been nothing short of astonishing. In 1961, when the Children's Bureau framed the first suggested model law, some professional persons were concerned at the amount of attention being paid to a phenomenon that seemed quite rare. By 1967 all the states had laws concerning the reporting of abuse. These have been constantly expanded as to the types of mistreatment to be reported and the range of professionals mandated to report; the volume of reports has climbed each year. Light[1] estimates that one in 100 children in the United States is abused, sexually molested, or neglected. And one eminent authority, Douglas Besharov, predicts that, in the near future, 1 million cases of suspected mistreatment will be reported each year in the United States.[2] It is impossible, of course, to determine whether the increase is due to more incidents of abuse, more effective identification, or expansion in the reporting requirements themselves.

Since the establishment in 1974 of the National Center on Child Abuse and Neglect, demonstration and research programs have sprung up on every side. Hot lines, Parents Anonymous, and many varieties of special projects abound. Among the objectives of these programs, three stand out: identification of high-risk families, identification and reporting of actual cases, and services to children and their families.

Curiously, comparatively little attention has been paid to the subsequent develop-

* Supported by grant MC-R-420336 from the Health Services Improvement Branch, Division of Clinical Services, Bureau of Community Health Services, DHEW, and by grants from the Maurice Falk Medical Fund, Pittsburgh, and the University of Pittsburgh Medical Alumni Association.

ment of abused children. It is reasonable to speculate that children exposed to parental rage and violence will sustain damage in a range of developmental areas. Unfortunately there are few hard data to support this possibility. Although a small number of follow-up studies have been published,[3-6] none of these studies employed a matched comparison group. The findings of the four studies tended to support each other, *i.e.*, abused children suffered disabilities in physical development, personality development, and intellectual achievement. Because of the lack of suitable comparison groups, however, these findings might have been due to uncontrolled variables such as social class.

A five-year follow-up study by Friedman and Morse[7] compared suspected abuse, suspected neglect, and accident cases. However, it was not possible to match the three study groups on demographic characteristics, and there was no comparison group from the general population, a drawback recognized by the authors.

The purpose of this paper is to report the results of a follow-up study of abused and accidentally injured children, utilizing matched comparison groups. Aside from medical care and placement in substitute homes of some abused children, the traumatized children received no specific treatment.

Summary of the Base Study

The traumatized children were first studied as infants of 12 months or less after their referral to the Department of Radiology, Children's Hospital of Pittsburgh, because of an impact event.* Each mother was interviewed at home to determine the circumstances of the index event; then the infant was brought to the outpatient department of the hospital for a pediatric and a developmental assessment. These initial data were the basis for a judgment of abuse or accident, which was made jointly by the pediatrician, the social work interviewer, and the author. A child was judged abused if one or more of the following criteria were present: report or admission of abuse of the patient or a sibling: injuries incurred more than once; or history conflicting or inadequate to explain the child's condition. Judgments of abuse had to be unanimous, otherwise the child was considered an accident victim.

Subsequent procedures in the Infant Accident Study included additional home visits, observations of mother-baby interaction, a mailed questionnaire, and a final evaluation of the baby in the outpatient clinic. The concluding procedure was a staff review of the original judgments (abuse or accident) in the light of the data gathered during the one-year investigation. New criteria were added concerning possible indicators of abuse such as marks on the body and observations of extremely harsh physical discipline. At the end of the study 24 children were judged abused and 77 were judged accident.

The Follow-up Study

Subject Selection

The follow-up study was conducted approximately eight years after the base study. Abused children were matched to accident children on age, race, sex, and

---

* "Impact event" means an accident or injury caused by an exchange of energy, *e.g.*, a fall or a blow. It excludes other types of accidents such as burns or ingestions.

socioeconomic status; 17 matching pairs could be identified and studied. In each group there were nine blacks (seven boys and two girls) and eight whites (five boys and three girls). The children were largely lower-class (classes IV and V) according to the Two-factor Index of Social Position.[8]

The comparison children had not been studied before. They were selected from hospital populations and were matched to the traumatized children on the same demographic variables. In addition we required that there be no history of abuse according to Child Welfare Services records and no history of accident resulting in referral to a hospital before the age of 12 months.

Many of the traumatized children had been hospitalized before age 12 months because of their injuries. Since hospitalization implies separation from the mother, and since very young children are considered especially vulnerable to such separation, it seemed possible that any group differences found between traumatized and untraumatized children might be attributable to differences in hospital experience during infancy. To avoid such a possibility, we decided to control for this variable.

The members of nine pairs of traumatized children were similar as to infantile hospitalization, *i.e.*, either both had been inpatients or neither had been. For each of these pairs we selected one untraumatized comparison child who was matched on early hospital experience as well as on the relevant demographic variables. The members of eight pairs of traumatized children were dissimilar as to infantile hospitalization. For each of these pairs we selected two comparison children. One matched the abused child as to infantile hospital experience and the other matched the accident child. The condition leading to inpatient care of comparison children had to be acute illness, not trauma.

To control for hospitalization, a total of 25 comparison subjects were chosen. The analyses to be described compare (1) abused children and untraumatized children, matched as to infantile hospital experience; (2) accident children and untraumatized children, matched as to infantile hospitalization; and (3) abused children and accident children. In the latter comparison, history of hospitalization could not be controlled as nine of the 17 abused children but only five of the 17 accident children had been inpatients before the age of 12 months.

Hypotheses

The hypotheses were that the abused would fall below the nonabused children in (1) height and weight, (2) language development, (3) self-concept, and (4) intellectual functioning; and that the abused would score higher than the non-abused children as to (5) impulsivity, (6) aggression, and (7) the number of interim illnesses and accidents. Children no longer in the abusive environment, *i.e.*, in foster or adoptive homes, were expected to function at a higher level than those who had remained with the abusive caretakers.

Procedures

The care-takers of all 34 traumatized children were located. At the time of follow-up, eight abused children were living with foster or adoptive families. Mothers were interviewed at home to gather demographic data and information about maternal health, perception of the child, and methods of reward and punishment. Black mothers were seen by a black female interviewer and white mothers by a white female interviewer.

Each child was brought to the laboratory for a half-day of evaluations. All clinicians were blind to the child's group identification (abuse, accident, or comparison).

Health was assessed by means of a pediatric examination that included history, anthropometric measures, systems review, and attention to behavioral symptoms and gross neurological signs. Anthropometric measures were later converted into percentiles for age and sex. Well-child care was assessed by examining the immunization record, last visit to the dentist and dental appearance, and physical care, *e.g.*, cleanliness of skin, hair, and clothes. Health data were rated on a five-point scale by a physician and a research assistant, both blind to the children's classification, working in concert.

An experienced speech pathologist performed the language evaluation, which consisted of ratings of articulation during testing[9] and during conversation. Expressive language was judged from the child's responses to the Blacky cards and from five stories that the child made up.

All the child's productions were recorded; articulation during testing and conversational articulation were judged from audio tapes and expressive language from transcripts. Both articulation and expressive language were scored on a five-point scale from 1, very poor, to 5, very good. Other communication disorders, *e.g.*, excessive nonfluency or voice deviations, were noted by the clinician during the testing.

Test-retest reliability was calculated after two months, using the tapes of 12 children and the transcripts of 12 others. For articulation during conversation the reliability was .89 and for expressive language, .96. Reliability with each of two other judges was .88 and .90 for articulation and the same for expressive language.

Self-concept was evaluated by means of the Piers-Harris Children's Self-concept Scale.[10] This is a paper-and-pencil test yielding numerical scores of self-concept in relation to six areas: behavior, intelligence, appearance, anxiety, popularity, and happiness. The overall score is the sum of the six subscales. The test has been widely used for children of approximately the same age as our subjects.

Intellectual standing was assessed by analyzing the entire school record of each child, including results of tests administered in school, grades, and grade placement. A senior psychologist who was familiar with the different school systems involved, and also with the tests commonly used, examined the de-identified data for each child. Achievement and ability were rated separately as either less than average or average. The ratio of achievement to ability was calculated.

A pre-coded teacher questionnaire modeled on that used by Werner *et al.*[11] was designed to obtain systematic data on all children concerning school behavior and attitudes.* Each item of the questionnaire was analyzed separately by assigning a numerical score of 0 to 2. Total scores were added to estimate the teacher's overall impressions of each child.

Impulsivity and aggression were assessed by means of a dramatic role-play procedure administered by an expressive arts clinician. The child verbalized and used

---

* A copy of the teacher questionnaire is available from author on request.

puppets to act out stories in response to five stimulus situations described by the clinician. A sixth story was entirely spontaneous.

The stories were transcribed, separated, and numbered according to a random table in order to scramble subjects and stories. Two judges independently rated the stories for each of the variables, using a scale that had previously been tested on the story productions of 20 other children. Reliability figures for the 354 stories (six stories for each of the 59 subjects) were impulsivity, .83 and aggression, .98.

Groups of children were compared as to the mean score for each behavioral quality on each story and across all stories, and on the difference between ratings for each behavior for story 5 minus story 1, and for story 6 minus story 1. The purpose was to assess possible changes in impulsivity and aggression as the child got into increasing fantasy material. Analysis of variance was used to assess changes in patterns between groups.

Several months after the conclusion of testing, all available record material concerning the child's behavior, past and present, was summarized in writing for each child. Possible comments about abuse were deleted as were all identifying data. The material formed the basis for clinical assessments of behavior by a senior psychiatrist, an experienced social worker, and a professional mental health worker with children. The children were rated on control of aggression: under, over, or about average; and on probable degree of disturbance using a five-point scale: 1, very disturbed, to 5, no apparent disturbance. References to nervous mannerisms were collected from teacher questionnaires and pediatric data.

Results

Although material is available for the families, in this paper the focus will be the children. All statistical tests are based on two-tailed estimates of probability.

Anthropometric measures for the children were compared by means of t-tests of the percentiles for height, weight, and head circumference. The only difference was in weight: the 17 abused children weighed significantly more than their nonabused comparisons ($t_{32} = 2.010$; $P < .05$).

Assessment of well-child care showed that immunizations and physical child care were adequate for the entire sample. The abused children were receiving poorer dental care than their comparison group but this was not a significant difference.

Data for injuries and illnesses showed that the abused children had had a greater number of such occurrences than their untraumatized comparisons, while the accident children exceeded both their untraumatized comparisons and the abused children. The only difference that was significant, however, was accident *vs.* untraumatized ($\chi^2 = 9.14$; $df = 2$; $P < .05$). No differences appeared as to ratings for systems review or operations and hospitalizations.

An interesting serendipitous finding was the extent of allergies in the sample. Twenty-four percent of all the children were subject to one or more of a long list of allergies or allergic manifestations, *e.g.*, asthma, hay fever, hives, or sensitivity to foods or plants. Asthma was a problem for seven children or 12% of all subjects. (Asthmatic children were also counted among those with allergies.) This contrasts with a figure of 2.8% reported for school children in Houston, Texas.[12] Since asthma has been categorized as a disease with strong emotional overtones, we compared the children with and without asthma on clinical ratings of aggression, estimated degree of disturbance, and tallies of nervous mannerisms. None of these showed any association with the disease.

Ratings of neurological findings showed that five abused and four accident children were at the lower points of the scale (poor or very poor). One of the comparison children for the abuse group also had a rating of poor. However, there were no significant differences between any of the major groups.

The groups were compared as to articulation in conversation, expressive language, other communication disorders, and combinations of these problems. No differences were found among the major groups. The surprising finding was the extent of language difficulties across all subjects. Seventy percent of the 56 children who could be rated had one or more language problems. Fifty-seven percent were poor or very poor in articulation; 39% were poor or very poor in expressive language; and 45% demonstrated other communication disorders, *e.g.*, stuttering or intermittent aphonia. The last figure is of particular interest since such problems are widely believed to be associated with tension and anxiety.

Abused children in foster or adoptive homes, compared to those in their natural homes, had a significantly greater number of problems in articulation ($P < .025$, Fisher's Exact Probability) and in combinations of communication problems ($P < .025$, Fisher's Exact Probability), and also tended to be poorer in expressive language. Goldfarb[13] noted that children placed away from a noxious environment recovered in most respects but did not improve substantially in language. Another possible explanation is that the difference in language skills were due to social status and ethnic differences. Foster/adoptive children and natural home children were of course not matched. Six of the eight children in substitute care were lower-class black children, while six of the nine children in natural homes were white; four of these were middle-class. Analyses of expressive language and conversational articulation among all the study children according to socioeconomic status showed that both skills were significantly associated with class: more children in the lower classes (four and five) were rated poor or very poor on expressive language ($\chi^2 = 8.32$; $P < .01$), and also on articulation ($\chi^2 = 8.77$; $P < .01$). Other investigators, for example Bernstein,[14] have also found that poorer language skills are a concomitant of lower class. In our sample, analyses of the same skills by ethnic origin indicated that whites had significantly better expressive language ($\chi^2 = 6.93$; $P < .01$). Although ratings of articulation favored whites, the difference was not significant. Thus, the only significant differences in language were between two subgroups of the major abuse group. In these comparisons the direction of the differences was contrary to expectations. (We expected that children in foster homes would perform better.)

Analysis of the Piers-Harris self-concept material showed no group differences on any of the subscales or on the overall scores.

School achievement ratings, combining the untraumatized comparison groups, are shown in Table I.

Although the proportion of less-than-average achievers was comparatively high in the abuse group, this was not significantly different. Ratings of ability showed even fewer differences: ten children, 16% of all subjects, were assessed as less than average in ability. Four of these were abused, three in the accident group, and three

TABLE I

School Achievement Ratings

Rating	Group		
	Abuse	Accident	Comparison
< average	9	5	7
≥ average	8	12	18

in the comparison group. No group differences appeared in the ratio of achievement to ability.

The range of scores on the teacher questionnaire was 12 to 38. Analysis of the results showed a tendency toward lower (less favorable) scores for the 17 abused children compared to their accident matches, but this was not a significant difference. Item analysis produced no differences between the major groups. Thus, teachers of the abused children appeared to perceive them as more troubled in general but there was no specific area that could be pinpointed.

Mean ratings of the children's scores for impulsivity and aggression were obtained for six stories for each child. There were no group differences on either of these variables considering either the mean score for each story or means across all stories. Further analyses of the ratings produced only three significant differences, all comparing the abused children with the matched accidents. One result showed a greater increase in aggression among abused children between stories one and six ($P < .05$), and one an increase in impulsivity among abused children between stories one and five ($P = .03$). Finally, analysis of variance showed that the abused group had a significantly different pattern of impulsivity from story one to six ($P = .04$).

These results are difficult to interpret. On one hand, marked increases in aggression and impulsivity under the pressure of ongoing provocative stimuli could well be one of the differences between abused and nonabused children; the consistency of the findings would seem to support this possibility. On the other hand, no differences appeared between the abused group and its untraumatized comparisons. Also, the percentage of significant findings was small compared to the number of tests on this material. The conclusions must therefore be considered equivocal: the findings may represent a fertile lead for exploration with a larger number of children but they also may be no more than chance findings.

Nervous mannerisms were assessed by means of pediatric data and also through systematic inquiry on the teacher questionnaire. These mannerisms included behaviors such as thumb-sucking, tics, biting fingers or nails, etc. The group with the fewest nervous mannerisms was the abused group (29%). More than one half the children in each of the other groups were listed as having one or more nervous mannerisms but comparisons with the abused group were not statistically significant. A plausible explanation is that the abused child might act out more and therefore have less need for this type of symptom. Neither the clinical assessment of behavior nor the ratings of impulsivity and aggression according to the dramatic role play stories supported this possibility.

Judgments based on the total behavioral history of the child concerned control of aggression and estimated degree of disturbance. Only five children (8%) were seen as dealing with aggression adequately. Twenty-one children (36%) were judged either variable or undercontrolled and 33 (56%) overcontrolled. The majority (58%) showed some degree of disturbance. Comparisons between the groups showed no differences for any of these ratings but the number of individual children with one or more behavior problems was obviously high.

Several clinicians observed a pronounced feminine identification among each of three abused black boys. During the speech evaluation one of these children began to imitate a girl's voice. When the clinician recognized verbally what he was doing, the child placed a towel over his head, calling it a wig, and continued to talk for the rest of the period in a high falsetto voice. He said that he enjoyed pretending to be a girl at home, and his foster mother confirmed this interest.

One can do no more than speculate about the meaning of these boys' feminine interests. In each case the natural mother was thought to be the abuser, which suggests as explanation a form of identification with the aggressor. Another possible explanation is that all three children were responding to their perception of the world as a matriarchal society. Until recent years one frequently encountered such an analysis of family structure among blacks, although the validity of this formulation has been disputed.[15]

To summarize the follow-up findings: when pertinent demographic variables were taken into account, few overall differences were found between abused, accident, and comparison children. Among the characteristics where no differences were detected were health, language development, intellectual status in school, self-concept, and behavior. The abused differed significantly from their peers only in weight (abused were heavier) and in a few measures of impulsivity and aggression. Each of these differences was in relation to *either* accident or untraumatized children, not to both groups, a fact that tends to weaken the results.

Differences were found in relation to certain subgroups. For example, ratings of language development favored abused children in their own homes compared with abused children in foster/adoptive homes. These findings, however, may stem from differences in social status or ethnicity.

Some differences were also found between another abused subgroup and its matched comparisons. Since this subgroup was characterized by gross neglect as well as abuse, these analyses are not included in this presentation.

Discussion

The absence of substantial differences between the abused children and their matched comparisons was strengthened by our clinical impressions concerning the families. No one group of families stood out: the majority appeared chaotic and poorly organized; many parents relied upon drugs or alcohol; and most were living in circumstances of daily violence. One mother described a recent break-in of her home which had caused her to shoot at the unknown intruder. Another woman talked of a neighborhood shoot-out when she and her children were forced to take refuge under beds and in stairwells. There were reports of fathers pushing mothers downstairs, women beating their children for minor infringements, and children attacking each other with knives and other deadly weapons.

Examples of violence were by no means confined to the abusive group but appeared equally in both the accident and the comparison groups. In one comparison family, the mother reported an incident when she had lunged at the father with a butcher knife. The father retaliated by breaking her arm and knocking out her front teeth. The same man had attacked his teen-age son with a knife because the boy crossed the street against orders. By the time we evaluated the 8-year-old, the parents had separated and scenes of violence were presumably reduced. But the mother had been on massive amounts of tranquilizers for six years, without medical supervision; she spoke of herself as a zombie who scarcely knew what was going on.

The examiners' clinical impressions of the children were alike in disbelief that so many could appear so handicapped psychologically. Overall, the children had an air of depression, sadness, and anxiety. One accident child voiced suicidal wishes. As part of many spontaneous stories told to the examiners, great concern was shown by the children that they might become the victims of attack. Most children of this age are involved with fantasies of witches, devils, and monsters that will eat up others or set fire to them, etc. These children, by contrast, linked their fears of injury or mutilation to real persons, not fantasy figures. The other persons might be parents, older children, or school teachers. Six of the black boys talked about being paddled in school.

Several children produced stories or fantasies that seemed to be associated with personal mistreatment. One child spent five minutes explaining and demonstrating with materials at hand just how a child might be tied with a lamp cord so he could be beaten.

One of the examiners observed that the terms used by Steele and Pollock[16] to describe abusive families match those used by Pavenstedt[17] to describe impoverished lower-class families: emotional problems, impoverished communication, isolation, self-devaluation, vulnerability to criticism, and separation anxiety. The majority of this study sample were identified with the lower classes (IV and V) and might be described in the same way.

The question remains why no systematic differences were found between abused children and their matched comparisons. Several explanations are possible. All but one of the children in the sample lived in the Greater Pittsburgh Metropolitan Area; all were known to a hospital; and the majority were identified with the lower classes. The first possible explanation concerns place of residence: perhaps children living in Pittsburgh are subjected to poorer methods of child-rearing than their peers living in other communities. Although this hypothesis appears unlikely, it cannot be disputed without studies of other children matched on the relevant variables and reared in other locations.

A second possible explanation for the absence of differences between abused and other study children is the fact that all came from hospital populations; their parents may therefore have utilized exceptionally harsh child-rearing methods. Like the first hypothesis, this one also seems unlikely. If social class is held constant, no valid reason exists to postulate a difference between hospital clients and non-hospital clients as to the use of aggression in child-rearing.

A third possibility is that the entire sample, not just the abused children, had been repeatedly subjected to uncontrolled aggression at the hands of their care-takers, who used such methods because of their lower-class membership. No conclusive data presently exist to confirm such an explanation.

The last hypothesis is that identification of a family with the lower classes may be as potent a factor as abuse for the development of a child. In a ten-year study, Werner *et al.*[11] found that the most powerful influence on development was social class membership. Whether or not the child is the target of physical insults, as part of the family he is inevitably caught up in the stress and privation to which his family is prey.

Any one of these explanations could account for the high proportion of children in our sample with developmental problems and also for their prevailing mood of sadness and anxiety. Validation of the results of this study await similar controlled investigations of children living in other communities, and from a range of socioeconomic status. The use of matched comparison groups to evaluate the outcome for abused children does offer a means to correct conclusions based on the study of abused children alone.

REFERENCES

1. LIGHT, R.: "Abused and neglected children in America: A study of alternative policies." *Harvard Educ. Rev.* 43:556, 1973.

2. "Child neglect an epidemic, study says." *New York Times*, November 30, 1975.

3. ELMER, E.: *Children in Jeopardy.* Pittsburgh, University of Pittsburgh Press, 1967.

4. SILVER, L. B., *et al.*: "Does violence breed violence? Contributions from a study of the child abuse syndrome." *Am. J. Psychiatry* 126:404, 1969.

5. MORSE, C. W., *et al.*: "A three year follow-up study of abused and neglected children." *Am. J. Dis. Child* 120:439, 1970.

6. MARTIN, H. P., *et al.*: "The development of abused children." In Schulman I (ed): *Advances in Pediatrics.* Chicago, Year Book Medical Publishers, 1974.

7. FRIEDMAN, S. B., MORSE, C. W.: "Child abuse: A five-year follow-up of early case finding in the emergency department." *Pediatrics* 54:404, 1974.

8. HOLLINGSHEAD, A. B. *Two Factor Index of Social Position.* Unpublished manuscript, 1956.

9. FUDALA, J.: *Arizona Articulation Proficiency Scale, Revised.* Los Angeles, Western Psychological Services, 1970.

10. PIERS, E. V., HARRIS, D. B.: *The Piers-Harris Children's Self-Concept Scale,* Nashville, Counselor Recordings & Tests, 1970.

11. WERNER, E. E., *et al.*: *The Children of Kauai: A Longitudinal Study from the Prenatal Period to Age Ten.* Honolulu, University of Hawaii Press, 1971.

12. SMITH, J.: "Incidence of atopic disease." *Med. Clin. North Am.* 58:3, 1974.

13. GOLDFARB, W. "Effects of psychological deprivation in infancy and subsequent stimulation." *Am. J. Psychiatry* 102:18, 1945.

14. BERNSTEIN, B.: "A public language: Some sociological implications of a linguistic form." *Br. J. Sociol.* 10:311, 1959.

15. BAUGHMAN, E. E.: *Black Americans: A Psychological Analysis.* New York, Academic Press, 1971.

16.   STEELE, B. F., POLLOCK, C. B.: "A psychiatric study of parents who abuse infants and small children." In, Helfer, R. E., Kempe, C. H. (eds.): *The Battered Child.* Chicago, University of Chicago Press, 1968.

17.   PAVENSTEDT, E. (ed.): *The Drifters: Children of Disorganized Lower-Class Families.* Boston, Little Brown, 1967.

38

Behavioral Observations of Abused Children*

Harold P. Martin
and Patricia Beezley

Introduction

The neurological and cognitive sequelae of physical abuse to children have been well documented over the past 13 years (Elmer 1967, Birrell and Birrell 1968, Gregg and Elmer 1969, Martin 1972, Martin *et al.* 1974, Franklin 1975, Sandgrund *et al.* 1975, Baher *et al.* 1976, Martin 1976). Considerably less attention has been given to the psychological wounds of the abused child.

The major reason for embarking on this study was to assess the physical status, the neurological function and the intellectual abilities of a group of abused children some years after abuse had been recognized. We also decided to make observations of the children's personality characteristics.

Our second concern had to do with the widespread assumption that the characteristics of abused children are primarily the result of the physical abuse itself. We have looked at a number of factors in the environment of the abused child, in addition to the physical trauma, which impinge upon his psychological development.

Method

Fifty abused children and their environments were assessed at a mean of 4½ years after physical abuse was first identified. The children ranged in age from 22 months

---

* Harold P. Martin and Patricia Beezley, "Behavioral Observations of Abused Children," *Developmental Medicine and Child Neurology*, Vol. 19, 1977: 373-387. Copyright © 1977 Spastics International Medical Publications. Reproduced by permission.

to 13 years (mean 6 years 5 months). A more complete description of the children can be found elsewhere (Martin *et al.* 1974), but a point to note is that these children were less severely battered than is usual in children reported in the literature. Over half of the children had suffered only soft-tissue trauma. As with any retrospective study which depends on the cooperation of parents, there are biases in the group selection. In this particular study the biases include our studying some of the 'best' of a random sample of abused children (*e.g.* less severely injured, families willing to allow researchers to interview and examine their children, less mobile families). Obviously the results reflect that bias and therefore are more optimistic than they might be from a random sample of abused children.

The children were brought to the University Medical Center for testing and interview. The research team consisted of a developmental pediatrician, a clinical social worker and a clinical child psychologist. While one of the three members of the team was in the interview room with the child, the other two researchers observed behind a one-way mirror. These observations were made during a physical examination, intelligence testing, interviews and a neuro-developmental assessment. In addition to the clinical observations of the three researchers, data about the child's behavior at home and at school were obtained by interviews with the parents during a home visit and from reports of teachers and social workers who had contact with the children and their families.

Findings

From previous clinical experience and earlier studies of abused children (Martin 1972, 1976), the authors arbitrarily decided to concentrate on nine characteristics in these children. The children were diagnosed independently by each examiner. A child was assessed as fitting a particular behavior category when: (*a*) all three examiners independently diagnosed the child as having one of the characteristics; and (*b*) there were corroborative data from parents, teachers or social workers that this characteristic was typical of the child and not a result of our examinations. The nine characteristics included:

(1) impaired ability for enjoyment;
(2) behavioral symptoms;
(3) low self-esteem;
(4) withdrawal;
(5) opposition;
(6) hypervigilance;
(7) compulsivity;
(8) precocious behavior;
(9) school learning problems.

Impaired Ability for Enjoyment

This was the characteristic most frequently diagnosed, being displayed by 33 of the 50 children. They lacked the capacity to play freely, to laugh and to enjoy themselves in an uninhibited fashion. They did not complain, even when frustrated or tired, which suggested that they had learned to accept an unrewarding world. Activities and games which most normal children enjoy under similar circumstances were met with sullenness, obsequious participation, opposition, or a stoical acceptance of the activity as a chore to be accomplished.

Behavioral Symptoms

These symptoms included behavior which parents and other adults complain of and which most professionals would agree are signs of emotional turmoil. They include enuresis, poor peer relationships (especially aggression and avoidance), temper tantrums, potentially delinquent behavior, sleep disturbance, hyperactivity and socially inappropriate behavior, occasionally accompanied by thought disorder. These symptoms were found in 31 children.

Self-esteem

Very few children thought well of themselves. 26 of the 50 children showed obviously low self-esteem. Self-deprecation, a lack of self-confidence and frequent comments of "I can't do it" or "I am bad" were the basis of such a judgment. Of the other 24 children, some of whom did appear to value themselves, it could not be determined whether theirs was a genuine feeling of worthiness or a defense against the opposite feelings of poor self-esteem. Two children were too young to assess. Only 11 of 26 children rated as low in self-esteem sought out or were noticeably affected by praise.

Withdrawal

The 12 withdrawn children were extremely fearful during the testing sessions, as well as in other settings (as reported by others). These children also tended to be inattentive, unco-operative, and had low tolerance of frustration.

Opposition

The 12 oppositional children showed either aggressive or passive-aggressive resistance in the testing situation and in their daily lives. They showed a lack of concern in completing any task and were unable to accept limits set by adults.

Hypervigilance

Eleven of the 50 children were unusually hypervigilant towards their surroundings, in scanning for cues and reading the moods of the people about them. These children's vigilance and heightened alertness to the environment appeared to be a wariness of external danger.

Compulsivity

The 11 children who demonstrated marked compulsivity in the testing sessions paid meticulous attention to details, redid tasks to perfection, and gave long, involved answers to questions. Such behavior was evident in other settings as well. They tended to have a high tolerance of frustration and were attentive and co-operative.

Precocious Behavior

The 10 pseudo-adult children demonstrated behavior which was precocious for their age. At home, such a child cared for his parents' emotional needs and performed household tasks one would expect of an older child. For example, one five-year-old did the family washing; a three-year-old prepared toast and juice and served his mother breakfast in bed; and a five-year-old baby-sat with an infant sibling. During the testing, such children might exhibit concern about the health of the examiners, discuss the appropriateness of the test questions, and quickly impress the examiners with interests, concerns and styles of behavior of an older child. This precocious behavior was involved in either 'caring' behavior towards adults—a sort of pseudo-empathy—or served to engage the adult on the adult's terms rather than on the developmental level of the child. In the testing sessions these children tended to be attentive and co-operative and often manifested high tolerance of frustration.

School Learning Problems

Nine of 34 children were not performing to expected capacity in school; often this was associated with destructive behavior or withdrawal. Children who were doing poorly in school because of brain damage or neurological deficits, as well as children not yet at school, were not included in this category of school learning problems.

Table I summarizes these data and Table II relates the personality characteristics of the 50 children to their median ages and IQ. The age and IQs of the oppositional children were the lowest of the subgroups. However, the lower IQ scores were partially the result of their opposition to the testing procedure: nine of the 12 children were considered to have more intellectual potential than the test scores indicated.

It has been suggested that almost all abused children are pleasant, co-operative, loving beings who, through rôle-reversal (Morris and Gould 1963a, b), obsequiously care for the adults in their surroundings. However, the present study shows there is considerable variation in how abuse and the abusive environment affect children's development: the common cause—physical abuse—does not have a common effect. It is impressive that over 50 per cent of these abused children had poor self-concepts, were sorrowful children and, despite the attendant danger, acted out in a manner upsetting to parents, teachers and peers; nonetheless, some took the path of withdrawal, while others were oppositional. Nine children with at least average intelligence were not learning adequately at school, while others performed well above average in their scholastic work. The bases for such variation are discussed elsewhere (Martin and Beezley 1974, Martin 1976).

TABLE I

Personality traits

Personality traits	Impaired ability to enjoy	Behavior adjustment symptoms	Low self-esteem	With-drawal	Oppo-sitional	Hyper-vigilance	Com-pulsivity	Pseudo-adult behavior	School learning problems
	No.	No.	No.	No.	No.	No.	No.	No.	No.
Impaired ability to enjoy	33	27	20	11	11	6	7	3	8
Behavioral adjustment symptoms		31	20	9	9	5	4	2	7
Low self-esteen			26	11	7	5	3	2	8
Withdrawal				12	3	3	1	0	4
Oppositional					12	1	0	0	4
Hypervigilance						11	3	3	2
Compulsivity							11	4	0
Pseudo-adult behavior								10	0
School learning problems									9

TABLE II

Personality traits in relation to age, IQ and neurological status

Personality traits	No. of children	Median age (yrs)	Median IQ	Neurological dysfunction*
No. of children	50	6·1	98·5	15
Impaired ability to enjoy	33	6·0	87·8	12
Behavioral adjustment symptoms	31	6·1	86·5	11
Low self-esteem	26	6·6	95	8
Withdrawal	12	5·7	93	3
Oppositional	12	5·2	86	1
Hypervigilance	11	7·0	106	4
Compulsivity	11	8·5	101	5
Pseudo-adult behavior	10	8·6	117	2
School learning problems	9	7·5	95·0	0

* Number of children with significant neurological dysfunction.

Home Environments of the Children

We were interested in the nature of the home environments and their relationship to personality characteristics and the modes of adaptation of the abused children. We do feel strongly that when assessing the effects of child abuse on the child's subsequent development, great care must be taken to separate out the effects of the abuse itself (the physical trauma) and the abusive environment (the environment in which the abuse occurred).

From records, home visits, and parental interviews, five environmental characteristics were found to occur frequently.

Home Changes

This included all moves the child made, such as natural home to foster home, foster home to foster home, or foster home to natural home. 17 children (34 per cent) had had from three to eight home changes from the time of the identified abuse to follow-up (mean period 4·5 years).

Unstable Home

This was characterized by poor household management, unemployment, multiple family moves, and chaotic social structure. 16 (32 per cent) of the 50 children were living in such a home. Over half the children in this type of home were also aware that their present home might not be a permanent one for them.

Parental Emotional Disturbance

Each parent's current personality functioning was assessed after several contacts. Additional data were obtained from therapists, public health nurses and welfare workers. Common personality traits included marked dependence, social isolation, low self-esteem, low tolerance of frustration and poor control of aggressive impulses. The degree of disturbance varied greatly, but only those parents whose emotional difficulties significantly interfered with their daily functioning were included in this category. 72 per cent of the natural parents were judged to fit this category.

Punitive Environment

This consisted of current excessive physical punishment (such as whippings with a belt or severe spankings) and/or obvious verbal rejection or hostility toward the child. Natural and foster parents spontaneously reported the excessive punishment, but no marks or bruises were found on any of the children. Rejection was defined as physical and verbal behavior by the parents which indicated a pervasive dislike of or dissatisfaction with the child. It was not uncommon for the parent to talk of the child, in their presence, as worthless or bad. The children also received this message through the parents' behavior. 24 of the 50 homes (48 per cent) were classified as highly punitive.

Divorce or Parental Separation

Fifty-eight per cent of the children at some stage had experienced the divorce or separation of their parents.

Table III summarizes the personality characteristics of the 50 children and their relationship to the factors in the home environments. It is notable that children who were oppositional, withdrawn, or who had behavioral problems are much more likely to be living in sub-optimal environments than the compulsive or pseudo-adult children. To examine more carefully the relationship of present home environment to the abused child's personality, the category of behavioral symptoms was looked at in more detail.

Differences in the behavior of the 50 children were noted and, according to the frequency and pervasiveness of their symptoms, the children were classified in one of four categories:

(1) no symptoms;

(2) few (1-2) symptoms;

(3) numerous (3-4) symptoms;

(4) severe disturbance (3 or more symptoms of severe intensity).

Five factors were found to be related to the severity and frequency of symptoms in the child: the number of home changes; a child's sense of impermanence in present home; instability of home; a punitive home; and parental emotional disturbance.

The more symptoms the child had, the more likely he was to have had three or more home changes (Table IV). Permanence of the present home was considered to be questionable when the child perceived the realistic possibility of losing his home at any time. He may have been subjected to sudden and frequent home changes in the past, and to his present caretaker's verbal threats to send him away. For example, several natural mothers and foster mothers threatened, as a means of discipline, to send their children to orphanages or to new foster homes. The more maladjusted a child was, the more likely he was to have perceived his present home as lacking permanence. There was also a significant relationship between behavioral maladjustment and instability of the child's present home environment. Additionally, the more maladjusted a child was, the more likely he was to be living in a punitive home and to have emotionally disturbed parents, although this relationship was not statistically significant.

There are two possible explanations for these relationships. A child's behavioral symptoms may increase as the result of experiencing frequent home changes, feeling a lack of permanence in his present home, living in an unstable home, or being subjected to punitive or emotionally disturbed parents. Alternatively, the home changes, impermanence, instability, punitiveness and parental emotional disturbance may be provoked or increased by the child's behavior. Most likely, there is an interaction between both of these factors, that is, the environment is reacted to by the child with symptoms, which in turn are reacted to by parents with more punishment, rejection and family chaos.

The adjustment of the children was also related to their present home placement (Table V). Many of the children with the most symptoms were in the care of foster parents, and no child with numerous or severe symptoms had been adopted. Children who remained in their natural homes were more likely to be living in

TABLE III

Personality Traits in relation to home environment

Personality traits	No. of children	Parental emotional problems	Divorce or separation of parents	Punitive environments	Present home might not be permanent	≥3 Home changes	Present home unstable
No. of children	50	36	29	24	19	17	16
Impaired ability to enjoy	33	23	21	17	14	14	11
Behavioral adjustment symptoms	31	25	21	19	16	15	13
Low self-esteem	26	19	15	14	12	11	7
Withdrawal	12	8	10	7	7	6	6
Oppositional	12	11	9	8	6	5	7
Hypervigilance	11	7	6	4	4	3	2
Compulsivity	11	7	3	5	1	2	0
Pseudo-adult behavior	10	5	5	1	2	1	1
School learning problems	9	7	5	4	5	5	3

TABLE IV

Behavioral adjustment in relation to home environment

Home environment	No symptoms		Few symptoms		Numerous symptoms††		Severe disturbance††	
	No.	%	No.	%	No.	%	No.	%
No. of children†	18		16		8		7	
≥3 home changes*	2	11·0	7	44·0	4	50·0	4	57·0
Present home might not be permanent**	3	17·0	4	25·0	6	75·0	6	86·0
Unstable home*	2	11·0	5	31·0	5	63·0	3	43·0

† One child excluded because of severe brain damage.
†† Numerous and severe categories combined for χ^2.
* $p < ·05$
** $p < ·001$

punitive and unstable environments than children in foster or adoptive homes (Table VI).

It appears from these findings that the abused child's development is related to the nature of the family with whom he lives *after* the identified abuse. The child's adjustment is also partially related to the number of home placements and the type of foster parents chosen. It would seem appropriate, then, to consider the relationship between the therapy the abusing parents had and the subsequent development of the abused child.

TABLE V

Behavioral adjustment in relation to home placement

Home placement	No symptoms		Few symptoms		Numerous symptoms		Severe disturbance	
	No.	%	No.	%	No.	%	No.	%
With natural parents (N= 31)	10	32·0	13	42·0	5	16·0	3	10·0
With foster parents (N= 11*)	3	27·0	1	9·0	3	27·0	4	37·0
With adoptive parents (N= 7)	5	71·0	2	29·0		0		0
Total (N = 49*)	18	37·0	16	33·0	8	16·0	7	14·0

* One child excluded because of severe brain damage.

TABLE VI

Quality of home placement

	Natural parents	Foster parents	Adoptive parents	Total
	No.	No.	No.	No.
Home placement	31	12	7	50
Excessive physical punishment and/or rejection	21	2	1	24
Excessive physical punishment	15	1	1	17
Instability of home	14	2	0	16

Intervention with Natural Parents

As soon as abuse of the children had been identified by a professional, the parents were offered considerable help to assist them through the temporary crisis. Usually they were also offered (or confronted with the need for) some type of longer-term professional intervention. For the purposes of this study, we have divided the treatment into three arbitrarily defined groups: psychotherapy, supportive care, or no formal intervention.

Psychotherapy is defined as treatment by a psychiatrist, a clinical psychologist or a psychiatric social worker. The therapy was given either in a mental-health clinic or in one of the general hospitals. The length, frequency and nature of the therapy varied, as did the experience and the style of the therapist, but generally the focus was on the intra-psychic problems of the parents, particularly the mother.

Supportive care is defined as professional assistance from either a welfare worker or a public-health nurse, who visited the home regularly and dealt directly with parent-child interaction and other marital, economic or social problems. These professionals usually were not able to deal with the intra-psychic problems of the mother, either because they were not trained to do so or their case-loads did not permit the time.

No intervention, obviously, means that no professional treatment and help were given. Either the parents had refused professional care or, inadvertently, were not offered it. They also appeared to have received little or no psychological assistance from non-professionals (*e.g.* friends, relatives, neighbors or religious ministers).

We acknowledge that this division of therapy is arbitrary. More valuable data might have been obtained by assessing factors such as frequency and length of therapy, the parents' perception of the help they were getting, or the commitment to change of both therapists and patients; however, because this study was retrospective, such information was not available. Accordingly, comparisons between the three types of intervention can only be in very general terms, but some impressions can be obtained by examining and comparing results in terms of the personality adjustment of the children whose parents had had intervention with those whose parents had not.

Psychotherapy

Almost half (21) of the parents* of the 50 children received psychotherapy (see Table VII). Eight (38 per cent) of these parents had inflicted severe injuries such as head trauma, fracture, or second or third-degree burns. 13 (62 per cent) had inflicted less severe injuries such as bruises, welts and bites. Parents receiving psychotherapy had a good chance of keeping their child with them or having him returned from foster care. Parents' willingness to accept psychotherapy was seen as an optimistic sign for changing parent-child interaction, so permanent placement of the child outside the natural home usually was not seriously considered. 90 per cent of the parents who received psychotherapy had their previously injured child living at home with them at the time of the follow-up. None of these released the child for adoption, whether or not this was recommended by professionals.

However, the incidence of excessive physical punishment and/or hostile rejection in these homes remains strikingly high. Even though the children were not being battered in the technical or legal sense, 68 per cent were still receiving excessive physical punishment and/or were experiencing overt rejection.

It was much easier to assess negative interaction between parent and child than to determine how much positive interaction had taken place at home. For example, beatings may have been occurring less frequently and there may have been the beginning of some mutual enjoyment between parent and child, but while we would have liked to document such improvement, the high incidence of continued excessive physical punishment and rejection was the more striking phenomenon. Furthermore, 38 per cent of the parents who received psychotherapy were still unable to provide a stable home for their child.

Supportive Intervention

Over one-fourth (14) of the total group of parents received only supportive care following their child's injury (see Table VII). 11 (79 per cent) of these parents had in-

---

* 'Parents' refers to both parents if both were present in the home, and to a single parent if it was a one-parent family.

TABLE VII

Parents' therapy

	Total	Psycho-therapy	Supportive therapy	No therapy
No. of children	50	21	14	15
Children with severe injuries	23	8	11	4
Now with foster parents	12	2	5	5
Now with adoptive parents	7	0	3	4
Now with natural parents	31	19	6	6
Excessive physical punishment or overt rejection*	21	13	3	5
Home unstable*	14	8	4	2

* These figures comprise only the 31 children living with natural parents at follow-up.

flicted severe injuries, whereas only three (21 per cent) had inflicted mild soft-tissue damage. The eventual home placement for the 14 children of these parents who had supportive care varied; at the time of the evaluation six were living with their natural parents, five were in foster homes and three had been adopted.

For the six children who were still with their natural parents, the incidence of excessive physical punishment was remarkably low; only one family was in question. However, verbal rejection continued and there remained a high incidence of instability in these homes.

No Intervention

Approximately one-third (15) of the total group of parents received no formal intervention (see Table VII). Four (27 per cent) of these parents had inflicted severe injuries on their child and 11 (73 per cent) had inflicted less severe injuries. At the time of evaluation six of these children were in their natural homes, five were in foster homes and four had been adopted. In almost all instances the parents of children in foster or adoptive homes had little interest in the child and were quite willing to let the welfare department or relatives take legal custody of him.

At follow-up, the amount of excessive punishment and rejection of these children was extremely high (83 per cent), and instability of the home remained a common problem. Children with numerous symptoms or severe disturbance did not remain in their own homes if their parents did not receive some formal type of help (Table VII). Many parents of these disturbed children were quite rejecting and indicated no interest in helping the children remain in their home. It is possible that such total rejection led to the child's behavioral difficulties in the first place or, alternatively, that the parent who received no intervention may be less able to tolerate the child's disruptive and irritating behavior than those parents who received either psychotherapy or supportive care.

Discussion

Abused children have both physical and psychological wounds. Children who have been struck and beaten by their primary love objects, their parents, have to

TABLE VIII

Children's behavior adjustment in relation to intervention
(31 children living with natural parents)

	No symptoms	Few symptoms	Numerous symptoms	Severe disturbance
	No.	No.	No.	No.
Parents received intervention (N= 25)	8	9	5	3
Parents received no intervention (N= 6)	2	4	0	0

deal with this psychological trauma, and such psychological wounds do not heal as readily as do fractures, bruises and lacerations. Anyone who has worked with physically battered children cannot help but be impressed by the differences between these children and most other children. However, abused children are not identical in their psychological profiles: the homes from which they come vary in many ways, and children themselves vary in their capacity to deal with psychological stress. Our object was not to describe a single, typical, personality profile of abused children; it was to identify those characteristics which are seen more commonly in abused children than in the general pediatric population and to identify the characteristics which handicap the child's growth and development.

Our findings are merely a beginning to understanding the psychological wounds of abused children. A number of practical issues prevented us from including a control group of children, so the data must be interpreted with some caution. We believe that the nine characteristics listed above are over-represented in the 50 abused children we studied, in comparison with most children, although we have no statistical evidence. However, even if these characteristics are *not* more prevalent in abused than in non-abused children, we must be concerned about a population of children with such a high preponderance of unhappiness, poor self-concept, learning problems and other psychological symptoms. Furthermore, this study gives some clues to the ways in which children adapt to the psychological trauma of assault from their parents, *e.g.* by withdrawal, opposition, hypervigilance, compulsivity, or by developing areas of precocious ego function.

Early in this century, Freud (1955a, b, c) noted the effect of both childhood and adult trauma (physical and psychological) in the inducement of psychopathology. Anna Freud's discussions (1958, 1969) include descriptions of British children during the Second World War: she notes that their emotional reactions were often due to separations, lack of mobility and deprivation of pleasure rather than to their memories of death and destruction. Our findings in this study, and our clinical experience with hundreds of other abused children, confirm this phenomenon. Physical pain and being assaulted by one's parents are psychologically traumatic events, but a host of other factors in the child's life are more important.

Our data do not confirm any relationship between the type of injury, nor the age at which it was inflicted, and subsequent emotional development. Rather, at an average of $4^{1}/_{2}$ years after the original abuse, psychiatric symptoms were strongly correlated with factors such as the impermanence of the subsequent home, instability of the family with whom the child was living, the acceptance or rejection the child was experiencing, and the emotional state of the parents or parent surrogates.

In a previous paper (Martin *et al.* 1974), we noted that the intelligence of abused children (when brain damage was allowed for) correlated quite highly with the subsequent stability and lack of physical punitiveness in the child's home. Adults are shocked and appalled by the knowledge of children being mistreated physically by their parents, but there is less reaction to a child being unloved, deprived, neglected or being raised by psychologically unfit parents.

A second issue of importance is the consequences of our management. It is not uncommon for professionals involved with the abused child to prescribe separation from the parents, admission to hospital, and foster-home placement. Through social incompetence, we often subject the child to a series of changing homes, which the child interprets as a series of parent losses. It is essential to consider ways of minimizing these stresses when separation or admission to hospital are essential to the child's safety and welfare. Two case descriptions emphasize this point.

Case 1:—We evaluated a six-year-old girl who had had fractures of the skull and tibia at age 12 months. She had subsequently been in 12 different foster homes, and in one adoptive home which did not meet with success. The professionals in this instance prevented a second bout of physical trauma, but they caused this girl to grow up in such a way that attachment, object constancy and trust are minimal, and probably no longer possible to achieve (Mahler *et al.* 1975). She is an attractive little girl with pre-psychotic behavior, learning handicaps, and problems which no longer make it possible for her to be a candidate for an adoptive home. Parental rights were not terminated until the girl was 4-1/2 years of age, 3-1/2 years after the physical abuse. This girl's developmental and psychological problems are not the result of a fractured tibia or skull: they are the result of inadequate, erratic and inconstant parenting. Therapy and good educational programs cannot make up for such a series of significant losses.

Case 2:—A second child (but not included in this study) was a 24-month-old boy who had been adopted at 19 months of age by excellent parents. The boy had been admitted to hospital at one month of age with several bruises about his face and because of failure to thrive, weighing less than his birthweight. From one to nine months of age he had lived in two different foster homes, and at age nine months he was returned to his natural parents. At 13 months of age he was again admitted to hospital with 80 per cent body burns after having been placed in an excessively hot bath. On discharge from hospital he went to a third foster home, and at 19 months of age he was adopted.

When seen at two years this boy had normal intelligence and a normal neurological system, but he is a very unhappy and disturbed child. He is extremely fearful of abandonment, panicking when mother leaves the room. He is extremely compliant and obedient. One day, shortly after his arrival at the adoptive parents' home, he began to cry with vehemence and anguish: the father said "stop crying", and the parents were amazed that he immediately stopped crying. He has an insatiable appetite, eating until he vomits and then continuing to eat until the parents remove all food from his surroundings. He takes no enjoyment in playing; and in fact has had to be taught how to play by his parents. His expressive language is delayed, although this developmental lag is quickly diminishing. He continues still to call all women 'mama' and to run up to strangers to hug and kiss them. The parents are troubled by his unhappiness; they feel an aloofness and distance with him, and they are at a loss to know how to relate to his strange behavior.

Not having seen this child during his first two years, we cannot be sure of all the events that have shaped his behavior. We *do* know that this little boy is now in his sixth home and has had to lose five previous sets of parents. This alone could explain his fearfulness, compliance and confusion about who is a 'mommy', and his tremendous need for food and to be loved, held and talked to.

In relation to therapy for abusive parents, while our data do not allow comparisons of the types of treatment given, there are several findings of interest. The families in this study may have had treatment assigned partially on the basis of the type of injuries they inflicted on their child, rather than on a more psychologically rational basis. Only 38 per cent of the parents who had been referred for psychotherapy had inflicted medically serious wounds on their children, while 79 per cent of the parents who had had supportive therapy had children with such serious medical wounds. The primary purpose of therapy for parents is to prevent recurrence of physical assault on the child; hence families who had inflicted the most severe injuries were considerably more likely to have had the services of a public-health nurse or social worker (who usually visit the home regularly to monitor the child), while those parents who had inflicted less serious damage were more likely to have been referred for intensive psychotherapy. We suggest that the type of injury is not a sound basis for determining the type of therapeutic approach to the parents.

It must be appreciated also that therapy, of whatever sort, for the abusive parent may or *may not* affect the parent-child interaction. This is certainly the case with psychotherapy: although it is often beneficial to the parent, it may only minimally affect the parent-child relationship:

> "Although protection of the infant is a main goal, direct interest in the infant should be avoided by the therapist, paradoxical as this may seem. Attention should be focused almost exclusively on the parent." (Steele and Pollock 1974, p. 126).

It now seems clear that a combination of various types of treatment for the parents is necessary (Steele 1970, 1975, Alexander 1972, Martin and Beezley 1974, Beezley *et al.* 1976, Helfer and Kempe 1976). Psychotherapy, services from a public-health nurse or social worker, groups such as 'Parents Anonymous' and nurturing from a lay therapist may all be required. The goals must be *not only* the physical protection of the child and improvement in the psychic life of the parent, but also alterations in the parent-child relationship.

Finally, we need to consider various forms of treatment for the child himself. Social planning for the abused child needs serious attention. While foster-home placements are often disappointing, they can be quite therapeutic for many children (Stone 1970, Kline and Overstreet 1972, Tizard 1974, Browder 1975, Moss and Moss 1975). In addition to social planning, we must offer the abused child direct help in dealing with his own feelings and reactions. He needs to be encouraged to develop autonomy and a feeling of self-worth. He needs to be shown that there are other relationships possible with adults than those he has experienced with his parents. Also, he needs help to enjoy himself and find pleasure in life. It is improbable that his parents by themselves will be able to help him achieve these goals: they have intra-psychic problems of their own to resolve, and they are doing well if they can control their impulses enough to prevent further serious physical injury to the child. They may be unable to make the necessary changes quickly enough to heal and protect their child's psyche.

Unfortunately, many professionals still assume that a child's emotional problems must be secondary to the parents' reactions to the child: they then erroneously assume that treatment of the parents will solve the child's problems. This is not so. The abused child needs help himself: he needs assistance in improving his self-concept, in loosening his inhibitions and in learning to enjoy life. He needs help in expressing and acknowledging his feelings about assault, neglect and separation from his parents. It may be necessary for him to learn how to live adaptively and to negotiate healthily in a family with parents who have numerous emotional problems themselves. Inasmuch as the parents usually cannot give this help, it must come from someone outside the family.

At The National Center for the Prevention and Treatment of Child Abuse and Neglect in Denver, Colorado, a number of treatment programs have been used in helping abused children deal with their psychological, cognitive and social wounds (Martin 1976). They include therapeutic pre-school groups, crisis nurseries, day-care programs, individual and group psychotherapy, treatment of developmental delays, and a specific program to intervene in the parent-child interaction by working with parents and children together.

SUMMARY

Since Kempe in 1962 first catalysed concern about child abuse, much effort has been expended to protect the lives of abused children and to help the parents. It has been found that many physically abused children can safely be returned to their parents following foster placements for the child and intensive intervention for the parents. But even though the repetition of serious physical injury may be prevented, data from the present follow-up study of 50 abused children points to the pervasive psychic injury that continues.

There was considerable variation in the personalities of the 50 children studied, with over half having low self-esteem and types of symptomatic behavior which made peers, parents and teachers reject them.

The most striking impression was that these abused children were not happy and had minimal ability to enjoy themselves in play or to interact socially as children in a manner appropriate to their ages. Whether inhibited, compulsive, angry, or socially pseudo-adult, they seemed unable to relax and enjoy themselves. The question of how these personality traits will change or be modified with time and maturation is of interest.

The factors which correlated with psychiatric symptoms were not the type or severity of the physical assault; rather, environmental factors such as emotional disturbance in parents, unstable family structure, the number of home changes, punitiveness and rejection by caretakers, and a child's perception of impermanence in his home setting were seen to be related to the effects of child abuse.

REFERENCES

ALEXANDER, H. (1972) "The social worker and the family." In Kempe, C. H., Helfer, R. E. (Eds.) *Helping the Battered Child and His Family*. Philadelphia: Lippincott, pp. 22-40.

BAHER, E., HYMAN, C., JONES, R., KERR, A., MITCHELL, R. (1976) *At Risk: An Account of the Work of the Battered Child Research Department of the N.S.P.C.C.* London: Routledge & Kegan Paul.

BEEZLEY, P., MARTIN, H. L., ALEXANDER, H. (1976) "Treatment for the family and the abused child" In Helfer, R. E., Kempe, C. H. (Eds.), *Child Abuse and Neglect: The Family and the Community*. Cambridge, Mass.: Ballinger Press.

BIRRELL, R. C., BIRRELL, J. H. W. (1968) "The maltreatment syndrome in children—a hospital survey." *Medica Journal of Australia*, 2, 1023-1029.

BROWDER, J. A. (1975) "Adoption and foster care of handicapped children in the United States." *Developmental Medicine and Child Neurology*, 17, 614-619.

ELMER, E. (1967) *Children in Jeopardy.* Pittsburgh: University of Pittsburgh Press.

FRANKLIN, A. W. (Ed.) (1975) *Concerning Child Abuse.* Edinburgh: Churchill Livingstone.

FREUD, A. (1958) "Child observation and prediction of development: a memorial lecture in honor of Ernst Kris." *Psychoanalytic Study of the Child,* 13, 92-124.

____(1969) "Comments on psychic trauma." In *The Writings of Anna Freud.* New York: International Universities Press, Vol. V, pp. 221-241.

FREUD, S. (1955a) "Introduction to psychoanalysis and the war neuroses." In *The Complete Psychological Works of Sigmund Freud.* London: Hogarth Press, Vol. XVII, pp. 205-211.

____(1955b) "Beyond the pleasure principle." In *The Complete Psychological Works of Sigmund Freud.* London: Hogarth Press, Vol. XVIII, pp. 3-64.

____(1955c) "An outline of psychoanalysis." In *The Complete Psychological Works of Sigmund Freud.* London: Hogarth Press, Vol. XXIII, pp. 139-208.

GREGG, G. S., ELMER, E. (1969) "Infant injuries: accident or abuse." *Pediatrics,* 44, 434-439.

HELFER, R. E., KEMPE, C. H. (1976) (Eds.) *Child Abuse and Neglect: The Family and the Community.* Cambridge, Mass.: Ballinger Press.

KLINE, D., OVERSTREET, H. F. (1972) *Foster Care of Children: Nurture and Treatment.* New York: Columbia University Press.

MAHLER, M. S., PINE, F., BERGMAN, A. (1975) *The Psychological Birth of the Human Infant: Symbiosis and Individuation.* New York: Basic Books.

MARTIN, H. P. (1972) "The child and his development." In Kempe, C. H., Helfer, R. E. (Eds.) *Helping the Battered Child and His Family.* Philadelphia: Lippincott, pp. 93-114.

____(Ed.) (1976) *The Abused Child: An Interdisciplinary Approach to Developmental Issues and Treatment.* Cambridge, Mass.: Ballinger Press.

____ BEEZLEY, P. (1974) "Prevention and the consequences of abuse." *Journal of Operational Psychiatry,* 6, 68-77.

____ ____ CONWAY, E. F., KEMPE, C. H. (1974) "The development of abused children: A review of the literature; Part II, Physical, neurologic and intellectual outcome." *Advances in Pediatrics,* 21, 25-73.

MOSS, S. Z., MOSS, M. S. (1975) "Surrogate mother-child relationships." *American Journal of Orthopsychiatry,* 45, 382-390.

SANDGRUND, A., GAINES, R. W., GREEN, A. H. (1975) "Child abuse and mental retardation: a problem of cause and effect." *American Journal of Mental Deficiency,* 19, 327-330.

STEELE, B. F. (1970) "Parental abuse of infants and small children." In Anthony, E. J., Benedek, T. (Eds.) *Parenthood: Its Psychology and Psychopathology.* Boston: Little, Brown, pp. 449-478.

____(1975) *Working with Abusive Parents from a Psychiatric Point of View.* Washington, D.C.: Dept. Health, Education and Welfare.

____ POLLOCK, C. B. (1974) "A psychiatric study of parents who abuse infants and small children." In Helfer, R. E., Kempe, C. H. (Eds.) *The Battered Child,* 2nd edn. Chicago: University of Chicago Press, pp. 89-133.

STONE, H. D. (Ed.) (1970) *Foster Care in Question: A National Reassessment by Twenty-one Experts.* New York: Child Welfare League of America.

TIZARD, J. (1974) "The upbringing of other people's children." *Journal of Child Psychology and Psychiatry,* 15, 161-173.

ACKNOWLEDGEMENTS

We wish to acknowledge the considerable support and professional assistance from Gaston E. Blom, M.D., Jacob G. Jacobson, M.D., and C. Henry Kempe, M.D. We also wish to acknowledge the psychological testing done by Esther Conway, Ph.D., on these children. This study was partially supported by grants from Maternal and Child Health (No. 926), The Grant Foundation, The Commonwealth Fund and the Robert Wood Johnson Foundation.

39

Consciously Rejected Children*

D. A. Pemberton
and D. R. Benady

Introduction

Children who are rejected give a clinical impression of making interpersonal relationships with difficulty. Wolberg (1944) described the consequences of parental rejection as depending upon the age of the child at the time of the rejection, the manner in which frustration was imposed by the parents, the nature and extent of compensatory gratification from others, and the success or failure of spontaneous reparative attempts on the part of the child to establish accepting relationships. Earlier studies of the child's reaction to rejection were marred by the tendency to define rejection too loosely, so that both conscious and unconscious forms were included as well as more frequent ambivalent parental attitudes, with a resultant wide scatter in the form of the children's responses. However, it has been shown by comparison with accepted children that the rejected child is uncommunicative, rebellious, less friendly, and bewildered about life (Symonds, 1938). Rejected children have been noted to be hypersensitive, and it has been speculated that this stems from feelings of insecurity and of not belonging to a permanent setting (Childers, 1935). The types of reaction to rejection were sub-divided into two broad groups—aggressive and submissive (Newell, 1934). Aggressive behaviour, including rebelliousness, disobedience, temper tantrums, quarrelsomeness, stealing and truancy occurred when the parental handling was consistently hostile; while submissive behaviour, including shyness, seclusiveness, cravings for attention, occurred more

* D. A. Pemberton and D. R. Benady, "Consciously Rejected Children," *British Journal of Psychiatry*, Vol. 123 (1973):575-578. Reproduced by permission.

frequently when the parental behaviour was consistently over-protective (Newell, 1936). The aggressive response to hostile rejection was confirmed by Wolberg, who also thought that the symptoms of delinquency, truancy, enuresis and frustration intolerance should be interpreted in the larger framework of the child's attitudes towards himself and the world.

The reasons for maternal rejection have been studied, and it has been found that rejection is primarily due to the mother's unhappy adjustment to marriage which, in turn, is usually a result of immaturity and emotional instability on the part of one or both parents (Newell, 1936).

At this clinic it became apparent that the consciously rejected child seemed to show clearcut clinical characteristics, whilst the parents themselves appeared to have common features. For the purpose of this study, consciously rejected children were defined as those children whose parents had excluded them from the family and had taken active steps to have them placed elsewhere; subsequently most of these parents had severed all contact with the child. We postulated that the consciously rejected child showed a specific behavior response to the insult of rejection.

Methods and Findings

The data concerning all the consciously rejected children, eight boys and four girls, who were seen at the clinic between 1967 and 1969 were collected in a retrospective and prospective study. Our controls were the next patient referred to the clinic of the same age and sex. Because of insufficient information, it was not possible to match for social class; we could postulate that social class as a random factor was equally distributed between both groups.

The Children

1. Age

The mean age of the sample group at referral was 9·0 years with a standard deviation of 3·25 years, and the control group 9·1 years with a standard deviation of 3·4 years.

2. Source of referral

The sample group children were referred to the clinic from various agencies, unlike the control group who were predominantly referred by doctors.

3. Ordinal position

In the sample group the mode was 2:4 and in the control group 2:3.
In the sample group the presenting child was never the youngest member of the family.

4. School career

The school careers of the children were studied from psychologists' reports and social histories. The difficulties they had in attending school, in continuing to attend school, in establishing working relationships with their teachers and their peers, and with school work revealed no significant difference between the sample and control groups.

5. Presenting Symptoms (Table I)

The symptoms of day wetting, nocturnal enuresis, encopresis, stealing, lying, aggression, negativistic attitude and rejecting attitude to parents which the consciously rejected children presented with are shown in Table I. These symptoms are significantly more common in the sample group, except for day and night wetting.

6. Intelligence

The educational psychologists measured the child's intellectual abilities with either the Stanford-Binet or the W.I.S.C. tests.

No statistical difference in intellectual abilities between the two groups was found.

The Parents

1. Mothers

The mother's descriptions of their own personality and of their childhood, as well as the presence of chronic or severe physical illness in the mother, the presence or absence of periods of separation from the child of greater or less than one month, and the mother's attitude to the other children differed little in the two groups.

The mothers of both groups of children had a high incidence of chronic or severe physical ill-health.

In only one family had the mother consciously rejected more than one child.

2. Fathers

In the sample group eight of the fathers also had rejecting attitudes towards the children.

3. The parents' marriage (Table II)

Marital disharmony was present and had been present for many years in every marriage of those parents who consciously rejected their child but was also present to a degree in the control group. However, the difference between the two groups is highly significant statistically.

In the sample group the parents tended to remain together with only one family being completely disrupted. However, in most cases there were either temporary

TABLE I

Presenting symptoms

		Sample (n = 12)	Control (n = 12)
Day wetting	Present (p > 0·05 n.s.)	5	2
Nocturnal enuresis	Present (p > 0·05 n.s.)	9	6
Encopresis	Present * (p = 0·002)	10	2
Stealing	Present * (p = 0·006)	9	2
Lying	Present * (p < 0·002)	10	1
Aggressive	Present * (p = 0·018)	10	4
Negative behaviour	Present * (p < 0·002)	10	1
Rejecting attitude	Present * (p = 0·006)	9	2

TABLE II

		Sample (n = 12)	Control (n = 12)
Marital disharmony	Present (p = 0·002)	12	5
Physical assaults on children	Present (p = 0·002)	12	2

separations of varying time duration or threats of departure. The origins of the marital difficulties were not satisfactorily elucidated in any of the families. This was due to a lack of co-operation and an unwillingness to attend the clinic on the part of the parents. Similarly, the families rejected any form of intervention by the social agencies including psychiatric social workers, education welfare officers and mental welfare officers who were trying to maintain contact once the child had left the home.

4. Assaults on children

The parents who consciously rejected their children assaulted them physically, but as far as is known they only inflicted 'soft' tissue injuries. These parents were vituperative in their description of their child. The following is a sample of their comments: 'She smells', 'He's destructive', 'A champion liar', 'Swears and is never satisfied'. The rejection of their child was expressed in many ways: 'I just hate that child', 'I can't stand her about the house', 'Not our child', 'He could have been changed at the hospital without us knowing', 'Not worth bothering about. I don't care where he goes', 'I don't care about him. I hate him.'

Disposal of Children (sample group only)

One child was able to be reintegrated with his family. Of the remainder, six ended up in the care of the local authority, five attended special schools for maladjusted children, two lived with grandparents and one was returned to her adoptive agency after 12 years. Three of the children in care also attended special schools.

Discussion

This survey confirms the earlier American studies that the consciously rejected child shows more symptoms of aggression, rejecting attitude to parents, negativistic attitude, stealing, lying and encopresis. Newell's studies on the pathology of the parents were supported with the evidence that the parents were unstable and had been so for years, and that the mothers were unsure of their role. This study also appears to demonstrate a reactive phenomenon to a clearly defined environmental stress which appears to be unrelated to the child's personality.

The origins of the scapegoating process were never fully elucidated in any family because of the parents' dislike of discussing their problems and their eagerness to focus attention on one child. The reasons for choosing one particular child were also obscure. However, the child's behaviour in every case served to strengthen the process of rejection. Prolonged emotional deprivation during the earliest years of life did happen to some children, but not all, and when it did occur some had brothers and sisters who had similar experiences yet did not show the same rejection picture. The lack of support from outside the family was noticeable, and it was our impression that the majority of the families were prone to frequent geographical moves.

The process of scapegoating appeared to produce a fragile kind of stability in the rest of the family. Even when the child was removed, the families in all but one case remained together and offered some care for the other children, without the process of scapegoating extending to them.

The consciously rejected children were subsequently seen to be severely damaged by their inability to establish close relationships with other significant persons in their life such as their peers and teachers. This observation was supported by the children's behaviour away from home. Initially they appeared to invite rejection, and only gradually did they show any warmth in their relationships with staff. However, under stress the symptoms returned, indicating the severity of their impairment. These children present a difficult therapeutic challenge where close co-operation between the people looking after them is essential. It is easy even for professionals to reject either the child or the child's family, perhaps needlessly polarizing the negative aspects of the relationships. In all honesty, it is sometimes extremely difficult to find any positive feeling from the family towards the child, and inescapable separation of the child from its family comes about. Whilst this separation may be beneficial in the short term, the difficulty these children have in establishing interpersonal relationships gives rise in their teens to a sense of emptiness and to acting-out behaviour which even whilst understood is extremely difficult to cope with.

It would appear that further studies are needed to assess the subsequent development of these children.

This study of consciously rejected children is incomplete in that it only includes the children referred to the clinic and does not include any children who were rejected in infancy.

Summary

A symptom-complex of aggression, rejecting attitude to parents, negativistic attitudes, stealing, lying and encopresis is described in twelve consciously rejected children. The parents of these children have unstable marriages and this instability antedates the rejection of the child.

ACKNOWLEDGEMENTS

We should like to express our gratitude to the whole Child Guidance staff of the Salop Clinic, and in particular to Mrs. Janice Hughes for her patience and help in preparing the manuscript.

REFERENCES

CHILDERS, A. T. (1935). "Hyperactivity in children having behaviour disorders." *American Journal of Orthopsychiatry*, 5, 227-43.

FINNEY, D. J. (1948). "Fischer-Yates days of significance in 2 x 2 contingency tables. *Biometrika*, vol. xxxv, Paris, 1 and 2.

NEWELL, H. W. (1934). "Psychodynamics of maternal rejection." *American Journal of Orthopsychiatry*, 4, 387-401.

——— (1936). "A further study of maternal rejection." *American Journal of Orthopsychiatry*, 6, 576-89.

SYMONDS, P. M. (1938). "A study of parental acceptance and rejection." *American Journal of Orthopsychiatry*, 8, 679-88.

WOLBERG, L. R. (1944). "The character structure of the rejected child." *Nervous Child*, 3, 74-88.

40

The Young Child as Victim of Sibling Attack*

Kay M. Tooley, Ph. D.

Child neglect and child abuse have received considerable attention in the past decade. The wall of privacy which shelters the nuclear family has been breached slightly to reveal some of the harsh extremes of intrafamilial behavior subsumed under the heading of "child rearing practices." In the past, the task of influencing, aiding, and controlling abusive parents fell to the extended family or the village. Now, with the increased isolation of the nuclear family, this responsibility falls to more remote social agencies. Their overview, necessarily more distant, is often vague and indistinct. If "child rearing practices" stretch from the giving of dollars for good marks at school to the fracturing of the skull of a crying infant, so "sibling rivalry" is also stretched to cover behavior from an artful lie intended to discredit a younger brother to murderous life-endangering aggression between siblings. Again, from the remote and impersonal distance of social agencies it is sometimes quite difficult to discern the details of the battle that can rage within the confines of the nuclear family.

Physicians, for example, have been sensitized to expect child abuse when they see certain patterns of multiple injuries over time. They have learned not to be totally accepting of parental reports of precipitating circumstances. All of the helping professions, however, have difficulty discerning child abuse when it happens at the

* Kay M. Tooley, "The Young Child as Victim of Sibling Attack," *Social Casework*, Vol. 58, No. 1 (Jan. 1977): 25-28. Copyright © 1977 Family Service Association of America. Reproduced by permission.

hands of another child. Further, having discerned such abuse, they seem much less sure about how to proceed from there.

When it is absolutely clear from both parental reports and examination of the victim that a life-endangering attack has been made on the child by a sibling, mental health professionals have followed the bias of the larger society; they bend their efforts toward providing treatment and rehabilitation of the aggressor.

Subsequent to the author's study of the family dynamics of murderously aggressive children[1] she found herself pulled up short by queries from professional colleagues. "But what about the victim child? What about his psychological difficulties?" In fact, very little attention had been paid to the impact on the little victim of such an enormous failure of parental protection as was involved in these cases. It was a particularly embarrassing and unexplainable oversight because the thesis pursued in that report is that the older siblings were acting out the mother's (only slightly) unconscious wish to be rid of the younger children—a rather drastic form of maternal rejection that must have been manifest in many other ways in addition to the murderous acting out of the older sibling. Because the attacks included such experiences as attempted drownings, poisonings, and setting fire to clothing, they could not be classified as minor. In a few opportunities to observe the child victims after a treatment alliance with the family had long been established, it was puzzling to note that in these cases there seemed to be no major sequelae to such frightening experiences. The author concluded, therefore, that the child victims were too young (two or three years old) to have a realistic perception of the danger to which they had been exposed because children of that age use their mother's reaction to gauge the threat of a given situation. These children received no such signals that their mothers were unduly alarmed or upset by the occurrences.

Impact on the Child Victim

The author then began to look for opportunities to study the impact on the child victim and some of the reasons for the "mysterious oversight" noted earlier became clearer: a boy accused by his parents of raping his six-year-old sister at knife point and of beating her was brought for admission to the inpatient service within hours. Months later, the parents were still successfully resisting hospital staff's efforts to talk with the little girl, resistant to the extent of breaking off contact with their hospitalized son for a considerable period. In another case, a boy accidentally shot his six-year-old sister, causing a serious abdominal wound. The circumstances of the accident were as follows. The gun and the ammunition were stored in opposite ends of the house. The accident happened in the week following a first parent-teacher conference. The parents had been upset and disappointed by the consistently poor school performance and poor behavior of the older boy. He was being treated by a local pediatrician for hyperkinesis. They were delighted by the first grade report of the excellent performance of their daughter. This information was the only glance at family dynamics that was permitted. Initially welcoming psychiatric help for the little girl in coping with her traumatic injury, the parents abruptly broke off contact as

---

[1] Kay M. Tooley, The Small Assassins: Clinical Notes on a Subgroup of Murderous Children, *Journal of the American Academy of Child Psychiatry*, 14:306-18 (Spring 1975).

soon as they perceived the tenor of the interviewer's questions. It was an accident; they were going to "forget" it. This latter family differs very much from the ones which first claimed the author's attention. There was not the covert compliance on the part of the parents that had been noted in those earlier cases. The above examples are offered to illustrate the unwillingness of parents to permit psychiatric attention for the "aggressed upon" child, an unwillingness which is not evident until one presses to see them and which may partially explain the oversight regarding the psychological difficulties of the victim—an oversight shared by some other writers on the subject.[2]

Subsequently, an opportunity both to examine and to see a "child victim" arose. The child was brought in for treatment, not because he had been badly hurt several times by his older sibling, but because he had begun to exhibit behavior which has been described as "prepsychotic." This victim, who was old enough and intelligent enough to have a vivid but imperfect comprehension that he was in danger, conveyed a strong sense of his nightmarish inability to convince anyone of the reality of the danger. He grew to doubt his own reality perceptions but still felt consistently vulnerable to attack. He was living day and night—weaponless and without safe refuge—in enemy territory. He was six years old.

Case illustration:—Allen was impelled into treatment at a local child guidance clinic at the insistence of his kindergarten teacher who found his behavior "wild, peculiar, aggressive and frightening." Allen's mother described him at that time with pride as "all boy—he stands up for himself." After a few months of treatment his behavior changed radically. He became very quiet and withdrawn, occupying himself for hours with intricate drawings of pipes and faucets and with any elongated collection of objects which he would designate as pipes. His behavior, while no longer threatening or disturbing, seemed to his therapist to be "prepsychotic." Allen reacted with obvious terror to the presence of his eight-year-old brother and to the threat of his three-year-old sister to "hit him with a sock." Allen was referred to Children's Psychiatric Hospital for inpatient treatment. The mother, Mrs. J, recounted without much evident concern that over a period of a year the older boy had: tried to drown Allen in the bathtub; pushed him down the stairs; cut his head to the degree that he required a dozen stitches to close the wound; and had set fire to the family home. In the last instance, which was never fully clarified by the parents, Allen had been trapped in his bedroom and had to be rescued by firemen "with hoses and axes." (At a later point in treatment, Allen told of turning the doorhandle and finding that it did not work—it came away in his hands. A vivid part of the symptomatic behavior had to do with his preoccupation with keys—which ones worked and which ones did not.)

Mrs. J further reported that she was often tired and left the three younger children in the elder boy's care. She never disciplines the children, she said. When she gets angry she just feels that she is going to kill someone and so does nothing. Mrs. J reported several dreams about killing her children and her husband. In one dream she soaked her husband's mattress with kerosene and ignited it as he slept. Mr. J had withdrawn psychologically from affective involvement with his wife and children. In Allen's period of psychotic-like withdrawal, when he was so good and quiet, Mrs. J saw him as very much like his father. She found him much more likeable, however, when he was acting out aggressively in kindergarten. She appreciates her elder son's babysitting and she finds him "spunky." The mother also reported, this time with mild disapproval, that her elder son had put a kitten in a school bag and had banged it again and again against a tree trunk and then had jumped up and down on it.

---

[2] William M. Easson and Richard M. Steinhibler, Murderous Aggression by Children and Adolescents, *Archives of General Psychiatry*, 4:1-9 (January 1961); and John M. MacDonald, The Threat to Kill, *American Journal of Psychiatry*, 120:125-30 (August 1963).

The hospital staff, of course, had the impression that the wrong child had been referred. The parents, however, were not willing to consider hospitalization for the older boy. The hospital agreed to accept Allen (for his own protection) with the stipulation that the older boy be entered into intensive treatment in his home community. The parents agreed to this arrangement.

It took a full year to coax Allen out of his fearful withdrawal and into the bare beginnings of warm and trusting relatedness. His therapist described several months in which he ignored her and busied himself with building Tinkertoy pipe systems. He spoke very little and met her comments with silence and a more pointed withdrawal. Her patient persistence, her demonstrated wish to protect his pipes and keep them safe, gradually convinced Allen that she would be helpful in expanding his plumbing project. The therapist was able to exploit this collaboration and the relationship warmed quite dramatically and was extended to other people in the milieu with surprising swiftness.

In his second year in the hospital Allen bloomed. He did well in school. His IQ test scores moved from the dull-normal range to well above average. He made friends, played, learned to joke and tease. At the beginning of the second year someone thought to include one of Allen's drawings in his chart notes. They show an intricate array of pipes jutting off busily in all directions and finally ending in a faucet delivering a drop of water to one small flower. At the end of the hospitalization Allen showed no sign of "psychotic preoccupations." He mastered his old fear by means of a very adaptive interest in biological and mechanical science. The family pathology was altered in several important ways and his post-hospital adjustment was excellent.

The previous paragraph is included to forestall questions which must come to mind when one studies the diagnostic evaluation of Allen during his first months in the hospital. Psychological testing revealed that Allen's extensive preoccupation with pipes was utilized rigidly across all situations to ward off a flood of anxious fantasies. He had schizophrenic Rorschach percepts. He said that his body was hollow inside and fitted with "pipe bones." "Most of my bones are gone." Looking down at his torso, he said, "I don't have any body." The examiner comments that "the content of Allen's fantasy is body damage and impending or remembered attack. A sibling is mixed up in the story but it is not clear whether he is the protector or aggressor." Another time Allen talks of the dragon bug which he has seen "out in the jungle in my backyard. It does not like me, it bites me, it helps me, it loves me, it *likes* boys." At times, while relating, Allen would "drift off into words and ideas which the examiner could not understand . . . there was a vague notion that Allen had done something wrong and was being punished." The examiner's impression was of a child with "broad early ego defects." The diagnosis of schizophrenia was made by other diagnosticians and then amended to preschizophrenia or prepsychosis. The point is that no one doubted that they saw in Allen a malignant psychotic process with poor prognosis. The discharge diagnosis was psychoneurosis exacerbated by a situational crisis, and the prognosis was thought to be good. The amended diagnosis was influenced by the swiftness and completeness with which Allen relinquished psychotic thinking and psychotic avoidance of and distortion of object relations.

Regarding the parents' relative lack of concern over what was happening to Allen, in retrospect, it must be noted that a fair number of both medical and mental health professionals also seemed slow to respond to an emergent situation and slow to speculate that Allen's problem might have current interpersonal as well as intrapsychic roots. Again with retrospective wisdom, if the attending physicians had suspected that a parent had inflicted those very same injuries on Allen they would have been considerably clearer on their right and responsibility to move to protect him instantly. Allen's parents were perfectly open in their reporting of the incidents. Professionals seem less sure about how to proceed when "child abuse" happens at the hands of another child.

Summary

It is commonly estimated that the actual number of child abuse cases far exceeds those identified and treated as such. Not only parents but older siblings may be implicated in repeated serious assaults on young children. Parents may hesitate to report or even to recognize such attacks for reasons which vary considerably. To maintain a degree of intra-familial solidarity and good feeling they may make a preconscious decision that the assault was "accidental" or a bit of normal horseplay gone wrong. They feel that overt recognition of such a high degree of hostility among family members would endanger the family's ability to function as such, and they utilize the defense of denial to a startling degree.

A second and different family arrangement involves the smoothing out of the life space around a "problem child." The parents are frightened by the overt and uncontrolled aggression of one of their children. Their mode is to placate and to "make allowances" in order to forestall temper outbursts and attacks. A younger child may be the family's sacrificial lamb bearing the brunt of considerable physical punishment from an older sibling and deflecting such abuse from other family members. Parents can refuse to "see" the resulting damage to the younger child or they can shrug it off. "Joey is tough." "He can take it." Or, "We warned Joey to stay away from his brother because he was in a bad mood." Again the mode is to manage the outbreak of hostility within the family circle.

A third and more serious family pathology involves the acting out by an older child of a parent's unconscious wish to be unencumbered by the younger children. A clinical example has been provided to illustrate not only the life endangering extremes of such behavior and parental complicity but also the possible serious psychological sequelae.

Behind the wall of privacy which surrounds the nuclear family, some children are living in frightening circumstances without sufficient protection, doing their desperate childish best to survive in "the jungle in their backyard." Mirroring the tendency of society in general to be concerned with the control and rehabilitation of the aggressor, the mental health professions, like the larger society, may need to attend more fully to the well-being of the victim.

41

Self-Chosen Victims:
Scapegoating Behavior Sequential to Battering*

Barbara Bender

In working with two boys who had been battered as young children, the writer was strongly impressed by a behavior pattern in both that seemed directly related to the abusive treatment they had received from their parents. Both boys, Tony, 8 years old, and Robbie, 10, had a compulsive need to provoke punishment from everyone they came in contact with, both peers and adults. This scapegoating behavior was most marked in Tony, who had been more frequently and consistently beaten over a longer time than Robbie. In both cases, however, the mistreatment they received, Robbie from his father and Tony from his mother and older sister, was serious enough so that doctors reported both to the Inflicted Injury Unit of the State Welfare Department, though neither was removed from his home. Each boy was the only child in his family to be abused this way; Tony's fraternal twin escaped mistreatment.

Robbie's tendency to get himself scapegoated was obvious in his activity group, from which he was chased home almost every afternoon by peers he had enraged, usually by saying something insulting about somebody's mother (a common way in his community to start trouble). Since he was a poor fighter, Robbie generally either got beaten or ended up having to be protected by his group leader. In casework he spent months in desperate attempts to provoke the worker into hitting him: insulting her mother and grandmother, screaming names, spitting, breaking toys, and attempting in a multitude of other ways to provoke retaliation. In the midst of these

* Barbara Bender, "Self-Chosen Victims: Scapegoating Behavior Sequential to Battering," *Child Welfare*, Vol. LV, No. 6: 417-422. Copyright © 1976 Child Welfare League of America. Reproduced by permission.

scenes he would scream: "Hit me! Go ahead and hit me!" Eventually this behavior was replaced by a calmer and more sublimated sort of testing in which Robbie asked endless questions about the worker's reaction to hypothetical situations: "What would you do if I spat on your mother's grave? What would do if I locked your desk and flushed the key down the toilet?" and so on. As he gradually felt safer with her, he no longer needed to try to provoke abuse.

Pattern of Provocations

Tony's problems were even more severe than Robbie's. He was beaten by peers many times a day, following episodes in which he broke their toys, insulted their mothers, or boasted that he could beat them. Invariably worsted, since he could not fight but cowered in terrified submission, Tony was back for more unbelievably quickly. He picked the strongest and most aggressive children to provoke, and many a time the worker dragged such a boy off him, when Tony groveled on the floor screaming for mercy while being stomped, only to hear Tony yelling obscenities at the same boy 2 minutes later, whereupon he was again attacked. Tony repeated this behavior compulsively day after day. His self-destructive behavior was also evident in his habit of deliberately running out in the street in front of cars when angry, or sticking metallic objects into an electric light socket. With adults he was equally provocative, and there was not one of the many staff members working with Tony who had not felt like slapping him at times. There were times when his teacher had to hand him over to another staff member to keep herself and/or his siblings from beating him. The worker herself was sorely tempted to hit him on occasion. She was convinced that Tony was one of those children who would "get battered in sequential foster home placements where no other child has ever been battered [2:30]," and for this reason did not want to make such a placement.

The Sense of Guilt

Some of the psychological mechanisms leading from physical abuse by parents to this kind of masochistic seeking out of punishment are described by Steele and Pollock [3:103ff.], who believe that aggression against the child causes him to identify with the aggressor and thus begin to develop a rudimentary superego; at the same time the frustration of his needs by the parent, as well as the pain inflicted, fills the child with aggression against the battering parent: "Stimulation of the aggressive drive with its accompanying anger toward the frustrating caretaker, coupled with the parallel development of strict superego rudiments, inevitably leads to a strong sense of guilt . . . (which) leads to turning much of the aggression inward toward the self . . . and contributes to the pervasive sense of inferiority and low self-esteem [3:122]."

This guilt appears to have been one of the strongest factors causing these boys to offer themselves so frequently as victims. Robbie's guilt about the anger he felt toward his father was evident in his inability to express negative feeling about him; his rare hostile comments were invariably followed by his pretending he was hurt and demanding that the worker bandage his leg or put a splint on his finger. Similarly Tony, in talking of his father, who deserted the family soon after he was born, showed the anger he felt at his father for not staying and protecting him by saying his father was dead, whereupon he pointed the toy gun at himself and pulled the trigger. Thus both boys felt that they must constantly atone for their angry impulses toward their parents.

The conflicts such children have about expressing aggression appropriately are described by Garland and Kolodny [1:46ff]: "The commonly observed characteristic of the scapegoat is his inability to deal with aggression. A strong passive and masochistic mode is usually evident; uncomfortable with, or inept at, direct expression of his own angry feelings or burdened with guilt, the potential scapegoat finds it necessary to seek ridicule or rejection from others [1:50]." As mentioned, both these boys were poor fighters, Tony ludicrously so. Peers accused both boys of "fighting like girls," and certainly in Tony one could see the confused sexual identity described by Garland and Kolodny as another characteristic of scapegoated children. At home he often dressed up in his mother's clothes and wigs and asked if he could paint his fingernails. The other boys referred to him as a "faggot" and he was singled out several times for homosexual assault by older boys. The feminine traits he evidenced may have been due in part to a sort of incorporative identification with the aggressor, as if by taking on mother's identity he could be powerful like her.

Symbolic Play

Low self-esteem and a sense of inferiority could be seen in both boys. Robbie frequently screamed: "I hate myself! I hate myself!" and Tony's characteristic response to failure at something he had tried to do was a miserably muttered: "Can't do nothing, don't know nothing." Both boys used a dog as a symbol of themselves in their play during casework sessions, underlining their debased self-image. In a puppet play Robbie acted out a scene where a father was beating a boy savagely; thereupon the boy began to growl and bite and father beat him all the more. A puppet policeman, happening upon the scene, asked father why he was beating the boy and father said it was because the boy thought he was a dog and was barking and biting like one. Playing with a dollhouse, Tony took a little toy dog and had him run wildly through the building, jumping up on the furniture, biting all the family members, and getting up on the table to eat everyone's food (Tony himself had an enormous appetite and frequently provoked the wrath of other children, including his siblings, by stealing food from them). Obviously a dog would be beaten for such behavior, just as Tony was.

With both Tony and Robbie, the casework process involved a long initial period of almost intolerable testing, full of frenzied acting out, in which they attempted to cast the worker in the role of the abusive parent. In Tony's case this lasted almost a year, during which he made no overt progress, and a residential placement was seriously considered because of the likelihood that he would be permanently injured by someone. Robbie, much the brighter of the boys, made more rapid progress in verbalizing and relating; a real turning point for him was a scene where he abreacted his original trauma provoked by his fear of the anger of a male teacher, which he initially handled by putting his fist through a window. When in the subsequent casework session the worker related this to his fear of father's anger in the past and powerlessness to protect himself, there was a dramatic reaction as Robbie leaped to his feet screaming at her to keep her hands off him. He spent the next half hour like a cornered animal, terrified and shrieking defiance: "You'd better not come any nearer, you bitch! Stay away from me! Don't you put your hands on me!" He got hold of a piece of extension cord and crouched with it in a corner, ready to fight her off and seeming to be reliving a situation in which he had been menaced by an adult, but was better able to defend himself. For a long time Robbie could not grasp repeated reassurances that the worker was not his father or mother and would not hurt him, but cried out the window to passersby: "Help! Murder! I'm going crazy! She'll kill me!"

Gradual Improvement

After a considerable period of intensive treatment during which they established some trust, both boys showed an encouraging diminution of their compulsive scapegoating behavior and masochistic need for punishment. In both cases this was linked to an increased ability to cope effectively with anger at their parents and consequent guilt. In casework sessions they symbolically punished their parents. Robbie did this in a puppet play in which a judge sentenced a father to 20 years in jail "for child abuse." However, following this the puppet boy broke down in tears crying: "It's all my fault! It's all my fault!" Tony acted out a similar retribution in a game of "police." In the game he was a strong and commanding police chief, relentlessly pursuing his man, barking out orders to his subordinates and engaging in frequent fierce and enemy-annihilating gun battles. In this role he burst into the office and arrested the worker "for putting scars on your kids!" He tongue-lashed her for a long time, saying that she must never again beat her children with a belt, and commenting over and over: "You should know better!" It is noteworthy that in both these situations the punishing agent was the law, acting on behalf of the child, rather than the child himself.

As Vogel and Bell state, the role of scapegoat causes serious personality impairment, as the child soon internalizes blame and conflict [4.382ff]. This certainly happened to Tony and Robbie. Picked out of their families, for reasons that are not clear, to receive the brunt of their parents' rage, they consequently suffered much emotional as well as physical damage. Most ironic of all was the manner in which they seemed doomed to repeat endlessly the original trauma, in compulsive behavior that elicited violence anew from all about them. It was most encouraging to see how far this process was reversible by means of intensive group and casework treatment, without removing either boy from his home.

REFERENCES

1.   GARLAND, James A., and KOLODNY, Ralph L., "Characteristics and Resolution of Scapegoating," in *Further Explorations in Groupwork*, edited by Saul Bernstein. Boston: Boston University School of Social Work, 1970.

2.   GIL, David. *Violence Against Children*. Cambridge, Mass.: Harvard University Press, 1970.

3.   STEELE, Brandt, F., and POLLOCK, Carl B. "A Psychiatric Study of Parents Who Abuse Infants and Young Children," in *The Battered Child*, edited by Ray Helfer and C. Henry Kempe. Chicago: University of Chicago Press, 1968.

4.   VOGEL, Ezra F., and BELL, Norman W. "The Emotionally Disturbed Child as the Family Scapegoat," in *A Modern Introduction to the Family*, edited by Ezra F. Vogel and Norman W. Bell. New York: Free Press of Glencoe, 1960.

42

The Aggressive Characteristics of Abused and Neglected Children*

During the past few years, child abuse has become a topic of increasing concern, especially because the reported incidence of child abuse has risen as a result of more enlightened laws and more stringent reporting procedures. One reflection of this increased awareness is the increase in research related to this topic. As Spinetta and Rigler (1972) point out in their review, however, most of these studies focus primarily on demographic and causal factors rather than on the abused child himself. This lack of attention to the relationship between abuse and the abused child's growth and development is unfortunate because the few observations that have been made suggest that physical abuse has serious psychological consequences. Specifically, abused children have been described as aggressive and full of hatred (Fontana, 1973); uncontrollable, negativistic, and subject to severe temper tantrums (Johnson & Morse, 1968); lacking in impulse control (Elmer, 1967); emotionally disturbed with behavior problems at home and at school (Morse, Sahler, & Friedman, 1970); and withdrawn and inhibited (Rolston, 1971). In addition, cognitive and neurological deficits have been noted (Martin, 1972; Martin, Beezley, Conway, & Kempe, 1974; McRae, Ferguson, & Lederman, 1973; Morse et al., 1970; Sandgrund, Gaines, & Green, 1974).

The problems of the abused child apparently do not disappear with adulthood; most disturbing is the frequent finding that abused children become abusive parents (Spinetta & Rigler, 1972). Thus, it seems that abused children need help to alleviate

* Thomas J. Reidy, "The Aggressive Characteristics of Abused and Neglected Children," *Journal of Clinical Psychology*, Vol. 33, No. 4 (Oct. 1977): 1140-1145. Copyright © 1977 Clinical Psychology Publishing Co. Inc. Reproduced by permission.

their current problems and to prevent further problems from developing in adulthood. If intervention is to be successful, however, it needs to rest on a firm knowledge of the abused child's development. Unfortunately, the present research on the abused child is difficult to interpret due to serious methodological problems, such as different definitions of abuse, inadequate descriptions of Ss, uncontrolled procedures, imprecise reports of results, and lack of matched control Ss. The present research considered, in an adequately controlled study, one aspect of the abused child's behavior that is relevant both to his present problems and to his potential as an abusive parent: the abused child's level of aggression.

The expectation that abused children would differ from other children in their level of aggression was based on past research with nonabused normal childen as well as on clinical observations of abused children. Past investigators of normal child development have reported a significant positive relationship between children's aggressiveness and the use of severe physical punishment in the home (Sears et al., 1957). Similarly, mothers who used physical and verbal aggression were found to have children who displayed such tactics in peer relationships (Hoffman, 1960). This evidence is consistent with the social learning formulation that children can acquire aggressive behavior by observing aggressive parental models, particularly in the context of disciplinary activities (Bandura, 1973). In addition, Ulrich (1967) indicates that physical pain, discomfort, or the blocking of positive reinforcement can lead to aggression in children. Because abused children have experienced extreme punishment at the hands of aggressive parental models, it was hypothesized that young abused children would exhibit more aggressive characteristics than their nonabused counterparts.

To test this hypothesis, both the aggressive fantasies and the overt aggressive behavior of young abused children were compared with two groups of matched controls: nonabused-neglected children and normal children. Aggressive fantasy was measured with the Thematic Apperception Test (TAT) (Murray, 1943), while two measures of overt aggressiveness were utilized: observers' ratings during free play and teachers' ratings on the Behavior Problem Checklist (BPC) (Quay & Peterson, 1967).

The nonabused-neglected group was included to provide a control for any potential effects produced by inadequate physical care and attention, common among abused children, as well as to help clarify the potential effects of child neglect. The normal group provided a reference point from which to demonstrate effects attributable to abuse or neglect. To the author's knowledge, no prior study has included a statistical comparison of abused with neglected and normal children on the variables used in this study.

Method

Subjects

Three groups of children were used in this study, which was part of a larger investigation: physically abused ($N = 20$), nonabused-neglected ($N = 16$), and normal ($N = 22$). The abused and neglected children were referred from the Illinois Department of Children and Family Services (IDCFS) and the Bowen Center for Abused and Neglected Children. Normal children were referred from neighborhood day care centers that serve low- and middle-income families.

An abused child was defined as a child who had suffered either bone fractures, contusions, abrasions, cuts or burns inflicted by a parental caretaker on more than one occasion. A neglected child was a child whose parents had failed to provide food, clothing, supervision, medical care, or sanitary living conditions, and for whom there was no evidence of physical abuse. Both the abused and neglected children had no known evidence of neurological impairment from abuse, neglect, or any other source. The criteria for abuse and neglect were validated for each child by IDCFS caseworkers.

At the time the study was conducted, 12 abused children were living in foster care and 8 in their natural homes. The neglected group consisted of 12 children in the natural homes and 4 in foster homes. Table 1 provides a summary of the demographic information gathered and indicates that the three groups were equated adequately on age, sex, SES, and race.

Procedure

All children were brought by the examiner to a playroom at the De Paul University Mental Health Center. Each child was administered cards 13B, 7GF, 3GF, 10, 6GF and 13MF from the TAT as a measure of aggressive imagery. The stories were rated by judges for aggressive content by the Hafner and Kaplan (1960) aggression scoring system. Interjudge reliability for this method was determined to be .91.

Immediately after the test situation, each child was brought into a playroom on which age- and sex-appropriate toys were present. The following instructions were given:

> In this playroom there are many different types of toys. See them all. You may play with any toy, but you must tell me a story or put on a show for me with each toy you play with.

The examiner remained in the room with the child for 20 minutes. Two observers situated behind a one-way mirror rated the occurrence of aggressive behavior, which was defined as any hostile action on the part of the child toward the toys or examiner, (e.g., throwing or hitting toys against the table or the examiner). Aggressive responses were rated by using a precise time sampling procedure in which the 20-minute observation period was divided into 15-second intervals by an electric interval timer. During the first 10 seconds of each interval the observer counted the number of aggressive responses made by the child, and in the subsequent 5-second interval the observer recorded the behaviors that occurred in the preceding 10 seconds. Any aggression that occured during this 5-second period was not recorded. Interrater reliability of .89 was established for this observation procedure.

The BPC was mailed to each child's teacher, who rated the child on the aggression scale and thus provided a measure of such behaviors as fighting, temper tantrums, uncooperativeness, anger and destructiveness. The total score for each child was the sum of aggressive behaviors checked by the teacher.

TABLE 1

Demographic Characteristics

	Age	Race		Annual parental income		Sex	
		Black	White	0-3000	4-8000	Male	Female
Abused							
Mean	77.8	11	9	10	10	16	4
SD	12.4						
Neglected							
Mean	82.8	9	7	5	11	7	9
SD	13.6						
Normal							
Mean	78.1	13	9	10	12	16	6
SD	12.0						

Note:—The groups did not differ in terms of age $F(2, 55) = .81$, $p > .05$; race $\chi^2(2) = .075$, $p > .05$; income $\chi^2(2) = 1.35$, $p > .05$; sex $\chi^2(2) = 5.79$, $p > .05$.

Results

Analysis of variance for the TAT aggression scores that used the Hafner and Kaplan (1960) scoring system revealed a statistically significant main effect for groups, $F(2,55) = 3.94$, $p < .05$. Additional comparisons demonstrated that the abused children expressed significantly more fantasy aggression in responding to the TAT as compared to both the neglected children, $t(34) = 1.98$, $p < .05$, and the normal children, $t(40) = 2.62$, $p < .01$. The neglected children did not differ significantly from the normal children. Table 2 provides the means and standard deviations for each group.

Because the data for aggression shown in the free play setting did not meet the requirement of homogeneity of variance necessary to perform an analysis of variance, an extension of the median test (Ferguson, 1966) was used for statistical purposes. Results demonstrated that there was a significant difference among the medians, $\chi^2(2) = 5.44$, $p < .05$. It is apparent (Table 2) that abused children used aggressive behavior with much greater frequency in this setting than did either neglected or normal children, whose mean frequency of aggression was less than one.

Behavior Problem Checklist ratings of aggression by teachers were analyzed by one-way analysis of variance. Results indicated a significant difference among groups on this measure, $F(2,53) = 6.70$, $p < .001$. Abused children were judged significantly more aggressive than normals, $t(38) = 3.45$, $p < .01$, as were the neglected children, $t(36) = 2.89$, $p < .01$. No significant difference was found between abused and neglected children. The means and standard deviations for teacher ratings are listed in Table 2.

Finally, abused children who were living in their natural homes were compared with abused children in foster care ($N = 12$) to see whether aggressiveness varied with place of residence. Although these two groups did not differ in amount of overt aggression as measured by the teachers' ratings on the BPC or by the amount of aggression displayed during free play, t-tests revealed that abused children in their

TABLE 2

Means and Standard Deviations for TAT Agression, Free Play Agression, and Teacher Ratings of Aggression

	TAT aggression	Free play aggression	Teacher ratings of aggression
Abused			
Mean	12.05	6.20	8.89
SD	6.56	9.42	4.68
Neglected			
Mean	7.94	.13	8.69
SD	5.67	.34	5.82
Normal			
Mean	6.82	.32	3.77
SD	6.37	1.09	4.65

natural homes expressed significantly more fantasy aggression than abused children in foster homes, $t(16) = 2.19, p < .05$. However, a large number of t-tests were performed within the context of the larger study, and very few significant differences were found. This suggests that the significant difference in fantasy aggression between abused children in foster care and abused children in their natural homes might result from Type I error alone. Because fantasy aggression was the only variable on which the two groups differed, a tentative interpretation could be that, in general, abused children who are living in foster care do not differ significantly from those who are living in their natural homes.

Discussion

The present study attempted to determine whether child abuse influences aggression in young children. The results clearly indicate that abused children are significantly more aggressive than nonabused, normal children in three distinct areas: fantasy, free play environment, and a school environment. Abused children expressed significantly more fantasies that contained themes of aggression and violence than did normal children. In addition, abused children showed more overt aggression during free play and were reported by their teachers to have more behavior problems at school than control Ss.

These findings support previous observations by others (Elmer, 1967; Fontana, 1973; Johnson & Morse, 1968; Morse et al., 1970) that abused children exhibit overly hostile and aggressive characteristics. The results also lend additional support to previous research that links physical punishment in the home and hyperaggressiveness in children (Hoffman, 1960; Sears et al., 1957). Finally, the data from this investigation are consistent with the social learning theory formulation that children exposed to extremely aggressive parental models will demonstrate aggressive characteristics in situations outside the home.

Given the tendency of abused children to become abusive parents in adulthood and the tendency of level of aggression to remain stable over time (Bloom, 1964; Kagan & Moss, 1962), it seems likely that the aggressiveness of abused children is frequently an enduring pattern of behavior perpetuated into adolescence and adulthood. This study thus strongly suggests that intervention should be initiated as soon as a child is identified as abused rather than waiting until his problems increase in severity.

The results that relate to differences between abused children who are in foster care and abused children in their natural homes also have implications with regard to the treatment of these children. It may be recalled that abused children in foster care expressed significantly less hostile fantasies than those in their natural homes, but showed as much overt aggression as abused children who remained in their natural homes. If there is little difference between children in foster care and those in their natural homes, at least in relation to direct expression of aggression, then simply removing a child from the abusive environment is inadequate to reduce his level of aggression and problems in school. This suggests that foster care placement alone is not an adequate remedy for the psychological damage suffered by abused children, but needs to be supplemented by treatment for the child and/or support for the foster parents. The impact of foster care placement on the characteristics of abused children is clearly an important area for further research, which ought to take into account relevant factors (such as the age at which abuse occurred, length of time in foster care, etc.) to see under what conditions foster homes are most effective in remediating the problems of the children placed in them.

The fact that neglected children were similar to abused children in terms of aggression at school, but resembled normals on fantasy and free play aggressiveness implies that neglect does influence aggressive behavior problems, but not to the same degree as child abuse. One interpretation for these findings is that neglectful parents, who are non-nurturant, may subject their children to more punishment and verbal abuse than normals, but may not punish with the same aggressive intensity or frequency as abusive parents. Thus, neglected children normally may be non-aggressive in unstructured environments such as fantasy or free play situations, but may have failed to learn the skills necessary to cope non-aggressively with the provocations and frustrations inherent in more structured environments such as the school. Part of the difficulty in interpreting differences between neglected and abused children is the lack of research that focuses on the characteristics of neglected children and the tendency of some authors to lump abused and neglected children together. The present study suggests that these two groups do differ and that further research is necessary to understand the neglected child and the school behavior problems that he appears to have.

REFERENCES

BANDURA, A. *Aggression: A social learning analysis.* Englewood Cliffs, N.J.: Prentice-Hall, 1973.

BLOOM, B. S. *Stability and change in human characteristics.* New York: John Wiley, 1964.

ELMER, E. *Children in jeopardy.* Pittsburgh: University of Pittsburgh Press, 1967.

EVANS, I., DUBANOSKI, R., & HIGUCHI, A. "Behavior therapy with child abusing parents: Initial concepts underlying predictive, preventive and analogue studies." Paper presented at the Eighth Annual Convention of the Association for the Advancement of Behavior Therapy, Chicago, November 1974.

FERGUSON, G. A. *Statistical analysis in psychology and education.* New York: McGraw Hill, 1966.

FONTANA, V. J. *Somewhere a child is crying.* New York: Macmillan, 1973.

HOFFMAN, M. "Power assertion by the parent and its impact on the child." *Child Development,* 1960, 31, 129-143.

HAFNER, A. J., & KAPLAN, A. M. "Hostility content analysis of the Rorschach and TAT." *Journal of Projective Techniques,* 1960, 24, 134-143.

JOHNSON, B., & MORSE, H. "Injured children and their parents." *Children,* 1968, 15, 147-152.

KAGAN, J., & MOSS, H. *Birth to maturity: A study in psychological development.* New York: John Wiley, 1962.

MARTIN, H. "The child and his development." In R. E. Helfer & C. H. Kempe (Eds.), *Helping the battered child and his family.* Philadelphia: Lippincott, 1972.

MARTIN, H., BEEZLEY, P., CONWAY, E., & KEMPE, C. H. "The development of abused children." *Advances in Pediatrics,* 1974, 21, 25-73.

McRAE, K., FERGUSON, C., & LEDERMAN, R. "The battered child syndrome." *Canadian Medical Association Journal,* 1973, 108, 859-866.

MORSE, C. W., SAHLER, O. J. Z., & FRIEDMAN, S. B. "A follow-up study of abused and neglected children." *American Journal of Diseases of Children,* 1970, 120, 439-446.

MURRAY, H. A. *Thematic Apperception Test.* Cambridge: Harvard University Press, 1943.

QUAY, H. C., & PETERSON, D. R. *Manual for the Behavior Problem Checklist.* Champaign, Ill.: University of Illinois, Children's Research Center, 1967.

ROLSTON, R. "The effect of prior physical abuse on the expression of overt and fantasy aggressive behavior in children" (Doctoral dissertation, Louisiana State University, 1971) *Dissertation Abstracts International,* 171, 32 (5), 2453B-3086B. (University Microfilms No. 71-29, 389).

SANDGRUND, A., GAINES, R. U., & GREEN, A. H. "Child abuse and mental retardation: A problem of cause and effect." *American Journal of Mental Deficiency,* 1974, 79, 327-329.

SEARS, R. R., MACCOBY, E. E., & LEVIN, H. *Patterns of child rearing.* Evanston, Ill.: Row, Peterson, 1957.

SPINETTA, J. J., & RIGLER, D. "The child abusing parent: A psychological review." *Psychological Bulletin,* 1972, 77, 296-304.

ULRICH, R. *The experimental analysis of aggression.* (Office of Naval Research, Group Psychology Branch, Contract Number N00014-67-A-0421-0001, N R 171-807). Kalamazoo: Western Michigan University, Department of Psychology, 1967.

43

Self-Destructive Behavior in Battered Children*

Arthur H. Green, M.D.

The phenomenon of self-destructive behavior in children, as in adults, has remained an enigma to behavioral scientists. In a recent survey of the literature on self-destructive behavior, Lester[1] described the common deficiencies of clinical investigation and research in this area. He cited the paucity of controlled studies, the lack of hypothesis testing, and the vain search for a unique trait or experience shared by all suicidal individuals. The absence of comprehensive research dealing with an interaction among numerous factors contributing to childhood self-destructive behavior prompted me to study children felt to be at risk for this symptom.

Various characteristics of the child and his environment have been previously associated with self-destructive behavior. There have been frequent reports of self-injury in children with marked ego impairment resulting from psychosis, brain damage, and mental retardation.[2-4] Poor impulse control has often been attributed to self-destructive children.[5-7] Traumatic environmental conditions that have been frequently associated with self-destructive behavior are object loss and maternal deprivation.[5, 8, 9] Parental rejection[10] and family disorganization[11] have also been observed as precipitants of self-destructive activity. The role of stimulus deprivation as a precursor to early self-mutilation and head banging has often been cited.[12-14]

One external factor that might possibly contribute to the development of self-destructive behavior has been generally overlooked. This is severe physical punishment or physical abuse. Primates and other animals have displayed unusually strong attachments to abusive mothers and artificial mother surrogates dispensing painful

* Arthur H. Green, "Self-destructive Behavior in Battered Children," *American Journal of Psychiatry*, Vol. 135, No. 5 (May 1978):579-582. Copyright © 1978 the American Psychiatric Association. Reproduced by permission.

stimulation.[15] I previously described the role of early painful stimuli (infantile head banging and excessive physical punishment) in the etiology of self-destructive behavior in schizophrenic children,[2, 16] stressing the complementary impact of painful stimulation and ego impairment. Others have inferred some association between physical punishment and self-destructive activity. Sears[17] reported preoccupation with self-punishment, accident proneness, and suicidal tendencies in 12-year-old boys who had been punitively handled during toilet training. Hendin[18] noted the frequent occurrence of physical abuse during childhood in case histories of suicidal black adults. Surprisingly, there are no studies of self-destructive behavior among physically abused children reported in the literature.

The purpose of this investigation is to test the hypothesis that a child's experience of repeated physical abuse potentiates his development of self-destructive behavior.

Method

The study included an experimental group of 60 abused children and control groups of 30 "neglected" and 30 "normal" children who were not maltreated. All of the children ranged in age between 5 years, 0 months, and 12 years, 11 months. The number of boys and girls in all groups were proportional, and the groups were comparable with respect to the mean age of the children (table 1). The children were predominantly black and Hispanic, an accurate reflection of the racial composition of the ghetto areas of the city from which the sample was drawn. All were from low-income families.

The abused children were referred by the Bureau of Child Welfare and the Family Court of New York City. Criteria for abuse specified that it be continuing or recurrent and confirmed. The majority of the abused children lived at home, although a few lived with a relative. The sample of neglected children was obtained from the Family Court. The criterion for neglect consisted of the court finding that the parent(s) failed to provide adequate physical care, i.e., food, clothing, medical care, and supervision. A reasonable suspicion of physical abuse disqualified children for the neglected sample. We chose a neglected group to control for the background of physical deprivation and neglect that often accompanies physical abuse in this ghetto population. Thus, the abused children selected for the study frequently manifested signs of neglect, whereas the neglected children were free of physical abuse. The normal control group children were randomly referred volunteers from the pediatric outpatient clinic at Kings County Hospital.

The presence of self-destructive behavior was determined by interviews with the mother or maternal guardian conducted by a psychiatrist or psychiatric social worker. The interview of 1 to 1-1/2 hours included detailed questions concerning possible forms of self-mutilation and self-destructive activity, such as self-biting, self-cutting, self-burning, hair pulling, head banging, suicide attempts, and suicidal threats and gestures. The presence or absence of self-destructive behavior and/or suicidal ideation was determined for each child, and differences across the three groups were tested by chi-square analysis. Of the 60 abused children and the 30 neglected children, statistical analyses were done on 59 and 29, respectively, because of incomplete or missing data on 1 child in each group.

TABLE 1

Descriptive Data for Abused, Neglected, and Normal Children

Children	Age (years) Mean	SD	Racial Composition (%) Black	White	Hispanic
Abused (N = 60)*	8.5	2.2	65.0	13.3	21.7
Neglected (N = 30)**	8.6	2.2	53.3	16.7	30.0
Normal (N = 30)**	8.3	2.3	66.7	6.7	26.6
Total (N = 120)	8.5	2.2	62.5	12.5	25.0

* 32 males, 28 females.
** 16 males, 14 females.

Results

A significantly higher incidence of self-destructive behavior was reported in the abused children. Of 59 abused children, 24 (40.6%) exhibited self-destructive behavior, and only 5 of 29 neglected children (17.2%) and 2 of 30 normal controls (6.7%) were self-destructive ($\chi^2 = 13.50$, $p < .01$). The difference between the abused and neglected children was also significant at the .05 level.

Five of the abused children were suicide attempters (4 girls and 1 boy), 2 made suicidal gestures (2 boys), and 12 were self-mutilators (5 girls and 7 boys). Six of the self-mutilators also manifested suicidal ideation, and 5 boys expressed suicidal ideation only. In the vast majority of cases self-destructive behavior was precipitated by parental beatings or occurred in response to actual or threatened separation from key parental figures.

Discussion

The results demonstrate the vulnerability of abused children to various forms of self-destructive behavior. Since the abused children displayed many of the behavioral impairments described in self-destructive children (and sustained the types of environmental trauma known to precipitate self-destructive behavior), it is likely that the cumulative effect of these variables and the physical abuse potentiated the self-destructive activity of these children. The high incidence of self-destructive activity in a predominantly latency and preadolescent population of abused children is especially noteworthy because these behaviors are rare in this age group in the general population: self-destructive activity only occurs in significant proportions after the onset of puberty. Several studies have demonstrated that many more adolescents than younger children are admitted to psychiatric facilities because of self-destructive behavior.[19, 20] Thus certain events occurring during the normal latency period seem to have a self-preservative function. The rapid growth of ego and superego structures, intellectual and cognitive development, and the establishment of stable identifications with loving parents contribute to better control over impulses, maintenance of normal self-esteem, and more effective ways of dealing with stress and conflict.

Components of the Child Abuse Syndrome

In our previous studies of abusing families[21, 23] child abuse was defined as a pathological syndrome of family interaction. Abuse-prone parents, when triggered by environmental stress, erupted into violence while interacting with a vulnerable child. Child abuse can be best understood as the repeated infliction of physical injury on a child by a parent within the context of a pathological parent-child and family relationship. The physical assault is superimposed on a harsh and punitive childrearing climate and is accompanied by long-standing humiliation, rejection, and scapegoating inflicted by the parent. Child abuse can be divided into the following major components.

Acute Physical and Psychological Assault

This exposes the child to the threat of annihilation and/or abandonment. The child may be overwhelmed by noxious stimulation that often cannot be adequately processed by the young victim's defensive structures, resulting in severe anxiety, painful affect, and ego disorganization. This situation corresponds to Freud's concept of "traumatic neurosis" associated with the breaching of the stimulus barrier.[24] Episodes of parental violence might increase the child's self-destructive potential. The child may attempt to escape from this intolerable situation by a suicidal gesture or attempt, often committed during or soon after an abusive episode. Each traumatic event adds to the cumulative damage to ego functions and defenses, producing aberrations in reality testing and impulsive control that facilitate self-destructive behavior.

Underlying Physical and Psychological Environment

Harsh and punitive childrearing atmosphere. Exposure of an infant or young child to a rejecting, harsh, and punitive parental figure may have numerous adverse sequelae. Our observations of abusing parent-abused child interaction have revealed a tendency of the child to imitate the parent's aggressive and impulsive characteristics. The abused child also learns to regard himself with the same hostility and criticism that his parents accorded him, forming the nucleus of a "bad" self-image. The introjection of parental hostility might represent an early stage in the formation of a punitive superego.

Early maternal deprivation and object loss. Child abuse, especially in our inner-city population, is usually associated with family disorganization and other signs of parental dysfunction, such as neglect, interruption of maternal care, and early experiences with object loss. These abusing parents fail to provide the child with average expectable psychological and physical nurturance. When the basic needs of these children for love, nurturance, and physical contact are generally unmet, the stimulation afforded them during the abusive interaction might reinforce further pain-seeking behavior. Severely deprived children seem to prefer beatings to abandonment. The early experience of separation and deprivation increases their sensitivity to the threat of abandonment during episodes of physical abuse. This deviant nurturance also acts as cumulative traumata[25] that undermine ego development.

Scapegoating. The abused child is usually blamed for the shortcomings and inadequacy of the parents. The scapegoated child reminds the parent of his/her own unacceptable traits and impulses that are projected onto the child. Unable to comprehend the scapegoating process, the child assumes that he is to blame and is deserving of the punishment. His self-hatred and low self-esteem increase and become the nucleus for subsequent self-destructive behavior. The child's acting out of parental hostility directed toward him has been described as an important factor in the etiology of adolescent suicidal behavior.[26]

Sequelae of Child Abuse

In addition to poor self-concept, the sequelae of the child abuse syndrome pertinent to the development of self-destructive behavior are overall impairment of ego functions and impulsive control.

Global ego function defects were demonstrated in abused children in a related study.[23] Such ego functions as reality testing, defensive operations, and body image were significantly impaired compared with those of normal controls. Intellectual functions of the abused children were also significantly depressed. It is likely that both the acute traumatic abusive episodes and the chronic harsh, rejecting, and neglectful childrearing practices contributed to these ego deficits. One may hypothesize an impairment in the ego functions that mediate self-preservation in the abused self-destructive children.

The same study reported that the abused children were often cited for aggressive and destructive behavior at home and in school. They were often described as hyperactive, with minimal frustration tolerance. Motor activity, rather than verbalization, was the preferred mode of expression. These children lacked the usual superego restraints found in normal latency children, because of inadequate superego models and faulty internalization.

To rule out the possibility that the self-destructive abused children represented a special subgroup of brain-damaged and/or psychotic children whose unique ego pathology was the major determinant of self-destructive behavior, their mean full-scale Wechsler Intelligence Scale in Children (WISC) and Wechsler Preschool and Primary Scale of Intelligence (WPPSI) scores were compared with those of the non-self-destructive abused children.[23] No significant differences were observed.

The high incidence of self-destructive behavior among the neglected children was not unexpected. These children shared many of the same environmental stresses and ego impairment with the abused children; however, rejection and deprivation was shared more equally with their siblings. They were seldom subjected to scapegoating or physical violence, which may account for their lower incidence of self-destructive behavior compared with the abused children.

Conclusions

The physically abused children demonstrated a significantly higher incidence of self-destructive behavior than the control groups of nonabused neglected and normal children. The self-destructive behavior, which included suicide attempts, self-mutilation, and suicidal ideation, was potentiated by a number of interrelated variables operating in the abused child and his environment. The abused child's sense of worthlessness, badness, and self-hatred as a consequence of parental assault, rejection, and scapegoating formed the nucleus for subsequent self-destructive behavior. The transformation of the child's self-hatred into self-destructive behavior was catalyzed by ego deficits and impaired impulse control. The self-destructive behavior satisfied numerous motivations and possessed varying psychodynamic significance.

In some children, suicidal behavior seemed to be an escape from a traumatic situation, while in others it represented a "cry for help," a fantasied means of rejoining a lost love object.

Self-destructive activity in abused children does not appear to be primarily related to self-punishment out of conflict, guilt, and superego pressure but rather to a more primitive, learned behavior pattern originating in the earliest painful encounters with hostile primary objects during the first months of life and prior to ego differentiation and verbalization.

REFERENCES

1. LESTER, D.: *Why People Kill Themselves.* Springfield, Ill., Charles C. Thomas, 1972.

2. GREEN, A.: "Self-mutilation in schizophrenic children." *Arch. Gen. Psychiatry* 17:234-244, 1967.

3. LOVASS, O., FREITAG, G., KINDER, M., et al.: *Experimental studies in childhood schizophrenia: developing social behaviors in autistic children using electric shock.* Presented at the annual meeting of the American Psychological Association, Los Angeles, September 5, 1964.

4. BERKSON, G., DAVENPORT, R.: "Stereotyped movements of mental defectives: 1. Initial survey." *Am. J. Ment. Defic.* 66:849-852, 1962.

5. TOOLAN, J.: "Suicide and suicide attempts in children and adolescents." *Am. J. Psychiatry* 118:719-727, 1962.

6. GOULD, R.: "Suicide problems in children and adolescents." *Am. J. Psychotherapy* 19:228-249, 1965.

7. LOURIE, R.: "Clinical studies of attempted suicide in childhood." *Clinical Proceedings of Children's Hospital* 22:163-173, 1966.

8. SPITZ, R., WOLF, K.: "Anaclitic depression." *Psychoanal Study Child* 2:213-241, 1946.

9. ACKERLY, W. "Latency-age children who threaten or attempt to kill themselves." *J. Child Psychiatry* 6:242-261, 1967.

10. CONNELL, P. H. "Suicidal attempts in childhood and adolescence," in *Modern Perspectives in Child Psychiatry.* Edited by Howells, J. G. New York, Brunner/Mazel, 1971, pp. 403-427.

11. TUCKMAN, J., CONNON, H.: "Attempted suicide in adolescents." *Am. J. Psychiatry*, 119: 228-232, 1962.

12. SILVERSTEIN, R., BLACKMAN, S. MANDELL, W.: "Autoerotic head-banging: a reflection on the opportunism of infants." *J. Child Psychiatry* 5:235-243, 1966.

13. LOURIE, R. "The role of rhythmic patterns in childhood." *Am. J. Psychiatry*, 105:653-660, 1949.

14. BERKSON, G., MASON, W.: "Stereotyped movements of mental defectives: IV. Effects of toys and the character of the acts." *Am. J. Ment. Defic.* 68:511-524, 1964.

15. SEAY, B., ALEXANDER, B. K., HARLOW, H. F.: "Maternal behavior of socially deprived rhesus monkeys." *J. Abnorm. Soc. Psychol.* 69:345-354, 1964.

16. GREEN, A.: "Self-destructive behavior in physically abused schizophrenic children." *Arch. Gen. Psychiatry*, 19:171-179, 1958.

17. SEARS, R.: "Relation of early socialization experience to aggression." *J. Abnorm. Soc. Psychol.* 63:466-492, 1961.

18. HENDIN, H.: "Black suicide." *Arch. Gen. Psychiatry*, 21:407-422, 1969.

19. MATTSON, A., HAWKINS, J., SEESE, I.: "Child psychiatric emergencies, clinical characteristics and follow-up results." *Arch. Gen. Psychiatry* 17:584-592, 1967.

20. SABOT, L., PECK, R., RASKIN, J.: "The waiting room society." *Arch. Gen. Psychiatry*, 21:25-32, 1969.

21. GREEN, A.: "A psychodynamic approach to the study and treatment of child-abusing parents." *Am. J. Child Psychiatry* 15:414-429, 1976.

22. GREEN, A., GAINES, R., SANDGRUND, A.: "Child abuse: a pathological syndrome of family interaction." *Am. J. Psychiatry* 131:882-886, 1974.

23. GREEN, A., SANDGRUND, A., GAINES, R., et al.: "Psychological sequelae of child abuse and neglect." Presented at the 127th annual meeting of the American Psychiatric Association, Detroit, Mich. May 6-10, 1974.

24. FREUD, S.: *Beyond the Pleasure Principle* (1920). Complete Psychological Works, standard ed., vol. 18. Translated and edited by Strachey, J. London, Hogarth Press, 1955.

25. KHAN, M.: "The concept of cumulative trauma." *Psychoanal Study Child* 18:286-306, 1963.

26. SABBETH, J.: "The suicidal adolescent." *J. Child Psychiatry*, 8:272-286, 1969.

Epilogue

Commission and Omission:
The Professionals

The consequences of the shift in professional interest from the abused child to those who abuse is acknowledged by many authors. But merely giving lip service to the problem with a few sentences recognizing both the lack of data on, and treatment resources for, the development of the abused child is an inadequate response. Social scientists "caught up in the politics which their work necessarily involves"[16] must surely assume some responsibility, both for the inadequacy and its solution.

It is not only the changing emphasis from victim to abuser that has affected both research and the allocation of resources. The academic frontiers themselves have been redrawn,[24] particularly in the last decade. There have been gradual but clearly perceptible changes in the descriptions of abuse, abusers and the abused. The boundaries of abusive behaviour have been broadened and softened. The syndrome now includes such actions as spanking[10] and even boredom in school[11] in contrast to the earlier descriptions of cruelty,[3] battery,[12] torture[26] and slaughter.[1] The abuser previously assessed psychologically as being hateful,[26] unconcerned[26, 8] and character disordered,[25, 7, 18, 23] is now more often described in terms of socio-environmental features[4, 14, 19, 21] which may cause stress. Moreover the abused child is currently viewed from the perspective of the responding adult thereby becoming less of a victim than a precipitator[9] of his own misfortune.

In effect, two of the essential ingredients of the child abuse pattern are being overlooked or reduced in importance by contemporary professionals: 1) the hostility of the perpetrator and 2) the vulnerability of the victim. The reluctance to acknowledge the possibility of hostile attitudes toward children could account for the lack of attention in the literature to abuse which occurs at the hands of non-relatives. The body of theoretical work on aggression toward targets who are incapable of retaliating[2] is similarly ignored. Yet the statistics on the incidence of abuse[10, 20, 22] indicate that the rate decreases as the age of the child increases and he becomes capable of striking back or reporting the assault.

The literature on abusing adults which downplays hostile attitudes in favour of a stress-reactive explanatory model is inconsistent with the research reports on the development of the abused child. In those studies emphasis is given, not to abusive incidents by themselves, but to the consequences of a generally hostile environment.[15] There seems to be an awareness of the existence of hatred, but an apparent unwillingness to acknowledge it.

The rationale for the softening of the description of the nature of abuse, the disregard of hostility and the changed role of the child from victim to provocateur appear to be related to the changes in social policy regarding the prevention and management of abuse. The prevalent practice is to maintain the integrity and autonomy of the family in contrast to previous policies of removal and foster placement for the child.[5, 6] Intervention now focuses on 'treatment' of the family by teaching alternate behaviours toward the child.[13, 19] However, the literature is very clear in stating that those with character disorders are not amenable to treatment.[7, 18, 21, 25]

In order to justify preserving the integrity of the family unit, the hostility inherent in the child abuse syndrome has been de-emphasized. Instead, the focus has been placed upon parenting behaviour which is more easily altered. In turn, the successful modification of parenting practice has been facilitated by broadening the definition of abuse to include culturally normative discipline[10] along with the truly abusive pattern of calculated, persistent, punishment for its own sake.[26] Further, altering parenting behaviour to prevent physical assault does not necessarily protect the child from damage due to continued rejection and neglect.[5, 7, 15] This brings into question the rationale for the shift in policy away from protective foster placement.

It is obvious from reading task force reports, newspapers and periodicals that the provision of monies to protect children and foster their development is inadequate. The currently "prevalent dogma that children must be kept with their families at all costs"[18] has economic benefits. It is much cheaper than paying for the establishment of good foster care.[5, 6, 17, 19] In short, it is the economics of social policy that has apparently provided the thrust for the changes in professional attitudes and research. Those who earn their living studying and servicing abusers and abused children have wittingly or unwittingly become accomplices to the policy of financial restraint. The parameters of research and service programmes have been circumscribed to fit economic priorities and practicalities. Unhappily for the abused child, it would appear that for the researchers and workers in this field the economic factor is more important than the human one.

Joanne Valiant Cook

REFERENCES

1.   BAKAN, David. 1971. *Slaughter of the Innocents*. Canadian Broadcasting Corporation, CBC Learning Systems, Toronto.

2.   BUSS, Arnold H. 1961. *The Psychology of Aggression*. John Wiley and Sons Inc., New York and London.

3.   CHESSER, E. 1952. *Cruelty to Children*. Philosophical Library, New York.

4.   CONGER, Rand D., BURGESS, Robert L., and BARRETT, Carol. "Child Abuse Related to Life Change and Perceptions of Illness: Some Preliminary Findings." Chapter 23 in this volume.

5. DERDEYN, Andre P. 1977. "Child Abuse and Neglect: The Rights of Parents and the Needs of Their Children." *Amer. J. Orthopsychiat.* 47(3), 377-385.

6. DERDEYN, Andre P. 1977. "A Case for Permanent Foster Placement of Dependent, Neglected and Abused Children." *Amer. J. Orthopsychiat.* 47(4), 604-614.

7. FISCHHOFF, Joseph, WHITTEN, Charles F., and PETTIT, Marvin C. "Psychiatric Study of Mothers of Infants With Growth Failure Secondary to Maternal Deprivation." Chapter 14 in this volume.

8. FONTANA, Vincent J. "The Diagnosis of the Maltreatment Syndrome in Children." Chapter 5 in this volume.

9. FRIEDRICH, William N. and BORISKIN, J. A. "The Role of the Child in Abuse: A Review of the Literature." Chapter 17 in this volume.

10. GELLES, Richard J. "Violence Toward Children in the United States." Chapter 2 in this volume.

11. GIL, David G. "Unraveling Child Abuse." Chapter 12 in this volume.

12. HELFER, R. E. and KEMPE, C. Henry, eds. 1974. *The Battered Child, 2nd edition.* University of Chicago Press.

13. KEMPE, C. Henry, and HELFER, Ray E., eds. 1972. *Helping the Battered Child and His Family.* J. B. Lippincott Company, Philadelphia and Toronto.

14. KERR, Mary Ann D., BOGUES, Jacqueline Landman, and KERR, Douglas S. "Psychosocial Functioning of Mothers of Malnourished Children." Chapter 19 in this volume.

15. MARTIN, Harold P., BEEZLEY, Patricia, CONWAY, Esther and KEMPE, C. Henry. 1974. "The Development of Abused Children." *Advances in Pediatrics.* 21:25-73.

16. MOYNIHAN, Daniel Patrick. 1979. "Social Science and the Courts." *Public Interest* 54:12-31.

17. NEWBERGER, Eli and BOURNE, R. "The Medicalization and Legalization of Child Abuse." Chapter 33 in this volume.

18. OLIVER, J. E., and COX, Jane. 1973. "A Family Kindred With Ill-Used Children: The Burden on the Community." *Brit. J. Psychiat.* 123: 81-90.

19. PARKE, Ross D. "Socialization into Child Abuse." Chapter 27 in this volume.

20. SCHLESINGER, Benjamin. 1977. *Child Abuse in Canada.* Guidance Centre, Faculty of Education, University of Toronto.

21. SMITH, Selwyn M., HANSON, Ruth, and NOBLE, Shiela. "Social Aspects of the Battered Baby Syndrome." Chapter 20 in this volume.

22. SOLOMON, Theo. "History and Demography of Child Abuse." Chapter 4 in this volume.

23. SPINETTA, John J., and RIGLER, David. "The Child Abusing Parent: A Psychological Review." Chapter 13 in this volume.

24. WOOTON, Barbara. 1959. *Social Science and Social Pathology.* George Allen and Unwin Ltd., Ltd., London.

25. WRIGHT, Logan. "The "Sick but Slick" Syndrome as a Personality Component of Parents of Battered Children." Chapter 15 in this volume.

26. YOUNG, Leontine. 1964. *Wednesday's Children: A Study of Child Neglect and Abuse.* McGraw-Hill Book Co., New York.

Appendix

A Selected Bibliography of Treatment, Prevention, and Protection Programmes

Books

1. BURGESS, Ann Wolbert, GROTH, A. Nicholas, HOLMSTROM, Lynda Lytle, and SGROI, Suzanne M.: *Sexual Assault of Children and Adolescents*. Lexington Books, Lexington, Mass., 1978.

   A comprehensive text, illustrated with case histories. Presents an interdisciplinary approach to the assault of children and adolescents. Part 1 concerns the offender; Part 2 focuses on victim related issues; Part 3 offers guidelines to those offering services to victims and their families, including directions for interviewing and counselling. Information on setting up a community treatment program is also given.

2. JUSTICE, Blair and JUSTICE, Rita: *The Abusing Family*, Human Sciences Press, New York, 1976.

   The authors examine the characteristics of abusing parents and their children. They describe rehabilitative techniques such as group therapy, transactional analysis, relaxation training and basic parenting information. The prevention of abuse through such mechanisms as a health visitors programme is discussed.

3. KEMPE, C. Henry and HELFER, Ray E., editors: *Helping the Battered Child and His Family*. J. B. Lippincott Company, Philadelphia and Toronto, 1972.

   17 Papers on caring for the parent and the abused child, including consideration of the school, medical consultation teams, community hospital programmes and the role of the courts.

4. SCHLESINGER, Benjamin: *Child Abuse in Canada*. Guidance Centre, Faculty of Education, University of Toronto, Toronto, 1977.

   A brief book which discusses the nature of abuse, abusers, and abused. He discusses the management of child abuse utilizing parent aides and groups such as Parents Anonymous. Discussions of legal responsibilities and recommendations for research are included.

5. SCHMITT, B. D., editor: *Child Protection Team Handbook*, A Multidisciplinary Approach to Managing Child Abuse and Neglect. Garland STPM Press, New York, 1978.

   Offers 29 papers on such topics as: organizing a child protection team, diagnostic tasks, child protection team conferences, treatment tasks, questionnaires and social worker evaluation forms.

6. FIRST NATIONAL SYMPOSIUM ON CHILD ABUSE. The American Humane Association, Childrens' Division, Denver, Colorado, 1976.

   Provides 29 papers on protection of the abused child including consideration of the professionals involved, the hospital, the community, the court, central abuse registries, model legislation and therapeutic groups.

Journal Articles

1. CARROL, N. A. and REICH, J. W.: "Issues in the Implementation of the Parent-aide Concept." *Social Casework*, 59(3), 1978, pp. 152-160.

   Description of how to develop such a programme to help abusing and neglecting parents using "empathic paraprofessionals" who provide a "nurturing friend relationship."

2. GALDSTON, Richard: "Preventing the Abuse of Little Children: The Parents' Center Project for the Study and Prevention of Child Abuse." *American Journal of Orthopsychiatry*, 45(3), April 1975, pp. 372-381.

   46 families with 73 children between the ages of 6 months and 4 years were treated in a project developed to preserve the integrity of the family while protecting the child from physical abuse. Improvement in the rate of growth and development was found among the children. There was much less improvement in the domestic functioning of their parents. However, it appeared that the parents would not have kept their children in the project if they had not been in concurrent treatment.

3. McNEIL, John S., and McBRIDE, Mary L.: "Group Therapy With Abusive Parents." *Social Casework*, Vol. 60, No. 1, January 1979, pp. 36-42.

   Discusses a 'couples group' as a means of treating abusers or hi-risk parents. Emphasis was placed on the quality of the marital relationship, the development of a mutual support system, decision-making and the role of the therapists as models.

4. MINDLIN, Rowland L.: "Child Abuse and Neglect: The Role of the Pediatrician and the Academy." *Pediatrics*, Vol. 54, No. 4, October 1974, pp. 393-395.

   Presents an appeal for increased mechanisms to deal with abused children and their families. The Academy of Pediatrics has available a set of audio-tape cassettes, each with an accompanying manual for a self-instructional course in the recognition, management and community aspects of child abuse and neglect.

5. SEEDHOUSE, C. A.: "The Social Problem of Child Abuse." *Journal of Applied Social Science*: 1(2), 1977, pp. 17-32.

   Describes a research project involving Parents Anonymous.

6. SEFCIK, T. R., and ORMSBY, N. J.: "Establishing a Rural Child Abuse/ Neglect Treatment Programme." *Child Welfare*, 57(3), 1978, pp. 187-195.

   Rural community attitudes such as "small-town conservatism" impede the development of programs. There are also problems in promoting co-operation between professionals. The most significant factor in a successful programme was learning to work with people, both professional and lay, in a manner non-threatening to the small community.

Information Agency

The National Center on Child Abuse and Neglect,
   P.O. Box 1182, Washington, D.C., 20013.

   This agency offers a booklet on the role of volunteers in child abuse and neglect treatment programmes. Its appendix lists 700 volunteer programmes in the United States.

*The Following References Were Obtained From The
Psychological Abstracts Information Service
American Psychological Association
1200 Seventeenth Street, N.W.
Washington, D.C. 20036*

1. ACCESSION NUMBER	53-05598(03)
TITLE	Protecting the children of life-threatening parents
AUTHOR	Alexander, Jerry
SOURCE	Journal of Clinical Child Psychology: 1974 Sum. Vol. 3(2) 53-54
ABSTRACT	Presents some of the statistics of child abuse and comments on how professionals can help to overcome this rapidly increasing problem.

2. ACCESSION NUMBER   60-12056(06)
TITLE   How psychologists can help stop child abuse
AUTHOR   Alexander, Jerry
ORGANIZATIONAL SOURCE   Citizens Committee for Battered Children, Chicago, Ill.
SOURCE   Journal of Clinical Child Psychology: 1976 Spr. Vol. 5(1) 13-14
ABSTRACT   Suggests strategies for psychologists to use in helping children. These include organizing interested professionals from social work, advertising, and law so as to produce effective state and local child advocacy activities; writing to legislators; and meeting with groups that are challenging uncooperative political incumbents, to provide professional information and support. (W. V. Adams)

3. ACCESSION NUMBER   60-05707(03)
TITLE   Parents Anonymous
AUTHOR   Bacon, Gertrude M.
ORGANIZATIONAL SOURCE   Parents Anonymous of New York, NY
SOURCE   Victimology: 1977 Sum. Vol. 2(2) 331-337
ABSTRACT   Presents the goals and guidelines of Parents Anonymous, a self-help group which offers immediate relief to parents who feel they are abusing or neglecting their children; discusses the methods of starting a Parents Anonymous Group; and describes some of the problems of members of these groups.

4. ACCESSION NUMBER   60-05403(03)
TITLE   Child abuse: Causes, effect and prevention
AUTHOR   Bailey, Bruce
ORGANIZATIONAL SOURCE   Stephen F. Austin State U
SOURCE   Victimology: 1977 Sum. Vol. 2(2) 337-342
ABSTRACT   Describes 3 research projects on child abuse which determined (a) etiological factors in child abuse, (b) developed a technique for the measurement of the effects of child abuse, and (c) analyzed a child abuse primary prevention project.

5. ACCESSION NUMBER   54-08081(04)
TITLE   Team treatment for abusive families
AUTHORS   Barnes, Geoffrey B.; Chabon, Robert S.; Hertzberg, Leonard, J.
ORGANIZATIONAL SOURCE   Woodbourne Ctr. Child Abuse Project, Baltimore, MD.
SOURCE   Social Casework: 1974 Dec. Vol. 55(10) 600-611
ABSTRACT   Reviews pertinent historical problems leading to innovative approaches in the management of abusive families and discusses the development and experience of the child abuse project of Sinai Hospital in Baltimore, Maryland. The team takes the view that child abuse is a social ill, the roots of which often stem from an unhealthy environment within the family of the victim. The team is composed of 2 full-time community aides, a half-time nurse, a consulting pediatrician, a consulting psychiatrist, and a full-time social worker. During the past 2 yrs. the team has served more than 30 families. Case illustrations are cited. A goal for each family is the definition and clarification of problems that can be dealt with in the family's future contacts with team members.

6. ACCESSION NUMBER   60-05404(03)
   TITLE   Child sexual abuse: What happens next?
   AUTHOR   Berliner, Lucy
   ORGANIZATIONAL SOURCE   Harborview Medical Ctr. Sexual Assault Ctr., Seattle, Washington
   SOURCE   Victimology: 1977 Sum. Vol. 2(2) 327-331
   ABSTRACT   Describes steps which can be taken when a child reports that he/she has been sexually molested, discusses some of the immediate problems of the sexually molested child (e.g., sleep disturbances, loss of appetite, and changes in behavior), and summarizes available data on the sexual abuse of children.

7. ACCESSION NUMBER   59-05860(03)
   TITLE   Treatment of the abused child and the child abuser
   AUTHOR   Blumberg, Marvin L.
   ORGANIZATIONAL SOURCE   Jamaica Hosp. Dept. of Pediatrics, NY.
   SOURCE   American Journal of Psychotherapy; 1977 Apr. Vol. 31(2) 204-215
   ABSTRACT   Considers that an abusing parent is not necessarily a criminal. He (or she) is usually an immature, lonely person with low self-esteem and a lack of ego strength as a result of neglectful or cruel parenting during his or her early childhood. Lacking normal ego mechanisms of reality testing and memory, the potential abuser employs self-defeating defense mechanisms of repression, denial, and projection. These prevent the realization of the consequence of the violence and permit the parent to vent anger on an inappropriate object in the person of the child. Therapeutic considerations require a multidisciplinary approach involving the psychotherapist, the social worker, the court, and child placement, temporary if possible. The maltreated child is traumatized emotionally as well as physically and often, like the abusing parent needs psychotherapy. Preventive measures under study are identifying questionnaires and various means of professional help for high-risk families. (Journal summary)

8. ACCESSION NUMBER   60-09901(05)
   TITLE   Development of an information system for the child abuse and neglect service system
   AUTHORS   Bommer, Michael; Goodgion, Gilbert; Pease, Victor; Zmud, Robert
   ORGANIZATIONAL SOURCE   Clarkson Coll. School of Management
   SOURCE   Community Mental Health Journal: 1977 Win. Vol. 13(4) 333-342
   ABSTRACT   Presents a plan for developing an information system that provides a basis for improved decision making and planning at all levels in a child abuse and neglect service system. The goal attainment scaling method (GAS) is suggested as a means for assisting the client and social worker in identifying needs and in developing a treatment plan for meeting these needs. The proposed information system is outlined using the GAS instrument as the basic information unit. (27 ref) (Journal abstract)

9. ACCESSION NUMBER 60-05407(03)
 TITLE Child sexual assault by a family member: Decisions following disclosure
 AUTHORS Burgess, Ann. W.; Holmstrom, Lynda, L.; McCausland, Maureen, P.
 ORGANIZATIONAL SOURCE Boston Coll.
 SOURCE Victimology: 1977 Sum. Vol. 2(2) 236-250
 ABSTRACT Analyzed 44 cases of child sexual assault by a family member to identify the key decision points and issues faced by the victim and family. In 8 cases, decisions were made for the family by the hospital for court-ordered foster placement. Decisions made by the family included handling the situation as a family matter, mental health intervention, and/or legal intervention. A major issue facing families is where to place their loyalty—to the child or to the offender. (25 ref) (Journal abstract)

10. ACCESSION NUMBER 60-05885(03)
 TITLE What can the schools do about child abuse?
 AUTHOR Broadhurst, Diane D.
 SOURCE Victimology: 1977 Sum. Vol. 2(2) 316-322
 ABSTRACT Maintains that there are at least 4 roles schools can play in the identification of child abuse and neglect: (a) reporter of suspected incidents, (b) partner in decision-making and treatment programs, (c) agency for primary prevention, and (d) child advocate. Case examples are presented to demonstrate how each role can be effected.

11. ACCESSION NUMBER 49-04277(03)
 TITLE Protecting children from their families and themselves: State laws and the Constitution
 AUTHOR Burt, Robert A.
 ORGANIZATIONAL SOURCE U. Michigan
 SOURCE Journal of Youth & Adolescence: 1972 Mar. Vol. 1(1) 91-111
 ABSTRACT Explores the rationale for court application, by constitutional mandate, of procedural safeguards to a broad range of child-protective legislation. It is suggested that some criminal-procedure rights are vitally important to protect children and their parents from inappropriate state interventions, but that wholesale application of all criminal rights, as if these laws were no different from criminal laws, unduly restricts proper application of these laws. Guidelines for determining what criminal rights should and should not be applied to child-protective legislation generally are suggested. (19 ref) (Journal abstract)

12. ACCESSION NUMBER 60-11912(06)
 TITLE Understanding and helping child-abusing parents
 AUTHORS Caskey, Owen L.; Richardson, Ivanna
 ORGANIZATIONAL SOURCE Texas Tech. U.
 SOURCE Elementary School Guidance & Counselling: 1975 Mar. Vol. 9(3) 196-208
 ABSTRACT Discusses legal, sociological, psychodynamic, and treatment aspects of child abuse. Statistics on incidence are presented, and legal definitions and reporting requirements which vary from state to state are summarized. The abusing

parent is one who has experienced emotional deprivation and often abuse in his or her own childhood. Treatment should help the abusing parent obtain gratification of his unmet needs through normal outlets. Group procedures should be used whenever feasible. Appropriately trained school personnel could play a key role in working with others to establish successful programs for preventing and treating child abuse. (L. H. Zaiden)

13.	ACCESSION NUMBER	54-12377(06)
	TITLE	Occupational therapy and child abuse
	AUTHOR	Colman, Wendy
	ORGANIZATIONAL SOURCE	Roosevelt Hosp., New York, NY
	SOURCE	American Journal of Occupational Therapy: 1975 Aug. Vol. 29(7) 412-417
	ABSTRACT	Describes the part occupational therapy played in a community-based research and demonstration project instituted to treat abusive parents and their children. The development of the project, designed to define characteristics of abusive parents and their children and to experiment with various forms of treatment, is discussed. The psychosocial and psychological dynamics of abusive parents are reviewed, including isolation, poor group and socialization skills, inability to set priorities or to develop order in most situations, a weak internalized ego structure as a basis for determining their needs and identity, the inability to perceive one's abilities and limitations accurately, and a great need for clear external structure. Finally, occupational therapy as a viable evaluative tool and treatment mode in child abuse is discussed wherein the parents learned and understood cause and effect and developed some measure of control of a situation. (Journal abstract)
14.	ACCESSION NUMBER	50-05280(03)
	TITLE	Protecting children from neglect and abuse
	AUTHOR	Costin, Lela B.
	ORGANIZATIONAL SOURCE	U. Illinois, School of Social Work
	SOURCE	In L. B. Costin, Child welfare: Policies and practice. New York, N.Y.: McGraw-Hill, 1972. xii, 423 p.
	ABSTRACT	Discusses the historical background, goals, and method of operation of child protective services. The causes and symptoms of child neglect and abuse are described, and the effectiveness of current programs is discussed.
15.	ACCESSION NUMBER	53-07822(04)
	TITLE	The use of the confrontation technique in the battered child syndrome
	AUTHOR	David, Charles A.
	ORGANIZATIONAL SOURCE	Dalhouise U., Victoria General Hosp., Halifax, Nova Scotia, Canada
	SOURCE	American Journal of Psychotherapy: 1974 Oct. Vol. 28(4) 543-552
	ABSTRACT	Presents a case in which the confrontation technique was used successfully to help a battering parent gain control over her punitive treatment of her child. Some causative factors in the development of the battered child syndrome are discussed. Treatment of the battering parent is a

psychiatric emergency since its primary goal, protection of the child, must be reached quickly. Once some patient-therapist rapport has been established, the use of authoritative confrontation statements which direct the patient to control battering impulses intensifies transference and relieves the anxiety and guilt of the patient by allowing him to rely on the therapist as an external source of control. It is concluded that the confrontation technique can be an effective tool in psychotherapy with battering parents. (J. Kelly)

16. ACCESSION NUMBER	60-02955(02)
TITLE	Child abuse and neglect: The rights of parents and the needs of their children
AUTHOR	Derdeyn, Andre P.
ORGANIZATIONAL SOURCE	U. Virginia Medical Ctr., Div. of Child & Adolescent Psychiatry
SOURCE	American Journal of Orthopsychiatry: 1977 Jul. Vol. 47(3) 377-387
ABSTRACT	Reviews the trends in treatment and in legal decisions with respect to custody of abused and neglected children. Parental rights, including a familial right to treatment, are discussed in terms of the needs of children for their parents and for a safe home environment. It is argued that the critical point for the assertion of parents' rights is not the ultimate custody hearing but the initial decision to remove the child from its home. (67 ref) (Journal abstract)

17. ACCESSION NUMBER	60-05048(03)
TITLE	A case for permanent foster placement of dependent, neglected, and abused children
AUTHOR	Derdeyn, Andre P.
ORGANIZATIONAL SOURCE	U. Virginia Medical School
SOURCE	American Journal of Orthopsychiatry: 1977 Oct. Vol. 47(4) 604-614
ABSTRACT	Since the number of children entering foster care continues to rise, and despite efforts to rehabilitate families and to place children for adoption, for many children foster care tends to be interminable. Return to the home is often impeded by a paucity of parental resources; adoption is often blocked by the courts' reluctance to terminate parental rights. Permanent foster placement is suggested as an alternative arrangement for better meeting the needs of some of these children. (49 ref) (Journal abstract)

18. ACCESSION NUMBER	59-01265(01)
TITLE	Child abuse in megalopolis
AUTHOR	Fontana, Vincent J.
ORGANIZATIONAL SOURCE	New York Foundling Hosp. Ctr. for Parent & Child Development, NY
SOURCE	New York State Journal of Medicine: 1976 Oct. Vol. 76(11) 1799-1802
ABSTRACT	Discusses and describes a multidimensional interdisciplinary approach to child abuse. Environmental factors such as strains created by social and/or cultural deprivation, depression, and anger contribute to the child abuse problem among minority groups in the megalopolis.

The health care system is charged with the responsibility of improving medical delivery services to allow parents to provide sufficient care for normal growth and development of children. Funding problems are discussed. The program described includes (a) a multidisciplinary team of professionals and nonprofessionals; (b) surrogate mothers or lay therapists; (c) a hotline service for crises; (d) in-resident facilities for mothers and children; (e) a Halfway House; and (f) an out-patient program. Successful components are not yet identified although the program as a whole is deemed successful by the author. (P. R. Sweet)

19. ACCESSION NUMBER	54-08480(04)
TITLE	Battered children and counselor responsibility
AUTHOR	Forrer, Stephen E.
ORGANIZATIONAL SOURCE	Northern Virginia Community Coll., Extended Learning Inst.
SOURCE	School Counselor: 1975 Jan. Vol. 22(3) 161-165
ABSTRACT	Discusses 3 general areas in which counselors can work to combat child abuse involving (a) interaction with the abusing parents with the goal of reeducating them to replace abusive behaviors with effective acceptable behaviors; (b) dealing with the psychological effects of abuse on the child (e.g., the abused child must relearn behavioral mechanisms for interacting with individuals and society); and (c) participation in the community response by involving the school in a child abuse council. A model of the function and community relationship of the child abuse council is illustrated. The development of a preventive approach through training and education is essential. (F. Beyer)

20. ACCESSION NUMBER	59-12862(06)
TITLE	Protective services: Coercive social control or mutual liberation
AUTHOR	Fortin, Alfred J.
ORGANIZATIONAL SOURCE	U Connecticut, School of Social Work, West Hartford
SOURCE	Journal of Sociology & Social Welfare: 1975 Sep. Vol. 3(1) 82-93
ABSTRACT	Discusses protective services for children (the prevention or control of child abuse or neglect) in terms of the general picture of social casework, which is based at present on a philosophy of elitist collectivism. This philosophy supports existing institutions by the very natures of its assumptions. To make casework more human, social workers must participate actively in efforts for change. Treatment of clients must be open, negotiable, teachable, and mutually self-revealing. Both workers and clients must be involved in making policy in social agencies. (19 ref) (T. T. Jackson)

21. ACCESSION NUMBER	48-01410(01)
TITLE	Violence begins at home: The Parents' Center Project for the Study and Prevention of Child Abuse
AUTHOR	Galdston, Richard
ORGANIZATIONAL SOURCE	Harvard Medical School, Boston, Mass.
SOURCE	Journal of the American Academy of Child Psychiatry, 1971. Apr. Vol. 10(2), 336-350
ABSTRACT	Discusses child abuse with a view toward prevention and

treatment. The Parents' Center Project is an institution which protects children from abuse, studies this problem, and seeks to help parents who are prone to violent behavior. Child care is provided for 8 or 10 hr., 5 days/wk. by adults who work in small research-oriented groups. Children adjust well to the separation but are initially listless and apathetic. They are uninterested in other children and activities and gain the attention of adults through violence. After many months children learn to play, to initiate activities, and to gain attention in a non-violent way but they remain unaware of other children. Parents attend group sessions. It was found that nonparticipants were likely to abuse their children again while participants had a better prognosis. It is believed that direct contacts with parents may be a working solution to the problem of child abuse. (H. Reiter)

22.	ACCESSION NUMBER	54-06068(03)
	TITLE	Breaking the communication barrier: The initial interview with an abusing parent
	AUTHOR	Goldberg, Gale
	ORGANIZATIONAL SOURCE	U Louisville, Raymond A. Kent School of Social Work
	SOURCE	Child Welfare: 1975 Apr. Vol. 54(4) 274-282
	ABSTRACT	Discusses 6 behaviors that can be used by the social worker in his initial and/or follow-up interview with the abusing parent: adjusting seating arrangement which, according to research, does not threaten the parent; reaching for feelings or using statements that verbalize nonverbal behavior; waiting for the parent to experience the emotions the previous behavior has elicited; expressing empathy for the patient's feelings; asking for information; and giving information. Examples of each behavior in use are provided. (17 ref) (M. E. Pounsel)

23.	ACCESSION NUMBER	59-05866(03)
	TITLE	A psychodynamic approach to the study and treatment of child-abusing parents
	AUTHOR	Green, Arthur, H.
	ORGANIZATIONAL SOURCE	State U. New York. Downstate Medical Ctr.
	SOURCE	Journal of the American Academy of Child Psychiatry, 1976. Sum. Vol. 15(3) 414-429
	ABSTRACT	Conducted structured interviews with 60 mothers of abused children, 30 neglecting mothers, and 30 normal controls to (a) identify the personality traits of the abusing parents, (b) explore the contributions of the child toward his/her abuse, (c) determine the environmental factors precipitating episodes of child abuse and (d) examine the key psychodynamics underlying the phenomenon of child abuse. Results indicate that child abuse is a dysfunction of parenting in which the parent misperceives the child due to his/her own frustrating childhood experiences. The beating represents the parent's attempt to master trauma passively experienced as a child. The child abuse syndrome is conceptualized as the product of 3 factors: the parent's abuse-prone personality, the child's abuse-provoking characteristics, and environmental stress. The techniques, aims, and pitfalls of psychotherapeutic intervention with abusing parents are described. (17 ref) (Journal abstract)

24. ACCESSION NUMBER 58-03538(02)
    TITLE Child abuse and neglect: The family and the community
    AUTHORS Helfer, Ray E.; Kempe, C. Henry
    ORGANIZATIONAL SOURCE Michigan State U., Coll. of Human Medicine
    SOURCE Cambridge, MA: Callinger, 1976 x. 438 p. $20
    ABSTRACT Presents a series of 20 theoretical and empirical articles on aspects of child abuse including dysfunctions in family interactions, methods of evaluating families, family-oriented therapy, community programs for studying and preventing child abuse, the family and the law, and early recognition and prevention of potential problems in family interaction.

25. ACCESSION NUMBER 54-06073(03)
    TITLE Working with the parent in child-abuse cases
    AUTHORS Holmes, Sally A.; Barnhart, Carol; Cantoni, Lucile; Reymer, Eva
    ORGANIZATIONAL SOURCE Family Service of Detroit & Wayne County, MI
    SOURCE Social Casework: 1975 Jan. Vol. 56(1) 3-12
    ABSTRACT Reports on the work of a study group formed to develop more responsible, sensitive, and skillful caseworkers in the treatment of child abuse cases. Some literature on child abuse is cited and excerpts from case histories presented. Maltreatment is considered to bear no relation to the child's behavior in many instances, but may relate to the parents' negative feelings about themselves or their situation. Resistance among caseworkers to treating abusive parents is discussed. Methods of developing a treatment relationship, defining precipitating factors, understanding rage, and helping parents modify behavior are discussed. (R. Tomasko)

26. ACCESSION NUMBER 59-06046(03)
    TITLE The treatment of child abuse: Play therapy with a 4-year-old child
    AUTHORS In, Peter A.; McDermott, John F.
    ORGANIZATIONAL SOURCE U Hawaii Medical School, Leahi Hosp.
    SOURCE Journal of the American Academy of Child Psychiatry, 1976, Sum. Vol. 15(3) 430-440
    ABSTRACT There are few reports on the follow-up of child-abuse victims or indications that these children need any special treatment beyond removal from the abusing situation. It is suggested these children may indeed suffer many sequelae and are in need of individual psychotherapy. A case study of play therapy with a severely regressed 3-yr-old girl is presented. Typical issues that need to be resolved to prevent crystallization of a chronically disturbed and arrested character structure in the children are discussed. (Journal abstract)

27. ACCESSION NUMBER 60-12183(06)
    TITLE A behavior modification program to remediate child abuse
    AUTHOR Jensen, Richard E.
    ORGANIZATIONAL SOURCE Mental Health Ctr. of Polk County Inc., Lakeland Ctr., Florida
    SOURCE Journal of Clinical Child Psychology, 1976, Spr. Vol. 5(1) 30-32
    ABSTRACT On the assumption that child abuse is contributed to by parents' lack of effective child management skills, training

in behavioral principles was developed for abusing parents. A general outline is given of the 12-session program. (W. V. Adams)

28. ACCESSION NUMBER
    TITLE
    AUTHORS
    ORGANIZATIONAL SOURCE
    SOURCE
    ABSTRACT

57-12958(06)
Physical abuse of children as a public health problem
Justice, Blair; Duncan, D. F.
U Texas School of Public Health, Houston
Public Health Reviews, 1975, Vol. 4(2) 183-200
Reviews studies of the physical abuse of children by their parents or other adults in an effort to present epidemiological data which can be used in a model for public health intervention. Child abuse is a public health problem of sizable proportions in many nations. Studies of the problem have been largely concentrated in the US but the problem has also been of concern in many other nations. Epidemiological findings are summarized, and major sociological and psychiatric theories of child abuse are discussed. A model of child abuse is presented in terms of the public health epidemiologist's concept of disease which involves host, environment, agent, and vector components. (47 ref) (Journal abstract)

29. ACCESSION NUMBER
    TITLE
    AUTHORS
    SOURCE
    ABSTRACT

55-00999(01)
TA work with child abuse
Justice, Rita; Justice, Blair
Transactional Analysis Journal, 1975, Jan. Vol. 5(1) 38-41
Used a transactional analysis approach to therapy with 10 couples legally charged with child abuse. The therapy focused on breaking up the destructive symbiosis between the parents and between parent and child. The confrontation of discounts and correction of misinformation about parenting were stressed. Kiresuk's Goal Attainment Scale was used to evaluate the therapy's impact on the couples. 8 couples had their children returned to them on the therapist's recommendation. (R. Tomasko)

30. ACCESSION NUMBER
    TITLE
    AUTHOR
    ORGANIZATIONAL SOURCE
    SOURCE

    ABSTRACT

47-01175(01)
Paediatric implications of the battered baby syndrome
Kempe, C. Henry
U. Colorado, Medical Center, Denver
Archives of Disease in Childhood, 1971, Vol. 46(245), 28-37
Presents an explication of the diagnosis and treatment of abused children based on the concept that child abuse is caused by a disturbance in mothering. (A. B. Warren)

31. ACCESSION NUMBER
    TITLE
    AUTHORS
    ORGANIZATIONAL SOURCE
    SOURCE
    ABSTRACT

55-05366(03)
Managing child abuse cases
Kristal, Helen F.; Tucker, Ford
U Rochester. Medical Ctr
Social Work: 1975 Sep Vol 20(5) 392-395
Describes a procedure coordinated by a social worker who works with a physician and helps train professionals from several disciplines. (29 ref)

32. ACCESSION NUMBER — 52-01216(01)

    TITLE — Abused and neglected children in America: A study of alternative policies

    AUTHOR — Light, Richard J.

    ORGANIZATIONAL SOURCE — Harvard U.

    SOURCE — Harvard Educational Review, 1973, Nov. Vol. 43(4) 556-598

    ABSTRACT — Examines several sources of data to estimate the incidence of abuse, its social and demographic features, and the nature of available child abuse case reports. 3 potential social policies are analyzed in detail; national health screening, education in child rearing, and the development of profiles of abusing families. (Journal abstract)

33. ACCESSION NUMBER — 54-10285(05)

    TITLE — A community approach to the prevention of child abuse

    AUTHORS — Lovens, Herbert D.; Rako, Jules

    ORGANIZATIONAL SOURCE — Massachusetts Society for the Prevention of Cruelty to Children, Brockton

    SOURCE — Child Welfare, 1975, Feb. Vol. 54(2) 83-87

    ABSTRACT — Discusses a suburban community's effort to identify and intervene in situations where children are designated as "vulnerable." The program operates through a coordinated system of interagency and hospital communication, a community cross-indexing register of vulnerable children, and a system of quality control.

34. ACCESSION NUMBER — 59-01448(01)

    TITLE — Review. Battered children, their parents, treatment and prevention

    AUTHOR — Margrain, Susan A.

    ORGANIZATIONAL SOURCE — Northern Ireland Polytechnic, Jordanstown

    SOURCE — Child Care, Health & Development, 1977, Jan-Feb. Vol. 3(1) 49-63

    ABSTRACT — Reviews the literature on battered children, their parents, management, treatment and prevention. It is suggested that socioeconomic factors are less important than the psychology of the parent, who has often been a battered child himself. Management and treatment of the syndrome in the United Kingdom and the US are indicated. An outline of the preventive and research projects in the field is presented. (34 ref.) (Journal abstract)

35. ACCESSION NUMBER — 58-03544(02)

    TITLE — The abused child: A multidisciplinary approach to developmental issues and treatment

    AUTHOR — Martin, Harold P.

    ORGANIZATIONAL SOURCE — U Colorado Medical School, Denver

    SOURCE — Cambridge, MA, Ballinger, 1976, xviii, 304 p.

    ABSTRACT — Presents a series of 22 papers on the nature, effects, and treatment of child abuse. Topics include the environment of the abused child; high-risk factors; relationships between abused children and their siblings; neurologic status of abused children; speech, language, learning, intelligence, and personality variables in abused children; special problems in developmental assessments of this population; and various strategies for dealing with the problem, such as psychotherapy, preschool programs, and crisis nurseries.

36. ACCESSION NUMBER — 60-05719(03)
    TITLE — Delicate inquiry: The investigator's role in child abuse
    AUTHOR — McGovern, James I.
    SOURCE — Victimology, 1977, Sum. Vol. 2(2) 277-284
    ABSTRACT — Examines the role that state investigators play in child abuse cases. Some of the special problems include the large volume of child abuse reports, the investigator's continual exposure to tragic situations, and the inability to treat them in as much depth as it would be necessary. Methods of approaching the family and interviewing techniques are also examined. Parents' reactions to the investigator; complicating factors such as cultural conflict or religious convictions; and the investigator's planning for the disposition of the case are discussed. The paper concludes with a consideration of child abuse prevention and of its relation to other social issues. (Journal abstract)

37. ACCESSION NUMBER — 57-13411(06)
    TITLE — At risk. An account of the work of the Battered Child Research Department NSPCC
    AUTHORS — NSPCC Battered Child Research Team
    SOURCE — London, England: Routledge & Kegan Paul, 1976, x. 246 p. $10.25
    ABSTRACT — Describes a total-family, multiple-modality approach to treatment of child abuse in 25 families. Chapters consider the overall management of cases, protection of children, the primary therapeutic relationship, the use of professional and untrained workers, evaluation of progress, psychological aspects of battering parents, and characteristics of battered children. (8 p ref) (A. C. Moltu)

38. ACCESSION NUMBER — 53-10193(05)
    TITLE — Aspects of bonding failure: The psychopathology and psychotherapeutic treatment of families of battered children
    AUTHORS — Ounsted, Christopher; Oppenheimer, Rhoda; Lindsay, Janet
    ORGANIZATIONAL SOURCE — Park Hosp. for Children, Headington, England
    SOURCE — Developmental Medicine & Child Neurology, 1974 Aug. Vol. 16(4) 447-456
    ABSTRACT — Effected notable improvement in parent-child relations by treating mothers and battered children conjointly in a special unit geared to provide what had been lacking in the home environment. Another group, in which the child was at risk of being battered, was treated preventively on an outpatient basis with small mutual support groups for the mothers and play groups for the children. Mothers kept diaries of explosive situations, and had a social worker on call at crisis points. No incidents of battering occurred and some small improvements were seen in the mothers. (Spanish, German, & French summaries) (P. W. Pruyser)

39. ACCESSION NUMBER — 55-12490(06)
    TITLE — Child trauma intervention: A community response to family violence
    AUTHOR — Paulson, Morris J.
    ORGANIZATIONAL SOURCE — U California, Ctr. for the Health Sciences, Los Angeles

SOURCE	Journal of Clinical Child Psychology, 1975, Fal. Vol. 4(3) 26-29
ABSTRACT	Briefly reviews child abuse, including history, theory, family concomitants, and a statement of the community's role in dealing with this problem. (W. V. Adams)

40.

ACCESSION NUMBER	53-01753(01)
TITLE	Parents of the battered child: A multidisciplinary group therapy approach to life-threatening behavior
AUTHOR	Paulson, Morris J., et al.
ORGANIZATIONAL SOURCE	U. California, Los Angeles
SOURCE	Life-Threatening Behavior: 1974 Spr. Vol. 4(1) 18-31
ABSTRACT	Reports the demographic findings and the experience of a 3-yr. multidisciplinary group psychotherapy program with 31 child-abusing families. No predictive demographic characteristics were identified. The abuse of children ranged from mild bruising to severe brain damage and multiple fractures. Group therapy as an intervention procedure had its successes and failures. The dynamics of male-female cotherapists, the peer group sharing, and the capacity to ultimately verbalize inadequacies in the parenting role were crucial factors in therapy. As an experiential encounter the study gives an insight into the personal and family pathology of parents who abuse their children. (Journal abstract)

41.

ACCESSION NUMBER	51-07714(04)
TITLE	Parent surrogate roles: A dynamic concept in understanding and treating abusive parents
AUTHORS	Paulson, Morris J.; Chaleff, Anne
ORGANIZATIONAL SOURCE	U. California, Medical School, Center for the Health Sciences, Los Angeles
SOURCE	Journal of Clinical Child Psychology, 1973, Fall Vol. 2(3) 38-40
ABSTRACT	Describes group therapy attempted with 61 parents admitting to or charged with child abuse or neglect. Cotherapists acted as parent surrogates in the group, emphasizing empathy rather than being judgmental. The therapists were used by the patients as sources of support, help, and attachment, often leading to cathartic emotional experiences of a positive nature. The parent-surrogate role is seen as a significant prophylactic factor in the rehabilitating of many of these parents to a more adequate and fulfilling role as parents. (A. Krionev)

42.

ACCESSION NUMBER	54-10245(05)
TITLE	Behavioral treatment of child abuse
AUTHORS	Polakow, Robert L.; Peabody, Dixie L.
ORGANIZATIONAL SOURCE	Los Angeles County Probation Dept., Behavior Research & Training Program, Reseda, CA.
SOURCE	International Journal of Offender Therapy & Comparative Criminology, 1975, Vol. 19(1) 100-103
ABSTRACT	Stresses that child abuse is often an inappropriate and desperate attempt to control severe acting-out behavior in children. Examples are presented of ways to control child abuse by teaching parents the skills necessary to deal with child control problems in a more adaptive manner.

Behavioral techniques suggested include contingency contracting and assertive and discrimination training. A case example of a 28-yr-old woman convicted of child abuse is presented. (R. Tomasko)

43. ACCESSION NUMBER — 54-05547(03)
    TITLE   A practice regimen for diagnosis and treatment of child abuse
    AUTHOR   Roth, Frederick
    ORGANIZATIONAL SOURCE Eau Claire County Dept. of Social Services, Juvenile Court Services, WI
    SOURCE   Child Welfare, 1975, Apr. Vol. 54(4) 268-273
    ABSTRACT   Describes a step-by-step system for identifying child abuse cases and delivering the services and treatment required by the families and their children.

44. ACCESSION NUMBER   46-07061(04)
    TITLE   A hospital program for the detection and registration of abused and neglected children
    AUTHORS   Rowe, Daniel S., et al.
    ORGANIZATIONAL SOURCE Yale U., Medical School
    SOURCE   New England Journal of Medicine, 1970, Apr. Vol. 282(17), 950-952
    ABSTRACT   Describes a program developed to facilitate early identification of abused and neglected children that includes a registry of such patients and a committee of staff members who are particularly qualified to deal with such problems. During the 18 mo. since the inception of the registry, 118 patients have been listed in the registry; 37 have evidence of abuse, 69 of neglect, and 12 are thought to be at high risk of maltreatment. The program appears to have increased the level of staff awareness of these problems, promoted early identification and led to thorough investigation, active intervention, and follow-up observation. A report to the Committee does not replace the mandatory formal report to the State Health or Welfare Department, and the Committee's tasks include assistance to the house officer in fulfillment of this responsibility. (Journal summary)

45. ACCESSION NUMBER   51-07795(04)
    TITLE   Community committee on child abuse
    AUTHORS   Sayre, James W.; Foley, Frank W.; Zingarella, Leonor S.; Kristal, Helen F.
    ORGANIZATIONAL SOURCE U. Rochester, Medical & Dental School
    SOURCE   New York State Journal of Medicine, 1973 Aug. Vol. 73(16) 2071-2075
    ABSTRACT   Describes a group of people representing medical, social services, and legal resources dealing with the identification, reporting, protective, and legal aspects of child abuse who have been holding regular monthly meetings to discuss their mutual concerns. This Monroe County Committee on Child Abuse has been successful in identifying interagency problems and misunderstandings, discussing them openly and constructively, and suggesting ways of improving care of these complex cases. The Committee provides a natural vehicle through which innovative programs may be implemented in the future. Its history, composition, and accomplishments are briefly discussed. (Journal summary)

46. ACCESSION NUMBER   55-10152(05)
    TITLE   Abused children are exceptional children
    AUTHOR   Soeffing, Marylane
    ORGANIZATIONAL SOURCE   Council for Exceptional Children, Reston, VA
    SOURCE   Exceptional Children, 1975, Nov. Vol. 42(3) 126-133
    ABSTRACT   Discusses child abuse as it relates to handicapped children. The susceptibility of these children to abuse is emphasized and the roles of teachers, schools, current programs, and resources are considered. Mental health consequences of abuse, such as low IQ and mild idiopathic mental retardation, are noted, and programs of the National Center on Child Abuse and Neglect are described. Communities are encouraged to provide counseling and support to abusive parents. (28 ref.) (R. Tomasko)

47. ACCESSION NUMBER   60-05729(03)
    TITLE   Reaching child abusers through target toddlers
    AUTHOR   Stephenson, P. Susan
    ORGANIZATIONAL SOURCE   U British Columbia, Vancouver, Canada
    SOURCE   Victimology, 1977, Sum. Vol. 2(2) 310-316
    ABSTRACT   Describes a demonstration project in which child abusing and neglecting parents voluntarily participated in an enrichment program for their toddlers. The program emphasized medical and nutritional care. The primary therapists were young preschool teachers who focused on the basic needs of very young children. As the children grew older, the enrichment program became similar to a regular preschool program. Follow-up evaluations of the program indicated that very disadvantaged, deprived, and alienated families who were neglecting or abusing their children could be successfully worked with on a voluntary basis. For example, there was no decline of IQ that is usually found with poverty children, suggesting that a comprehensive evaluation of all "high-risk" toddlers with referral to appropriate resources would be a useful preventive measure. (19 ref.) (M. Ellison-Pounsel)

48. ACCESSION NUMBER   53-03838(02)
    TITLE   Counseling the abusing parent by telephone
    AUTHORS   Tapp, Jack T.; Ryken, Virginia; Kaltwasser, Carl
    SOURCE   Crisis Intervention, 1974, Vol. 5(3) 27-37
    ABSTRACT   Discusses procedures and issues involved in operating a 24-hr crisis service dealing with child abuse. The focus is on ways in which phone workers can help potentially abusing parents; special problems to be anticipated with this population are identified.

49. ACCESSION NUMBER   55-05126(03)
    TITLE   Child abuse project: A follow-up
    AUTHOR   Tracy, James J.; Ballard, Carolyn M.; Clark, Elizabeth H.
    ORGANIZATIONAL SOURCE   U Washington, Medical School, Seattle
    SOURCE   Social Work, 1975, Sep. Vol. 20(5) 398-399
    ABSTRACT   Presents results of a project designed to (a) identify families with an abused child, (b) increase effective parental behavior, and (c) decrease abusive behavior. Principles of behavior modification and social learning theory were used.

50. ACCESSION NUMBER   52-08381(04)
    TITLE   Treatment for child abusers
    AUTHOR   Tracy, James J.; Clark, Elizabeth H.
    ORGANIZATIONAL SOURCE U. Washington
    SOURCE   Social Work, 1974, May, Vol. 19(3) 338-342
    ABSTRACT   Describes the use of methods derived from social learning theory and some techniques of behavior modification as treatment for child abusers. The program was located in a predominantly black neighborhood and was staffed primarily by 4 female black family health workers, 3 full-time social workers, and a black registered nurse. The program encompasses 5 basic steps: (a) identify the cause of injury; (b) conduct a precise behavioral analysis of the parent's child management techniques; (c) decide whether the child can be returned to the family if the program provides continued assistance; and (d) introduce the family to the staff, usually when the child leaves the hospital. Treatment involves using specific procedures for certain problem areas in parent-child relationships, establishing a continuity of service between the child's hospitalization and the parent's treatment, and evaluating behavioral changes. Problems and limitations of the program are briefly noted. (L. Gorsey)

51. ACCESSION NUMBER   59-01845(01)
    TITLE   Interdisciplinary education in child abuse and neglect
    AUTHORS   Venters, Maurine; ten Bensel, Robert
    ORGANIZATIONAL SOURCE U Minnesota School of Public Health
    SOURCE   Journal of Medical Education, 1977, Apr. Vol. 52(4) 334-337
    ABSTRACT   The increased need for professionals working with children and their families to understand, identify, and in some cases treat and follow up situations of child abuse and neglect has led to the offering of a structured graduate interdisciplinary course to students in various types of professional training. A description is presented of the objectives, content, methodology, problems, and short-term evaluation of this course. (Journal abstract)

52. ACCESSION NUMBER   57-01439(01)
    TITLE   Physical and sexual abuse of children: Causes and treatment
    AUTHOR   Walters, David R.
    ORGANIZATIONAL SOURCE Indiana C
    SOURCE   Bloomington, In., Indiana U Press, 1975, xii, 192 p. $7.95
    ABSTRACT   Presents an overview of current thinking about child abuse for psychologists, psychiatrists, and social workers treating abused children and/or abusive adults, and for other professionals dealing with child abuse cases. Topics include (a) the nature and extent of child abuse, (b) the cultural causes and history, (c) a typology of physical abusers, (d) treatment for the abuser, (e) sexual abuse of children, (f) treatment of the sexual abuser, and (g) strategies for change.

53. ACCESSION NUMBER   55-05240(03)
    TITLE   Case management of child abuse
    AUTHOR   Weinbach, Robert W.

ORGANIZATIONAL SOURCE	U South Carolina, Coll. of Social Work, Columbia
SOURCE	Social Work, 1975, Sep. Vol. 20(5) 396-397
ABSTRACT	Discusses problems related to the identification of child abuse cases, procedural ambiguity in dealing with them, and the lack of relevant treatment and central registries. The coordinating role of the medical social worker is noted.

54.
ACCESSION NUMBER	58-05989(03)
TITLE	Evolution of a program for the management of child abuse
AUTHOR	Wolkenstein, Alan S.
ORGANIZATIONAL SOURCE	Milwaukee Children's Hosp, WI
SOURCE	Social Casework, 1976, May, Vol. 57(5) 309-316
ABSTRACT	Describes the development in Milwaukee Children's Hospital of an interdisciplinary committee for abused children. The committee is a coordinating and referral agency providing a variety of services, including psychosocial assessment, limited diagnostic evaluation, and therapy and re-evaluation after 6 mo. (E. D. Hillenbrand)

55.
ACCESSION NUMBER	59-03842(02)
TITLE	The fear of committing child abuse: A discussion of eight families
AUTHOR	Wolkenstein, Alan S.
ORGANIZATIONAL SOURCE	St. Luke's Hosp. Family Practice Ctr. Behavioral Science, Milwaukee, WI
SOURCE	Child Welfare, 1977, Apr. Vol. 56(4) 249-257
ABSTRACT	Presents case examples of 8 families who volunteered to participate in a program for potentially abusive parents. During their admissions procedure, the families described their overwhelming fear of hurting their children. A lifeline procedure was used in which a therapist was available to clients on a 24-hr. 7 day/wk basis for as long as necessary. Four stages developed in the therapeutic process—emotional release, outburst of rage at other family members, denial of the initial problem, and integration and resolution of reality. Each of these stages is described. (M. Ellison-Pounsel)